Foreword by
GARETH BATTY

Editor
BENJ MOOREHEAD

Compiled by
JO HARMAN
& BEN GARDNER

Design
ROB WHITEHOUSE

This edition first published in the UK by Cricket Properties Ltd

ISBN: 978-1-909811-48-5

 A CIP Catalogue record for this book is available from the British Library.

Published by Jellyfish Publishing
www.jellyfishsolutions.co.uk

Editor: *Benj Moorehead;* Research and editorial: *Jo Harman, Ben Gardner*
Design: *Rob Whitehouse;* Images: *Getty Images unless stated;*
Print: *Jellyfish Print Solutions*

Acknowledgements
The publishers would like to thank the county clubs and the players for their assistance in helping to put together this book. Additional information has been gathered from espncricinfo.com and cricketarchive.com. Thanks also to Mike Vimpany for providing images.

CONTENTS

The
Cricketers'
Who's Who
2019

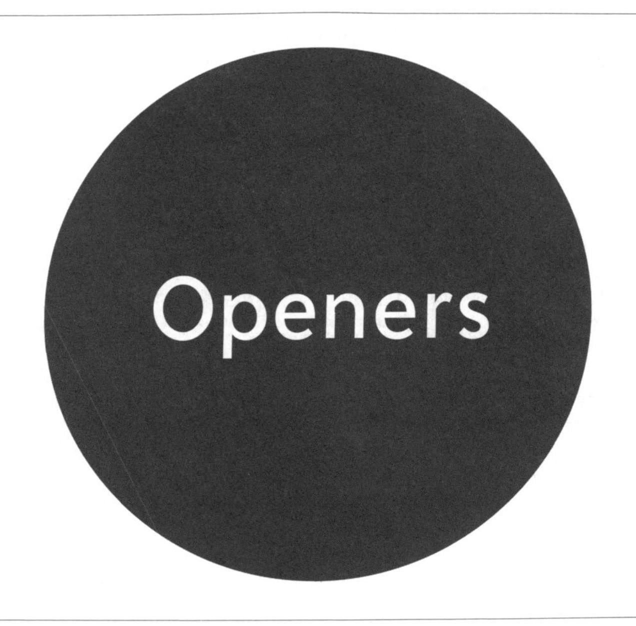
Openers

FOREWORD

By Gareth Batty

Welcome to the 2019 edition of *The Cricketers' Who's Who*, a book which always used to be knocking around the county dressing rooms when I started playing in the 1990s and still is all these years later.

This will be my 23rd season as a professional cricketer and I am looking forward to it as much as I did my first in 1997. County cricket is a way of life. It challenges you but it gives you so much fulfilment and joy and a real sense of belonging to something bigger: the great game of cricket. After a full county season a lot of overseas pros will say: "Wow. I don't know how you do that every year. But I'm glad I've done it because it's an amazing thing to be part of."

You could ask my Surrey colleagues from last year or the Essex boys in 2017 about what's it's like to go through an English season and absolutely break yourself to then win something at the end of it – particularly the County Championship. The Championship is a wonderful tradition. I understand that traditions have to change for the better, but we also have to understand we have an incredible product. Our first-class system is the best in the world.

Surrey winning the title in 2018 was a culmination of a lot of things, not least the club's hard work to get the finances in such a good state. We have excellent coaching and facilities. Alec Stewart, Surrey's director of cricket, also spent a lot of time making sure that young players weren't on their own but that there was a crossover between seniors and youngsters. And he made a great effort to instil the identity of the club within the players.

Then last summer, the captain Rory Burns grabbed it by the horns. He drove the lads forward and got the best out of everybody. The best thing about Rory is that he's a Surrey boy through and through. He's been through the good and the bad times and understands what you need to play for the club, and he passes that down to the younger players.

Looking at the broader picture from an English spinner's perspective, it does concern me that there is a lack of desire among counties to get spinners involved in Championship cricket. This is largely because it's all about getting results, which I understand. Clubs think: 'We'll just get four big lads on a green seamer, and the ball will swing, that's our best chance of winning.' A lot of people complain about all the 70-75mph seamers in England, but if you're playing in April then those sort of bowlers are going to be very successful.

The only way to change it is somehow to have more four-day cricket played in the middle of the summer. That way teams would need spinners to get results. We need to be mindful that the beauty of our game requires it to have different skillsets for it to have an attraction to everybody.

It's the job of everybody in county cricket to produce good players and I am delighted to see my old club Worcestershire doing such a magnificent job to bring through local youngsters and create a unique bond between them. That's why they were so successful last summer, winning the T20 Blast. I tell you what: even if all those guys at Worcester don't see each other for 10 years, when they get together again it will be like they saw each other yesterday. That's the bond you get and that's the thing I will miss most when I retire.

A lot of you who have played club cricket will know exactly what I am talking about, and I wish you all the best of luck for the 2019 season. For all us England supporters, it's shaping up to be an exciting summer, with good reason to believe the team can triumph in the World Cup and then the Ashes series which follows. Fingers crossed.

Gareth Batty
March 2019

EDITOR'S NOTES

By Benj Moorehead

Welcome to the 40th edition of *The Cricketers' Who's Who*.

That's four decades of cajoling, nagging, pleading and blackmailing county cricketers up and down the land to fill in our unique questionnaire. Once, a pair of Surrey players, whose misfortune it was that our headquarters are located on their home ground, were frogmarched into the office a day before deadline and told they could not leave until it was done. Full, proper answers please boys. We'll stop at nothing.

It's a formidable operation, but one can only imagine what it was like when Iain Sproat, the Conservative MP and founder of this annual, first went about the business in the 1980s. No internet. No media managers to do all that nagging on our behalf. No formalised pre-season photo sessions to provide a picture for each player; in the preface to the first edition in 1980, Sproat thanks a "Mr. Bill Smith, F.R.P.S., who personally took most of the photographs". We tip our hat to you sirs.

Elsewhere in that understated preface, Sproat talks about respecting the players' wishes: "Some cricketers, for example, are prepared to give both their address and their phone number, others prefer to give one and not the other." We live in different times. Certainly we didn't have the gall to ask, say, Joe Root for his number or full postal address (ideally both) so that we could tell the rest of the world.

The annual has evolved over the years; where once it was more of a formal, information-gathering exercise, now it seeks to unearth an anecdote or two to embellish the facts. But the essence remains the same: to bring to life all those hundreds of cricketers who might otherwise be merely a name on a scorecard. And, who knows, to provide the odd giggle along the way.

It tells you something about a person when you know they plan "to run an international not-for-profit scaling-up development program in Sub-Saharan Africa" (see page 418); that their favourite quote comes from Roosevelt's 'The Man in the Arena' speech in 1910 (page 492); that they built the local clubhouse with their own bare hands (page 247); that they cried when Alastair Cook was dismissed in his final Test innings (page 519). Or to know which book means most to them, a spectrum which includes *1984*, *The God Delusion*, the Quran, Jack Shantry's benefit brochure, *Kama Sutra* and *Cats Galore: A Compendium of Cultured Cats*.

We are hugely grateful to all the players who completed their questionnaire, and to all the county press officers who spurred them to do it. This book would not be what it is without them.

* * *

Our 40th edition coincides with what some have billed the biggest cricketing summer in a generation. First England host a World Cup for which they will be most people's favourites (we kick-off our Comment section with Matt Thacker's whistle-stop tour of the four previous World Cups held in this country). Then follows an Ashes series which, unlike recent contests between England and Australia, feels timely and hard to call. The Aussies are undergoing some sort of ethical cleansing after that ball-tampering row, with the chief culprits – Steve Smith, David Warner and Cameron Bancroft – due to come back into the fold this summer. For their part, England appear to be trying to steal the "mercurial" tag from Pakistan. Meanwhile England Women will be attempting to win back the Ashes for the first time since 2014 and avenge their home defeat of four years ago.

There is also a sense that this will be the last English summer as we know it, with the ECB's city-based 100-ball competition due to begin next year (in case you hadn't heard). New teams and a new format are significant changes, but the endless tweaking of the summer calendar has hardened fans and players as much as a stint at fine leg on a blustery day at Derby. We are used to the earth moving below our feet; as long as there are bowlers and batsmen – and space for some red-ball cricket – then we are content enough.

That said, the arrival of The Hundred does leave an uncertain future for the T20 Blast competition, which could be forgiven for feeling like an older sibling having to contend with a new-born rival. Surely there is space for only one upstart in English cricket's family? With this in mind, we celebrate 10 iconic moments of our domestic T20 competition since it began in 2003, from a shirt-wielding Mark Ramprakash to a Paul Nixon wonder catch. Not forgetting the day when a jam-packed Rose Bowl crowd cheered on a man with a bucket of paint.

Our Comment section concludes with Emma John's beautiful tribute to James Anderson, the man who has taken more wickets than any other fast bowler in the history of Test cricket and, no less uniquely, has become entrenched in English hearts and minds as Our Jimmy. Can't you already hear it? That slurred chant on a warm evening in late summer at The Oval, the final day of the fifth Test, with the Ashes on the line and England needing one wicket to win. Oh Jimmy, Jimmy…

Benj Moorehead
March 2019

COMMENT

HOME DISCOMFORTS

It's coming home, it's coming home, it's coming... cricket's coming home. You can just hear it, can't you? Sunday 14 July, Lord's, packed house, the champers and beer started to kick in some time ago. The noise swells, buffeting the members' ears in the Pavilion, subsides, then stirs again, relentless, coming from somewhere deep inside. Matt Thacker *on why it's still something of a long shot*

A home win appears all very possible, despite the fact that England, famously, have never won any of the 11 editions of the cricket World Cup. We have fared marginally better in rugby (one from eight) and football (one from 21) – those solitary wins might be slim pickings but the fans of those sports don't half go on about them. Still. Winning a World Cup is a big thing.

When I say England (and we), I mean it in a wrong-headed, sexist kind of way, i.e. the men, because it hasn't been 44 years of hurt for our women's cricketers, far from it. Back in 1973, before the men had the nous to multitask their way to long-form *and* short-form cricket, the inaugural cricket World Cup was held in England, the hosts pipping Australia on points in what was a *de facto* final at Edgbaston. And they won three more of the next 10 editions besides, for a more-than-handy record of four from 11.

The last of those wins, in 2017, took place on another blissful July day at Lord's, with England overcoming India by nine runs in a thriller that has changed the course of women's cricket in the competing nations forever. Apart from those two instances, which bookmark the history of the women's tournament, England have been hosts on only one other occasion, 1993, when they beat New Zealand in the final at Lord's. So, three World Cups on home soil, three wins. Easy-peasy.

Which bring us to the men. This year will be their fifth attempt at lifting the trophy at Lord's and over the years it's been a story, by and large, of diminishing returns. Semi-finalists; finalists; semi-finalists; laughing stocks. The only way, it would seem, is up.

Back when it all began in 1975, the world of cricket was a very different place. As Madan Lal came jogging in to John Jameson in the 19th one-day international *ever* played, there was little understanding that short-form cricket was anything more than a hit-and-giggle diversion from the proper first-class stuff. England's 334 in 60 overs in that first World Cup game was monstrous, mountainous. In new money, it was probably worth 500. India's opening bat, the great Sunil Gavaskar, was so disheartened that he didn't bother putting on his hiking boots, preferring to carpet-slipper his was to a bat-carrying 36 not out from 174 balls. Genius.

Over a sun-kissed two weeks, things got better, but not much better. The eight competing teams included East Africa and Sri Lanka, who were blown away by West Indies but showed real

fight against Australia, despite Duleep Mendis copping a sickening blow on the head from Jeff Thomson, who hospitalised Sunil Wettimuny in the same innings, leading an uncomprehending policeman to ask the latter if he wanted to press charges against his assailant.

There was only one really close game, when West Indies pulled off a one-wicket win against Pakistan at Edgbaston, and the semi-final between England and Australia at Headingley was notable for Garry Gilmour's 6-14 from 12 overs. Gilmour went on to take five in the final but played only one more ODI. Weird game, cricket.

Clive Lloyd lit up Lord's in that final, stroking and bludgeoning his way to a sublime hundred and following it up with 12 tidy overs. The Aussies were never quite out of it, but never quite in it either. Five run-outs, three of them effortlessly effected by Viv Richards, hardly helped their cause.

When Dennis Lillee joins Jeff Thomson at the fall of the ninth wicket, 59 are required. The pair slaps and scraps 34 of them when Thommo spoons the ball straight to a grateful Roy Fredericks at cover and the crowd invades the field. Nobody registers that a no-ball has been called. Then it dawns on Fredericks, who shies at the non-striker's end with Lillee way out of his ground. The ball misses and is engulfed by the sea of onrushing fans. Ever the pragmatists, Lillee and Thomson simply get their heads down and keep on running. When things quieten down, the batsmen ask umpires Bird and Spencer how many runs they are going to award. "Two," guesses Spencer. Thomson explodes and Lillee suggests to Bird that they have run about 17. The decision of four seems about right. Three balls later, it's all over, with a run-out of course.

Four years on, we were back to do it all again. By the start of this tournament, 60 ODIs had been and gone. This edition also contained eight teams and was played in the same, two-groups-of-four, all-over-in-a-fortnight format. Why change a winning formula? It was almost as if, in the gap between the two World Cups, we had not seen the most seismic change there had ever been in the sport: Kerry Packer's World Series Cricket, with its floodlights, helmets and coloured clothing.

Back in the land where change came more slowly (although the month before the World Cup we had just elected our first female PM), Canada came in for East Africa and had about as much success, their nadir being bowled out by the hosts in 40.3 painstaking overs for 45, then the lowest total in an ODI. India lost every game, taking their World Cup record to played six, won one. England, having squeezed past New Zealand in the semi-final, found themselves up against the mighty West Indies at Lord's in the June showpiece. Mike Brearley opted to bowl first and West Indies were struggling at 99-4. Enter the King. Supported by King. Viv Richards was magisterial, his unbeaten 138 a lesson in one-day batting, and Collis King was even more brutal, a 66-ball 86 giving him a strike-rate that in the '70s was pretty much unheard of. In reply to 286-9, Brearley and Boycott bedded in, took the shine off the new ball, set the platform. It took our Geoffrey 17 overs to reach double figures, at which point he was dropped by Clive Lloyd. It is not known whether Boycs wandered over to the West Indies captain to tell him he'd just dropped the World Cup. Reaching 129 runs in 38 overs left England needing another 160 in 22. Gettable. In 2019. But this was 1979 and, with Joel Garner's yorkers spearing in from above the sightscreen, England lost their last eight wickets for 11 runs.

In 1983 there was still no real thought that the World Cup would take place anywhere other than Blighty. And there was to be no tinkering with the formula. ODIs were now a 'thing' but there had still been less than 200 of them by the time England and New Zealand faced off at Lord's on 9 June. There was a definite improvement in the standard of the smaller nations – it's often forgotten that India beat West Indies at Old Trafford in the group stage – with Zimbabwe shocking Australia and Sri Lanka beating New Zealand. And there was a dawning understanding that ODIs did not have to be played like mini-Test matches. India's battery of miserly dibbly-dobblies squeezed the life out of England in the semi-final at Old Trafford and then did the same to West Indies at Lord's after Roberts, Marshall, Garner and Holding had restricted them to 183. Kapil Dev's over-the-shoulder catch to get rid of Viv, who had come to see St John's Wood as his personal fiefdom for World Cup final day, was the pivotal moment (Richards had made just 33). And when India's captain lifted the trophy, the cricket world changed forever. It is no exaggeration to say that the make-up of the modern game stems from 25 June, 1983, the day India fell head-over-heels in love with one-day cricket.

The balance of cricketing power now altered completely. The next World Cup took place on the subcontinent and it was to be 16 years before the trophy rocked up on these shores again, a very different beast from when we last saw it close-up. Coloured clothing, pinch-hitters, slower balls, leg-side wides, a Duke's ball, 50 overs rather than 60, a cast list of 12 teams and, sigh, Australian dominance. The world had moved on. And there was a whole new concept to deal with – the Super Sixes, when sides carried forward points gained in the group stages. Oh, and 21 venues, including Cardiff, Edinburgh, Dublin and Amstelveen.

England started well, beating defending champions Sri Lanka in the tournament-opener (ODI No.1443) and then crushing Kenya, but it was downhill thereafter. Batterings at the hands of South Africa and India sandwiched a win against Zimbabwe, but the dawdle to their target in that match ultimately saw the home side lose out on net run-rate to the Zimbabweans, who went through to the next stage at England's expense by upsetting South Africa at Chelmsford.

England were out. Out, in fact, before their official Word Cup song was. But the party goes on even if the host is absent and the Super Sixes saw some thrilling cricket, including a game between sub-continental superpowers India and Pakistan at a time when the two nations were officially at war. The second stage culminated in Australia's stunning five-wicket win against South Africa, powered by an unbeaten Steve Waugh ton, and the same two sides came face to face at Edgbaston in the second semi-final (after Pakistan had breezed past New Zealand) for what may be the most tense game of ODI cricket ever played.

Australia are defending 213 and, thanks to Shane Warne's 4-29 – including a ball to get rid of Herschelle Gibbs which recalled Gatting in '93 – they manage to leave the last pair of Lance Klusener and Allan Donald with nine to get off the final over. Brutal boundaries from Klusener off Fleming's first two deliveries leave the scores tied. One needed off four to send South Africa through. Dot ball (and a missed run-out). And then, the mix-up of all mix-ups. Klusener calls; Donald doesn't respond; then does; then drops his bat; the ball is relayed back to Gilchrist; the bails are off. The match is tied and the Aussies are through, based on their superior net run-rate in the Super Sixes.

The final was a huge anticlimax, a Warne-inspired Australia routing Pakistan, their win coming in one ball over 20 overs. A taste of things to come...

And so to this year, two decades on. Personally, I can't wait for Bastille Day, when there will be approximately 1.5 billion people tuning in to see cricket coming home... I hope it delivers.

TEN ICONIC MOMENTS OF ENGLISH T20 CRICKET

With a 100-ball domestic competition starting next summer, the T20 Blast will no longer stand alone as county cricket's box-office attraction. The tournament has been an unqualified success since it was launched as the Twenty20 Cup in 2003, drawing bumper crowds and producing some logic-defying cricket. To celebrate its final year in the limelight, we have chosen 10 moments over the last 16 years that define what this competition is all about. Note that these are iconic moments, not necessarily best moments, so we make no apologies for including a Bumble-Flintoff duet

MARK RAMPS IT UP

Hampshire v Surrey, Southampton, 2006

Throw together Mark Ramprakash's intense competitive instincts, a boisterous home crowd at Hampshire and a knife-edge clash between two cocksure heavyweights, and you get this: a tetchy tear-up that turned postal at the death, with Ramprakash getting shirty after running out last-man Billy Taylor to seal a 10-run win. Wound-up after sparring with the crowd all night, Ramps' final act tipped him over the edge. He whipped off his Surrey shirt and set off around the outfield, veins throbbing, face contorted, swirling the offending garment around his head. Later regaining some semblance of the plot, Ramprakash was savvy enough to request security after the game, and though he escaped to tell the tale and triumph later that year in *Strictly*, the resurrected 'Bloodaxe' nickname, which had followed him around since his early days at Middlesex, would stick right through till the end of his garlanded career.

NAPIER'S RAPIER

Essex v Sussex, Chelmsford, 2008

Graham Napier never quite knew his own strength. He always seemed more at ease as a quality seamer and merry lower-order hitter than a bona fide county allrounder. And yet with the bat, on his day, there were few in the world who could match his explosiveness. On this occasion, Napier was blessed with two slices of fortune. One, Essex were experimenting with their line-up and just that morning had decided to throw him in at No.3; and two, this group match happened to be on TV. Striding out in the third over, Napier was quickly into his work, eyeing the short straight boundaries at Chelmsford and in particular the river behind the Tom Pearce Stand. Once he got going, he was unstoppable. His century came up in 44 balls, and the next 52 runs were pummelled from 14 deliveries. In the final analysis, his unbeaten 152 had been found to contain 16 sixes – a T20 world record and since surpassed only by Chris Gayle (twice). For a time, before Gayle got busy, Napier held perhaps the coolest record: he was the only man to have hit 16 sixes twice in a professional innings, after repeating the feat against Surrey at Guildford in 2011 – in a County Championship match.

BRING OUT THE WHITEWASH

Hampshire v Somerset, Final, Edgbaston, 2010

This was all the drama and perversion of T20 cricket rolled into the last ball of the tournament. Hampshire require one run to tie and win on fewer wickets lost, but on-strike batsman Dan Christian needs a runner. Problem: no crease lines for the runner. "Bring out the whitewash!" calls David Lloyd from the commentary box, and moments later the groundsman is painting lines on the adjacent strip, each stroke of his brush cheered by a sell-out Rose Bowl crowd. Finally the job is done, Jimmy Adams has emerged as Christian's runner, and Somerset seamer Zander de Bruyn is ready. Thud. Huge cry for lbw. Very close. Not out. At which point Christian forgets everything and scrambles to the other end for the winning leg-bye. So does his runner.

The Hampshire team pour onto the pitch, then halt: *is* the game over? There are two batsmen at the non-striker's end. Somerset need merely to break the wicket at the striker's end to run out Christian and *they* will win. Yet in all the chaos, this fact does not occur to any one of the fielding side. The umpires wait to see if the penny drops, and then call time. "It'll probably haunt me for a few years," says Marcus Trescothick once the dust has settled.

SUPPIAH ON FIRE

Glamorgan v Somerset, Cardiff, 2011

The T20 competition has been awash with big stars over the years, but it never ceases to produce unlikely heroes. Look at Worcestershire's Pat Brown: a virtual unknown until he bowled his club to T20 glory last summer with 31 wickets, the second-most in the competition's history. Brown is likely to play for England, but for Arul Suppiah in 2011 it was a case of one fleeting and glorious moment on top of the world. An allrounder born in Kuala Lumpur, Suppiah was predominantly an opening batsman who bowled some left-arm spin. This was his 10th season at Somerset and he had never taken a five-for in any format of the game. His career had stuttered along at Taunton, 1,000 first-class runs in 2009 an exception to a modest record. In 2013 a chronic knee condition would force him to retire at the age of 29 with first-class batting and bowling averages of 32 and 58. But he remains the man with the best T20 figures on the planet: 6-5! No matter that it was against Glamorgan on a raging turner at Cardiff; no matter that only one of his wickets was a top-five batsman. Let no one dare topple King Suppiah and ruin a brilliant quiz question.

FANTASTIC MR FOX

Leicestershire v Somerset, Final, Edgbaston 2011

Victory and a spectacular one-handed grab to dismiss Kieron Pollard provided the perfect climax to 40-year-old Paul Nixon's professional career in England as he helped his beloved Foxes secure their third T20 triumph by defeating Somerset at Edgbaston. Leicestershire, who had posted a modest 145-6, believed the comeback was on from the moment that edge nestled into Nixon's mitts. Foxes skipper Matthew Hoggard would later describe the catch as a "sprinkling of magic in a fairytale". Somerset were now 89-4 with their West Indian big gun back in the pavilion, and Josh Cobb went on to claim 4-22 with his part-time off-spin as Leicestershire won by 18 runs. It was a timely boost for the financially-stricken county, who had also triumphed in 2004 and 2006. Leicestershire's unrivalled success in the T20 Cup is the best example of how this competition has been an inspiration for some of the humble underdogs, including Northamptonshire (2013 and 2016) and Worcestershire (2018), to overcome the swanky powerhouses.

BIG WILLEY STYLE

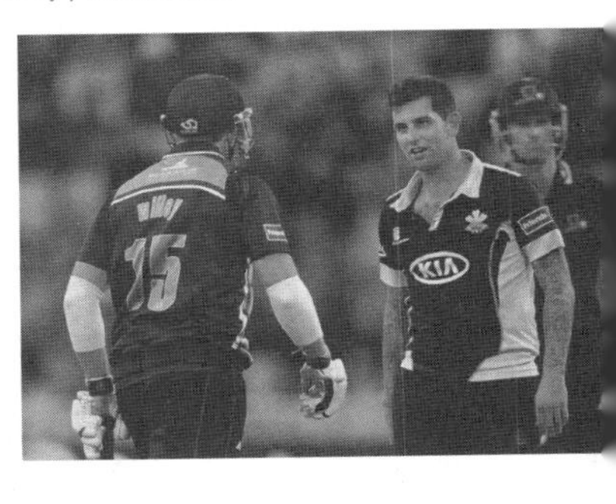

Northamptonshire v Surrey, Final, Edgbaston, 2013

Fondly described as a "loose cannon" by his Northants captain Alex Wakely, David Willey came out all guns blazing in a one-sided final, dishing out some verbals to Jade Dernbach – "I don't really like the bloke, to be honest," admitted Willey – before slamming Surrey's attack for a 19-ball fifty. He was then a man possessed in the field, clean-bowling Jason Roy and running out Steven Davies with a direct hit from the boundary before sealing the trophy with a hat-trick, finishing with figures of 4-9 in a shock win for the unfancied Steelbacks. Willey has continued to be one of the competition's most iconic performers and personalities, smashing a 40-ball century in the 2015 quarter-final against Sussex and hitting a club record 118 off 55 balls two years later for his new side Yorkshire versus Worcestershire, all the time displaying the sort of ferocious commitment which has been a hallmark of English domestic T20 cricket.

IT TAKES TWO

Lancashire v Yorkshire, Old Trafford, 2018

Boundary 'relay' fielding was once a gentler thing, one player producing a sliding save on the floor while another mopped up the loose ball and sent it back to the wicketkeeper. However, the all-action nature of T20 has stirred the players to perform the sort of acrobatics that has the crowd gasping. The 'relay catch' typically involves a flying fielder parrying the ball just as it sails over the rope while an accomplice stands by to pounce. Not uncommon these days, but in 2014 the same two fielders completed two of the greatest relay catches in the space of two weeks. First at Old Trafford, the Roses match no less. Tom Smith smites the ball back over the bowler's head, and Yorkshire's Adam Lyth leaps backward on the boundary, catches the ball and then releases it mid-air before he has crossed the line. Aaron Finch collects a simple catch. Then to Headingley against Leicestershire. Another straight hit, same Houdini act from Lyth, only this time Finch has to dive low to scoop up the rebound with his right hand. It beggared belief, just as much as the fact that Lyth has no mention on the scorecard for either dismissal.

GAYLE FORCE

Somerset v Kent, Taunton, 2015

It took the undisputed king of T20 a long time to make his way to the T20 Blast, but he looked a man determined to make up for lost time when he got there in 2015. Signed by Somerset for a three-game stint, Gayle tallied 328 runs and 29 maximums in three innings before slipping off again, presumably to some other lucrative T20 tournament in a far point of the globe. He warmed up with 92 off 59 against Kent and finished off with 85 off 49 against Hampshire, but the pièce de résistance was 151 off 62 on his Taunton debut, at the time the fifth-highest T20 score in history and still third for sixes in an innings (15). Amazingly, Somerset lost a high-scoring match, Gayle able to muster only 12 runs from the last four balls when 16 were needed. "I thought Sam Northeast [115] played a sensational innings [for Kent], but then the World Boss came in and it's different gravy," said Matthew Maynard, then Somerset coach. "However good Sam's innings was, it just pales a little bit… Words can't explain exactly what we have seen today. He makes it looks so easy and strikes the ball so cleanly."

UH-HUH

Bumble and Freddie, Finals Day, Edgbaston, 2017

Finals Day has rarely been all, or even much, about the cricket, with three back-to-back T20s serving as a backdrop to a binge of off-pitch revelry including the annual mascot race and fire cannons galore. And, in 2017, a sing-off between David Lloyd and Andrew Flintoff, Bumble and Freddie, who dressed up as Johnny Cash and Elvis to serenade the Edgbaston crowd in the build-up the final. This may not be everybody's cuppa, but it was quintessential T20 froth. First we had a gravelly Bumble doing Cash's 'Folsom Prison Blues' and then an uneven Freddie treated us to 'Suspicious Minds' before the two came together for a 'Sweet Caroline' duet. Bumble's Cash impression wasn't bad at all, though the mock-guitar playing needs a bit of work, but Flintoff, moonlighting as Elvis, was never going to be put in the shade. Like an intern at karaoke night, he started nervously but grew into his performance, and soon the natural showman was on full display. A stumble over a speaker as he proceeded on a backwards lap of honour was a reminder of a famous escapade in a pedalo, but by that point the crowd were too pissed to notice.

GAME OF ROSES

Lancashire v Yorkshire, Old Trafford, 2018

It's been said that county cricket's local derbies have lost a little of their lustre in recent times but the rivalries are alive and kicking in the domestic T20 competition, with bumper crowds regularly turning out to watch their team lock horns with their neighbours. Matches between Middlesex and Surrey attract in excess of 25,000 fans. Last summer a crowd of 22,515 packed into Emirates Old Trafford – a record figure outside London – to watch the 'Game of Roses' fixture, and they were treated to yet another nail-biting thriller between two star-studded line-ups. Some early rain did nothing to dampen the spirits of the crowd, who created a cacophonous atmosphere and witnessed more than 350 runs in a 14-overs-a-side smash which went down to the final delivery. Yorkshire needed four off the last ball but Kane Williamson could only scramble two as the hosts claimed a one-run victory and the local bragging rights.

FROM FROSTED TIPS TO GRIZZLED GREY

Emma John *on growing up with James Anderson*

I missed the wicket [pictured, right]. There are few places on earth, now, where sports scores can't reach you, but I wasn't strictly *on* earth. As I'd sat in Gatwick airport, eating my pre-flight Pret baguette, India had been 300-5, and KL Rahul was dug in like an obstinate aardvark. I'd listened as long as I could, until the air steward, wearing a surprisingly loud plaid jacket and a tight little smile, had marched down the aisle doing his take-off checks.

It was too much to hope that the flight deck might keep us clued in. I've flown a couple of times during football and rugby World Cups, when partisan pilots have announced their team's victory over the public-address system and it's been the best entertainment on offer. I was travelling Air New Zealand when the All Blacks beat France in the 2011 World Cup final and the plane broke into spontaneous applause. But I didn't imagine that the crew of our Norwegian Air vessel, bound for Boston, Massachusetts, were pestering air-traffic control for updates from the final day of England's fifth Test against India at The Oval.

It was the middle of the night in Britain when I landed and hastily agreed to whatever terms and conditions Logan airport's wifi was demanding of me. There is a reckless incontinence to the sports fan unwillingly separated from an important game, and as I stood in the port-of-entry line I furiously flouted the signs forbidding cellphone use. At least, until I had the information I wanted. James Anderson had taken his 564th wicket with the last ball of the match.

A few days later I tried to explain to some American friends the significance of his achievement. It was historic, I said. No other pace bowler in Test cricket had dismissed so many batsmen. And the *real* significance was in overtaking Glenn McGrath because he was an Australian icon who… I had forgotten that other people's sporting statistics are very rarely interesting. They listened politely and went back to talking about the Red Sox, who it turned out were having their own record-breaking season.

Usually I'm not that bothered about figures, and lists, and rankings. In fact, before Jimmy started making his charge, my instant recall of the all-time top-10 wicket-takers probably wouldn't have extended far beyond Warne and Murali. The more we were told that their figures were untouchable, never to be replicated, the less attention I paid to the rest.

Anderson's own rise through the ranks had snuck up on me. He was the solid core of a bowling attack that sometimes struggled at its periphery; the man whose return always

felt the best hope of a breakthrough. But there was something about his presence in the England team that was so dependable and understated that it was easy to take his wickets for granted. But still they came. His contribution to the team – to the sport – had become so large as to be almost impossible to see any more. He wasn't the greatest pace bowler in the world. He was just our Jimmy.

For me the best way to get some perspective on James Anderson isn't to look at numbers on a page, but pictures on a screen. One glance at the frosted tips with which he greeted the international scene demonstrates how far he's travelled. Nothing against that haircut, you understand (if it worked for Justin Timberlake, why would there be any reason to doubt it?). But the young face with its hedgehog topping is a powerful reminder of how sportspeople tend to grow up on the job.

For a start, it's a reminder that his first sensational appearances came considerably before the 2005 Ashes. There's such a sense of legacy about that series that Anderson is, rightly, deemed an inheritor of their mantle. It's a jolt to think that two years before that series, he was one of the few England bowlers to emerge from a World Cup in credit.

I've always thought the narrative around his early England career was a little unfair. But then, I was biased from the start. The moment he fizzed onto my TV screen, I was a believer. His raw energy, combined with the banana splits he could perform with the ball, held me spellbound. No matter that Andy Bichel and Michael Bevan took 12 runs off his final over at Port Elizabeth, ensuring that England failed to reach the Super Sixes. If he hadn't already taken 10 wickets in that 2003 tournament, we wouldn't have been in with a hope.

Three months later he took a five-for on his Test debut. And yes, it was only against Zimbabwe, and yes, it was at an overcast Lord's in May. But neither of those factors were Anderson's choosing. He took five wickets for 73, and 17 of those came off his first over. All of them were won with his peculiar head-down bowling action, which meant that at the moment of releasing the ball, Anderson was actually looking at the ground. If Paul Adams was a frog in a blender, Jimmy was a hamster whose feet were sellotaped to the bottom of his wheel.

I remember how quickly the tide of popular opinion turned against him, and how angry I was when it did. Anderson had been propelled into the international set-up, aged 20, with only a single Second-XI season behind him; he still played many of his games for Burnley and had barely been involved in Lancashire age-group cricket. But a combination of that admittedly unsustainable bowling style, and an indisputably expensive Test account – in his first four years he went for 3.74 runs an over – were enough for many to lose patience and write him off.

Certain bona fide cricket experts, amused by my ardent defence of his natural talent, told me that he was a busted flush, and that he'd never amount to anything. Stories swirled that the England bowling coaches, in trying to correct his action, had broken him entirely. The Anderson narrative, to the gossipy outside world, became that of a precocious child-star who hadn't got what it took for the grown-up game. Those who had been suspicious of his fashion-forward haircuts and his t-shirted James Dean 'tude were now at liberty to interpret these as the superficial trappings of a sulky teen.

* * *

Many of us fall for our sporting heroes pretty early. This footballer or that pole vaulter takes our fancy – for whatever reason – and we're committed to them for the rest of their careers, and potentially the rest of our lives. When I started following cricket, my idols were all a good 10 to 20 years older than me. But as the years go by, the age-gap closes, descending with the slow yet ruthless inevitability of one of those stone walls threatening to crush Indiana Jones, or at least to separate him from his fedora.

And yet the men representing the team I loved always seemed so much more adult than me. You notice I don't use the word mature – it would be hard to argue that Andrew Flintoff's pedalo escapades or Kevin Pietersen's, well, anything, spoke particularly well of their wisdom or decision-making at the time. But it never occurred to me, when that 2005 Ashes team were in their pomp, that we were comparable in age – I didn't even notice that Steve Harmison and I were born a month apart.

The men I saw on the field belonged to a world far removed from my own late-20s experiences. These guys were married. They had kids. They drove Volkswagen Touaregs. They probably didn't come home and make "vegetable surprise" with the half-an-onion and partially mouldy carrot they found in the bottom of their fridge.

So yes, James Anderson was the first England cricketer who didn't make me feel like an ingénue (OK, fine, a student) by comparison. He was four years younger than me, and he looked it. I was sent to interview him by the *Wisden Cricketer* magazine in 2003, and our hour together was a slightly awkward session of fumbled questions and mumbled replies.

He had the red streak in his hair, then, and 11 Test wickets. I remember feeling very self-conscious, and sorry for him, that he'd been forced to sit in an airless hotel room talking to a woman with whom he had absolutely nothing in common.

I also remember how very hard he was trying, in the long pauses where he looked away at the flimsy beige walls surrounding us, to think about his responses, to offer something acceptable. He was nothing like as cocksure as his hair. And his reticence wasn't sullenness, it was shyness. I wanted to tell him it would all be OK. It was possibly the first maternal twinge I'd ever had.

It was that experience with James Anderson that made me such a passionate advocate for Andy Murray too, back in the late 2000s when the common belief was that he was a grouchy, petulant kid who choked when the heat was on. It infuriated me that the very qualities that made Murray Britain's first real contender in world tennis in 70 years – his single-minded focus, his indifference to image, his lack of interest in much outside his sport – were the very traits everyone wanted to knock.

Anderson improved, of course. Like Murray, it took years, and it took dedication. The people who knew him best weren't surprised. Mike Watkinson, who was Anderson's coach in the Lancashire Second XI, and one of the first to talk to him about swing, encountered a young man who was quick to listen and act on what he was told. Watkinson could recall a particular game against Middleton, when he'd discussed some bowling theories with Anderson just before play. He watched as his protégé put them into practice that very day.

"He picked things up fast," Watkinson told me. "But he also had his own thoughts on his game, and put a lot of time into analysing the opposition. He was quietly thorough in his personal preparation – a real thinker on the game." It's an attribute that people are quick to credit him with today; less so back then.

Anderson has changed in very few fundamentals. The many characteristics that he is lauded for today – his aggressive intent on the field, his laidback humour off it, his lack of ego, his determination to perfect every art of swing bowling – were all there, in embryonic form, in the 25-year-old with a Test bowling average of nearly 40. The transformative element has been nothing more than time itself.

And that, I think, is why his greatness has crept up on us. Or maybe it's just on me. I've always considered myself his biggest fan – short of anyone who's got a tattoo, or a shrine,

or a restraining order. I've always been primed to sing his praises to the unconverted – often at stages in his career when many would argue he hadn't yet earned them.

But when you're growing up alongside your heroes, it's hard to spot that they're growing up too. Just like it's hard to recognise a golden age when you're the one basking in its glow. I spent far too much of the past decade worrying about whether England were going to come away with a first-innings lead, or who was the best choice of fourth seamer, or why there was such a dearth of spin in the UK, to fully appreciate Anderson's incredible journey to the top.

Swing bowling is a deceptive craft in more than one way. There's the magic of the ball in flight and the mystery of the physics behind it. There's the bowler's own sleight of hand – literally, in Anderson's case, when he hides the ball in his run-up to cloak his intent. But there's another misleading element too – the fact that many of a bowler's best deliveries are the ones never immortalised on the scoreboard. All those brilliant outswingers and devastating inswingers that bamboozle the batsmen too much to touch his bat or take his wicket.

Anderson may have upward of 500 scalps in his satchel but his true worth cannot be counted in those alone. His world-beating achievement in 2018 has come about because of the 148 Tests he has played, and the 32,335 balls he has delivered. Because of the 15 years that he has given, unstintingly, to his pursuit of excellence. A little less than half his life, spent in the colours of his national team. Somehow, that's as inspiring to me as any top-10 list.

This article appeared in the 2019 spring edition of The Nightwatchman, *the Wisden Cricket Quarterly which specialises in long-form articles by an array of international authors*

CAPTAIN: Joe Root (Test), Eoin Morgan (ODI/T20I)
COACH: Trevor Bayliss

2019 SUMMER FIXTURES

May 3
Ireland vs England
Only ODI
Dublin

May 5
England vs Pakistan
Only T20I
Cardiff

May 8
England vs Pakistan
1st ODI
The Oval

May 11
England vs Pakistan
2nd ODI
Southampton

May 14
England vs Pakistan
3rd ODI
Bristol

May 17
England vs Pakistan
4th ODI
Trent Bridge

May 19
England vs Pakistan
5th ODI
Headingley

May 25
England vs Australia
ICC World Cup Warm-up
Southampton

May 27
England vs Afghanistan
ICC World Cup Warm-up
The Oval

May 30
England vs South Africa
ICC World Cup
The Oval

June 3
England vs Pakistan
ICC World Cup
Trent Bridge

June 8
England vs Bangladesh
ICC World Cup
Cardiff

June 14
England vs West Indies
ICC World Cup
Southampton

June 18
England vs Afghanistan
ICC World Cup
Old Trafford

June 21
England vs Sri Lanka
ICC World Cup
Headingley

June 25
England vs Australia
ICC World Cup
Lord's

June 30
England vs India
ICC World Cup
Edgbaston

July 3
England vs New Zealand
ICC World Cup
Chester-le-Street

July 24
England vs Ireland
Only Test
Lord's

August 1
England vs Australia
1st Test
Edgbaston

August 14
England vs Australia
2nd Test
Lord's

August 22
England vs Australia
3rd Test
Headingley

September 4
England vs Australia
4th Test
Old Trafford

September 12
England vs Australia
5th Test
The Oval

KEY

THE PLAYERS

LHB – Left-hand batsman
LB – Leg-break bowler
LF – Left-arm fast bowler
LFM – Left-arm fast-medium bowler
LM – Left-arm medium bowler
LMF – Left-arm medium-fast bowler
MCCU – Marylebone Cricket Club University
MVP – Denotes a player's presence in the top 100 places of the 2018 PCA County MVP Rankings (the number next to 'MVP' denotes the player's specific placing)
OB – Off-break bowler
R – 1,000 or more first-class runs in an English season (the number next to 'R' denotes how many times the player has achieved this feat)
RF – Right-arm fast bowler
RFM – Right-arm fast-medium bowler
RHB – Right-hand batsman
RM – Right-arm medium bowler
RMF – Right-arm medium-fast bowler
SLA – Slow left-arm orthodox bowler
SLW – Slow left-arm wrist-spin bowler
UCCE – University Centre of Cricketing Excellence
W – 50 or more first-class wickets in an English season (the number next to 'W' denotes how many times the player has achieved this feat)
WK – Wicketkeeper
* – Not-out innings (e.g. 137*)

THE TEAMS

(s) – A competition has been shared between two or more winners
C&G – Cheltenham & Gloucester Trophy (English domestic 50-over competition, 2001-2006)
CB40 – Clydesdale Bank 40 (English domestic 40-over competition, 2010-2012)
CC1/CC2 – County Championship Division One/Division Two
FP Trophy – Friends Provident Trophy (English domestic 50-over competition, 2007-2009)
Gillette – Gillette Cup (English domestic limited-overs competition, 1963-1980)
NatWest – NatWest Trophy (English domestic limited-overs competition, 1981-2000)
Pro40 – NatWest Pro40 (English domestic 40-over competition, 2005-09)
REL – A player has been released by the relevant county
RET – A player has retired
RL50 – Royal London One-Day Cup (English domestic 50-over competition, 2014-19)
T20 Cup – English domestic T20 competition (2003-19)
YB40 – Yorkshire Bank 40 (English domestic 40-over competition, 2013)

NOTES: The statistics given for a player's best batting and best bowling performance are limited to first-class cricket. A field within a player's career statistics which is marked with an '-' indicates that a particular statistic is inapplicable, e.g. a player has never bowled a ball in first-class cricket. All stats correct as of March 11, 2019

The Teams

DERBYSHIRE

FORMED: 1870
HOME GROUND: The Pattonair County Ground, Derby
ONE-DAY NAME: Derbyshire Falcons
CAPTAIN: Billy Godleman (Championship and RL50), TBC (T20)
2018 RESULTS: CC2: 7/10; RL50: 5/9 North Group; T20: 7/9 North Group
HONOURS: Championship: 1936; Gillette/NatWest/C&G/FP Trophy: 1981; Benson & Hedges Cup: 1993; Sunday League: 1990

THE LOWDOWN

Revamping the coaching set-up is becoming an annual tradition at Derby. Following Kim Barnett's resignation last July, Dave Houghton has returned to the club as head of cricket, with previous T20 coach John Wright taking up an advisory role. Backroom support will ease the strain on captain Billy Godleman, who effectively ran the first team after Barnett's departure. Houghton arrives at a time when Derbyshire are the mid-table masters, but it's also true that the club were competitive in T20 and 50-over cricket last summer, while in Division Two they were 29 points off a third-placed finish which this season would earn promotion. As one of the game's most respected batting coaches, Houghton should stiffen a fragile top-order which has lost Ben Slater, one of its more consistent performers, to Nottinghamshire. Wayne Madsen cannot do it on his own, while Godleman will want to channel his white-ball form into the Championship. Keeper Harvey Hosein, 22, takes the gloves on a long-term basis following Gary Wilson's release. Hardus Viljoen has left but Kiwi allrounder Logan van Beek will sharpen the seam attack in all formats.

IN: Logan van Beek (NZ), Tom Lace (Mid, loan), Kane Richardson (Aus, T20)
OUT: Will Davis (Lei), Ben Slater (Not), Callum Brodrick, Hardus Viljoen, Gary Wilson (all REL)

HEAD OF CRICKET: DAVE HOUGHTON

A former Zimbabwe captain, Houghton averaged 43 from 22 Tests after his country acquired Test status in 1992. He has vast experience on the county circuit, with previous stints as batting coach for Derbyshire, Somerset and most recently Middlesex. He was head coach at Derbyshire between 2004 and 2007. Houghton will be supported by former Gloucestershire quick Steve Kirby, who has been appointed assistant and bowling coach. Dominic Cork is another addition to the backroom staff – the ex-Derbyshire allrounder will be head coach for the T20 campaign.

www.derbyshireccc.com / tel: 01332 388 101

COUNTY CHAMPIONSHIP AVERAGES 2018

Batting

	Mat	Inns	NO	Runs	HS	Ave	SR	100	50	4s	6s
BT Slater	9	17	1	676	99	42.25	48.11	0	6	93	1
WL Madsen	14	27	0	1016	144	37.62	62.29	2	7	133	2
DM Wheeldon	1	2	1	35	33*	35.00	48.61	0	0	2	1
LM Reece	6	11	1	349	157*	34.90	46.72	1	1	39	1
AF Gleadall	1	2	1	29	27*	29.00	47.54	0	0	1	0
AL Hughes	14	27	1	737	103	28.34	46.49	1	5	98	2
MJJ Critchley	14	26	1	705	105	28.20	62.33	1	4	86	2
GC Wilson	8	14	1	357	66	27.46	48.11	0	2	39	2
TC Lace	4	8	0	219	43	27.37	36.80	0	0	33	0
HR Hosein	8	16	2	376	66*	26.85	41.91	0	3	43	0
BA Godleman	14	27	2	658	122	26.32	48.92	2	3	84	3
D Smit	4	8	2	129	45*	21.50	41.34	0	0	13	0
GC Viljoen	12	22	2	386	60*	19.30	70.05	0	1	41	16
AP Palladino	12	23	6	317	32	18.64	39.72	0	0	38	2
AK Dal	4	7	0	107	25	15.28	34.96	0	0	8	1
SM Ervine	2	4	0	51	26	12.75	34.22	0	0	5	0
CAJ Brodrick	1	2	0	19	19	9.50	26.76	0	0	2	0
D Olivier	7	11	2	78	40*	8.66	44.82	0	0	12	0
R Rampaul	8	11	5	51	18*	8.50	47.66	0	0	4	1
LH Ferguson	5	10	2	51	16	6.37	55.43	0	0	4	2
WS Davis	1	1	0	6	6	6.00	35.29	0	0	0	0
Hamidullah Qadri	4	8	2	33	15*	5.50	27.73	0	0	3	0
MK Andersson	1	2	0	11	11	5.50	26.19	0	0	1	0
MHA Footitt	1	2	1	0	0*	0.00	0.00	0	0	0	0

Bowling

	Overs	Mdns	Runs	Wkts	BBI	BBM	Ave	Econ	SR	5w	10w
MK Andersson	14.0	3	41	4	4/25	4/41	10.25	2.92	21.0	0	0
LM Reece	64.1	13	186	11	7/20	7/38	16.90	2.89	35.0	1	0
WS Davis	11.0	3	39	2	2/39	2/39	19.50	3.54	33.0	0	0
AP Palladino	369.0	94	1006	51	6/29	10/81	19.72	2.72	43.4	3	1
AL Hughes	87.0	19	255	10	4/57	4/79	25.50	2.93	52.2	0	0
D Olivier	251.3	47	852	31	5/20	10/125	27.48	3.38	48.6	2	1
GC Viljoen	356.1	55	1225	38	4/51	6/128	32.23	3.43	56.2	0	0
LH Ferguson	164.3	22	618	18	4/56	5/86	34.33	3.75	54.8	0	0
WL Madsen	42.4	9	152	4	1/9	1/9	38.00	3.56	64.0	0	0
MJJ Critchley	285.5	14	1218	32	6/106	10/194	38.06	4.26	53.5	1	1
Hamidullah Qadri	78.1	7	319	8	3/66	3/96	39.87	4.08	58.6	0	0
DM Wheeldon	13.0	2	48	1	1/12	1/48	48.00	3.69	78.0	0	0
R Rampaul	183.3	35	651	13	3/53	4/113	50.07	3.54	84.6	0	0
MHA Footitt	15.0	2	57	1	1/57	1/57	57.00	3.80	90.0	0	0
AF Gleadall	13.3	1	59	1	1/20	1/59	59.00	4.37	81.0	0	0

Catches/Stumpings:

25 Madsen, 11 Hosein (inc 1st), Smit, 9 Critchley, Hughes, Wilson, 8 Godleman, 7 Wilson, 4 Ferguson, 3 Slater, 2 Andersson, Brodrick, Dal, Ervine, Hosein, Qadri, Rampaul, Reece, 1 Footitt, Lace, Palladino, Viljoen

ROYAL LONDON ONE-DAY CUP AVERAGES 2018

Batting

	Mat	Inns	NO	Runs	HS	Ave	SR	100	50	4s	6s
BA Godleman	8	8	1	509	137	72.71	88.83	2	3	44	3
BT Slater	8	8	1	386	109*	55.14	101.31	1	2	45	5
LM Reece	5	5	1	174	92	43.50	88.32	0	2	19	0
WL Madsen	8	8	0	231	87	28.87	94.28	0	2	21	6
GC Wilson	6	6	1	137	49	27.40	82.03	0	0	8	3
D Smit	8	7	2	99	30	19.80	116.47	0	0	10	1
AL Hughes	8	7	1	114	47	19.00	110.67	0	0	11	4
D Olivier	8	5	3	35	23*	17.50	57.37	0	0	2	1
MJJ Critchley	8	7	0	100	35	14.28	78.74	0	0	9	2
GC Viljoen	7	6	2	56	50*	14.00	94.91	0	1	2	4
CAJ Brodrick	2	1	0	11	11	11.00	91.66	0	0	1	0
Hamidullah Qadri	2	1	0	4	4	4.00	50.00	0	0	1	0
SM Sharif	2	2	0	3	2	1.50	33.33	0	0	0	0
R Rampaul	8	3	3	4	4*	-	80.00	0	0	1	0

Bowling

	Overs	Mdns	Runs	Wkts	BBI	Ave	Econ	SR	4w	5w
D Olivier	53.0	3	247	13	3/31	19.00	4.66	24.4	0	0
WL Madsen	28.0	4	136	3	1/21	45.33	4.85	56.0	0	0
LM Reece	28.0	0	144	8	3/37	18.00	5.14	21.0	0	0
Hamidullah Qadri	10.0	1	60	1	1/31	60.00	6.00	60.0	0	0
AL Hughes	36.0	1	217	5	2/49	43.40	6.02	43.2	0	0
GC Viljoen	40.4	1	258	4	2/55	64.50	6.34	61.0	0	0
R Rampaul	56.0	3	375	13	5/48	28.84	6.69	25.8	0	1
MJJ Critchley	47.0	0	323	8	3/35	40.37	6.87	35.2	0	0
SM Sharif	11.3	0	93	3	2/31	31.00	8.08	23.0	0	0

Catches/Stumpings:
14 Smit, 5 Wilson, 3 Hughes, Madsen, 2 Brodrick, Olivier, Rampaul, Reece, Slater, Viljoen, 1 Critchley, Godleman, Qadri

VITALITY BLAST AVERAGES 2018

Batting

	Mat	Inns	NO	Runs	HS	Ave	SR	100	50	4s	6s
BA Godleman	9	8	2	309	77	51.50	125.10	0	3	25	7
WL Madsen	13	12	2	328	76*	32.80	142.60	0	3	41	6
CS MacLeod	13	12	0	324	104	27.00	121.80	1	0	37	7
GC Wilson	13	11	3	199	35	24.87	119.16	0	0	15	4
Wahab Riaz	12	8	0	152	53	19.00	138.18	0	1	17	7
MJJ Critchley	13	11	2	154	38*	17.11	121.25	0	0	15	3
AL Hughes	13	8	4	67	18	16.75	124.07	0	0	3	2
AK Dal	9	8	2	94	35	15.66	122.07	0	0	7	2
D Smit	4	3	0	44	28	14.66	118.91	0	0	5	0
GC Viljoen	10	6	1	56	32	11.20	130.23	0	0	5	2
BT Slater	5	5	0	53	33	10.60	126.19	0	0	7	1
LH Ferguson	13	4	3	5	5*	5.00	100.00	0	0	0	0
R Rampaul	13	3	3	12	8*	-	171.42	0	0	2	0
MH McKiernan	1	1	1	1	1*	-	100.00	0	0	0	0
HM Nicholls	1	-	-	-	-	-	-	-	-	-	-
SM Sharif	1	-	-	-	-	-	-	-	-	-	-

Bowling

	Overs	Mdns	Runs	Wkts	BBI	Ave	Econ	SR	4w	5w
LH Ferguson	48.0	0	319	16	4/26	19.93	6.64	18.0	1	0
MH McKiernan	4.0	0	27	0	-	-	6.75	-	0	0
Wahab Riaz	43.0	1	313	15	3/27	20.86	7.27	17.2	0	0
GC Viljoen	35.0	0	270	13	3/25	20.76	7.71	16.1	0	0
AL Hughes	40.0	0	324	17	4/42	19.05	8.10	14.1	1	0
SM Sharif	3.0	0	25	0	-	-	8.33	-	0	0
R Rampaul	41.5	0	359	14	4/19	25.64	8.58	17.9	1	0
MJJ Critchley	14.4	0	150	4	2/15	37.50	10.22	22.0	0	0
WL Madsen	9.0	0	98	1	1/20	98.00	10.88	54.0	0	0

Catches/Stumpings:
11 Wilson, 8 MacLeod, 5 Critchley, Ferguson, 4 Dal, Hughes, Rampaul, 3 Madsen,
2 Godleman, Riaz, Smit (1st), Viljoen

DURHAM

FORMED: 1882
HOME GROUND: Emirates Riverside, Chester-le-Street
CAPTAIN: TBC
2018 RESULTS: CC2: 8/10; RL50: 9/9 North Group; T20: Quarter-finalists
HONOURS: Championship: (3) 2008, 2009, 2013; Gillette/NatWest/C&G/FP Trophy: 2007; Pro40/National League/ CB40/YB40/RL50: 2014

THE LOWDOWN

In trying times, it was something for Durham to have avoided the Championship wooden spoon last summer, and there was an uplifting run to the T20 knockout stages. Little more can be expected in 2019, when the club will be without two pillars of the north-east: Paul Collingwood, who retired after 22 seasons at Chester-le-Street, and Geoff Cook, who stood down as director of cricket to end a 27-year association with Durham. Cook's replacement is the ex-Australia batsman Marcus North, with former New Zealand and Middlesex allrounder James Franklin heading the coaching staff. Their main task is to develop, and keep hold of, the club's emerging players. Among them are Cameron Steel, their only batsman to pass 500 Championship runs last summer, and Gareth Harte, who scored his first two hundreds in first-class cricket. The departure of Kiwi international Tom Latham is cushioned by the arrival of Cameron Bancroft, who will not be short of incentive as he returns from his ball-tampering ban ahead of this summer's Ashes. The bowling looks capable, with Chris Rushworth still going strong and Matt Salisbury enjoying a breakthrough season in 2018. Seamer Ben Raine, who has re-signed from Leicestershire, is an excellent addition. As for Mark Wood, who knows?

IN: Alex Lees (Yor), Ben Raine (Lei), Cameron Bancroft (Aus), D'Arcy Short (Aus, T20)
OUT: Ryan Davies, Barry McCarthy (both REL), Paul Collingwood (RET)

DIRECTOR OF CRICKET: MARCUS NORTH

North, who turns 40 in July, played 21 Tests for Australia as well as scoring over 4,000 first-class runs for six different counties, including a successful season for Durham in 2004. He spent the past three seasons as CEO at South Northumberland CC. Jon Lewis has left after six rollercoaster seasons as head coach, with James Franklin taking the role of lead high performance coach as part of a structural overhaul overseen by North.

COUNTY CHAMPIONSHIP AVERAGES 2018

Batting

	Mat	Inns	NO	Runs	HS	Ave	SR	100	50	4s	6s
TWM Latham	4	8	0	366	147	45.75	44.36	1	2	46	0
WJ Weighell	3	5	0	185	84	37.00	72.83	0	1	16	4
CT Steel	12	22	0	638	160	29.00	37.46	1	4	69	0
GJ Harte	8	15	0	382	114	25.46	41.61	2	0	39	0
SW Poynter	11	20	1	475	170	25.00	67.09	1	1	58	0
AK Markram	3	5	0	124	94	24.80	59.61	0	1	20	0
AR Patel	4	7	1	147	95*	24.50	80.32	0	1	18	2
AZ Lees	6	11	0	256	69	23.27	52.24	0	1	40	0
MA Wood	4	7	2	115	61*	23.00	50.43	0	1	18	0
NJ Rimmington	7	13	1	255	61	21.25	62.96	0	1	34	2
WR Smith	9	17	0	357	90	21.00	44.18	0	2	49	0
MJ Richardson	10	18	0	377	115	20.94	53.78	1	1	44	0
G Clark	12	22	0	460	64	20.90	48.47	0	2	70	0
RD Pringle	1	2	0	37	34	18.50	61.66	0	0	6	0
PD Collingwood	11	20	0	299	47	14.95	50.42	0	0	39	2
BJ McCarthy	6	11	1	111	43	11.10	40.65	0	0	12	0
J Coughlin	2	4	0	42	19	10.50	36.20	0	0	5	0
MET Salisbury	10	19	5	141	37	10.07	29.87	0	0	14	0
C Rushworth	12	22	12	72	11*	7.20	48.97	0	0	10	0
MA Jones	1	2	0	13	10	6.50	28.26	0	0	2	0
BA Stokes	1	2	0	12	9	6.00	26.08	0	0	1	0
RC Davies	3	6	0	27	20	4.50	40.29	0	0	4	0

Bowling

	Overs	Mdns	Runs	Wkts	BBI	BBM	Ave	Econ	SR	5w	10w
AR Patel	99.4	33	235	18	7/54	9/130	13.05	2.35	33.2	1	0
BA Stokes	43.0	11	118	8	5/52	8/118	14.75	2.74	32.2	1	0
MA Wood	109.1	24	293	17	6/46	8/117	17.23	2.68	38.5	2	0
PD Collingwood	49.0	15	116	6	2/25	2/25	19.33	2.36	49.0	0	0
C Rushworth	386.4	83	1201	60	8/51	12/100	20.01	3.10	38.6	3	1
WJ Weighell	108.3	23	304	15	7/32	9/138	20.26	2.80	43.4	1	0
CT Steel	46.2	4	202	9	2/7	4/99	22.44	4.35	30.8	0	0
RD Pringle	28.0	2	74	3	3/31	3/74	24.66	2.64	56.0	0	0
MET Salisbury	293.1	54	1090	44	6/37	7/107	24.77	3.71	39.9	1	0
G Clark	13.5	0	51	2	1/10	1/10	25.50	3.68	41.5	0	0
BJ McCarthy	130.3	21	460	14	4/58	6/108	32.85	3.52	55.9	0	0
MJ Potts	5.0	0	37	1	1/37	1/37	37.00	7.40	30.0	0	0
J Coughlin	35.0	3	139	3	2/31	2/49	46.33	3.97	70.0	0	0
GJ Harte	45.1	7	148	3	2/26	2/26	49.33	3.27	90.3	0	0
WR Smith	66.1	6	204	4	2/10	2/33	51.00	3.08	99.2	0	0
MW Dixon	28.2	6	108	2	2/99	2/108	54.00	3.81	85.0	0	0
NJ Rimmington	167.4	34	606	11	3/39	4/67	55.09	3.61	91.4	0	0

Catches/Stumpings:
35 Poynter (inc 1st), 12 Collingwood, 9 Clark, Steel, 8 Latham, 7 Davies, 5 Smith, 4 Harte, Markram, 3 Lees, Richardson, 2 McCarthy, Rushworth, Stokes, 1 Coughlin, Patel, Pringle, Rimmington, Salisbury, Weighell, Wood

ROYAL LONDON ONE-DAY CUP AVERAGES 2018

Batting

	Mat	Inns	NO	Runs	HS	Ave	SR	100	50	4s	6s
MJ Richardson	8	8	0	392	111	49.00	82.35	1	2	35	2
BJ McCarthy	1	1	0	43	43	43.00	87.75	0	0	2	1
GJ Harte	5	5	1	140	48	35.00	85.36	0	0	12	2
WR Smith	8	8	0	266	119	33.25	80.60	1	0	21	1
TWM Latham	8	8	0	255	86	31.87	80.18	0	2	23	2
NJ Rimmington	6	6	3	72	22	24.00	90.00	0	0	5	1
C Rushworth	5	4	2	35	16*	17.50	97.22	0	0	2	2
G Clark	8	8	0	131	45	16.37	64.53	0	0	19	0
MJ Potts	2	2	0	31	30	15.50	62.00	0	0	3	0
SW Poynter	8	8	0	110	36	13.75	79.71	0	0	9	0
WJ Weighell	2	2	0	26	23	13.00	78.78	0	0	2	0
CT Steel	4	4	0	49	24	12.25	55.05	0	0	5	0
RD Pringle	8	8	0	77	30	9.62	81.05	0	0	7	0
PD Collingwood	3	3	0	19	12	6.33	50.00	0	0	3	0
MA Wood	2	2	0	6	6	3.00	42.85	0	0	0	0
MW Dixon	5	3	2	1	1	1.00	33.33	0	0	0	0
MET Salisbury	1	1	0	1	1	1.00	25.00	0	0	0	0
RC Davies	1	1	1	61	61*	-	108.92	0	1	6	1
GHI Harding	3	2	2	3	3*	-	27.27	0	0	0	0

Bowling

	Overs	Mdns	Runs	Wkts	BBI	Ave	Econ	SR	4w	5w
C Rushworth	45.3	3	202	9	3/39	22.44	4.43	30.3	0	0
RD Pringle	53.0	1	236	4	2/39	59.00	4.45	79.5	0	0
G Clark	4.0	1	18	3	3/18	6.00	4.50	8.0	0	0
PD Collingwood	25.0	0	124	1	1/56	124.00	4.96	150.0	0	0
WR Smith	27.0	0	143	2	2/33	71.50	5.29	81.0	0	0
GJ Harte	17.0	1	91	3	2/35	30.33	5.35	34.0	0	0
NJ Rimmington	53.0	2	295	9	3/36	32.77	5.56	35.3	0	0
MA Wood	20.0	1	114	1	1/52	114.00	5.70	120.0	0	0
MET Salisbury	7.0	0	45	0	-	-	6.42	-	0	0
MW Dixon	43.4	0	296	9	3/42	32.88	6.77	29.1	0	0
GHI Harding	26.0	0	180	2	1/44	90.00	6.92	78.0	0	0
WJ Weighell	19.0	1	133	2	2/59	66.50	7.00	57.0	0	0
BJ McCarthy	7.2	0	54	0	-	-	7.36	-	0	0
MJ Potts	10.0	0	83	3	3/69	27.66	8.30	20.0	0	0

Catches/Stumpings:
7 Poynter (1st), 4 Richardson, 3 Rushworth, 2 Clark, Latham, Pringle, Rimmington, Smith, 1 Collingwood, Dixon, Potts, Steel, Wood

VITALITY BLAST AVERAGES 2018

Batting

	Mat	Inns	NO	Runs	HS	Ave	SR	100	50	4s	6s
BA Stokes	4	4	1	177	90*	59.00	138.28	0	1	20	6
SW Poynter	14	10	6	177	31	44.25	131.11	0	0	14	2
TWM Latham	14	14	1	470	98*	36.15	136.62	0	4	43	16
G Clark	14	14	0	408	65	29.14	139.72	0	3	49	10
PD Collingwood	12	12	2	257	50*	25.70	112.71	0	1	16	7
RD Pringle	6	4	1	75	35	25.00	125.00	0	0	8	2
WR Smith	11	11	2	154	37*	17.11	111.59	0	0	9	5
RC Davies	13	11	3	136	27	17.00	146.23	0	0	11	6
MA Wood	3	3	1	33	17*	16.50	86.84	0	0	2	0
NJ Rimmington	14	6	4	32	14*	16.00	118.51	0	0	1	1
WJ Weighell	12	10	3	85	28	12.14	130.76	0	0	2	6
L Trevaskis	8	7	1	54	26	9.00	108.00	0	0	3	2
C Rushworth	13	1	0	2	2	2.00	40.00	0	0	0	0
BJ McCarthy	2	1	1	7	7*	-	175.00	0	0	1	0
BG Whitehead	6	1	1	2	2*	-	66.66	0	0	0	0
Imran Tahir	8	-	-	-	-	-	-	-	-	-	-

Bowling

	Overs	Mdns	Runs	Wkts	BBI	Ave	Econ	SR	4w	5w
BA Stokes	4.0	0	16	4	4/16	4.00	4.00	6.0	1	0
L Trevaskis	7.0	0	37	4	4/16	9.25	5.28	10.5	1	0
MA Wood	12.0	0	76	5	2/22	15.20	6.33	14.4	0	0
Imran Tahir	32.0	0	203	15	4/14	13.53	6.34	12.8	2	0
WR Smith	16.0	1	107	5	2/20	21.40	6.68	19.2	0	0
BG Whitehead	20.0	0	144	5	2/23	28.80	7.20	24.0	0	0
C Rushworth	43.0	0	326	11	3/22	29.63	7.58	23.4	0	0
PD Collingwood	42.0	0	324	10	3/25	32.40	7.71	25.2	0	0
BJ McCarthy	7.0	0	55	4	4/31	13.75	7.85	10.5	1	0
NJ Rimmington	45.3	1	408	22	4/28	18.54	8.96	12.4	1	0
WJ Weighell	36.0	0	328	13	2/7	25.23	9.11	16.6	0	0
RD Pringle	6.0	0	57	2	1/17	28.50	9.50	18.0	0	0
G Clark	0.2	0	8	0	-	-	24.00	-	0	0

Catches/Stumpings:

16 Poynter (3st), 11 Latham, 9 Clark, Trevaskis, Weighell, 5 Collingwood, Davies, 4 Smith, 3 Pringle, Whitehead, 2 Rimmington, Tahir, 1 Rushworth, Stokes, Wood

ESSEX

FORMED: 1876
HOME GROUND: The Cloudfm County Ground, Chelmsford
ONE-DAY NAME: Essex Eagles
CAPTAIN: Ryan ten Doeschate
2018 RESULTS: CC1: 3/8; RL50: Quarter-finalists; T20: 7/9 South Group
HONOURS: Championship: (7) 1979, 1983, 1984, 1986, 1991, 1992, 2017; Gillette/NatWest/C&G/FP Trophy: (3) 1985, 1997, 2008; Benson & Hedges Cup: (2) 1979, 1998; Pro40/National League/CB40/YB40/RL50: (2) 2005, 2006; Sunday League: (3) 1981, 1984, 1985

THE LOWDOWN

Winning the Championship can leave quite a hangover – just ask Middlesex – but Essex finished comfortably in the top three last summer and produced a thrilling victory at The Oval to deny the champions an unbeaten record. The rivalry with Surrey is shaping up very nicely. The Porter-Harmer axis was irresistible again in 2018 (262 wickets between them across the last two seasons), while 21-year-old seamer Sam Cook is rising fast. Peter Siddle, who signed a two-year contract in September, completes a potent attack. Runs were harder to come by, though Essex were hardly alone in that regard. Alastair Cook's decision to play on until at least 2021 will have sent a chill through county bowlers. For such a multi-dimensional side, the Eagles' annual T20 failure is a mystery; they won two of 14 matches in 2018. Varun Chopra led the way with 503 runs – to go with 528 in the One-Day Cup – but, Adam Zampa apart, the bowling was a collective failure. Thus the return of Zampa and Mohammad Amir is welcome. For the first time this century Essex will be without James Foster, who retired after the club did not renew his contract.

IN: Peter Siddle (Aus), Mohammad Amir (Pak, T20), Cameron Delport (Lei, T20), Adam Zampa (Aus, T20)
OUT: Matt Dixon, Callum Taylor, Ashar Zaidi (all REL), James Foster (RET)

HEAD COACH: ANTHONY MCGRATH

McGrath helped deliver back-to-back titles in Division Two and Division One as assistant coach and took over the reins in 2017 after Chris Silverwood's appointment as England bowling coach. McGrath spent an 18-year playing career at Yorkshire, for whom he scored more than 23,000 runs and took 240 wickets in all formats. He played four Tests and 14 ODIs for England. Former South Africa and Essex fast bowler Andre Nel has replaced Dimitri Mascarenhas as assistant coach.

COUNTY CHAMPIONSHIP AVERAGES 2018

Batting

	Mat	Inns	NO	Runs	HS	Ave	SR	100	50	4s	6s
M Vijay	3	5	0	323	100	64.60	62.59	1	3	48	1
RS Bopara	13	22	4	751	133*	41.72	53.49	2	4	87	4
RN ten Doeschate	12	20	2	680	173*	37.77	64.63	1	4	84	6
AN Cook	6	11	0	412	96	37.45	54.93	0	4	63	0
AJA Wheater	8	13	3	340	68*	34.00	57.14	0	3	44	1
T Westley	13	23	1	687	134	31.22	47.41	2	2	106	0
SR Harmer	13	20	3	460	102*	27.05	60.76	1	1	54	3
N Wagner	3	4	1	80	37	26.66	70.79	0	0	10	4
MR Quinn	3	5	4	26	16	26.00	32.91	0	0	5	0
NLJ Browne	10	17	0	414	86	24.35	43.94	0	3	69	0
JS Foster	4	7	0	165	69	23.57	59.13	0	1	22	1
DW Lawrence	12	21	1	468	124	23.40	45.13	1	1	57	3
PM Siddle	7	11	2	158	33*	17.55	61.24	0	0	14	4
V Chopra	7	13	0	201	61	15.46	45.89	0	1	30	0
SJ Cook	10	11	7	56	14	14.00	45.90	0	0	7	0
MS Pepper	2	4	0	53	22	13.25	42.06	0	0	7	0
PI Walter	1	2	0	21	14	10.50	48.83	0	0	2	0
MT Coles	4	5	1	37	10*	9.25	60.65	0	0	5	0
JA Porter	13	17	3	88	31	6.28	25.95	0	0	12	0

Bowling

	Overs	Mdns	Runs	Wkts	BBI	BBM	Ave	Econ	SR	5w	10w
PM Siddle	234.4	47	607	37	5/37	8/72	16.40	2.58	38.0	3	0
PI Walter	11.0	1	39	2	2/21	2/39	19.50	3.54	33.0	0	0
T Westley	26.0	9	65	3	1/0	1/1	21.66	2.50	52.0	0	0
SR Harmer	526.2	136	1394	57	6/87	7/69	24.45	2.64	55.4	3	0
JA Porter	432.3	81	1429	58	7/41	11/98	24.63	3.30	44.7	3	1
SJ Cook	219.3	60	684	27	5/28	5/84	25.33	3.11	48.7	1	0
MR Quinn	101.0	19	306	12	3/23	5/75	25.50	3.02	50.5	0	0
MT Coles	124.0	27	393	13	5/123	5/123	30.23	3.16	57.2	1	0
RS Bopara	80.2	9	304	9	3/30	3/36	33.77	3.78	53.5	0	0
N Wagner	109.0	9	421	9	3/122	4/178	46.77	3.86	72.6	0	0
NLJ Browne	1.0	0	4	0	-	-	-	4.00	-	0	0
DW Lawrence	3.0	0	15	0	-	-	-	5.00	-	0	0

Catches/Stumpings:

24 Wheater (inc 1st), 14 Foster (inc 1st), 13 Harmer, ten Doeschate, 10 Lawrence, 8 Bopara, Browne, 7 Chopra, 6 A Cook, 3 Wagner, 2 Porter, Westley, 1 Coles, S Cook, Vijay

ROYAL LONDON ONE-DAY CUP AVERAGES 2018

Batting

	Mat	Inns	NO	Runs	HS	Ave	SR	100	50	4s	6s
V Chopra	9	9	1	528	160	66.00	86.98	1	3	45	13
RS Bopara	9	8	1	401	125	57.28	95.93	1	4	26	9
T Westley	9	9	1	387	134	48.37	99.23	1	3	37	7
AJA Wheater	9	9	0	390	88	43.33	97.25	0	4	44	4
Ashar Zaidi	8	7	1	188	82	31.33	101.07	0	2	16	5
DW Lawrence	9	8	0	241	115	30.12	88.92	1	0	16	4
RN ten Doeschate	8	7	2	112	28	22.40	99.11	0	0	11	2
MT Coles	4	2	1	20	13	20.00	117.64	0	0	1	1
SR Harmer	9	7	4	50	34*	16.66	100.00	0	0	3	1
N Wagner	8	3	0	36	35	12.00	90.00	0	0	1	2
AN Cook	1	1	0	11	11	11.00	50.00	0	0	2	0
SJ Cook	8	2	1	2	1*	2.00	100.00	0	0	0	0
S Snater	3	2	2	12	9*	-	133.33	0	0	2	0
JA Porter	5	1	1	2	2*	-	20.00	0	0	0	0

Bowling

	Overs	Mdns	Runs	Wkts	BBI	Ave	Econ	SR	4w	5w
SJ Cook	66.0	3	278	5	1/21	55.60	4.21	79.2	0	0
JA Porter	40.1	3	170	12	4/29	14.16	4.23	20.0	2	0
RN ten Doeschate	9.0	0	42	3	2/23	14.00	4.66	18.0	0	0
Ashar Zaidi	44.0	0	209	2	2/32	104.50	4.75	132.0	0	0
SR Harmer	63.0	1	339	7	2/38	48.42	5.38	54.0	0	0
MT Coles	34.3	3	188	9	3/41	20.88	5.44	23.0	0	0
RS Bopara	71.2	4	404	11	3/30	36.72	5.66	38.9	0	0
N Wagner	70.0	0	445	12	3/40	37.08	6.35	35.0	0	0
S Snater	17.3	0	134	5	5/60	26.80	7.65	21.0	0	1
DW Lawrence	8.0	0	72	0	-	-	9.00	-	0	0

Catches/Stumpings:
13 Wheater (inc 1st), 4 Bopara, Harmer, ten Doeschate, 3 Snater, Zaidi, 2 Chopra, Lawrence, Wagner, 1 Coles, S Cook, Westley

VITALITY BLAST AVERAGES 2018

Batting

	Mat	Inns	NO	Runs	HS	Ave	SR	100	50	4s	6s
MS Pepper	4	3	2	53	27	53.00	98.14	0	0	5	0
V Chopra	13	13	0	503	67	38.69	128.97	0	6	42	16
Ashar Zaidi	6	5	2	95	24*	31.66	163.79	0	0	11	3
DW Lawrence	9	9	1	233	86	29.12	157.43	0	1	17	9
RS Bopara	13	12	3	240	45*	26.66	157.89	0	0	14	11
N Wagner	3	3	1	43	16*	21.50	215.00	0	0	5	2
T Westley	6	6	0	124	26	20.66	119.23	0	0	12	2
RN ten Doeschate	12	11	0	216	43	19.63	127.81	0	0	15	6
AJA Wheater	13	13	0	250	45	19.23	152.43	0	0	32	8
PI Walter	7	7	0	128	40	18.28	143.82	0	0	15	4
MT Coles	8	6	2	45	19	11.25	136.36	0	0	6	0
SR Harmer	13	10	1	98	15	10.88	144.11	0	0	4	6
A Zampa	10	7	4	13	4*	4.33	72.22	0	0	0	0
JA Porter	7	4	3	4	1*	4.00	66.66	0	0	0	0
SJ Cook	7	2	1	0	0*	0.00	0.00	0	0	0	0
PM Siddle	6	2	0	0	0	0.00	0.00	0	0	0	0
ASS Nijjar	1	-	-	-	-	-	-	-	-	-	-
MR Quinn	4	-	-	-	-	-	-	-	-	-	-
S Snater	1	-	-	-	-	-	-	-	-	-	-

Bowling

	Overs	Mdns	Runs	Wkts	BBI	Ave	Econ	SR	4w	5w
JA Porter	22.2	0	171	3	2/26	57.00	7.65	44.6	0	0
A Zampa	31.3	0	249	12	3/17	20.75	7.90	15.7	0	0
Ashar Zaidi	10.0	0	86	2	2/27	43.00	8.60	30.0	0	0
SR Harmer	29.0	0	257	7	2/43	36.71	8.86	24.8	0	0
RS Bopara	27.0	0	253	5	2/26	50.60	9.37	32.4	0	0
PM Siddle	16.0	0	152	3	1/21	50.66	9.50	32.0	0	0
SJ Cook	19.0	0	184	4	1/27	46.00	9.68	28.5	0	0
ASS Nijjar	3.0	0	30	1	1/30	30.00	10.00	18.0	0	0
N Wagner	7.0	0	75	3	2/50	25.00	10.71	14.0	0	0
MT Coles	22.5	0	263	5	2/33	52.60	11.51	27.4	0	0
PI Walter	6.0	0	70	0	-	-	11.66	-	0	0
MR Quinn	9.0	0	126	4	3/61	31.50	14.00	13.5	0	0
S Snater	3.0	0	42	1	1/42	42.00	14.00	18.0	0	0
RN ten Doeschate	2.0	0	28	0	-	-	14.00	-	0	0

Catches/Stumpings:
13 Wheater (inc 2st), 8 Harmer, 5 Lawrence, 2 Bopara, Chopra, Coles, Siddle, Walter, Zampa,
1 Pepper, Porter, Snater, Zaidi

GLAMORGAN

FORMED: 1888
HOME GROUND: Sophia Gardens, Cardiff
CAPTAIN: Chris Cooke (Championship and RL50), Colin Ingram (T20)
2018 RESULTS: CC2: 10/10; RL50: 9/9 South Group; T20: 6/9 South Group
HONOURS: Championship: (3) 1948, 1969, 1997; Pro40/National League/ CB40/YB40/ RL50: (2) 2002, 2004; Sunday League: 1993

THE LOWDOWN

Something had to give after a season in which Glamorgan finished bottom of Division Two – by 34 points – and bottom of their One-Day Cup group, losing 17 of 22 matches across both formats. Robert Croft has gone after three difficult years as coach, with Matthew Maynard stepping in on an interim basis, and former captain Mark Wallace is the new director of cricket, leaving Hugh Morris to focus on his role as chief executive. Chris Cooke has replaced Michael Hogan as the Championship and 50-over captain. Glamorgan's faith in homegrown youngsters is admirable but patience is wearing thin – no batsman who played more than four Championship matches averaged 30 last summer and there were only six hundreds in all, three of them by Usman Khawaja. Aneurin Donald, once the great hope of Welsh cricket, is starting afresh at Hampshire while Shaun Marsh's availability is uncertain. The bowling was the problem in 50-over cricket but that department will be boosted by a fit-again Marchant de Lange. Yorkshire-born Charlie Hemphrey, who resurrected his career in Australia after playing Second XI county cricket, will add depth to the batting. Colin Ingram, bought by Delhi Capitals for this year's IPL, will skipper the side in the T20 Blast but is not expected to appear in four-day or 50-over cricket.

IN: Billy Root (Not), Charlie Hemphrey (unattached)
OUT: Aneurin Donald (Ham)

HEAD COACH: MATTHEW MAYNARD

Maynard had a three-year spell as Glamorgan coach between 2008 and 2010 and returned as a batting consultant last season following a stint as Somerset's director of cricket. His appointment is on an interim basis, with a long-term replacement for Robert Croft to be sought after the season. A dashing batsman for Glamorgan during a 20-year career, Maynard made a club-record 54 centuries and was a key figure in the side that won the County Championship in 1997. He played four Tests and 14 ODIs.

COUNTY CHAMPIONSHIP AVERAGES 2018

Batting

	Mat	Inns	NO	Runs	HS	Ave	SR	100	50	4s	6s
UT Khawaja	4	8	0	420	126	52.50	72.16	3	0	58	5
M de Lange	3	5	1	142	90	35.50	103.64	0	2	6	10
DL Lloyd	10	18	2	474	119	29.62	64.31	1	1	69	5
SE Marsh	4	7	0	203	111	29.00	58.16	1	1	30	1
JR Murphy	12	23	2	533	80	25.38	40.50	0	2	81	0
CB Cooke	14	26	1	606	69	24.24	55.09	0	4	87	2
KS Carlson	13	25	1	567	152	23.62	57.21	1	1	87	0
CAJ Meschede	4	8	1	151	55	21.57	49.50	0	2	22	1
RAJ Smith	7	14	2	246	52*	20.50	67.58	0	1	42	2
NJ Selman	12	23	0	403	42	17.52	43.00	0	0	53	0
T van der Gugten	10	18	5	217	60*	16.69	57.86	0	2	33	0
KA Bull	4	8	3	76	30	15.20	18.40	0	0	8	0
SC Cook	4	8	0	120	36	15.00	44.28	0	0	13	0
AO Morgan	3	6	0	89	36	14.83	28.16	0	0	12	0
AG Salter	10	17	3	204	72*	14.57	43.40	0	1	26	2
P Sisodiya	2	4	1	41	38	13.66	54.66	0	0	6	0
GG Wagg	4	8	0	102	33	12.75	48.11	0	0	12	2
MG Hogan	13	21	8	152	28	11.69	77.15	0	0	14	8
AHT Donald	4	7	1	67	27	11.16	55.37	0	0	9	1
JL Lawlor	3	6	0	49	21	8.16	29.16	0	0	5	0
CR Brown	6	12	0	95	33	7.91	28.70	0	0	13	0
LJ Carey	6	8	0	58	28	7.25	63.73	0	0	7	3
TN Cullen	2	4	0	29	20	7.25	32.22	0	0	4	0

Bowling

	Overs	Mdns	Runs	Wkts	BBI	BBM	Ave	Econ	SR	5w	10w
P Sisodiya	63.2	12	151	7	3/54	5/73	21.57	2.38	54.2	0	0
T van der Gugten	287.0	69	936	43	7/42	8/71	21.76	3.26	40.0	2	0
MG Hogan	393.3	101	1014	45	5/49	8/102	22.53	2.57	52.4	2	0
M de Lange	114.4	22	383	16	5/62	8/160	23.93	3.34	43.0	1	0
KA Bull	85.4	14	278	11	3/36	4/69	25.27	3.24	46.7	0	0
JL Lawlor	29.1	3	110	4	3/59	3/59	27.50	3.77	43.7	0	0
RAJ Smith	155.3	24	593	20	5/87	7/148	29.65	3.81	46.6	1	0
GG Wagg	82.4	13	258	8	3/25	3/52	32.25	3.12	62.0	0	0
CAJ Meschede	76.0	8	327	9	2/30	4/85	36.33	4.30	50.6	0	0
DL Lloyd	105.3	19	343	9	2/31	2/16	38.11	3.25	70.3	0	0
AG Salter	245.0	45	759	18	4/80	6/145	42.16	3.09	81.6	0	0
LJ Carey	172.0	36	592	13	4/105	7/177	45.53	3.44	79.3	0	0
JR Murphy	16.3	2	73	1	1/41	1/41	73.00	4.42	99.0	0	0
KS Carlson	1.0	0	5	0	-	-	-	5.00	-	0	0
NJ Selman	1.0	0	6	0	-	-	-	6.00	-	0	0
AO Morgan	12.1	2	46	0	-	-	-	3.78	-	0	0

Catches/Stumpings:

42 Cooke (inc 1st), 21 Selman, 8 Salter, 7 Hogan, 5 Carlson, 4 Murphy, 3 Brown, Cook, Lawlor, Lloyd, 2 Bull, Cullen, Donald, Khawaja, van der Gugten, 1 de Lange, Marsh, Morgan, Sisodiya, Smith

ROYAL LONDON ONE-DAY CUP AVERAGES 2018

GLAMORGAN

Batting

	Mat	Inns	NO	Runs	HS	Ave	SR	100	50	4s	6s
CA Ingram	8	8	1	402	95*	57.42	98.04	0	3	35	11
CR Brown	3	3	0	163	98	54.33	63.67	0	1	16	1
KS Carlson	3	3	1	93	59*	46.50	113.41	0	1	9	5
SE Marsh	4	4	0	143	57	35.75	78.57	0	1	17	1
GG Wagg	8	7	0	210	49	30.00	106.06	0	0	12	11
NJ Selman	8	8	0	236	92	29.50	68.80	0	1	24	0
DL Lloyd	8	8	0	233	92	29.12	86.94	0	1	16	6
CB Cooke	8	7	0	168	59	24.00	79.24	0	1	9	4
M de Lange	3	3	0	60	40	20.00	133.33	0	0	3	3
AHT Donald	6	6	0	115	48	19.16	86.46	0	0	16	1
AG Salter	8	7	1	89	43	14.83	100.00	0	0	5	3
RAJ Smith	3	3	0	37	14	12.33	108.82	0	0	3	1
LJ Carey	7	5	3	23	12	11.50	76.66	0	0	3	0
T van der Gugten	7	6	3	29	19*	9.66	96.66	0	0	4	0
JR Murphy	2	2	0	19	10	9.50	52.77	0	0	3	0
MG Hogan	2	2	2	5	4*	-	100.00	0	0	0	0

Bowling

	Overs	Mdns	Runs	Wkts	BBI	Ave	Econ	SR	4w	5w
MG Hogan	19.0	0	93	0	-	-	4.89	-	0	0
GG Wagg	63.0	0	348	9	2/33	38.66	5.52	42.0	0	0
LJ Carey	57.4	2	321	5	2/57	64.20	5.56	69.2	0	0
CA Ingram	39.4	0	221	4	3/24	55.25	5.57	59.5	0	0
AG Salter	63.0	1	358	6	2/50	59.66	5.68	63.0	0	0
DL Lloyd	25.0	0	154	2	1/17	77.00	6.16	75.0	0	0
T van der Gugten	49.2	1	316	6	3/58	52.66	6.40	49.3	0	0
RAJ Smith	17.2	0	114	2	2/41	57.00	6.57	52.0	0	0
M de Lange	26.0	1	221	5	3/65	44.20	8.50	31.2	0	0
KS Carlson	2.0	0	17	0	-	-	8.50	-	0	0

Catches/Stumpings:
11 Cooke (inc 1st), 4 Lloyd, 3 Donald, Ingram, 2 Salter, Selman, 1 Brown, Carey, de Lange, Wagg

VITALITY BLAST AVERAGES 2018

Batting

	Mat	Inns	NO	Runs	HS	Ave	SR	100	50	4s	6s
CA Ingram	11	11	3	430	89	53.75	164.75	0	3	40	23
KS Carlson	11	11	1	295	58	29.50	143.20	0	1	27	10
CAJ Meschede	12	10	1	247	77*	27.44	153.41	0	1	18	15
CB Cooke	13	12	3	238	60*	26.44	147.82	0	1	15	13
MG Hogan	13	4	3	25	17*	25.00	113.63	0	0	1	1
DL Lloyd	7	6	1	122	39	24.40	112.96	0	0	6	4
UT Khawaja	7	7	0	168	44	24.00	136.58	0	0	25	3
T van der Gugten	13	6	4	43	21*	21.50	143.33	0	0	1	2
RAJ Smith	9	5	3	42	22*	21.00	150.00	0	0	2	4
GG Wagg	13	10	2	130	53*	16.25	144.44	0	1	10	5
AHT Donald	13	13	0	206	37	15.84	138.25	0	0	18	10
NJ Selman	4	3	1	28	16	14.00	147.36	0	0	1	2
SE Marsh	2	2	0	25	15	12.50	78.12	0	0	3	0
AG Salter	13	10	3	66	21	9.42	120.00	0	0	4	4
JA Burns	2	2	0	6	5	3.00	50.00	0	0	0	0

Bowling

	Overs	Mdns	Runs	Wkts	BBI	Ave	Econ	SR	4w	5w
DL Lloyd	1.0	0	6	1	1/6	6.00	6.00	6.0	0	0
KS Carlson	0.1	0	1	0	-	-	6.00	-	0	0
RAJ Smith	26.0	1	195	9	4/6	21.66	7.50	17.3	1	0
AG Salter	37.0	1	285	11	3/34	25.90	7.70	20.1	0	0
CA Ingram	18.5	0	151	4	2/15	37.75	8.01	28.2	0	0
GG Wagg	37.5	0	331	14	2/17	23.64	8.74	16.2	0	0
MG Hogan	46.0	0	416	13	3/31	32.00	9.04	21.2	0	0
CAJ Meschede	31.0	0	288	6	3/21	48.00	9.29	31.0	0	0
T van der Gugten	42.4	1	427	19	4/31	22.47	10.00	13.4	1	0

Catches/Stumpings:
13 Cooke (inc 3st), 10 Donald, 6 Carlson, van der Gugten, 5 Hogan, 4 Lloyd, Salter, Smith, 3 Ingram, 2 Wagg, 1 Khawaja, Meschede, Selman

GLOUCESTERSHIRE

FORMED: 1871
HOME GROUND: The Brightside Ground, Bristol
CAPTAIN: Chris Dent (Championship and RL50), Michael Klinger (T20)
2018 RESULTS: CC2: 5/10; RL50: 7/9 South Group; T20: Quarter-finalists
HONOURS: Gillette/NatWest/C&G/FP Trophy: (5) 1973, 1999, 2000, 2003, 2004; Benson & Hedges Cup: (3) 1977, 1999, 2000; Pro40/National League/CB40/YB40/RL50: (2) 2000, 2015

THE LOWDOWN

Something appears to be brewing at Gloucestershire, another county making the most of thin resources. Last year a number of their protegés caught the eye: James Bracey (21) scored nearly 800 Championship runs in his first full season; Miles Hammond (23) made an astonishing transition from off-spinner to opening bat; George Hankins (22) was the club's leading run-scorer in the One-Day Cup; and 18-year-old allrounder Ben Charlesworth sparkled in a handful of Championship matches in late summer. Meanwhile the club are held together by a strong nucleus of Bristol loyalists including Chris Dent, Ian Cockbain, Benny Howell, David Payne and the Taylor brothers, Jack and Matt. (Off-spinner Jack will bowl leg-spin in 2019 having served his third ban for an illegal action.) Throw in dynamic allrounder Ryan Higgins and experienced Aussie seamer Dan Worrall and the portents look good. But losing Liam Norwell and Craig Miles – the club's leading Championship wicket-takers in 2017 and 2018 – will test their bowling depth, while Kieran Noema-Barnett will also be missed after the allrounder decided to return to his native New Zealand. The prolific Michael Klinger, now 38, will play in the T20 Blast as captain.

IN: Stuart Whittingham (Sus), Dan Worrall (Aus)
OUT: Craig Miles, Liam Norwell (both War), Kieran Noema-Barnett (REL)

HEAD COACH: RICHARD DAWSON

Dawson was appointed in early 2015 after gaining some coaching experience with Yorkshire's Second XI and inspired Gloucestershire to win the One-Day Cup in his first season. A former Yorkshire and Gloucestershire off-spinner who played seven Tests, Dawson worked as a spin-bowling and one-day coach at Bristol following his retirement in 2011. Assistant coach Ian Harvey won six one-day trophies at the club between 1999 and 2003. T20 captain Michael Klinger will also serve as a batting consultant.

COUNTY CHAMPIONSHIP AVERAGES 2018

	Mat	Inns	NO	Runs	HS	Ave	SR	100	50	4s	6s
K Noema-Barnett	8	14	5	323	73*	35.88	44.12	0	2	38	3
CDJ Dent	14	28	3	851	214*	34.04	45.72	1	4	110	2
MAH Hammond	8	16	2	476	123*	34.00	42.34	2	2	69	1
JR Bracey	14	27	3	785	125*	32.70	40.63	2	2	98	0
BAC Howell	13	24	1	604	67	26.26	57.52	0	4	86	1
BG Charlesworth	6	9	1	194	77*	24.25	41.10	0	2	24	1
GH Roderick	12	22	1	500	67	23.80	44.52	0	4	56	2
DJ Worrall	4	5	1	94	50	23.50	51.93	0	1	14	0
RF Higgins	14	24	2	482	105	21.90	58.00	1	2	65	0
JMR Taylor	10	18	0	384	112	21.33	43.83	1	0	49	3
GL van Buuren	7	14	1	275	83	21.15	44.07	0	2	36	0
DA Payne	7	11	6	86	31	17.20	40.00	0	0	11	1
CN Miles	13	20	5	201	38*	13.40	36.67	0	0	29	0
MD Taylor	14	19	3	177	48	11.06	41.64	0	0	21	0
GS Drissell	5	9	0	76	19	8.44	31.53	0	0	11	0
GT Hankins	1	2	0	13	10	6.50	26.00	0	0	2	0
CJ Liddle	2	4	2	11	6*	5.50	28.94	0	0	2	0
LC Norwell	1	2	0	3	2	1.50	18.75	0	0	0	0
IA Cockbain	1	1	0	0	0	0.00	0.00	0	0	0	0

Batting

	Overs	Mdns	Runs	Wkts	BBI	BBM	Ave	Econ	SR	5w	10w
BG Charlesworth	21.1	7	47	4	3/25	3/25	11.75	2.22	31.7	0	0
RF Higgins	353.5	99	882	48	5/21	8/54	18.37	2.49	44.2	2	0
CN Miles	328.1	61	1180	56	5/50	8/90	21.07	3.59	35.1	2	0
DJ Worrall	119.1	33	348	16	4/45	6/85	21.75	2.92	44.6	0	0
MD Taylor	344.0	61	1171	46	5/81	7/133	25.45	3.40	44.8	1	0
DA Payne	204.2	42	573	22	4/25	5/71	26.04	2.80	55.7	0	0
BAC Howell	28.0	5	122	4	2/54	2/54	30.50	4.35	42.0	0	0
K Noema-Barnett	78.0	13	260	7	2/34	2/34	37.14	3.33	66.8	0	0
CJ Liddle	31.0	5	99	2	2/52	2/52	49.50	3.19	93.0	0	0
GL van Buuren	72.0	8	246	4	3/74	3/74	61.50	3.41	108.0	0	0
GS Drissell	83.0	10	272	4	2/38	2/58	68.00	3.27	124.5	0	0
CDJ Dent	4.0	3	2	0	-	-	-	0.50	-	0	0
MAH Hammond	3.0	0	14	0	-	-	-	4.66	-	0	0
LC Norwell	9.0	3	20	0	-	-	-	2.22	-	0	0

Bowling

Catches/Stumpings:
48 Roderick, 14 Bracey, 11 Dent, Noema-Barnett, 9 Howell, 6 Hammond, Higgins, 4 J Taylor, M Taylor, 3 Miles, 2 Charlesworth, van Buuren, Worrall, 1 Cockbain, Hankins, Payne

ROYAL LONDON ONE-DAY CUP AVERAGES 2018

Batting

	Mat	Inns	NO	Runs	HS	Ave	SR	100	50	4s	6s
IA Cockbain	6	4	1	208	106*	69.33	97.65	1	1	12	6
RF Higgins	6	4	1	195	81*	65.00	117.46	0	2	15	5
GT Hankins	6	6	1	291	92	58.20	78.43	0	3	29	0
GH Roderick	6	5	2	155	87*	51.66	91.17	0	1	13	2
CDJ Dent	6	6	1	225	80	45.00	108.17	0	2	29	3
BAC Howell	6	5	1	165	68*	41.25	85.49	0	2	9	5
JMR Taylor	6	4	0	146	54	36.50	94.19	0	2	9	5
TMJ Smith	5	3	2	23	18*	23.00	176.92	0	0	3	0
DA Payne	1	1	0	6	6	6.00	66.66	0	0	1	0
GL van Buuren	1	1	0	3	3	3.00	50.00	0	0	0	0
CJ Liddle	6	1	0	1	1	1.00	33.33	0	0	0	0
GS Drissell	1	1	0	0	0	0.00	0.00	0	0	0	0
MD Taylor	5	1	1	1	1*	-	100.00	0	0	0	0
CN Miles	3	1	1	0	0*	-	-	0	0	0	0
DJ Worrall	2	-	-	-	-	-	-	-	-	-	-

Bowling

	Overs	Mdns	Runs	Wkts	BBI	Ave	Econ	SR	4w	5w
DJ Worrall	20.0	0	94	3	3/47	31.33	4.70	40.0	0	0
DA Payne	6.0	0	31	0	-	-	5.16	-	0	0
BAC Howell	55.0	1	298	5	2/24	59.60	5.41	66.0	0	0
RF Higgins	38.0	0	210	4	1/11	52.50	5.52	57.0	0	0
TMJ Smith	37.0	0	211	2	2/24	105.50	5.70	111.0	0	0
MD Taylor	38.4	0	224	1	1/36	224.00	5.79	232.0	0	0
GS Drissell	7.0	0	45	0	-	-	6.42	-	0	0
CJ Liddle	50.0	0	337	13	4/57	25.92	6.74	23.0	2	0
CN Miles	23.1	2	162	6	3/31	27.00	6.99	23.1	0	0
GL van Buuren	7.0	0	55	0	-	-	7.85	-	0	0

Catches/Stumpings:
5 Hankins, Roderick, 3 Cockbain, 2 Howell, Smith, J Taylor, M Taylor, 1 Dent, Liddle, Miles, van Buuren, Worrall

VITALITY BLAST AVERAGES 2018

Batting

	Mat	Inns	NO	Runs	HS	Ave	SR	100	50	4s	6s
M Klinger	14	13	1	431	77*	35.91	114.93	0	3	38	8
IA Cockbain	14	13	2	362	123	32.90	137.12	1	0	34	14
JMR Taylor	13	12	4	247	52	30.87	199.19	0	1	24	15
K Noema-Barnett	11	9	2	198	57*	28.28	172.17	0	1	11	15
MAH Hammond	14	13	0	313	51	24.07	155.72	0	1	43	13
RF Higgins	14	11	1	240	55	24.00	129.03	0	1	15	11
BAC Howell	11	9	1	137	28	17.12	130.47	0	0	12	4
GH Roderick	14	10	3	89	24	12.71	128.98	0	0	8	2
AJ Tye	11	5	2	29	12	9.66	181.25	0	0	0	4
GL van Buuren	4	2	1	8	8	8.00	133.33	0	0	1	0
JB Lintott	3	3	2	1	1*	1.00	50.00	0	0	0	0
NLTC Perera	2	1	1	13	13*	-	118.18	0	0	2	0
MD Taylor	4	1	1	7	7*	-	77.77	0	0	1	0
TMJ Smith	10	2	2	2	1*	-	66.66	0	0	0	0
DA Payne	14	2	2	0	0*	-	-	0	0	0	0
LC Norwell	1	-	-	-	-	-	-	-	-	-	-

Bowling

	Overs	Mdns	Runs	Wkts	BBI	Ave	Econ	SR	4w	5w
JB Lintott	11.5	0	83	3	2/26	27.66	7.01	23.6	0	0
AJ Tye	41.2	1	307	13	3/17	23.61	7.42	19.0	0	0
BAC Howell	41.5	0	328	17	3/31	19.29	7.84	14.7	0	0
DA Payne	51.0	1	436	18	3/29	24.22	8.54	17.0	0	0
K Noema-Barnett	21.0	0	180	6	3/18	30.00	8.57	21.0	0	0
TMJ Smith	26.5	0	234	9	3/39	26.00	8.72	17.8	0	0
GL van Buuren	10.0	0	89	2	1/26	44.50	8.90	30.0	0	0
RF Higgins	34.4	0	334	10	3/34	33.40	9.63	20.8	0	0
MD Taylor	13.4	0	135	4	2/36	33.75	9.87	20.5	0	0
NLTC Perera	7.0	0	74	2	1/37	37.00	10.57	21.0	0	0
LC Norwell	1.3	0	22	0	-	-	14.66	-	0	0

Catches/Stumpings:

11 Roderick, 9 Hammond, 8 Klinger, 7 Howell, 6 Tye, 5 J Taylor, 4 Cockbain, Higgins, 3 Payne, 2 Noema-Barnett, Smith, 1 M Taylor, van Buuren

HAMPSHIRE

FORMED: 1863
HOME GROUND: The Ageas Bowl, Southampton
CAPTAIN: James Vince
2018 RESULTS: CC1: 5/8; RL50: Winners; T20: 8/9 South Group
HONOURS: Championship: (2) 1961, 1973; Gillette/NatWest/C&G/FP Trophy: (3) 1991, 2005, 2009; Benson & Hedges Cup: (2) 1988, 1992; Pro40/National League/CB40/YB40/RL50: (2) 2012, 2018; Sunday League: (3) 1975, 1978, 1986; T20 Cup: (2) 2010, 2012

THE LOWDOWN

Hampshire can stride confidently into the new campaign following a first trophy in six seasons and another escape from Championship relegation. Indeed, with a pace attack of Kyle Abbott, Dale Steyn (possibly in late summer), Fidel Edwards and new recruit Keith Barker, there is reason to believe they can challenge for the title. Seamer James Fuller also comes into the reckoning after signing from Middlesex. But the key will be the batting. James Vince had an outstanding season but most of the rest struggled in 2018. Sam Northeast averaged 25 in his first season following a high-profile move from Kent. With Jimmy Adams and Sean Ervine retired, there are spaces in the batting order for youngsters such as Joe Weatherley, who notched his maiden first-class and List A hundreds last summer, and Aneurin Donald, who has the chance to start over after a lean time at Glamorgan. Hampshire will also hope to find their T20 mojo after winning just two of 14 group matches in 2018, with batting again the chief concern.

IN: Keith Barker (War), Aneurin Donald (Gla), James Fuller (Mid), Dimuth Karunaratne (SL)
OUT: Calvin Dickinson, Asher Hart, Chris Sole, Reece Topley (all REL), Jimmy Adams, Sean Ervine (both RET)

FIRST-TEAM MANAGER: ADRIAN BIRRELL

After six years on the backroom staff, including the last two as head coach, Craig White left last October to spend more time with his family. Birrell, a former first-class cricketer from South Africa's Eastern Province, made his name as coach of Ireland, whom he guided to a famous victory over Pakistan in the 2007 World Cup. More recently he was coach of England U19 before a four-year stint as South Africa's assistant coach. The retired Jimmy Adams and former Somerset bowler Alfonso Thomas have joined as assistant coaches.

COUNTY CHAMPIONSHIP AVERAGES 2018

Batting

	Mat	Inns	NO	Runs	HS	Ave	SR	100	50	4s	6s
HM Amla	5	9	0	492	112	54.66	53.71	2	3	65	0
JM Vince	14	25	1	962	201*	40.08	57.22	3	2	147	3
RR Rossouw	9	17	3	489	120*	34.92	50.62	1	1	71	2
TP Alsop	8	14	1	397	99	30.53	38.95	0	4	53	1
GK Berg	9	14	2	335	84*	27.91	50.83	0	2	44	3
LA Dawson	10	17	2	385	72	25.66	56.36	0	1	38	2
KJ Abbott	14	22	5	436	60*	25.64	47.85	0	2	62	2
SA Northeast	10	18	0	451	129	25.05	43.28	1	1	60	0
JHK Adams	14	25	1	582	147	24.25	40.00	1	1	88	0
JJ Weatherley	12	21	1	459	126*	22.95	43.38	1	2	60	0
LD McManus	7	12	1	211	66	19.18	40.89	0	1	28	3
CP Wood	3	5	1	56	26	14.00	41.48	0	0	9	0
IG Holland	7	11	1	135	31	13.50	34.97	0	0	17	0
DW Steyn	5	7	1	65	25	10.83	57.52	0	0	11	1
BTJ Wheal	5	7	1	63	25*	10.50	32.14	0	0	10	0
BJ Taylor	1	2	0	21	16	10.50	52.50	0	0	3	0
OC Soames	4	7	0	69	29	9.85	32.70	0	0	9	0
SM Ervine	1	2	0	18	10	9.00	40.00	0	0	3	0
FH Edwards	14	20	9	75	14	6.81	30.48	0	0	9	0
OP Rayner	2	2	0	0	0	0.00	0.00	0	0	0	0

Bowling

	Overs	Mdns	Runs	Wkts	BBI	BBM	Ave	Econ	SR	5w	10w
TP Alsop	3.0	0	12	1	1/12	1/12	12.00	4.00	18.0	0	0
DW Steyn	142.3	30	382	20	5/66	7/71	19.10	2.68	42.7	1	0
KJ Abbott	348.3	70	1182	51	6/39	11/71	23.17	3.39	41.0	4	1
BJ Taylor	16.0	4	50	2	2/50	2/50	25.00	3.12	48.0	0	0
IG Holland	151.0	42	389	15	3/48	3/58	25.93	2.57	60.4	0	0
FH Edwards	362.2	55	1443	54	6/50	7/122	26.72	3.98	40.2	2	0
LA Dawson	205.2	36	627	20	4/30	6/115	31.35	3.05	61.6	0	0
JJ Weatherley	14.0	1	65	2	1/2	1/2	32.50	4.64	42.0	0	0
OP Rayner	72.0	17	196	5	4/54	4/79	39.20	2.72	86.4	0	0
BTJ Wheal	114.5	17	462	11	2/46	4/131	42.00	4.02	62.6	0	0
GK Berg	200.1	41	654	15	5/130	5/130	43.60	3.26	80.0	1	0
CP Wood	72.0	13	268	6	2/56	3/121	44.66	3.72	72.0	0	0
JHK Adams	1.0	0	3	0	-	-	-	3.00	-	0	0
JM Vince	5.0	1	17	0	-	-	-	3.40	-	0	0

Catches/Stumpings:
22 Alsop, 15 Adams, 9 McManus, 8 Rossouw, 7 Wheal, 6 Dawson, 5 Northeast, Vince, Weatherley, 4 Berg, 3 Edwards, Holland, 2 Amla, Rayner, Wood, 1 Steyn

ROYAL LONDON ONE-DAY CUP AVERAGES 2018

Batting

	Mat	Inns	NO	Runs	HS	Ave	SR	100	50	4s	6s
SA Northeast	2	2	1	133	75*	133.00	114.65	0	2	10	3
JM Vince	9	9	0	527	171	58.55	109.79	2	2	58	5
TP Alsop	5	5	0	248	95	49.60	89.53	0	2	33	0
RR Rossouw	9	9	0	394	125	43.77	105.34	2	1	38	6
GK Berg	9	6	2	163	65	40.75	134.71	0	2	18	5
HM Amla	3	3	0	109	63	36.33	87.20	0	1	11	0
JJ Weatherley	9	9	2	250	105*	35.71	79.11	1	0	24	0
LA Dawson	3	3	0	101	76	33.66	138.35	0	1	8	3
BJ Taylor	7	7	2	155	56	31.00	68.88	0	2	10	0
JHK Adams	7	7	2	142	51*	28.40	77.59	0	1	11	2
LD McManus	9	8	3	140	41	28.00	106.06	0	0	8	7
DW Steyn	3	3	2	8	6	8.00	114.28	0	0	1	0
CP Wood	7	2	0	15	13	7.50	214.28	0	0	3	0
MS Crane	8	2	2	30	21*	-	90.90	0	0	4	0
RJW Topley	6	2	2	11	6*	-	122.22	0	0	0	1
FH Edwards	2	-	-	-	-	-	-	-	-	-	-
BTJ Wheal	1	-	-	-	-	-	-	-	-	-	-

Bowling

	Overs	Mdns	Runs	Wkts	BBI	Ave	Econ	SR	4w	5w
BJ Taylor	61.0	1	294	6	2/35	49.00	4.81	61.0	0	0
JM Vince	8.0	0	40	1	1/19	40.00	5.00	48.0	0	0
CP Wood	64.2	1	325	6	3/46	54.16	5.05	64.3	0	0
RJW Topley	55.3	1	291	7	4/40	41.57	5.24	47.5	1	0
LA Dawson	28.0	1	147	7	4/47	21.00	5.25	24.0	1	0
GK Berg	82.1	1	481	13	3/46	37.00	5.85	37.9	0	0
MS Crane	74.0	0	437	15	4/46	29.13	5.90	29.6	1	0
FH Edwards	19.0	0	124	4	2/56	31.00	6.52	28.5	0	0
DW Steyn	26.0	1	170	3	1/34	56.66	6.53	52.0	0	0
BTJ Wheal	10.0	0	71	2	2/71	35.50	7.10	30.0	0	0

Catches/Stumpings:
8 McManus (inc 2st), 7 Vince, 4 Adams, Berg, Taylor, 3 Alsop, Weatherley, 2 Topley, 1 Amla, Crane, Northeast, Rossouw, Steyn

VITALITY BLAST AVERAGES 2018

Batting

	Mat	Inns	NO	Runs	HS	Ave	SR	100	50	4s	6s
C Munro	8	8	0	211	63	26.37	154.01	0	2	20	10
LA Dawson	13	12	1	289	82	26.27	129.59	0	2	24	7
KJ Abbott	3	3	1	48	29	24.00	133.33	0	0	5	1
SA Northeast	13	12	1	256	73*	23.27	106.22	0	1	20	4
JM Vince	13	12	1	248	74	22.54	140.11	0	1	31	7
RR Rossouw	13	12	0	217	50	18.08	158.39	0	1	26	8
LD McManus	8	7	2	83	38	16.60	143.10	0	0	5	3
TP Alsop	13	12	2	165	41	16.50	105.09	0	0	10	4
GK Berg	9	7	1	76	26	12.66	120.63	0	0	7	2
CP Wood	13	8	2	52	13*	8.66	113.04	0	0	5	0
JJ Weatherley	6	5	0	36	12	7.20	83.72	0	0	3	0
FH Edwards	3	2	1	7	7	7.00	87.50	0	0	0	1
Mujeeb Ur Rahman	12	5	3	10	8*	5.00	83.33	0	0	1	0
RA Stevenson	10	6	3	12	4*	4.00	100.00	0	0	1	0
CM Dickinson	1	1	0	1	1	1.00	25.00	0	0	0	0
DW Steyn	4	2	2	19	11*	-	95.00	0	0	2	0
TAR Scriven	1	-	-	-	-	-	-	-	-	-	-

Bowling

	Overs	Mdns	Runs	Wkts	BBI	Ave	Econ	SR	4w	5w
DW Steyn	15.2	0	108	5	2/29	21.60	7.04	18.4	0	0
Mujeeb Ur Rahman	44.5	1	318	9	2/31	35.33	7.09	29.8	0	0
LA Dawson	47.0	0	335	9	2/22	37.22	7.12	31.3	0	0
CP Wood	44.0	0	335	19	5/32	17.63	7.61	13.8	1	1
C Munro	10.0	0	77	4	2/20	19.25	7.70	15.0	0	0
TAR Scriven	1.0	0	8	0	-	-	8.00	-	0	0
RA Stevenson	31.5	0	289	9	2/28	32.11	9.07	21.2	0	0
GK Berg	22.0	1	222	2	2/33	111.00	10.09	66.0	0	0
FH Edwards	12.0	0	123	3	2/30	41.00	10.25	24.0	0	0
KJ Abbott	10.2	0	119	3	2/24	39.66	11.51	20.6	0	0

Catches/Stumpings:
10 Alsop (inc 2st), 9 Dawson, Rossouw, 4 Northeast, 3 Munro, Vince, Wood, 2 Dickinson, McManus (inc 1st), 1 Berg, Mujeeb, Stevenson, Steyn, Weatherley

KENT

FORMED: 1870
HOME GROUND: The Spitfire Ground, Canterbury
ONE-DAY NAME: Kent Spitfires
CAPTAIN: Sam Billings
2018 RESULTS: CC2: 2/10; RL50: Runners-up; T20: Quarter-finalists
HONOURS: Championship: (7) 1906, 1909, 1910, 1913, 1970, 1977(s), 1978; Gillette/NatWest/C&G/FP Trophy: (2) 1967, 1974; Pro40/National League/CB40/RL50: 2001; Benson & Hedges Cup: (3) 1973, 1976, 1978; Sunday League: (4) 1972, 1973, 1976, 1995; T20 Cup: 2007

THE LOWDOWN

Last season was Kent's best since they last won a trophy in 2007. In fact it was probably better: promotion to Division One, quarter-finalists in the T20 Blast, and runners-up in the One-Day Cup. PCA Player of the Year Joe Denly had another stunning season across all formats, while youngsters Zak Crawley, Grant Stewart and Harry Podmore produced some excellent displays. But Denly aside, Kent were heavily dependent on the miracles of two foreign imports: South African Kolpak Heino Kuhn amassed 696 runs at 87 in the One-Day Cup, including four centuries in five innings leading up to the final, while Kiwi seamer Matt Henry waltzed through Championship batting line-ups with an astonishing 75 wickets at 15.48. Henry will be missed, although Kent have brought in Dutch left-armer Fred Klaassen and former Notts seamer Matt Milnes as cover. And there is always Darren Stevens, who in his 43rd year took 42 wickets at 19 in the Championship. Australian batsman Matthew Renshaw, so impressive for Somerset last season, has signed for the early season, softening the blow of losing Denly and captain Sam Billings to the IPL.

IN: Fred Klaassen (Net, EU passport), Matt Milnes (Not), Matthew Renshaw (Aus), Adam Milne (NZ, T20), Mohammad Nabi (Afg, T20)
OUT: Will Gidman, Matt Hunn, James Tredwell (all RET)

HEAD COACH: MATT WALKER

Walker was assistant to Jimmy Adams before his promotion to the top job ahead of the 2017 season, having previously worked with Essex and England Lions. A left-handed batsman, he scored nearly 20,000 runs for Kent and Essex between 1992 and 2011, including 275 not out against Somerset in 1996. His assistant is Allan Donald. Simon Storey has joined as CEO after stepping down from the same role at Derbyshire.

COUNTY CHAMPIONSHIP AVERAGES 2018

Batting

	Mat	Inns	NO	Runs	HS	Ave	SR	100	50	4s	6s
JL Denly	14	24	0	828	119	34.50	54.58	3	3	110	2
HG Kuhn	14	26	3	780	96*	33.91	58.47	0	6	108	4
Z Crawley	14	24	0	755	168	31.45	58.89	1	4	100	4
SW Billings	8	14	2	370	85	30.83	57.45	0	2	46	0
SR Dickson	14	26	1	710	134*	28.40	56.98	3	1	87	7
G Stewart	10	17	1	414	103	25.87	70.28	1	2	60	7
MJ Henry	11	17	3	303	81	21.64	93.51	0	2	29	14
DJ Bell-Drummond	13	24	2	436	61	19.81	48.60	0	1	58	1
DI Stevens	11	18	2	310	89	19.37	66.81	0	2	48	1
HW Podmore	14	22	7	285	53	19.00	43.05	0	1	29	1
AEN Riley	4	6	3	56	23	18.66	37.08	0	0	5	1
AP Rouse	7	11	0	187	55	17.00	57.18	0	1	27	0
OG Robinson	3	4	0	59	26	14.75	56.19	0	0	9	0
CJ Haggett	2	4	0	53	31	13.25	33.97	0	0	6	0
WRS Gidman	3	4	0	27	19	6.75	34.61	0	0	3	0
IAA Thomas	11	14	8	17	4*	2.83	11.88	0	0	1	0
ME Claydon	1	2	0	5	5	2.50	27.77	0	0	0	0

Bowling

	Overs	Mdns	Runs	Wkts	BBI	BBM	Ave	Econ	SR	5w	10w
DJ Bell-Drummond	7.0	3	8	2	1/1	1/1	4.00	1.14	21.0	0	0
CJ Haggett	18.0	7	44	4	2/6	3/32	11.00	2.44	27.0	0	0
ME Claydon	11.4	0	27	2	2/27	2/27	13.50	2.31	35.0	0	0
MJ Henry	382.4	83	1161	75	7/42	12/73	15.48	3.03	30.6	5	3
JL Denly	160.1	28	426	23	4/36	5/121	18.52	2.65	41.7	0	0
DI Stevens	295.4	76	799	42	6/26	8/83	19.02	2.70	42.2	2	0
G Stewart	164.5	26	505	22	6/22	8/58	22.95	3.06	44.9	1	0
HW Podmore	339.2	80	1002	43	6/36	8/110	23.30	2.95	47.3	1	0
IAA Thomas	183.0	31	630	24	5/91	9/126	26.25	3.44	45.7	1	0
WRS Gidman	18.4	2	56	2	1/10	1/18	28.00	3.00	56.0	0	0
AEN Riley	134.2	33	334	9	4/68	7/146	37.11	2.48	89.5	0	0

Catches/Stumpings:
25 Dickson, 24 Rouse, 22 Billings (inc 2st), 21 Kuhn, 11 Crawley, 6 Riley, Thomas, 3 Bell-Drummond, Denly, Stewart, 2 Gidman, Henry, Podmore, Robinson, Stevens

ROYAL LONDON ONE-DAY CUP AVERAGES 2018

Batting

	Mat	Inns	NO	Runs	HS	Ave	SR	100	50	4s	6s
HG Kuhn	11	11	3	696	127	87.00	101.45	4	1	61	10
JL Denly	11	11	4	492	150*	70.28	94.61	2	2	49	12
DJ Bell-Drummond	11	11	0	485	90	44.09	88.34	0	4	50	3
AJ Blake	11	9	1	326	61	40.75	121.18	0	2	21	21
AP Rouse	5	4	1	114	70	38.00	82.60	0	1	9	2
SR Dickson	9	6	1	173	68*	34.60	92.02	0	2	10	5
SW Billings	6	4	0	85	75	21.25	101.19	0	1	9	1
Z Crawley	4	4	0	73	29	18.25	66.36	0	0	9	0
CJ Haggett	11	6	2	64	31	16.00	83.11	0	0	1	3
DI Stevens	11	8	1	95	26*	13.57	104.39	0	0	8	2
Imran Qayyum	8	5	2	26	9*	8.66	48.14	0	0	1	0
MJ Henry	11	6	0	46	23	7.66	106.97	0	0	5	2
HW Podmore	4	2	1	7	6*	7.00	116.66	0	0	1	0
ME Claydon	8	3	3	7	7*	-	77.77	0	0	0	0

Bowling

	Overs	Mdns	Runs	Wkts	BBI	Ave	Econ	SR	4w	5w
DJ Bell-Drummond	0.5	0	3	0	-	-	3.60	-	0	0
DI Stevens	93.1	1	421	16	6/25	26.31	4.51	34.9	0	1
Imran Qayyum	66.0	0	364	6	2/45	60.66	5.51	66.0	0	0
MJ Henry	99.1	7	551	16	3/37	34.43	5.55	37.1	0	0
JL Denly	73.0	2	431	14	4/56	30.78	5.90	31.2	2	0
ME Claydon	62.0	2	402	8	3/73	50.25	6.48	46.5	0	0
HW Podmore	34.0	1	227	6	4/57	37.83	6.67	34.0	1	0
CJ Haggett	83.2	0	560	14	3/42	40.00	6.72	35.7	0	0

Catches/Stumpings:
7 Blake, Henry, Kuhn, 6 Billings (inc 1st), 5 Denly, 4 Bell-Drummond, Dickson, 3 Haggett, Rouse, 2 Claydon, Qayyum, Stevens, 1 Crawley, Podmore

VITALITY BLAST AVERAGES 2018

Batting

	Mat	Inns	NO	Runs	HS	Ave	SR	100	50	4s	6s
SW Billings	13	12	5	372	95*	53.14	144.74	0	3	33	12
JL Denly	13	12	1	409	102	37.18	145.03	1	2	48	11
CJ Haggett	13	5	3	63	20	31.50	143.18	0	0	6	2
DJ Bell-Drummond	13	12	0	372	80	31.00	145.31	0	3	39	9
HG Kuhn	13	12	2	310	67*	31.00	145.53	0	1	26	8
SR Dickson	13	8	4	112	32	28.00	115.46	0	0	5	4
AF Milne	12	4	3	23	17*	23.00	135.29	0	0	3	0
MP Stoinis	5	4	0	80	47	20.00	119.40	0	0	3	3
AJ Blake	13	10	1	161	57	17.88	161.00	0	1	13	9
CR Brathwaite	5	3	1	13	11*	6.50	118.18	0	0	1	1
G Stewart	2	2	1	5	5*	5.00	166.66	0	0	1	0
Z Crawley	1	1	0	3	3	3.00	75.00	0	0	0	0
Imran Qayyum	13	1	1	21	21*	-	150.00	0	0	4	0
ME Claydon	9	2	2	5	5*	-	71.42	0	0	0	0
HW Podmore	1	-	-	-	-	-	-	-	-	-	-
IAA Thomas	4	-	-	-	-	-	-	-	-	-	-

Bowling

	Overs	Mdns	Runs	Wkts	BBI	Ave	Econ	SR	4w	5w
AF Milne	41.3	0	297	13	4/15	22.84	7.15	19.1	1	0
JL Denly	43.1	0	335	20	3/25	16.75	7.76	12.9	0	0
MP Stoinis	13.5	0	118	4	4/17	29.50	8.53	20.7	1	0
Imran Qayyum	33.1	0	296	10	3/40	29.60	8.92	19.9	0	0
CR Brathwaite	18.0	0	170	9	4/21	18.88	9.44	12.0	1	0
CJ Haggett	36.0	0	349	11	2/26	31.72	9.69	19.6	0	0
ME Claydon	31.0	0	311	8	2/36	38.87	10.03	23.2	0	0
DJ Bell-Drummond	2.0	0	21	0	-	-	10.50	-	0	0
IAA Thomas	7.0	0	75	2	1/10	37.50	10.71	21.0	0	0
G Stewart	5.2	0	68	1	1/40	68.00	12.75	32.0	0	0
HW Podmore	2.0	0	37	0	-	-	18.50	-	0	0

Catches/Stumpings:
13 Billings (inc 4st), 10 Dickson, 7 Denly, 6 Blake, Kuhn, 3 Bell-Drummond, Thomas,
2 Brathwaite, Qayyum, Stewart, 1 Haggett, Podmore, Stoinis

FORMED: 1864
HOME GROUND: Emirates Old Trafford, Manchester
ONE-DAY NAME: Lancashire Lightning
CAPTAIN: Dane Vilas
2018 RESULTS: CC1: 7/8; RL50: 6/9 North Group; T20: Semi-finalists
HONOURS: Championship: (9) 1897, 1904, 1926, 1927, 1928, 1930, 1934, 1950(s), 2011; Gillette/NatWest/C&G/FP Trophy: (7) 1970, 1971, 1972, 1985, 1990, 1996, 1998; Benson & Hedges Cup: (4) 1984, 1990, 1995, 1996; Pro40/National League/CB40/YB40/RL50: 1999; Sunday League: (4) 1969, 1970, 1989, 1998; T20 Cup: 2015

THE LOWDOWN

Lancashire appear to have fallen off the cliff edge just as they seemed to be climbing the summit. In 2017 they finished second in the Championship and there was hope they could go one better last summer. Relegation followed instead. Liam Livingstone failed to make a Championship fifty in 16 innings and resigned the captaincy after one season, with the experienced Dane Vilas taking charge. With the exception of Vilas and Keaton Jennings, the batting misfired badly. Even Shiv Chanderpaul, who won't be returning this season, hardly made a run. This wasn't fair on an outstanding seam attack led by Tom Bailey and Graham Onions, who between them shared 121 wickets. Reaching T20 Finals Day was a bright spot, and leggie Matthew Parkinson produced a stellar season across all formats, although a back injury over the winter meant he could not play for England Lions or in the Big Bash. Aussie duo Joe Burns and Glenn Maxwell will share the overseas spot and, with Ashes places at stake, neither will be short on incentive. Richard Gleeson has joined from Northants but dynamic allrounder Jordan Clark was lured by first-division cricket at Surrey.

IN: Richard Gleeson (Nor), Joe Burns, Glenn Maxwell (both Aus)
OUT: Jordan Clark (Sur), Arron Lilley (Lei), Karl Brown, Simon Kerrigan (both REL)

HEAD COACH: GLEN CHAPPLE

Chapple endured a tough first year as head coach after stepping into the breach ahead of the 2018 season following Ashley Giles's decision to return to Warwickshire. Chapple took 1,373 wickets in 664 appearances during a 23-year playing career at Old Trafford and captained the club to the Championship title in 2011. Assistant coach Mark Chilton and former Derbyshire keeper Karl Krikken have taken on new 'performance' roles to smooth the path to the top for Lancashire's brightest talents.

COUNTY CHAMPIONSHIP AVERAGES 2018

Batting

	Mat	Inns	NO	Runs	HS	Ave	SR	100	50	4s	6s
KK Jennings	10	16	1	709	177	47.26	48.46	3	1	110	0
DJ Vilas	14	23	2	792	235*	37.71	54.69	3	1	104	5
J Clark	10	16	0	538	82	33.62	60.24	0	5	68	3
JM Mennie	7	11	4	232	68*	33.14	47.73	0	2	23	3
JJ Bohannon	5	9	1	255	78*	31.87	45.69	0	2	34	1
JC Buttler	1	2	0	62	59	31.00	83.78	0	1	8	1
AL Davies	14	24	0	732	115	30.50	64.89	1	5	125	1
AM Lilley	1	1	0	28	28	28.00	90.32	0	0	5	0
LS Livingstone	10	16	2	336	48*	24.00	63.15	0	0	54	2
SJ Croft	8	13	0	276	62	21.23	42.52	0	2	32	1
S Chanderpaul	8	13	0	257	65	19.76	38.82	0	2	38	0
RP Jones	5	8	0	137	68	17.12	50.00	0	1	21	1
KR Brown	2	4	0	67	43	16.75	31.60	0	0	12	0
TE Bailey	14	22	2	308	66	15.40	51.76	0	1	45	2
DJ Lamb	4	6	2	57	20*	14.25	30.31	0	0	9	0
KA Maharaj	3	5	0	66	38	13.20	98.50	0	0	8	3
H Hameed	10	17	0	165	31	9.70	33.06	0	0	21	1
G Onions	12	19	4	135	41	9.00	69.58	0	0	16	3
TJ Lester	1	2	0	16	8	8.00	32.00	0	0	3	0
MW Parkinson	6	11	5	35	9*	5.83	24.13	0	0	2	0
BD Guest	1	2	0	8	8	4.00	27.58	0	0	1	0
JM Anderson	3	4	0	14	8	3.50	25.45	0	0	2	0
SD Parry	3	4	0	7	6	1.75	38.88	0	0	1	0

Bowling

	Overs	Mdns	Runs	Wkts	BBI	BBM	Ave	Econ	SR	5w	10w
KA Maharaj	103.4	23	283	17	7/37	11/102	16.64	2.72	36.5	1	1
RP Jones	6.0	0	19	1	1/18	1/18	19.00	3.16	36.0	0	0
RJ Gleeson	57.0	15	196	10	3/34	6/91	19.60	3.43	34.2	0	0
TE Bailey	439.4	106	1258	64	5/53	8/67	19.65	2.86	41.2	1	0
JJ Bohannon	27.0	3	103	5	3/46	4/82	20.60	3.81	32.4	0	0
JM Mennie	192.5	44	601	28	4/43	6/50	21.46	3.11	41.3	0	0
G Onions	379.3	72	1241	57	6/55	9/77	21.77	3.27	39.9	2	0
TJ Lester	27.1	2	78	3	2/51	3/78	26.00	2.87	54.3	0	0
S Mahmood	21.0	4	57	2	2/39	2/57	28.50	2.71	63.0	0	0
J Clark	198.3	22	688	24	5/58	7/97	28.66	3.46	49.6	1	0
MW Parkinson	155.1	23	481	16	5/101	8/181	30.06	3.09	58.1	1	0
LS Livingstone	86.5	18	214	7	3/27	3/27	30.57	2.46	74.4	0	0
JM Anderson	100.0	29	280	9	4/26	6/53	31.11	2.80	66.6	0	0
AM Lilley	28.3	6	89	2	2/52	2/89	44.50	3.12	85.5	0	0
SD Parry	97.0	14	274	3	2/101	3/151	91.33	2.82	194.0	0	0

Catches/Stumpings:
54 Vilas (inc 4st), 15 Davies (inc 1st), Livingstone, 10 Croft, 9 Jennings, 6 Hameed, Jones, 5 Bailey, Davies, 2 Bohannon, Buttler, Clark, Maharaj, 1 Anderson, Brown, Lamb, Mennie, Onions, Parkinson

ROYAL LONDON ONE-DAY CUP AVERAGES 2018

Batting

	Mat	Inns	NO	Runs	HS	Ave	SR	100	50	4s	6s
KK Jennings	6	6	1	375	136	75.00	95.41	1	3	34	2
LS Livingstone	8	7	1	362	90*	60.33	122.71	0	4	29	17
H Hameed	3	3	1	113	55*	56.50	77.39	0	1	11	0
AL Davies	8	8	0	339	147	42.37	94.42	1	1	40	2
DJ Vilas	8	6	1	210	83*	42.00	119.31	0	1	18	2
J Clark	8	6	1	149	51	29.80	100.00	0	1	12	2
KR Brown	4	4	1	89	48	29.66	77.39	0	0	7	2
TE Bailey	4	4	2	47	33	23.50	117.50	0	0	3	0
JJ Bohannon	5	3	0	54	25	18.00	87.09	0	0	5	0
SJ Croft	5	4	0	68	33	17.00	63.55	0	0	1	0
AM Lilley	1	1	0	16	16	16.00	123.07	0	0	1	0
SD Parry	6	4	2	23	20	11.50	100.00	0	0	2	0
RP Jones	3	2	0	19	17	9.50	55.88	0	0	1	0
JM Mennie	7	5	0	29	11	5.80	74.35	0	0	3	0
G Onions	4	2	2	32	30*	-	145.45	0	0	3	2
MW Parkinson	8	3	3	9	6*	-	50.00	0	0	0	0

Bowling

	Overs	Mdns	Runs	Wkts	BBI	Ave	Econ	SR	4w	5w
LS Livingstone	43.0	1	193	4	2/30	48.25	4.48	64.5	0	0
JM Mennie	52.5	4	251	8	3/56	31.37	4.75	39.6	0	0
SD Parry	41.1	1	209	7	2/20	29.85	5.07	35.2	0	0
MW Parkinson	63.4	3	328	18	5/68	18.22	5.15	21.2	1	1
G Onions	28.0	1	151	5	2/31	30.20	5.39	33.6	0	0
KK Jennings	19.0	0	105	5	2/19	21.00	5.52	22.8	0	0
AM Lilley	3.0	0	18	0	-	-	6.00	-	0	0
J Clark	37.0	2	241	2	2/61	120.50	6.51	111.0	0	0
JJ Bohannon	10.0	0	66	0	-	-	6.60	-	0	0
TE Bailey	30.0	1	200	6	2/16	33.33	6.66	30.0	0	0

Catches/Stumpings:
7 Livingstone, 6 Vilas (inc 3st), 5 Davies (inc 1st), Jennings, Parry, 2 Bohannon, Clark, Croft, Jones, Lilley, 1 Bailey

VITALITY BLAST AVERAGES 2018

Batting

	Mat	Inns	NO	Runs	HS	Ave	SR	100	50	4s	6s
KK Jennings	9	7	3	239	51*	59.75	117.15	0	2	17	5
AL Davies	15	14	4	534	94*	53.40	129.61	0	6	58	11
J Clark	13	10	6	191	41*	47.75	143.60	0	0	8	9
LS Livingstone	7	7	0	318	100	45.42	188.16	1	1	31	21
KR Brown	7	7	0	204	61	29.14	150.00	0	2	19	8
DJ Vilas	15	11	1	192	30*	19.20	134.26	0	0	16	4
AM Lilley	15	15	2	246	47	18.92	156.68	0	0	25	11
SJ Croft	13	9	2	108	30	15.42	112.50	0	0	8	3
JP Faulkner	15	9	3	86	23	14.33	122.85	0	0	4	4
DJ Lamb	6	2	0	28	24	14.00	90.32	0	0	2	2
JJ Bohannon	2	2	0	27	23	13.50	93.10	0	0	1	0
JC Buttler	3	3	0	28	16	9.33	112.00	0	0	0	1
TJ Lester	11	4	2	8	7*	4.00	88.88	0	0	0	0
MRJ Watt	4	1	0	4	4	4.00	57.14	0	0	0	0
MW Parkinson	15	3	0	4	4	1.33	57.14	0	0	1	0
SD Parry	4	1	1	7	7*	-	175.00	0	0	1	0
Zahir Khan	7	3	3	2	1*	-	40.00	0	0	0	0
G Onions	3	1	1	1	1*	-	33.33	0	0	0	0
JM Mennie	1	-	-	-	-	-	-	-	-	-	-

Bowling

	Overs	Mdns	Runs	Wkts	BBI	Ave	Econ	SR	4w	5w
SJ Croft	11.0	0	77	3	1/4	25.66	7.00	22.0	0	0
Zahir Khan	26.2	0	185	9	2/8	20.55	7.02	17.5	0	0
MW Parkinson	56.4	0	415	25	3/19	16.60	7.32	13.6	0	0
JP Faulkner	45.5	2	352	20	3/24	17.60	7.68	13.7	0	0
SD Parry	12.0	0	96	3	2/19	32.00	8.00	24.0	0	0
KK Jennings	2.0	0	16	1	1/8	16.00	8.00	12.0	0	0
AM Lilley	13.0	0	105	1	1/27	105.00	8.07	78.0	0	0
LS Livingstone	16.0	0	132	6	4/17	22.00	8.25	16.0	1	0
DJ Lamb	12.0	0	100	5	2/19	20.00	8.33	14.4	0	0
MRJ Watt	12.1	0	106	1	1/42	106.00	8.71	73.0	0	0
J Clark	24.5	0	218	7	2/26	31.14	8.77	21.2	0	0
TJ Lester	37.4	2	335	15	4/25	22.33	8.89	15.0	1	0
G Onions	9.0	0	99	3	2/54	33.00	11.00	18.0	0	0
JM Mennie	3.0	0	34	1	1/34	34.00	11.33	18.0	0	0

Catches/Stumpings:
19 Vilas (inc 6st), 8 Croft, 7 Clark, Lilley, 5 Davies, Faulkner, 4 Brown, Buttler (inc 2st), Livingstone, Watt, 2 Jennings, Lester, Parkinson, 1 Bohannon

LEICESTERSHIRE

FORMED: 1879
HOME GROUND: Fischer County Ground, Leicester
ONE-DAY NAME: Leicestershire Foxes
CAPTAIN: Paul Horton
2018 RESULTS: CC2: 6/10; RL50: 8/9 North Group; T20: 8/9 North Group
HONOURS: Championship: (3) 1975, 1996, 1998; Benson & Hedges Cup: (3) 1972, 1975, 1985; Sunday League: (2) 1974, 1977; T20 Cup: (3) 2004, 2006, 2011

THE LOWDOWN

If we put aside their white-ball cricket, Leicestershire appear to have made strides a year into Paul Nixon's tenure as coach. Halfway through last season they even had an outside chance of promotion. Their four-day campaign derailed thereafter, the top-order folding all too easily, but five wins and sixth place was a significant improvement on no wins and last in 2017, a decent send-off for outgoing chief executive Wasim Khan. It'll be tough this summer without the club's Player of the Season Ben Raine, who decided to return to his native Durham, while young Zak Chappell's defection to Nottinghamshire left a sour taste. Will Davis and Chris Wright will add pace and experience to the attack. Pakistan's Mohammad Abbas – signed as a little-known Pakistan seamer, now regarded among the best in the world – returns for a second summer. Runs, though, will be the key, with Colin Ackermann the only batsman to make a Championship hundred last summer. In October the club officially cut ties with Michael Carberry, who was replaced by Paul Horton as captain last year after just two months in charge.

IN: Will Davis (Der), Arron Lilley (Lan), Chris Wright (War)
OUT: Zak Chappell (Not), Ben Raine (Dur), Michael Carberry, Cameron Delport, Ned Eckersley, Richard Jones, Mark Pettini, Rob Sayer, Tom Wells (all REL)

HEAD COACH: PAUL NIXON

Leicestershire went back to the boot room by appointing Nixon ahead of the 2018 season. A former England wicketkeeper, he has lived in Leicester for 30 years and won two Championship titles in the 1990s. He won the Caribbean Premier League twice as coach of Jamaica Tallawahs. Wasim Khan stepped down after four years as chief executive to become managing director of the Pakistan Cricket Board. Khan is credited with keeping the club's fragile finances afloat, a task that now falls to former England netball commercial director Karen Rothery.

COUNTY CHAMPIONSHIP AVERAGES 2018

Batting

	Mat	Inns	NO	Runs	HS	Ave	SR	100	50	4s	6s
ZJ Chappell	4	5	2	145	40	48.33	61.18	0	0	18	0
CN Ackermann	14	24	2	876	196*	39.81	54.17	2	3	116	8
NJ Dexter	12	20	3	585	87	34.41	49.03	0	3	81	2
D Klein	5	9	3	202	94	33.66	84.16	0	1	33	1
MA Carberry	4	6	0	193	73	32.16	48.37	0	1	31	1
PJ Horton	12	22	1	594	88	28.28	48.01	0	5	84	0
GT Griffiths	12	18	8	225	40	22.50	36.76	0	0	30	0
HE Dearden	10	18	2	357	74	22.31	45.82	0	2	53	1
BA Raine	11	17	0	371	65	21.82	66.48	0	1	52	4
LJ Hill	9	15	2	241	85	18.53	40.16	0	1	29	0
MJ Cosgrove	14	24	0	440	75	18.33	49.71	0	3	58	0
EJH Eckersley	7	12	0	220	74	18.33	45.54	0	2	28	0
A Javid	6	10	0	157	58	15.70	38.19	0	1	20	0
TAI Taylor	1	2	0	31	26	15.50	46.26	0	0	5	0
CF Parkinson	12	19	1	252	48	14.00	39.43	0	0	24	0
BWM Mike	4	7	0	96	39	13.71	54.23	0	0	10	3
DW Sayer	1	2	0	27	21	13.50	87.09	0	0	4	0
ST Evans	3	5	0	50	29	10.00	32.67	0	0	5	0
Mohammad Abbas	10	15	6	84	32*	9.33	30.65	0	0	7	1
U Arshad	1	2	0	9	9	4.50	36.00	0	0	1	0
VR Aaron	3	5	1	14	8	3.50	26.41	0	0	3	0
RA Jones	1	1	0	0	0	0.00	0.00	0	0	0	0

Bowling

	Overs	Mdns	Runs	Wkts	BBI	BBM	Ave	Econ	SR	5w	10w
CN Ackermann	43.3	5	137	9	2/26	3/29	15.22	3.14	29.0	0	0
TAI Taylor	34.0	11	92	6	4/15	6/92	15.33	2.70	34.0	0	0
ZJ Chappell	76.0	13	255	16	6/44	6/53	15.93	3.35	28.5	1	0
Mohammad Abbas	345.1	101	886	50	6/48	10/52	17.72	2.56	41.4	5	1
BWM Mike	87.2	10	385	19	5/37	9/94	20.26	4.40	27.5	1	0
BA Raine	395.1	90	1146	51	4/44	7/89	22.47	2.90	46.4	0	0
GT Griffiths	269.0	67	882	36	6/49	10/83	24.50	3.27	44.8	1	1
NJ Dexter	169.0	40	494	18	3/17	4/18	27.44	2.92	56.3	0	0
A Javid	26.2	3	78	2	1/30	2/73	39.00	2.96	79.0	0	0
VR Aaron	86.0	11	359	9	4/65	6/131	39.88	4.17	57.3	0	0
RA Jones	13.0	1	44	1	1/39	1/44	44.00	3.38	78.0	0	0
D Klein	94.0	17	400	5	2/23	3/83	80.00	4.25	112.8	0	0
CF Parkinson	239.0	42	824	10	3/50	4/72	82.40	3.44	143.4	0	0
MA Carberry	2.0	0	7	0	-	-	-	3.50	-	0	0
MJ Cosgrove	3.0	0	8	0	-	-	-	2.66	-	0	0
DW Sayer	5.0	1	28	0	-	-	-	5.60	-	0	0
U Arshad	16.0	2	81	0	-	-	-	5.06	-	0	0

Catches/Stumpings:

29 Hill, 26 Eckersley, 10 Ackermann, 9 Dexter, 6 Cosgrove, Dearden, 5 Raine, 3 Horton, 2 Griffiths, Javid, Klein, Mike, Sayer, 1 Abbas, Carberry, Chappell, Evans, Jones, Parkinson

ROYAL LONDON ONE-DAY CUP AVERAGES 2018

Batting

	Mat	Inns	NO	Runs	HS	Ave	SR	100	50	4s	6s
TJ Wells	7	7	3	198	69	49.50	106.45	0	1	13	5
MJ Cosgrove	7	7	0	317	84	45.28	95.77	0	4	28	6
CN Ackermann	8	8	1	286	71*	40.85	89.09	0	3	27	4
CF Parkinson	7	5	2	119	52*	39.66	82.63	0	1	9	0
EJH Eckersley	6	5	1	145	50	36.25	81.00	0	1	9	2
PJ Horton	8	8	0	284	103	35.50	79.55	1	1	31	0
A Javid	2	2	1	35	21	35.00	64.81	0	0	0	0
CS Delport	5	5	0	174	122	34.80	95.60	1	0	22	4
BA Raine	6	6	0	166	83	27.66	114.48	0	1	14	5
VR Aaron	6	3	2	25	14*	25.00	83.33	0	0	4	0
NJ Dexter	7	6	1	121	50*	24.20	87.68	0	1	8	3
MA Carberry	2	2	0	31	25	15.50	79.48	0	0	3	0
LJ Hill	3	2	0	24	21	12.00	64.86	0	0	1	0
D Klein	2	2	0	16	11	8.00	106.66	0	0	3	0
HE Dearden	1	1	0	6	6	6.00	42.85	0	0	0	0
ZJ Chappell	3	2	0	8	5	4.00	34.78	0	0	0	0
RA Jones	2	1	0	0	0	0.00	0.00	0	0	0	0
GT Griffiths	5	2	2	17	15*	-	65.38	0	0	2	0
HJ Swindells	1	-	-	-	-	-	-	-	-	-	-

Bowling

	Overs	Mdns	Runs	Wkts	BBI	Ave	Econ	SR	4w	5w
RA Jones	16.0	0	83	2	2/40	41.50	5.18	48.0	0	0
ZJ Chappell	23.0	2	124	5	3/45	24.80	5.39	27.6	0	0
BA Raine	52.4	3	285	7	3/31	40.71	5.41	45.1	0	0
D Klein	14.0	1	76	1	1/37	76.00	5.42	84.0	0	0
NJ Dexter	25.2	0	160	6	2/46	26.66	6.31	25.3	0	0
A Javid	8.5	1	56	1	1/34	56.00	6.33	53.0	0	0
VR Aaron	51.0	1	326	7	4/31	46.57	6.39	43.7	1	0
CF Parkinson	57.0	0	377	1	1/34	377.00	6.61	342.0	0	0
GT Griffiths	32.0	0	223	8	4/30	27.87	6.96	24.0	1	0
TJ Wells	21.0	0	148	2	2/54	74.00	7.04	63.0	0	0
CN Ackermann	13.4	0	106	1	1/40	106.00	7.75	82.0	0	0
CS Delport	12.5	0	111	1	1/38	111.00	8.64	77.0	0	0

Catches/Stumpings:
6 Eckersley, 5 Ackermann, 4 Horton, 3 Delport, Hill, 2 Raine, Swindells, 1 Carberry, Cosgrove, Dexter, Griffiths, Parkinson, Wells

VITALITY BLAST AVERAGES 2018

Batting

	Mat	Inns	NO	Runs	HS	Ave	SR	100	50	4s	6s
HE Dearden	1	1	0	61	61	61.00	152.50	0	1	5	2
CN Ackermann	14	14	3	343	74	31.18	137.75	0	2	26	11
A Javid	6	6	3	78	28*	26.00	95.12	0	0	5	1
BA Raine	13	13	0	332	113	25.53	168.52	1	1	28	21
Mohammad Nabi	13	12	2	246	86*	24.60	143.85	0	1	18	13
Mohammad Abbas	9	5	4	24	15*	24.00	171.42	0	0	3	1
NJ Dexter	13	13	0	296	56	22.76	137.03	0	1	40	7
CS Delport	9	9	0	177	33	19.66	126.42	0	0	19	6
EJH Eckersley	11	7	2	95	39*	19.00	106.74	0	0	7	0
MJ Cosgrove	13	13	0	234	65	18.00	113.59	0	1	20	5
AM Ali	1	1	0	14	14	14.00	155.55	0	0	2	0
TJ Wells	8	7	2	59	19	11.80	103.50	0	0	3	2
CF Parkinson	14	7	3	47	27*	11.75	106.81	0	0	4	0
LJ Hill	4	4	2	23	12*	11.50	92.00	0	0	1	1
HJ Swindells	5	3	0	31	15	10.33	91.17	0	0	4	0
ZJ Chappell	12	9	2	67	16	9.57	134.00	0	0	3	4
GT Griffiths	7	2	2	4	3*	-	40.00	0	0	0	0
D Klein	1	-	-	-	-	-	-	-	-	-	-

Bowling

	Overs	Mdns	Runs	Wkts	BBI	Ave	Econ	SR	4w	5w
D Klein	4.0	1	23	2	2/23	11.50	5.75	12.0	0	0
Mohammad Nabi	44.2	0	323	9	2/13	35.88	7.28	29.5	0	0
CF Parkinson	42.0	0	323	15	4/20	21.53	7.69	16.8	1	0
GT Griffiths	21.0	0	171	5	3/28	34.20	8.14	25.2	0	0
CN Ackermann	9.4	0	80	4	1/7	20.00	8.27	14.5	0	0
NJ Dexter	12.0	0	101	2	2/18	50.50	8.41	36.0	0	0
Mohammad Abbas	31.0	0	278	7	3/32	39.71	8.96	26.5	0	0
ZJ Chappell	35.4	0	342	12	3/23	28.50	9.58	17.8	0	0
A Javid	4.0	0	39	0	-	-	9.75	-	0	0
BA Raine	38.1	0	409	10	2/28	40.90	10.71	22.9	0	0
CS Delport	2.0	0	34	0	-	-	17.00	-	0	0

Catches/Stumpings:
6 Ackermann, Eckersley (inc 4st), 5 Chappell, Wells, 4 Delport, Raine, 3 Dexter, 2 Abbas, Cosgrove, Nabi, Swindells, 1 Dearden, Griffiths, Hill, Javid

MIDDLESEX

FORMED: 1864
HOME GROUND: Lord's Cricket Ground, London
CAPTAIN: Dawid Malan
2018 RESULTS: CC2: 4/10; RL50: 6/9 South Group; T20: 9/9 South Group
HONOURS: Championship: (13) 1903, 1920, 1921, 1947, 1949(s), 1976, 1977(s), 1980, 1982, 1985, 1990, 1993, 2016; Gillette/NatWest/C&G/FP Trophy: (4) 1977, 1980, 1984, 1998; Benson & Hedges Cup: (2) 1983, 1986; Sunday League: 1992; T20 Cup: 2008

THE LOWDOWN

It seems only yesterday that hat-trick hero Toby Roland-Jones was wheeling away in delight, but how things have changed since Middlesex won the Championship in 2016. Roland-Jones missed most of last season with a stress fracture of the back, while the club's attempt to bounce back from relegation ended in mid-table mediocrity. Richard Scott left last July after nine years as head coach and ex-Australia batsman Stuart Law has been charged with taking over across all formats, with T20 coach Dan Vettori departing after another torrid Blast in which Middlesex lost 12 of 14 matches. The arrival of AB de Villiers for his first stint in county cricket – the South African has signed up for a minimum of seven T20 games – should kick-start this summer's campaign. Law will need to instill consistency among the batsmen but can still rely on strong fast-bowling reserves, despite injuries to Roland-Jones and Steven Finn. James Harris was in outstanding form in 2018 and Tim Murtagh took 58 wickets at a staggering 15.31; Murtagh is now ninth on the list of all-time Middlesex wicket-takers and has the chance to leapfrog Angus Fraser (679 wickets) and Wayne Daniel (685) this summer.

IN: AB de Villiers (SA, T20), Mujeeb ur Rahman (Afg, T20)
OUT: James Fuller (Ham), Ravi Patel (REL), James Franklin, Nick Compton (both RET), Tom Lace (Der, loan)

HEAD COACH: STUART LAW

Middlesex have shaken up a coaching structure which had been in place for some time. Both head coach Richard Scott and bowling guru Richard Johnson left after nearly a decade, while batting assistant Dave Houghton joined Derbyshire as head coach. T20 specialist Dan Vettori also moved on. Law, a Queenslander who scored 65 hundreds across all formats for Essex and Lancashire between 1996 and 2008, is fresh from a two-year stint as West Indies coach. Former Hampshire keeper Nic Pothas will be Law's assistant.

COUNTY CHAMPIONSHIP AVERAGES 2018

Batting

	Mat	Inns	NO	Runs	HS	Ave	SR	100	50	4s	6s
SS Eskinazi	12	22	1	740	97	35.23	58.22	0	5	102	0
NRT Gubbins	9	17	0	585	107	34.41	52.00	1	2	90	1
JAR Harris	12	22	8	454	79*	32.42	39.37	0	3	59	0
MDE Holden	13	24	3	632	119*	30.09	53.87	1	3	84	1
DJ Malan	12	22	1	613	119	29.19	52.79	1	4	78	1
SD Robson	13	24	1	633	134	27.52	49.03	1	2	89	0
TG Helm	4	6	2	102	52	25.50	60.00	0	1	16	1
JA Simpson	8	14	0	309	39	22.07	47.75	0	0	51	0
TS Roland-Jones	2	4	0	79	46	19.75	54.86	0	0	12	1
JK Fuller	8	16	3	242	71	18.61	58.17	0	1	26	2
PR Stirling	6	11	0	199	52	18.09	53.63	0	1	36	0
MK Andersson	3	6	2	72	34	18.00	45.28	0	0	6	0
HWR Cartwright	7	12	0	204	80	17.00	52.44	0	1	28	1
TJ Murtagh	11	19	4	200	40	13.33	79.36	0	0	33	2
OP Rayner	9	15	2	172	28	13.23	44.44	0	0	21	1
EJG Morgan	6	11	0	121	76	11.00	37.93	0	1	15	1
ER Bamber	6	10	3	76	27*	10.85	29.92	0	0	7	0
ST Finn	4	6	0	50	27	8.33	76.92	0	0	8	0
RH Patel	2	4	0	33	20	8.25	39.75	0	0	6	0
GFB Scott	1	2	0	16	13	8.00	43.24	0	0	3	0
RG White	5	10	0	71	35	7.10	33.33	0	0	10	0
TE Barber	2	3	1	3	3	1.50	21.42	0	0	0	0

Bowling

	Overs	Mdns	Runs	Wkts	BBI	BBM	Ave	Econ	SR	5w	10w
TJ Murtagh	359.5	95	888	58	5/38	8/63	15.31	2.46	37.2	2	0
ER Bamber	203.5	37	567	28	4/81	6/70	20.25	2.78	43.6	0	0
JAR Harris	384.5	67	1253	61	7/83	9/48	20.54	3.25	37.8	3	0
HWR Cartwright	122.2	16	410	19	4/33	5/62	21.57	3.35	38.6	0	0
MK Andersson	56.0	2	198	8	2/15	3/60	24.75	3.53	42.0	0	0
RH Patel	48.2	9	177	6	3/58	4/74	29.50	3.66	48.3	0	0
JK Fuller	227.2	25	845	28	4/49	7/102	30.17	3.71	48.7	0	0
TG Helm	74.5	12	236	7	3/46	4/98	33.71	3.15	64.1	0	0
PR Stirling	24.0	3	81	2	2/62	2/62	40.50	3.37	72.0	0	0
ST Finn	108.0	9	395	9	2/34	3/71	43.88	3.65	72.0	0	0
OP Rayner	146.5	35	334	7	2/23	3/76	47.71	2.27	125.8	0	0
DJ Malan	48.0	3	145	3	1/15	2/80	48.33	3.02	96.0	0	0
TS Roland-Jones	21.0	0	98	2	1/35	2/73	49.00	4.66	63.0	0	0
MDE Holden	40.0	3	145	1	1/15	1/15	145.00	3.62	240.0	0	0
GFB Scott	12.0	3	23	0	-	-	-	1.91	-	0	0
SD Robson	4.0	0	27	0	-	-	-	6.75	-	0	0
TE Barber	34.0	4	131	0	-	-	-	3.85	-	0	0

Catches/Stumpings:

26 Simpson (inc 3st), 16 Eskinazi, 14 Rayner, White, 12 Malan, 7 Cartwright, Robson, 6 Harris, 4 Holden, Morgan, Stirling, 3 Fuller, Murtagh, 2 Bamber, Gubbins, Helm, 1 Patel

ROYAL LONDON ONE-DAY CUP AVERAGES 2018

MIDDLESEX
CRICKET

Batting

	Mat	Inns	NO	Runs	HS	Ave	SR	100	50	4s	6s
PR Stirling	8	8	1	515	127*	73.57	89.25	3	1	49	10
JEC Franklin	8	7	4	148	62*	49.33	90.79	0	1	16	1
EJG Morgan	7	7	0	300	100	42.85	96.46	1	2	23	12
MDE Holden	1	1	0	38	38	38.00	65.51	0	0	1	1
NRT Gubbins	8	8	0	246	86	30.75	87.85	0	3	34	2
RH Patel	8	4	3	30	24*	30.00	150.00	0	0	5	0
SS Eskinazi	7	6	0	167	49	27.83	71.06	0	0	11	1
JA Simpson	8	7	1	166	77	27.66	77.20	0	1	15	3
HWR Cartwright	8	8	1	189	60*	27.00	94.97	0	1	11	7
NA Sowter	7	5	2	78	29	26.00	81.25	0	0	5	1
TG Helm	8	5	0	79	30	15.80	82.29	0	0	5	1
ST Finn	7	5	1	43	17	10.75	104.87	0	0	5	1
DJ Malan	1	1	0	10	10	10.00	55.55	0	0	1	0
TE Barber	1	1	0	0	0	0.00	0.00	0	0	0	0
JAR Harris	1	-	-	-	-	-	-	-	-	-	-

Bowling

	Overs	Mdns	Runs	Wkts	BBI	Ave	Econ	SR	4w	5w
JEC Franklin	45.0	0	213	4	3/42	53.25	4.73	67.5	0	0
RH Patel	77.0	0	378	15	4/58	25.20	4.90	30.8	1	0
NA Sowter	60.4	0	298	10	3/43	29.80	4.91	36.4	0	0
PR Stirling	19.0	0	95	2	2/38	47.50	5.00	57.0	0	0
JAR Harris	9.0	0	45	1	1/45	45.00	5.00	54.0	0	0
ST Finn	60.4	2	322	12	4/65	26.83	5.30	30.3	1	0
MDE Holden	2.0	0	12	0	-	-	6.00	-	0	0
TG Helm	66.1	2	441	13	4/49	33.92	6.66	30.5	1	0
HWR Cartwright	16.4	1	124	1	1/31	124.00	7.44	100.0	0	0
TE Barber	8.0	0	65	0	-	-	8.12	-	0	0

Catches/Stumpings:
13 Simpson (inc 4st), 5 Stirling, 4 Finn, Franklin, Sowter, 3 Eskinazi, 2 Gubbins, 1 Cartwright, Helm, Morgan, Patel

VITALITY BLAST AVERAGES 2018

MIDDLESEX
CRICKET

Batting

	Mat	Inns	NO	Runs	HS	Ave	SR	100	50	4s	6s
HWR Cartwright	3	3	1	89	38	44.50	125.35	0	0	9	1
JK Fuller	14	13	7	224	46*	37.33	158.86	0	0	17	10
PR Stirling	14	14	0	498	109	35.57	160.12	1	4	61	21
MDE Holden	6	6	0	169	84	28.16	137.39	0	1	23	2
SS Eskinazi	12	11	1	262	55	26.20	130.34	0	2	20	7
DJ Bravo	6	6	1	131	38	26.20	148.86	0	0	8	8
EJG Morgan	11	11	1	259	90	25.90	143.09	0	2	11	18
JA Simpson	11	11	0	246	62	22.36	130.15	0	1	11	13
AC Agar	6	6	4	40	23*	20.00	129.03	0	0	1	3
JEC Franklin	6	5	1	71	27	17.75	126.78	0	0	4	4
NRT Gubbins	8	8	0	123	25	15.37	126.80	0	0	14	4
GFB Scott	6	5	1	48	32	12.00	100.00	0	0	2	2
RH Patel	8	1	0	12	12	12.00	120.00	0	0	2	0
DJ Malan	6	6	0	68	36	11.33	141.66	0	0	7	4
RG White	3	2	1	11	11*	11.00	100.00	0	0	1	0
ST Finn	7	3	2	6	3	6.00	75.00	0	0	0	0
NA Sowter	8	3	1	9	6	4.50	75.00	0	0	1	0
TE Barber	7	2	0	2	2	1.00	66.66	0	0	0	0
TG Helm	6	3	3	41	28*	-	146.42	0	0	6	0
JAR Harris	5	2	2	12	12*	-	92.30	0	0	1	0

Bowling

	Overs	Mdns	Runs	Wkts	BBI	Ave	Econ	SR	4w	5w
TG Helm	21.4	0	191	7	2/29	27.28	8.81	18.5	0	0
DJ Bravo	22.2	0	199	7	2/24	28.42	8.91	19.1	0	0
GFB Scott	5.0	0	46	1	1/14	46.00	9.20	30.0	0	0
NA Sowter	24.0	0	221	3	1/24	73.66	9.20	48.0	0	0
PR Stirling	20.5	0	193	6	3/26	32.16	9.26	20.8	0	0
ST Finn	23.0	0	216	9	3/21	24.00	9.39	15.3	0	0
AC Agar	22.0	0	208	9	3/17	23.11	9.45	14.6	0	0
DJ Malan	5.0	0	48	1	1/8	48.00	9.60	30.0	0	0
RH Patel	25.0	0	241	5	2/27	48.20	9.64	30.0	0	0
JAR Harris	16.2	0	162	6	3/32	27.00	9.91	16.3	0	0
JK Fuller	44.1	0	478	15	6/28	31.86	10.82	17.6	0	1
JEC Franklin	8.0	0	89	1	1/53	89.00	11.12	48.0	0	0
TE Barber	22.0	0	273	9	4/28	30.33	12.40	14.6	1	0

Catches/Stumpings:
8 Fuller, Stirling, 7 Morgan, 6 Eskinazi, Simpson (inc 2st), 3 Finn, Gubbins, Holden, Malan, 2 Agar, Patel, Sowter, 1 Andersson, Barber, Bravo, Cartwright, Franklin, Scott, White

NORTHAMPTONSHIRE

FORMED: 1878
HOME GROUND: County Ground, Northampton
ONE-DAY NAME: Northamptonshire Steelbacks
CAPTAIN: Alex Wakely
2018 RESULTS: CC2: 9/10; RL50: 7/9 North Group; T20: 9/9 North Group
HONOURS: Gillette/NatWest/C&G/FP Trophy: (2) 1976, 1992; Benson & Hedges Cup: 1980; T20 Cup: (2) 2013, 2016

THE LOWDOWN

Tough times at Northampton. The club weren't able to make an impression in any format last summer and finished bottom of the class in their specialist subject: the T20 Blast. Since then they have lost two of their best performers (Ben Duckett to Notts and Richard Gleeson to Lancashire), as well as two mainstays of the side in Rory Kleinveldt and Steven Crook. In the Championship, runs are needed to back up a capable seam attack led by the rejuvenated Ben Sanderson. Ricardo Vasconcelos had an encouraging first season and has signed on until 2021, while Ben Curran looks to be another jewel in the family, but otherwise only captain Alex Wakely was consistent with the bat. A spate of international signings offers hope for the new season. South Africa Test batsman Temba Bavuma is available from mid-May to mid-July and the 6ft 6in Zimbabwean fast bowler Blessing Muzarabani, just 22, is an exciting prospect. West Indies captain Jason Holder will provide impetus in the first month of the season, while Pakistan allrounder Faheem Ashraf offers some much-needed clout in the T20 Blast.

IN: Ben Cotton (unattached), Blessing Muzarabani (Zim, Kolpak), Temba Bavuma (SA), Jason Holder (WI), Faheem Ashraf (Pak, T20)
OUT: Ben Duckett (Not), Richard Gleeson (Lan), Rory Kleinveldt (REL), Steven Crook (RET)

HEAD COACH: DAVID RIPLEY

A Northamptonshire stalwart, Ripley led the club to their maiden T20 title in 2013 – their first trophy in two decades – and repeated the trick in 2016. In a 17-year playing career he scored over 10,000 runs for the county with more than 1,000 dismissals as wicketkeeper. After retiring in 2001 he became Second XI coach before his promotion in 2012. David Sales, the former captain who scored more than 22,000 runs for Northamptonshire, is the batting coach.

www.northantscricket.com / tel: 01604 514455

COUNTY CHAMPIONSHIP AVERAGES 2018

	Mat	Inns	NO	Runs	HS	Ave	SR	100	50	4s	6s
SP Crook	5	9	0	351	92	39.00	61.57	0	3	45	0
BJ Curran	5	9	1	251	83*	31.37	53.74	0	2	34	0
R Vasconcelos	10	18	0	554	140	30.77	52.66	1	4	76	1
AG Wakely	12	22	1	600	106	28.57	54.20	1	4	75	7
RI Newton	4	7	0	183	46	26.14	47.65	0	0	20	0
RE Levi	11	20	1	492	75	25.89	66.39	0	2	72	5
BM Duckett	8	16	1	375	133	25.00	79.61	1	1	58	0
AM Rossington	11	19	1	419	58	23.27	57.31	0	3	57	2
LA Procter	10	20	1	442	70	23.26	48.46	0	3	59	1
DAJ Bracewell	3	6	1	113	81	22.60	48.49	0	1	17	1
CO Thurston	2	4	0	78	29	19.50	56.52	0	0	10	0
SA Zaib	7	11	1	163	57	16.30	37.90	0	1	13	3
BD Cotton	3	4	2	32	24*	16.00	36.78	0	0	3	0
JJ Cobb	5	10	0	140	30	14.00	53.23	0	0	14	3
S Prasanna	2	4	0	42	27	10.50	80.76	0	0	3	3
NL Buck	9	15	2	135	20	10.38	37.19	0	0	18	1
BA Hutton	12	20	2	184	27	10.22	45.43	0	0	17	1
RI Keogh	4	7	0	69	29	9.85	31.08	0	0	7	0
BW Sanderson	13	21	13	72	36	9.00	41.37	0	0	11	1
RK Kleinveldt	3	5	0	45	21	9.00	69.23	0	0	7	0
RJ Gleeson	4	7	1	38	26	6.33	33.62	0	0	3	0

Batting

	Overs	Mdns	Runs	Wkts	BBI	BBM	Ave	Econ	SR	5w	10w
BD Cotton	44.0	13	101	10	5/48	7/58	10.10	2.29	26.4	1	0
RJ Gleeson	90.3	19	256	16	6/79	9/95	16.00	2.82	33.9	1	0
BW Sanderson	422.0	112	1002	60	5/16	8/108	16.70	2.37	42.2	2	0
SP Crook	32.2	5	146	8	4/51	4/51	18.25	4.51	24.2	0	0
RK Kleinveldt	95.1	14	282	14	4/51	7/89	20.14	2.96	40.7	0	0
LA Procter	101.1	20	341	14	5/33	5/49	24.35	3.37	43.3	1	0
S Prasanna	72.0	7	247	10	4/49	6/164	24.70	3.43	43.2	0	0
NL Buck	196.5	22	782	31	4/51	7/124	25.22	3.97	38.0	0	0
BA Hutton	367.2	86	1143	45	8/57	9/65	25.40	3.11	48.9	3	0
SA Zaib	26.4	8	52	2	2/24	2/24	26.00	1.95	80.0	0	0
DAJ Bracewell	93.0	19	304	11	4/71	4/92	27.63	3.26	50.7	0	0
RI Keogh	53.0	5	205	2	1/40	2/109	102.50	3.86	159.0	0	0
JJ Cobb	3.4	0	28	0	-	-	-	7.63	-	0	0

Bowling

Catches/Stumpings:
34 Rossington, 15 Levi, Vasconcelos (inc 1st), 9 Hutton, 5 Duckett, 4 Wakely, 3 Curran, Keogh, Sanderson, 2 Bracewell, Cotton, Crook, Procter, 1 Kleinveldt, Newton, Thurston

ROYAL LONDON ONE-DAY CUP AVERAGES 2018

Batting

	Mat	Inns	NO	Runs	HS	Ave	SR	100	50	4s	6s
CO Thurston	1	1	0	53	53	53.00	85.48	0	1	6	1
RE Levi	3	3	0	127	90	42.33	90.71	0	1	11	3
JJ Cobb	6	5	0	203	78	40.60	87.12	0	3	22	6
AG Wakely	8	7	0	280	79	40.00	86.68	0	2	22	5
AM Rossington	7	7	0	271	66	38.71	86.85	0	3	23	4
RI Newton	4	3	0	86	61	28.66	85.14	0	1	10	2
BA Hutton	4	4	1	80	34*	26.66	101.26	0	0	9	2
RK Kleinveldt	6	5	0	132	41	26.40	126.92	0	0	8	8
RI Keogh	5	4	0	92	51	23.00	78.63	0	1	8	1
SP Crook	3	3	1	46	45*	23.00	117.94	0	0	3	2
GG White	8	7	1	119	41*	19.83	92.96	0	0	12	3
BM Duckett	8	7	0	133	57	19.00	71.50	0	1	14	0
NL Buck	6	5	3	30	10	15.00	142.85	0	0	3	1
R Vasconcelos	3	2	0	30	20	15.00	85.71	0	0	4	1
LA Procter	6	5	1	54	43*	13.50	85.71	0	0	7	0
BD Cotton	1	1	0	8	8	8.00	47.05	0	0	1	0
SA Zaib	2	2	0	12	10	6.00	60.00	0	0	1	0
BW Sanderson	7	4	2	11	7	5.50	68.75	0	0	0	1

Bowling

	Overs	Mdns	Runs	Wkts	BBI	Ave	Econ	SR	4w	5w
RI Keogh	29.0	1	137	3	2/26	45.66	4.72	58.0	0	0
BD Cotton	5.0	0	24	0	-	-	4.80	-	0	0
LA Procter	32.0	1	164	5	3/45	32.80	5.12	38.4	0	0
RK Kleinveldt	46.0	2	237	6	2/39	39.50	5.15	46.0	0	0
GG White	63.0	1	332	8	3/63	41.50	5.26	47.2	0	0
SA Zaib	14.0	0	76	1	1/38	76.00	5.42	84.0	0	0
SP Crook	6.0	0	34	2	2/27	17.00	5.66	18.0	0	0
JJ Cobb	11.0	0	63	1	1/28	63.00	5.72	66.0	0	0
BW Sanderson	59.0	3	355	6	2/60	59.16	6.01	59.0	0	0
NL Buck	46.0	3	278	4	2/70	69.50	6.04	69.0	0	0
BA Hutton	34.2	0	224	6	2/37	37.33	6.52	34.3	0	0

Catches/Stumpings:
9 Rossington (inc 1st), 6 Wakely, 4 Duckett, 2 Buck, Vasconcelos, 1 Cobb, Cotton, Hutton, Kleinveldt

VITALITY BLAST AVERAGES 2018

Batting

	Mat	Inns	NO	Runs	HS	Ave	SR	100	50	4s	6s
JJ Cobb	14	14	2	448	103	37.33	147.36	1	4	31	28
BM Duckett	14	14	0	414	96	29.57	144.75	0	2	53	10
RE Levi	9	9	1	233	95*	29.12	150.32	0	1	27	11
AG Wakely	14	14	3	292	54*	26.54	132.72	0	2	24	10
CO Thurston	6	5	0	87	41	17.40	112.98	0	0	4	3
GG White	9	6	3	52	21*	17.33	144.44	0	0	4	3
BJ Curran	3	3	0	46	29	15.33	127.77	0	0	6	1
BA Hutton	8	6	3	46	18*	15.33	104.54	0	0	2	2
SP Crook	11	11	2	128	33	14.22	143.82	0	0	11	6
S Prasanna	13	11	0	149	38	13.54	134.23	0	0	11	10
RK Kleinveldt	9	7	0	92	36	13.14	187.75	0	0	8	7
R Vasconcelos	8	7	1	73	25	12.16	105.79	0	0	8	1
LA Procter	6	5	1	48	14*	12.00	106.66	0	0	3	1
BW Sanderson	9	5	4	9	7*	9.00	100.00	0	0	0	1
NL Buck	10	5	2	18	11*	6.00	85.71	0	0	2	0
KJ Coetzer	3	2	0	6	6	3.00	50.00	0	0	0	0
TB Sole	1	1	1	7	7*	-	140.00	0	0	1	0
RJ Gleeson	6	2	2	3	2*	-	75.00	0	0	0	0
G Wade	1	-	-	-	-	-	-	-	-	-	-

Bowling

	Overs	Mdns	Runs	Wkts	BBI	Ave	Econ	SR	4w	5w
TB Sole	4.0	0	32	0	-	-	8.00	-	0	0
RJ Gleeson	23.3	0	200	7	2/21	28.57	8.51	20.1	0	0
BA Hutton	26.4	0	231	4	2/28	57.75	8.66	40.0	0	0
S Prasanna	46.0	0	399	9	2/22	44.33	8.67	30.6	0	0
JJ Cobb	14.0	0	124	1	1/13	124.00	8.85	84.0	0	0
NL Buck	37.1	0	340	11	3/38	30.90	9.14	20.2	0	0
LA Procter	19.0	0	188	4	2/20	47.00	9.89	28.5	0	0
BW Sanderson	29.0	0	299	7	2/41	42.71	10.31	24.8	0	0
GG White	18.0	0	191	3	1/22	63.66	10.61	36.0	0	0
RK Kleinveldt	29.4	0	338	8	2/53	42.25	11.39	22.2	0	0
SP Crook	4.0	0	59	0	-	-	14.75	-	0	0
KJ Coetzer	1.0	0	19	0	-	-	19.00	-	0	0
G Wade	0.1	0	9	0	-	-	54.00	-	0	0

Catches/Stumpings:
6 Duckett (inc 1st), 3 Cobb, Crook, Hutton, Levi, Prasanna, Procter, Thurston, Wakely, White, 2 Curran, Gleeson, Kleinveldt, Vasconcelos, 1 Buck, Duckett, Sole, Wade

NOTTINGHAMSHIRE

FORMED: 1841
HOME GROUND: Trent Bridge, Nottingham
ONE-DAY NAME: Notts Outlaws
CAPTAIN: Steven Mullaney (Championship and RL50), Dan Christian (T20)
2018 RESULTS: CC1: 6/8; RL50: Quarter-finalists; T20: Quarter-finalists
HONOURS: County Championship: (6) 1907, 1929, 1981, 1987, 2005, 2010; Gillette/NatWest/C&G/FP Trophy: 1987; Pro40/National League/CB40/YB40/RL50: (2) 2013, 2017; Benson & Hedges Cup: 1989; Sunday League: 1991; T20 Cup: 2017

THE LOWDOWN

White-ball kings in 2017, Notts came down with a bump last summer, and the club survived an immediate return to Division Two only by dint of having won more matches than relegated Lancashire. They made the quarter-finals of both knockout competitions but were well beaten on each occasion. There appeared to be a collective hangover from the highs of the previous summer and there weren't enough outstanding performers to carry the burden. Injuries also took their toll. On a positive note, Harry Gurney returned to his best form – although he will be a latecomer in 2019 after landing an IPL contract – and 22-year-old off-spinner Matt Carter looks a fine prospect. Special mention also goes to Tom Moores, who made the task of replacing Chris Read look easy. As is their custom, Notts have been skimming the cream off the smaller counties, with the addition of Joe Clarke, Ben Duckett and Ben Slater bolstering the top-order significantly. But the most exciting signing may be the much-touted 22-year-old fast bowler Zak Chappell. Naturally a few players have had to make way, among them Riki Wessels, who scored more than 11,000 runs across eight seasons at the club.

IN: Zak Chappell (Lei), Joe Clarke (Wor), Ben Duckett (Nor), Ben Slater (Der)
OUT: Will Fraine (Yor), Matt Milnes (Ken), Billy Root (Gla), Riki Wessels (Wor), Ben Kitt (REL)

HEAD COACH: PETER MOORES

Moores replaced the long-serving Mick Newell (who remains at the club as director of cricket) as head coach in 2016 and immediately led the club to the cup double as well as Championship promotion. Moores has had two spells as England head coach and won the Championship with Sussex in 2003 and Lancashire in 2011. As a wicketkeeper-batsman, he scored 7,000 first-class runs and claimed 517 dismissals for Sussex between 1985 and 1998.

COUNTY CHAMPIONSHIP AVERAGES 2018

Batting

	Mat	Inns	NO	Runs	HS	Ave	SR	100	50	4s	6s
BT Slater	4	8	0	349	109	43.62	53.94	1	1	57	0
KC Brathwaite	4	8	1	296	71	42.28	40.38	0	3	41	0
LRPL Taylor	8	15	0	506	146	33.73	76.09	1	4	68	6
SJ Mullaney	11	20	0	601	130	30.05	57.73	1	4	80	7
TJ Moores	13	22	1	616	103	29.33	57.46	1	2	88	14
MH Wessels	12	23	3	568	75*	28.40	59.22	0	4	79	2
BM Duckett	3	5	0	133	80	26.60	65.84	0	1	23	0
JD Libby	14	27	2	662	100*	26.48	46.88	1	4	79	1
SR Patel	14	26	1	639	76	25.56	61.20	0	6	90	4
WAR Fraine	1	2	0	49	30	24.50	35.50	0	0	8	0
CD Nash	9	17	0	383	139	22.52	49.86	1	2	60	0
ME Milnes	6	10	5	100	43	20.00	44.44	0	0	13	1
MHA Footitt	3	5	3	38	21*	19.00	59.37	0	0	5	1
L Wood	6	10	2	137	35*	17.12	69.54	0	0	26	0
WT Root	6	12	0	196	36	16.33	45.47	0	0	21	5
JT Ball	6	10	2	130	44*	16.25	70.27	0	0	20	1
SCJ Broad	5	8	0	123	38	15.37	66.84	0	0	13	2
LJ Fletcher	13	23	1	304	43	13.81	46.69	0	0	40	4
HF Gurney	11	16	10	73	29*	12.16	55.72	0	0	11	1
M Carter	4	8	0	76	22	9.50	55.88	0	0	9	3
LW James	1	2	0	14	13	7.00	51.85	0	0	3	0

Bowling

	Overs	Mdns	Runs	Wkts	BBI	BBM	Ave	Econ	SR	5w	10w
WT Root	9.3	1	55	3	3/37	3/37	18.33	5.78	19.0	0	0
SCJ Broad	117.3	31	352	18	4/41	6/102	19.55	2.99	39.1	0	0
CD Nash	22.0	1	66	3	2/4	3/52	22.00	3.00	44.0	0	0
JT Ball	171.5	38	623	28	5/43	9/57	22.25	3.62	36.8	2	0
LW James	15.0	1	68	3	3/54	3/68	22.66	4.53	30.0	0	0
LJ Fletcher	347.3	86	977	38	5/27	7/55	25.71	2.81	54.8	1	0
HF Gurney	325.3	52	1137	42	6/25	8/43	27.07	3.49	46.5	2	0
M Carter	153.2	28	525	16	5/113	8/195	32.81	3.42	57.5	1	0
SJ Mullaney	114.0	21	402	11	4/68	4/92	36.54	3.52	62.1	0	0
JD Libby	11.5	0	40	1	1/23	1/23	40.00	3.38	71.0	0	0
L Wood	110.1	15	411	10	3/66	3/66	41.10	3.73	66.1	0	0
MHA Footitt	66.4	9	276	6	3/69	4/136	46.00	4.14	66.6	0	0
SR Patel	305.5	66	896	19	6/114	6/114	47.15	2.92	96.5	1	0
ME Milnes	153.0	26	527	11	4/44	5/64	47.90	3.44	83.4	0	0
KC Brathwaite	2.0	0	10	0	-	-	-	5.00	-	0	0

Catches/Stumpings:

39 Moores, 14 Wessels, 13 Taylor, 11 Mullaney, 6 Libby, 5 Patel, Wood, 4 Carter, Fletcher, Milnes, Nash, 3 Root, 2 Broad, 1 Ball, Brathwaite, Duckett, Footitt, Gurney, Slater

ROYAL LONDON ONE-DAY CUP AVERAGES 2018

Batting

	Mat	Inns	NO	Runs	HS	Ave	SR	100	50	4s	6s
SJ Mullaney	8	7	0	406	124	58.00	103.04	1	3	34	11
TJ Moores	8	8	1	263	76	37.57	101.54	0	1	26	9
MH Wessels	8	8	0	273	76	34.12	109.63	0	3	29	9
LRPL Taylor	8	8	1	235	58	33.57	87.68	0	2	27	1
LJ Fletcher	8	7	3	133	53*	33.25	107.25	0	1	15	5
SR Patel	8	7	0	208	100	29.71	96.29	1	0	24	2
CD Nash	8	7	0	169	56	24.14	70.41	0	2	17	1
WT Root	7	6	0	128	41	21.33	85.90	0	0	10	2
WAR Fraine	3	3	1	27	13	13.50	122.72	0	0	4	0
AD Hales	3	3	0	38	21	12.66	60.31	0	0	5	0
M Carter	5	4	0	28	17	7.00	82.35	0	0	0	2
JT Ball	8	5	1	20	13	5.00	105.26	0	0	2	1
HF Gurney	4	2	1	2	2*	2.00	50.00	0	0	0	0
JM Blatherwick	2	2	2	5	3*	-	27.77	0	0	0	0

Bowling

	Overs	Mdns	Runs	Wkts	BBI	Ave	Econ	SR	4w	5w
M Carter	43.0	2	198	13	4/40	15.23	4.60	19.8	2	0
SJ Mullaney	53.0	0	245	4	2/42	61.25	4.62	79.5	0	0
SR Patel	74.1	1	372	10	2/33	37.20	5.01	44.5	0	0
LJ Fletcher	60.0	3	325	9	4/20	36.11	5.41	40.0	1	0
CD Nash	11.0	0	62	2	1/18	31.00	5.63	33.0	0	0
JT Ball	69.0	4	391	14	4/29	27.92	5.66	29.5	1	0
HF Gurney	33.0	0	216	9	4/58	24.00	6.54	22.0	1	0
WT Root	21.0	0	153	3	1/27	51.00	7.28	42.0	0	0
JM Blatherwick	2.0	0	17	0	-	-	8.50	-	0	0

Catches/Stumpings:
10 Moores (inc 2st), Taylor, 7 Wessels, 6 Mullaney, 3 Hales, 2 Ball, Carter, Fletcher, Root, 1 Fraine, Nash, Patel

VITALITY BLAST AVERAGES 2018

Batting

	Mat	Inns	NO	Runs	HS	Ave	SR	100	50	4s	6s
DT Christian	15	14	4	415	113*	41.50	172.91	1	1	29	24
JD Libby	11	11	3	284	58	35.50	142.71	0	1	25	5
AD Hales	6	6	1	173	71*	34.60	132.06	0	1	21	3
TJ Moores	15	15	2	445	80*	34.23	146.86	0	3	35	25
WT Root	13	11	3	199	40	24.87	109.94	0	0	16	2
MH Wessels	14	14	0	307	58	21.92	163.29	0	2	29	22
SR Patel	15	14	2	228	52	19.00	118.75	0	1	29	2
SJ Mullaney	15	14	0	263	55	18.78	152.02	0	1	24	11
LJ Fletcher	12	7	1	56	27	9.33	136.58	0	0	3	4
WAR Fraine	7	7	1	49	14	8.16	116.66	0	0	8	0
IS Sodhi	15	9	5	27	8*	6.75	103.84	0	0	3	0
P Coughlin	3	3	0	13	5	4.33	76.47	0	0	0	0
JT Ball	6	3	1	8	8*	4.00	80.00	0	0	0	1
HF Gurney	15	5	2	7	6	2.33	77.77	0	0	1	0
CD Nash	1	1	0	0	0	0.00	0.00	0	0	0	0
M Carter	2	1	1	16	16*	-	266.66	0	0	1	1

Bowling

	Overs	Mdns	Runs	Wkts	BBI	Ave	Econ	SR	4w	5w
HF Gurney	50.4	0	387	20	3/24	19.35	7.63	15.2	0	0
IS Sodhi	54.0	0	441	19	4/17	23.21	8.16	17.0	1	0
M Carter	6.0	0	51	2	1/25	25.50	8.50	18.0	0	0
LJ Fletcher	42.1	0	375	12	3/21	31.25	8.89	21.0	0	0
SR Patel	42.5	0	393	8	2/26	49.12	9.17	32.1	0	0
JT Ball	17.1	0	159	3	3/40	53.00	9.26	34.3	0	0
SJ Mullaney	32.0	0	309	11	2/29	28.09	9.65	17.4	0	0
WT Root	2.0	0	20	0	-	-	10.00	-	0	0
DT Christian	35.1	0	354	10	3/34	35.40	10.06	21.1	0	0

Catches/Stumpings:
10 Christian, 7 Hales, 5 Moores, Mullaney, 4 Coughlin, Fraine, Patel, Wessels, 3 Gurney, Root, 2 Sodhi, 1 Ball, Libby

SOMERSET

FORMED: 1875
HOME GROUND: The Cooper Associates County Ground, Taunton
CAPTAIN: Tom Abell (Championship and RL50), Lewis Gregory (T20)
2018 RESULTS: CC1: 2/8; RL50: 4/9 South Group; T20: Semi-finalists
HONOURS: Gillette/NatWest/C&G/FP Trophy: (3) 1979, 1983, 2001; Benson & Hedges Cup: (2) 1981, 1982; Sunday League: 1979; T20 Cup: 2005

THE LOWDOWN

We could hark on about Somerset being everybody's favourite runners-up after another titillating Championship campaign, but this is a thriving club who are competitive across all formats and always entertaining along the way. Their young captain, Tom Abell, has come of age following a tough baptism in 2017, when he even dropped himself. James Hildreth, outstanding last summer, must be the best current English batsman not to have played international cricket. The pace attack, led by the underrated Lewis Gregory, is very strong when the Overton twins are fit and available, with Josh Davey impressing in the last campaign and Jack Brooks brought in over the winter. Gregory shone in his first year as T20 captain, leading the club to Finals Day. And, of course, there are spinners aplenty, although Dom Bess will want to return to form after a bizarre summer in which he made his Test debut but struggled to make the Championship XI. Peter Trego and Max Waller have agreed white-ball deals, while Marcus Trescothick has signed on for his 27th season. Pakistan batsman Azhar Ali returns to play Championship and 50-over cricket. Meanwhile a new day-night era dawns, with the installation of floodlights at Taunton due to be complete by the start of the season.

IN: Jack Brooks (Yor), Azhar Ali (Pak), Jerome Taylor (WI, T20)
OUT: Fin Trenouth (REL), Johann Myburgh (RET)

HEAD COACH: JASON KERR

A new management structure was put in place when director of cricket Matthew Maynard left after the 2017 season, with former Somerset allrounder Kerr promoted from bowling to head coach. Kerr has been part of the coaching staff since 2005, grooming the club's brightest talent as Academy director. He works alongside director of cricket Andy Hurry, who had a successful spell as coach between 2006 and 2013 before taking charge of the England Development Programme until his return to Taunton in 2017.

COUNTY CHAMPIONSHIP AVERAGES 2018

Batting

	Mat	Inns	NO	Runs	HS	Ave	SR	100	50	4s	6s
MT Renshaw	6	11	1	513	112	51.30	63.17	3	1	69	9
JC Hildreth	14	26	2	1089	184	45.37	65.56	3	6	155	4
TB Abell	14	26	4	883	132*	40.13	51.12	1	5	124	2
Azhar Ali	7	13	1	402	125	33.50	52.54	1	2	53	2
SM Davies	14	25	2	756	92*	32.86	57.14	0	5	115	1
GA Bartlett	6	11	0	306	110	27.81	54.64	1	0	36	3
ME Trescothick	10	18	0	491	100	27.27	51.73	1	4	78	2
DM Bess	7	11	1	226	92	22.60	55.39	0	1	37	0
L Gregory	12	21	2	411	65	21.63	65.55	0	3	48	13
EJ Byrom	8	15	0	309	54	20.60	38.33	0	2	44	0
J Overton	8	12	2	197	55	19.70	78.80	0	1	33	3
C Overton	11	18	1	331	80	19.47	71.64	0	1	46	4
JH Davey	11	17	6	206	36	18.72	48.93	0	0	23	3
TD Groenewald	7	11	5	91	36*	15.16	61.07	0	0	11	3
MJ Leach	11	16	2	174	66	12.42	39.45	0	1	26	1
T Banton	2	3	0	37	30	12.33	48.68	0	0	4	1
PD Trego	2	4	0	46	39	11.50	45.09	0	0	4	1
BGF Green	2	4	0	43	26	10.75	40.18	0	0	6	0
PA van Meekeren	1	2	1	6	6	6.00	75.00	0	0	1	0
RE van der Merwe	1	1	0	0	0	0.00	0.00	0	0	0	0
MTC Waller	1	1	0	0	0	0.00	0.00	0	0	0	0

Bowling

	Overs	Mdns	Runs	Wkts	BBI	BBM	Ave	Econ	SR	5w	10w
BGF Green	7.0	3	17	1	1/8	1/17	17.00	2.42	42.0	0	0
Azhar Ali	11.0	3	20	1	1/5	1/5	20.00	1.81	66.0	0	0
MJ Leach	255.4	57	722	30	8/85	12/102	24.06	2.82	51.1	3	2
TD Groenewald	173.0	41	509	21	4/85	5/63	24.23	2.94	49.4	0	0
J Overton	177.3	34	646	26	4/25	8/143	24.84	3.63	40.9	0	0
L Gregory	305.5	75	928	37	4/33	7/86	25.08	3.03	49.5	0	0
JH Davey	290.4	73	862	34	5/65	7/111	25.35	2.96	51.2	1	0
TB Abell	121.4	23	492	19	4/43	4/43	25.89	4.04	38.4	0	0
C Overton	321.3	72	1014	37	4/27	7/95	27.40	3.15	52.1	0	0
RE van der Merwe	51.0	13	143	5	4/138	5/143	28.60	2.80	61.2	0	0
PD Trego	41.0	7	146	3	2/63	3/106	48.66	3.56	82.0	0	0
DM Bess	204.1	51	602	11	3/81	5/213	54.72	2.94	111.3	0	0
PA van Meekeren	20.0	3	67	1	1/67	1/67	67.00	3.35	120.0	0	0
MT Renshaw	3.0	1	11	0	-	-	-	3.66	-	0	0
GA Bartlett	3.2	0	27	0	-	-	-	8.10	-	0	0
EJ Byrom	10.0	1	39	0	-	-	-	3.90	-	0	0

Catches/Stumpings:

41 Davies (inc 3st), 16 Trescothick, 13 Hildreth, 12 Gregory, 9 C Overton, 5 Leach, J Overton, Renshaw, 3 Bess, Davey, Green, 2 Abell, Azhar, Bartlett, Byrom, Davey, Groenewald, 1 Banton, Trego

ROYAL LONDON ONE-DAY CUP AVERAGES 2018

Batting

	Mat	Inns	NO	Runs	HS	Ave	SR	100	50	4s	6s
JC Hildreth	8	8	1	438	159	62.57	98.20	1	2	35	12
PD Trego	8	8	0	376	100	47.00	89.52	1	4	33	5
TB Abell	2	1	0	40	40	40.00	160.00	0	0	7	0
RE van der Merwe	8	7	2	195	61	39.00	107.73	0	2	14	4
L Gregory	5	4	0	151	60	37.75	102.72	0	2	8	5
BGF Green	3	3	2	35	26*	35.00	79.54	0	0	1	1
JG Myburgh	8	8	1	218	75*	31.14	110.65	0	2	34	4
MT Renshaw	6	6	0	180	56	30.00	103.44	0	2	16	3
PA van Meekeren	4	3	2	20	10*	20.00	83.33	0	0	2	0
SM Davies	8	8	0	158	56	19.75	105.33	0	1	16	7
C Overton	6	5	2	59	23*	19.66	120.40	0	0	5	2
TD Groenewald	4	3	1	30	24	15.00	136.36	0	0	2	2
MTC Waller	4	2	1	12	6*	12.00	80.00	0	0	2	0
T Banton	7	6	0	70	40	11.66	55.11	0	0	4	0
J Overton	5	5	0	39	23	7.80	82.97	0	0	5	0
DM Bess	1	-	-	-	-	-	-	-	-	-	-
JH Davey	1	-	-	-	-	-	-	-	-	-	-

Bowling

	Overs	Mdns	Runs	Wkts	BBI	Ave	Econ	SR	4w	5w
JH Davey	10.0	0	47	1	1/47	47.00	4.70	60.0	0	0
PD Trego	50.0	3	244	7	2/23	34.85	4.88	42.8	0	0
L Gregory	33.0	1	186	6	2/41	31.00	5.63	33.0	0	0
TD Groenewald	34.0	0	198	9	3/43	22.00	5.82	22.6	0	0
PA van Meekeren	17.1	1	101	3	3/32	33.66	5.88	34.3	0	0
C Overton	56.2	3	336	12	4/27	28.00	5.96	28.1	1	0
BGF Green	11.0	0	70	1	1/52	70.00	6.36	66.0	0	0
MTC Waller	15.0	0	98	3	3/52	32.66	6.53	30.0	0	0
J Overton	22.0	0	145	2	1/42	72.50	6.59	66.0	0	0
RE van der Merwe	41.3	0	287	6	2/64	47.83	6.91	41.5	0	0
DM Bess	3.0	0	34	0	-	-	11.33	-	0	0

Catches/Stumpings:
10 Davies, 7 Waller, 4 Hildreth, 3 Banton, van der Merwe, 2 C Overton, J Overton, Renshaw, 1 Groenewald, Myburgh, Trego, van Meekeren

VITALITY BLAST AVERAGES 2018

	Mat	Inns	NO	Runs	HS	Ave	SR	100	50	4s	6s
RE van der Merwe	16	10	8	118	34*	59.00	173.52	0	0	13	4
L Gregory	16	13	6	328	62	46.85	202.46	0	3	28	19
CJ Anderson	16	15	3	514	72	42.83	169.07	0	3	31	34
T Banton	2	2	1	38	29*	38.00	105.55	0	0	4	1
TB Abell	16	15	5	292	48	29.20	132.12	0	0	23	7
JC Hildreth	16	15	1	403	57	28.78	139.93	0	4	35	13
JG Myburgh	16	16	2	372	103*	26.57	151.21	1	1	48	12
PD Trego	16	15	1	328	72*	23.42	138.98	0	3	38	11
SM Davies	14	14	0	213	60	15.21	141.05	0	1	31	3
J Overton	16	5	3	17	7*	8.50	141.66	0	0	2	0
C Overton	3	1	0	0	0	0.00	-	0	0	0	0
JE Taylor	11	1	1	1	1*	-	100.00	0	0	0	0
JH Davey	2	-	-	-	-	-	-	-	-	-	-
MTC Waller	16	-	-	-	-	-	-	-	-	-	-

Batting

	Overs	Mdns	Runs	Wkts	BBI	Ave	Econ	SR	4w	5w
MTC Waller	56.0	1	382	16	4/25	23.87	6.82	21.0	1	0
TB Abell	2.0	0	17	0	-	-	8.50	-	0	0
JG Myburgh	2.0	0	17	1	1/5	17.00	8.50	12.0	0	0
RE van der Merwe	58.3	0	502	12	2/26	41.83	8.58	29.2	0	0
JE Taylor	41.0	0	366	22	5/15	16.63	8.92	11.1	1	1
L Gregory	58.0	0	574	18	4/28	31.88	9.89	19.3	1	0
CJ Anderson	4.0	0	40	1	1/11	40.00	10.00	24.0	0	0
J Overton	52.4	0	540	24	5/47	22.50	10.25	13.1	1	1
C Overton	9.1	0	97	3	2/31	32.33	10.58	18.3	0	0
JH Davey	4.0	0	45	3	2/35	15.00	11.25	8.0	0	0
PD Trego	4.0	0	47	1	1/10	47.00	11.75	24.0	0	0

Bowling

Catches/Stumpings:
13 Waller, 12 Abell, 10 J Overton, 9 Davies (inc 1st), van der Merwe, 6 Myburgh, 5 Gregory, Hildreth, 3 Anderson, Taylor, 2 Trego, 1 Banton (inc 1st)

SURREY

FORMED: 1845
GROUND: The Kia Oval, London
CAPTAIN: Rory Burns (Championship and RL50), Jade Dernbach (T20)
2018 RESULTS: CC1: Winners; RL50: 5/9 South Group; T20: 5/9 South Group
HONOURS: Championship: (20) 1890, 1891, 1892, 1894, 1895, 1899, 1914, 1950, 1952, 1953, 1954, 1955, 1956, 1957, 1958, 1971, 1999, 2000, 2002, 2018; Gillette/NatWest/C&G/FP Trophy: 1982; Benson & Hedges Cup: (3) 1974, 1997, 2001; Pro40/National League/CB40/YB40/RL50: (2) 2003, 2011; Sunday League: 1996; T20 Cup: 2003

THE LOWDOWN

It says much about Surrey's depth of talent that their first Championship title since 2002 came without the runs of Kumar Sangakkara and that the Curran brothers played just 11 four-day matches between them. There is a feeling at The Oval that this could be the start of another Surrey dynasty. The question they must answer is much the same as that which faced the great Adam Hollioake side at the turn of the century: can they cope with all the England call-ups? Rory Burns, Jason Roy, Ollie Pope, Ben Foakes and the Currans are all likely to be unavailable for chunks of the season. Mind you, it may not matter if you've got Morne Morkel – surely the most glamorous Kolpak signing ever made, except from the view of those who face him. In March Morkel signed on to play for the club until the end of next season. South Africa opener Dean Elgar returns, while the arrival of Jordan Clark and Liam Plunkett will strengthen Surrey's pursuit of a first white-ball trophy since 2011.

IN: Jordan Clark (Lan), Liam Plunkett (Yor), Dean Elgar (SA)
OUT: Mathew Pillans (Yor)

HEAD COACH: MICHAEL DI VENUTO

A prolific Australian batsmen for Sussex, Derbyshire and Durham between 1999 and 2012, di Venuto took over from Graham Ford before the 2016 season, having been Australia's batting coach for three years. He led the club to two Lord's finals in his first two seasons before landing the holy grail last summer. Vikram Solanki is his deputy, while Richard Johnson will work with the bowling attack after being lured across the river from Middlesex.

COUNTY CHAMPIONSHIP AVERAGES 2018

Batting

	Mat	Inns	NO	Runs	HS	Ave	SR	100	50	4s	6s
OJ Pope	13	16	2	986	158*	70.42	63.81	4	1	148	2
JJ Roy	2	3	0	196	128	65.33	79.67	1	1	26	4
RJ Burns	14	22	1	1359	193	64.71	51.53	4	7	178	1
SG Borthwick	8	12	1	444	83	40.36	55.91	0	5	57	2
D Elgar	7	10	0	387	110	38.70	46.18	1	2	51	1
BT Foakes	12	18	1	624	90	36.70	49.64	0	4	80	1
MD Stoneman	13	21	1	660	144	33.00	57.94	1	4	101	1
R Clarke	13	17	1	500	111	31.25	68.02	1	2	79	6
AJ Finch	2	3	0	77	43	25.66	73.33	0	0	6	3
RS Patel	9	13	3	255	48	25.50	34.88	0	0	29	0
SM Curran	7	10	1	209	70	23.22	60.93	0	1	30	1
TB de Bruyn	2	3	1	46	38	23.00	51.11	0	0	4	0
C McKerr	5	5	2	64	29	21.33	46.37	0	0	9	0
WG Jacks	6	8	0	168	53	21.00	45.40	0	1	20	3
A Harinath	2	3	0	56	48	18.66	44.44	0	0	9	1
TK Curran	4	5	0	81	43	16.20	59.12	0	0	10	0
M Morkel	10	13	2	172	29	15.63	64.41	0	0	24	3
SC Meaker	1	1	0	13	13	13.00	41.93	0	0	1	0
JW Dernbach	10	13	2	129	31	11.72	82.69	0	0	18	2
A Virdi	14	16	8	68	21*	8.50	64.15	0	0	11	2
MP Dunn	2	3	1	10	9*	5.00	22.72	0	0	1	0

Bowling

	Overs	Mdns	Runs	Wkts	BBI	BBM	Ave	Econ	SR	5w	10w
M Morkel	315.4	82	845	59	6/57	9/120	14.32	2.67	32.1	4	0
TK Curran	120.4	30	312	19	5/28	6/59	16.42	2.58	38.1	1	0
C McKerr	67.2	13	246	13	4/26	7/47	18.92	3.65	31.0	0	0
R Clarke	363.1	87	1012	47	5/29	8/75	21.53	2.78	46.3	1	0
SM Curran	192.2	37	608	25	6/54	10/101	24.32	3.16	46.1	1	1
JW Dernbach	285.5	65	929	32	4/49	7/138	29.03	3.25	53.5	0	0
A Virdi	360.3	46	1184	39	6/105	6/105	30.35	3.28	55.4	1	0
RS Patel	87.1	14	279	8	6/5	6/12	34.87	3.20	65.3	1	0
MP Dunn	44.3	10	171	3	2/41	3/83	57.00	3.84	89.0	0	0
SG Borthwick	18.0	1	67	0	-	-	-	3.72	-	0	0
SC Meaker	22.0	1	93	0	-	-	-	4.22	-	0	0

Catches/Stumpings:

38 Foakes (inc 1st), 21 Pope, 19 Clarke, 13 Borthwick, 11 Burns, 8 Jacks, 6 Elgar, 5 Virdi, 4 Patel, Stoneman, 2 S Curran, de Bruyn, Dernbach, Dunn, 1 Finch, Harinath, Meaker, Morkel

ROYAL LONDON ONE-DAY CUP AVERAGES 2018

Batting

	Mat	Inns	NO	Runs	HS	Ave	SR	100	50	4s	6s
D Elgar	4	4	0	229	91	57.25	91.60	0	3	14	5
BT Foakes	8	7	2	279	86	55.80	81.10	0	3	28	3
SG Borthwick	4	2	1	46	46*	46.00	95.83	0	0	5	1
OJ Pope	8	7	4	119	57*	39.66	79.86	0	1	9	2
RJ Burns	8	7	0	270	68	38.57	86.53	0	1	20	1
WG Jacks	8	7	0	254	121	36.28	118.13	1	1	36	6
JJ Roy	6	5	0	181	86	36.20	119.07	0	2	20	7
SM Curran	6	3	1	67	30	33.50	76.13	0	0	7	0
GJ Batty	8	3	1	29	15	14.50	76.31	0	0	2	0
R Clarke	8	4	1	42	22	14.00	77.77	0	0	5	0
MD Stoneman	4	3	0	26	18	8.66	76.47	0	0	5	0
TK Curran	4	1	0	8	8	8.00	57.14	0	0	0	0
JW Dernbach	6	2	0	14	12	7.00	82.35	0	0	0	1
SC Meaker	2	1	1	18	18*	-	75.00	0	0	2	0
M Morkel	4	1	1	1	1*	-	33.33	0	0	0	0

Bowling

	Overs	Mdns	Runs	Wkts	BBI	Ave	Econ	SR	4w	5w
M Morkel	30.0	2	138	4	2/39	34.50	4.60	45.0	0	0
GJ Batty	54.0	0	304	5	1/33	60.80	5.62	64.8	0	0
R Clarke	61.0	1	352	13	4/48	27.07	5.77	28.1	1	0
WG Jacks	17.0	0	99	1	1/12	99.00	5.82	102.0	0	0
SM Curran	41.0	2	242	7	2/37	34.57	5.90	35.1	0	0
TK Curran	30.0	2	188	8	4/33	23.50	6.26	22.5	2	0
JW Dernbach	50.5	0	322	6	2/57	53.66	6.33	50.8	0	0
SG Borthwick	13.0	0	83	4	2/32	20.75	6.38	19.5	0	0
SC Meaker	7.3	0	60	0	-	-	8.00	-	0	0

Catches/Stumpings:
8 Foakes, 5 Clarke, 4 Roy, 3 Dernbach, Morkel, 2 Borthwick, Burns, T Curran, Pope, 1 Batty, S Curran, Jacks, Meaker

VITALITY BLAST AVERAGES 2018

Batting

	Mat	Inns	NO	Runs	HS	Ave	SR	100	50	4s	6s
AJ Finch	9	9	5	589	131*	147.25	182.35	2	3	60	31
R Clarke	14	8	3	235	50	47.00	176.69	0	1	14	18
OJ Pope	9	7	3	159	34	39.75	167.36	0	0	15	5
BT Foakes	14	10	2	310	75*	38.75	149.03	0	3	32	9
NJ Maddinson	12	10	3	245	70	35.00	138.41	0	1	17	12
SM Curran	4	2	1	29	16*	29.00	131.81	0	0	2	1
RJ Burns	9	8	1	176	50	25.14	154.38	0	1	28	2
JJ Roy	8	7	0	163	84	23.28	179.12	0	1	14	12
TK Curran	8	1	0	21	21	21.00	175.00	0	0	2	1
WG Jacks	10	5	0	100	53	20.00	142.85	0	1	4	9
FOE van den Bergh	4	3	1	27	19*	13.50	103.84	0	0	2	0
JL Smith	2	2	1	7	7*	7.00	70.00	0	0	0	0
MW Pillans	9	2	1	5	5*	5.00	71.42	0	0	0	0
M Morkel	9	3	1	7	3*	3.50	46.66	0	0	0	0
GJ Batty	14	2	0	4	2	2.00	36.36	0	0	0	0
JW Dernbach	14	2	1	1	1*	1.00	25.00	0	0	0	0
SG Borthwick	4	1	1	7	7*	-	58.33	0	0	0	0
MD Stoneman	1	-	-	-	-	-	-	-	-	-	-

Bowling

	Overs	Mdns	Runs	Wkts	BBI	Ave	Econ	SR	4w	5w
SM Curran	9.0	2	58	2	1/14	29.00	6.44	27.0	0	0
GJ Batty	42.0	0	330	11	3/36	30.00	7.85	22.9	0	0
R Clarke	45.1	0	377	16	2/19	23.56	8.34	16.9	0	0
JW Dernbach	44.4	0	385	12	3/31	32.08	8.61	22.3	0	0
M Morkel	34.0	0	320	12	3/30	26.66	9.41	17.0	0	0
MW Pillans	24.0	0	238	10	3/20	23.80	9.91	14.4	0	0
TK Curran	28.0	0	280	12	3/30	23.33	10.00	14.0	0	0
FOE van den Bergh	6.0	0	67	0	-	-	11.16	-	0	0
WG Jacks	2.0	0	26	0	-	-	13.00	-	0	0
SG Borthwick	3.0	0	49	1	1/31	49.00	16.33	18.0	0	0

Catches/Stumpings:
9 Clarke, 8 Foakes, 7 Dernbach, 6 Jacks, 5 Batty, 4 Borthwick, Burns, Maddinson, Roy, 3 T Curran, Finch, Pope, 1 Pillans, Smith, van den Bergh

SUSSEX

FORMED: 1839
HOME GROUND: The 1st Central County Ground, Hove
ONE-DAY NAME: Sussex Sharks
CAPTAIN: Ben Brown
2018 RESULTS: CC2: 3/10; RL50: 8/9 South Group; T20: Runners-up
HONOURS: Championship: (3) 2003, 2006, 2007; Gillette/NatWest/C&G/FP Trophy: (5) 1963, 1964, 1978, 1986, 2006; Pro40/ National League/CB40/YB40/RL50: (2) 2008, 2009; Sunday League: 1982; T20 Cup: 2009

THE LOWDOWN

Still no trophy this decade, but Sussex are going well after making the final of the T20 Blast and just missing out on Championship promotion in Jason Gillespie's first year in charge. Ben Brown appears to have been inspired by the captaincy, and having six batsmen who averaged more than 30 was some achievement in a bowler's summer. Among them were the young pair of Phil Salt (22) and Tom Haines (20), both of whom made their maiden Championship hundreds. Salt's explosive hitting also spiced up Sussex's T20 campaign, in which the old pros Laurie Evans and Luke Wright amassed 1,066 between them. The bowling resources are rich. Ollie Robinson hit the form of his life in 2018 (74 Championship wickets) and Pakistan left-armer Mir Hamza has signed for eight Championship matches between May and July. A T20 attack of Jofra Archer, Chris Jordan, Tymal Mills, Rashid Khan (for the group phase only) and a rejuvenated Danny Briggs could be the best in the land. Archer may soon be gobbled up by England – he qualified for selection in March – but watch out for 21-year-old Bermudan allrounder Delray Rawlins.

IN: Mir Hamza (Pak), Rashid Khan (Afg, T20)
OUT: Stuart Whittingham (Glo)

HEAD COACH: JASON GILLESPIE

Gillespie, a serial winner, was appointed by chief executive Rob Andrew to replace Mark Davis in October 2017. In five seasons at Headingley, Gillespie led Yorkshire to Championship promotion and then back-to-back titles in 2014 and 2015. He also coached the Adelaide Strikers to victory at the 2017/18 Big Bash. Gillespie took 402 international wickets as a fast bowler and was an integral part of the great Australian team of the late 1990s and early 2000s.

COUNTY CHAMPIONSHIP AVERAGES 2018

Batting

	Mat	Inns	NO	Runs	HS	Ave	SR	100	50	4s	6s
BC Brown	14	24	3	912	116	43.42	59.29	1	7	117	0
D Wiese	13	20	4	538	106	33.62	78.77	1	2	68	6
TJ Haines	7	10	0	319	124	31.90	62.79	1	1	50	1
PD Salt	14	24	0	739	148	30.79	77.54	2	2	102	8
MGK Burgess	12	19	1	551	101*	30.61	71.46	1	2	70	2
HZ Finch	14	24	0	722	103	30.08	53.16	1	5	103	5
LWP Wells	14	24	1	607	102*	26.39	45.23	1	4	78	5
S van Zyl	5	9	0	237	45	26.33	46.65	0	0	36	0
I Sharma	4	6	2	102	66	25.50	47.88	0	1	11	2
CJ Jordan	8	13	0	299	68	23.00	58.05	0	2	44	0
LJ Wright	9	16	0	338	88	21.12	60.24	0	1	52	3
DR Briggs	12	20	7	234	46	18.00	53.42	0	0	35	0
JC Archer	8	13	3	170	33	17.00	51.35	0	0	19	2
LJ Evans	1	2	0	34	34	17.00	56.66	0	0	4	0
OE Robinson	14	22	3	294	52	15.47	59.51	0	1	32	1
DMW Rawlins	1	2	0	0	0	0.00	0.00	0	0	0	0
GHS Garton	1	1	1	22	22*	-	64.70	0	0	2	1
A Sakande	1	2	2	1	1*	-	11.11	0	0	0	0
SG Whittingham	1	1	1	0	0*	-	0.00	0	0	0	0
WAT Beer	1	-	-	-	-	-	-	-	-	-	-

Bowling

	Overs	Mdns	Runs	Wkts	BBI	BBM	Ave	Econ	SR	5w	10w
JC Archer	273.5	67	750	42	5/69	8/46	17.85	2.73	39.1	1	0
OE Robinson	485.0	92	1381	74	7/58	10/67	18.66	2.84	39.3	4	1
I Sharma	114.3	19	346	15	4/52	7/114	23.06	3.02	45.8	0	0
D Wiese	339.1	65	1041	41	5/48	6/75	25.39	3.06	49.6	1	0
DR Briggs	279.5	51	764	28	4/70	6/118	27.28	2.73	59.9	0	0
CJ Jordan	191.1	32	598	20	3/23	5/37	29.90	3.12	57.3	0	0
A Sakande	22.0	1	91	3	3/44	3/91	30.33	4.13	44.0	0	0
SG Whittingham	16.0	2	61	2	2/56	2/61	30.50	3.81	48.0	0	0
PD Salt	9.0	2	32	1	1/32	1/32	32.00	3.55	54.0	0	0
S van Zyl	48.0	12	127	3	3/16	3/28	42.33	2.64	96.0	0	0
LWP Wells	125.2	11	378	8	4/81	4/81	47.25	3.01	94.0	0	0
TJ Haines	29.0	8	74	1	1/13	1/13	74.00	2.55	174.0	0	0
WAT Beer	26.0	3	88	1	1/88	1/88	88.00	3.38	156.0	0	0
GHS Garton	27.0	2	103	1	1/46	1/103	103.00	3.81	162.0	0	0
BC Brown	3.0	2	1	0	-	-	-	0.33	-	0	0
MGK Burgess	6.0	1	14	0	-	-	-	2.33	-	0	0

Catches/Stumpings:
53 Brown (inc 1st), 23 Finch, 11 Salt, 6 Archer, 5 Briggs, Jordan, Robinson, 4 Burgess, 3 Wells, 2 Haines, Wiese, 1 Evans, Garton, Sharma, van Zyl, Wright

ROYAL LONDON ONE-DAY CUP AVERAGES 2018

Batting

	Mat	Inns	NO	Runs	HS	Ave	SR	100	50	4s	6s
LJ Evans	7	6	2	243	107*	60.75	78.38	1	0	20	3
D Wiese	7	5	1	214	67	53.50	118.23	0	3	15	9
JC Archer	3	2	1	52	33*	52.00	162.50	0	0	3	3
LJ Wright	6	5	0	229	105	45.80	106.01	1	1	30	4
CJ Jordan	3	2	1	42	35	42.00	95.45	0	0	1	3
HZ Finch	7	6	0	250	108	41.66	68.49	1	1	21	2
MGK Burgess	7	5	0	162	58	32.40	122.72	0	2	12	6
BC Brown	7	6	1	131	73*	26.20	71.97	0	1	9	0
LWP Wells	7	6	0	121	62	20.16	69.54	0	1	19	1
OE Robinson	5	3	0	33	17	11.00	113.79	0	0	3	0
I Sharma	6	2	1	11	7*	11.00	110.00	0	0	1	0
PD Salt	1	1	0	5	5	5.00	45.45	0	0	1	0
DR Briggs	7	3	1	3	2	1.50	30.00	0	0	0	0
DMW Rawlins	1	1	0	0	0	0.00	0.00	0	0	0	0
A Sakande	2	1	1	1	1*	-	50.00	0	0	0	0
GHS Garton	1	-	-	-	-	-	-	-	-	-	-

Bowling

	Overs	Mdns	Runs	Wkts	BBI	Ave	Econ	SR	4w	5w
I Sharma	44.0	3	212	8	3/47	26.50	4.81	33.0	0	0
DR Briggs	57.0	1	278	9	3/23	30.88	4.87	38.0	0	0
D Wiese	48.0	0	246	6	3/46	41.00	5.12	48.0	0	0
OE Robinson	44.0	3	244	9	3/31	27.11	5.54	29.3	0	0
JC Archer	19.0	0	106	2	2/53	53.00	5.57	57.0	0	0
CJ Jordan	20.0	0	115	3	2/55	38.33	5.75	40.0	0	0
LWP Wells	28.0	0	162	2	2/30	81.00	5.78	84.0	0	0
DMW Rawlins	4.0	0	26	0	-	-	6.50	-	0	0
A Sakande	13.0	0	86	2	2/53	43.00	6.61	39.0	0	0
GHS Garton	5.0	0	36	0	-	-	7.20	-	0	0

Catches/Stumpings:
4 Brown, 3 Briggs, Burgess, Evans, 2 Finch, Wells, 1 Robinson, Wiese, Wright

VITALITY BLAST AVERAGES 2018

	Mat	Inns	NO	Runs	HS	Ave	SR	100	50	4s	6s
LJ Evans	15	14	5	614	96	68.22	135.84	0	7	55	17
LJ Wright	13	12	0	452	92	37.66	151.17	0	5	47	15
HZ Finch	2	2	0	55	33	27.50	117.02	0	0	6	1
DMW Rawlins	9	9	1	203	49	25.37	146.04	0	0	15	10
PD Salt	15	14	0	355	74	25.35	172.33	0	4	42	16
MGK Burgess	15	11	4	160	56	22.85	128.00	0	1	9	9
D Wiese	13	10	2	167	52	20.87	130.46	0	1	15	4
JC Archer	15	10	4	120	26*	20.00	139.53	0	0	8	5
TC Bruce	10	8	2	62	21	10.33	95.38	0	0	7	1
CJ Jordan	13	5	1	19	13	4.75	67.85	0	0	0	0
DR Briggs	15	3	2	3	2	3.00	60.00	0	0	0	0
Rashid Khan	11	4	1	6	4	2.00	75.00	0	0	1	0
OE Robinson	4	1	1	5	5*	-	100.00	0	0	0	0
WAT Beer	6	1	1	1	1*	-	100.00	0	0	0	0
TS Mills	9	-	-	-	-	-	-	-	-	-	-

Batting

	Overs	Mdns	Runs	Wkts	BBI	Ave	Econ	SR	4w	5w
Rashid Khan	37.0	0	244	17	3/9	14.35	6.59	13.0	0	0
DR Briggs	48.0	0	339	18	3/29	18.83	7.06	16.0	0	0
WAT Beer	17.0	0	129	7	2/17	18.42	7.58	14.5	0	0
CJ Jordan	37.5	1	300	13	2/9	23.07	7.92	17.4	0	0
TS Mills	26.3	0	224	7	3/20	32.00	8.45	22.7	0	0
JC Archer	51.1	0	438	22	3/24	19.90	8.56	13.9	0	0
OE Robinson	13.0	0	114	0	-	-	8.76	-	0	0
D Wiese	30.0	0	285	7	5/24	40.71	9.50	25.7	0	1

Bowling

Catches/Stumpings:
10 Burgess (inc 5st), 7 Bruce, 6 Rawlins, 4 Evans, Jordan, Salt, Wiese, 3 Archer, Briggs, Finch, 2 Wright, 1 Khan, Mills, Robinson

WARWICKSHIRE

FORMED: 1882
HOME GROUND: Edgbaston Stadium, Birmingham
T20 BLAST NAME: Birmingham Bears
CAPTAIN: Jeetan Patel
2018 RESULTS: CC2: Winners; RL50: 4/9 North Group; T20: 6/9 North Group
HONOURS: Championship: (7) 1911, 1951, 1972, 1994, 1995, 2004, 2012; Gillette/NatWest/C&G/FP Trophy: (5) 1966, 1968, 1989, 1993, 1995; Benson & Hedges Cup: (2) 1994, 2002; Pro40/National League/CB40/YB40/RL50: (2) 2010, 2016; Sunday League: (3) 1980, 1994, 1997; T20 Cup: 2014

THE LOWDOWN

Warwickshire return to Division One with a new sporting director, Paul Farbrace, after Ashley Giles was appointed as England's director of cricket in December. Farbrace arrives at a time when the club are undergoing a delicate generational transition. Ian Bell is still there to oil the batting but the retirement of Jonathan Trott leaves a big hole. Opening rookies Will Rhodes and Dom Sibley impressed last summer, sharing eight first-class hundreds between them, but it'll be tougher in the top tier. Sam Hain, prolific in white-ball cricket, will need to come of age in the Championship. The bowling is just as hard to forecast. Keith Barker, who took 359 wickets at 24.50 in 10 seasons at Edgbaston, will be sorely missed. Stalwarts Chris Wright and Boyd Rankin have also moved on while Chris Woakes and Olly Stone are likely to have international commitments. But the club have captured the prolific Gloucestershire seam pair of Liam Norwell and Craig Miles, while 19-year-old Henry Brookes is a pacy prospect. The insatiable Jeetan Patel will lead again, with Australian spinner Ashton Agar offering support throughout the T20 Blast campaign.

IN: Liam Norwell, Craig Miles (both Glo), Ashton Agar (Aus, T20)
OUT: Keith Barker (Ham), Josh Poysden (Yor), Chris Wright (Lei), Boyd Rankin, Sunny Singh, Andy Umeed (all REL), Grant Elliott, Jonathan Trott (both RET)

FIRST-TEAM COACH: JIM TROUGHTON

Involved with Warwickshire since the age of 11, Troughton scored more than 13,000 runs for the club between 2001 and 2014 and played six ODIs for England. In 2012 he captained Warwickshire to the Championship title. Troughton became fielding coach immediately after a back injury curtailed his playing career and was appointed first-team coach in 2016, working under former sport director Ashley Giles as part of the club's management overhaul. He will work alongside Paul Farbrace, who in February left his position as England's assistant coach to replace Giles.

COUNTY CHAMPIONSHIP AVERAGES 2018

Batting

	Mat	Inns	NO	Runs	HS	Ave	SR	100	50	4s	6s
IR Bell	14	23	4	1027	204	54.05	55.87	5	2	140	3
MJ Lamb	3	4	1	151	79	50.33	44.41	0	1	14	1
IJL Trott	14	23	3	935	170*	46.75	56.66	2	6	113	0
WMH Rhodes	14	23	1	972	137	44.18	53.14	4	4	124	3
CR Woakes	2	3	1	86	73*	43.00	86.00	0	1	12	1
DP Sibley	14	23	2	777	144*	37.00	42.57	4	1	82	0
SR Hain	12	17	1	566	90	35.37	49.04	0	6	75	0
TR Ambrose	14	20	1	656	103	34.52	52.06	1	3	80	1
HJH Brookes	5	6	1	165	70	33.00	61.11	0	2	16	3
AJ Hose	3	6	1	126	65	25.20	43.29	0	1	18	0
CJC Wright	14	18	2	342	72	21.37	42.37	0	2	39	0
KHD Barker	10	14	2	218	58	18.16	52.15	0	1	28	1
OP Stone	7	8	2	86	42*	14.33	55.48	0	0	10	2
JS Patel	14	19	3	184	32	11.50	64.33	0	0	22	1
RN Sidebottom	9	12	6	30	10*	5.00	23.43	0	0	1	0
OJ Hannon-Dalby	4	7	0	29	13	4.14	24.78	0	0	4	0
JE Poysden	1	1	0	0	0	0.00	0.00	0	0	0	0

Bowling

	Overs	Mdns	Runs	Wkts	BBI	BBM	Ave	Econ	SR	5w	10w
OP Stone	160.2	26	525	43	8/80	11/96	12.20	3.27	22.3	3	1
JE Poysden	23.2	2	73	5	5/29	5/73	14.60	3.12	28.0	1	0
KHD Barker	254.1	69	672	40	5/32	9/96	16.80	2.64	38.1	2	0
OJ Hannon-Dalby	103.4	22	329	15	4/61	5/80	21.93	3.17	41.4	0	0
HJH Brookes	142.0	22	470	21	4/54	8/119	22.38	3.30	40.5	0	0
JS Patel	431.4	108	1276	56	7/83	10/106	22.78	2.95	46.2	4	2
RN Sidebottom	185.0	40	637	25	6/35	10/96	25.48	3.44	44.4	1	1
CJC Wright	373.2	67	1279	41	5/32	7/65	31.19	3.42	54.6	1	0
CR Woakes	51.0	6	225	4	2/27	2/86	56.25	4.41	76.5	0	0
WMH Rhodes	56.0	12	182	1	1/0	1/0	182.00	3.25	336.0	0	0
MJ Lamb	6.0	1	22	0	-	-	-	3.66	-	0	0

Catches/Stumpings:
57 Ambrose, 18 Sibley, 13 Bell, 11 Trott, 9 Hain, 5 Rhodes, Sidebottom, 4 Patel, 3 Brookes, Wright, 1 Barker, Hose, Lamb, Woakes

Batting

	Mat	Inns	NO	Runs	HS	Ave	SR	100	50	4s	6s
SR Hain	8	6	2	426	108	106.50	88.93	2	3	42	1
WMH Rhodes	1	1	0	69	69	69.00	123.21	0	1	9	0
IR Bell	8	5	1	226	145*	56.50	86.59	1	0	18	2
IJL Trott	8	6	1	271	102*	54.20	79.00	2	1	26	0
AJ Hose	7	4	0	139	51	34.75	96.52	0	1	12	3
TR Ambrose	8	5	0	123	75	24.60	96.09	0	1	9	0
AD Thomason	7	4	2	48	15*	24.00	94.11	0	0	4	1
OP Stone	8	2	1	23	16	23.00	82.14	0	0	2	0
DP Sibley	1	1	0	22	22	22.00	84.61	0	0	1	1
EJ Pollock	8	6	0	127	56	21.16	144.31	0	1	17	6
CR Woakes	1	1	0	9	9	9.00	112.50	0	0	1	0
JS Patel	8	3	1	14	11	7.00	127.27	0	0	2	0
OJ Hannon-Dalby	1	1	0	5	5	5.00	100.00	0	0	1	0
KHD Barker	7	2	2	64	48*	-	152.38	0	0	9	1
HJH Brookes	7	1	1	1	1*	-	100.00	0	0	0	0

Bowling

	Overs	Mdns	Runs	Wkts	BBI	Ave	Econ	SR	4w	5w
CR Woakes	6.0	2	18	1	1/18	18.00	3.00	36.0	0	0
JS Patel	56.0	3	266	10	4/33	26.60	4.75	33.6	1	0
KHD Barker	51.0	1	271	6	2/28	45.16	5.31	51.0	0	0
HJH Brookes	44.3	2	245	9	3/57	27.22	5.50	29.6	0	0
OP Stone	59.5	3	338	12	4/71	28.16	5.64	29.9	1	0
AD Thomason	36.4	0	238	9	4/45	26.44	6.49	24.4	1	0
IJL Trott	17.2	0	118	4	4/65	29.50	6.80	26.0	1	0
OJ Hannon-Dalby	10.0	0	70	0	-	-	7.00	-	0	0
DP Sibley	1.0	0	9	0	-	-	9.00	-	0	0
WMH Rhodes	3.4	0	34	0	-	-	9.27	-	0	0

Catches/Stumpings:
8 Ambrose (inc 2st), 6 Stone, 4 Hose, 3 Patel, Trott, 2 Barker, Bell, Pollock, Thomason, 1 Brookes, Hannon-Dalby, Sibley

VITALITY BLAST AVERAGES 2018

Batting

	Mat	Inns	NO	Runs	HS	Ave	SR	100	50	4s	6s
CR Woakes	4	2	1	78	57*	78.00	177.27	0	1	9	4
IR Bell	14	14	2	580	131	48.33	139.08	1	4	60	15
C de Grandhomme	14	11	4	254	63*	36.28	170.46	0	1	17	18
SR Hain	14	14	3	371	95	33.72	133.45	0	2	34	12
AJ Hose	14	14	2	377	66*	31.41	140.67	0	3	39	12
WMH Rhodes	2	1	0	21	21	21.00	123.52	0	0	1	0
TR Ambrose	14	5	2	62	23*	20.66	121.56	0	0	4	1
DP Sibley	3	2	1	19	11*	19.00	118.75	0	0	1	0
EJ Pollock	14	14	0	251	39	17.92	185.92	0	0	23	19
AT Thomson	1	1	0	14	14	14.00	200.00	0	0	0	1
JS Patel	14	5	3	24	11	12.00	150.00	0	0	1	2
GD Elliott	14	10	3	80	29	11.42	114.28	0	0	7	3
AD Thomason	8	5	1	24	14	6.00	77.41	0	0	1	0
HJH Brookes	5	2	0	10	9	5.00	142.85	0	0	1	0
JE Poysden	4	1	0	0	0	0.00	0.00	0	0	0	0
OJ Hannon-Dalby	8	2	2	16	14*	-	160.00	0	0	3	0
OP Stone	5	1	1	1	1*	-	100.00	0	0	0	0
WB Rankin	2	-	-	-	-	-	-	-	-	-	-

Bowling

	Overs	Mdns	Runs	Wkts	BBI	Ave	Econ	SR	4w	5w
JS Patel	56.0	2	420	11	2/17	38.18	7.50	30.5	0	0
JE Poysden	16.0	0	122	4	3/41	30.50	7.62	24.0	0	0
GD Elliott	47.0	0	372	19	3/16	19.57	7.91	14.8	0	0
HJH Brookes	20.0	1	170	7	2/28	24.28	8.50	17.1	0	0
OP Stone	19.0	0	163	7	3/22	23.28	8.57	16.2	0	0
AT Thomson	4.0	0	35	4	4/35	8.75	8.75	6.0	1	0
DP Sibley	6.0	0	56	1	1/25	56.00	9.33	36.0	0	0
OJ Hannon-Dalby	32.0	0	302	16	4/20	18.87	9.43	12.0	1	0
WMH Rhodes	3.0	0	29	1	1/15	29.00	9.66	18.0	0	0
CR Woakes	15.3	0	150	4	2/18	37.50	9.67	23.2	0	0
WB Rankin	8.0	1	80	3	2/56	26.66	10.00	16.0	0	0
C de Grandhomme	22.0	0	239	5	2/24	47.80	10.86	26.4	0	0
AD Thomason	30.0	0	350	12	3/55	29.16	11.66	15.0	0	0

Catches/Stumpings:
12 Ambrose (inc 1st), 9 Hose, 7 Thomason, 6 de Grandhomme, Hain, 5 Elliott, Patel, 4 Hannon-Dalby, 3 Bell, Pollock, Sibley, Stone, Woakes, 2 Rankin, 1 Brookes, Poysden

WORCESTERSHIRE

FORMED: 1865
HOME GROUND: Blackfinch New Road, Worcester
ONE-DAY NAME: Worcestershire Rapids
CAPTAIN: Joe Leach
2018 RESULTS: CC1: 8/8; RL50: Semi-finalists; T20: Winners
HONOURS: Championship: (5) 1964, 1965, 1974, 1988, 1989; Gillette/NatWest/C&G/FP Trophy: 1994; Benson & Hedges Cup: 1991; Pro40/National League/CB40/YB40/RL50: 2007; Sunday League: (3) 1971, 1987, 1988; T20 Cup: 2018

THE LOWDOWN

Even Championship relegation could not dampen a glorious 2018 for Worcestershire, whose unexpected T20 victory brought the club their second trophy in nearly a quarter of a century. The headlines were stolen by Pat Brown's meteoric rise – only Alfonso Thomas has taken more wickets (33) than Brown (31) in a T20 season – but Worcestershire's triumph was built on the overall depth of their bowling attack, right down to the supposed part-timer Daryl Mitchell. Moeen Ali sprinkled his magic whenever he appeared, although he will be even busier with England this summer. The club should see more, though, of captain Joe Leach, whose absence with injury for most of last season weighed on the Championship campaign. In fairness, the young pace duo of Ed Barnard (23) and Josh Tongue (21) were outstanding, sharing 89 wickets between them. Kolpak signing Wayne Parnell adds more firepower. Beyond Mitchell, it is harder to see where the runs will come from without the departed Joe Clarke. Much will rest on new arrivals Riki Wessels and Callum Ferguson, and on whether Tom Fell can deliver on his undoubted talent.

IN: Riki Wessels (Not), Wayne Parnell (SA, Kolpak), Callum Ferguson (Aus), Martin Guptill (NZ, T20)
OUT: Joe Clarke (Not), Alex Hepburn (REL), Steve Magoffin (RET)

FIRST-TEAM COACH: ALEX GIDMAN

Brought in as Second XI coach as part of a reshuffle following Steve Rhodes' departure in December 2017, Gidman ended up taking responsibility for the first team in white-ball cricket alongside bowling coach Alan Richardson. His promotion is recognition of the success of the club in the short formats last year, with previous incumbent Kevin Sharp taking on a developmental role. A former Gloucestershire captain, Gidman turned to coaching in 2016 after spending one season as a player at New Road.

COUNTY CHAMPIONSHIP AVERAGES 2018

Batting

	Mat	Inns	NO	Runs	HS	Ave	SR	100	50	4s	6s
L Wood	1	2	1	78	65*	78.00	82.97	0	1	12	0
MM Ali	3	5	0	383	219	76.60	78.48	1	2	54	8
MJ Guptill	2	4	0	170	111	42.50	70.83	1	0	21	4
WD Parnell	6	10	3	273	58*	39.00	58.08	0	3	41	3
DKH Mitchell	14	26	0	957	178	36.80	50.55	4	1	130	0
JM Clarke	14	26	1	853	177*	34.12	62.76	3	1	116	0
TM Head	6	11	1	339	62	33.90	67.66	0	2	56	0
RA Whiteley	6	11	0	364	91	33.09	69.86	0	2	49	7
TC Fell	13	24	0	652	89	27.16	49.84	0	4	88	0
EG Barnard	13	24	2	516	66	23.45	53.69	0	3	67	2
AG Milton	7	13	2	250	104*	22.72	46.12	1	0	35	1
OB Cox	12	22	1	372	65	17.71	65.14	0	2	53	5
CAJ Morris	4	7	5	31	9*	15.50	28.18	0	0	2	0
BL D'Oliveira	10	19	0	276	65	14.52	50.92	0	1	40	1
BJ Twohig	7	13	2	145	35	13.18	36.89	0	0	19	0
JC Tongue	11	19	3	201	34	12.56	48.78	0	0	33	0
OE Westbury	2	4	0	49	22	12.25	32.66	0	0	8	0
SJ Magoffin	6	10	3	65	43	9.28	28.63	0	0	12	0
DY Pennington	8	14	3	94	37	8.54	36.86	0	0	14	0
J Leach	5	9	0	66	18	7.33	58.92	0	0	11	0
GH Rhodes	3	6	0	22	12	3.66	17.46	0	0	2	0
PR Brown	1	1	1	2	2*	-	66.66	0	0	0	0

Bowling

	Overs	Mdns	Runs	Wkts	BBI	BBM	Ave	Econ	SR	5w	10w
MJ Guptill	4.0	1	17	1	1/12	1/17	17.00	4.25	24.0	0	0
MM Ali	107.5	20	334	18	6/49	8/89	18.55	3.09	35.9	2	0
J Leach	157.5	28	508	23	4/42	7/97	22.08	3.21	41.1	0	0
EG Barnard	368.3	93	1138	49	6/37	11/89	23.22	3.08	45.1	4	1
JC Tongue	304.4	52	1011	40	5/53	9/98	25.27	3.31	45.7	2	0
WD Parnell	154.4	22	582	18	4/23	6/54	32.33	3.76	51.5	0	0
DY Pennington	187.0	34	778	22	4/53	6/80	35.36	4.16	51.0	0	0
SJ Magoffin	202.0	55	593	16	3/70	4/121	37.06	2.93	75.7	0	0
RA Whiteley	36.2	4	115	3	1/2	1/2	38.33	3.16	72.6	0	0
CAJ Morris	108.4	15	372	9	3/20	5/119	41.33	3.42	72.4	0	0
DKH Mitchell	62.0	9	200	4	2/21	2/35	50.00	3.22	93.0	0	0
BL D'Oliveira	51.0	3	208	4	2/44	2/68	52.00	4.07	76.5	0	0
BJ Twohig	161.0	18	598	10	2/47	3/84	59.80	3.71	96.6	0	0
PR Brown	20.0	3	67	1	1/53	1/67	67.00	3.35	120.0	0	0
L Wood	32.0	6	108	1	1/59	1/108	108.00	3.37	192.0	0	0
TM Head	43.0	6	162	1	1/30	1/30	162.00	3.76	258.0	0	0
OE Westbury	1.0	0	6	0	-	-	-	6.00	-	0	0

Catches/Stumpings:

35 Cox, 21 Mitchell, 9 Barnard, 8 Clarke, Whiteley, 7 Fell, Milton (inc 1st), 4 Pennington, 3 Guptill, Twohig, 2 Head, Rhodes, Tongue, 1 Brown, D'Oliveira, Leach, Parnell, Westbury

ROYAL LONDON ONE-DAY CUP AVERAGES 2018

Batting

	Mat	Inns	NO	Runs	HS	Ave	SR	100	50	4s	6s
CJ Ferguson	5	5	1	377	192	94.25	117.81	2	0	38	8
OB Cox	9	8	3	396	122*	79.20	107.02	1	3	43	7
EG Barnard	9	7	5	153	50*	76.50	100.00	0	1	13	3
BL D'Oliveira	9	9	2	265	78	37.85	92.98	0	2	23	4
DKH Mitchell	9	8	1	260	102*	37.14	82.53	1	2	24	0
JM Clarke	9	9	0	306	122	34.00	89.21	1	2	31	5
RA Whiteley	9	8	2	195	66*	32.50	126.62	0	2	23	8
TM Head	4	4	0	127	77	31.75	80.89	0	1	13	1
MM Ali	5	5	0	148	114	29.60	126.49	1	0	18	5
TC Fell	3	3	0	88	56	29.33	80.73	0	1	10	0
J Leach	7	3	1	49	42*	24.50	76.56	0	0	4	1
CAJ Morris	9	2	1	6	6	6.00	50.00	0	0	0	0
DY Pennington	2	1	0	3	3	3.00	15.00	0	0	0	0
GH Rhodes	1	1	0	2	2	2.00	28.57	0	0	0	0
PR Brown	6	1	1	0	0*	-	0.00	0	0	0	0
JC Tongue	3	-	-	-	-	-	-	-	-	-	-

Bowling

	Overs	Mdns	Runs	Wkts	BBI	Ave	Econ	SR	4w	5w
MM Ali	47.0	1	233	11	4/33	21.18	4.95	25.6	1	0
BL D'Oliveira	72.0	1	380	10	2/28	38.00	5.27	43.2	0	0
DKH Mitchell	40.1	0	217	5	2/19	43.40	5.40	48.2	0	0
J Leach	51.3	0	315	7	2/28	45.00	6.11	44.1	0	0
EG Barnard	75.0	0	462	16	3/64	28.87	6.16	28.1	0	0
TM Head	12.0	0	74	2	2/48	37.00	6.16	36.0	0	0
JC Tongue	22.0	0	137	4	2/48	34.25	6.22	33.0	0	0
CAJ Morris	60.0	0	381	11	4/33	34.63	6.35	32.7	1	0
PR Brown	37.4	1	241	7	3/53	34.42	6.39	32.2	0	0
DY Pennington	17.0	0	111	3	2/50	37.00	6.52	34.0	0	0

Catches/Stumpings:
18 Cox, 5 D'Oliveira, Leach, 4 Ferguson, Mitchell, Whiteley, 3 Fell, 2 Barnard, Clarke, Morris, 1 Ali, Brown, Head, Rhodes, Tongue

www.wccc.co.uk / tel: 01905 748474

VITALITY BLAST AVERAGES 2018

Batting

	Mat	Inns	NO	Runs	HS	Ave	SR	100	50	4s	6s
WD Parnell	9	5	4	57	22*	57.00	154.05	0	0	5	2
CJ Ferguson	10	10	2	390	102*	48.75	141.81	1	2	36	7
MM Ali	9	8	0	334	115	41.75	175.78	1	1	37	18
TM Head	4	4	1	120	40	40.00	144.57	0	0	13	5
MJ Guptill	7	7	0	253	102	36.14	147.09	1	2	28	11
EG Barnard	16	11	7	115	28*	28.75	133.72	0	0	12	1
JM Clarke	15	15	1	396	76	28.28	151.72	0	2	47	14
OB Cox	16	14	4	274	55*	27.40	120.70	0	1	23	8
RA Whiteley	16	15	3	313	60	26.08	152.68	0	1	27	15
OE Westbury	1	1	0	24	24	24.00	150.00	0	0	5	0
BL D'Oliveira	15	11	2	171	64	19.00	143.69	0	1	20	3
TC Fell	3	2	0	24	23	12.00	100.00	0	0	3	0
L Wood	14	3	1	24	11	12.00	109.09	0	0	2	1
DKH Mitchell	15	7	2	46	18	9.20	80.70	0	0	3	0
DY Pennington	4	2	1	6	6*	6.00	75.00	0	0	1	0
PR Brown	16	1	0	0	0	0.00	0.00	0	0	0	0
GH Rhodes	3	2	2	14	8*	-	116.66	0	0	1	0
A Carter	3	-	-	-	-	-	-	-	-	-	-

Bowling

	Overs	Mdns	Runs	Wkts	BBI	Ave	Econ	SR	4w	5w
DY Pennington	12.0	0	86	7	4/9	12.28	7.16	10.2	1	0
PR Brown	54.1	1	414	31	4/21	13.35	7.64	10.4	1	0
DKH Mitchell	31.0	0	239	10	2/7	23.90	7.70	18.6	0	0
WD Parnell	32.2	0	257	14	3/20	18.35	7.94	13.8	0	0
L Wood	40.4	0	328	8	2/20	41.00	8.06	30.5	0	0
BL D'Oliveira	32.0	0	269	8	4/26	33.62	8.40	24.0	1	0
MM Ali	31.0	0	265	11	3/30	24.09	8.54	16.9	0	0
EG Barnard	51.0	0	462	12	3/29	38.50	9.05	25.5	0	0
TM Head	2.0	0	20	1	1/20	20.00	10.00	12.0	0	0
A Carter	7.0	0	77	1	1/48	77.00	11.00	42.0	0	0
GH Rhodes	6.0	0	66	3	2/27	22.00	11.00	12.0	0	0

Catches/Stumpings:
15 Barnard, 14 Cox (inc 5st), 7 Whiteley, 6 Ali, Clarke, Guptill, 5 Wood, 4 Mitchell, 3 Brown, D'Oliveira, Ferguson, Head, 2 Fell, Rhodes, 1 Parnell

YORKSHIRE

FORMED: 1863
HOME GROUND: Emerald Headingley Stadium, Leeds
ONE-DAY NAME: Yorkshire Vikings
CAPTAIN: Steven Patterson
2018 RESULTS: CC1: 4/8; RL50: Semi-finalists; T20: 5/9 North Group
HONOURS: County Championship: (33) 1893, 1896, 1898, 1900, 1901, 1902, 1905, 1908, 1912, 1919, 1922, 1923, 1924, 1925, 1931, 1932, 1933, 1935, 1937, 1938, 1939, 1946, 1949, 1959, 1960, 1962, 1963, 1966, 1967, 1968, 2001, 2014, 2015; Gillette/ NatWest/C&G/FP Trophy: (3) 1965, 1969, 2002; Benson & Hedges Cup: 1987; Sunday League: 1983

THE LOWDOWN

Yorkshire have been dizzy ever since the Gillespie era came to an end in 2017. There was another brush with relegation last summer, as well as a mid-season change of captain when Gary Ballance took time out for personal reasons. Ballance has since returned – and how Yorkshire need his runs – but Steven Patterson will lead in 2019. Losing Jack Brooks – their leading Championship wicket-taker in 2018 – as well as Liam Plunkett, both to key rivals, is a sign of the times. David Willey's future is uncertain following last year's bust-up with the club over playing in the IPL. Their white-ball cricket looks rosier, after reaching the One-Day Cup semi-finals last summer. Tom Kohler-Cadmore has been a revelation since his move from Worcestershire and progress was made by batsman Harry Brook (20) and keeper Jonathan Tattersall (24). Ben Coad, 25, is now the leader of the seam attack and will benefit hugely from the arrival of South African pace bowler Duanne Olivier, who turned his back on international cricket at the age of 26 to sign a three-year Kolpak deal in February. New signing Josh Poysden has a key role to play as the main spinner.

IN: Will Fraine (Not), Mathew Pillans (Sur), Josh Poysden (War), Duanne Olivier (SA, Kolpak)
OUT: Jack Brooks (Som), Alex Lees (Dur), Liam Plunkett (Sur), Azeem Rafiq (REL), Andy Hodd (RET)

HEAD COACH: ANDREW GALE

Gale has had a rough ride after making the transition from captain to coach following Jason Gillespie's departure in 2017. He knows better than anyone that he will need to deliver this summer, having spent a 14-year career at Yorkshire, eight of them as skipper. Former Essex and Yorkshire allrounder Paul Grayson was appointed as a batting specialist coach in January. Grayson was Essex head coach between 2007 and 2015 and has been in charge of the Yorkshire Diamonds women's team for the past two summers.

COUNTY CHAMPIONSHIP AVERAGES 2018

Batting

	Mat	Inns	NO	Runs	HS	Ave	SR	100	50	4s	6s
T Kohler-Cadmore	6	11	2	414	106	46.00	54.76	2	2	53	4
JM Bairstow	3	6	0	263	95	43.83	93.26	0	3	35	1
GS Ballance	12	23	0	906	194	39.39	60.27	3	4	142	3
KS Williamson	3	6	0	218	87	36.33	56.18	0	3	33	2
JA Tattersall	7	12	1	350	70	31.81	37.15	0	2	49	0
AJ Hodd	3	6	0	175	85	29.16	53.03	0	2	25	0
A Lyth	13	25	1	656	134*	27.33	47.57	1	2	98	1
JA Leaning	8	16	2	371	68	26.50	33.03	0	2	45	0
HC Brook	12	23	0	575	124	25.00	58.73	1	3	79	3
J Shaw	3	6	1	104	42	20.80	40.94	0	0	17	0
TT Bresnan	12	22	3	385	80	20.26	40.06	0	2	47	1
SA Patterson	8	13	2	205	45*	18.63	52.16	0	0	31	0
BO Coad	9	15	7	135	33	16.87	66.50	0	0	21	1
JE Root	3	6	0	97	35	16.16	50.00	0	0	11	0
MJ Waite	4	6	0	96	42	16.00	50.79	0	0	11	2
JA Brooks	13	22	3	303	82	15.94	68.24	0	1	45	3
CA Pujara	6	12	0	172	41	14.33	33.14	0	0	23	1
DJ Willey	2	4	1	42	34*	14.00	49.41	0	0	8	0
MD Fisher	2	4	1	39	20*	13.00	31.96	0	0	5	0
JA Raval	4	7	0	84	21	12.00	45.40	0	0	13	0
JE Poysden	3	5	2	25	20*	8.33	26.31	0	0	2	0
MW Pillans	1	1	0	8	8	8.00	72.72	0	0	1	0
AZ Lees	4	8	0	50	39	6.25	42.73	0	0	10	0
JEG Logan	1	1	0	6	6	6.00	16.66	0	0	0	0
K Carver	1	2	2	1	1*	-	2.77	0	0	0	0

Bowling

	Overs	Mdns	Runs	Wkts	BBI	BBM	Ave	Econ	SR	5w	10w
JE Root	20.4	7	37	5	4/5	4/5	7.40	1.79	24.8	0	0
BO Coad	272.5	87	784	48	6/81	10/130	16.33	2.87	34.1	3	1
SA Patterson	235.0	63	594	24	6/40	7/63	24.75	2.52	58.7	1	0
MJ Waite	61.0	14	221	8	3/91	3/97	27.62	3.62	45.7	0	0
TT Bresnan	279.5	48	969	35	5/28	5/28	27.68	3.46	47.9	1	0
JA Brooks	346.3	51	1430	51	6/94	9/113	28.03	4.12	40.7	5	0
DJ Willey	67.2	13	217	6	3/72	6/146	36.16	3.22	67.3	0	0
JE Poysden	52.2	1	259	7	3/128	3/94	37.00	4.94	44.8	0	0
JA Leaning	19.0	3	57	1	1/16	1/16	57.00	3.00	114.0	0	0
A Lyth	68.0	8	246	4	2/97	2/97	61.50	3.61	102.0	0	0
J Shaw	63.0	5	265	4	2/72	2/114	66.25	4.20	94.5	0	0
MD Fisher	54.0	6	219	2	2/80	2/135	109.50	4.05	162.0	0	0
HC Brook	22.1	5	67	0	-	-	-	3.02	-	0	0
MW Pillans	30.0	5	130	0	-	-	-	4.33	-	0	0

Catches/Stumpings:

19 Tattersall, 16 Lyth, 12 Hodd, 9 Bairstow, Bresnan, Leaning, 7 Brook, 4 Ballance, Kohler-Cadmore, Pujara, 3 Raval, Williamson, 2 Patterson, Root, 1 Brooks, Fisher, Lees, Logan

ROYAL LONDON ONE-DAY CUP AVERAGES 2018

Batting

	Mat	Inns	NO	Runs	HS	Ave	SR	100	50	4s	6s
DJ Willey	3	3	0	202	131	67.33	107.44	1	1	19	9
A Lyth	9	9	1	433	144	54.12	99.08	2	0	54	5
CA Pujara	8	8	1	370	101	52.85	90.02	1	3	36	1
T Kohler-Cadmore	9	9	0	472	164	52.44	101.50	1	3	42	17
GS Ballance	6	5	0	247	91	49.40	100.40	0	2	24	4
JA Tattersall	6	4	1	143	89	47.66	103.62	0	2	9	0
MD Fisher	6	4	2	85	35*	42.50	132.81	0	0	8	1
JA Leaning	5	5	1	114	57	28.50	67.05	0	1	9	0
TT Bresnan	7	7	2	140	41	28.00	97.90	0	0	11	5
AJ Hodd	3	2	1	18	17*	18.00	138.46	0	0	1	1
JE Root	1	1	0	18	18	18.00	45.00	0	0	0	0
JC Wainman	3	2	1	18	18*	18.00	90.00	0	0	1	1
AU Rashid	7	4	1	42	24	14.00	175.00	0	0	8	0
HC Brook	6	5	0	68	24	13.60	89.47	0	0	7	0
BO Coad	6	2	1	12	9	12.00	109.09	0	0	1	0
SA Patterson	9	3	0	24	17	8.00	88.88	0	0	4	0
LE Plunkett	3	2	2	9	6*	-	112.50	0	0	0	0
K Carver	2	1	1	3	3*	-	75.00	0	0	0	0

Bowling

	Overs	Mdns	Runs	Wkts	BBI	Ave	Econ	SR	4w	5w
BO Coad	54.0	0	271	9	2/40	30.11	5.01	36.0	0	0
DJ Willey	23.5	2	130	11	4/47	11.81	5.45	13.0	2	0
SA Patterson	73.4	2	409	13	4/36	31.46	5.55	34.0	1	0
MD Fisher	48.1	2	268	9	3/40	29.77	5.56	32.1	0	0
A Lyth	15.0	0	86	1	1/35	86.00	5.73	90.0	0	0
TT Bresnan	57.0	3	338	7	2/39	48.28	5.92	48.8	0	0
JC Wainman	25.0	0	150	2	2/53	75.00	6.00	75.0	0	0
AU Rashid	64.0	1	405	14	4/47	28.92	6.32	27.4	1	0
JE Root	6.0	0	39	0	-	-	6.50	-	0	0
LE Plunkett	23.0	0	167	2	1/50	83.50	7.26	69.0	0	0
K Carver	16.0	0	131	2	2/65	65.50	8.18	48.0	0	0

Catches/Stumpings:
11 Kohler-Cadmore, 6 Rashid, Tattersall (inc 1st), 5 Patterson, 4 Hodd, Pujara, 3 Brook, 2 Bresnan, Fisher, Leaning, 1 Coad, Lyth, Plunkett

VITALITY BLAST AVERAGES 2018

Batting

	Mat	Inns	NO	Runs	HS	Ave	SR	100	50	4s	6s
KS Williamson	10	10	3	280	77	40.00	148.14	0	2	25	10
DJ Willey	10	10	0	386	80	38.60	142.96	0	4	27	22
A Lyth	14	14	1	401	92*	30.84	153.05	0	3	37	20
HC Brook	8	8	2	165	44	27.50	144.73	0	0	13	7
T Kohler-Cadmore	13	13	0	321	73	24.69	140.17	0	3	32	12
JA Tattersall	14	9	2	165	53*	23.57	135.24	0	1	15	1
GS Ballance	14	13	1	269	79	22.41	141.57	0	1	19	12
LE Plunkett	5	3	1	37	19	18.50	160.86	0	0	2	2
MD Fisher	6	3	2	18	17*	18.00	150.00	0	0	0	2
TT Bresnan	11	9	3	106	28*	17.66	134.17	0	0	8	4
JA Leaning	4	3	0	28	11	9.33	80.00	0	0	0	0
JA Thompson	8	6	3	22	12*	7.33	129.41	0	0	2	1
Azeem Rafiq	12	5	4	5	2*	5.00	55.55	0	0	0	0
AU Rashid	3	2	1	1	1*	1.00	33.33	0	0	0	0
SA Patterson	11	2	0	0	0	0.00	0.00	0	0	0	0
JE Root	1	1	1	51	51*	-	231.81	0	1	5	2
JA Brooks	10	-	-	-	-	-	-	-	-	-	-

Bowling

	Overs	Mdns	Runs	Wkts	BBI	Ave	Econ	SR	4w	5w
A Lyth	8.0	0	61	1	1/23	61.00	7.62	48.0	0	0
LE Plunkett	18.0	0	138	4	2/25	34.50	7.66	27.0	0	0
JA Brooks	34.3	0	268	9	3/21	29.77	7.76	23.0	0	0
SA Patterson	42.0	0	335	12	3/35	27.91	7.97	21.0	0	0
AU Rashid	10.0	0	82	3	2/19	27.33	8.20	20.0	0	0
JA Thompson	23.0	0	192	8	3/23	24.00	8.34	17.2	0	0
DJ Willey	35.0	1	296	9	3/30	32.88	8.45	23.3	0	0
Azeem Rafiq	37.0	0	334	8	2/28	41.75	9.02	27.7	0	0
MD Fisher	23.0	0	236	7	2/26	33.71	10.26	19.7	0	0
TT Bresnan	29.5	0	312	5	3/38	62.40	10.45	35.8	0	0
HC Brook	1.0	0	13	0	-	-	13.00	-	0	0

Catches/Stumpings:

10 Tattersall (inc 2st), 7 Brooks, 6 Lyth, 5 Bresnan, 4 Kohler-Cadmore, Patterson, Thompson, 3 Ballance, Leaning, Willey, 2 Rafiq, Williamson, 1 Fisher, Root

The
Players

MOHAMMAD ABBAS RHB / RMF / R0 / W1 / MVP84

FULL NAME: Mohammad Abbas
BORN: March 10, 1990, Sialkot, Pakistan
SQUAD NO: 26
TEAMS: Pakistan, Leicestershire, Khan Research Laboratories, Islamabad, Multan Sultans, Pakistan Television, Rawalpindi, Sialkot, Sui Northern Gas Pipelines Limited
ROLE: Bowler
DEBUT: Test: 2017; First-class: 2009; List A: 2009; T20: 2013

BEST BATTING: 40 Khan Research Laboratories vs Karachi Whites, Karachi, 2016
BEST BOWLING: 8-46 Khan Research Laboratories vs Karachi Whites, Karachi, 2016
COUNTY CAP: 2018

TWITTER: @Mohmmadabbas11
NOTES: After a stellar first season in which he took 50 Championship wickets at 17.72, Abbas returns for a second summer as Leicestershire's overseas player to play in all formats. Though a leader of Pakistan's Test attack, the right-arm seamer has not played an ODI and he is unlikely to be required for his country's 50-over schedule in England this summer. Abbas's career has progressed rapidly in the past few years. He made his first-class debut in 2009 but until the start of 2014 had taken just 74 wickets at an average of 35.45, working in a leather factory, as a welder, and as a helper in a law firm to support his cricket career. Since then he has emerged as one of the most skilful seamers in the world. In the 2016 Quaid-e-Azam Trophy he claimed 71 wickets in 10 games at an average of 12.74. He recorded his maiden Test five-for on the 2017 tour of West Indies, his debut series, and took 10 wickets in two Tests in England last summer. In October he became the joint-second-fastest to take 50 Test wickets for Pakistan (10 matches), behind only Yasir Shah (9)

Batting	Mat	Inns	NO	Runs	HS	Ave	SR	100	50	Ct	St
Tests	14	21	11	63	11	6.30	17.45	0	0	4	0
First-class	90	132	50	602	40	7.34	28.99	0	0	24	0
List A	47	28	12	124	15*	7.75	51.23	0	0	11	0
T20s	23	9	6	32	15*	10.66	152.38	0	0	5	0
Bowling	**Mat**	**Balls**	**Runs**	**Wkts**	**BBI**	**BBM**	**Ave**	**Econ**	**SR**	**5w**	**10**
Tests	14	3036	1245	66	5/33	10/95	18.86	2.46	46.0	4	1
First-class	90	18068	8231	413	8/46	14/93	19.92	2.73	43.7	34	10
List A	47	2238	1756	63	4/31	4/31	27.87	4.70	35.5	0	0
T20s	23	468	663	17	3/32	3/32	39.00	8.50	27.5	0	0

KYLE ABBOTT RHB / RFM / R0 / W2 / MVP39

FULL NAME: Kyle John Abbott
BORN: June 18, 1987, Empangeni, KwaZulu-Natal, South Africa
SQUAD NO: 11
NICKNAME: Jimmy
EDUCATION: Kearsney College, KwaZulu-Natal
TEAMS: South Africa, Hampshire, Dolphins, Durban Heat, Kings XI Punjab, KwaZulu-Natal, Middlesex, Worcestershire
ROLE: Bowler
DEBUT: Test: 2013; ODI: 2013; T20I: 2013; First-class: 2009; List A: 2009; T20: 2011

BEST BATTING: 97* Hampshire vs Lancashire, Old Trafford, 2017
BEST BOWLING: 8-45 Dolphins vs Cape Cobras, Cape Town, 2013

TWITTER: Kyle_Abbott87
NOTES: A well-built South African fast bowler, Abbott interrupted his international career to sign a four-year Kolpak deal with Hampshire in January 2017 and had an immediate impact with 60 Championship wickets at 18.20 to help save the county from relegation. He followed this up with 51 wickets at 23.18 last summer, forming one of county cricket's most potent pace duos with West Indian fast bowler Fidel Edwards. Abbott's Test debut figures of 7-29 are the second-best for South Africa, behind only Lance Klusener's 8-64 at Eden Gardens in 1996. He previously played for Hampshire as an overseas player in 2014, impressing with 36 wickets at 20.33

Batting	Mat	Inns	NO	Runs	HS	Ave	SR	100	50	Ct	St
Tests	11	14	0	95	17	6.78	28.10	0	0	4	0
ODIs	28	13	4	76	23	8.44	60.31	0	0	7	0
T20Is	21	6	4	23	9*	11.50	115.00	0	0	7	0
First-class	100	139	26	2198	97*	19.45	47.00	0	8	17	0
List A	94	44	18	470	56	18.07	88.18	0	1	26	0
T20s	134	50	27	299	30	13.00	115.44	0	0	31	0
Bowling	**Mat**	**Balls**	**Runs**	**Wkts**	**BBI**	**BBM**	**Ave**	**Econ**	**SR**	**5w**	**10**
Tests	11	2081	886	39	7/29	9/68	22.71	2.55	53.3	3	0
ODIs	28	1303	1051	34	4/21	4/21	30.91	4.83	38.3	0	0
T20Is	21	436	579	26	3/20	3/20	22.26	7.96	16.7	0	0
First-class	100	17402	8093	370	8/45	12/96	21.87	2.79	47.0	24	3
List A	94	4217	3627	121	4/21	4/21	29.97	5.16	34.8	0	0
T20s	134	2805	3833	130	5/14	5/14	29.48	8.19	21.5	1	0

TOM ABELL RHB / RM / R0 / W0 / MVP48

FULL NAME: Thomas Benjamin Abell
BORN: March 5, 1994, Taunton
SQUAD NO: 28
HEIGHT: 5ft 11in
NICKNAME: Tabes
EDUCATION: Taunton School; Exeter University
TEAMS: Somerset
ROLE: Batsman
DEBUT: First-class: 2014; List A: 2015; T20: 2016

BEST BATTING: 135 Somerset vs Lancashire, Old Trafford, 2016
BEST BOWLING: 4-43 Somerset vs Lancashire, Old Trafford, 2018
COUNTY CAP: 2018

WHAT WAS YOUR FIRST CRICKET CLUB? Taunton CC, Somerset. My first and hopefully my last club team
WHICH BOWLER WOULD YOU LEAST LIKE TO FACE? Jack Brooks – he doesn't let me forget it when he gets me out
BEST INNINGS YOU'VE SEEN? James Hildreth's T20 hundred against Glamorgan in 2012. We had our backs against the wall, and he played on a different level
WHICH RULE WOULD YOU CHANGE ABOUT CRICKET? The one that says you need to wait until 5pm before the captains can shake hands on a draw
YOUR BIGGEST CRICKETING REGRET? Losing to Warwickshire by eight runs in the semi-finals of the 2016 50-over competition
FAVOURITE QUOTE OR SAYING? I've failed over and over and over again in my life. And that is why I succeed (Michael Jordan)
WHICH BOOK MEANS MOST TO YOU? The Obstacle is the Way – The Timeless Art of Turning Trials into Triumph by Ryan Holiday
TWITTER: @tomabell1

Batting	Mat	Inns	NO	Runs	HS	Ave	SR	100	50	Ct	St
First-class	59	107	12	3055	135	32.15	48.83	4	18	35	0
List A	14	11	1	383	106	38.30	75.24	1	1	4	0
T20s	20	18	5	305	48	23.46	125.00	0	0	12	0
Bowling	**Mat**	**Balls**	**Runs**	**Wkts**	**BBI**	**BBM**	**Ave**	**Econ**	**SR**	**5w**	**10**
First-class	59	938	621	22	4/43	4/43	28.22	3.97	42.6	0	0
List A	14	-	-	-	-	-	-	-	-	-	-
T20s	20	12	17	0	-	-	-	8.50	-	0	0

COLIN ACKERMANN RHB / OB / R0 / W0 / MVP36

FULL NAME: Colin Niel Ackermann
BORN: April 4, 1991, George, Cape Province, South Africa
SQUAD NO: 48
HEIGHT: 6ft 1in
NICKNAME: Ackers
EDUCATION: Grey High School, Port Elizabeth; University of South Africa
TEAMS: Leicestershire, Eastern Province, Warriors
ROLE: Batsman
DEBUT: First-class: 2010; List A: 2010; T20: 2011

BEST BATTING: 196* Leicestershire vs Middlesex, Leicester, 2018
BEST BOWLING: 3-45 Leicestershire vs Northamptonshire, Northampton, 2017

WHAT GOT YOU INTO CRICKET? My dad played a bit and by the age of three I had a bat in my hands
BEST ADVICE EVER RECEIVED? Watch the ball
'ROY OF THE ROVERS' MOMENT? Walking on to the field at Centurion for the 2016 T20 Challenge final in South Africa
BEST THING ABOUT YOUR HOME GROUND? Grace Road has the best net facilities on the county circuit
IF YOU WEREN'T A CRICKETER? I'd be involved in property
WHERE IS PARADISE? Anywhere in Italy
CRICKETING HERO? Jacques Kallis
TWITTER: @ackers38

Batting	Mat	Inns	NO	Runs	HS	Ave	SR	100	50	Ct	St
First-class	111	194	19	7189	196*	41.08	49.87	17	41	93	0
List A	75	68	13	1832	92	33.30	76.17	0	14	53	0
T20s	82	78	13	1864	79*	28.67	118.19	0	11	45	0
Bowling	**Mat**	**Balls**	**Runs**	**Wkts**	**BBI**	**BBM**	**Ave**	**Econ**	**SR**	**5w**	**10**
First-class	111	3713	1904	48	3/45	4/54	39.66	3.07	77.3	0	0
List A	75	1855	1453	37	4/48	4/48	39.27	4.69	50.1	0	0
T20s	82	808	956	30	3/21	3/21	31.86	7.09	26.9	0	0

ASHTON AGAR

LHB / SLA / R0 / W0

FULL NAME: Ashton Charles Agar
BORN: October 14, 1993, Melbourne, Australia
SQUAD NO: 46
EDUCATION: De La Salle College, Melbourne
TEAMS: Australia, Warwickshire, Middlesex, Perth Scorchers, Western Australia
ROLE: Allrounder
DEBUT: Test: 2013; ODI: 2015; T20I: 2016; First-class: 2013; List A: 2013; T20: 2013

BEST BATTING: 106 Western Australia vs Tasmania, Perth, 2015
BEST BOWLING: 6-110 Western Australia vs New South Wales, Sydney, 2016

NOTES: Birmingham Bears have signed the Australian left-arm spinner for the duration of the T20 Blast. Agar made his first appearance in county cricket last summer when he played six T20 matches for Middlesex and was a teammate of Ian Bell in the Perth Scorchers side which won the 2016/17 Big Bash. He burst on the scene in 2013 as a 19-year-old when he made 98 batting at No.11 on his Test debut at Trent Bridge but has played only three Tests since then. He is on the fringes of Australia's T20 and one-day side. Bears first-team coach Jim Troughton said: "Ashton has won major T20 trophies and possesses quality international experience. [He] gives us an excellent spin pairing with Jeetan Patel [and] has also proven himself to be a very capable and powerful batsman who can clear the ropes, whilst also being an excellent fielder"

Batting	Mat	Inns	NO	Runs	HS	Ave	SR	100	50	Ct	St
Tests	4	7	1	195	98	32.50	55.55	0	1	0	0
ODIs	9	8	1	144	46	20.57	86.74	0	0	4	0
T20Is	15	7	1	82	29	13.66	103.79	0	0	10	0
First-class	52	77	9	1742	106	25.61	52.62	2	9	19	0
List A	40	32	6	603	64	23.19	93.19	0	1	17	0
T20s	71	52	16	673	68	18.69	115.43	0	1	39	0
Bowling	**Mat**	**Balls**	**Runs**	**Wkts**	**BBI**	**BBM**	**Ave**	**Econ**	**SR**	**5w**	**10**
Tests	4	874	410	9	3/46	5/101	45.55	2.81	97.1	0	0
ODIs	9	432	414	8	2/48	2/48	51.75	5.75	54.0	0	0
T20Is	15	264	329	10	3/27	3/27	32.90	7.47	26.4	0	0
First-class	52	10410	5359	137	6/110	10/141	39.11	3.08	75.9	5	2
List A	40	1963	1643	47	5/39	5/39	34.95	5.02	41.7	1	0
T20s	71	1142	1428	46	3/17	3/17	31.04	7.50	24.8	0	0

AADIL ALI RHB / OB / R0 / W0

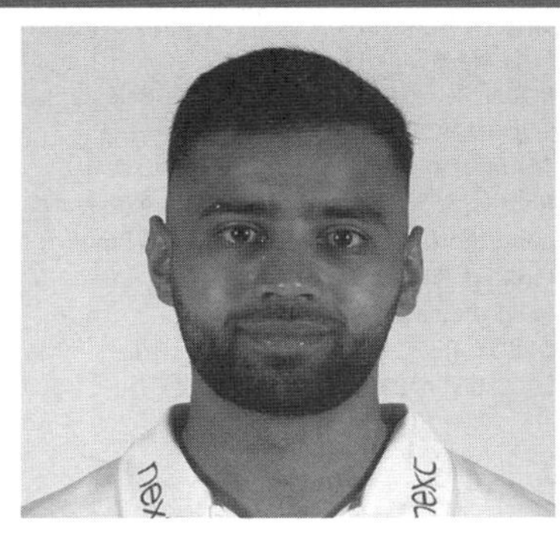

FULL NAME: Aadil Masud Ali
BORN: December 29, 1994, Leicester
SQUAD NO: 14
HEIGHT: 6ft
NICKNAME: Dil
EDUCATION: Lancaster School, Leicester; Wyggeston & Queen Elizabeth I College, Leicester
TEAMS: Leicestershire
ROLE: Batsman
DEBUT: First-class: 2015; List A: 2015; T20: 2015

BEST BATTING: 80 Leicestershire vs Gloucestershire, Leicester, 2015
BEST BOWLING: 1-10 Leicestershire vs Worcestershire, Worcester, 2017

WHAT FIRST GOT YOU INTO CRICKET? One day my dad's team were a player short so I was made to field. And watching Sachin Tendulkar
FAMILY TIES? My dad came over 25 years ago to play as an overseas player and then settled here. Biggest cricket badger around
BEST ADVICE EVER RECEIVED? See ball, hit ball
'ROY OF THE ROVERS' MOMENT? Making my first-class debut
BEST THING ABOUT YOUR HOME GROUND? The Stench & Benno Stand
IF YOU WEREN'T A CRICKETER? I'd be a striker for Arsenal
SURPRISING FACT ABOUT YOU? I dropped out of Cambridge to live the dream
NON-CRICKETING HERO? My dad – he's been there for me through thick and thin
TWITTER: @aadil_ali94

Batting	Mat	Inns	NO	Runs	HS	Ave	SR	100	50	Ct	St
First-class	15	25	1	639	80	26.62	39.08	0	3	6	0
List A	16	14	0	313	88	22.35	73.64	0	3	9	0
T20s	12	8	1	112	35*	16.00	107.69	0	0	4	0
Bowling	**Mat**	**Balls**	**Runs**	**Wkts**	**BBI**	**BBM**	**Ave**	**Econ**	**SR**	**5w**	**10**
First-class	15	78	86	1	1/10	1/31	86.00	6.61	78.0	0	0
List A	16	114	124	1	1/31	1/31	124.00	6.52	114.0	0	0
T20s	12	72	93	4	2/22	2/22	23.25	7.75	18.0	0	0

AZHAR ALI

RHB / LB / R0 / W0

FULL NAME: Azhar Ali
BORN: February 19, 1985, Lahore, Pakistan
SQUAD NO: 79
TEAMS: Pakistan, Somerset, Abbottabad Rhinos, Baluchistan Warriors, Khan Research Laboratories, Lahore, Northern Gas Pipelines Limited, Punjab, Rawalpindi
ROLE: Batsman
DEBUT: Test: 2010; ODI: 2011; First-class: 2002; List A: 2001; T20: 2006

BEST BATTING: 302* Pakistan vs West Indies, Dubai, 2016
BEST BOWLING: 4-34 Khan Research Laboratories vs Peshawar, Peshawar, 2003

TWITTER: @AzharAli_
NOTES: Somerset re-signed the Pakistan top-order batsman after a brief spell at Taunton last season in which he scored 402 Championship runs at 33.50, including 125 on debut against Worcestershire. Azhar is due to be available for the duration of the Championship and One-Day Cup campaigns. He boasts a formidable Test record for his country, most notably in 2016 when he scored 1,198 runs at 63.05. "Azhar fitted in seamlessly during his time with us towards the back end of the 2018 season," said Andy Hurry, Somerset's director of cricket. "Knowing the positive impact that he will have both on and off the field, alongside his availability all summer, were key factors in wanting to secure him"

Batting	Mat	Inns	NO	Runs	HS	Ave	SR	100	50	Ct	St
Tests	73	139	8	5669	302*	43.27	41.42	15	31	61	0
ODIs	53	53	3	1845	102	36.90	74.45	3	12	8	0
First-class	177	310	26	11182	302*	39.37	42.63	35	48	136	0
List A	160	144	22	5827	132*	47.76	77.03	16	34	40	0
T20s	49	49	4	985	72	21.88	104.67	0	3	24	0
Bowling	**Mat**	**Balls**	**Runs**	**Wkts**	**BBI**	**BBM**	**Ave**	**Econ**	**SR**	**5w**	**10**
Tests	73	848	602	8	2/35	2/49	75.25	4.25	106.0	0	0
ODIs	53	258	260	4	2/26	2/26	65.00	6.04	64.5	0	0
First-class	177	3203	1979	47	4/34	4/34	42.10	3.70	68.1	0	0
List A	160	2400	2173	62	5/23	5/23	35.04	5.43	38.7	3	0
T20s	49	267	283	15	3/10	3/10	18.86	6.35	17.8	0	0

MOEEN ALI LHB / OB / R2 / W0 / MVP8

FULL NAME: Moeen Munir Ali
BORN: June 18, 1987, Birmingham
SQUAD NO: 8
HEIGHT: 6ft
NICKNAME: Brother Mo
EDUCATION: Moseley School, Birmingham
TEAMS: England, Worcestershire, Duronto Rajshahi, Matabeleland Tuskers, Moors Sports Club, Royal Challengers Bangalore, Warwickshire
ROLE: Allrounder
DEBUT: Test: 2014; ODI: 2014; T20I: 2014; First-class: 2005; List A: 2006; T20: 2007

BEST BATTING: 250 Worcestershire vs Glamorgan, Worcester, 2013
BEST BOWLING: 6-29 Worcestershire vs Lancashire, Old Trafford, 2012
COUNTY CAP: 2007 (Worcestershire)

FAMILY TIES? My cousin Kabir played for England and my brother Kadeer played for Worcestershire, Gloucestershire and Leicestershire
'ROY OF THE ROVERS' MOMENT? Playing for England
CRICKETING HERO? Saeed Anwar
NON-CRICKETING HERO? Muhammad Ali
IF YOU WEREN'T A CRICKETER? I'd be working in a chippy
NOTES: Retained by Royal Challengers Bangalore for the 2019 edition of the IPL which runs until mid-May

Batting	Mat	Inns	NO	Runs	HS	Ave	SR	100	50	Ct	St
Tests	58	100	8	2769	155*	30.09	51.44	5	14	32	0
ODIs	92	74	11	1645	128	26.11	103.52	3	5	28	0
T20Is	25	22	6	235	72*	14.68	118.68	0	1	7	0
First-class	190	324	27	11063	250	37.24	55.10	20	69	110	0
List A	209	185	13	4940	158	28.72	102.42	11	20	61	0
T20s	126	118	9	2583	115	23.69	134.88	1	13	42	0
Bowling	**Mat**	**Balls**	**Runs**	**Wkts**	**BBI**	**BBM**	**Ave**	**Econ**	**SR**	**5w**	**10**
Tests	58	10694	6438	177	6/53	10/112	36.37	3.61	60.4	5	1
ODIs	92	4216	3668	78	4/46	4/46	47.02	5.22	54.0	0	0
T20Is	25	362	519	15	2/21	2/21	34.60	8.60	24.1	0	0
First-class	190	23091	13569	357	6/29	12/96	38.00	3.52	64.6	12	2
List A	209	7327	6551	153	4/33	4/33	42.81	5.36	47.8	0	0
T20s	126	1817	2330	84	5/34	5/34	27.73	7.69	21.6	1	0

TOM ALSOP

LHB / WK / R0 / W0

FULL NAME: Thomas Philip Alsop
BORN: November 27, 1995, High Wycombe, Buckinghamshire
SQUAD NO: 9
HEIGHT: 5ft 11in
NICKNAME: Deeney, Alsop, Sloppy, T
EDUCATION: Lavington School; The John Bentley School, Wiltshire
TEAMS: Hampshire, England Lions
ROLE: Batsman
DEBUT: First-class: 2014; List A: 2014; T20: 2016

BEST BATTING: 117 Hampshire vs Surrey, The Oval, 2016
BEST BOWLING: 2-59 Hampshire vs Yorkshire, Headingley, 2016

FAMILY TIES? Dad played for Merchant Taylors' School and my older brother Owen played for Wiltshire CCC and was in the Hampshire Academy. My little (not so little) brother plays for Wiltshire age-groups
BEST ADVICE EVER RECEIVED? Stay in the present
'ROY OF THE ROVERS' MOMENT? Receiving my England Lions cap
IF YOU WEREN'T A CRICKETER? I'd be doing something in the car or watch industry
SURPRISING FACT ABOUT YOU? I played hockey to a reasonable standard
WHERE IS PARADISE? Rome
CRICKETING HERO? Shikhar Dhawan – if only I was half as good as him!
NON-CRICKETING HERO? My mother – she's the head of an NHS intensive care unit saving lives (I've got huge respect for anyone within the NHS)
UNUSUAL OBJECT AT HOME? A watch-winder

Batting	Mat	Inns	NO	Runs	HS	Ave	SR	100	50	Ct	St
First-class	33	56	1	1482	117	26.94	45.65	1	12	46	0
List A	38	38	2	1114	116	30.94	74.61	2	6	19	0
T20s	31	29	4	575	85	23.00	114.77	0	2	13	2
Bowling	**Mat**	**Balls**	**Runs**	**Wkts**	**BBI**	**BBM**	**Ave**	**Econ**	**SR**	**5w**	**10**
First-class	33	78	78	3	2/59	2/59	26.00	6.00	26.0	0	0
List A	38	-	-	-	-	-	-	-	-	-	-
T20s	31	-	-	-	-	-	-	-	-	-	-

TIM AMBROSE RHB / WK / R0 / W0

FULL NAME: Timothy Raymond Ambrose
BORN: December 1, 1982, Newcastle, New South Wales, Australia
SQUAD NO: 11
HEIGHT: 5ft 7in
NICKNAME: Amby, Shambrose
EDUCATION: Merewether Selective High, NSW; Training and Further Education College, NSW
TEAMS: England, Warwickshire, Sussex
ROLE: Wicketkeeper
DEBUT: Test: 2008; ODI: 2008; T20I: 2008; First-class: 2001; List A: 2001; T20: 2003

BEST BATTING: 251* Warwickshire vs Worcestershire, Worcester, 2007
BEST BOWLING: 1-0 Warwickshire vs Middlesex, Lord's, 2016
COUNTY CAP: 2003 (Sussex), 2007 (Warwickshire); **BENEFIT:** 2016 (Warwickshire)

FAMILY TIES? My father played for Nelson Bay CC in Australia
'ROY OF THE ROVERS' MOMENT? County Championship titles in 2003 and 2012 and becoming T20 champions in 2014. Anytime playing for England
CRICKETING HEROES? Ian Healy for his attention to detail in wicketkeeping. Steve Waugh and Sachin Tendulkar for mental strength and concentration
NON-CRICKETING HERO? Michael Jordan – for his ability to deliver under pressure
SURPRISING FACT? I have a Puggle named Frank
TWITTER: @timambrose2016

Batting	Mat	Inns	NO	Runs	HS	Ave	SR	100	50	Ct	St
Tests	11	16	1	447	102	29.80	46.41	1	3	31	0
ODIs	5	5	1	10	6	2.50	29.41	0	0	3	0
T20Is	1	-	-	-	-	-	-	-	-	1	1
First-class	239	363	34	10950	251*	33.28	51.87	17	65	639	40
List A	178	144	20	4006	135	32.30	79.56	3	23	170	34
T20s	106	66	19	1138	77	24.21	112.45	0	3	66	24
Bowling	**Mat**	**Balls**	**Runs**	**Wkts**	**BBI**	**BBM**	**Ave**	**Econ**	**SR**	**5w**	**10**
Tests	11	-	-	-	-	-	-	-	-	-	-
ODIs	5	-	-	-	-	-	-	-	-	-	-
T20Is	1	-	-	-	-	-	-	-	-	-	-
First-class	239	17	1	1	1/0	1/0	1.00	0.35	17.0	0	0
List A	178	-	-	-	-	-	-	-	-	-	-
T20s	106	-	-	-	-	-	-	-	-	-	-

MOHAMMAD AMIR LHB / LFM / R0 / W0

FULL NAME: Mohammad Amir
BORN: April 13, 1992, Gujjar Khan, Pakistan
SQUAD NO: 5
HEIGHT: 6ft 2in
TEAMS: Pakistan, Essex, Chittagong Vikings, Federal Areas, Karachi Kings, National Bank of Pakistan, Rawalpindi, Sindh, Sui Southern Gas Corperation
ROLE: Bowler
DEBUT: Test: 2009; ODI: 2009; T20I: 2009; First-class: 2008; List A: 2008; T20: 2008

BEST BATTING: 66 Sui Southern Gas Corporation vs Lahore Blues, Lahore, 2015
BEST BOWLING: 7-61 National Bank of Pakistan vs Lahore Shalimar, Lahore, 2009

TWITTER: @iamamirofficial
NOTES: Once the most exciting teenage fast bowler in the world, Amir was found guilty of spot-fixing at Lord's in 2010 and subsequently banned from all cricket for five years. Repentant and now rehabilitated, the left-armer is back at the heart of Pakistan's attack. He was a key part of Pakistan's Test team that snatched a 2-2 draw in England in 2017. Amir first signed for Essex in 2017, when he impressed with 14 wickets and an economy-rate of 6.77 in 13 T20 games. He will be available for eight T20 Blast matches this summer

Batting	Mat	Inns	NO	Runs	HS	Ave	SR	100	50	Ct	St
Tests	36	67	11	751	48	13.41	37.92	0	0	5	0
ODIs	49	27	9	352	73*	19.55	81.86	0	2	6	0
T20Is	42	11	4	44	21*	6.28	75.86	0	0	4	0
First-class	66	100	15	1334	66	15.69	44.36	0	2	15	0
List A	71	35	15	402	73*	20.10	80.40	0	2	11	0
T20s	120	43	20	177	21*	7.69	92.67	0	0	11	0
Bowling	**Mat**	**Balls**	**Runs**	**Wkts**	**BBI**	**BBM**	**Ave**	**Econ**	**SR**	**5w**	**10**
Tests	36	7619	3627	119	6/44	7/64	30.47	2.85	64.0	4	0
ODIs	49	2419	1912	60	4/28	4/28	31.86	4.74	40.3	0	0
T20Is	42	936	1066	55	4/13	4/13	19.38	6.83	17.0	0	0
First-class	66	12214	5786	254	7/61	10/72	22.77	2.84	48.0	13	2
List A	71	3596	2746	101	5/36	5/36	27.18	4.58	35.6	1	0
T20s	120	2643	2966	143	4/13	4/13	20.74	6.73	18.4	0	0

JAMES ANDERSON

LHB / RFM / R0 / W3

FULL NAME: James Michael Anderson
BORN: July 30, 1982, Burnley, Lancashire
SQUAD NO: 9
HEIGHT: 6ft 2in
NICKNAME: Jimmy, Jimbo, Jimbob
EDUCATION: St Theodore's Roman Catholic High School, Burnley
TEAMS: England, Lancashire, Auckland
ROLE: Bowler
DEBUT: Test: 2003; ODI: 2002; T20I: 2007; First-class: 2002; List A: 2000; T20: 2004

BEST BATTING: 81 England vs India, Trent Bridge, 2014
BEST BOWLING: 7-42 England vs West Indies, Lord's, 2017
COUNTY CAP: 2003; BENEFIT: 2012

FAMILY TIES? My dad played for Burnley CC
'ROY OF THE ROVERS' MOMENT? Ashes wins, County Championship winners' medal
CRICKETING HERO? Peter Martin
NON-CRICKETING HERO? Steve Davis (ex-Burnley FC)
IF YOU WEREN'T A CRICKETER? I'd be busking with my recorder
SURPRISING FACT? I can peel a potato in 2.4 seconds and I'm allergic to mushrooms
TWITTER: @jimmy9

Batting	Mat	Inns	NO	Runs	HS	Ave	SR	100	50	Ct	St
Tests	148	207	86	1174	81	9.70	39.93	0	1	91	0
ODIs	194	79	43	273	28	7.58	48.66	0	0	53	0
T20Is	19	4	3	1	1*	1.00	50.00	0	0	3	0
First-class	239	308	124	1790	81	9.72		0	1	140	0
List A	255	102	62	371	28	9.27		0	0	65	0
T20s	44	10	6	23	16	5.75	88.46	0	0	8	0
Bowling	**Mat**	**Balls**	**Runs**	**Wkts**	**BBI**	**BBM**	**Ave**	**Econ**	**SR**	**5w**	**10**
Tests	148	32335	15490	575	7/42	11/71	26.93	2.87	56.2	27	3
ODIs	194	9584	7861	269	5/23	5/23	29.22	4.92	35.6	2	0
T20Is	19	422	552	18	3/23	3/23	30.66	7.84	23.4	0	0
First-class	239	48503	23446	920	7/42		25.48	2.90	52.7	45	6
List A	255	12414	10003	352	5/23	5/23	28.41	4.83	35.2	2	0
T20s	44	933	1318	41	3/23	3/23	32.14	8.47	22.7	0	0

MARTIN ANDERSSON

RHB / RM / R0 / W0

FULL NAME: Martin Kristoffer Andersson
BORN: September 6, 1996, Reading
SQUAD NO: 24
HEIGHT: 6ft 1in
NICKNAME: Tino, Pasty
EDUCATION: Reading Blue Coat School; University of Leeds
TEAMS: Middlesex, Derbyshire
ROLE: Allrounder
DEBUT: First-class: 2017; T20: 2018

BEST BATTING: 34 Middlesex vs Durham, Chester-le-Street, 2018
BEST BOWLING: 4-25 Derbyshire vs Glamorgan, Derby, 2018

WHAT WAS YOUR FIRST CRICKET CLUB? Reading CC, Berkshire
CRICKETING HERO? Hashim Amla
WHICH BOWLER WOULD YOU LEAST LIKE TO FACE? Vernon Philander – gets too much nip
BEST INNINGS YOU'VE SEEN? Kusal Perera's 153 not out for Sri Lanka against South Africa at Durban earlier this year. He single-handedly chased down the target against a great attack
SURPRISING FACT ABOUT YOU? My karaoke song of choice is Basshunter's 'Now You're Gone' in Swedish. I have 90% of my middle finger left – the other 10% was left in a door frame in a building at school
FAVOURITE QUOTE OR SAYING? I've missed more than 9,000 shots in my career. I've lost almost 300 games. Twenty-six times, I've been trusted to take the game-winning shot and missed. I've failed over and over and over again in my life. And that is why I succeed (Michael Jordan)
WHICH BOOK MEANS MOST TO YOU? Bounce – The Myth of Talent and the Power of Practice by Matthew Syed
TWITTER: @MartinAnderss11

Batting	Mat	Inns	NO	Runs	HS	Ave	SR	100	50	Ct	St
First-class	6	12	2	99	34	9.90	38.97	0	0	6	0
T20s	1	1	0	1	1	1.00	33.33	0	0	1	0
Bowling	**Mat**	**Balls**	**Runs**	**Wkts**	**BBI**	**BBM**	**Ave**	**Econ**	**SR**	**5w**	**10**
First-class	6	420	239	12	4/25	4/41	19.91	3.41	35.0	0	0
T20s	1	6	7	0	-	-	-	7.00	-	0	0

JOFRA ARCHER RHB / RF / R0 / W1 / MVP50

FULL NAME: Jofra Chioke Archer
BORN: April 1, 1995, Bridgetown, Barbados
SQUAD NO: 22
HEIGHT: 6ft 2in
NICKNAME: Regi
EDUCATION: Christ Church Foundation School, Barbados
TEAMS: Sussex, Hobart Hurricanes, Khulna Titans, Quetta Gladiators, Rajasthan Royals
ROLE: Allrounder
DEBUT: First-class: 2016; List A: 2016; T20: 2016

BEST BATTING: 81* Sussex vs Northamptonshire, Northampton, 2017
BEST BOWLING: 7-67 Sussex vs Kent, Hove, 2017

BEST ADVICE EVER RECEIVED? Be the best in your own way
'ROY OF THE ROVERS' MOMENT? Dismissing Eoin Morgan in a televised T20 match against Middlesex in 2017
BEST THING ABOUT YOUR HOME GROUND? The slope at Hove gives that extra push to fast bowlers
IF YOU WEREN'T A CRICKETER? I'd be a Nat Geo Wild presenter
SURPRISING FACT ABOUT YOU? I'm ambidextrous
WHERE IS PARADISE? Barbados
CRICKETING HERO? Don't have one
NON-CRICKETING HEROES? My parents
TWITTER: @craig_arch
NOTES: One of the game's hottest young talents, the Barbados-born allrounder becomes eligible to play for England in March on account of his English father and the ECB's revised residency criteria. He was retained by Rajasthan Royals for the 2019 IPL

Batting	Mat	Inns	NO	Runs	HS	Ave	SR	100	50	Ct	St
First-class	28	41	9	1003	81*	31.34	71.33	0	6	19	0
List A	14	11	3	192	45	24.00	121.51	0	0	4	0
T20s	81	43	21	351	36	15.95	136.57	0	0	23	0
Bowling	**Mat**	**Balls**	**Runs**	**Wkts**	**BBI**	**BBM**	**Ave**	**Econ**	**SR**	**5w**	**10**
First-class	28	5953	3071	131	7/67	11/137	23.44	3.09	45.4	5	1
List A	14	731	645	21	5/42	5/42	30.71	5.29	34.8	1	0
T20s	81	1760	2350	105	4/18	4/18	22.38	8.01	16.7	0	0

FAHEEM ASHRAF

RHB / RM / R0 / W0

FULL NAME: Faheem Ashraf
BORN: January 16, 1994, Kasur, Punjab, Pakistan
SQUAD NO: TBC
TEAMS: Pakistan, Northamptonshire, Faisalabad Wolves, Habib Bank Limited, Islamabad United, Khyber Pakhtunkhwa, Lahore Blues, National Bank of Pakistan
ROLE: Allrounder
DEBUT: Test: 2018; ODI: 2017; T20I: 2017; First-class: 2013; List A: 2013; T20: 2015

BEST BATTING: 116 Faisalabad vs Multan, Faisalabad, 2013
BEST BOWLING: 6-65 Habib Bank Limited vs Khan Research Laboratories, Karachi, 2016

TWITTER: @iFaheemAshraf
NOTES: Northamptonshire have signed the Pakistan allrounder for the whole of the T20 Blast. At the time of writing Faheem is ninth in the ICC's T20I bowling rankings and his canny medium-pacers should suit English conditions. He made his Test debut last May against Ireland and offered a telling contribution with the bat, hitting 83 in Pakistan's first innings. Two months later Faheem claimed his first five-wicket haul in ODIs, taking 5-22 against Zimbabwe in Bulawayo. "Faheem is a proven white-ball cricketer with the variety and subtle bowling skills required in Twenty20," said Northants head coach David Ripley

Batting	Mat	Inns	NO	Runs	HS	Ave	SR	100	50	Ct	St
Tests	4	6	0	138	83	23.00	70.05	0	1	0	0
ODIs	18	11	2	104	23	11.55	74.28	0	0	5	0
T20Is	25	16	6	108	21	10.80	117.39	0	0	7	0
First-class	40	58	8	1478	116	29.56	66.21	2	5	18	0
List A	60	45	7	625	71	16.44	80.23	0	2	18	0
T20s	63	44	19	403	54*	16.12	129.16	0	1	14	0
Bowling	**Mat**	**Balls**	**Runs**	**Wkts**	**BBI**	**BBM**	**Ave**	**Econ**	**SR**	**5w**	**10**
Tests	4	540	287	11	3/42	6/99	26.09	3.18	49.0	0	0
ODIs	18	675	505	18	5/22	5/22	28.05	4.48	37.5	1	0
T20Is	25	409	483	24	3/5	3/5	20.12	7.08	17.0	0	0
First-class	40	6263	3172	117	6/65	9/115	27.11	3.03	53.5	5	0
List A	60	2551	2153	85	5/22	5/22	25.32	5.06	30.0	2	0
T20s	63	1177	1494	71	6/19	6/19	21.04	7.61	16.5	1	0

GUS ATKINSON

RHB / RM / R0 / W0

FULL NAME: Angus Alexander Patrick Atkinson
BORN: January 19, 1998, Chelsea, London
SQUAD NO: 37
HEIGHT: 6ft 2in
NICKNAME: G-bus
EDUCATION: Northcote Lodge, London; Bradfield College, Berkshire
TEAMS: Surrey
ROLE: Bowler

WHAT WAS YOUR FIRST CRICKET CLUB? Spencer CC, London. Still play for them
FAVOURITE CRICKET BAT? Chase Vortex – lovely weight and it really pings off the bat
CRICKETING HERO? Andrew Flintoff
'ROY OF THE ROVERS' MOMENT? Taking 6-64 for Surrey Second XI against Middlesex Second XI at Richmond in 2017
WHICH BOWLER WOULD YOU LEAST LIKE TO FACE? Morne Morkel
BEST INNINGS YOU'VE SEEN? Aaron Finch's 117 not out from 52 balls against Middlesex at The Oval in last year's T20 Blast. Never seen anything like it
WHO WOULD YOU ASK TO BAT FOR YOUR LIFE? Alastair Cook
WHICH RULE WOULD YOU CHANGE ABOUT CRICKET? You can be out lbw even if you are hit outside the line of off stump while playing a shot
SURPRISING FACT ABOUT YOU? I had a rugby trial for Harlequins aged 13
FAVOURITE QUOTE OR SAYING? Don't be afraid to fail
WHICH BOOK MEANS MOST TO YOU? A Clockwork Orange by Anthony Burgess
ODDEST SPORT YOU'VE PLAYED? Hurling
TWITTER: @gus_atkinson1

TOM BAILEY

RHB / RFM / R0 / W1 / MVP19

FULL NAME: Thomas Ernest Bailey
BORN: April 21, 1991, Preston, Lancashire
SQUAD NO: 8
HEIGHT: 6ft 4in
NICKNAME: Jebby, Bails
EDUCATION: Myerscough College, Lancashire
TEAMS: Lancashire, England Lions
ROLE: Bowler
DEBUT: First-class: 2012; List A: 2014; T20: 2015

BEST BATTING: 66 Lancashire vs Surrey, Old Trafford, 2018
BEST BOWLING: 5-12 Lancashire vs Leicestershire, Leicester, 2015
COUNTY CAP: 2018

FAMILY TIES? My dad played for a local side and I used to watch him every weekend as a kid
BEST ADVICE EVER RECEIVED? You're only young once
'ROY OF THE ROVERS' MOMENT? Winning the T20 Blast with Lancashire in 2015
BEST THING ABOUT YOUR HOME GROUND? Good wicket for both batsmen and bowlers
IF YOU WEREN'T A CRICKETER? I'd be a nuclear scientist
SURPRISING FACT? I'm actually really smart
WHERE IS PARADISE? Dubai
CRICKETING HERO? Steve Harmison – bowled fast and won the Ashes for England in 2005
NON-CRICKETING HERO? Tom Webster
TWITTER: @TomBaildog

Batting	Mat	Inns	NO	Runs	HS	Ave	SR	100	50	Ct	St
First-class	47	66	12	921	66	17.05	49.38	0	3	9	0
List A	15	11	6	81	33	16.20	89.01	0	0	2	0
T20s	13	4	1	18	10	6.00	112.50	0	0	6	0
Bowling	**Mat**	**Balls**	**Runs**	**Wkts**	**BBI**	**BBM**	**Ave**	**Econ**	**SR**	**5w**	**10**
First-class	47	8221	4096	156	5/12	10/98	26.25	2.98	52.6	6	1
List A	15	679	660	20	3/31	3/31	33.00	5.83	33.9	0	0
T20s	13	216	351	11	2/24	2/24	31.90	9.75	19.6	0	0

JONNY BAIRSTOW

RHB / WK / R3 / W0

FULL NAME: Jonathan Marc Bairstow
BORN: September 26, 1989, Bradford
SQUAD NO: 21
HEIGHT: 5ft 10in
NICKNAME: Bluey
EDUCATION: St Peter's School, York; Leeds Metropolitan University
TEAMS: England, Yorkshire, Peshawar Zalmi, Sunrisers Hyderabad
ROLE: Batsman/wicketkeeper
DEBUT: Test: 2012; ODI: 2011; T20I: 2011; First-class: 2009; List A: 2009; T20: 2010

BEST BATTING: 246 Yorkshire vs Hampshire, Headingley, 2016

COUNTY CAP: 2011

FAMILY TIES? My father David played for Yorkshire and England
CRICKETING HERO? Sachin Tendulkar
NON-CRICKETING HERO? Steve Irwin
IF YOU WEREN'T A CRICKETER? I'd be a rugby player
SURPRISING FACT? I played football for the Leeds United Academy for seven years
TWITTER: @jbairstow21
NOTES: In December Bairstow was bought for 240,000 by Sunrisers Hyderabad to play in the 2019 IPL, which runs until mid-May

Batting	Mat	Inns	NO	Runs	HS	Ave	SR	100	50	Ct	St
Tests	63	109	6	3806	167*	36.95	55.65	6	20	160	11
ODIs	59	54	8	2118	141*	46.04	105.00	6	8	24	2
T20Is	30	25	6	513	68	27.00	130.20	0	3	28	0
First-class	174	285	32	11352	246	44.86	63.10	24	61	446	22
List A	127	116	14	4040	174	39.60	103.56	9	18	75	8
T20s	99	87	17	1766	102*	25.22	127.69	1	7	61	10
Bowling	**Mat**	**Balls**	**Runs**	**Wkts**	**BBI**	**BBM**	**Ave**	**Econ**	**SR**	**5w**	**10**
Tests	63	-	-	-	-	-	-	-	-	-	-
ODIs	59	-	-	-	-	-	-	-	-	-	-
T20Is	30	-	-	-	-	-	-	-	-	-	-
First-class	174	6	1	0	-	-	-	1.00	-	0	0
List A	127	-	-	-	-	-	-	-	-	-	-
T20s	99	-	-	-	-	-	-	-	-	-	-

GEORGE BALDERSON LHB / RM / R0 / W0

FULL NAME: George Philip Balderson
BORN: October 11, 2000, Manchester
SQUAD NO: 10
HEIGHT: 5ft 11in
NICKNAME: Balders
EDUCATION: Cheadle Hulme High School, Greater Manchester
TEAMS: Lancashire, England U19
ROLE: Allrounder

WHAT WAS YOUR FIRST CRICKET CLUB? Cheadle Hulme CC, Greater Manchester. I'd watch my dad play there every Saturday
FAVOURITE CRICKET BAT? GM Icon – the first bat I scored a hundred with
WHICH BOWLER WOULD YOU LEAST LIKE TO FACE? Morne Morkel – his height and his record against left-handers speak for themselves
WHO WOULD YOU ASK TO BAT FOR YOUR LIFE? Alastair Cook
YOUR BIGGEST CRICKETING REGRET? Bowling leg-spin until I was 14
TWITTER: @BaldersonGeorge
NOTES: Balderson is a top-order batsman and right-arm seamer who signed his first professional contract with Lancashire in November 2018. The 18-year-old left-hander made four appearances for Lancashire in the Second XI Championship last summer and featured in both games at the victorious Second XI T20 Finals Day. He was selected for the England Young Lions squad for winter training camps in the UK and for the 2018/19 tour of Bangladesh, scoring 65 as an opener in the first youth Test and taking 3-40 in the second. He said: "It's a dream come true to sign my first professional contract with Lancashire. This is just the start of my journey now. My aim in 2019 is to consistently perform for the Second XI and push my case for first-team selection"

JAKE BALL RHB / RFM / R0 / W1 / MVP77

FULL NAME: Jacob Timothy Ball
BORN: March 14, 1991, Mansfield, Nottinghamshire
SQUAD NO: 28
HEIGHT: 6ft 3in
NICKNAME: Yak
EDUCATION: Meden School, Mansfield
TEAMS: England, Nottinghamshire
ROLE: Bowler
DEBUT: Test: 2016; ODI: 2016; T20I: 2018; First-class: 2011; List A: 2009; T20: 2011

BEST BATTING: 49* Nottinghamshire vs Warwickshire, Trent Bridge, 2015
BEST BOWLING: 6-49 Nottinghamshire vs Sussex, Trent Bridge, 2015
COUNTY CAP: 2016

FAMILY TIES? My uncle Bruce French played for England
WHAT WAS YOUR FIRST CRICKET CLUB? Welbeck Colliery CC, Nottinghamshire
BEST INNINGS YOU'VE SEEN? Alastair Cook's double century at the MCG in the 2017/18 Ashes. As a member of the squad I got to see how hard he worked for that innings over the whole tour
WHO WOULD YOU ASK TO BAT FOR YOUR LIFE? The Wymeswold Wall – Harry Gurney
SURPRISING FACT ABOUT YOU? I was a batter till the age of 15
WHAT WILL YOU BE DOING IN THE YEAR 2040? I'll be sat in the Radcliffe Road Stand shouting at the players
TWITTER: @Jakeball30

Batting	Mat	Inns	NO	Runs	HS	Ave	SR	100	50	Ct	St
Tests	4	8	0	67	31	8.37	53.60	0	0	1	0
ODIs	18	6	2	38	28	9.50	77.55	0	0	5	0
T20Is	2	-	-	-	-	-	-	-	-	1	0
First-class	52	79	12	897	49*	13.38	75.95	0	0	7	0
List A	88	35	14	184	28	8.76	102.79	0	0	18	0
T20s	60	14	9	33	8*	6.60	91.66	0	0	15	0
Bowling	**Mat**	**Balls**	**Runs**	**Wkts**	**BBI**	**BBM**	**Ave**	**Econ**	**SR**	**5w**	**10**
Tests	4	612	343	3	1/47	1/47	114.33	3.36	204.0	0	0
ODIs	18	947	980	21	5/51	5/51	46.66	6.20	45.0	1	0
T20Is	2	42	83	2	1/39	1/39	41.50	11.85	21.0	0	0
First-class	52	7850	4530	173	6/49	9/57	26.18	3.46	45.3	6	0
List A	88	3736	3626	104	5/51	5/51	34.86	5.82	35.9	1	0
T20s	60	1190	1722	66	3/27	3/27	26.09	8.68	18.0	0	0

GARY BALLANCE

LHB / LB / R3 / W0 / MVP41

FULL NAME: Gary Simon Ballance
BORN: November 22, 1989, Harare, Zimbabwe
SQUAD NO: 19
NICKNAME: Gazza, Gaz
EDUCATION: Peterhouse School, Marondera, Zimbabwe; Harrow School, London
TEAMS: England, Yorkshire, Derbyshire, Mid West Rhinos
ROLE: Batsman
DEBUT: Test: 2014; ODI: 2013; First-class: 2008; List A: 2006; T20: 2010

BEST BATTING: 210 Mid West Rhinos vs Southern Rocks, Masvingo, 2011

COUNTY CAP: 2012 (Yorkshire)

NOTES: A close family friend of former Zimbabwe skipper David Houghton, Ballance signed for Derbyshire aged 16 before joining the Yorkshire Academy in 2008. He played for Zimbabwe at the 2006 U19 World Cup before qualifying to play for England. His ODI debut was in 2013 before his Test debut at Sydney in the 2013/14 Ashes. He had an exceptional summer in Test cricket in 2014, hitting three centuries to cement his place at No.3. Ballance lost his Test spot during the 2015 Ashes and was in and out the side over the next two years. His most recent Test was in 2017. He was made captain of Yorkshire across all formats that year but stood down last summer when he took a brief break from cricket for personal reasons. Ballance has been the club's leading run-scorer in the Championship for the past two seasons. He has signed a new contract which ties him to Yorkshire until the end of the 2021 season

Batting	Mat	Inns	NO	Runs	HS	Ave	SR	100	50	Ct	St
Tests	23	42	2	1498	156	37.45	47.16	4	7	22	0
ODIs	16	15	1	297	79	21.21	67.04	0	2	8	0
First-class	145	238	22	10268	210	47.53	52.03	35	48	116	0
List A	103	96	14	4066	152*	49.58	88.99	7	25	41	0
T20s	85	76	9	1624	79	24.23	123.21	0	6	43	0
Bowling	**Mat**	**Balls**	**Runs**	**Wkts**	**BBI**	**BBM**	**Ave**	**Econ**	**SR**	**5w**	**10**
Tests	23	12	5	0	-	-	-	2.50	-	0	0
ODIs	16	-	-	-	-	-	-	-	-	-	-
First-class	145	162	154	0	-	-	-	5.70	-	0	0
List A	103	-	-	-	-	-	-	-	-	-	-
T20s	85	-	-	-	-	-	-	-	-	-	-

ETHAN BAMBER RHB / RFM / R0 / W0

FULL NAME: Ethan Read Bamber
BORN: December 17, 1998, Westminster
SQUAD NO: 54
HEIGHT: 5ft 11in
NICKNAME: Sorry, Bambs
EDUCATION: Mill Hill School, London; University of Exeter
TEAMS: Middlesex
ROLE: Bowler
DEBUT: First-class: 2018

BEST BATTING: 27* Middlesex vs Gloucestershire, Bristol, 2018
BEST BOWLING: 4-81 Middlesex vs Gloucestershire, Bristol, 2018

WHAT WAS YOUR FIRST CRICKET CLUB? North Middlesex CC, London. It was about 400 metres from my house
FAVOURITE CRICKET BAT? Gray-Nicolls Powerbow, though I never found the middle. Nothing's changed...
WHICH BOWLER WOULD YOU LEAST LIKE TO FACE? Allan Donald
BEST INNINGS YOU'VE SEEN? Alastair Cook's final Test innings
WHO WOULD YOU ASK TO BAT FOR YOUR LIFE? My friend Matti Thal – solid as a rock
WHICH RULE WOULD YOU CHANGE ABOUT CRICKET? An edge for a four should go down as extras
YOUR BIGGEST CRICKETING REGRET? Getting out with a shocking shot when the other batter was on 98
WHAT WILL YOU BE DOING IN THE YEAR 2040? I'll be a teacher perhaps
FAVOURITE QUOTE OR SAYING? Lynn, would you call Bill Oddie? (Alan Partridge)
ODDEST SPORT YOU'VE PLAYED? Kabaddi
TWITTER: @etbamber

Batting	Mat	Inns	NO	Runs	HS	Ave	SR	100	50	Ct	St
First-class	6	10	3	76	27*	10.85	29.92	0	0	2	0
Bowling	**Mat**	**Balls**	**Runs**	**Wkts**	**BBI**	**BBM**	**Ave**	**Econ**	**SR**	**5w**	**10**
First-class	6	1223	567	28	4/81	6/70	20.25	2.78	43.6	0	0

CAMERON BANCROFT RHB / WK / R0 / W0

DURHAM

FULL NAME: Cameron Timothy Bancroft
BORN: November 19, 1992, Perth, Australia
SQUAD NO: TBC
HEIGHT: 5ft 10in
EDUCATION: Aquinas College, Perth
TEAMS: Australia, Durham, Gloucestershire, Perth Scorchers, Western Australia
ROLE: Batsman/wicketkeeper
DEBUT: Test: 2017; T20I: 2016; First-class: 2013; List A: 2011; T20: 2014

BEST BATTING: 228* Western Australia vs South Australia, Perth, 2017
BEST BOWLING: 1-67 Gloucestershire vs Sussex, Hove, 2017

TWITTER: @cbancroft4
NOTES: Durham have signed the Australian opener to play across all formats, international commitments permitting. Bancroft, who can also keep wicket, has previous experience of county cricket having played 16 first-class matches and scored 877 runs at 33.73 for Gloucestershire across 2016 and 2017. He was due to play for Somerset last season only to have his contract terminated following the ball-tampering scandal in Cape Town which led to him being suspended for nine months by Cricket Australia. Having served his ban, Bancroft will be hoping a successful spell with Durham can put him in the reckoning for Ashes selection this summer. He scored 82 not out in the first Test of the 2017/18 Ashes at Brisbane and hit two impressive half-centuries against South Africa in March 2018 before his Test career was brought to a halt

Batting	Mat	Inns	NO	Runs	HS	Ave	SR	100	50	Ct	St
Tests	8	14	1	402	82*	30.92	45.68	0	3	11	0
T20Is	1	1	1	0	0*	-	-	0	0	1	0
First-class	78	143	12	5197	228*	39.67	43.06	12	22	102	1
List A	41	39	5	1224	176	36.00	77.81	1	9	35	1
T20s	36	31	7	800	87*	33.33	127.18	0	6	16	5
Bowling	**Mat**	**Balls**	**Runs**	**Wkts**	**BBI**	**BBM**	**Ave**	**Econ**	**SR**	**5w**	**10**
Tests	8	-	-	-	-	-	-	-	-	-	-
T20Is	1	-	-	-	-	-	-	-	-	-	-
First-class	78	48	67	1	1/67	1/67	67.00	8.37	48.0	0	0
List A	41	-	-	-	-	-	-	-	-	-	-
T20s	36	-	-	-	-	-	-	-	-	-	-

LIAM BANKS

RHB / RM / R0 / W0

FULL NAME: Liam Banks
BORN: March 27, 1999, Stoke-on-Trent
SQUAD NO: 8
HEIGHT: 5ft 10in
NICKNAME: Banksy
EDUCATION: Newcastle-under-Lyme School and Sixth Form College
TEAMS: Warwickshire
ROLE: Batsman
DEBUT: First-class: 2017

BEST BATTING: 29 Warwickshire vs Yorkshire, Headingley, 2017

WHAT WAS YOUR FIRST CRICKET CLUB? Silverdale CC, Staffordshire
FAVOURITE CRICKET BAT? Spyder Venom
CRICKETING HERO? Ricky Ponting
WHICH BOWLER WOULD YOU LEAST LIKE TO FACE? Mitchell Johnson
BEST INNINGS YOU'VE SEEN? Alastair Cook's Test hundred on debut against India at Nagpur in 2006. Nerveless
WHO WOULD YOU ASK TO BAT FOR YOUR LIFE? Kane Williamson
WHICH RULE WOULD YOU CHANGE ABOUT CRICKET? Bring DRS into domestic cricket
YOUR BIGGEST CRICKETING REGRET? Getting in and getting out
SURPRISING FACT ABOUT YOU? I love animals and fishing
WHAT WILL YOU BE DOING IN THE YEAR 2040? Hopefully still playing for Warwickshire
FAVOURITE QUOTE OR SAYING? You won't have to force anything that's truly meant to be
WHICH BOOK MEANS MOST TO YOU? The Subtle Art of Not Giving a F*** – A Counterintuitive Approach to Living a Good Life by Mark Manson
ODDEST SPORT YOU'VE PLAYED? Polo

Batting	Mat	Inns	NO	Runs	HS	Ave	SR	100	50	Ct	St
First-class	2	4	0	57	29	14.25	37.25	0	0	1	0
Bowling	**Mat**	**Balls**	**Runs**	**Wkts**	**BBI**	**BBM**	**Ave**	**Econ**	**SR**	**5w**	**10**
First-class	2	-	-	-	-	-	-	-	-	-	-

TOM BANTON

RHB / WK / R0 / W0

FULL NAME: Thomas Banton
BORN: November 11, 1998, Chiltern, Buckinghamshire
SQUAD NO: 18
HEIGHT: 6ft 2in
NICKNAME: Bants
EDUCATION: King's College, Taunton
TEAMS: Somerset
ROLE: Wicketkeeper/batsman
DEBUT: First-class: 2018; List A: 2018; T20: 2017

BEST BATTING: 30 Somerset vs Surrey, Taunton, 2018

WHAT WAS YOUR FIRST CRICKET CLUB? Sutton CC, London
CRICKETING HERO? Virat Kohli
WHICH BOWLER WOULD YOU LEAST LIKE TO FACE? Dale Steyn
BEST INNINGS YOU'VE SEEN? Johann Myburgh smashing 103 off 44 balls against Essex in the 2018 T20 Blast. I was batting at the other end as we chased down 136 without losing a wicket
WHO WOULD YOU ASK TO BAT FOR YOUR LIFE? My dog – love him so much
YOUR BIGGEST CRICKETING REGRET? Not playing for Somerset at the age of 10
SURPRISING FACT ABOUT YOU? I love playing hockey
WHAT WILL YOU BE DOING IN THE YEAR 2040? I'll be married and commentating
ODDEST SPORT YOU'VE PLAYED? Aussie Rules
TWITTER: @tombanton18

Batting	Mat	Inns	NO	Runs	HS	Ave	SR	100	50	Ct	St
First-class	2	3	0	37	30	12.33	48.68	0	0	1	0
List A	7	6	0	70	40	11.66	55.11	0	0	3	0
T20s	4	3	1	42	29*	21.00	97.67	0	0	0	2
Bowling	**Mat**	**Balls**	**Runs**	**Wkts**	**BBI**	**BBM**	**Ave**	**Econ**	**SR**	**5w**	**10**
First-class	2	-	-	-	-	-	-	-	-	-	-
List A	7	-	-	-	-	-	-	-	-	-	-
T20s	4	-	-	-	-	-	-	-	-	-	-

TOM BARBER

RHB / LF / R0 / W0

FULL NAME: Thomas Edward Barber
BORN: August 8, 1995, Poole, Dorset
SQUAD NO: 25
HEIGHT: 6ft 3in
NICKNAME: Barbs
EDUCATION: Bournemouth Grammar School
TEAMS: Middlesex, Hampshire
ROLE: Bowler
DEBUT: First-class: 2018; List A: 2014; T20: 2017

BEST BATTING: 3 Middlesex vs Sussex, Hove, 2018

WHAT WAS YOUR FIRST CRICKET CLUB? Parley CC, Dorset. The club also produced David Payne of Gloucestershire
CRICKETING HERO? Andrew Flintoff
BEST ADVICE EVER RECEIVED? Hit the top of off stump
WHICH BOWLER WOULD YOU LEAST LIKE TO FACE? Anyone who bowls 85mph-plus
BEST INNINGS YOU'VE SEEN? Paul Stirling's 66 off 36 balls for us against Surrey in the 2018 T20 Blast. Sixes all over the place
WHO WOULD YOU ASK TO BAT FOR YOUR LIFE? Alastair Cook
WHICH RULE WOULD YOU CHANGE ABOUT CRICKET? Allow more bouncers per over
SURPRISING FACT ABOUT YOU? I broke the record for the fastest ball bowled in the Vicon testing at Loughborough – 89.6mph
TWITTER: @Tom_Barber20

Batting	Mat	Inns	NO	Runs	HS	Ave	SR	100	50	Ct	St
First-class	2	3	1	3	3	1.50	21.42	0	0	0	0
List A	7	6	0	1	1	0.16	5.88	0	0	0	0
T20s	9	3	0	2	2	0.66	40.00	0	0	1	0
Bowling	**Mat**	**Balls**	**Runs**	**Wkts**	**BBI**	**BBM**	**Ave**	**Econ**	**SR**	**5w**	**10**
First-class	2	204	131	0	-	-	-	3.85	-	0	0
List A	7	300	322	9	3/62	3/62	35.77	6.44	33.3	0	0
T20s	9	174	342	10	4/28	4/28	34.20	11.79	17.4	0	0

KEITH BARKER LHB / LFM / R0 / W3 / MVP95

FULL NAME: Keith Hubert Douglas Barker
BORN: October 21, 1986, Manchester
SQUAD NO: 10
HEIGHT: 6ft 3in
NICKNAME: Barks, Barky, Barksy
EDUCATION: Moorhead High School, Accrington; Preston College
TEAMS: Hampshire, Warwickshire
ROLE: Allrounder
DEBUT: First-class: 2009; List A: 2009; T20: 2009

BEST BATTING: 125 Warwickshire vs Surrey, Guildford, 2013
BEST BOWLING: 6-40 Warwickshire vs Somerset, Taunton, 2012
COUNTY CAP: 2013 (Warwickshire)

FAMILY TIES? My father, godfather and brothers all played various levels of cricket
WHAT WAS YOUR FIRST CRICKET CLUB? Enfield CC, Lancashire
FAVOURITE CRICKET BAT? Gray-Nicolls Scoop
CRICKETING HERO? My father
BEST ADVICE EVER RECEIVED? It's only a game
WHICH BOWLER WOULD YOU LEAST LIKE TO FACE? Keith Barker (my father)
WHO WOULD YOU ASK TO BAT FOR YOUR LIFE? Alastair Cook
WHICH RULE WOULD YOU CHANGE ABOUT CRICKET? The ECB should stop making things easier for batters
SURPRISING FACT ABOUT YOU? I never scored a hundred for the Enfield first team
WHICH BOOK MEANS MOST TO YOU? Rich Dad Poor Dad – What the Rich Teach Their Kids About Money that the Poor and Middle Classes Do Not by Robert Kiyosaki

Batting	Mat	Inns	NO	Runs	HS	Ave	SR	100	50	Ct	St
First-class	113	150	25	3554	125	28.43	58.10	6	16	33	0
List A	62	39	11	560	56	20.00	94.59	0	1	14	0
T20s	65	35	7	383	46	13.67	111.01	0	0	17	0
Bowling	**Mat**	**Balls**	**Runs**	**Wkts**	**BBI**	**BBM**	**Ave**	**Econ**	**SR**	**5w**	**10**
First-class	113	18436	9122	359	6/40	10/70	25.40	2.96	51.3	14	1
List A	62	2342	2263	69	4/33	4/33	32.79	5.79	33.9	0	0
T20s	65	1206	1588	69	4/19	4/19	23.01	7.90	17.4	0	0

ED BARNARD RHB / RFM / R0 / W0 / MVP3

FULL NAME: Edward George Barnard
BORN: November 20, 1995, Shrewsbury
SQUAD NO: 30
HEIGHT: 6ft 1in
NICKNAME: Barndoor, Earthworm Jim
EDUCATION: Meole Brace School, Shrewsbury; Shrewsbury School
TEAMS: Worcestershire, England Lions
ROLE: Allrounder
DEBUT: First-class: 2015; List A: 2015; T20: 2015

BEST BATTING: 75 Worcestershire vs Durham, Worcester, 2017
BEST BOWLING: 6-37 Worcestershire vs Somerset, Taunton, 2018

FAMILY TIES? Dad (Andy) played for Shropshire; brother (Mike) played for Shropshire and first-class cricket for Oxford MCCU; brother (Steve) played for Shropshire
WHAT WAS YOUR FIRST CRICKET CLUB? Shrewsbury CC, Shropshire. National Knockout champions 1983 and 2011
FAVOURITE CRICKET BAT? Gray-Nicolls Dynadrive
CRICKETING HERO? Andrew Flintoff
WHICH BOWLER WOULD YOU LEAST LIKE TO FACE? Morne Morkel isn't pleasant
BEST INNINGS YOU'VE SEEN? Ben Cox's 46 not out to beat Sussex in the 2018 T20 final
WHO WOULD YOU ASK TO BAT FOR YOUR LIFE? Daryl Mitchell
WHAT WILL YOU BE DOING IN THE YEAR 2040? I'll be a school teacher
ODDEST SPORT YOU'VE PLAYED? Eton Fives – a brilliant sport. Like squash but using your hands
TWITTER: @EdBarn95

Batting	Mat	Inns	NO	Runs	HS	Ave	SR	100	50	Ct	St
First-class	46	69	12	1599	75	28.05	57.80	0	10	24	0
List A	35	25	10	464	51	30.93	102.20	0	2	16	0
T20s	52	30	14	275	34*	17.18	131.57	0	0	31	0
Bowling	**Mat**	**Balls**	**Runs**	**Wkts**	**BBI**	**BBM**	**Ave**	**Econ**	**SR**	**5w**	**10**
First-class	46	7035	4093	143	6/37	11/89	28.62	3.49	49.1	4	1
List A	35	1512	1504	46	3/37	3/37	32.69	5.96	32.8	0	0
T20s	52	734	1120	26	3/29	3/29	43.07	9.15	28.2	0	0

ED BARNES RHB / RFM / R0 / W0

FULL NAME: Edward Barnes
BORN: November 26, 1997, York
SQUAD NO: 62
NICKNAME: Barnesy
EDUCATION: King James School, Knaresborough, North Yorkshire
TEAMS: Yorkshire, England U19
ROLE: Bowler

NOTES: The 21-year-old seam-bowling allrounder has been a consistent performer for Yorkshire's Academy and Second XI for a number of seasons, one of several players from York to make the grade along with Jonny Bairstow, Matthew Fisher and Jack Leaning. He helped the Yorkshire Academy win the league-and-cup double in 2014 and a year later hit a run-a-ball 177 against Derbyshire U17. Barnes is yet to make his first-team debut but played two 'Tests' and two 'ODIs' for England U19s against Sri Lanka in 2016, taking nine wickets and playing in the same side as future Test cricketers Ollie Pope and Dom Bess. Up until the start of this season, Barnes had taken 51 wickets and scored three half-centuries in 48 Second XI appearances across all formats

GEORGE BARTLETT

RHB / OB / R0 / W0

FULL NAME: George Anthony Bartlett
BORN: March 14, 1998, Frimley, Surrey
SQUAD NO: 14
EDUCATION: Millfield School, Somerset
TEAMS: Somerset
ROLE: Batsman
DEBUT: First-class: 2017

BEST BATTING: 110 Somerset vs Lancashire, Old Trafford, 2018

TWITTER: @georgebartlett9
NOTES: A batsman who bowls off-spin, Bartlett is a product of the Somerset Academy and signed a contract with the club in October 2016. In early 2017 he made 179 for England U19 against India U19 in a four-day match at Nagpur, taking Nasser Hussain's record for the highest score by an England U19 batsman overseas. Bartlett made his debut for Somerset Second XI in 2014 and featured in the 2016 U19 World Cup. He made a hundred in the U19 Test against Sri Lanka in 2016 and earned a senior contract on the back of consistent performances for the Second XI. He made his first-class debut in 2017 and scored his maiden Championship hundred last season against Lancashire at Old Trafford

Batting	Mat	Inns	NO	Runs	HS	Ave	SR	100	50	Ct	St
First-class	10	19	1	406	110	22.55	54.93	1	0	5	0
Bowling	**Mat**	**Balls**	**Runs**	**Wkts**	**BBI**	**BBM**	**Ave**	**Econ**	**SR**	**5w**	**10**
First-class	10	20	27	0	-	-	-	8.10	-	0	0

GARETH BATTY

RHB / OB / R0 / W2

FULL NAME: Gareth Jon Batty
BORN: October 13, 1977, Bradford
SQUAD NO: 13
HEIGHT: 5ft 11in
NICKNAME: Bats, Stuta
EDUCATION: Bingley Grammar School
TEAMS: England, Surrey, Worcestershire, Yorkshire
ROLE: Bowler
DEBUT: Test: 2003; ODI: 2002; T20I: 2009; First-class: 1997; List A: 1998; T20: 2003

BEST BATTING: 133 Worcestershire vs Surrey, The Oval, 2004
BEST BOWLING: 8-68 Surrey vs Essex, Chelmsford, 2014
COUNTY CAP: 2011 (Surrey); **BENEFIT:** 2017 (Surrey)

FAMILY TIES? Dad played for Yorkshire Second XI, brother Jeremy played for Yorkshire and Somerset
CRICKETING HERO? Joel Garner
NON-CRICKETING HEROES? Winston Churchill and Maggie Thatcher – people who had the courage to make decisions
IF YOU WEREN'T A CRICKETER? I'd be a fireman
SURPRISING FACT? This is my 23rd year as a pro
UNUSUAL OBJECT AT HOME? A carrier pigeon

Batting	Mat	Inns	NO	Runs	HS	Ave	SR	100	50	Ct	St
Tests	9	12	2	149	38	14.90	25.68	0	0	3	0
ODIs	10	8	2	30	17	5.00	41.09	0	0	4	0
T20Is	1	1	0	4	4	4.00	57.14	0	0	0	0
First-class	253	374	64	7276	133	23.47	52.01	3	30	161	0
List A	265	194	42	2354	83*	15.48	73.43	0	5	82	0
T20s	158	87	29	608	87	10.48	101.84	0	1	47	0
Bowling	**Mat**	**Balls**	**Runs**	**Wkts**	**BBI**	**BBM**	**Ave**	**Econ**	**SR**	**5w**	**10**
Tests	9	1714	914	15	3/55	5/153	60.93	3.19	114.2	0	0
ODIs	10	440	366	5	2/40	2/40	73.20	4.99	88.0	0	0
T20Is	1	18	17	0	-	-	-	5.66	-	0	0
First-class	253	44776	21678	656	8/68	10/113	33.04	2.90	68.2	26	3
List A	265	10359	8016	246	5/35	5/35	32.58	4.64	42.1	3	0
T20s	158	2797	3432	124	4/13	4/13	27.67	7.36	22.5	0	0

TEMBA BAVUMA

RHB / RM / R0 / W0

FULL NAME: Temba Bavuma
BORN: May 17, 1990, Cape Town, South Africa
SQUAD NO: TBC
HEIGHT: 5ft 4in
TEAMS: South Africa, Northamptonshire, Cape Cobras, Durban Heat, Gauteng, Lions
ROLE: Batsman
DEBUT: Test: 2014; ODI: 2016; First-class: 2008; List A: 2008; T20: 2011

BEST BATTING: 162 South Africa A vs Australia A, Townsville, 2014
BEST BOWLING: 2-34 Gauteng vs North West, Potchefstroom, 2011

TWITTER: @tbavuma10
NOTES: The South African middle-order batsman has signed for Northamptonshire for eight Championship fixtures across May, June and July. Bavuma became the first black African cricketer to score a century for South Africa when he hit 102 against England at Cape Town in January 2016. He was an ever-present during the Test series in England in 2017, hitting two half-centuries. "Signing a player of Temba's international stature underlines our ambitions as a club," said Northants chief executive Ray Payne. "We are keen to return to the Championship's top division and hopefully his runs will help us achieve that. His Test experience will bring an added dimension to the team"

Batting	Mat	Inns	NO	Runs	HS	Ave	SR	100	50	Ct	St
Tests	36	59	7	1716	102*	33.00	47.93	1	13	16	0
ODIs	2	2	0	161	113	80.50	94.70	1	0	1	0
First-class	132	219	29	7014	162	36.91	51.44	12	39	69	0
List A	83	70	8	1940	117*	31.29	82.09	3	7	19	0
T20s	51	44	8	953	79*	26.47	123.44	0	4	21	0
Bowling	**Mat**	**Balls**	**Runs**	**Wkts**	**BBI**	**BBM**	**Ave**	**Econ**	**SR**	**5w**	**10**
Tests	36	96	61	1	1/29	1/29	61.00	3.81	96.0	0	0
ODIs	2	-	-	-	-	-	-	-	-	-	-
First-class	132	476	311	7	2/34	2/34	44.42	3.92	68.0	0	0
List A	83	3	4	0	-	-	-	8.00	-	0	0
T20s	51	-	-	-	-	-	-	-	-	-	-

AARON BEARD

LHB / RMF / R0 / W0

FULL NAME: Aaron Paul Beard
BORN: October 15, 1997, Chelmsford
SQUAD NO: 14
HEIGHT: 5ft 11in
NICKNAME: Beardo, AB
EDUCATION: The Boswells School, Chelmsford; Great Baddow High School, Chelmsford
TEAMS: Essex
ROLE: Bowler
DEBUT: First-class: 2016

BEST BATTING: 58* Essex vs Durham MCCU, Chelmsford, 2017
BEST BOWLING: 4-62 Essex vs Sri Lankans, Chelmsford, 2016

WHAT WAS YOUR FIRST CRICKET CLUB? Writtle CC, Essex
FAVOURITE CRICKET BAT? Warsop – got my first-ever hundred with it
WHICH BOWLER WOULD YOU LEAST LIKE TO FACE? Jamie Porter – nips them sideways
BEST INNINGS YOU'VE SEEN? Dan Lawrence hitting 141 against Lancashire at Chelmsford in 2017. He batted out the final day to get Essex a draw after we had lost some early wickets
WHO WOULD YOU ASK TO BAT FOR YOUR LIFE? Alastair Cook
WHICH RULE WOULD YOU CHANGE ABOUT CRICKET? For DRS and lbws: if it's hitting the stumps it is out, regardless of whether the whole ball or part of the ball is hitting
WHAT WILL YOU BE DOING IN THE YEAR 2040? Hopefully finishing a happy career in cricket
FAVOURITE QUOTE OR SAYING? Hard work beats talent when talent doesn't work hard (Tim Notke)
WHICH BOOK MEANS MOST TO YOU? My passport
ODDEST SPORT YOU'VE PLAYED? Aussie Rules
TWITTER: @aaronbeard_14

Batting	Mat	Inns	NO	Runs	HS	Ave	SR	100	50	Ct	St
First-class	9	9	5	79	58*	19.75	58.95	0	1	1	0
Bowling	**Mat**	**Balls**	**Runs**	**Wkts**	**BBI**	**BBM**	**Ave**	**Econ**	**SR**	**5w**	**10**
First-class	9	1256	783	17	4/62	5/81	46.05	3.74	73.8	0	0

WILL BEER RHB / LB / R0 / W0

FULL NAME: William Andrew Thomas Beer
BORN: October 8, 1988, Crawley, Sussex
SQUAD NO: 18
HEIGHT: 5ft 10in
NICKNAME: Beery
EDUCATION: Reigate Grammar School; Collyer's Sixth Form College, Horsham
TEAMS: Sussex
ROLE: Bowler
DEBUT: First-class: 2008; List A: 2009; T20: 2008

BEST BATTING: 50* Sussex vs Loughborough MCCU, Hove, 2018
BEST BOWLING: 6-29 Sussex vs South Africa A, Arundel, 2017

WHAT WAS YOUR FIRST CRICKET CLUB? Horsham CC, West Sussex. Best wicket in the UK
CRICKETING HERO? Shane Warne
BEST INNINGS YOU'VE SEEN? No.9 Ollie Robinson hitting 41 off 37 balls for a one-wicket win at Colwyn Bay in the Championship in 2017
WHO WOULD YOU ASK TO BAT FOR YOUR LIFE? Michael Thornely – he has the best technique I have ever seen
WHICH RULE WOULD YOU CHANGE ABOUT CRICKET? White-ball games should begin early or be shortened if the weather looks really bad – as long as both captains agree
WHAT WILL YOU BE DOING IN THE YEAR 2040? Buying horses for Johnson & Beer Bloodstock
FAVOURITE QUOTE OR SAYING? Goonyella
WHICH BOOK MEANS MOST TO YOU? Racing Post Guide to the Jumps 2018–2019 by David Dew
TWITTER: @willbeer18

Batting	Mat	Inns	NO	Runs	HS	Ave	SR	100	50	Ct	St
First-class	16	17	4	338	50*	26.00	33.00	0	1	5	0
List A	53	32	9	349	45*	15.17	83.29	0	0	10	0
T20s	105	53	18	329	37	9.40	127.51	0	0	21	0
Bowling	**Mat**	**Balls**	**Runs**	**Wkts**	**BBI**	**BBM**	**Ave**	**Econ**	**SR**	**5w**	**10**
First-class	16	1847	1002	32	6/29	11/91	31.31	3.25	57.7	2	1
List A	53	2226	1919	47	3/27	3/27	40.82	5.17	47.3	0	0
T20s	105	1866	2291	84	3/14	3/14	27.27	7.36	22.2	0	0

IAN BELL

RHB / RM / R5 / W0 / MVP15

FULL NAME: Ian Ronald Bell
BORN: April 11, 1982, Walsgrave, Coventry
SQUAD NO: 4
HEIGHT: 5ft 10in
NICKNAME: Belly
EDUCATION: Princethorpe College, Rugby
TEAMS: England, Warwickshire, Perth Scorchers
ROLE: Batsman
DEBUT: Test: 2004; ODI: 2004; T20I: 2006; First-class: 1999; List A: 1999; T20: 2003

BEST BATTING: 262* Warwickshire vs Sussex, Horsham, 2004
BEST BOWLING: 4-4 Warwickshire vs Middlesex, Lord's, 2004
COUNTY CAP: 2001; BENEFIT: 2011

'ROY OF THE ROVERS' MOMENT? Winning the County Championship with Warwickshire and Ashes victories
CRICKETING HERO? Dominic Ostler
NON-CRICKETING HERO? Gordon Cowans
IF YOU WEREN'T A CRICKETER? I'd be sitting at the Holte End watching the Villa
SURPRISING FACT? I have an honorary doctorate at Coventry University
TWITTER: @Ian_Bell

Batting	Mat	Inns	NO	Runs	HS	Ave	SR	100	50	Ct	St
Tests	118	205	24	7727	235	42.69	49.46	22	46	100	0
ODIs	161	157	14	5416	141	37.87	77.16	4	35	54	0
T20Is	8	8	1	188	60*	26.85	115.33	0	1	4	0
First-class	307	516	55	20256	262*	43.93	51.80	57	103	233	0
List A	318	301	31	11130	158	41.22	80.49	13	79	109	0
T20s	104	100	12	2749	131	31.23	124.72	1	18	36	0
Bowling	**Mat**	**Balls**	**Runs**	**Wkts**	**BBI**	**BBM**	**Ave**	**Econ**	**SR**	**5w**	**10**
Tests	118	108	76	1	1/33	1/33	76.00	4.22	108.0	0	0
ODIs	161	88	88	6	3/9	3/9	14.66	6.00	14.6	0	0
T20Is	8	-	-	-	-	-	-	-	-	-	-
First-class	307	2875	1615	47	4/4	6/45	34.36	3.37	61.1	0	0
List A	318	1290	1138	33	5/41	5/41	34.48	5.29	39.0	1	0
T20s	104	132	186	3	1/12	1/12	62.00	8.45	44.0	0	0

DANIEL BELL-DRUMMOND RHB / RM / R1 / W0 / MVP66

FULL NAME: Daniel James Bell-Drummond
BORN: August 4, 1993, Lewisham, London
SQUAD NO: 23
HEIGHT: 5ft 11in
NICKNAME: DBD, Deebz
EDUCATION: Millfield School, Somerset; Anglia Ruskin University
TEAMS: Kent, Auckland, England Lions, Rajshahi Kings
ROLE: Batsman
DEBUT: First-class: 2011; List A: 2011; T20: 2011

BEST BATTING: 206* Kent vs Loughborough MCCU, Canterbury, 2016
BEST BOWLING: 1-1 Kent vs Gloucestershire, Bristol, 2018
COUNTY CAP: 2015

FAMILY TIES? My father got me into cricket. I've always really enjoyed spending time at my local club Catford Wanderers CC
CRICKETING HERO? Marcus Trescothick
NON-CRICKETING HERO? Thierry Henry
IF YOU WEREN'T A CRICKETER? I'd be a musician
TWITTER: @deebzz23
NOTES: A stylish strokeplayer, Bell-Drummond had been tipped to open the batting for England since he was a teenager but hasn't been able to establish the sort of four-day consistency to attract the national selectors. His last first-class hundred was in 2016, although he has been a key member of the Kent side in the short formats. In November he signed to play for the club until the end of the 2021 season. Kent director of cricket Paul Downton said: "We are building a squad that will compete in all formats and Daniel is an integral part of our plans. I'm confident he can thrive in Division One next season"

Batting	Mat	Inns	NO	Runs	HS	Ave	SR	100	50	Ct	St
First-class	97	164	14	4825	206*	32.16	49.77	9	24	40	0
List A	85	84	7	3197	171*	41.51	81.20	5	22	31	0
T20s	78	77	6	2152	112*	30.30	133.74	1	16	22	0
Bowling	**Mat**	**Balls**	**Runs**	**Wkts**	**BBI**	**BBM**	**Ave**	**Econ**	**SR**	**5w**	**10**
First-class	97	89	72	2	1/1	1/1	36.00	4.85	44.5	0	0
List A	85	17	18	0	-	-	-	6.35	-	0	0
T20s	78	30	47	0	-	-	-	9.40	-	0	0

GARETH BERG RHB / RMF / R0 / W0 / MVP87

FULL NAME: Gareth Kyle Berg
BORN: January 18, 1981, Cape Town, South Africa
SQUAD NO: 13
HEIGHT: 6ft
NICKNAME: Iceman, Batman, Greb
EDUCATION: South African College School, Cape Town
TEAMS: Italy, Hampshire, Middlesex
ROLE: Allrounder
DEBUT: First-class: 2008; List A: 2008; T20: 2009

BEST BATTING: 130* Middlesex vs Leicestershire, Leicester, 2011
BEST BOWLING: 6-56 Hampshire vs Yorkshire, Southampton, 2016
COUNTY CAP: 2010 (Middlesex); 2016 (Hampshire)

WHAT WAS YOUR FIRST CRICKET CLUB? My first English club was Southgate CC, London
FAVOURITE CRICKET BAT? A Brian Lara 501 I brought back from a tour in the UK in my younger days. It was the first of its kind in South Africa
CRICKETING HERO? I've never had a hero
WHICH BOWLER WOULD YOU LEAST LIKE TO FACE? Neil Dexter – only because he wouldn't stop sledging me
WHICH RULE WOULD YOU CHANGE ABOUT CRICKET? A longer tea break please
YOUR BIGGEST CRICKETING REGRET? Missing out on playing professional sport from the age of 20 to 27
FAVOURITE QUOTE OR SAYING? Precious few are born with it, even fewer know what to do with it
ODDEST SPORT YOU'VE PLAYED? Nothing competes with cricket on that score
TWITTER: @Bergy646

Batting	Mat	Inns	NO	Runs	HS	Ave	SR	100	50	Ct	St
First-class	122	184	22	4845	130*	29.90	65.05	2	27	64	0
List A	90	67	12	1314	75	23.89	93.72	0	7	34	0
T20s	89	68	22	1063	90	23.10	127.00	0	3	22	0
Bowling	**Mat**	**Balls**	**Runs**	**Wkts**	**BBI**	**BBM**	**Ave**	**Econ**	**SR**	**5w**	**10**
First-class	122	16031	8057	254	6/56	7/45	31.72	3.01	63.1	5	0
List A	90	3042	2761	77	4/24	4/24	35.85	5.44	39.5	0	0
T20s	89	1549	2067	70	4/20	4/20	29.52	8.00	22.1	0	0

DOM BESS RHB / OB / R0 / W0

FULL NAME: Dominic Mark Bess
BORN: July 22, 1997, Exeter, Devon
SQUAD NO: 22
HEIGHT: 5ft 11in
NICKNAME: Calf, Bessy
EDUCATION: Blundell's School, Tiverton, Devon
TEAMS: England, Somerset
ROLE: Allrounder
DEBUT: Test: 2018; First-class: 2016; List A: 2018; T20: 2016

BEST BATTING: 107 MCC vs Essex, Barbados, 2018
BEST BOWLING: 7-117 Somerset vs Hampshire, Taunton, 2017

WHAT WAS YOUR FIRST CRICKET CLUB? Sidmouth CC, Devon. A beautiful coastal cricket club with a thatched roof
CRICKETING HERO? Graeme Swann
BEST INNINGS YOU'VE SEEN? James Hildreth scoring a hundred on one leg against Nottinghamshire in 2016
WHO WOULD YOU ASK TO BAT FOR YOUR LIFE? Marcus Trescothick – but only if he has got his glasses on
YOUR BIGGEST CRICKETING REGRET? Right now? Not playing with all three of my cousins at my home club
WHAT WILL YOU BE DOING IN THE YEAR 2040? I'll be a lifelong member of the Barmy Army
FAVOURITE QUOTE OR SAYING? I don't trust anyone who's nice to me and rude to a waiter. Because they would treat me the same way if I were in that position (Muhammad Ali)
TWITTER: @DomBess99

Batting	Mat	Inns	NO	Runs	HS	Ave	SR	100	50	Ct	St
Tests	2	3	0	111	57	37.00	51.62	0	1	1	0
First-class	26	41	5	845	107	23.47	54.97	1	3	16	0
List A	13	10	1	81	24*	9.00	62.30	0	0	5	0
T20s	2	1	0	1	1	1.00	50.00	0	0	0	0
Bowling	**Mat**	**Balls**	**Runs**	**Wkts**	**BBI**	**BBM**	**Ave**	**Econ**	**SR**	**5w**	**10**
Tests	2	190	121	3	3/33	3/33	40.33	3.82	63.3	0	0
First-class	26	4443	2353	84	7/117	10/162	28.01	3.17	52.8	7	1
List A	13	618	584	11	3/35	3/35	53.09	5.66	56.1	0	0
T20s	2	36	42	1	1/31	1/31	42.00	7.00	36.0	0	0

SAM BILLINGS

RHB / WK / R0 / W0 / MVP90

FULL NAME: Samuel William Billings
BORN: June 15, 1991, Pembury, Kent
SQUAD NO: 7
HEIGHT: 6ft
NICKNAME: Bilbo, Skittles
EDUCATION: Haileybury and Imperial College, Hertfordshire; Loughborough University
TEAMS: England, Kent, Chennai Super Kings, Delhi Daredevils, Sydney Sixers
ROLE: Batsman/wicketkeeper
DEBUT: ODI: 2015; T20I: 2015; First-class: 2011; List A: 2011; T20: 2011

BEST BATTING: 171 Kent vs Gloucestershire, Bristol, 2016

COUNTY CAP: 2015

'ROY OF THE ROVERS' MOMENT? Making my England debut
CRICKETING HEROES? Adam Gilchrist and Sachin Tendulkar
NON-CRICKETING HEROES? Lewis Hamilton, David Beckham, Cristiano Ronaldo
IF YOU WEREN'T A CRICKETER? I'd be working for the family business or in the City. I'm very driven – if I want something I'll work tirelessly to get it
TWITTER: @sambillings

Batting	Mat	Inns	NO	Runs	HS	Ave	SR	100	50	Ct	St
ODIs	15	12	0	271	62	22.58	90.93	0	2	13	0
T20Is	21	18	0	314	87	17.44	142.08	0	2	13	1
First-class	64	95	10	2792	171	32.84	58.84	3	14	164	11
List A	90	80	13	2708	175	40.41	105.41	6	18	82	8
T20s	159	148	20	3030	95*	23.67	131.16	0	17	93	14
Bowling	**Mat**	**Balls**	**Runs**	**Wkts**	**BBI**	**BBM**	**Ave**	**Econ**	**SR**	**5w**	**10**
ODIs	15	-	-	-	-	-	-	-	-	-	-
T20Is	21	-	-	-	-	-	-	-	-	-	-
First-class	64	1	4	0	-	-	-	24.00	-	0	0
List A	90	-	-	-	-	-	-	-	-	-	-
T20s	159	-	-	-	-	-	-	-	-	-	-

ALEX BLAKE

LHB / RM / R0 / W0

FULL NAME: Alexander James Blake
BORN: January 25, 1989, Farnborough, Kent
SQUAD NO: 10
HEIGHT: 6ft 2in
NICKNAME: Blakey, Butler, TS
EDUCATION: Hayes Secondary School, Kent; Leeds Metropolitan University
TEAMS: Kent
ROLE: Batsman
DEBUT: First-class: 2008; List A: 2007; T20: 2010

BEST BATTING: 105* Kent vs Yorkshire, Headingley, 2010
BEST BOWLING: 2-9 Kent vs Pakistanis, Canterbury, 2010
COUNTY CAP: 2017

WHAT WAS YOUR FIRST CRICKET CLUB? Bromley Town CC, London
CRICKETING HERO? Graham Thorpe
WHICH BOWLER WOULD YOU LEAST LIKE TO FACE? Jonny Darke
BEST INNINGS YOU'VE SEEN? Matt Coles's hundred in the 2015 50-over quarter-final against Surrey. He was switch-hitting sixes
WHO WOULD YOU ASK TO BAT FOR YOUR LIFE? Steve Waugh
WHICH RULE WOULD YOU CHANGE ABOUT CRICKET? Double plays, like you have in baseball – if you catch a batsman you can also run out the non-striker in the same play
SURPRISING FACT ABOUT YOU? I can name every player's squad number in county cricket (give or take)
SURPRISING FACT ABOUT A TEAMMATE? Adam Riley is an avid trainspotter
FAVOURITE QUOTE OR SAYING? It's definitely Tottenham's year
TWITTER: @aj_blake10

Batting	Mat	Inns	NO	Runs	HS	Ave	SR	100	50	Ct	St
First-class	40	62	6	1374	105*	24.53	57.68	1	6	23	0
List A	97	81	17	1924	116	30.06	99.17	1	11	49	0
T20s	105	90	23	1397	71*	20.85	133.55	0	6	56	0
Bowling	**Mat**	**Balls**	**Runs**	**Wkts**	**BBI**	**BBM**	**Ave**	**Econ**	**SR**	**5w**	**10**
First-class	40	204	129	3	2/9	2/9	43.00	3.79	68.0	0	0
List A	97	84	74	3	2/13	2/13	24.66	5.28	28.0	0	0
T20s	105	-	-	-	-	-	-	-	-	-	-

JACK BLATHERWICK RHB / RFM / R0 / W0

FULL NAME: Jack Morgan Blatherwick
BORN: June 4, 1998, Nottingham
SQUAD NO: 80
HEIGHT: 6ft 3in
NICKNAME: Blathers
EDUCATION: Holgate Academy, Hucknall; Central College, Nottingham
TEAMS: Nottinghamshire
ROLE: Bowler
DEBUT: List A: 2018

WHAT GOT YOU INTO CRICKET? My family. And Andrew Flintoff in 2005
WHAT WAS YOUR FIRST CRICKET CLUB? Kimberley Institute CC, Nottingham. There's a very steep hill on the run-up at one end
BEST ADVICE EVER RECEIVED? Be yourself, don't follow the crowd
FAVOURITE CRICKET BAT? B3. It's a family company so I always get the best ones – ha!
WHICH BOWLER WOULD YOU LEAST LIKE TO FACE? Pat Cummins
BEST INNINGS YOU'VE SEEN? Jos Buttler's 150 from 77 balls in the ODI at Grenada earlier this year. Twelves sixes and a 360-degree wagon wheel
WHO WOULD YOU ASK TO BAT FOR YOUR LIFE? Monty Panesar – he was a barn door in the Cardiff Test of the 2009 Ashes
WHICH RULE WOULD YOU CHANGE ABOUT CRICKET? In T20 it should be a wide rather than a no-ball when it goes over the batsman's head
YOUR BIGGEST CRICKETING REGRET? Leaving it until I was 17 years old to really knuckle down with my game
SURPRISING FACT ABOUT A TEAMMATE? Luke Wood gets through three cans of hairspray every month
FAVOURITE QUOTE OR SAYING? Hard work beats talent when talent doesn't work hard (Tim Notke)
TWITTER: @BlatherwickJM

Batting	Mat	Inns	NO	Runs	HS	Ave	SR	100	50	Ct	St
List A	2	2	2	5	3*	-	27.77	0	0	0	0
Bowling	**Mat**	**Balls**	**Runs**	**Wkts**	**BBI**	**BBM**	**Ave**	**Econ**	**SR**	**5w**	**10**
List A	2	12	17	0	-	-	-	8.50	-	0	0

JOSH BOHANNON

RHB / RMF / R0 / W0

FULL NAME: Joshua James Bohannon
BORN: April 9, 1997, Bolton, Lancashire
SQUAD NO: 20
HEIGHT: 5ft 8in
NICKNAME: Bo'ey, Bosh
EDUCATION: Harper Green High School, Bolton
TEAMS: Lancashire
ROLE: Allrounder
DEBUT: First-class: 2018; List A: 2018; T20: 2018

BEST BATTING: 78* Lancashire vs Worcestershire, Southport, 2018
BEST BOWLING: 3-46 Lancashire vs Hampshire, Southampton, 2018

WHAT WAS YOUR FIRST CRICKET CLUB? Farnworth CC, Greater Manchester
FAVOURITE CRICKET BAT? Slazenger V500
CRICKETING HERO? Joe Root
WHICH BOWLER WOULD YOU LEAST LIKE TO FACE? Liam Hurt – I've no clue where it's going
BEST INNINGS YOU'VE SEEN? Alastair Cook's last Test innings
WHO WOULD YOU ASK TO BAT FOR YOUR LIFE? Richard Gleeson – I'd back his technique
SURPRISING FACT ABOUT YOU? I played junior cricket alongside Haseeb Hameed at Farnworth Social Circle CC (Bolton League)
FAVOURITE QUOTE OR SAYING? You can't catch sixes
ODDEST SPORT YOU'VE PLAYED? Volleyball
TWITTER: @joshbo97

Batting	Mat	Inns	NO	Runs	HS	Ave	SR	100	50	Ct	St
First-class	5	9	1	255	78*	31.87	45.69	0	2	2	0
List A	5	3	0	54	25	18.00	87.09	0	0	2	0
T20s	2	2	0	27	23	13.50	93.10	0	0	1	0
Bowling	**Mat**	**Balls**	**Runs**	**Wkts**	**BBI**	**BBM**	**Ave**	**Econ**	**SR**	**5w**	**10**
First-class	5	162	103	5	3/46	4/82	20.60	3.81	32.4	0	0
List A	5	60	66	0	-	-	-	6.60	-	0	0
T20s	2	-	-	-	-	-	-	-	-	-	-

RAVI BOPARA RHB / RM / R1 / W0 / MVP24

FULL NAME: Ravinder Singh Bopara
BORN: May 4, 1985, Forest Gate, London
SQUAD NO: 25
HEIGHT: 5ft 10in
NICKNAME: Puppy
EDUCATION: Brampton Manor, London
TEAMS: England, Essex, Auckland, Chittagong Kings, Dhaka Dynamites, Gloucestershire, Karachi Kings, Kings XI Punjab, Sunrisers Hyderabad, Sydney Sixers
ROLE: Allrounder
DEBUT: Test: 2007; ODI: 2007; T20I: 2008; First-class: 2002; List A: 2002; T20: 2003

BEST BATTING: 229 Essex vs Northamptonshire, Chelmsford, 2007
BEST BOWLING: 5-49 Essex vs Derbyshire, Chelmsford, 2016
COUNTY CAP: 2005 (Essex); BENEFIT: 2015 (Essex)

FAMILY TIES? My brother played Essex age-group cricket
'ROY OF THE ROVERS' MOMENT? Scoring 201* against Leicestershire in a one-day match, playing in the IPL, and scoring three centuries in a row for England
CRICKETING HERO? Sachin Tendulkar
SURPRISING FACT? I have a fast-food business
TWITTER: @ravibopara

Batting	Mat	Inns	NO	Runs	HS	Ave	SR	100	50	Ct	St
Tests	13	19	1	575	143	31.94	52.89	3	0	6	0
ODIs	120	109	21	2695	101*	30.62	77.84	1	14	35	0
T20Is	38	35	10	711	65*	28.44	118.69	0	3	7	0
First-class	210	341	39	12251	229	40.56	51.55	29	52	108	0
List A	315	293	56	9666	201*	40.78	84.09	15	59	103	0
T20s	319	293	59	6355	105*	27.15	119.72	1	31	109	0
Bowling	**Mat**	**Balls**	**Runs**	**Wkts**	**BBI**	**BBM**	**Ave**	**Econ**	**SR**	**5w**	**10**
Tests	13	434	290	1	1/39	1/39	290.00	4.00	434.0	0	0
ODIs	120	1860	1523	40	4/38	4/38	38.07	4.91	46.5	0	0
T20Is	38	322	387	16	4/10	4/10	24.18	7.21	20.1	0	0
First-class	210	14958	9107	248	5/49	7/23	36.72	3.65	60.3	3	0
List A	315	7773	6871	240	5/63	5/63	28.62	5.30	32.3	1	0
T20s	319	4211	5274	209	6/16	6/16	25.23	7.51	20.1	1	0

SCOTT BORTHWICK

LHB / LB / R3 / W0

FULL NAME: Scott George Borthwick
BORN: April 19, 1990, Sunderland, County Durham
SQUAD NO: 6
HEIGHT: 5ft 10in
NICKNAME: Badger
EDUCATION: Farringdon Community Sports College, Sunderland
TEAMS: England, Surrey, Chilaw Marians, Durham, Wellington
ROLE: Allrounder
DEBUT: Test: 2014; ODI: 2011; T20I: 2011; First-class 2009; List A: 2009; T20: 2008

BEST BATTING: 216 Durham vs Middlesex, Chester-le-Street, 2014
BEST BOWLING: 6-70 Durham vs Surrey, The Oval, 2013

WHAT WAS YOUR FIRST CRICKET CLUB? Eppleton CC, Sunderland. Made my first-team debut aged 13 and I got a 44-ball duck (on a poor pitch)
FAVOURITE CRICKET BAT? The one my grandad made for me when I was a kid. That was my first-ever bat
BEST INNINGS YOU'VE SEEN? Kevin Pietersen's double ton at Adelaide in the 2010/11 Ashes
SURPRISING FACT ABOUT YOU? I know Only Fools and Horses word for word
WHICH BOOK MEANS MOST TO YOU? The Girl on the Train by Paula Hawkins. That was the first time I'd read the book before watching the film (the book is better)
ODDEST SPORT YOU'VE PLAYED? The one where you hit the little ball through the hoops
TWITTER: @Borthwick16

Batting	Mat	Inns	NO	Runs	HS	Ave	SR	100	50	Ct	St
Tests	1	2	0	5	4	2.50	26.31	0	0	2	0
ODIs	2	2	0	18	15	9.00	112.50	0	0	0	0
T20Is	1	1	0	14	14	14.00	87.50	0	0	1	0
First-class	150	251	25	8375	216	37.05	54.39	17	46	200	0
List A	99	72	11	1350	87	22.13	78.67	0	7	32	0
T20s	91	49	18	548	62	17.67	95.47	0	1	42	0
Bowling	**Mat**	**Balls**	**Runs**	**Wkts**	**BBI**	**BBM**	**Ave**	**Econ**	**SR**	**5w**	**10**
Tests	1	78	82	4	3/33	4/82	20.50	6.30	19.5	0	0
ODIs	2	54	72	0	-	-	-	8.00	-	0	0
T20Is	1	24	15	1	1/15	1/15	15.00	3.75	24.0	0	0
First-class	150	11653	7708	202	6/70	8/84	38.15	3.96	57.6	3	0
List A	99	2750	2773	69	5/38	5/38	40.18	6.05	39.8	1	0
T20s	91	1106	1506	64	4/18	4/18	23.53	8.16	17.2	0	0

JAMES BRACEY LHB / WK / R0 / W0

FULL NAME: James Robert Bracey
BORN: May 3, 1997, Bristol
SQUAD NO: 25
HEIGHT: 6ft 1in
NICKNAME: Bob, Brace, Dagger
EDUCATION: The Ridings High School, Bristol; SGS Filton College; Loughborough University
TEAMS: Gloucestershire
ROLE: Wicketkeeper/batsman
DEBUT: First-class: 2016

BEST BATTING: 156 Gloucestershire vs Glamorgan, Cardiff, 2017

WHAT GOT YOU INTO CRICKET? My local cricket club is outside my back gate
FAMILY TIES? My older brother Sam has played first-class cricket for Cardiff MCCU
BEST ADVICE EVER RECEIVED? Make the most of every opportunity
'ROY OF THE ROVERS' MOMENT? Winning the National Schools T20 region with SGS Filton College. I scored 115 not out as we beat Millfield in the regional final – the first time the college had ever beaten Millfield
BEST THING ABOUT YOUR HOME GROUND? The new flats at one end and the new stands enhance the atmosphere
IF YOU WEREN'T A CRICKETER? I'd be an elite sport psychologist
SURPRISING FACT ABOUT YOU? I was probably the only child ever who did not like Ketchup or baked beans
CRICKETING HERO? Alastair Cook
NON-CRICKETING HERO? Rickie Lambert – Bristol Rovers legend
TWITTER: @bobbybracey114

Batting	Mat	Inns	NO	Runs	HS	Ave	SR	100	50	Ct	St
First-class	23	40	4	1282	156	35.61	43.79	3	5	22	0
Bowling	**Mat**	**Balls**	**Runs**	**Wkts**	**BBI**	**BBM**	**Ave**	**Econ**	**SR**	**5w**	**10**
First-class	23	-	-	-	-	-	-	-	-	-	-

TIM BRESNAN RHB / RMF / R0 / W0 / MVP43

FULL NAME: Timothy Thomas Bresnan
BORN: February 28, 1985, Pontefract, Yorkshire
SQUAD NO: 16
HEIGHT: 6ft
NICKNAME: Brez, Brezzylad
EDUCATION: Castleford High School, West Yorkshire; New College Pontefract
TEAMS: England, Yorkshire, Hobart Hurricanes, Perth Scorchers, Sylhet Sixers
ROLE: Allrounder
DEBUT: Test: 2009; ODI: 2006; T20I: 2006; First-class: 2003; List A: 2001; T20: 2003

BEST BATTING: 169* Yorkshire vs Durham, Chester-le-Street, 2015
BEST BOWLING: 5-28 Yorkshire vs Hampshire, Headingley, 2018
COUNTY CAP: 2006; **BENEFIT:** 2014

'ROY OF THE ROVERS' MOMENT? The MCG on Boxing Day in the 2010/11 Ashes, with 96,000 people in the ground at 11am singing the national anthem
CRICKETING HEROES? Shaun Pollock, Jacques Kallis – great allrounders who played the game in the right way
NON-CRICKETING HEROES? Anyone in the armed forces – fighting to protect our rights and way of life while endangering themselves
IF YOU WEREN'T A CRICKETER? I'd be a builder
SURPRISING FACT? I'm a fully qualified scuba-diver
TWITTER: @timbresnan

Batting	Mat	Inns	NO	Runs	HS	Ave	SR	100	50	Ct	St
Tests	23	26	4	575	91	26.13	39.43	0	3	8	0
ODIs	85	64	20	871	80	19.79	90.25	0	1	20	0
T20Is	34	22	9	216	47*	16.61	127.05	0	0	10	0
First-class	194	264	41	6456	169*	28.95	47.26	6	33	101	0
List A	273	199	54	3104	95*	21.40	90.65	0	9	72	0
T20s	165	121	49	1535	51	21.31	131.75	0	1	58	0
Bowling	**Mat**	**Balls**	**Runs**	**Wkts**	**BBI**	**BBM**	**Ave**	**Econ**	**SR**	**5w**	**10**
Tests	23	4674	2357	72	5/48	8/141	32.73	3.02	64.9	1	0
ODIs	85	4221	3813	109	5/48	5/48	34.98	5.42	38.7	1	0
T20Is	34	663	887	24	3/10	3/10	36.95	8.02	27.6	0	0
First-class	194	32356	16830	546	5/28	8/51	30.82	3.12	59.2	9	0
List A	273	12074	10535	309	5/48	5/48	34.09	5.23	39.0	1	0
T20s	165	3182	4301	160	6/19	6/19	26.88	8.10	19.8	1	0

DANNY BRIGGS RHB / SLA / R0 / W0 / MVP56

FULL NAME: Danny Richard Briggs
BORN: April 30, 1991, Newport, Isle of Wight
SQUAD NO: 21
HEIGHT: 6ft 2in
NICKNAME: Briggsy
EDUCATION: Carisbrooke High School
TEAMS: England, Sussex, Hampshire
ROLE: Bowler
DEBUT: ODI: 2012; T20I: 2012; First-class: 2009; List A: 2009; T20: 2010

BEST BATTING: 120* Sussex vs South Africa A, Arundel, 2017
BEST BOWLING: 6-45 England Lions vs Windward Islands, Roseau, 2011
COUNTY CAP: 2012 (Hampshire)

WHAT WAS YOUR FIRST CRICKET CLUB? Ventnor CC, Isle of Wight. Gets more sun than anywhere else in the UK
CRICKETING HERO? Daniel Vettori
WHICH BOWLER WOULD YOU LEAST LIKE TO FACE? Jofra Archer – fast and accurate
BEST INNINGS YOU'VE SEEN? AB de Villiers's record 31-ball hundred in the 2015 ODI against West Indies in Johannesburg
WHO WOULD YOU ASK TO BAT FOR YOUR LIFE? Alastair Cook
ODDEST SPORT YOU'VE PLAYED? Dodgeball
TWITTER: @DannyBriggs19

Batting	Mat	Inns	NO	Runs	HS	Ave	SR	100	50	Ct	St
ODIs	1	-	-	-	-	-	-	-	-	0	0
T20Is	7	1	1	0	0*	-	-	0	0	1	0
First-class	104	133	36	1689	120*	17.41		1	1	36	0
List A	99	50	21	352	25	12.13	90.02	0	0	32	0
T20s	144	28	19	81	13	9.00	106.57	0	0	25	0
Bowling	**Mat**	**Balls**	**Runs**	**Wkts**	**BBI**	**BBM**	**Ave**	**Econ**	**SR**	**5w**	**10**
ODIs	1	60	39	2	2/39	2/39	19.50	3.90	30.0	0	0
T20Is	7	108	199	5	2/25	2/25	39.80	11.05	21.6	0	0
First-class	104	18141	9135	266	6/45	9/96	34.34	3.02	68.1	8	0
List A	99	4472	3772	101	4/32	4/32	37.34	5.06	44.2	0	0
T20s	144	2923	3492	166	5/19	5/19	21.03	7.16	17.6	1	0

STUART BROAD LHB / RFM / R0 / W0

FULL NAME: Stuart Christopher John Broad
BORN: June 24, 1986, Nottingham
SQUAD NO: 8
HEIGHT: 6ft 5in
NICKNAME: Broady
EDUCATION: Oakham School, Rutland
TEAMS: England, Nottinghamshire, Hobart Hurricanes, Kings XI Punjab, Leicestershire
ROLE: Bowler
DEBUT: Test: 2007; ODI: 2006; T20I: 2006; First-class: 2005; List A: 2005; T20: 2006

BEST BATTING: 169 England vs Pakistan, Lord's, 2010
BEST BOWLING: 8-15 England vs Australia, Trent Bridge, 2015
COUNTY CAP: 2007 (Leicestershire); 2008 (Nottinghamshire)

FAMILY TIES? My father Chris played for England, Nottinghamshire and Gloucestershire and is now an ICC match official
SUPERSTITIONS? Three warm-up balls before I bowl a new spell
CRICKETING HERO? Shaun Pollock
NON-CRICKETING HERO? Brian Clough
IF YOU WEREN'T A CRICKETER? I'd be a traffic warden
SURPRISING FACT? I often dream in French
TWITTER: @StuartBroad8

Batting	Mat	Inns	NO	Runs	HS	Ave	SR	100	50	Ct	St
Tests	126	183	24	3064	169	19.27	65.05	1	12	42	0
ODIs	121	68	25	529	45*	12.30	74.61	0	0	27	0
T20Is	56	26	10	118	18*	7.37	100.00	0	0	21	0
First-class	202	280	40	4910	169	20.45	63.65	1	24	73	0
List A	151	80	28	620	45*	11.92	75.88	0	0	32	0
T20s	85	32	12	152	18*	7.60	102.01	0	0	26	0
Bowling	**Mat**	**Balls**	**Runs**	**Wkts**	**BBI**	**BBM**	**Ave**	**Econ**	**SR**	**5w**	**10**
Tests	126	25737	12698	437	8/15	11/121	29.05	2.96	58.8	16	2
ODIs	121	6109	5364	178	5/23	5/23	30.13	5.26	34.3	1	0
T20Is	56	1173	1491	65	4/24	4/24	22.93	7.62	18.0	0	0
First-class	202	38302	19603	710	8/15	11/121	27.60	3.07	53.9	27	3
List A	151	7496	6591	216	5/23	5/23	30.51	5.27	34.7	1	0
T20s	85	1788	2144	100	4/24	4/24	21.44	7.19	17.8	0	0

HARRY BROOK RHB / RMF / R0 / W0

FULL NAME: Harry Cherrington Brook
BORN: February 22, 1999, Keighley, Yorkshire
SQUAD NO: 88
HEIGHT: 6ft
NICKNAME: Brooky
EDUCATION: Sedbergh School, Cumbria
TEAMS: Yorkshire
ROLE: Batsman
DEBUT: First-class: 2016; List A: 2017; T20: 2018

BEST BATTING: 124 Yorkshire vs Essex, Chelmsford, 2018
BEST BOWLING: 1-54 Yorkshire vs Somerset, Scarborough, 2017

BEST ADVICE EVER RECEIVED? What will be will be
'ROY OF THE ROVERS' MOMENT? My first-class debut for Yorkshire against Pakistan A at Headingley in 2016
BEST THING ABOUT YOUR HOME GROUND? The players and the people
SURPRISING FACT ABOUT YOU? I love Tinder
WHERE IS PARADISE? Home
CRICKETING HERO? Jacques Kallis
NON-CRICKETING HERO? Tommy Shelby (Peaky Blinders)
TWITTER: @harry_brook88

Batting	Mat	Inns	NO	Runs	HS	Ave	SR	100	50	Ct	St
First-class	17	30	0	657	124	21.90	55.77	1	3	8	0
List A	7	5	0	68	24	13.60	89.47	0	0	3	0
T20s	9	9	2	202	44	28.85	145.32	0	0	0	0
Bowling	**Mat**	**Balls**	**Runs**	**Wkts**	**BBI**	**BBM**	**Ave**	**Econ**	**SR**	**5w**	**10**
First-class	17	247	132	1	1/54	1/65	132.00	3.20	247.0	0	0
List A	7	-	-	-	-	-	-	-	-	-	-
T20s	9	6	13	0	-	-	-	13.00	-	0	0

HENRY BROOKES

RHB / RFM / R0 / W0

FULL NAME: Henry James Hamilton Brookes
BORN: August 21, 1999, Solihull, Warwickshire
SQUAD NO: 10
HEIGHT: 6ft 4in
NICKNAME: Brookesy
EDUCATION: Tudor Grange Academy, Solihull
TEAMS: Warwickshire
ROLE: Bowler
DEBUT: First-class: 2017; List A: 2018; T20: 2018

BEST BATTING: 70 Warwickshire vs Northamptonshire, Northampton, 2018
BEST BOWLING: 4-54 Warwickshire vs Northamptonshire, Edgbaston, 2018

FAMILY TIES? My two brothers Ben and Ethan have both played age-group cricket for Warwickshire
WHAT WAS YOUR FIRST CRICKET CLUB? Olton CC, West Midlands
CRICKETING HERO? Ian Botham
'ROY OF THE ROVERS' MOMENT? My County Championship debut for Warwickshire in 2017
WHICH BOWLER WOULD YOU LEAST LIKE TO FACE? Brett Lee
WHO WOULD YOU ASK TO BAT FOR YOUR LIFE? Rahul Dravid
WHICH RULE WOULD YOU CHANGE ABOUT CRICKET? Allow free hits in all cricket
IF YOU WEREN'T A CRICKETER? I'd be an engineer
FAVOURITE QUOTE OR SAYING? If you don't back yourself then who is going to back you?
ODDEST SPORT YOU'VE PLAYED? Windsurfing
TWITTER: @BrookesHenry

Batting	Mat	Inns	NO	Runs	HS	Ave	SR	100	50	Ct	St
First-class	6	8	1	180	70	25.71	57.32	0	2	3	0
List A	7	1	1	1	1*	-	100.00	0	0	1	0
T20s	5	2	0	10	9	5.00	142.85	0	0	1	0
Bowling	**Mat**	**Balls**	**Runs**	**Wkts**	**BBI**	**BBM**	**Ave**	**Econ**	**SR**	**5w**	**10**
First-class	6	918	513	21	4/54	8/119	24.42	3.35	43.7	0	0
List A	7	267	245	9	3/57	3/57	27.22	5.50	29.6	0	0
T20s	5	120	170	7	2/28	2/28	24.28	8.50	17.1	0	0

JACK BROOKS RHB / RFM / R0 / W4 / MVP29

FULL NAME: Jack Alexander Brooks
BORN: June 4, 1984, Oxford
SQUAD NO: 70
HEIGHT: 6ft 2in
NICKNAME: Animal, Ferret, SuBo, Headband Warrior, King of Oxford, Therapist
EDUCATION: Wheatley Park School, South Oxfordshire
TEAMS: Somerset, England Lions, Northamptonshire, Yorkshire
ROLE: Bowler
DEBUT: First-class: 2009; List A: 2009; T20: 2010

BEST BATTING: 109* Yorkshire vs Lancashire, Old Trafford, 2017
BEST BOWLING: 6-65 Yorkshire vs Middlesex, Lord's, 2016
COUNTY CAP: 2012 (Northamptonshire); 2013 (Yorkshire)

WHAT WAS YOUR FIRST CRICKET CLUB? Tiddington CC, Oxfordshire. AKA: Oxfordshire's Premier Nightspot
CRICKETING HERO? Dennis Lillee
WHICH BOWLER WOULD YOU LEAST LIKE TO FACE? Dale Steyn
BEST INNINGS YOU'VE SEEN? It's entertaining any time when Steve Patterson bats
WHO WOULD YOU ASK TO BAT FOR YOUR LIFE? Joe Root – the best I've played with
WHICH RULE WOULD YOU CHANGE ABOUT CRICKET? A longer tea break
SURPRISING FACT ABOUT YOU? I breed ferrets
FAVOURITE QUOTE OR SAYING? Don't ask, don't get
WHICH BOOK MEANS MOST TO YOU? The dictionary
ODDEST SPORT YOU'VE PLAYED? Aussie Rules – had no idea what was going on
TWITTER: @brooksyferret

Batting	Mat	Inns	NO	Runs	HS	Ave	SR	100	50	Ct	St
First-class	119	145	49	1609	109*	16.76	56.73	1	4	29	0
List A	36	15	5	49	10	4.90	52.12	0	0	4	0
T20s	56	10	6	59	33*	14.75	134.09	0	0	16	0
Bowling	**Mat**	**Balls**	**Runs**	**Wkts**	**BBI**	**BBM**	**Ave**	**Econ**	**SR**	**5w**	**10**
First-class	119	20079	11869	434	6/65	9/84	27.34	3.54	46.2	19	0
List A	36	1584	1276	37	3/30	3/30	34.48	4.83	42.8	0	0
T20s	56	1029	1282	47	5/21	5/21	27.27	7.47	21.8	1	0

BEN BROWN

RHB / WK / R1 / W0

FULL NAME: Ben Christopher Brown
BORN: November 23, 1988, Crawley, Sussex
SQUAD NO: 26
HEIGHT: 5ft 8in
NICKNAME: Goblin
EDUCATION: Ardingly College
TEAMS: Sussex
ROLE: Wicketkeeper/batsman
DEBUT: First-class: 2007; List A: 2007; T20: 2008

BEST BATTING: 163 Sussex vs Durham, Hove, 2014
BEST BOWLING: 1-48 Sussex vs Essex, Colchester, 2016
COUNTY CAP: 2014

WHAT WAS YOUR FIRST CRICKET CLUB? Balcombe CC, West Sussex. My dad won the Sally Miller Trophy when he played for them and hasn't kept quiet about it ever since
CRICKETING HERO? Adam Gilchrist
WHICH BOWLER WOULD YOU LEAST LIKE TO FACE? Me – appalling spin is tough to manage
BEST INNINGS YOU'VE SEEN? Maiden first-class hundreds by Phil Salt and Tom Haines at Arundel last summer. Particularly special because they are homegrown lads
WHO WOULD YOU ASK TO BAT FOR YOUR LIFE? Murray Goodwin – best batsman I've seen at Sussex
WHICH RULE WOULD YOU CHANGE ABOUT CRICKET? Scrap The Hundred!
SURPRISING FACT ABOUT YOU? I don't like cheese
WHAT WILL YOU BE DOING IN THE YEAR 2040? Moaning about people like Jofra Archer who cannot look away from their phones
TWITTER: @Ben_brown26

Batting	Mat	Inns	NO	Runs	HS	Ave	SR	100	50	Ct	St
First-class	125	195	30	6495	163	39.36	61.96	15	36	343	16
List A	66	50	11	930	73*	23.84	87.81	0	6	61	10
T20s	74	61	8	797	68	15.03	111.62	0	1	36	7
Bowling	**Mat**	**Balls**	**Runs**	**Wkts**	**BBI**	**BBM**	**Ave**	**Econ**	**SR**	**5w**	**10**
First-class	125	108	94	1	1/48	1/48	94.00	5.22	108.0	0	0
List A	66	-	-	-	-	-	-	-	-	-	-
T20s	74	-	-	-	-	-	-	-	-	-	-

CONNOR BROWN

RHB / OB / R0 / W0

FULL NAME: Connor Rhys Brown
BORN: April 28, 1997, Caerphilly, Wales
SQUAD NO: 28
HEIGHT: 6ft
NICKNAME: Browntown, Browny
EDUCATION: Y Pant Comprehensive School, Llantrisant; Cardiff Metropolitan University
TEAMS: Glamorgan
ROLE: Batsman
DEBUT: First-class: 2017; List A: 2018

BEST BATTING: 35 Glamorgan vs Gloucestershire, Cardiff, 2017

WHAT WAS YOUR FIRST CRICKET CLUB? Pentyrch CC, South Wales. My dad also played there for 10 years
FAVOURITE CRICKET BAT? My first-ever: a Slazenger V500
CRICKETING HERO? Mitchell Starc
WHICH BOWLER WOULD YOU LEAST LIKE TO FACE? James Anderson – because of his ability to swing the ball both ways
BEST INNINGS YOU'VE SEEN? AB de Villiers hitting the fastest-ever ODI hundred against West Indies in 2015
WHO WOULD YOU ASK TO BAT FOR YOUR LIFE? Kieran Bull – trusty forward defence
WHICH RULE WOULD YOU CHANGE ABOUT CRICKET? Free hits for a wide or a no-ball in every format
YOUR BIGGEST CRICKETING REGRET? Falling two runs short of my first List A hundred
ODDEST SPORT YOU'VE PLAYED? Footgolf
TWITTER: @connorbrown_97

Batting	Mat	Inns	NO	Runs	HS	Ave	SR	100	50	Ct	St
First-class	10	19	0	249	35	13.10	32.80	0	0	3	0
List A	3	3	0	163	98	54.33	63.67	0	1	1	0
Bowling	**Mat**	**Balls**	**Runs**	**Wkts**	**BBI**	**BBM**	**Ave**	**Econ**	**SR**	**5w**	**10**
First-class	10	24	14	0	-	-	-	3.50	-	0	0
List A	3	-	-	-	-	-	-	-	-	-	-

PAT BROWN

RHB / RFM / R0 / W0

FULL NAME: Patrick Rhys Brown
BORN: August 23, 1998, Peterborough, Cambridgeshire
SQUAD NO: 36
HEIGHT: 6ft 2in
NICKNAME: Browny, Brownfish
EDUCATION: Bourne Grammar School, Lincolnshire; University of Worcester
TEAMS: Worcestershire
ROLE: Bowler
DEBUT: First-class: 2017; List A: 2018; T20: 2017

BEST BATTING: 5* Worcestershire vs Sussex, Worcester, 2017
BEST BOWLING: 2-15 Worcestershire vs Gloucestershire, Worcester, 2017

WHAT WAS YOUR FIRST CRICKET CLUB? Market Deeping CC, Lincolnshire
CRICKETING HERO? Brett Lee – he offers a fantastic technical framework for bowling fast
WHICH BOWLER WOULD YOU LEAST LIKE TO FACE? Mitchell Johnson
BEST INNINGS YOU'VE SEEN? Callum Ferguson scoring 192 on his Worcestershire debut to chase down 377 against Leicestershire last season
WHO WOULD YOU ASK TO BAT FOR YOUR LIFE? Daryl Mitchell – always finds a way
WHICH RULE WOULD YOU CHANGE ABOUT CRICKET? The lbw rule should be simpler. If it's hitting the stumps, it's out, right?
YOUR BIGGEST CRICKETING REGRET? Losing in the final over of the 2018 One-Day Cup semi-final when I was bowling
SURPRISING FACT ABOUT YOU? I'm not as grumpy as I seem when I am bowling
WHICH BOOK MEANS MOST TO YOU? My Story by Steven Gerrard
TWITTER: @patbrowny6

Batting	Mat	Inns	NO	Runs	HS	Ave	SR	100	50	Ct	St
First-class	5	6	4	14	5*	7.00	25.00	0	0	2	0
List A	6	1	1	0	0*	-	0.00	0	0	1	0
T20s	22	3	0	0	0	0.00	0.00	0	0	6	0
Bowling	**Mat**	**Balls**	**Runs**	**Wkts**	**BBI**	**BBM**	**Ave**	**Econ**	**SR**	**5w**	**10**
First-class	5	376	266	7	2/15	3/70	38.00	4.24	53.7	0	0
List A	6	226	241	7	3/53	3/53	34.42	6.39	32.2	0	0
T20s	22	397	541	32	4/21	4/21	16.90	8.17	12.4	0	0

NICK BROWNE

LHB / LB / R3 / W0

ESSEX

FULL NAME: Nicholas Laurence Joseph Browne
BORN: March 24, 1991, Leytonstone, Essex
SQUAD NO: 10
HEIGHT: 6ft 3in
NICKNAME: Brownie, Orse
EDUCATION: Trinity Catholic High School, London
TEAMS: Essex
ROLE: Batsman
DEBUT: First-class: 2013; List A: 2015; T20: 2015

BEST BATTING: 255 Essex vs Derbyshire, Chelmsford, 2016

COUNTY CAP: 2015

WHAT WAS YOUR FIRST CRICKET CLUB? South Woodford CC, London. My parents met each other for the first time at the club, and I was practically born into it. I'm lucky that I can play with my two brothers when I get the chance to play for the club
FAVOURITE CRICKET BAT? Aged 14 I bought a GM Maxi with money from my paper round because of being a huge fan of Marcus Trescothick
WHICH BOWLER WOULD YOU LEAST LIKE TO FACE? David Masters – I used to face him in the nets most days and he was an unbelievably skilful bowler who could seam the ball both ways and never missed his length
BEST INNINGS YOU'VE SEEN? Alastair Cook's in his final Test. The amount of people who wanted him to score a hundred was a testament to him as a person
YOUR BIGGEST CRICKETING REGRET? The quarter-final against Yorkshire at Chelmsford in the 2015 One-Day Cup. Chasing a low total, Tom Westley and I were flying before we both got out in quick succession. We lost by 20 runs
FAVOURITE QUOTE OR SAYING? Not all superheroes wear capes
TWITTER: @NickBrowne4

Batting	Mat	Inns	NO	Runs	HS	Ave	SR	100	50	Ct	St
First-class	76	124	9	4821	255	41.92	50.35	14	20	56	0
List A	21	18	0	557	99	30.94	89.83	0	3	7	0
T20s	14	12	2	165	38	16.50	114.58	0	0	6	0
Bowling	**Mat**	**Balls**	**Runs**	**Wkts**	**BBI**	**BBM**	**Ave**	**Econ**	**SR**	**5w**	**10**
First-class	76	268	175	0	-	-	-	3.91	-	0	0
List A	21	-	-	-	-	-	-	-	-	-	-
T20s	14	-	-	-	-	-	-	-	-	-	-

NATHAN BUCK

RHB / RFM / R0 / W0

FULL NAME: Nathan Liam Buck
BORN: April 26, 1991, Leicester
SQUAD NO: 11
HEIGHT: 6ft 3in
NICKNAME: Bucky, Top Bag
EDUCATION: Ashby Grammar School, Ashby-de-la-Zouch
TEAMS: Northamptonshire, England Lions, Lancashire, Leicestershire
ROLE: Bowler
DEBUT: First-class: 2009; List A: 2009; T20: 2010

BEST BATTING: 43 Northamptonshire vs Derbyshire, Derby, 2017
BEST BOWLING: 6-34 Northamptonshire vs Durham, Chester-le-Street, 2017
COUNTY CAP: 2011 (Leicestershire)

WHAT WAS YOUR FIRST CRICKET CLUB? Grace Dieu Park CC, Leicestershire. I got hit into the forest on many occasions
WHICH BOWLER WOULD YOU LEAST LIKE TO FACE? Ben Sanderson – he doesn't miss the top of off stump
WHO WOULD YOU ASK TO BAT FOR YOUR LIFE? Chris Martin – get it over with
WHICH RULE WOULD YOU CHANGE ABOUT CRICKET? Bowlers should be allowed more than two bouncers per over
YOUR BIGGEST CRICKETING REGRET? Not getting 'off 'em' on debut
SURPRISING FACT ABOUT YOU? I got seven A stars and three As in my GCSEs
WHAT WILL YOU BE DOING IN THE YEAR 2040? Working for Hotdog Haulage
WHICH BOOK MEANS MOST TO YOU? Of Mice and Men by John Steinbeck (the only book I've read as it was compulsory for my GCSEs)
ODDEST SPORT YOU'VE PLAYED? Ultimate Frisbee (Leicestershire U12)
TWITTER: @nathanbuck17

Batting	Mat	Inns	NO	Runs	HS	Ave	SR	100	50	Ct	St
First-class	83	117	31	1058	43	12.30	38.16	0	0	15	0
List A	53	25	11	122	21	8.71	71.34	0	0	12	0
T20s	45	12	7	37	11*	7.40	82.22	0	0	6	0
Bowling	**Mat**	**Balls**	**Runs**	**Wkts**	**BBI**	**BBM**	**Ave**	**Econ**	**SR**	**5w**	**10**
First-class	83	12941	7684	225	6/34	7/79	34.15	3.56	57.5	7	0
List A	53	2149	2236	57	4/39	4/39	39.22	6.24	37.7	0	0
T20s	45	958	1379	56	4/26	4/26	24.62	8.63	17.1	0	0

KIERAN BULL RHB / OB / R0 / W0

FULL NAME: Kieran Andrew Bull
BORN: April 5, 1995, Haverfordwest, Pembrokeshire
SQUAD NO: 11
HEIGHT: 6ft 1in
NICKNAME: Bully
EDUCATION: Queen Elizabeth High School, Haverfordwest; Cardiff Metropolitan University
TEAMS: Glamorgan
ROLE: Bowler
DEBUT: First-class: 2014; List A: 2015

BEST BATTING: 31 Glamorgan vs Gloucestershire, Swansea, 2015
BEST BOWLING: 4-62 Glamorgan vs Kent, Canterbury, 2014

WHAT GOT YOU INTO CRICKET? Watching my brother play at our local club
STRANGEST THING SEEN IN A GAME? Play suspended due to a helicopter landing on the field
'ROY OF THE ROVERS' MOMENT? Making my first-class debut at Canterbury
CRICKETING HERO? Darren Gough
NON-CRICKETING HERO? Ron Burgundy
SURPRISING FACT? I set off an alarm every time I walk into a shop due to the metal screw in my back. Aged 10 I moved to Spain to take up a place in a tennis academy and lived there for two years, representing Spain at age-group level. I was also ball boy for Rafael Nadal
UNUSUAL OBJECT AT HOME? A singing fish on the wall
TWITTER: @Kieran_Bull89

Batting	Mat	Inns	NO	Runs	HS	Ave	SR	100	50	Ct	St
First-class	11	18	6	145	31	12.08	20.39	0	0	3	0
List A	2	-	-	-	-	-	-	-	-	0	0
Bowling	**Mat**	**Balls**	**Runs**	**Wkts**	**BBI**	**BBM**	**Ave**	**Econ**	**SR**	**5w**	**10**
First-class	11	1258	761	20	4/62	4/62	38.05	3.62	62.9	0	0
List A	2	52	48	1	1/40	1/40	48.00	5.53	52.0	0	0

MICHAEL BURGESS

RHB / WK / R0 / W0

FULL NAME: Michael Gregory Kerran Burgess
BORN: July 8, 1994, Epsom
SQUAD NO: 5
HEIGHT: 6ft 1in
NICKNAME: Burge
EDUCATION: Cranleigh School; Loughborough University
TEAMS: Sussex, Leicestershire
ROLE: Wicketkeeper
DEBUT: First-class: 2014; List A: 2015; T20: 2016

BEST BATTING: 146 Sussex vs Nottinghamshire, Hove, 2017

WHAT WAS YOUR FIRST CRICKET CLUB? Reigate Priory CC, Surrey
FAVOURITE CRICKET BAT? My Puma Ballistic – that was my garden cricket bat as a kid
WHICH BOWLER WOULD YOU LEAST LIKE TO FACE? Rashid Khan
BEST INNINGS YOU'VE SEEN? Brendon McCullum's last Test innings when he scored the fastest-ever Test hundred (54 balls), against Australia at Christchurch in 2016
WHICH RULE WOULD YOU CHANGE ABOUT CRICKET? Seven runs should be awarded if you hit it out the ground
YOUR BIGGEST CRICKETING REGRET? Not learning to bowl mystery spin
WHAT WILL YOU BE DOING IN THE YEAR 2040? I'll be suited-up in London
FAVOURITE QUOTE OR SAYING? Hey, there are skittles in there! (The Hangover)
ODDEST SPORT YOU'VE PLAYED? Eton Fives
TWITTER: @mgkburgess

Batting	Mat	Inns	NO	Runs	HS	Ave	SR	100	50	Ct	St
First-class	26	38	3	1336	146	38.17	66.86	2	6	27	0
List A	18	16	0	352	58	22.00	100.57	0	2	9	0
T20s	16	11	4	160	56	22.85	128.00	0	1	5	5
Bowling	**Mat**	**Balls**	**Runs**	**Wkts**	**BBI**	**BBM**	**Ave**	**Econ**	**SR**	**5w**	**10**
First-class	26	36	14	0	-	-	-	2.33	-	0	0
List A	18	-	-	-	-	-	-	-	-	-	-
T20s	16	-	-	-	-	-	-	-	-	-	-

JACK BURNHAM RHB / RM / R0 / W0

FULL NAME: Jack Tony Arthur Burnham
BORN: January 18, 1997, Durham
SQUAD NO: 8
HEIGHT: 6ft 2in
NICKNAME: Burny
EDUCATION: Deerness Valley Comprehensive School, Durham; The Durham Federation
TEAMS: Durham
ROLE: Batsman
DEBUT: First-class: 2015; List A: 2016; T20: 2016

BEST BATTING: 135 Durham vs Surrey, The Oval, 2016

WHAT WAS YOUR FIRST CRICKET CLUB? Esh Winning CC, County Durham. My mum and dad coached the U13 team for three years
FAVOURITE CRICKET BAT? Newbery Uzi – got my first hundred with it aged 10
CRICKETING HERO? Stephen Harmison
WHICH BOWLER WOULD YOU LEAST LIKE TO FACE? Brett Lee – too fast
WHO WOULD YOU ASK TO BAT FOR YOUR LIFE? Sachin Tendulkar
WHICH RULE WOULD YOU CHANGE ABOUT CRICKET? Left-handed batsmen should not be permitted in the game!
YOUR BIGGEST CRICKETING REGRET? Getting a one-year ban
FAVOURITE QUOTE OR SAYING? Howay lads
ODDEST SPORT YOU'VE PLAYED? Badminton
TWITTER: @BurnhamMorton

Batting	Mat	Inns	NO	Runs	HS	Ave	SR	100	50	Ct	St
First-class	26	44	4	1018	135	25.45	47.95	1	6	9	0
List A	5	4	0	69	26	17.25	66.34	0	0	0	0
T20s	16	13	1	150	53*	12.50	88.75	0	1	4	0
Bowling	**Mat**	**Balls**	**Runs**	**Wkts**	**BBI**	**BBM**	**Ave**	**Econ**	**SR**	**5w**	**10**
First-class	26	-	-	-	-	-	-	-	-	-	-
List A	5	-	-	-	-	-	-	-	-	-	-
T20s	16	1	0	0	-	-	-	0.00	-	0	0

JOE BURNS

RHB / RM / R0 / W0

FULL NAME: Joseph Anthony Burns
BORN: September 6, 1989, Herston, Brisbane, Australia
SQUAD NO: 14
TEAMS: Australia, Lancashire, Brisbane Heat, Glamorgan, Leicestershire, Middlesex, Queensland
ROLE: Batsman
DEBUT: Test: 2014; ODI: 2015; First-class: 2011; List A: 2010; T20: 2012

BEST BATTING: 202* Queensland vs South Australia, Cairns, 2017
BEST BOWLING: 1-0 Queensland vs Tasmania, Brisbane, 2017

TWITTER: @joeburns441
NOTES: Burns returns to county cricket having previously represented Leicestershire, Glamorgan and Middlesex and is expected to be available for 10 of Lancashire's Championship fixtures. He will be hoping to improve upon a modest first-class record in the English domestic game: he scored 214 runs at 30.57 for Leicestershire in 2013 and 320 runs at 29.09 for Middlesex in 2015. He has proven his class at international level though, scoring four centuries in his first 16 Tests, including 180 against Sri Lanka at Canberra on his recall to the side in February. A positive stint with Lancashire could well rubber-stamp his selection for this summer's Ashes series. Burns has scored more than 5,000 first-class runs for Queensland since hitting a century on his Sheffield Shield debut in 2011

Batting	Mat	Inns	NO	Runs	HS	Ave	SR	100	50	Ct	St
Tests	16	28	0	1123	180	40.10	59.92	4	4	18	0
ODIs	6	6	0	146	69	24.33	79.34	0	1	2	0
First-class	106	187	13	7149	202*	41.08	54.61	16	41	96	0
List A	68	68	9	2146	154	36.37	80.43	3	12	28	0
T20s	62	59	9	1255	81*	25.10	121.60	0	5	19	0
Bowling	**Mat**	**Balls**	**Runs**	**Wkts**	**BBI**	**BBM**	**Ave**	**Econ**	**SR**	**5w**	**10**
Tests	16	-	-	-	-	-	-	-	-	-	-
ODIs	6	-	-	-	-	-	-	-	-	-	-
First-class	106	114	48	1	1/0	1/1	48.00	2.52	114.0	0	0
List A	68	18	33	1	1/20	1/20	33.00	11.00	18.0	0	0
T20s	62	54	71	3	1/8	1/8	23.66	7.88	18.0	0	0

RORY BURNS

LHB / RM / R5 / W0 / MVP17

FULL NAME: Rory Joseph Burns
BORN: August 26, 1990, Epsom, Surrey
SQUAD NO: 17
HEIGHT: 5ft 10in
NICKNAME: Fong, The Cat (goalkeeper)
EDUCATION: Whitgift School; City of London Freemen's; Cardiff Metropolitan University
TEAMS: England, Surrey
ROLE: Batsman
DEBUT: Test: 2018; First-class: 2011; List A: 2012; T20: 2012

BEST BATTING: 219* Surrey vs Hampshire, The Oval, 2017
BEST BOWLING: 1-18 Surrey vs Middlesex, Lord's, 2013
COUNTY CAP: 2014

'ROY OF THE ROVERS' MOMENT? Being off the field for only 30 mins during the whole of the Championship game against Hampshire in 2017, when I was captaining the side
BEST THING ABOUT YOUR HOME GROUND? The history. From FA Cups to the Ashes, The Oval has had it all
IF YOU WEREN'T A CRICKETER? I'd be a digital marketer
SURPRISING FACT ABOUT YOU? I love Smartwater
SURPRISING FACT ABOUT A TEAMMATE? Matthew Dunn labels his socks left and right and always wears them the wrong way round
CRICKETING HERO? Kumar Sangakkara – The King
NON-CRICKETING HERO? Chris and Christine Burns, for raising me and my brothers
UNUSUAL OBJECT AT HOME? A strong whisky collection
TWITTER: @roryburns17

Batting	Mat	Inns	NO	Runs	HS	Ave	SR	100	50	Ct	St
Tests	6	12	0	300	84	25.00	47.77	0	2	4	0
First-class	113	196	14	7901	219*	43.41	49.30	15	44	97	0
List A	49	47	6	1524	95	37.17	86.00	0	11	25	0
T20s	40	35	4	452	50	14.58	118.63	0	1	13	1
Bowling	**Mat**	**Balls**	**Runs**	**Wkts**	**BBI**	**BBM**	**Ave**	**Econ**	**SR**	**5w**	**10**
Tests	6	-	-	-	-	-	-	-	-	-	-
First-class	113	180	127	2	1/18	1/18	63.50	4.23	90.0	0	0
List A	49	-	-	-	-	-	-	-	-	-	-
T20s	40	-	-	-	-	-	-	-	-	-	-

JOS BUTTLER RHB / WK / R0 / W0

FULL NAME: Joseph Charles Buttler
BORN: September 8, 1990, Taunton
SQUAD NO: 6
NICKNAME: Jose
EDUCATION: King's College, Taunton
TEAMS: England, Lancashire, Comilla Victorians, Melbourne Renegades, Mumbai Indians, Rajasthan Royals, Somerset, Sydney Thunder
ROLE: Batsman/wicketkeeper
DEBUT: Test: 2014; ODI: 2012; T20I: 2011; First-class: 2009; List A: 2009; T20: 2009

BEST BATTING: 144 Somerset vs Hampshire, Southampton, 2013

COUNTY CAP: 2013 (Somerset)

TWITTER: @josbuttler
NOTES: Buttler signed for Lancashire in September 2013 to pursue more opportunities as a keeper after sharing duties with Craig Kieswetter at Somerset. Called up for England's limited-overs squads in 2012, he usurped Matt Prior as England's No.1 Test wicketkeeper two years later, scoring 85 on Test debut against India at Southampton. He hit England's fastest ODI hundred (46 balls) against Pakistan at Dubai in 2015. Buttler lost his Test place to Jonny Bairstow following a poor 2015 Ashes series, returned to the side on the 2016/17 tour of India but again couldn't hold on to his spot. He is now a regular across all three formats for his country and unlikely to play much county cricket in 2019 (he played just four matches for Lancashire last summer). Buttler has been retained by Rajasthan Royals for the 2019 IPL

Batting	Mat	Inns	NO	Runs	HS	Ave	SR	100	50	Ct	St
Tests	31	54	6	1722	106	35.87	59.87	1	14	68	0
ODIs	127	105	22	3387	150	40.80	118.34	7	18	155	28
T20Is	66	58	11	1260	73*	26.80	138.15	0	7	23	4
First-class	95	152	13	4593	144	33.04	60.03	5	29	184	2
List A	198	165	42	5553	150	45.14	119.34	9	34	207	33
T20s	241	220	41	5397	95*	30.15	144.03	0	36	127	27
Bowling	**Mat**	**Balls**	**Runs**	**Wkts**	**BBI**	**BBM**	**Ave**	**Econ**	**SR**	**5w**	**10**
Tests	31	-	-	-	-	-	-	-	-	-	-
ODIs	127	-	-	-	-	-	-	-	-	-	-
T20Is	66	-	-	-	-	-	-	-	-	-	-
First-class	95	12	11	0	-	-	-	5.50	-	0	0
List A	198	-	-	-	-	-	-	-	-	-	-
T20s	241	-	-	-	-	-	-	-	-	-	-

EDDIE BYROM

LHB / OB / R0 / W0

FULL NAME: Edward James Byrom
BORN: June 17, 1997, Harare, Zimbabwe
SQUAD NO: 97
HEIGHT: 6ft
NICKNAME: Quady
EDUCATION: King's College, Taunton
TEAMS: Somerset, Rising Stars
ROLE: Batsman
DEBUT: First-class: 2017

BEST BATTING: 152 Rising Stars vs Tuskers, Kwekwe, 2017

WHAT WAS YOUR FIRST CRICKET CLUB? Taunton St Andrews CC, Somerset
FAVOURITE CRICKET BAT? The old Kookaburra Kahuna
CRICKETING HERO? Brian Lara. Whenever West Indies were playing I would watch him bat and as soon as he got out I would change the channel
WHICH BOWLER WOULD YOU LEAST LIKE TO FACE? Mohammad Abbas
BEST INNINGS YOU'VE SEEN? Any century by James Hildreth
WHO WOULD YOU ASK TO BAT FOR YOUR LIFE? Virat Kohli
WHICH RULE WOULD YOU CHANGE ABOUT CRICKET? We should use the same type of ball all over the world
YOUR BIGGEST CRICKETING REGRET? Diving for a ball I was never going to get to and dislocating my shoulder
WHAT WILL YOU BE DOING IN THE YEAR 2040? I'll be a strength and conditioning coach
FAVOURITE QUOTE OR SAYING? Trying to be perfect is an excuse not to do
WHICH BOOK MEANS MOST TO YOU? Crushing It! How Great Entrepreneurs Build Their Business and Influence – and How You Can, Too by Gary Vaynerchuk
ODDEST SPORT YOU'VE PLAYED? Water polo
TWITTER: @EddieByrom

Batting	Mat	Inns	NO	Runs	HS	Ave	SR	100	50	Ct	St
First-class	19	36	0	915	152	25.41	41.40	1	3	7	0
Bowling	**Mat**	**Balls**	**Runs**	**Wkts**	**BBI**	**BBM**	**Ave**	**Econ**	**SR**	**5w**	**10**
First-class	19	60	39	0	-	-	-	3.90	-	0	0

HARRY CAME RHB / OB / R0 / W0

FULL NAME: Harry Robert Charles Came
BORN: August 27, 1998, Hampshire
SQUAD NO: 4
HEIGHT: 5ft 9in
NICKNAME: Hazza, Camey, Cameo
EDUCATION: Bradfield College, Berkshire
TEAMS: Hampshire
ROLE: Batsman

WHAT WAS YOUR FIRST CRICKET CLUB? Odiham and Greywell CC
FAVOURITE CRICKET BAT? Chase Four Leaf Clover. I hit one of my biggest sixes with that bat
WHICH BOWLER WOULD YOU LEAST LIKE TO FACE? Rashid Khan – he's just so hard to pick
BEST INNINGS YOU'VE SEEN? Kusal Perera's match-winning 153 not out for Sri Lanka against South Africa in the Test at Durban earlier this year. It was such a gutsy innings and he batted so well with the Sri Lankan tail
WHO WOULD YOU ASK TO BAT FOR YOUR LIFE? Sachin Tendulkar
WHICH RULE WOULD YOU CHANGE ABOUT CRICKET? If you are trying to leave the ball and it hits you, 'dead ball' should be called
YOUR BIGGEST CRICKETING REGRET? Getting run out for 99 for the Hampshire Academy when I was 16 years old
WHAT WILL YOU BE DOING IN THE YEAR 2040? Hopefully I'll still be playing
FAVOURITE QUOTE OR SAYING? Be great (Adam Rouse)
ODDEST SPORT YOU'VE PLAYED? Curling
TWITTER: @HarryCame4
NOTES: The 20-year-old batsman thrived in the Kent Second XI last summer but turned down a contract at Canterbury last October to sign a two-year deal with Hampshire, his home county. Came had come through the age-group ranks at Hampshire and was a key member of the side which won the U17 County Championship in 2015

JACK CAMPBELL RHB / LMF / R0 / W0

FULL NAME: Jack Oliver Ian Campbell
BORN: November 11, 1999, Portsmouth
SQUAD NO: 21
EDUCATION: Churcher's College, Petersfield, Hampshire
TEAMS: Durham, England U19
ROLE: Bowler

NOTES: The 19-year-old left-arm seamer signed his first professional contract with Durham last September. Campbell played in the Durham Second XI last season but has also played second-team cricket for Kent and Hampshire. He has also represented Hampshire U17 as well as the county's Academy, taking 42 wickets at an average of just over 23 in 2017. Last summer he made his England U19 debut, playing in the youth ODI against South Africa at Gosforth. "I found out I was making my debut the night before the match at a team meeting," said Campbell. "I had a very nice feeling when I knew I was playing. Andy Flower did a little speech when he gave me my cap, which was nice"

LUKAS CAREY RHB / RFM / R0 / W0

FULL NAME: Lukas John Carey
BORN: July 17, 1997, Carmarthen, Wales
SQUAD NO: 17
EDUCATION: Pontarddulais Comprehensive School, Swansea; Gower College Swansea
TEAMS: Glamorgan
ROLE: Bowler
DEBUT: First-class: 2016; List A: 2017; T20: 2017

BEST BATTING: 54 Glamorgan vs Worcestershire, Worcester, 2017
BEST BOWLING: 4-85 Glamorgan vs Northamptonshire, Northampton, 2017

TWITTER: @LukasCarey
NOTES: Hailing from Robert Croft's club Pontarddulais, Carey made a promising start to his Glamorgan career in August 2016, picking up seven wickets against Northants with his skiddy fast-medium seamers. He had a breakthrough season in 2017, taking 35 wickets at 30.03 in 10 Championship matches as well as making his maiden first-class half-century. Last year he played six matches in the Championship and seven in the One-Day Cup but wasn't able to have the same impact. A graduate from Glamorgan's Academy, Carey is another in the ranks of talented local products looking to reinvigorate the Welsh club

Batting	Mat	Inns	NO	Runs	HS	Ave	SR	100	50	Ct	St
First-class	20	27	3	289	54	12.04	70.31	0	1	4	0
List A	11	6	4	32	12	16.00	71.11	0	0	1	0
T20s	4	-	-	-	-	-	-	-	-	1	0
Bowling	**Mat**	**Balls**	**Runs**	**Wkts**	**BBI**	**BBM**	**Ave**	**Econ**	**SR**	**5w**	**10**
First-class	20	3217	1982	61	4/85	7/151	32.49	3.69	52.7	0	0
List A	11	526	504	8	2/57	2/57	63.00	5.74	65.7	0	0
T20s	4	42	61	2	1/19	1/19	30.50	8.71	21.0	0	0

KIRAN CARLSON RHB / OB / R0 / W0

FULL NAME: Kiran Shah Carlson
BORN: May 16, 1998, Cardiff
SQUAD NO: 5
HEIGHT: 5ft 8in
NICKNAME: Peter Dinklage
EDUCATION: Whitchurch High School, Cardiff; Cardiff University
TEAMS: Glamorgan
ROLE: Allrounder
DEBUT: First-class: 2016; List A: 2016; T20: 2017

BEST BATTING: 191 Glamorgan vs Gloucestershire, Cardiff, 2017
BEST BOWLING: 5-28 Glamorgan vs Northamptonshire, Northampton, 2016

WHAT WAS YOUR FIRST CRICKET CLUB? Cardiff CC
FAVOURITE CRICKET BAT? Gray-Nicolls Powerbow from when I was 14
CRICKETING HERO? Sachin Tendulkar
WHICH BOWLER WOULD YOU LEAST LIKE TO FACE? Morne Morkel – he's double my height
WHO WOULD YOU ASK TO BAT FOR YOUR LIFE? Jack Murphy – known as the Rahul Dravid of Wales
WHICH RULE WOULD YOU CHANGE ABOUT CRICKET? You should get 12 runs for hitting the ball out of the ground
YOUR BIGGEST CRICKETING REGRET? Not being 6ft 5in and bowling 90mph
SURPRISING FACT ABOUT YOU? I'm half-Indian
WHAT WILL YOU BE DOING IN THE YEAR 2040? I'll be sat watching cricket and saying: "Back in my day..."
WHICH BOOK MEANS MOST TO YOU? Kama Sutra by Vatsyayana
TWITTER: @kiran_carlson

Batting	Mat	Inns	NO	Runs	HS	Ave	SR	100	50	Ct	St
First-class	26	47	2	1263	191	28.06	56.30	3	3	10	0
List A	12	12	1	316	63	28.72	103.26	0	2	2	0
T20s	16	13	1	298	58	24.83	139.90	0	1	8	0
Bowling	**Mat**	**Balls**	**Runs**	**Wkts**	**BBI**	**BBM**	**Ave**	**Econ**	**SR**	**5w**	**10**
First-class	26	276	183	6	5/28	5/78	30.50	3.97	46.0	1	0
List A	12	42	47	1	1/30	1/30	47.00	6.71	42.0	0	0
T20s	16	1	1	0	-	-	-	6.00	-	0	0

BRYDON CARSE RHB / RF / R0 / W0

FULL NAME: Brydon Alexander Carse
BORN: July 31, 1995, Port Elizabeth, South Africa
SQUAD NO: 99
HEIGHT: 6ft 2in
NICKNAME: Cheesy, Carsie
EDUCATION: Pearson High School, Port Elizabeth
TEAMS: Durham, Eastern Province
ROLE: Bowler
DEBUT: First-class: 2016; T20: 2014

BEST BATTING: 61* Durham vs Sussex, Chester-le-Street, 2017
BEST BOWLING: 3-38 Durham vs Lancashire, Chester-le-Street, 2016

FAMILY TIES? My dad James played for Northants, Rhodesia, Eastern Province, Border and Western Province
WHAT WAS YOUR FIRST CRICKET CLUB? Union CC, South Africa. Best traditional song for newcomers: 'Buffalo Soildier'
FAVOURITE CRICKET BAT? As a kid I loved my Bellingham and Smith. It had a huge curve
WHICH BOWLER WOULD YOU LEAST LIKE TO FACE? Shane Warne
BEST INNINGS YOU'VE SEEN? Herschelle Gibbs in the 438 game at Johannesburg in 2006
WHICH RULE WOULD YOU CHANGE ABOUT CRICKET? You should be allowed four fielders out in the first six overs in T20
FAVOURITE QUOTE OR SAYING? I'm Sunderland till I die
WHICH BOOK MEANS MOST TO YOU? To the Point – The No-Holds-Barred Autobiography by Herschelle Gibbs
ODDEST SPORT YOU'VE PLAYED? Water polo. Hated it
TWITTER: @CarseBrydon

Batting	Mat	Inns	NO	Runs	HS	Ave	SR	100	50	Ct	St
First-class	11	11	4	267	61*	38.14	50.85	0	1	2	0
T20s	3	3	1	5	3	2.50	83.33	0	0	1	0
Bowling	**Mat**	**Balls**	**Runs**	**Wkts**	**BBI**	**BBM**	**Ave**	**Econ**	**SR**	**5w**	**10**
First-class	11	1298	798	20	3/38	4/86	39.90	3.68	64.9	0	0
T20s	3	47	75	2	1/11	1/11	37.50	9.57	23.5	0	0

MATT CARTER

RHB / OB / R0 / W0

FULL NAME: Matthew Carter
BORN: May 26, 1996, Lincoln
SQUAD NO: 20
HEIGHT: 6ft 6in
NICKNAME: Carts
EDUCATION: Branston Community Academy, Lincolnshire
TEAMS: Nottinghamshire
ROLE: Bowler
DEBUT: First-class: 2015; List A: 2018; T20: 2018

BEST BATTING: 33 Nottinghamshire vs Sussex, Hove, 2017
BEST BOWLING: 7-56 Nottinghamshire vs Somerset, Taunton, 2015

FAMILY TIES? My dad and oldest brother played at village level. My brother Andrew played for Notts, Derby and Hampshire before retiring in 2016
BEST ADVICE EVER RECEIVED? If it's to be, it's up to me
'ROY OF THE ROVERS' MOMENT? Taking seven wickets in the first innings on my first-class debut
BEST THING ABOUT YOUR HOME GROUND? The atmosphere on T20 nights
IF YOU WEREN'T A CRICKETER? I'd be doing a lot of shooting (see below)
SURPRISING FACT ABOUT YOU? Any chance I get, whether for an hour or a full day, it's spent with the dog in the middle of a field shooting. I've had a lot of swimming achievements but now I'm scared of swimming
WHERE IS PARADISE? Home
CRICKETING HERO? Andrew Flintoff in the 2005 Ashes
UNUSUAL OBJECT AT HOME? A cabinet full of guns

Batting	Mat	Inns	NO	Runs	HS	Ave	SR	100	50	Ct	St
First-class	9	16	1	140	33	9.33	52.04	0	0	8	0
List A	8	6	0	32	17	5.33	69.56	0	0	3	0
T20s	2	1	1	16	16*	-	266.66	0	0	0	0
Bowling	**Mat**	**Balls**	**Runs**	**Wkts**	**BBI**	**BBM**	**Ave**	**Econ**	**SR**	**5w**	**10**
First-class	9	1824	1197	33	7/56	10/195	36.27	3.93	55.2	2	1
List A	8	393	322	16	4/40	4/40	20.12	4.91	24.5	0	0
T20s	2	36	51	2	1/25	1/25	25.50	8.50	18.0	0	0

KARL CARVER LHB / SLA / R0 / W0

FULL NAME: Karl Carver
BORN: March 26, 1996, Northallerton, Yorkshire
SQUAD NO: 29
HEIGHT: 5ft 11in
NICKNAME: Keith, Carves, Curly
EDUCATION: Thirsk School and Sixth Form College, North Yorkshire
TEAMS: Yorkshire
ROLE: Bowler
DEBUT: First-class: 2014; List A: 2015; T20: 2015

BEST BATTING: 20 Yorkshire vs Somerset, Taunton, 2017
BEST BOWLING: 4-106 Yorkshire vs MCC, Abu Dhabi, 2016

WHAT GOT YOU INTO CRICKET? Watching my grandad and dad play every week
STRANGEST THING SEEN IN A GAME? Our fine-leg fielder at Sheriff Hutton Bridge having his lunch stolen and his coffee knocked over by a bird
'ROY OF THE ROVERS' MOMENT? Making my full debuts in all formats for my home county Yorkshire. Getting the wicket of Kumar Sangakkara on my List A debut in 2015
SUPERSTITIONS? Wearing my sunglasses when bowling. I often bat in a long-sleeved shirt
CRICKETING HERO? Joe Root – because even though he's the best player in the world he's a nice guy too
SURPRISING FACT? I went on tour to India in February 2016 and ended up playing for Hong Kong in a T20 because they were short on numbers
TWITTER: @Carver_Karl

Batting	Mat	Inns	NO	Runs	HS	Ave	SR	100	50	Ct	St
First-class	8	13	6	108	20	15.42	32.43	0	0	4	0
List A	15	4	4	52	35*	-	76.47	0	0	2	0
T20s	9	2	1	2	2	2.00	50.00	0	0	5	0
Bowling	**Mat**	**Balls**	**Runs**	**Wkts**	**BBI**	**BBM**	**Ave**	**Econ**	**SR**	**5w**	**10**
First-class	8	946	543	18	4/106	6/194	30.16	3.44	52.5	0	0
List A	15	486	440	14	3/5	3/5	31.42	5.43	34.7	0	0
T20s	9	108	179	6	3/40	3/40	29.83	9.94	18.0	0	0

ZAK CHAPPELL RHB / RFM / R0 / W0

FULL NAME: Zachariah John Chappell
BORN: August 21, 1996, Grantham, Lincolnshire
SQUAD NO: 32
HEIGHT: 6ft 6in
NICKNAME: Smasher
EDUCATION: Stamford School, Lincolnshire
TEAMS: Nottinghamshire, England Lions, Leicestershire
ROLE: Allrounder
DEBUT: First-class: 2015; List A: 2015; T20: 2015

BEST BATTING: 96 Leicestershire vs Derbyshire, Derby, 2015
BEST BOWLING: 6-44 Leicestershire vs Northamptonshire, Northampton, 2018

BEST ADVICE EVER RECEIVED? Play across, be a boss
WHICH BOWLER WOULD YOU LEAST LIKE TO FACE? Brett Lee
'ROY OF THE ROVERS' MOMENT? Scoring 96 on my Championship debut batting at No.10
WHICH RULE WOULD YOU CHANGE ABOUT CRICKET? No cricket when it goes below 10 degrees
IF YOU WEREN'T A CRICKETER? I'd be a nutritionist
SURPRISING FACT ABOUT YOU? I can walk on my hands
TWITTER: @ZakkChappell
NOTES: Another talented young cricketer to beat a path from Grace Road to Trent Bridge, Chappell described signing for Notts last September as a "dream move". He said: "Nottinghamshire have a top-quality squad and I think it will be the perfect place for me to take my game to the next level"

Batting	Mat	Inns	NO	Runs	HS	Ave	SR	100	50	Ct	St
First-class	16	24	4	538	96	26.90	58.60	0	2	1	0
List A	15	13	5	133	59*	16.62	63.33	0	1	2	0
T20s	13	9	2	67	16	9.57	134.00	0	0	5	0
Bowling	**Mat**	**Balls**	**Runs**	**Wkts**	**BBI**	**BBM**	**Ave**	**Econ**	**SR**	**5w**	**10**
First-class	16	1813	1191	38	6/44	6/53	31.34	3.94	47.7	1	0
List A	15	677	698	17	3/45	3/45	41.05	6.18	39.8	0	0
T20s	13	226	367	12	3/23	3/23	30.58	9.74	18.8	0	0

BEN CHARLESWORTH LHB / RMF / R0 / W0

FULL NAME: Ben Geoffrey Charlesworth
BORN: November 19, 2000, Oxford
SQUAD NO: 64
HEIGHT: 6ft 3in
NICKNAME: Charlie
EDUCATION: St Edward's School, Oxford
TEAMS: Gloucestershire
ROLE: Allrounder
DEBUT: First-class: 2018

BEST BATTING: 77* Gloucestershire vs Middlesex, Bristol, 2018
BEST BOWLING: 3-25 Gloucestershire vs Middlesex, Bristol, 2018

WHAT WAS YOUR FIRST CRICKET CLUB? Abingdon Vale CC, Oxfordshire. It was 10 minutes down the road from my house. I played and trained there from the age of five to 16
FAVOURITE CRICKET BAT? GM sent me their Noir bat for my recent tour of Bangladesh with England U19 and it went absolutely beautifully. Unfortunately it cracked right at the end of the tour but I've sent it back asking for more of the same!
CRICKETING HERO? Kumar Sangakkara. I used to love watching him on TV. He would score so effortlessly and make it look like he didn't have to take any risks to score a hundred. He's been my idol ever since I was a kid
WHICH BOWLER WOULD YOU LEAST LIKE TO FACE? Shane Warne – he would consistently beat both edges of my bat and give me nothing to score off. Oh, and there's the massive rip he gets on the ball
WHICH RULE WOULD YOU CHANGE ABOUT CRICKET? Free hits in red-ball cricket to bring more excitement into the longer format – and to punish bowlers for no-balls
YOUR BIGGEST CRICKETING REGRET? Not speaking to Eoin Morgan last year when I played against Middlesex. I could have learned a thing or two by having a chat with him
WHICH BOOK MEANS MOST TO YOU? Rafa – My Story by Rafael Nadal with John Carlin
ODDEST SPORT YOU'VE PLAYED? Paddle tennis
TWITTER: @Ben_1289

Batting	Mat	Inns	NO	Runs	HS	Ave	SR	100	50	Ct	St
First-class	6	9	1	194	77*	24.25	41.10	0	2	2	0
Bowling	**Mat**	**Balls**	**Runs**	**Wkts**	**BBI**	**BBM**	**Ave**	**Econ**	**SR**	**5w**	**10**
First-class	6	127	47	4	3/25	3/25	11.75	2.22	31.7	0	0

VARUN CHOPRA RHB / LB / R3 / W0 / MVP70

FULL NAME: Varun Chopra
BORN: June 21, 1987, Barking, Essex
SQUAD NO: 6
HEIGHT: 6ft 1in
NICKNAME: Tiddles, Chops
EDUCATION: Ilford County High School
TEAMS: Essex, England Lions, Tamil Union Cricket & Athletic Club, Warwickshire
ROLE: Batsman
DEBUT: First-class: 2006; List A: 2006; T20: 2006

BEST BATTING: 233* Tamil Union vs Sinhalese Sports Club, Colombo, 2012

COUNTY CAP: 2012 (Warwickshire)

WHAT GOT YOU INTO CRICKET? Dad taking me to Joe Hussain's Ilford Cricket School
BEST ADVICE EVER RECEIVED? It's not how, it's how many
'ROY OF THE ROVERS' MOMENT? Winning the T20 competition in 2014 off the last ball in front of a packed house at Edgbaston
BEST THING ABOUT YOUR HOME GROUND? The crowd
IF YOU WEREN'T A CRICKETER? I'd be an architect
SURPRISING FACT ABOUT YOU? I love a chin-up
CRICKETING HERO? Sachin Tendulkar
TWITTER: @vchops06

Batting	Mat	Inns	NO	Runs	HS	Ave	SR	100	50	Ct	St
First-class	186	305	20	9977	233*	35.00	50.81	20	50	220	0
List A	109	106	7	4368	160	44.12	76.08	9	28	38	0
T20s	106	103	12	2781	116	30.56	119.66	2	20	22	0
Bowling	**Mat**	**Balls**	**Runs**	**Wkts**	**BBI**	**BBM**	**Ave**	**Econ**	**SR**	**5w**	**10**
First-class	186	204	128	0	-	-	-	3.76	-	0	0
List A	109	18	18	0	-	-	-	6.00	-	0	0
T20s	106	-	-	-	-	-	-	-	-	-	-

DAN CHRISTIAN

RHB / RMF / R0 / W0

FULL NAME: Daniel Trevor Christian
BORN: May 4, 1983, Sydney, Australia
SQUAD NO: 54
HEIGHT: 6ft
EDUCATION: St Gregory's College, Sydney
TEAMS: Australia, Nottinghamshire, Brisbane Heat, Deccan Chargers, Gloucestershire, Hampshire, Hobart Hurricanes, Jozi Stars, Melbourne Renegades, Middlesex, NSW, RC Bangalore, South Australia, Victoria
ROLE: Allrounder
DEBUT: ODI: 2012; T20I: 2010; First-class: 2008; List A: 2006; T20: 2006

BEST BATTING: 131* South Australia vs New South Wales, Adelaide, 2011
BEST BOWLING: 5-24 South Australia vs Western Australia, Perth, 2010
COUNTY CAP: 2013 (Gloucestershire); 2015 (Nottinghamshire)

WHAT WAS YOUR FIRST CRICKET CLUB? Narrandera CC, New South Wales, Australia
FAVOURITE CRICKET BAT? My current Kookaburra Ghost. Two years old and still going
BEST INNINGS YOU'VE SEEN? Chris Gayle's 175 not out in the 2013 IPL (I was carrying the drinks for Bangalore). He took down the Pune Warriors with the cleanest hitting I have ever seen
WHO WOULD YOU ASK TO BAT FOR YOUR LIFE? Steve Waugh
WHICH RULE WOULD YOU CHANGE ABOUT CRICKET? Balls over head height to be no-balls in the T20 Blast
YOUR BIGGEST CRICKETING REGRET? Not nailing down a spot in the Australia team
TWITTER: @danchristian54

Batting	Mat	Inns	NO	Runs	HS	Ave	SR	100	50	Ct	St
ODIs	19	18	5	273	39	21.00	88.92	0	0	10	0
T20Is	16	7	3	27	9	6.75	96.42	0	0	5	0
First-class	83	141	17	3783	131*	30.50	53.77	5	16	90	0
List A	119	108	21	2844	117	32.68	101.64	2	14	43	0
T20s	281	241	59	4296	129	23.60	138.40	2	13	118	0
Bowling	**Mat**	**Balls**	**Runs**	**Wkts**	**BBI**	**BBM**	**Ave**	**Econ**	**SR**	**5w**	**10**
ODIs	19	727	595	20	5/31	5/31	29.75	4.91	36.3	1	0
T20Is	16	213	317	11	3/27	3/27	28.81	8.92	19.3	0	0
First-class	83	10301	5679	163	5/24	9/87	34.84	3.30	63.1	3	0
List A	119	3896	3585	107	6/48	6/48	33.50	5.52	36.4	3	0
T20s	281	4339	6063	214	5/14	5/14	28.33	8.38	20.2	2	0

GRAHAM CLARK RHB / LB / R0 / W0 / MVP80

FULL NAME: Graham Clark
BORN: March 16, 1993, Whitehaven, Cumbria
SQUAD NO: 7
HEIGHT: 6ft 2in
NICKNAME: Sparky, Schnoz
EDUCATION: St Benedict's Catholic High School, Whitehaven
TEAMS: Durham
ROLE: Batsman
DEBUT: First-class: 2015; List A: 2015; T20: 2015

BEST BATTING: 109 Durham vs Glamorgan, Chester-le-Street, 2017
BEST BOWLING: 1-10 Durham vs Sussex, Arundel, 2018

FAMILY TIES? My older brother Jordan plays for Lancashire
WHAT WAS YOUR FIRST CRICKET CLUB? Cleator CC, Cumbria. They won the National Village Cup at Lord's in 2013 and my dad (Ian) was man of the match
FAVOURITE CRICKET BAT? GM Icon – it was the first bat that felt right in my hands
WHICH BOWLER WOULD YOU LEAST LIKE TO FACE? Rashid Khan – he bowls as fast as a medium-pacer but spins it both ways and disguises it well
BEST INNINGS YOU'VE SEEN? Cameron Steel's 224 at Leicester in 2017. He showed great patience and determination for over eight hours
WHICH RULE WOULD YOU CHANGE ABOUT CRICKET? The lbw rule – then I might not get dismissed so often that way!
YOUR BIGGEST CRICKETING REGRET? Not believing myself in my first years as a professional cricketer
FAVOURITE QUOTE OR SAYING? Money don't make the world go round, I'm reaching out to a higher ground (Des'ree)
TWITTER: @GrahamClark16

Batting	Mat	Inns	NO	Runs	HS	Ave	SR	100	50	Ct	St
First-class	30	55	0	1464	109	26.61	53.90	1	10	21	0
List A	26	26	1	576	114	23.04	81.24	1	1	8	0
T20s	37	37	2	865	91*	24.71	137.73	0	6	16	0
Bowling	**Mat**	**Balls**	**Runs**	**Wkts**	**BBI**	**BBM**	**Ave**	**Econ**	**SR**	**5w**	**10**
First-class	30	83	51	2	1/10	1/10	25.50	3.68	41.5	0	0
List A	26	24	18	3	3/18	3/18	6.00	4.50	8.0	0	0
T20s	37	14	29	0	-	-	-	12.42	-	0	0

JORDAN CLARK RHB / RMF / R0 / W0 / MVP46

FULL NAME: Jordan Clark
BORN: October 14, 1990, Whitehaven, Cumbria
SQUAD NO: 8
HEIGHT: 6ft 4in
NICKNAME: Clarky
EDUCATION: Sedbergh School, Cumbria
TEAMS: Surrey, Hobart Hurricanes, Lancashire
ROLE: Allounder
DEBUT: First-class: 2015; List A: 2010; T20: 2011

BEST BATTING: 140 Lancashire vs Surrey, The Oval, 2017
BEST BOWLING: 5-58 Lancashire vs Yorkshire, Old Trafford, 2018

FAMILY TIES? My younger brother Graham plays for Durham. My older brother Darren has played Minor Counties with Cumberland and together with dad won the National Village Cup with Cleator CC in 2013
FAVOURITE CRICKET BAT? It has to be a GM – the only bat I can clear the ropes with
WHICH BOWLER WOULD YOU LEAST LIKE TO FACE? Darren Stevens – he lands it on a sixpence
BEST INNINGS YOU'VE SEEN? Ashwell Prince's 261 for Lancashire against Glamorgan at Colwyn Bay in 2015. He was playing one-handed reverse-sweeps
WHO WOULD YOU ASK TO BAT FOR YOUR LIFE? Dane Vilas – he always gets his body in the way, especially his shin
SURPRISING FACT ABOUT YOU? I once split a testicle when pole dancing
WHAT WILL YOU BE DOING IN THE YEAR 2040? I'll be on the east coast of Australia
FAVOURITE QUOTE OR SAYING? My way
TWITTER: @Clarksy16

Batting	Mat	Inns	NO	Runs	HS	Ave	SR	100	50	Ct	St
First-class	42	59	4	1616	140	29.38	56.60	1	9	6	0
List A	46	34	8	835	79*	32.11	101.82	0	4	7	0
T20s	72	52	20	711	44	22.21	132.64	0	0	28	0
Bowling	**Mat**	**Balls**	**Runs**	**Wkts**	**BBI**	**BBM**	**Ave**	**Econ**	**SR**	**5w**	**10**
First-class	42	4714	2728	78	5/58	7/97	34.97	3.47	60.4	1	0
List A	46	1258	1309	31	4/34	4/34	42.22	6.24	40.5	0	0
T20s	72	851	1249	46	4/22	4/22	27.15	8.80	18.5	0	0

JOE CLARKE RHB / WK / R1 / W0 / MVP30

FULL NAME: Joseph Michael Clarke
BORN: May 26, 1996, Shrewsbury, Shropshire
SQUAD NO: 33
HEIGHT: 5ft 11in
NICKNAME: Clarkey
EDUCATION: Llanfyllin High School, Powys
TEAMS: Nottinghamshire, England Lions, Worcestershire
ROLE: Batsman
DEBUT: First-class: 2015; List A: 2015; T20: 2015

BEST BATTING: 194 Worcestershire vs Derbyshire, Worcester, 2016

WHAT WAS YOUR FIRST CRICKET CLUB? Oswestry CC, Shropshire
FAVOURITE CRICKET BAT? Gray-Nicolls Maverick – scored my first double hundred with it
CRICKETING HERO? Adam Gilchrist
WHICH BOWLER WOULD YOU LEAST LIKE TO FACE? Murali – men round the bat, not having a clue which way it's turning…
BEST INNINGS YOU'VE SEEN? Callum Ferguson's 192 for Worcestershire against Leicestershire in the 2018 One-Day Cup. Pure skill, and so good to watch from the other end
WHO WOULD YOU ASK TO BAT FOR YOUR LIFE? Daryl Mitchell
WHICH RULE WOULD YOU CHANGE ABOUT CRICKET? If you get a duck in the first innings then you should start on one in the second innings
YOUR BIGGEST CRICKETING REGRET? Being not out overnight before Bank Holiday Monday
SURPRISING FACT ABOUT YOU? I can speak (some) Welsh
FAVOURITE QUOTE OR SAYING? You can never stop improving
TWITTER: @joeclarke10

Batting	Mat	Inns	NO	Runs	HS	Ave	SR	100	50	Ct	St
First-class	62	107	8	3943	194	39.82	61.73	13	14	30	0
List A	53	51	5	1506	131*	32.73	87.25	3	8	21	2
T20s	44	43	3	1034	124*	25.85	150.07	1	5	13	0

Bowling	Mat	Balls	Runs	Wkts	BBI	BBM	Ave	Econ	SR	5w	10
First-class	62	12	22	0	-	-	-	11.00	-	0	0
List A	53	-	-	-	-	-	-	-	-	-	-
T20s	44	-	-	-	-	-	-	-	-	-	-

RIKKI CLARKE RHB / RMF / R1 / W0 / MVP2

FULL NAME: Rikki Clarke
BORN: September 29, 1981, Orsett, Essex
SQUAD NO: 81
HEIGHT: 6ft 5in
NICKNAME: Clarkey, Crouchy, Rock
EDUCATION: Broadwater Secondary, Surrey; Godalming College
TEAMS: England, Surrey, Derbyshire, Warwickshire
ROLE: Allrounder
DEBUT: Test: 2003; ODI: 2003; First-class: 2002; List A: 2001; T20: 2003

BEST BATTING: 214 Surrey vs Somerset, Guildford, 2006
BEST BOWLING: 7-55 Surrey vs Somerset, The Oval, 2017
COUNTY CAP: 2005 (Surrey); 2011 (Warwickshire)

WHAT WAS YOUR FIRST CRICKET CLUB? Godalming CC, Surrey. Mum did the teas and Dad played. I was nine when I played my first men's game
BEST INNINGS YOU'VE SEEN? I was 12th man when Brian Lara made 400 at Antigua
WHICH RULE WOULD YOU CHANGE ABOUT CRICKET? On the last day of a Championship match the captains can shake hands on a draw an hour after lunch
YOUR BIGGEST CRICKETING REGRET? That I didn't know earlier what I know now. When I was younger I made mistakes. If I was the person I am now when I was 21 then things might have been better
FAVOURITE QUOTE OR SAYING? If not now, when? If not you, who? (Always helps me to stay motivated – if I'm not doing it someone else will be)
TWITTER: @rikkiclarke81

Batting	Mat	Inns	NO	Runs	HS	Ave	SR	100	50	Ct	St
Tests	2	3	0	96	55	32.00	37.94	0	1	1	0
ODIs	20	13	0	144	39	11.07	62.06	0	0	11	0
First-class	238	358	40	10426	214	32.78	61.06	17	54	356	0
List A	229	186	27	4061	98*	25.54	90.19	0	21	105	0
T20s	160	139	38	2245	79*	22.22	123.82	0	6	79	0
Bowling	**Mat**	**Balls**	**Runs**	**Wkts**	**BBI**	**BBM**	**Ave**	**Econ**	**SR**	**5w**	**10**
Tests	2	174	60	4	2/7	3/11	15.00	2.06	43.5	0	0
ODIs	20	469	415	11	2/28	2/28	37.72	5.30	42.6	0	0
First-class	238	26123	14459	460	7/55	9/83	31.43	3.32	56.7	5	0
List A	229	6278	5684	150	5/26	5/26	37.89	5.43	41.8	1	0
T20s	160	2148	2650	112	4/16	4/16	23.66	7.40	19.1	0	0

MITCHELL CLAYDON LHB / RMF / R0 / W2

FULL NAME: Mitchell Eric Claydon
BORN: November 25, 1982, Fairfield, New South Wales, Australia
SQUAD NO: 8
HEIGHT: 6ft 3in
NICKNAME: Ellen, Precious, Lips
EDUCATION: Westfield Sports High School, Sydney
TEAMS: Kent, Canterbury, Central Districts, Durham, Yorkshire
ROLE: Bowler
DEBUT: First-class: 2005; List A: 2006; T20: 2006

BEST BATTING: 77 Kent vs Leicestershire, Leicester, 2014
BEST BOWLING: 6-104 Durham vs Somerset, Taunton, 2011
COUNTY CAP: 2016 (Kent)

'ROY OF THE ROVERS' MOMENT? Winning three County Championship titles with Durham and being voted as the players' player of the year at Kent in 2014
CRICKETING HERO? Ricky Ponting
NON-CRICKETING HERO? Tiger Woods
IF YOU WEREN'T A CRICKETER? I'd be a policeman
SURPRISING FACT? I'm a magician, a keen surfer and I love to play a prank or two
TWITTER: @mitchellclaydon

Batting	Mat	Inns	NO	Runs	HS	Ave	SR	100	50	Ct	St
First-class	102	130	28	1561	77	15.30	60.29	0	4	11	0
List A	107	49	16	271	19	8.21	83.38	0	0	9	0
T20s	143	47	28	186	19	9.78	89.42	0	0	26	0
Bowling	**Mat**	**Balls**	**Runs**	**Wkts**	**BBI**	**BBM**	**Ave**	**Econ**	**SR**	**5w**	**10**
First-class	102	15241	9129	280	6/104		32.60	3.59	54.4	8	0
List A	107	4667	4349	136	5/31	5/31	31.97	5.59	34.3	1	0
T20s	143	2947	4155	158	5/26	5/26	26.29	8.45	18.6	2	0

BEN COAD RHB / RFM / R0 / W1 / MVP62

FULL NAME: Benjamin Oliver Coad
BORN: January 10, 1994, Harrogate, Yorkshire
SQUAD NO: 10
HEIGHT: 6ft 3in
NICKNAME: Coady, Hench
EDUCATION: Thirsk School and Sixth Form College, North Yorkshire
TEAMS: Yorkshire
ROLE: Bowler
DEBUT: First-class: 2016; List A: 2013; T20: 2015

BEST BATTING: 33 Yorkshire vs Nottinghamshire, Headingley, 2018
BEST BOWLING: 6-25 Yorkshire vs Lancashire, Headingley, 2017
COUNTY CAP: 2018

FAMILY TIES? My brothers played representative cricket at junior levels. My dad played Minor Counties cricket for Suffolk
'ROY OF THE ROVERS' MOMENT? My second T20 game in 2015, playing against Warwickshire at home in front of a very good crowd and managing to take two wickets and winning the game against the defending champions
SUPERSTITIONS? When playing at Headingley I touch the White Rose on the stairs as I walk out
SURPRISING FACT? I'm a Newcastle United fan
TWITTER: @bencoad10

Batting	Mat	Inns	NO	Runs	HS	Ave	SR	100	50	Ct	St
First-class	24	33	13	281	33	14.05	58.66	0	0	1	0
List A	17	6	5	15	9	15.00	62.50	0	0	5	0
T20s	7	2	1	3	2*	3.00	60.00	0	0	5	0
Bowling	**Mat**	**Balls**	**Runs**	**Wkts**	**BBI**	**BBM**	**Ave**	**Econ**	**SR**	**5w**	**10**
First-class	24	4275	2030	103	6/25	10/102	19.70	2.84	41.5	7	2
List A	17	764	748	20	4/63	4/63	37.40	5.87	38.2	0	0
T20s	7	109	186	6	2/24	2/24	31.00	10.23	18.1	0	0

JOSH COBB RHB / OB / R0 / W0

FULL NAME: Joshua James Cobb
BORN: August 17, 1990, Leicester
SQUAD NO: 4
HEIGHT: 6ft 1in
NICKNAME: Cobby, Tuck Shop, Lord
EDUCATION: Oakham School, Rutland
TEAMS: Northamptonshire, Barisal Bulls, Central Districts, Dhaka Gladiators, Leicestershire, Prime Doleshwar Sporting Club, Sylhet Superstars
ROLE: Batsman
DEBUT: First-class: 2007; List A: 2008; T20: 2008

BEST BATTING: 148* Leicestershire vs Middlesex, Lord's, 2008
BEST BOWLING: 2-11 Leicestershire vs Gloucestershire, Leicester, 2011
COUNTY CAP: 2018 (Northamptonshire)

FAMILY TIES? My dad Russell played for Leicestershire
WHAT WAS YOUR FIRST CRICKET CLUB? Kibworth CC, Leicestershire
CRICKETING HERO? Brad Hodge
WHICH BOWLER WOULD YOU LEAST LIKE TO FACE? Ben Sanderson – nibbles it both ways
BEST INNINGS YOU'VE SEEN? Abdul Razzaq's 62 from 30 balls for Leicestershire at Old Trafford in a T20 match in 2011
WHO WOULD YOU ASK TO BAT FOR YOUR LIFE? James Taylor
SURPRISING FACT ABOUT YOU? At Oakham I was a member of the debating society and took an active interest in historical and modern British politics. I take a number of books and papers with me to away games which keep me busy during rain delays, much to the dismay of my teammates
WHICH BOOK MEANS MOST TO YOU? The Art of Captaincy by Mike Brearley
TWITTER: @Cobby24

Batting	Mat	Inns	NO	Runs	HS	Ave	SR	100	50	Ct	St
First-class	119	205	22	4702	148*	25.69	49.00	3	27	50	0
List A	89	84	6	2908	137	37.28	92.93	6	19	26	0
T20s	136	129	14	2911	103	25.31	133.83	1	17	64	0
Bowling	**Mat**	**Balls**	**Runs**	**Wkts**	**BBI**	**BBM**	**Ave**	**Econ**	**SR**	**5w**	**10**
First-class	119	2554	1516	17	2/11	2/11	89.17	3.56	150.2	0	0
List A	89	1632	1597	32	3/34	3/34	49.90	5.87	51.0	0	0
T20s	136	1191	1649	54	4/22	4/22	30.53	8.30	22.0	0	0

IAN COCKBAIN

RHB / RM / R0 / W0

FULL NAME: Ian Andrew Cockbain
BORN: February 17, 1987, Liverpool
SQUAD NO: 28
HEIGHT: 6ft
NICKNAME: Coey, Bird's Nest, Gramps, Mini
EDUCATION: Maghull High School, Sefton; Liverpool John Moores University
TEAMS: Gloucestershire
ROLE: Batsman
DEBUT: First-class: 2011; List A: 2011; T20: 2011

BEST BATTING: 151* Gloucestershire vs Surrey, Bristol, 2014
BEST BOWLING: 1-23 Gloucestershire vs Durham MCCU, Bristol, 2016
COUNTY CAP: 2011

FAMILY TIES? My dad Ian played for Lancashire
WHAT WAS YOUR FIRST CRICKET CLUB? Bootle CC, Merseyside. My grandad, dad and uncle all played there when they were kids
FAVOURITE CRICKET BAT? GM Maestro, my first bat. I used it so much that it had pieces missing and cracks all over it
WHICH BOWLER WOULD YOU LEAST LIKE TO FACE? Ryan Higgins – he bowls horrible little nippers
WHO WOULD YOU ASK TO BAT FOR YOUR LIFE? Kane Williamson – best defence I've seen
WHICH RULE WOULD YOU CHANGE ABOUT CRICKET? Introduce a free hit for a wide or no-ball in red-ball cricket. 'Double play' in white-ball cricket (for example, two wickets can fall when there is a catch and a run-out off the same delivery)
FAVOURITE QUOTE OR SAYING? There is one thing you do know. And that's that you never know

Batting	Mat	Inns	NO	Runs	HS	Ave	SR	100	50	Ct	St
First-class	51	86	6	2382	151*	29.77	42.81	4	13	35	0
List A	65	56	11	1539	108*	34.20	89.42	2	9	41	0
T20s	98	91	15	2388	123	31.42	127.56	1	12	45	0
Bowling	**Mat**	**Balls**	**Runs**	**Wkts**	**BBI**	**BBM**	**Ave**	**Econ**	**SR**	**5w**	**10**
First-class	51	47	44	1	1/23	1/23	44.00	5.61	47.0	0	0
List A	65	-	-	-	-	-	-	-	-	-	-
T20s	98	-	-	-	-	-	-	-	-	-	-

MATT COLES

LHB / RFM / R0 / W2

FULL NAME: Matthew Thomas Coles
BORN: May 26, 1990, Maidstone, Kent
SQUAD NO: 1
HEIGHT: 6ft 3in
NICKNAME: Colesy
EDUCATION: Maplesden Noakes School, Maidstone; MidKent College
TEAMS: Essex, Dhaka Dynamites, England Lions, Hampshire, Kent
ROLE: Allrounder
DEBUT: First-class: 2009; List A: 2009; T20: 2010

BEST BATTING: 103* Kent vs Yorkshire, Headingley, 2012
BEST BOWLING: 6-51 Kent vs Northamptonshire, Northampton, 2012
COUNTY CAP: 2012 (Kent)

WHAT GOT YOU INTO CRICKET? Playing six-a-side indoor cricket when I was five
BEST ADVICE EVER RECEIVED? Play with a smile on your face
'ROY OF THE ROVERS' MOMENT? Taking 100 wickets for Kent across all formats in 2015
IF YOU WEREN'T A CRICKETER? I'd be a gardener
SURPRISING FACT ABOUT YOU? I took two white-ball hat-tricks for Kent – the first in a 50-over game against Nottinghamshire at Trent Bridge in 2015 and the second in a T20 match against Middlesex at Richmond in 2017
WHERE IS PARADISE? In front of a plate of roast lamb
CRICKETING HERO? Andrew Flintoff
TWITTER: @MattColes_90

Batting	Mat	Inns	NO	Runs	HS	Ave	SR	100	50	Ct	St
First-class	111	147	20	2508	103*	19.74	68.78	1	12	58	0
List A	76	44	6	545	100	14.34	112.37	1	1	29	0
T20s	94	66	11	530	54	9.63	133.83	0	1	30	0
Bowling	**Mat**	**Balls**	**Runs**	**Wkts**	**BBI**	**BBM**	**Ave**	**Econ**	**SR**	**5w**	**10**
First-class	111	17098	10255	348	6/51	10/98	29.46	3.59	49.1	12	2
List A	76	3114	2925	130	6/32	6/32	22.50	5.63	23.9	2	0
T20s	94	1828	2756	87	4/27	4/27	31.67	9.04	21.0	0	0

SAM CONNORS

RHB / RFM / R0 / W0

FULL NAME: Sam Connors
BORN: February 13, 1999, Nottingham
SQUAD NO: 59
HEIGHT: 6ft
NICKNAME: Sammy
EDUCATION: George Spencer Academy, Nottingham
TEAMS: Derbyshire, England U19
ROLE: Bowler

WHAT WAS YOUR FIRST CRICKET CLUB? Attenborough CC, Nottingham
FAVOURITE CRICKET BAT? GM Octane F2 DXM
WHICH BOWLER WOULD YOU LEAST LIKE TO FACE? Steve Harmison
BEST INNINGS YOU'VE SEEN? Ben Stokes hitting 258 against South Africa at Cape Town in 2016. Every ball seemed like it was going to the boundary
WHO WOULD YOU ASK TO BAT FOR YOUR LIFE? Virat Kohli
WHICH RULE WOULD YOU CHANGE ABOUT CRICKET? It should be 10 runs if you hit the ball out of the ground
YOUR BIGGEST CRICKETING REGRET? Bowling two no-balls in a national quarter-final, which meant that I had to be brought off
FAVOURITE QUOTE OR SAYING? Fail to prepare, prepare to fail
WHICH BOOK MEANS MOST TO YOU? Firestarter – Me, Cricket and the Heat of the Moment by Ben Stokes
ODDEST SPORT YOU'VE PLAYED? Bocce

ALASTAIR COOK LHB / RM / R8 / W0 / MVP50

FULL NAME: Alastair Nathan Cook
BORN: December 25, 1984, Gloucester
SQUAD NO: 26
HEIGHT: 6ft 2in
NICKNAME: Cookie, Chef
EDUCATION: Bedford School
TEAMS: England, Essex
ROLE: Batsman
DEBUT: Test: 2006; ODI: 2006; T20I: 2007; First-class: 2003; List A: 2003; T20: 2005

BEST BATTING: 294 England vs India, Edgbaston, 2011
BEST BOWLING: 3-13 Essex vs Northamptonshire, Chelmsford, 2005
COUNTY CAP: 2005; BENEFIT: 2014

FAMILY TIES? Dad played for the local club side and was a very good opening bat, while my mum made the teas. My brothers played for Maldon Cricket Club
CRICKETING HEROES? Graham Gooch – I watched him playing for Essex at Chelmsford
IF YOU WEREN'T A CRICKETER? I'd be a farmer
NOTES: Following his retirement from international cricket in September, Cook signed a three-year contract with Essex that keeps him at the club until the end of the 2021 season

Batting	Mat	Inns	NO	Runs	HS	Ave	SR	100	50	Ct	St
Tests	161	291	16	12472	294	45.35	46.95	33	57	175	0
ODIs	92	92	4	3204	137	36.40	77.13	5	19	36	0
T20Is	4	4	0	61	26	15.25	112.96	0	0	1	0
First-class	289	513	36	22604	294	47.38	50.87	63	107	306	0
List A	160	158	11	5851	137	39.80	79.80	12	34	66	0
T20s	32	30	2	892	100*	31.85	127.61	1	5	13	0
Bowling	**Mat**	**Balls**	**Runs**	**Wkts**	**BBI**	**BBM**	**Ave**	**Econ**	**SR**	**5w**	**10**
Tests	161	18	7	1	1/6	1/6	7.00	2.33	18.0	0	0
ODIs	92	-	-	-	-	-	-	-	-	-	-
T20Is	4	-	-	-	-	-	-	-	-	-	-
First-class	289	282	211	7	3/13	3/13	30.14	4.48	40.2	0	0
List A	160	18	10	0	-	-	-	3.33	-	0	0
T20s	32	-	-	-	-	-	-	-	-	-	-

SAM COOK

RHB / RFM / R0 / W0

FULL NAME: Samuel James Cook
BORN: August 4, 1997, Chelmsford, Essex
SQUAD NO: 16
HEIGHT: 6ft 2in
NICKNAME: Glen
EDUCATION: Great Baddow High School, Chelmsford; Loughborough University
TEAMS: Essex
ROLE: Bowler
DEBUT: First-class: 2016; List A: 2018; T20: 2018

BEST BATTING: 14 Essex vs Hampshire, Chelmsford, 2018
BEST BOWLING: 5-18 Essex vs Hampshire, Southampton, 2017

WHAT WAS YOUR FIRST CRICKET CLUB? Writtle CC, Essex. The team was made up of kids from the football team who played at the same ground
CRICKETING HERO? Glenn McGrath
WHICH BOWLER WOULD YOU LEAST LIKE TO FACE? Pat Cummins – skiddy, horrible, get off me!
BEST INNINGS YOU'VE SEEN? Ben Stokes's 258 at Cape Town in 2016 – an I-was-there moment
WHO WOULD YOU ASK TO BAT FOR YOUR LIFE? Me – at least it would be over quickly
WHICH RULE WOULD YOU CHANGE ABOUT CRICKET? Allow three men out in T20 powerplays (it's a batsman's game)
SURPRISING FACT ABOUT YOU? I don't like cheese
WHAT WILL YOU BE DOING IN THE YEAR 2040? I'll be a world-famous international DJ
WHICH BOOK MEANS MOST TO YOU? Origin by Dan Brown
TWITTER: @samcook09

Batting	Mat	Inns	NO	Runs	HS	Ave	SR	100	50	Ct	St
First-class	19	19	11	60	14	7.50	37.50	0	0	1	0
List A	8	2	1	2	1*	2.00	100.00	0	0	1	0
T20s	7	2	1	0	0*	0.00	0.00	0	0	0	0
Bowling	**Mat**	**Balls**	**Runs**	**Wkts**	**BBI**	**BBM**	**Ave**	**Econ**	**SR**	**5w**	**10**
First-class	19	2702	1395	53	5/18	7/102	26.32	3.09	50.9	3	0
List A	8	396	278	5	1/21	1/21	55.60	4.21	79.2	0	0
T20s	7	114	184	4	1/27	1/27	46.00	9.68	28.5	0	0

CHRIS COOKE RHB / WK / R0 / W0 / MVP68

GLAMORGAN

FULL NAME: Christopher Barry Cooke
BORN: May 30, 1986, Johannesburg, South Africa
SQUAD NO: 46
HEIGHT: 5ft 11in
NICKNAME: Chris Jelly, Dough, Beans, Minty, Shapeless, Cookie
EDUCATION: Bishops School, Cape Town; University of Cape Town
TEAMS: Glamorgan, Western Province
ROLE: Batsman/wicketkeeper
DEBUT: First-class: 2009; List A: 2009; T20: 2011

BEST BATTING: 171 Glamorgan vs Kent, Canterbury, 2014

WHAT WAS YOUR FIRST CRICKET CLUB? Cape Town CC, South Africa. Cheap beer and I made lots of friends there
FAVOURITE CRICKET BAT? Black Widow (brand based in Cape Town), aka The Railway Sleeper
CRICKETING HERO? Hylton Ackerman
WHICH BOWLER WOULD YOU LEAST LIKE TO FACE? Any non-bowler who comes on for an over
BEST INNINGS YOU'VE SEEN? Usman Khawaja's Championship hundred on his Glamorgan debut last summer, coming up against Jeetan Patel on a turning Edgbaston pitch. I was watching at the other end
WHO WOULD YOU ASK TO BAT FOR YOUR LIFE? Kieran Bull – The Wall
WHICH RULE WOULD YOU CHANGE ABOUT CRICKET? No runs allowed off a direct hit
WHICH BOOK MEANS MOST TO YOU? Spud by John van de Ruit
ODDEST SPORT YOU'VE PLAYED? Picigin (a Croatian form of volleyball played in the sea)
TWITTER: @Cooky_24

Batting	Mat	Inns	NO	Runs	HS	Ave	SR	100	50	Ct	St
First-class	77	133	16	4110	171	35.12	52.99	4	27	123	2
List A	80	73	9	2270	137*	35.46	98.69	2	14	47	3
T20s	92	77	16	1463	65*	23.98	140.53	0	4	54	5
Bowling	**Mat**	**Balls**	**Runs**	**Wkts**	**BBI**	**BBM**	**Ave**	**Econ**	**SR**	**5w**	**10**
First-class	77	-	-	-	-	-	-	-	-	-	-
List A	80	-	-	-	-	-	-	-	-	-	-
T20s	92	-	-	-	-	-	-	-	-	-	-

MARK COSGROVE

LHB / RM / R3 / W0

FULL NAME: Mark James Cosgrove
BORN: June 14, 1984, Adelaide, Australia
SQUAD NO: 55
HEIGHT: 5ft 9in
NICKNAME: Cozzie
EDUCATION: Trinity College, Adelaide
TEAMS: Australia, Leicestershire, Glamorgan, Hobart Hurricanes, South Australia, Sydney Sixers, Sydney Thunder, Tasmania
ROLE: Batsman
DEBUT: ODI: 2006; First-class: 2002; List A: 2002; T20: 2006

BEST BATTING: 233 Glamorgan vs Derbyshire, Derby, 2006
BEST BOWLING: 3-3 South Australia vs Tasmania, Adelaide, 2007
COUNTY CAP: 2006 (Glamorgan)

WHAT GOT YOU INTO CRICKET? Playing in the back yard
'ROY OF THE ROVERS' MOMENT? Receiving the Man of the Match award in my first ODI
SUPERSTITIONS? Listening to music before I go out to bat
IF YOU WEREN'T A CRICKETER? I'd be an Aussie Rules player
SURPRISING FACT? I grew up at the same club as Darren Lehmann, Ryan Harris and Graham Manou
CRICKETING HERO? Brian Lara
NON-CRICKETING HERO? Steven Gerrard
UNUSUAL OBJECT AT HOME? A swimming pool
TWITTER: @Cozzie99

Batting	Mat	Inns	NO	Runs	HS	Ave	SR	100	50	Ct	St
ODIs	3	3	0	112	74	37.33	96.55	0	1	0	0
First-class	208	370	19	14279	233	40.68	62.64	35	81	131	0
List A	152	146	4	4637	121	32.65	89.10	4	38	46	0
T20s	126	122	9	2774	89	24.54	122.14	0	14	25	0
Bowling	**Mat**	**Balls**	**Runs**	**Wkts**	**BBI**	**BBM**	**Ave**	**Econ**	**SR**	**5w**	**10**
ODIs	3	30	13	1	1/1	1/1	13.00	2.60	30.0	0	0
First-class	208	4204	2357	52	3/3	3/3	45.32	3.36	80.8	0	0
List A	152	1067	1141	18	2/21	2/21	63.38	6.41	59.2	0	0
T20s	126	197	320	10	2/11	2/11	32.00	9.74	19.7	0	0

BEN COTTON

RHB / RMF / R0 / W0

FULL NAME: Benjamin David Cotton
BORN: September 13, 1993, Stoke-on-Trent, Staffordshire
SQUAD NO: 36
HEIGHT: 6ft 5in
NICKNAME: Dot, Big Lad
EDUCATION: Clayton Hall Business and Language College, Newcastle-under-Lyme; Staffordshire University
TEAMS: Northamptonshire, Derbyshire
ROLE: Bowler
DEBUT: First-class: 2014; List A: 2014; T20: 2014

BEST BATTING: 43 Derbyshire vs Leicestershire, Derby, 2015
BEST BOWLING: 5-48 Northamptonshire vs Sussex, Northampton, 2018

WHAT WAS YOUR FIRST CRICKET CLUB? Porthill Park CC, Staffordshire. SF Barnes played for the club
FAVOURITE CRICKET BAT? Puma Ballistic 5000
BEST INNINGS YOU'VE SEEN? AB de Villiers hitting the fastest-ever ODI hundred (31 balls) against West Indies at Johannesburg in 2015
WHO WOULD YOU ASK TO BAT FOR YOUR LIFE? Adam Rossington – because it would be quickly over and done with
WHICH RULE WOULD YOU CHANGE ABOUT CRICKET? Make the tea break longer
YOUR BIGGEST CRICKETING REGRET? Being a bowler
SURPRISING FACT ABOUT YOU? I'm hoping to become a groundsman when I finish playing
WHAT WILL YOU BE DOING IN THE YEAR 2040? Rolling the wicket at Porthill Park
FAVOURITE QUOTE OR SAYING? Paddy, can you hear me?!
TWITTER: @cotts1993

Batting	Mat	Inns	NO	Runs	HS	Ave	SR	100	50	Ct	St
First-class	23	33	11	346	43	15.72	58.84	0	0	5	0
List A	30	11	7	71	18*	17.75	69.60	0	0	4	0
T20s	18	6	4	45	30*	22.50	121.62	0	0	3	0

Bowling	Mat	Balls	Runs	Wkts	BBI	BBM	Ave	Econ	SR	5w	10
First-class	23	3191	1741	47	5/48	7/58	37.04	3.27	67.8	1	0
List A	30	1271	1186	32	4/43	4/43	37.06	5.59	39.7	0	0
T20s	18	334	497	20	2/14	2/14	24.85	8.92	16.7	0	0

JOSH COUGHLIN

LHB / RM / R0 / W0

FULL NAME: Josh Coughlin
BORN: September 29, 1997, Sunderland
SQUAD NO: 29
HEIGHT: 6ft 5in
NICKNAME: Coggers
EDUCATION: St Robert of Newminster Catholic School, Sunderland
TEAMS: Durham
ROLE: Allrounder
DEBUT: First-class: 2016

BEST BATTING: 19 Durham v Derbyshire, Chester-le-Street, 2018
BEST BOWLING: 2-31 Durham v Derbyshire, Chester-le-Street, 2018

FAMILY TIES? My gran's brother played Minor Counties and my older brother Paul plays for Nottinghamshire
WHAT WAS YOUR FIRST CRICKET CLUB? Eppington CC, Sunderland
WHICH BOWLER WOULD YOU LEAST LIKE TO FACE? Billy Stanlake – fast with steep bounce
BEST INNINGS YOU'VE SEEN? Alex Hales's 171 against Pakistan at Trent Bridge in 2016
WHO WOULD YOU ASK TO BAT FOR YOUR LIFE? Paul Collingwood – summed up by his innings against Australia at Cardiff in 2009 which rescued a draw
WHICH RULE WOULD YOU CHANGE ABOUT CRICKET? Allow more fielders outside the circle in one-day and T20 cricket
YOUR BIGGEST CRICKETING REGRET? Getting hit on the head with no helmet
ODDEST SPORT YOU'VE PLAYED? Benchball
TWITTER: @Coughlin97

Batting	Mat	Inns	NO	Runs	HS	Ave	SR	100	50	Ct	St
First-class	3	5	0	42	19	8.40	35.59	0	0	1	0
Bowling	**Mat**	**Balls**	**Runs**	**Wkts**	**BBI**	**BBM**	**Ave**	**Econ**	**SR**	**5w**	**10**
First-class	3	366	184	5	2/31	2/45	36.80	3.01	73.2	0	0

PAUL COUGHLIN

RHB / RFM / R0 / W0

FULL NAME: Paul Coughlin
BORN: October 23, 1992, Sunderland
SQUAD NO: 28
HEIGHT: 6ft 2in
NICKNAME: Coggers
EDUCATION: St Robert of Newminster Catholic School, Sunderland
TEAMS: Nottinghamshire, Durham, England Lions
ROLE: Allrounder
DEBUT: First-class: 2012; List A: 2012; T20: 2014

BEST BATTING: 85 Durham vs Lancashire, Chester-le-Street, 2014
BEST BOWLING: 5-49 Durham vs Northamptonshire, Chester-le-Street, 2017

WHAT GOT YOU INTO CRICKET? Playing in my uncle's homemade net in his back garden
FAMILY TIES? A different uncle, Tommy Harland, played for Durham as a Minor County. My younger brother Josh is currently at Durham
STRANGEST THING SEEN IN A GAME? A fielder placed directly behind the bowler's arm
'ROY OF THE ROVERS' MOMENT? Winning the One-Day Cup at Lord's in 2014
CRICKETING HERO? Andrew Flintoff – amazing to watch. Kept the crowd entertained in all aspects of the game
SURPRISING FACT? I started out aiming to be a wicketkeeper. Then I tried myself as a batter. Ended up being more of a bowler
TWITTER: @Coughlin92

Batting	Mat	Inns	NO	Runs	HS	Ave	SR	100	50	Ct	St
First-class	32	51	7	1168	85	26.54	57.08	0	7	13	0
List A	26	17	3	166	22	11.85	95.95	0	0	7	0
T20s	33	22	7	433	53	28.86	137.89	0	1	10	0
Bowling	**Mat**	**Balls**	**Runs**	**Wkts**	**BBI**	**BBM**	**Ave**	**Econ**	**SR**	**5w**	**10**
First-class	32	3951	2244	75	5/49	10/133	29.92	3.40	52.6	2	1
List A	26	977	915	18	3/36	3/36	50.83	5.61	54.2	0	0
T20s	33	493	768	34	5/42	5/42	22.58	9.34	14.5	1	0

BEN COX

RHB / WK / R0 / W0 / MVP44

FULL NAME: Oliver Benjamin Cox
BORN: February 2, 1992, Wordsley, Stourbridge, Worcestershire
SQUAD NO: 10
HEIGHT: 5ft 11in
NICKNAME: Cocko, Coxy, Benji
EDUCATION: Bromsgrove School, Worcestershire
TEAMS: Worcestershire
ROLE: Wicketkeeper
DEBUT: First-class: 2009; List A: 2010; T20: 2010

BEST BATTING: 124 Worcestershire vs Gloucestershire, Cheltenham, 2017

WHAT WAS YOUR FIRST CRICKET CLUB? Belbroughton CC, Worcestershire. Tiny village which I had to leave because I couldn't get in the first team as a wicketkeeper
WHICH BOWLER WOULD YOU LEAST LIKE TO FACE? Rashid Khan – for his variation of googlies and leg-breaks bowled at a ridiculous pace
BEST INNINGS YOU'VE SEEN? Callum Ferguson's 192 on his Worcestershire debut in the One-Day Cup last summer
WHO WOULD YOU ASK TO BAT FOR YOUR LIFE? Daryl Mitchell
WHICH RULE WOULD YOU CHANGE ABOUT CRICKET? I'd introduce a 'double play': if the batsman nicks it and also gets stumped then the next allocated batsman is out too. Same applies with being caught and run out
WHAT WILL YOU BE DOING IN THE YEAR 2040? Hopefully having a business and property portfolio to my name. I'd definitely like to be a businessman rather than staying in cricket
ODDEST SPORT YOU'VE PLAYED? Beer-pong
TWITTER: @bencox10

Batting	Mat	Inns	NO	Runs	HS	Ave	SR	100	50	Ct	St
First-class	101	165	22	3981	124	27.83	62.81	3	23	267	12
List A	66	50	8	1133	122*	26.97	98.26	1	4	69	8
T20s	97	84	33	1406	59*	27.56	125.76	0	3	41	24
Bowling	**Mat**	**Balls**	**Runs**	**Wkts**	**BBI**	**BBM**	**Ave**	**Econ**	**SR**	**5w**	**10**
First-class	101	-	-	-	-	-	-	-	-	-	-
List A	66	-	-	-	-	-	-	-	-	-	-
T20s	97	-	-	-	-	-	-	-	-	-	-

JORDAN COX RHB / WK / R0 / W0

FULL NAME: Jordan Matthew Cox
BORN: October 21, 2000, Portsmouth
SQUAD NO: 22
EDUCATION: Felsted School, Essex
TEAMS: Kent, England U19
ROLE: Wicketkeeper/batsman

NOTES: The 18-year-old wicketkeeper/batsman signed a three-year contract with Kent in October after being a regular in the Second XI last year. "I'm honoured to have the opportunity to join the club, it really is a dream come true," he said. "Having been here since the age of 10 going up through the Academy, to sign my first professional contract is unbelievable and hopefully will be the start of something special." Cox was selected for the England U19 tour of Bangladesh over the winter, making his debut in the youth T20I at Cox's Bazar in January. He also played in the second youth Test later in the tour, making a quick-fire 30 in the second innings and claiming three catches and one stumping

MASON CRANE

RHB / LB / R0 / W0

FULL NAME: Mason Sidney Crane
BORN: February 18, 1997, Shoreham-by-Sea, Sussex
SQUAD NO: 32
HEIGHT: 5ft 9in
EDUCATION: Lancing College, West Sussex
TEAMS: England, Hampshire, New South Wales
ROLE: Bowler
DEBUT: Test: 2018; T20I: 2017; First-class: 2015; List A: 2015; T20: 2015

BEST BATTING: 29 Hampshire vs Somerset, Taunton, 2017
BEST BOWLING: 5-35 Hampshire vs Warwickshire, Southampton, 2015

WHAT GOT YOU INTO CRICKET? The 2005 Ashes
BEST ADVICE EVER RECEIVED? Never leave a birdie-putt short
BEST THING ABOUT YOUR HOME GROUND? Everything – it's awesome!
IF YOU WEREN'T A CRICKETER? I'd be wishing I tried harder at school
SURPRISING FACT ABOUT YOU? To walk back to my mark I always go past the stumps the same side I'm bowling and always turn left at my mark
WHERE IS PARADISE? Home
CRICKETING HERO? Shane Warne
UNUSUAL OBJECT AT HOME? Two tortoises
TWITTER: @masoncrane32

Batting	Mat	Inns	NO	Runs	HS	Ave	SR	100	50	Ct	St
Tests	1	2	0	6	4	3.00	54.54	0	0	0	0
T20Is	2	-	-	-	-	-	-	-	-	0	0
First-class	32	45	17	321	29	11.46	34.59	0	0	9	0
List A	30	11	7	68	21*	17.00	74.72	0	0	10	0
T20s	20	5	4	11	3*	11.00	52.38	0	0	4	0
Bowling	**Mat**	**Balls**	**Runs**	**Wkts**	**BBI**	**BBM**	**Ave**	**Econ**	**SR**	**5w**	**10**
Tests	1	288	193	1	1/193	1/193	193.00	4.02	288.0	0	0
T20Is	2	48	62	1	1/38	1/38	62.00	7.75	48.0	0	0
First-class	32	5563	3607	77	5/35	6/89	46.84	3.89	72.2	2	0
List A	30	1537	1563	53	4/30	4/30	29.49	6.10	29.0	0	0
T20s	20	420	512	22	3/15	3/15	23.27	7.31	19.0	0	0

ZAK CRAWLEY

RHB / RM / R0 / W0

FULL NAME: Zak Crawley
BORN: February 3, 1998, Bromley, Kent
SQUAD NO: 16
HEIGHT: 6ft 5in
NICKNAME: Creepy, Orangutan
EDUCATION: Tonbridge School, Kent
TEAMS: Kent
ROLE: Batsman
DEBUT: First-class: 2017; List A: 2017; T20: 2018

BEST BATTING: 168 Kent vs Glamorgan, Canterbury, 2018

WHAT WAS YOUR FIRST CRICKET CLUB? Holmesdale CC, Sevenoaks, Kent
FAVOURITE CRICKET BAT? Kookaburra Beast – I loved the stickers on the back
WHICH BOWLER WOULD YOU LEAST LIKE TO FACE? Kagiso Rabada
BEST INNINGS YOU'VE SEEN? Ricky Ponting's 156 at Old Trafford in 2005
WHO WOULD YOU ASK TO BAT FOR YOUR LIFE? Rahul Dravid
WHICH RULE WOULD YOU CHANGE ABOUT CRICKET? You should be able to spray the umpire for giving you a bad decision. They should be allowed to spray you for complaining if it turns out to be plum
YOUR BIGGEST CRICKETING REGRET? My last over in the JET Cup U13 semi-final went for 11 runs. Let the side down
FAVOURITE QUOTE OR SAYING? Everyone has the will to win, the best have the will to prepare to win
WHICH BOOK MEANS MOST TO YOU? The Day After Tomorrow by Allan Folsom
TWITTER: @zakcrawley

Batting	Mat	Inns	NO	Runs	HS	Ave	SR	100	50	Ct	St
First-class	21	33	0	934	168	28.30	57.44	1	5	15	0
List A	14	14	1	342	99*	26.30	62.40	0	2	6	0
T20s	1	1	0	3	3	3.00	75.00	0	0	0	0
Bowling	**Mat**	**Balls**	**Runs**	**Wkts**	**BBI**	**BBM**	**Ave**	**Econ**	**SR**	**5w**	**10**
First-class	21	-	-	-	-	-	-	-	-	-	-
List A	14	-	-	-	-	-	-	-	-	-	-
T20s	1	-	-	-	-	-	-	-	-	-	-

MATT CRITCHLEY RHB / LB / R0 / W0 / MVP37

FULL NAME: Matthew James John Critchley
BORN: August 13, 1996, Preston, Lancashire
SQUAD NO: 20
HEIGHT: 6ft 2in
NICKNAME: Critch
EDUCATION: St Michael's CE High School, Chorley; Cardinal Newman College, Preston; University of Derby
TEAMS: Derbyshire, England Lions
ROLE: Allrounder
DEBUT: First-class: 2015; List A: 2015; T20: 2016

BEST BATTING: 137* Derbyshire vs Northamptonshire, Derby, 2015
BEST BOWLING: 6-106 Derbyshire vs Northamptonshire, Chesterfield, 2018

WHAT WAS YOUR FIRST CRICKET CLUB? Chorley CC, Lancashire
FAVOURITE CRICKET BAT? A Kippax – scored my maiden first-class hundred with it
WHICH BOWLER WOULD YOU LEAST LIKE TO FACE? Stuart MacGill. He still gets me out now
BEST INNINGS YOU'VE SEEN? Kevin Pietersen's 158 at The Oval in the 2005 Ashes
WHO WOULD YOU ASK TO BAT FOR YOUR LIFE? Kevin Pietersen – either way, it would be interesting to watch
FAVOURITE QUOTE OR SAYING? I've missed more than 9,000 shots in my career. I've lost almost 300 games. Twenty-six times I've been trusted to take the game-winning shot and missed. I've failed over and over and over again in my life. And that is why I succeed (Michael Jordan)
WHICH BOOK MEANS MOST TO YOU? No Spin by Shane Warne
ODDEST SPORT YOU'VE PLAYED? Ultimate Frisbee
TWITTER: @mattcritchley96

Batting	Mat	Inns	NO	Runs	HS	Ave	SR	100	50	Ct	St
First-class	32	54	5	1480	137*	30.20	61.41	3	6	16	0
List A	34	25	4	461	64	21.95	101.09	0	1	4	0
T20s	37	27	6	430	72*	20.47	129.12	0	1	10	0
Bowling	**Mat**	**Balls**	**Runs**	**Wkts**	**BBI**	**BBM**	**Ave**	**Econ**	**SR**	**5w**	**10**
First-class	32	2968	2286	42	6/106	10/194	54.42	4.62	70.6	1	1
List A	34	1170	1296	25	4/48	4/48	51.84	6.64	46.8	0	0
T20s	37	423	581	22	3/32	3/32	26.40	8.24	19.2	0	0

STEVEN CROFT

RHB / RM / OB / R0 / W0

FULL NAME: Steven John Croft
BORN: October 11, 1984, Blackpool
SQUAD NO: 15
HEIGHT: 5ft 11in
NICKNAME: Crofty
EDUCATION: Highfield High School, Blackpool; Myerscough College, Lancashire
TEAMS: Lancashire, Auckland, Northern Districts
ROLE: Allrounder
DEBUT: First-class: 2005; List A: 2003; T20: 2006

BEST BATTING: 156 Lancashire vs Northamptonshire, Old Trafford, 2014
BEST BOWLING: 6-41 Lancashire vs Worcestershire, Old Trafford, 2012
COUNTY CAP: 2010

WHAT GOT YOU INTO CRICKET? Living in Sri Lanka as an eight-year-old (there was nothing else to do)
'ROY OF THE ROVERS' MOMENT? Hitting a six off the last ball of the match to beat Leicestershire in 2006 in my second T20 appearance
BEST THING ABOUT YOUR HOME GROUND? The mix of modernity and tradition
IF YOU WEREN'T A CRICKETER? I'd be involved with the armed forces
WHERE IS PARADISE? Home with family
CRICKETING HERO? Andrew Flintoff – he was from around my area and played in the same league as me
TWITTER: @Stevenjcroft

Batting	Mat	Inns	NO	Runs	HS	Ave	SR	100	50	Ct	St
First-class	165	258	23	7791	156	33.15	50.64	13	44	172	0
List A	147	131	22	3736	127	34.27	85.37	2	28	73	0
T20s	173	159	38	3629	94*	29.99	122.47	0	21	103	0
Bowling	**Mat**	**Balls**	**Runs**	**Wkts**	**BBI**	**BBM**	**Ave**	**Econ**	**SR**	**5w**	**10**
First-class	165	5213	2914	71	6/41	9/105	41.04	3.35	73.4	1	0
List A	147	2583	2350	60	4/24	4/24	39.16	5.45	43.0	0	0
T20s	173	1540	1919	66	3/6	3/6	29.07	7.47	23.3	0	0

TOM CULLEN

RHB / WK / R0 / W0

FULL NAME: Thomas Nicholas Cullen
BORN: January 4, 1992, Perth, Australia
SQUAD NO: 54
HEIGHT: 5ft 10in
NICKNAME: TC, Culley
EDUCATION: Cardiff Metropolitan University
TEAMS: Glamorgan
ROLE: Wicketkeeper
DEBUT: First-class: 2015

BEST BATTING: 42 Glamorgan vs Sussex, Colwyn Bay, 2017

WHAT GOT YOU INTO CRICKET? Growing up in Australia, cricket was everywhere
BEST ADVICE EVER RECEIVED? Nothing worth experiencing comes easy
'ROY OF THE ROVERS' MOMENT? Winning the University Challenge final at Lord's with Cardiff MCCU, then getting a call from Robert Croft the next morning (when I had a bit of a sore head) telling me to race back to Cardiff to travel with Glamorgan and make my debut. Two days later I was receiving my Glamorgan cap from Michael Hogan
BEST THING ABOUT YOUR HOME GROUND? It's in the heart of Cardiff
IF YOU WEREN'T A CRICKETER? I'd be doing something with my degree
SURPRISING FACT ABOUT YOU? When I was younger I wanted to be a fighter pilot
SURPRISING FACT ABOUT A TEAMMATE? Connor Brown has a lot of stories and will make a great grandad one day
CRICKETING HERO? I loved watching Ricky Ponting and Adam Gilchrist come to play at the WACA every year
NON-CRICKETING HERO? My mum, who sadly passed away four years ago. She gave me the confidence to pursue my dreams. I try to honour her by giving everything to cricket
TWITTER: @thomascullen186

Batting	Mat	Inns	NO	Runs	HS	Ave	SR	100	50	Ct	St
First-class	8	13	0	183	42	14.07	34.33	0	0	15	1
Bowling	**Mat**	**Balls**	**Runs**	**Wkts**	**BBI**	**BBM**	**Ave**	**Econ**	**SR**	**5w**	**10**
First-class	8	-	-	-	-	-	-	-	-	-	-

BEN CURRAN

LHB / OB / R0 / W0

NORTHAMPTONSHIRE

FULL NAME: Benjamin Jack Curran
BORN: June 7, 1996, Northampton
SQUAD NO: 57
HEIGHT: 5ft 9in
NICKNAME: Lord, BC
EDUCATION: Wellington College, Berkshire
TEAMS: Northamptonshire
ROLE: Batsman
DEBUT: First-class: 2018; T20: 2018

BEST BATTING: 83* Northamptonshire vs Sussex, Northampton, 2018

FAMILY TIES? My father Kevin played for Zimbabwe, Gloucestershire and Northamptonshire. My older brother Tom and younger brother Sam both play for Surrey
WHAT WAS YOUR FIRST CRICKET CLUB? Weybridge CC, Surrey
WHICH BOWLER WOULD YOU LEAST LIKE TO FACE? Brett Lee
BEST INNINGS YOU'VE SEEN? Adam Gilchrist's 149 in the 2007 World Cup final
WHICH RULE WOULD YOU CHANGE ABOUT CRICKET? Make lunch half an hour and tea half an hour
YOUR BIGGEST CRICKETING REGRET? Not bowling left-arm
WHAT WILL YOU BE DOING IN THE YEAR 2040? Still opening the batting for Northamptonshire CCC
FAVOURITE QUOTE OR SAYING? Stay in your lane
ODDEST SPORT YOU'VE PLAYED? Eton Fives
TWITTER: @curranjb_57

Batting	Mat	Inns	NO	Runs	HS	Ave	SR	100	50	Ct	St
First-class	5	9	1	251	83*	31.37	53.74	0	2	3	0
T20s	3	3	0	46	29	15.33	127.77	0	0	2	0
Bowling	**Mat**	**Balls**	**Runs**	**Wkts**	**BBI**	**BBM**	**Ave**	**Econ**	**SR**	**5w**	**10**
First-class	5	-	-	-	-	-	-	-	-	-	-
T20s	3	-	-	-	-	-	-	-	-	-	-

SAM CURRAN

LHB / LMF / R0 / W0

FULL NAME: Samuel Matthew Curran
BORN: June 3, 1998, Northampton
SQUAD NO: 58
HEIGHT: 5ft 9in
NICKNAME: Junior, Sammy
EDUCATION: Wellington College, Berkshire
TEAMS: England, Surrey, Auckland, Kings XI Punjab
ROLE: Allrounder
DEBUT: Test: 2018; ODI: 2018; First-class: 2015; List A: 2015; T20: 2015

BEST BATTING: 96 Surrey vs Lancashire, The Oval, 2016
BEST BOWLING: 7-58 Surrey vs Durham, Chester-le-Street, 2016
COUNTY CAP: 2018

FAMILY TIES? My father Kevin played for Zimbabwe, and my brother Tom plays with me at Surrey. Ben, my other brother, plays for Northants. We have always been a competitive family
BEST THING ABOUT YOUR HOME GROUND? Big crowds, great atmosphere
WHERE IS PARADISE? Cape Town
CRICKETING HERO? Brian Lara
TWITTER: @CurranSM

Batting	Mat	Inns	NO	Runs	HS	Ave	SR	100	50	Ct	St
Tests	9	16	2	454	78	32.42	58.73	0	3	0	0
ODIs	2	2	0	17	15	8.50	58.62	0	0	0	0
First-class	51	78	10	1952	96	28.70	58.02	0	14	13	0
List A	51	34	5	597	57	20.58	84.20	0	1	20	0
T20s	47	36	6	478	50	15.93	118.90	0	1	11	0
Bowling	**Mat**	**Balls**	**Runs**	**Wkts**	**BBI**	**BBM**	**Ave**	**Econ**	**SR**	**5w**	**10**
Tests	9	893	513	15	4/74	5/92	34.20	3.44	59.5	0	0
ODIs	2	72	90	2	2/44	2/44	45.00	7.50	36.0	0	0
First-class	51	6980	3995	133	7/58	10/101	30.03	3.43	52.4	6	1
List A	51	2292	2129	68	4/32	4/32	31.30	5.57	33.7	0	0
T20s	47	870	1196	42	4/13	4/13	28.47	8.24	20.7	0	0

TOM CURRAN

RHB / RFM / R0 / W1

FULL NAME: Thomas Kevin Curran
BORN: March 12, 1995, Cape Town, South Africa
SQUAD NO: 59
HEIGHT: 6ft
NICKNAME: TC
EDUCATION: Wellington College, Berkshire
TEAMS: England, Surrey, Kolkata Knight Riders, Sydney Sixers
ROLE: Allrounder
DEBUT: Test: 2017; ODI: 2017; T20I: 2017; First-class: 2014; List A: 2013; T20: 2014

BEST BATTING: 60 Surrey vs Leicestershire, Leicester, 2015
BEST BOWLING: 7-20 Surrey vs Gloucestershire, The Oval, 2015
COUNTY CAP: 2016

FAMILY TIES? My father Kevin played for Northants and Zimbabwe, my brother Sam also plays for Surrey, and my other younger brother Ben is at Northants
CRICKETING HERO? Hamilton Masakadza
IF YOU WEREN'T A CRICKETER? I would be fishing or playing the guitar in a bar somewhere exotic
SURPRISING FACT? I have a degree in Law
TWITTER: @_TC59

Batting	Mat	Inns	NO	Runs	HS	Ave	SR	100	50	Ct	St
Tests	2	3	1	66	39	33.00	55.00	0	0	0	0
ODIs	13	8	5	71	35	23.66	109.23	0	0	4	0
T20Is	10	4	3	10	6	10.00	125.00	0	0	1	0
First-class	58	79	10	1211	60	17.55	50.45	0	5	20	0
List A	69	45	17	491	44	17.53	96.27	0	0	23	0
T20s	82	44	15	593	62	20.44	131.19	0	2	24	0
Bowling	**Mat**	**Balls**	**Runs**	**Wkts**	**BBI**	**BBM**	**Ave**	**Econ**	**SR**	**5w**	**10**
Tests	2	396	200	2	1/65	1/82	100.00	3.03	198.0	0	0
ODIs	13	557	581	18	5/35	5/35	32.27	6.25	30.9	1	0
T20Is	10	186	280	11	4/36	4/36	25.45	9.03	16.9	0	0
First-class	58	10173	5495	192	7/20	10/176	28.61	3.24	52.9	7	1
List A	69	3044	2861	104	5/16	5/16	27.50	5.63	29.2	3	0
T20s	82	1647	2320	95	4/35	4/35	24.42	8.45	17.3	0	0

ANUJ DAL RHB / RM / R0 / W0

FULL NAME: Anuj Kailash Dal
BORN: July 8, 1996, Newcastle-under-Lyme, Staffordshire
SQUAD NO: 65
HEIGHT: 5ft 9in
NICKNAME: Nuj
EDUCATION: Nottingham High School
TEAMS: Derbyshire
ROLE: Batsman
DEBUT: First-class: 2018; T20: 2018

BEST BATTING: 25 Derbyshire vs Sussex, Hove, 2018

WHAT WAS YOUR FIRST CRICKET CLUB? Kimberley Institute CC, Nottinghamshire
FAVOURITE CRICKET BAT? My first Bradbury Players bat. I chose the willow and watched the whole process from start to finish. Best bat I've ever used as a pro
WHICH BOWLER WOULD YOU LEAST LIKE TO FACE? Mitchell Starc – horrible combination of pace and late swing
BEST INNINGS YOU'VE SEEN? Harvey Hosein's fifty to get us over the line by one wicket in the Championship match at Northampton last summer. He showed a lot of character in that innings
WHO WOULD YOU ASK TO BAT FOR YOUR LIFE? Jonny Buttler (old schoolmate) – couldn't hit the ball off the square but had the best-looking and most effective defence I've ever seen
WHICH RULE WOULD YOU CHANGE ABOUT CRICKET? A longer lunch and a longer tea of course!
YOUR BIGGEST CRICKETING REGRET? Not doubling up when I get past 50
FAVOURITE QUOTE OR SAYING? 99 per cent concentration = 100 per cent failure
TWITTER: @AnujDal

Batting	Mat	Inns	NO	Runs	HS	Ave	SR	100	50	Ct	St
First-class	4	7	0	107	25	15.28	34.96	0	0	2	0
T20s	9	8	2	94	35	15.66	122.07	0	0	4	0
Bowling	**Mat**	**Balls**	**Runs**	**Wkts**	**BBI**	**BBM**	**Ave**	**Econ**	**SR**	**5w**	**10**
First-class	4	6	1	0	-	-	-	1.00	-	0	0
T20s	9	-	-	-	-	-	-	-	-	-	-

JOSH DAVEY

RHB / RMF / R0 / W0

FULL NAME: Joshua Henry Davey
BORN: August 3, 1990, Aberdeen, Scotland
SQUAD NO: 38
HEIGHT: 6ft
NICKNAME: JD
EDUCATION: Culford School, Bury St Edmunds; Oxford Brookes University
TEAMS: Scotland, Somerset, Hampshire, Middlesex
ROLE: Allrounder
DEBUT: ODI: 2010; T20I: 2012; First-class: 2010; List A: 2010; T20: 2010

BEST BATTING: 72 Middlesex vs Oxford MCCU, Oxford, 2010
BEST BOWLING: 5-65 Somerset vs Yorkshire, Headingley, 2018

WHAT WAS YOUR FIRST CRICKET CLUB? Bury St Edmunds CC, Suffolk
BEST INNINGS YOU'VE SEEN? Chris Gayle's 151 not out against Kent at Taunton in 2015
WHO WOULD YOU ASK TO BAT FOR YOUR LIFE? Brian Lara – anyone who can score 500 in an innings has my trust
ODDEST SPORT YOU'VE PLAYED? Pub skittles
TWITTER: @JoshDavey38
NOTES: After four years at Middlesex, Davey was released at the end of 2013 and excelled for Somerset Second XI in 2014, which led to a full contract at the county. The seam-bowling allrounder played for Scotland in the 2015 World Cup, finishing as his team's highest wicket-taker. He was a peripheral figure at Somerset for a few seasons until making the breakthrough last summer with 34 Championship wickets at 25.35

Batting	Mat	Inns	NO	Runs	HS	Ave	SR	100	50	Ct	St
ODIs	29	26	5	471	64	22.42	65.87	0	2	9	0
T20Is	14	7	2	55	24	11.00	127.90	0	0	9	0
First-class	26	42	8	626	72	18.41	44.42	0	3	11	0
List A	73	60	11	1132	91	23.10	65.66	0	5	23	0
T20s	37	20	9	173	24	15.72	124.46	0	0	21	0
Bowling	**Mat**	**Balls**	**Runs**	**Wkts**	**BBI**	**BBM**	**Ave**	**Econ**	**SR**	**5w**	**10**
ODIs	29	1199	1014	47	6/28	6/28	21.57	5.07	25.5	2	0
T20Is	14	298	422	14	4/34	4/34	30.14	8.49	21.2	0	0
First-class	26	3271	1637	59	5/65	7/111	27.74	3.00	55.4	1	0
List A	73	2591	2361	89	6/28	6/28	26.52	5.46	29.1	2	0
T20s	37	544	825	31	4/34	4/34	26.61	9.09	17.5	0	0

ALEX DAVIES RHB / WK / R1 / W0 / MVP9

FULL NAME: Alexander Luke Davies
BORN: August 23, 1994, Darwen, Lancashire
SQUAD NO: 17
HEIGHT: 5ft 8in
NICKNAME: Davo, Chikwambo, Little Boy
EDUCATION: Queen Elizabeth's Grammar School, Blackburn
TEAMS: Lancashire, England Lions
ROLE: Batsman/wicketkeeper
DEBUT: First-class: 2012; List A: 2011; T20: 2014

BEST BATTING: 140* Lancashire vs Essex, Chelmsford, 2017

FAMILY TIES? Dad played club cricket all his life
'ROY OF THE ROVERS' MOMENT? Winning the T20 Blast with Lancashire in 2015
CRICKETING HEROES? Sachin Tendulkar – he timed the ball amazingly. Adam Gilchrist – he was the first high-quality aggressive batsman-keeper. AB de Villiers – for his 360-degree gameplay
NON-CRICKETING HEROES? Alan Shearer
SURPRISING FACT? Despite being a wicketkeeper, I can bowl with both arms
TWITTER: @aldavies23

Batting	Mat	Inns	NO	Runs	HS	Ave	SR	100	50	Ct	St
First-class	65	100	4	3298	140*	34.35	56.46	4	21	156	15
List A	49	46	3	1380	147	32.09	90.49	1	7	48	11
T20s	41	38	6	833	94*	26.03	129.95	0	6	25	4
Bowling	**Mat**	**Balls**	**Runs**	**Wkts**	**BBI**	**BBM**	**Ave**	**Econ**	**SR**	**5w**	**10**
First-class	65	-	-	-	-	-	-	-	-	-	-
List A	49	-	-	-	-	-	-	-	-	-	-
T20s	41	-	-	-	-	-	-	-	-	-	-

JACK DAVIES LHB / WK / R0 / W0

FULL NAME: Jack Leo Benjamin Davies
BORN: March 30, 2000, Reading
SQUAD NO: 23
HEIGHT: 5ft 9in
NICKNAME: Davo
EDUCATION: Wellington College, Berkshire
TEAMS: Middlesex, England U19
ROLE: Wicketkeeper/batsman

WHAT WAS YOUR FIRST CRICKET CLUB? Henley CC, Oxfordshire
FAVOURITE CRICKET BAT? My first one, a Salix Pod
WHICH BOWLER WOULD YOU LEAST LIKE TO FACE? Tom Barber – he bowls off 17 yards and likes the bumper option
BEST INNINGS YOU'VE SEEN? Any one of Kane Williamson's great innings
WHO WOULD YOU ASK TO BAT FOR YOUR LIFE? Martin Andersson – he bats with arrogance
WHICH RULE WOULD YOU CHANGE ABOUT CRICKET? The minimum number of overs a day in Second XI cricket should be less than 96
YOUR BIGGEST CRICKETING REGRET? Plenty of leaves which have blown my pads off
FAVOURITE QUOTE OR SAYING? If it's in the 'V', it's in the tree
ODDEST SPORT YOU'VE PLAYED? Real tennis
TWITTER: @daviesjlb
NOTES: The 19-year-old wicketkeeper-batsman signed his first professional contract in November when he agreed a two-year deal with Middlesex. Davies inspired Berkshire to the Minor Counties double in 2017, hitting an unbeaten 127 in the one-day final against Lincolnshire. He made his Middlesex Second XI debut that summer and was selected by England for last year's U19 World Cup in New Zealand. Managing director of cricket Angus Fraser said: "We have been aware of and excited by Jack's potential for quite some time through his performances at Wellington College, Berkshire CCC and in our youth sides. This potential has been recognised by England too, who selected Jack for the last U19 World Cup, a tournament where he highlighted his talent"

STEVEN DAVIES LHB / WK / R6 / W0 / MVP60

FULL NAME: Steven Michael Davies
BORN: June 17, 1986, Bromsgrove, Worcestershire
SQUAD NO: 11
HEIGHT: 6ft
NICKNAME: Davos
EDUCATION: King Charles High School, Kidderminster
TEAMS: England, Somerset, Surrey, Worcestershire
ROLE: Batsman/wicketkeeper
DEBUT: ODI: 2009; T20I: 2009; First-class: 2005; List A: 2003; T20: 2006

BEST BATTING: 200* Surrey vs Glamorgan, Cardiff, 2015

COUNTY CAP: 2011 (Surrey)

WHAT WAS YOUR FIRST CRICKET CLUB? Victoria Carpets CC, Kidderminster, Worcestershire
FAVOURITE CRICKET BAT? Kookaburra Kahuna – big and light
WHO WOULD YOU ASK TO BAT FOR YOUR LIFE? Rahul Dravid
WHICH RULE WOULD YOU CHANGE ABOUT CRICKET? Make the wickets taller
YOUR BIGGEST CRICKETING REGRET? Getting to Finals Day and not winning
SURPRISING FACT ABOUT YOU? I'm a session harp player
WHICH BOOK MEANS MOST TO YOU? Open by Andre Agassi
ODDEST SPORT YOU'VE PLAYED? Walking football
TWITTER: @SteveDavies43

Batting	Mat	Inns	NO	Runs	HS	Ave	SR	100	50	Ct	St
ODIs	8	8	0	244	87	30.50	105.62	0	1	8	0
T20Is	5	5	0	102	33	20.40	124.39	0	0	2	1
First-class	210	348	34	12409	200*	39.51	61.36	23	58	484	30
List A	184	173	14	5645	127*	35.50	101.86	9	35	147	42
T20s	142	133	8	2644	99*	21.15	142.15	0	15	65	23
Bowling	**Mat**	**Balls**	**Runs**	**Wkts**	**BBI**	**BBM**	**Ave**	**Econ**	**SR**	**5w**	**10**
ODIs	8	-	-	-	-	-	-	-	-	-	-
T20Is	5	-	-	-	-	-	-	-	-	-	-
First-class	210	-	-	-	-	-	-	-	-	-	-
List A	184	-	-	-	-	-	-	-	-	-	-
T20s	142	-	-	-	-	-	-	-	-	-	-

WILL DAVIS

RHB / RFM / R0 / W0

FULL NAME: William Samuel Davis
BORN: March 6, 1996, Stafford
SQUAD NO: 44
HEIGHT: 6ft 2in
NICKNAME: Thumb, Spaceman
EDUCATION: Stafford Grammar School
TEAMS: Leicestershire, Derbyshire
ROLE: Bowler
DEBUT: First-class: 2015; List A: 2016

BEST BATTING: 25 Derbyshire vs Sussex, Hove, 2017
BEST BOWLING: 7-146 Derbyshire vs Glamorgan, Colwyn Bay, 2016

STRANGEST THING SEEN IN A GAME? Greg Cork's field placements
'ROY OF THE ROVERS' MOMENT? Taking my maiden five-wicket haul in first-class cricket against Glamorgan at Colwyn Bay in 2016
CRICKETING HERO? Andrew Flintoff
NON-CRICKETING HERO? Cristiano Ronaldo
IF YOU WEREN'T A CRICKETER? I'd be a professional gamer
TWITTER: @W_Davis44
NOTES: Leicestershire signed the 23-year-old fast bowler from Derbyshire on a two-year contract last September. Head coach Paul Nixon said: "Will burst on to the county scene with a number of quality performances but had his chances limited due to Derbyshire's experienced pace attack. [He] is a highly promising young quick bowler who we have been tracking for a while"

Batting	Mat	Inns	NO	Runs	HS	Ave	SR	100	50	Ct	St
First-class	13	17	4	112	25	8.61	56.85	0	0	2	0
List A	1	-	-	-	-	-	-	-	-	-	-
Bowling	**Mat**	**Balls**	**Runs**	**Wkts**	**BBI**	**BBM**	**Ave**	**Econ**	**SR**	**5w**	**10**
First-class	13	1843	1263	40	7/146	8/204	31.57	4.11	46.0	1	0
List A	1	-	-	-	-	-	-	-	-	-	-

LIAM DAWSON RHB / SLA / R1 / W0 / MVP47

FULL NAME: Liam Andrew Dawson
BORN: March 1, 1990, Swindon
SQUAD NO: 8
HEIGHT: 5ft 8in
NICKNAME: Daws, Lemmy, Chav, Stomper
EDUCATION: The John Bentley School, Wiltshire
TEAMS: England, Hampshire, Comilla Victorians, Essex, Mountaineers, Peshawar Zalmi, Rangpur Riders
ROLE: Allrounder
DEBUT: Test: 2016; ODI: 2016; T20I: 2016; First-class: 2007; List A: 2007; T20: 2008

BEST BATTING: 169 Hampshire vs Somerset, Southampton, 2011
BEST BOWLING: 7-51 Mountaineers vs Mashonaland Eagles, Mutare Sports Club, 2011
COUNTY CAP: 2013 (Hampshire)

WHAT GOT YOU INTO CRICKET? Watching my dad play for Goatacre CC in Wiltshire
FAMILY TIES? My brother Brad has played Minor Counties for Wiltshire
STRANGEST THING SEEN IN A GAME? Benny Howell
'ROY OF THE ROVERS' MOMENT? My England debut in 2016
CRICKETING HERO? Shane Warne
IF YOU WEREN'T A CRICKETER? I'd be an umpire
TWITTER: @daws128

Batting	Mat	Inns	NO	Runs	HS	Ave	SR	100	50	Ct	St
Tests	3	6	2	84	66*	21.00	42.63	0	1	2	0
ODIs	3	2	0	14	10	7.00	82.35	0	0	0	0
T20Is	6	2	1	17	10	17.00	212.50	0	0	2	0
First-class	142	233	25	6677	169	32.10	48.60	8	35	138	0
List A	151	123	22	3255	113*	32.22	94.75	2	17	67	0
T20s	150	109	26	1619	82	19.50	115.47	0	5	66	0
Bowling	**Mat**	**Balls**	**Runs**	**Wkts**	**BBI**	**BBM**	**Ave**	**Econ**	**SR**	**5w**	**10**
Tests	3	526	298	7	2/34	4/101	42.57	3.39	75.1	0	0
ODIs	3	84	96	3	2/70	2/70	32.00	6.85	28.0	0	0
T20Is	6	120	152	5	3/27	3/27	30.40	7.60	24.0	0	0
First-class	142	13095	6632	189	7/51	8/129	35.08	3.03	69.2	3	0
List A	151	5672	4524	144	6/47	6/47	31.41	4.78	39.3	1	0
T20s	150	2366	2876	110	5/17	5/17	26.14	7.29	21.5	1	0

MARCHANT DE LANGE

RHB / RF / R0 / W0

FULL NAME: Marchant de Lange
BORN: October 13, 1990, Tzaneen, Transvaal, South Africa
SQUAD NO: 90
HEIGHT: 6ft 7in
NICKNAME: Shanna
TEAMS: South Africa, Glamorgan, Barbados Tridents, Durban Heat, Easterns, Free State, Guyana Amazon Warriors, Knights, Kolkata Knight Riders, Mumbai Indians, Titans
ROLE: Bowler
DEBUT: Test: 2011; ODI: 2012; T20I: 2012; First-class: 2010; List A: 2010; T20: 2011

BEST BATTING: 90 Glamorgan vs Leicestershire, Leicester, 2018
BEST BOWLING: 7-23 Knights vs Titans, Centurion, 2016

BEST ADVICE EVER RECEIVED? To bowl top of off stump
'ROY OF THE ROVERS' MOMENT? Taking seven wickets on my Test debut
IF YOU WEREN'T A CRICKETER? I'd be a MotoGP rider or Formula 1 driver
SURPRISING FACT ABOUT YOU? I love art and building
WHERE IS PARADISE? Santorini
CRICKETING HERO? Dale Steyn
NON-CRICKETING HERO? Valentino Rossi – the best-ever MotoGP rider

Batting	Mat	Inns	NO	Runs	HS	Ave	SR	100	50	Ct	St
Tests	2	2	0	9	9	4.50	47.36	0	0	1	0
ODIs	4	-	-	-	-	-	-	-	-	0	0
T20Is	6	-	-	-	-	-	-	-	-	1	0
First-class	74	99	15	1323	90	15.75	71.78	0	3	32	0
List A	83	58	16	580	53	13.80	99.14	0	1	20	0
T20s	82	28	14	160	27*	11.42	133.33	0	0	18	0

Bowling	Mat	Balls	Runs	Wkts	BBI	BBM	Ave	Econ	SR	5w	10
Tests	2	448	277	9	7/81	8/126	30.77	3.70	49.7	1	0
ODIs	4	209	198	10	4/46	4/46	19.80	5.68	20.9	0	0
T20Is	6	140	228	7	2/26	2/26	32.57	9.77	20.0	0	0
First-class	74	13758	8218	279	7/23	11/62	29.45	3.58	49.3	11	2
List A	83	4118	3693	148	5/49	5/49	24.95	5.38	27.8	4	0
T20s	82	1649	2376	93	4/23	4/23	25.54	8.64	17.7	0	0

AB DE VILLIERS

RHB / RM / WK / R0 / W0

FULL NAME: Abraham Benjamin de Villiers
BORN: February 17, 1984, Pretoria, South Africa
SQUAD NO: 11
TEAMS: South Africa, Middlesex, Barbados Tridents, Delhi Daredevils, Lahore Qalandars, Northerns, Rangpur Riders, Royal Challengers Banglaore, Titans, Tshwane Spartans
ROLE: Batsman
DEBUT: Test: 2004; ODI: 2005; T20I: 2006; First-class: 2003; List A: 2003; T20: 2004

BEST BATTING: 278* South Africa vs Pakistan, Abu Dhabi, 2010
BEST BOWLING: 2-49 South Africa vs West Indies, Antigua, 2005

TWITTER: @ABdeVilliers17
NOTES: Middlesex have signed the 35-year-old de Villiers – one of the greatest players of his generation – for the first seven matches of the T20 Blast and if needed for the latter stages of the tournament. The South African has participated in every IPL, scoring almost 4,000 runs at an average of just under 40. De Villiers retired from international cricket in May 2018 to end an extraordinary career which produced more than 20,000 runs across all formats for his country. Of late he has been playing T20 cricket in South Africa, Bangladesh and Pakistan. "I have always wanted to play county cricket," said de Villiers. "Playing at Lord's is always a wonderful privilege, and I'm looking forward to the match at Richmond, a beautiful ground in south-west London"

Batting	Mat	Inns	NO	Runs	HS	Ave	SR	100	50	Ct	St
Tests	114	191	18	8765	278*	50.66	54.51	22	46	222	5
ODIs	228	218	39	9577	176	53.50	101.09	25	53	176	5
T20Is	78	75	11	1672	79*	26.12	135.16	0	10	65	7
First-class	141	238	23	10689	278*	49.71	56.18	25	60	275	6
List A	263	252	44	11123	176	53.47	99.46	29	63	203	5
T20s	274	256	51	7396	133*	36.07	148.36	4	48	188	16
Bowling	**Mat**	**Balls**	**Runs**	**Wkts**	**BBI**	**BBM**	**Ave**	**Econ**	**SR**	**5w**	**10**
Tests	114	204	104	2	2/49	2/49	52.00	3.05	102.0	0	0
ODIs	228	192	202	7	2/15	2/15	28.85	6.31	27.4	0	0
T20Is	78	-	-	-	-	-	-	-	-	-	-
First-class	141	234	138	2	2/49	2/49	69.00	3.53	117.0	0	0
List A	263	192	202	7	2/15	2/15	28.85	6.31	27.4	0	0
T20s	274	-	-	-	-	-	-	-	-	-	-

HARRY DEARDEN LHB / OB / R0 / W0

FULL NAME: Harry Edward Dearden
BORN: May 7, 1997, Bury, Lancashire
SQUAD NO: 5
HEIGHT: 5ft 8in
NICKNAME: H, Haz, Deards
EDUCATION: Tottington High School, Bury; Bury College
TEAMS: Leicestershire
ROLE: Batsman
DEBUT: First-class: 2016; List A: 2018; T20: 2018

BEST BATTING: 87 Leicestershire vs Glamorgan, Leicester, 2017
BEST BOWLING: 1-0 Leicestershire vs Kent, Leicester, 2017

WHAT GOT YOU INTO CRICKET? The 2005 Ashes. I still have the box set at home and get it out from time to time
FAMILY TIES? Dad played for the Lancashire Cricket Board and still plays now
'ROY OF THE ROVERS' MOMENT? My first-class debut for Leicestershire in 2016
STRANGEST THING SEEN IN A GAME? It happened during a T20 on a wet Friday night for my club team. The ball was pretty soggy before an opposition batter hit it out the ground. We gave a replacement ball to the umpire, who proceeded to wipe it along the wet outfield, claiming the substitute ball had to be in the exact same state as the lost one. Madness
SURPRISING FACT? I was on a Channel 4 roadshow for the 2001 Ashes series, having a split-screen with Shane Warne
CRICKETING HERO? Brian Lara
NON-CRICKETING HERO? Roy Keane
TWITTER: @HarryDearden97

Batting	Mat	Inns	NO	Runs	HS	Ave	SR	100	50	Ct	St
First-class	23	43	2	838	87	20.43	41.05	0	4	20	0
List A	2	2	0	37	31	18.50	61.66	0	0	2	0
T20s	1	1	0	61	61	61.00	152.50	0	1	1	0
Bowling	**Mat**	**Balls**	**Runs**	**Wkts**	**BBI**	**BBM**	**Ave**	**Econ**	**SR**	**5w**	**10**
First-class	23	112	95	2	1/0	1/0	47.50	5.08	56.0	0	0
List A	2	-	-	-	-	-	-	-	-	-	-
T20s	1	-	-	-	-	-	-	-	-	-	-

JOSH DELL

RHB / RM / R0 / W0

FULL NAME: Joshua Jamie Dell
BORN: September 26, 1997, Tenbury Wells, Worcestershire
SQUAD NO: TBC
HEIGHT: 6ft 3in
NICKNAME: Dellboy, Squire
EDUCATION: Abberley Hall School, Worcestershire; Cheltenham College
TEAMS: Worcestershire
ROLE: Batsman
DEBUT: List A: 2018

WHAT WAS YOUR FIRST CRICKET CLUB? Ombersley CC, Worcestershire. I've been playing there since I was 11
WHICH BOWLER WOULD YOU LEAST LIKE TO FACE? Morne Morkel – because of that bounce
BEST INNINGS YOU'VE SEEN? AB de Villiers's 162 not out off 66 balls against West Indies at Sydney in the 2015 World Cup
WHO WOULD YOU ASK TO BAT FOR YOUR LIFE? Tom Fell
WHAT WILL YOU BE DOING IN THE YEAR 2040? I'll be working in London
WHICH BOOK MEANS MOST TO YOU? Bounce – The Myth of Talent and the Power of Practice by Matthew Syed
ODDEST SPORT YOU'VE PLAYED? Racquets
NOTES: The 21-year-old batsman has come through the Worcestershire Academy and signed a professional contract in June 2018 shortly after scoring his maiden Second XI hundred against Lancashire. Later that month he made an impressive 46 on his List A debut against a strong West Indies A attack at New Road. Dell played two unofficial Tests and one ODI for England U19 in 2016

Batting	Mat	Inns	NO	Runs	HS	Ave	SR	100	50	Ct	St
List A	1	1	0	46	46	46.00	102.22	0	0	1	0

Bowling	Mat	Balls	Runs	Wkts	BBI	BBM	Ave	Econ	SR	5w	10
List A	1	-	-	-	-	-	-	-	-	-	-

CAMERON DELPORT

LHB / RMF / R0 / W0

FULL NAME: Cameron Scott Delport
BORN: May 12, 1989, Durban, South Africa
SQUAD NO: 89
HEIGHT: 5ft 10in
NICKNAME: Camo, Delpo, Goose
EDUCATION: Kloof Senior School, Durban; Westville Boys' High School, Durban
TEAMS: Essex, Dolphins, KwaZulu-Natal, Lahore Qalandars, Leicestershire, Sydney Thunder, Trinidad & Tobago Red Steel
ROLE: Allrounder
DEBUT: First-class: 2009; List A: 2009; T20: 2010

BEST BATTING: 163 KwaZulu-Natal vs Northerns, Centurion, 2011
BEST BOWLING: 2-10 KwaZulu-Natal vs Northern Cape, Chatsworth, 2016

BEST ADVICE EVER RECEIVED? See ball, hit ball
'ROY OF THE ROVERS' MOMENT? In general terms, playing and sharing dressing rooms with international cricketers in various T20 tournaments around the world – getting their advice and hearing about how their careers have been shaped through good and bad times
BEST THING ABOUT YOUR HOME GROUND? I have many home grounds at the moment! As long as they are batter-friendly then I am happy
IF YOU WEREN'T A CRICKETER? I'd be a surfer-traveller-businessman
SURPRISING FACT ABOUT YOU? I am a great BBQ chef and entertainer
NON-CRICKETING HERO? Kelly Slater – amazing pro surfer and an amazing man
TWITTER: @Cam12Delport
NOTES: The South African batsman left Leicestershire in November with a year to run on his contract and signed a two-year deal to play for Essex in the T20 Blast. He holds a UK passport and qualifies as a non-overseas player

Batting	Mat	Inns	NO	Runs	HS	Ave	SR	100	50	Ct	St
First-class	61	106	6	3206	163	32.06	88.29	3	19	36	0
List A	107	97	6	2765	169*	30.38	105.93	3	15	38	0
T20s	193	185	13	4464	117*	25.95	137.43	4	22	65	0
Bowling	**Mat**	**Balls**	**Runs**	**Wkts**	**BBI**	**BBM**	**Ave**	**Econ**	**SR**	**5w**	**10**
First-class	61	1183	723	14	2/10	2/10	51.64	3.66	84.5	0	0
List A	107	1572	1596	38	4/42	4/42	42.00	6.09	41.3	0	0
T20s	193	1156	1493	57	4/17	4/17	26.19	7.74	20.2	0	0

JOE DENLY

RHB / LB / R4 / W0 / MVP1

FULL NAME: Joseph Liam Denly
BORN: March 16, 1986, Canterbury, Kent
SQUAD NO: 6
HEIGHT: 6ft
NICKNAME: JD, Denners, No Pants
EDUCATION: Chaucer Technology School, Canterbury
TEAMS: England, Kent, Barisal Burners, Brothers Union, Karachi Kings, Kolkata Knight Riders, Middlesex, Sydney Sixers
ROLE: Batsman
DEBUT: Test: 2019; ODI: 2009; T20I: 2009; First-class: 2004; List A: 2004; T20: 2004

BEST BATTING: 227 Kent vs Worcestershire, Worcester, 2017
BEST BOWLING: 3-43 Kent vs Surrey, The Oval, 2011
COUNTY CAP: 2008 (Kent); 2012 (Middlesex); BENEFIT: 2019 (Kent)

WHAT WAS YOUR FIRST CRICKET CLUB? Whitstable CC, Kent
WHO WOULD YOU ASK TO BAT FOR YOUR LIFE? Not Mitch Claydon. Probably Rob Key – he was one of the toughest to get out
WHICH RULE WOULD YOU CHANGE ABOUT CRICKET? They should introduce specialist fielders that just field and do nothing else
YOUR BIGGEST CRICKETING REGRET? Not got any... yet
ODDEST SPORT YOU'VE PLAYED? Tedball
TWITTER: @joed1986

Batting	Mat	Inns	NO	Runs	HS	Ave	SR	100	50	Ct	St
Tests	2	4	0	112	69	28.00	47.86	0	1	0	0
ODIs	9	9	0	268	67	29.77	65.52	0	2	5	0
T20Is	9	8	0	72	30	9.00	88.88	0	0	2	0
First-class	191	329	23	11098	227	36.26	56.28	27	55	78	0
List A	151	145	16	4668	150*	36.18	76.63	8	23	52	0
T20s	202	195	16	5033	127	28.11	122.07	4	30	80	0
Bowling	**Mat**	**Balls**	**Runs**	**Wkts**	**BBI**	**BBM**	**Ave**	**Econ**	**SR**	**5w**	**10**
Tests	2	24	17	0	-	-	-	4.25	-	0	0
ODIs	9	-	-	-	-	-	-	-	-	-	-
T20Is	9	60	70	7	4/19	4/19	10.00	7.00	8.5	0	0
First-class	191	4286	2312	62	4/36	6/114	37.29	3.23	69.1	0	0
List A	151	1304	1098	46	4/35	4/35	23.86	5.05	28.3	0	0
T20s	202	475	622	31	4/19	4/19	20.06	7.85	15.3	0	0

GLOUCESTERSHIRE

CHRIS DENT

LHB / SLA / WK / R3 / W0

FULL NAME: Christopher David James Dent
BORN: January 20, 1991, Bristol
SQUAD NO: 15
HEIGHT: 5ft 9in
NICKNAME: Denty
EDUCATION: Backwell School, North Somerset; SGS Filton College, Bristol
TEAMS: Gloucestershire
ROLE: Batsman
DEBUT: First-class: 2010; List A: 2009; T20: 2010

BEST BATTING: 268 Gloucestershire vs Glamorgan, Bristol, 2015
BEST BOWLING: 2-21 Gloucestershire vs Sussex, Hove, 2016
COUNTY CAP: 2010

WHAT WAS YOUR FIRST CRICKET CLUB? Cleeve CC, Somerset
WHICH BOWLER WOULD YOU LEAST LIKE TO FACE? Darren Stevens – always hits my shin
BEST INNINGS YOU'VE SEEN? Michael Klinger's 137 not out in the 2015 One-Day Cup semi-final at Headingley. I was so nervous but he and Hamish Marshall calmly knocked the runs off
WHO WOULD YOU ASK TO BAT FOR YOUR LIFE? Kane Williamson. Even when he was playing for us when he was younger, he was a step above the rest
WHICH RULE WOULD YOU CHANGE ABOUT CRICKET? If you hit the ball against the stumps at the other end, it's worth five runs (unless the bowler touches it)
YOUR BIGGEST CRICKETING REGRET? Every time I was out in the 90s trying to hit a six
WHAT WILL YOU BE DOING IN THE YEAR 2040? I'll be renovating houses
FAVOURITE QUOTE OR SAYING? There's no failure – just feedback
WHICH BOOK MEANS MOST TO YOU? Mind Gym – Achieve More by Thinking Differently by Sebastian Bailey and Octavius Black
TWITTER: @cdent15

Batting	Mat	Inns	NO	Runs	HS	Ave	SR	100	50	Ct	St
First-class	129	232	22	7894	268	37.59	51.86	14	47	148	0
List A	61	56	5	1559	151*	30.56	95.06	3	4	20	0
T20s	49	43	7	725	63*	20.13	116.37	0	3	17	0

Bowling	Mat	Balls	Runs	Wkts	BBI	BBM	Ave	Econ	SR	5w	10
First-class	129	1206	795	8	2/21	2/21	99.37	3.95	150.7	0	0
List A	61	438	412	12	4/43	4/43	34.33	5.64	36.5	0	0
T20s	49	120	168	5	1/4	1/4	33.60	8.40	24.0	0	0

JADE DERNBACH RHB / RFM / R0 / W1 / MVP78

FULL NAME: Jade Winston Dernbach
BORN: March 3, 1986, Johannesburg, South Africa
SQUAD NO: 16
HEIGHT: 6ft 2in
NICKNAME: El Jefe
EDUCATION: St John the Baptist School, Woking
TEAMS: England, Surrey, Melbourne Stars, Wellington
ROLE: Bowler
DEBUT: ODI: 2011; T20I: 2011; First-class: 2003; List A: 2005; T20: 2005

BEST BATTING: 56* Surrey vs Northamptonshire, Northampton, 2011
BEST BOWLING: 6-47 Surrey vs Leicestershire, Leicester, 2010
COUNTY CAP: 2011

WHAT WAS YOUR FIRST CRICKET CLUB? Old Woking Remnants CC, Surrey. Where dreams are made
FAVOURITE CRICKET BAT? My first love, an SS Turbo
WHICH BOWLER WOULD YOU LEAST LIKE TO FACE? Morne Morkel
BEST INNINGS YOU'VE SEEN? Kumar Sangakkara's 130 not out to take us to a one-wicket win in the quarter-final of the 2016 One-Day Cup
WHO WOULD YOU ASK TO BAT FOR YOUR LIFE? Kumar – he has it all
YOUR BIGGEST CRICKETING REGRET? Not being a batsman
WHAT WILL YOU BE DOING IN THE YEAR 2040? I'll be Santa's right-hand man
WHICH BOOK MEANS MOST TO YOU? ECB Rules and Regulations
ODDEST SPORT YOU'VE PLAYED? Synchronised swimming
TWITTER: @jwd_16

Batting	Mat	Inns	NO	Runs	HS	Ave	SR	100	50	Ct	St
ODIs	24	8	1	19	5	2.71	48.71	0	0	5	0
T20Is	34	7	2	24	12	4.80	114.28	0	0	8	0
First-class	113	139	47	871	56*	9.46	49.91	0	1	17	0
List A	144	51	19	242	31	7.56	82.59	0	0	31	0
T20s	145	33	15	143	24*	7.94	109.16	0	0	34	0
Bowling	**Mat**	**Balls**	**Runs**	**Wkts**	**BBI**	**BBM**	**Ave**	**Econ**	**SR**	**5w**	**10**
ODIs	24	1234	1308	31	4/45	4/45	42.19	6.35	39.8	0	0
T20Is	34	702	1020	39	4/22	4/22	26.15	8.71	18.0	0	0
First-class	113	18222	10139	311	6/47	9/138	32.60	3.33	58.5	10	0
List A	144	6283	6181	228	6/35	6/35	27.10	5.90	27.5	3	0
T20s	145	2935	4149	158	4/22	4/22	26.25	8.48	18.5	0	0

NEIL DEXTER

RHB / RM / R0 / W0

LEICESTERSHIRE

FULL NAME: Neil John Dexter
BORN: August 21, 1984, Johannesburg, South Africa
SQUAD NO: 17
HEIGHT: 5ft 11in
NICKNAME: Dexy, Dex, Sexy Dexy
EDUCATION: Northwood School, Durban; University of South Africa
TEAMS: Leicestershire, Essex, Kent, Middlesex
ROLE: Allrounder
DEBUT: First-class: 2005; List A: 2005; T20: 2006

BEST BATTING: 163* Middlesex vs Northamptonshire, Northampton, 2014
BEST BOWLING: 6-63 Middlesex vs Lancashire, Lord's, 2014
COUNTY CAP: 2010 (Middlesex)

'ROY OF THE ROVERS' MOMENT? Taking six wickets against Lancashire and reaching my PB with the bat against Northants in 2014
CRICKETING HEROES? Brett Lee – fast and aggressive but played the game in the right spirit. AB de Villiers – the best player in the world and very humble
NON-CRICKETING HEROES? My family, as they are my No.1 fans
IF YOU WEREN'T A CRICKETER? I'd be a scientist
TWITTER: @dexy214
NOTES: The former Middlesex allrounder signed a one-year extension to his contract in October. Leicestershire head coach Paul Nixon said: "Dex has shown his quality in all formats of the game. He played nicely in the middle order in first-class cricket and took on a new role at the top of the order in the T20 Blast. He is a calming influence at the crease, a good bowler who has shown that he can adapt to different roles, and a fine fielder"

Batting	Mat	Inns	NO	Runs	HS	Ave	SR	100	50	Ct	St
First-class	153	257	30	7875	163*	34.69	51.15	17	37	97	0
List A	108	90	20	2070	135*	29.57	81.75	2	9	27	0
T20s	130	107	15	1846	73	20.06	113.53	0	3	47	0
Bowling	**Mat**	**Balls**	**Runs**	**Wkts**	**BBI**	**BBM**	**Ave**	**Econ**	**SR**	**5w**	**10**
First-class	153	10348	5385	166	6/63	6/47	32.43	3.12	62.3	6	0
List A	108	2457	2316	48	4/22	4/22	48.25	5.65	51.1	0	0
T20s	130	1487	1876	66	4/21	4/21	28.42	7.56	22.5	0	0

SEAN DICKSON RHB / RM / R0 / W0

FULL NAME: Sean Robert Dickson
BORN: September 2, 1991, Johannesburg, South Africa
SQUAD NO: 58
HEIGHT: 5ft 10in
NICKNAME: Dicko
EDUCATION: King Edward VII School, Johannesburg; University of Pretoria
TEAMS: Kent, Northerns
ROLE: Batsman
DEBUT: First-class: 2013; List A: 2013; T20: 2014

BEST BATTING: 318 Kent vs Northamptonshire, Beckenham, 2017
BEST BOWLING: 1-15 Northerns vs Griqualand West, Centurion, 2015

FAVOURITE CRICKET BAT? GM Neon LE – the bat that stuck with me through my triple hundred against Northants in 2017. It's framed and will be on my wall forever
WHICH BOWLER WOULD YOU LEAST LIKE TO FACE? Curtly Ambrose
BEST INNINGS YOU'VE SEEN? Herschelle Gibbs against Australia in the 438 game
WHO WOULD YOU ASK TO BAT FOR YOUR LIFE? Gary Kirsten – an absolute master act. He took shots in the trenches all day and still battled on
WHICH RULE WOULD YOU CHANGE ABOUT CRICKET? Offer eight runs for hitting the ball out of the ground
FAVOURITE QUOTE OR SAYING? Every struggle you had in your life shaped you into the person you are today. Be thankful for the hard times – they can only make you stronger
WHICH BOOK MEANS MOST TO YOU? Legacy – What the All Blacks Can Teach Us About the Business of Life by James Kerr
TWITTER: @Seano_146

Batting	Mat	Inns	NO	Runs	HS	Ave	SR	100	50	Ct	St
First-class	57	94	7	3068	318	35.26	52.09	7	13	46	0
List A	38	34	2	956	99	29.87	75.93	0	8	13	0
T20s	17	12	4	226	53	28.25	126.25	0	1	11	0
Bowling	**Mat**	**Balls**	**Runs**	**Wkts**	**BBI**	**BBM**	**Ave**	**Econ**	**SR**	**5w**	**10**
First-class	57	72	44	2	1/15	2/40	22.00	3.66	36.0	0	0
List A	38	-	-	-	-	-	-	-	-	-	-
T20s	17	6	9	1	1/9	1/9	9.00	9.00	6.0	0	0

ANEURIN DONALD

RHB / OB / R1 / W0

FULL NAME: Aneurin Henry Thomas Donald
BORN: December 20, 1996, Swansea, Wales
SQUAD NO: 12
HEIGHT: 6ft 3in
NICKNAME: Sir Don, The Don
EDUCATION: Pontarddulais Comprehensive School, Swansea; Gower College Swansea
TEAMS: Hampshire, Glamorgan
ROLE: Batsman
DEBUT: First-class: 2014; List A: 2015; T20: 2015

BEST BATTING: 234 Glamorgan vs Derbyshire, Colwyn Bay, 2016

FAMILY TIES? My grand-uncle, Bernard Hedges, scored the first one-day century for Glamorgan. My brother Gafyn played Wales age-group cricket and plays in the Welsh Premier League for Pontarddulais CC
CRICKETING HERO? Kevin Pietersen
SURPRISING FACT? When I used to net with my brother and father on a Saturday morning, rugby international Leigh Halfpenny would be there every week practising his goal-kicking. I never had the courage to ask him to feed the bowling machine
TWITTER: @AneurinDonald12
NOTES: Seen as the brightest of Glamorgan's young Welsh talents, Donald made an extraordinary 234 from 136 balls against Derbyshire at Colwyn Bay in 2016 when he was 19. It equalled the record for the fastest double century in first-class cricket (123 balls). But he has been unable to live up to those expectations since and turned down a three-year contract renewal last August to sign a two-year deal with Hampshire in the hope of reviving his career. At 22 years old, there is plenty of time

Batting	Mat	Inns	NO	Runs	HS	Ave	SR	100	50	Ct	St
First-class	39	71	4	2056	234	30.68	71.01	2	13	31	0
List A	23	20	0	293	53	14.65	80.71	0	1	10	0
T20s	43	39	3	724	76	20.11	136.09	0	4	26	0
Bowling	**Mat**	**Balls**	**Runs**	**Wkts**	**BBI**	**BBM**	**Ave**	**Econ**	**SR**	**5w**	**10**
First-class	39	-	-	-	-	-	-	-	-	-	-
List A	23	-	-	-	-	-	-	-	-	-	-
T20s	43	-	-	-	-	-	-	-	-	-	-

GEORGE DRISSELL

RHB / OB / R0 / W0

FULL NAME: George Samuel Drissell
BORN: January 20, 1999, Bristol
SQUAD NO: 20
HEIGHT: 6ft 2in
NICKNAME: Dris, Lemon, Lethal
EDUCATION: Bedminster Down Secondary School, Bristol; SGS Filton College
TEAMS: Gloucestershire
ROLE: Allrounder
DEBUT: First-class: 2017; List A: 2018

BEST BATTING: 19 Gloucestershire vs Warwickshire, Edgbaston, 2018
BEST BOWLING: 2-38 Gloucestershire vs Sussex, Cheltenham, 2018

WHAT WAS YOUR FIRST CRICKET CLUB? Bedminster CC, Bristol, where you can see the Clifton Suspension Bridge in the background. I also played football for Bedminster Cricketers FC
FAVOURITE CRICKET BAT? Gray-Nicolls Dynadrive – played with it for two seasons and it's still alive and well today
CRICKETING HERO? Graeme Swann
WHICH BOWLER WOULD YOU LEAST LIKE TO FACE? Mitchell Starc
BEST INNINGS YOU'VE SEEN? Alastair Cook's final Test innings
WHO WOULD YOU ASK TO BAT FOR YOUR LIFE? Kane Williamson – technical genius
SURPRISING FACT ABOUT YOU? I'm a big fan of Bristol City FC
WHAT WILL YOU BE DOING IN THE YEAR 2040? I'll be the captain of Bedminster CC and winning the West of England Premier League for the 20th time
TWITTER: @GeorgeDrissell

Batting	Mat	Inns	NO	Runs	HS	Ave	SR	100	50	Ct	St
First-class	6	10	0	76	19	7.60	31.02	0	0	0	0
List A	1	1	0	0	0	0.00	0.00	0	0	0	0
Bowling	**Mat**	**Balls**	**Runs**	**Wkts**	**BBI**	**BBM**	**Ave**	**Econ**	**SR**	**5w**	**10**
First-class	6	570	330	4	2/38	2/58	82.50	3.47	142.5	0	0
List A	1	42	45	0	-	-	-	6.42	-	0	0

BEN DUCKETT LHB / OB / WK / R2 / W0 / MVP97

FULL NAME: Ben Matthew Duckett
BORN: October 17, 1994, Farnborough, Kent
SQUAD NO: 17
HEIGHT: 5ft 9in
NICKNAME: Ducky, Tyrian
EDUCATION: Millfield School, Somerset; Winchester House School; Stowe School
TEAMS: England, Nottinghamshire, Hobart Hurricanes, Nelson Mandela Bay Giants, Northamptonshire, Islamabad United
ROLE: Batsman
DEBUT: Test: 2016; ODI: 2016; First-class: 2013; List A: 2013; T20: 2012

BEST BATTING: 282* Northamptonshire vs Sussex, Northampton, 2016
BEST BOWLING: 1-21 Northamptonshire vs Kent, Beckenham, 2017
COUNTY CAP: 2016 (Northamptonshire)

WHAT WAS YOUR FIRST CRICKET CLUB? Glastonbury CC, Somerset
BEST INNINGS YOU'VE SEEN? Ben Stokes's double hundred at Cape Town in 2016
WHO WOULD YOU ASK TO BAT FOR YOUR LIFE? Cheteshwar Pujara
WHICH RULE WOULD YOU CHANGE ABOUT CRICKET? Bring in free hits in four-day cricket
YOUR BIGGEST CRICKETING REGRET? Coming back a few weeks earlier than I should have done after my hand operation in 2018
SURPRISING FACT ABOUT YOU? I have a tattoo of a duck with the number 17 and a cricket bat on one side of my bottom
WHICH BOOK MEANS MOST TO YOU? Horrid Henry by Francesca Simon (that was the last book I read)
TWITTER: @benduckett1

Batting	Mat	Inns	NO	Runs	HS	Ave	SR	100	50	Ct	St
Tests	4	7	0	110	56	15.71	57.89	0	1	1	0
ODIs	3	3	0	123	63	41.00	80.92	0	2	0	0
First-class	76	131	7	4818	282*	38.85	71.71	14	23	59	3
List A	66	61	7	2196	220*	40.66	98.60	3	15	32	3
T20s	83	78	16	1836	96	29.61	132.37	0	9	29	2
Bowling	**Mat**	**Balls**	**Runs**	**Wkts**	**BBI**	**BBM**	**Ave**	**Econ**	**SR**	**5w**	**10**
Tests	4	-	-	-	-	-	-	-	-	-	-
ODIs	3	-	-	-	-	-	-	-	-	-	-
First-class	76	59	49	1	1/21	1/32	49.00	4.98	59.0	0	0
List A	66	-	-	-	-	-	-	-	-	-	-
T20s	83	-	-	-	-	-	-	-	-	-	-

MATT DUNN

LHB / RFM / R0 / W0

FULL NAME: Matthew Peter Dunn
BORN: May 5, 1992, Egham, Surrey
SQUAD NO: 4
HEIGHT: 6ft 1in
NICKNAME: Dunny
EDUCATION: Bishopsgate School; Bearwood College, Wokingham
TEAMS: Surrey
ROLE: Bowler
DEBUT: First-class: 2010; List A: 2011; T20: 2013

BEST BATTING: 31* Surrey vs Kent, Guildford, 2014
BEST BOWLING: 5-48 Surrey vs Gloucestershire, The Oval, 2014

WHAT WAS YOUR FIRST CRICKET CLUB? Egham CC, Surrey
FAVOURITE CRICKET BAT? Kookaburra Bubble
WHICH BOWLER WOULD YOU LEAST LIKE TO FACE? Fidel Edwards – he has already broken my rib once
BEST INNINGS YOU'VE SEEN? Aaron Finch's hundred against Middlesex at The Oval in the 2018 T20 Blast
WHO WOULD YOU ASK TO BAT FOR YOUR LIFE? Rory Burns
YOUR BIGGEST CRICKETING REGRET? Not working on my batting from a younger age
SURPRISING FACT ABOUT YOU? I lived in Norway when I was younger, and I can breakdance. And I absolutely love coffee
WHAT WILL YOU BE DOING IN THE YEAR 2040? Hopefully I'll own a coffee shop
FAVOURITE QUOTE OR SAYING? You wouldn't want a warm beer, would you?
ODDEST SPORT YOU'VE PLAYED? Egg-tossing
TWITTER: @MatthewDunn05

Batting	Mat	Inns	NO	Runs	HS	Ave	SR	100	50	Ct	St
First-class	36	38	18	143	31*	7.15	20.75	0	0	7	0
List A	1	-	-	-	-	-	-	-	-	1	0
T20s	16	2	0	3	2	1.50	60.00	0	0	4	0
Bowling	**Mat**	**Balls**	**Runs**	**Wkts**	**BBI**	**BBM**	**Ave**	**Econ**	**SR**	**5w**	**10**
First-class	36	5329	3576	99	5/48	6/84	36.12	4.02	53.8	3	0
List A	1	36	32	2	2/32	2/32	16.00	5.33	18.0	0	0
T20s	16	300	450	22	3/8	3/8	20.45	9.00	13.6	0	0

BRETT D'OLIVEIRA RHB / LB / R0 / W0 / MVP85

FULL NAME: Brett Louis D'Oliveira
BORN: February 28, 1992, Worcester
SQUAD NO: 15
HEIGHT: 5ft 8in
NICKNAME: Dolly
EDUCATION: Blessed Edward Oldcorne Catholic College, Worcester; Worcester Sixth Form College
TEAMS: Worcestershire, England Lions
ROLE: Allrounder
DEBUT: First-class: 2012; List A: 2011; T20: 2012

BEST BATTING: 202* Worcestershire vs Glamorgan, Cardiff, 2016
BEST BOWLING: 5-48 Worcestershire vs Durham, Chester-le-Street, 2015

FAMILY TIES? My grandad Basil played for England and Worcestershire and also went on to coach Worcestershire. My dad Damian played for Worcestershire and went on to be assistant coach and Academy director
WHAT WAS YOUR FIRST CRICKET CLUB? Worcester Dominies and Guild CC
FAVOURITE CRICKET BAT? A Duncan Fearnley Gold given to me by Vikram Solanki
CRICKETING HERO? Shane Warne
WHICH BOWLER WOULD YOU LEAST LIKE TO FACE? Saeed Ajmal
WHO WOULD YOU ASK TO BAT FOR YOUR LIFE? Virat Kohli
SURPRISING FACT ABOUT YOU? I've got a coaching qualification in basketball
SURPRISING FACT ABOUT A TEAMMATE? There are rumours that Joe Leach puts sprinkles in his hair
FAVOURITE QUOTE OR SAYING? The more I practise, the luckier I get
TWITTER: @Bdolly09

Batting	Mat	Inns	NO	Runs	HS	Ave	SR	100	50	Ct	St
First-class	52	92	2	2495	202*	27.72	54.40	6	6	25	0
List A	57	47	11	919	79	25.52	87.85	0	5	23	0
T20s	78	55	18	922	64	24.91	127.34	0	4	17	0
Bowling	**Mat**	**Balls**	**Runs**	**Wkts**	**BBI**	**BBM**	**Ave**	**Econ**	**SR**	**5w**	**10**
First-class	52	3348	1981	37	5/48	7/133	53.54	3.55	90.4	1	0
List A	57	2174	1901	44	3/35	3/35	43.20	5.24	49.4	0	0
T20s	78	1050	1344	40	4/26	4/26	33.60	7.68	26.2	0	0

FIDEL EDWARDS RHB / RF / R0 / W1 / MVP74

FULL NAME: Fidel Henderson Edwards
BORN: February 6, 1982, Gays, Barbados
SQUAD NO: 82
HEIGHT: 5ft 8in
NICKNAME: Castro
TEAMS: West Indies, Hampshire, Barbados, Deccan Chargers, Dolphins, Rajasthan Royals, St Lucia Zouks, Sydney Thunder, Sylhet Superstars, Trinidad & Tobago Red Steel
ROLE: Bowler
DEBUT: Test: 2003; ODI: 2003; T20I: 2007; First-class: 2001; List A: 2003; T20: 2007

BEST BATTING: 40 Barbados vs Jamaica, Bridgetown, 2008
BEST BOWLING: 7-87 West Indies vs New Zealand, Napier, 2008

TWITTER: @EdwardsFidel
NOTES: The slingy Barbadian fast bowler is entering his fifth season at Hampshire as a Kolpak player. In January he signed a contract to play only red-ball cricket in 2019. Edwards was first drafted into Hampshire's squad in 2015 and took 45 wickets in eight games to help his county stave off relegation in the Championship. The following year was blighted by injury but he came back to collect 30 Championship wickets in 2017. Last summer he was an ever-present in the four-day side, taking 54 wickets at 26.72. Edwards took five wickets on Test debut in 2003 after playing just one match for Barbados and being spotted in the nets by Brian Lara. He played the last of his 55 Tests in 2012

Batting	Mat	Inns	NO	Runs	HS	Ave	SR	100	50	Ct	St
Tests	55	88	28	394	30	6.56	28.20	0	0	10	0
ODIs	50	22	14	73	13	9.12	45.62	0	0	4	0
T20Is	20	4	2	10	7*	5.00	111.11	0	0	5	0
First-class	123	173	65	757	40	7.00	30.34	0	0	23	0
List A	89	36	20	138	21*	8.62	40.76	0	0	11	0
T20s	93	30	14	102	11*	6.37	86.44	0	0	12	0
Bowling	**Mat**	**Balls**	**Runs**	**Wkts**	**BBI**	**BBM**	**Ave**	**Econ**	**SR**	**5w**	**10**
Tests	55	9602	6249	165	7/87	8/132	37.87	3.90	58.1	12	0
ODIs	50	2138	1812	60	6/22	6/22	30.20	5.08	35.6	2	0
T20Is	20	360	497	16	3/23	3/23	31.06	8.28	22.5	0	0
First-class	123	19333	12485	405	7/87	10/83	30.82	3.87	47.7	23	2
List A	89	3984	3440	115	6/22	6/22	29.91	5.18	34.6	3	0
T20s	93	1870	2399	87	5/22	5/22	27.57	7.69	21.4	1	0

DEAN ELGAR LHB / SLA / R0 / W0

FULL NAME: Dean Elgar
BORN: June 11, 1987, Welkom, Orange Free State, South Africa
SQUAD NO: 64
TEAMS: South Africa, Surrey, Eagles, Free State, Knights, Northerns, Somerset, Titans, Tshwane Spartans
ROLE: Batsman
DEBUT: Test: 2012; ODI: 2012; First-class: 2006; List A: 2006; T20: 2008

BEST BATTING: 268 South Africa A vs Australia A, Pretoria, 2013
BEST BOWLING: 4-22 South Africa vs India, Mohali, 2015

TWITTER: @deanelgar
NOTES: South Africa's Test opening batsman returns for a third stint at Surrey, for whom he made 387 runs in seven Championship matches last season, including one century. The gritty left-hander, who has captained his country at Test level, is due to arrive at the end of April and remain at The Oval until the end of the season as the club's overseas player, subject to international commitments. Elgar has also played county cricket for Somerset, making 519 runs at an average of 103.80 in the 2017 One-Day Cup, along with another 517 runs in six Championship matches that summer

Batting	Mat	Inns	NO	Runs	HS	Ave	SR	100	50	Ct	St
Tests	56	96	8	3412	199	38.77	45.29	11	13	59	0
ODIs	8	7	1	104	42	17.33	58.75	0	0	4	0
First-class	188	326	26	12909	268	43.03	49.47	39	47	153	0
List A	149	143	21	5170	137	42.37	80.17	6	38	46	0
T20s	66	61	15	1633	79*	35.50	112.46	0	9	27	0
Bowling	**Mat**	**Balls**	**Runs**	**Wkts**	**BBI**	**BBM**	**Ave**	**Econ**	**SR**	**5w**	**10**
Tests	56	987	623	14	4/22	4/56	44.50	3.78	70.5	0	0
ODIs	8	96	67	2	1/11	1/11	33.50	4.18	48.0	0	0
First-class	188	4002	2693	53	4/22	5/141	50.81	4.03	75.5	0	0
List A	149	2741	2493	52	3/43	3/43	47.94	5.45	52.7	0	0
T20s	66	615	701	29	4/23	4/23	24.17	6.83	21.2	0	0

STEVIE ESKINAZI

RHB / WK / R0 / W0

FULL NAME: Stephen Sean Eskinazi
BORN: March 28, 1994, Johannesburg, South Africa
SQUAD NO: 28
HEIGHT: 6ft 2in
NICKNAME: Eski, Esk, GOAT
EDUCATION: Christ Church Grammar School, Perth; University of Western Australia; University of Hertfordshire
TEAMS: Middlesex
ROLE: Batsman/wicketkeeper
DEBUT: First-class: 2015; List A: 2018; T20: 2016

BEST BATTING: 179 Middlesex vs Warwickshire, Edgbaston, 2017

FAMILY TIES? My dad played a good standard of club cricket in South Africa
WHAT WAS YOUR FIRST CRICKET CLUB? Fair Oak CC, Hampshire. I drive past it every time I go to the Ageas Bowl but haven't been back there since I was seven
FAVOURITE CRICKET BAT? Gray-Nicolls Predator – it lasted 24 backyard seasons
BEST INNINGS YOU'VE SEEN? Tim Murtagh's 47 against Yorkshire at Scarborough in 2016 which helped set up victory by an innings
YOUR BIGGEST CRICKETING REGRET? Giving up my medium-pace bowling
SURPRISING FACT ABOUT YOU? I could have four passports (if that was legal)
WHAT WILL YOU BE DOING IN THE YEAR 2040? Telling people how hard it was in my day
FAVOURITE QUOTE OR SAYING? We are the music makers and we are the dreamers of the dreams (Arthur O'Shaughnessy)
WHICH BOOK MEANS MOST TO YOU? Make Your Bed – Little Things That Can Change Your Life... And Maybe the World by William McRaven
ODDEST SPORT YOU'VE PLAYED? Floorball
TWITTER: @seskinazi

Batting	Mat	Inns	NO	Runs	HS	Ave	SR	100	50	Ct	St
First-class	38	67	4	2346	179	37.23	55.63	5	11	32	0
List A	8	7	0	169	49	24.14	70.41	0	0	3	0
T20s	18	17	2	456	57*	30.40	129.54	0	3	7	0

Bowling	Mat	Balls	Runs	Wkts	BBI	BBM	Ave	Econ	SR	5w	10
First-class	38	-	-	-	-	-	-	-	-	-	-
List A	8	-	-	-	-	-	-	-	-	-	-
T20s	18	-	-	-	-	-	-	-	-	-	-

LAURIE EVANS RHB / RM / R0 / W0 / MVP99

FULL NAME: Laurie John Evans
BORN: October 12, 1987, Lambeth, London
SQUAD NO: 32
HEIGHT: 6ft
NICKNAME: Loz
EDUCATION: Whitgift School; The John Fisher School, Purley; Durham University
TEAMS: Sussex, Kabul Zwanan, Multan Sultans, Northamptonshire, Rajshahi Kings, Surrey, Warwickshire
ROLE: Batsman
DEBUT: First-class: 2007; List A: 2009; T20: 2009

BEST BATTING: 213* Warwickshire vs Sussex, Edgbaston, 2015
BEST BOWLING: 1-29 Warwickshire vs Sussex, Edgbaston, 2015

FAVOURITE CRICKET BAT? A size-six Salix which I used when I was 13
CRICKETING HERO? Brian Lara
WHICH BOWLER WOULD YOU LEAST LIKE TO FACE? Darren Stevens
BEST INNINGS YOU'VE SEEN? Brendon McCullum's 158 not out in the first-ever IPL match
WHO WOULD YOU ASK TO BAT FOR YOUR LIFE? Jonathan Trott
WHICH RULE WOULD YOU CHANGE ABOUT CRICKET? The T20 time-restrictions by which the fielding side must have bowled 20 overs
YOUR BIGGEST CRICKETING REGRET? Not batting higher up the order in T20 cricket
FAVOURITE QUOTE OR SAYING? Everything but the kitchen sink
WHICH BOOK MEANS MOST TO YOU? A book about the rules of golf
ODDEST SPORT YOU'VE PLAYED? Tiddlywinks
TWITTER: @laurieevans32

Batting	Mat	Inns	NO	Runs	HS	Ave	SR	100	50	Ct	St
First-class	60	103	6	3020	213*	31.13	45.28	5	16	49	0
List A	55	49	11	1400	134*	36.84	97.02	2	4	24	0
T20s	118	105	26	2555	104*	32.34	129.56	1	18	51	0
Bowling	**Mat**	**Balls**	**Runs**	**Wkts**	**BBI**	**BBM**	**Ave**	**Econ**	**SR**	**5w**	**10**
First-class	60	354	259	2	1/29	1/29	129.50	4.38	177.0	0	0
List A	55	36	53	0	-	-	-	8.83	-	0	0
T20s	118	22	35	1	1/5	1/5	35.00	9.54	22.0	0	0

SAM EVANS RHB / R0 / W0

FULL NAME: Samuel Thomes Evans
BORN: December 20, 1997, Leicester
SQUAD NO: 21
HEIGHT: 5ft 8in
NICKNAME: Smevs
EDUCATION: Lancaster Boys School, Leicester; Wyggeston QE I College; Loughborough University
TEAMS: Leicestershire
ROLE: Batsman
DEBUT: First-class: 2017; List A: 2018

BEST BATTING: 114 Loughborough MCCU vs Northamptonshire, Northampton, 2017

WHAT GOT YOU INTO CRICKET? Playing cricket in the garden with my dad
BEST ADVICE EVER RECEIVED? You'll have more bad days than good so enjoy the good ones
'ROY OF THE ROVERS' MOMENT? Making my first-class debut in 2017
BEST THING ABOUT YOUR HOME GROUND? The lovely food
IF YOU WEREN'T A CRICKETER? I'd be a student
SURPRISING FACT ABOUT YOU? I go to Loughborough University and am one of the few who is not studying sports science
CRICKETING HERO? Ricky Ponting – he made batting look elegant and easy
NON-CRICKETING HERO? Jamie Vardy – for his tenacity and desire. He started at the bottom and made it to the top
TWITTER: @SamEvans97

Batting	Mat	Inns	NO	Runs	HS	Ave	SR	100	50	Ct	St
First-class	8	12	1	248	114	22.54	43.05	1	0	2	0
List A	1	1	0	20	20	20.00	71.42	0	0	0	0
Bowling	**Mat**	**Balls**	**Runs**	**Wkts**	**BBI**	**BBM**	**Ave**	**Econ**	**SR**	**5w**	**10**
First-class	8	36	24	0	-	-	-	4.00	-	0	0
List A	1	-	-	-	-	-	-	-	-	-	-

JAMES FAULKNER

RHB / LFM / R0 / W0

FULL NAME: James Peter Faulkner
BORN: April 29, 1990, Launceston, Tasmania, Australia
SQUAD NO: 44
HEIGHT: 6ft 1in
TEAMS: Australia, Lancashire, Gujarat Lions, Hobart Hurricanes, Kings XI Punjab, Melbourne Stars, Pune Warriors, Rajasthan Royals, Tasmania
ROLE: Allrounder
DEBUT: Test: 2013; ODI: 2013; T20I: 2012; First-class: 2008; List A: 2008; T20: 2009

BEST BATTING: 121 Lancashire vs Surrey, The Oval, 2015
BEST BOWLING: 5-5 Tasmania vs South Australia, Hobart, 2010

TWITTER: @JamesFaulkner44
NOTES: The Australian allrounder played a starring role in Lancashire's 2015 T20 title win, scoring 302 runs and taking 25 wickets, and in December 2017 he signed a two-year T20 contract with the club. He struggled with the bat last summer but was typically effective with the ball, taking 20 wickets with an economy-rate of 7.68. Faulkner, a canny left-arm seamer who excels as a death bowler, was Man of the Match in the 2015 World Cup final against New Zealand and was the first Australian to take a five-for in T20Is, claiming 5-27 against Pakistan at the 2016 World T20. He is no slouch with the bat, hitting 116 from 57 balls in an ODI against India in Bangalore in 2013. His sole Test appearance was in the final game of the 2013 Ashes

Batting	Mat	Inns	NO	Runs	HS	Ave	SR	100	50	Ct	St
Tests	1	2	0	45	23	22.50	104.65	0	0	0	0
ODIs	69	52	22	1032	116	34.40	104.24	1	4	21	0
T20Is	24	18	7	159	41*	14.45	115.21	0	0	11	0
First-class	63	95	12	2566	121	30.91	50.91	2	15	26	0
List A	121	94	30	1936	116	30.25	91.45	1	10	34	0
T20s	187	136	58	1689	73	21.65	122.39	0	1	59	0
Bowling	**Mat**	**Balls**	**Runs**	**Wkts**	**BBI**	**BBM**	**Ave**	**Econ**	**SR**	**5w**	**10**
Tests	1	166	98	6	4/51	6/98	16.33	3.54	27.6	0	0
ODIs	69	3211	2962	96	4/32	4/32	30.85	5.53	33.4	0	0
T20Is	24	515	684	36	5/27	5/27	19.00	7.96	14.3	1	0
First-class	63	9776	4759	192	5/5	8/97	24.78	2.92	50.9	5	0
List A	121	5719	5102	168	4/20	4/20	30.36	5.35	34.0	0	0
T20s	187	3782	5019	214	5/16	5/16	23.45	7.96	17.6	3	0

TOM FELL

RHB / OB / R1 / W0

FULL NAME: Thomas Charles Fell
BORN: October 17, 1993, Hillingdon, Middlesex
SQUAD NO: 29
HEIGHT: 6ft 1in
NICKNAME: Lord, Feltch
EDUCATION: Tettenhall College, Wolverhampton; Oakham School, Rutland; Oxford Brookes University
TEAMS: Worcestershire
ROLE: Batsman
DEBUT: First-class: 2013; List A: 2013; T20: 2018

BEST BATTING: 171 Worcestershire vs Middlesex, Worcester, 2015

WHAT WAS YOUR FIRST CRICKET CLUB? Wolverhampton CC, West Midlands. Joined when I was nine and still playing there today
FAVOURITE CRICKET BAT? GM Purist
WHICH BOWLER WOULD YOU LEAST LIKE TO FACE? Joe Leach on a green seamer. Thankfully he's on my team
BEST INNINGS YOU'VE SEEN? Moeen Ali's hundred against Warwickshire at Edgbaston last season. That was my T20 debut and it was a pleasure to watch
WHO WOULD YOU ASK TO BAT FOR YOUR LIFE? Daryl Mitchell – he'd be grubby and find a way to bat all day
TWITTER: @TomFell_29

Batting	Mat	Inns	NO	Runs	HS	Ave	SR	100	50	Ct	St
First-class	73	126	5	3672	171	30.34	50.64	5	16	56	0
List A	36	35	4	1149	116*	37.06	81.60	1	10	11	0
T20s	3	2	0	24	23	12.00	100.00	0	0	2	0
Bowling	**Mat**	**Balls**	**Runs**	**Wkts**	**BBI**	**BBM**	**Ave**	**Econ**	**SR**	**5w**	**10**
First-class	73	20	17	0	-	-	-	5.10	-	0	0
List A	36	-	-	-	-	-	-	-	-	-	-
T20s	3	-	-	-	-	-	-	-	-	-	-

CALLUM FERGUSON RHB / RM / R0 / W0

FULL NAME: Callum James Ferguson
BORN: November 21, 1984, North Adelaide, Australia
SQUAD NO: 5
TEAMS: Australia, Worcestershire, Adelaide Strikers, Melbourne Renegades, Pune Warriors, South Australia, Sydney Thunder
ROLE: Batsman
DEBUT: Test: 2016; ODI: 2009; T20I: 2009; First-class: 2004; List A: 2003; T20: 2006

BEST BATTING: 213 South Australia vs Tasmania, Hobart, 2015
BEST BOWLING: 2-32 South Australia vs Tasmania, Hobart, 2014

TWITTER: @calferguson12
NOTES: Worcestershire have re-signed the 34-year-old Australian batsman to be their overseas player across all formats in 2019. Ferguson made an instant impact at New Road last summer, hitting 192 not out on his debut for the club against Leicestershire – the highest score by a Worcestershire player in one-day cricket. Another One-Day Cup century followed and then a third hundred in the T20 Blast, his 390 runs in 10 innings crucial to Worcestershire lifting the trophy. Ferguson made his ODI and T20I debuts back in 2009 but recurring knee troubles derailed his international career until he was called up for his one and only Test to date in 2016. He has been a very consistent performer for South Australia in the Sheffield Shield over the past few seasons

Batting	Mat	Inns	NO	Runs	HS	Ave	SR	100	50	Ct	St
Tests	1	2	0	4	3	2.00	17.39	0	0	0	0
ODIs	30	25	9	663	71*	41.43	85.32	0	5	7	0
T20Is	3	3	0	16	8	5.33	84.21	0	0	1	0
First-class	127	237	20	8249	213	38.01	52.08	18	43	70	0
List A	160	151	26	5312	192	42.49	86.86	11	30	47	0
T20s	107	99	12	2307	113*	26.51	125.51	2	9	41	0
Bowling	**Mat**	**Balls**	**Runs**	**Wkts**	**BBI**	**BBM**	**Ave**	**Econ**	**SR**	**5w**	**10**
Tests	1	-	-	-	-	-	-	-	-	-	-
ODIs	30	-	-	-	-	-	-	-	-	-	-
T20Is	3	-	-	-	-	-	-	-	-	-	-
First-class	127	149	99	2	2/32	2/32	49.50	3.98	74.5	0	0
List A	160	30	22	1	1/8	1/8	22.00	4.40	30.0	0	0
T20s	107	-	-	-	-	-	-	-	-	-	-

AARON FINCH

RHB / SLA / R0 / W0

FULL NAME: Aaron James Finch
BORN: November 17, 1986, Colac, Victoria, Australia
SQUAD NO: 15
HEIGHT: 5ft 8in
TEAMS: Australia, Surrey, Auckland, Delhi Daredevils, Gujarat Lions, Kings XI Punjab, Melbourne Renegades, Mumbai Indians, Pune Warriors, Rajasthan Royals, Sunrisers Hyderabad, Victoria, Yorkshire
ROLE: Batsman
DEBUT: Test: 2018; ODI: 2013; T20I: 2011; First-class: 2007; List A: 2007; T20: 2009

BEST BATTING: 288* Cricket Australia XI vs New Zealand, Sydney, 2015
BEST BOWLING: 1-0 Victoria vs Western Australia, Perth, 2013

TWITTER: @AaronFinch5
NOTES: The Australia batsman returns to Surrey for his fourth consecutive summer to play in the T20 Blast. A powerful hitter with a simple technique, Finch has been the county's leading run-scorer for the past two seasons, including last summer's extraordinary tally of 589 runs at an average of 147.25. A former T20I captain, Finch became the fastest batsman to score 10 ODI hundreds for Australia (83 innings) in 2018. Despite his white-ball reputation, Finch made his Test debut last October and made two fifties in his first five matches. With the Ashes following the World Cup, Surrey may see less of him this summer

Batting	Mat	Inns	NO	Runs	HS	Ave	SR	100	50	Ct	St
Tests	5	10	0	278	62	27.80	44.98	0	2	7	0
ODIs	103	99	1	3574	148	36.46	88.72	11	19	50	0
T20Is	52	52	7	1671	172	37.13	155.87	2	9	23	0
First-class	83	139	6	4721	288*	35.49	61.39	7	31	78	0
List A	182	178	6	6463	154	37.57	87.97	15	39	77	0
T20s	253	248	27	7835	172	35.45	142.50	6	53	111	0
Bowling	**Mat**	**Balls**	**Runs**	**Wkts**	**BBI**	**BBM**	**Ave**	**Econ**	**SR**	**5w**	**10**
Tests	5	12	8	0	-	-	-	4.00	-	0	0
ODIs	103	176	159	2	1/2	1/2	79.50	5.42	88.0	0	0
T20Is	52	12	27	0	-	-	-	13.50	-	0	0
First-class	83	464	318	5	1/0	1/0	63.60	4.11	92.8	0	0
List A	182	371	340	7	2/44	2/44	48.57	5.49	53.0	0	0
T20s	253	221	340	7	1/9	1/9	48.57	9.23	31.5	0	0

WORCESTERSHIRE

ADAM FINCH RHB / RMF / R0 / W0

FULL NAME: Adam William Finch
BORN: May 28, 2000, Wordsley, Stourbridge, Worcestershire
SQUAD NO: 61
HEIGHT: 6ft 4in
NICKNAME: Finchy
EDUCATION: Kingswinford School, West Midlands; Oldswinford Hospital Sixth Form College, Stourbridge
TEAMS: Worcestershire, England U19
ROLE: Bowler

WHAT WAS YOUR FIRST CRICKET CLUB? Himley CC, Staffordshire. It has one of the best youth systems in the area
FAVOURITE CRICKET BAT? Gray-Nicolls Supernova
WHICH BOWLER WOULD YOU LEAST LIKE TO FACE? Mitchell Johnson
BEST INNINGS YOU'VE SEEN? Alastair Cook's final Test innings
WHO WOULD YOU ASK TO BAT FOR YOUR LIFE? Joe Root
WHICH RULE WOULD YOU CHANGE ABOUT CRICKET? Overthrows being marked down against the bowler
FAVOURITE QUOTE OR SAYING? It's not the size of the dog in the fight, it's the size of the fight in the dog
WHICH BOOK MEANS MOST TO YOU? Harry Potter
ODDEST SPORT YOU'VE PLAYED? Judo
NOTES: The tall seamer, who turns 19 this May, signed a professional contract with Worcestershire in March 2018 after being a member of the England squad in the U19 World Cup in New Zealand earlier that year. Finch made his England U19 debut in 2017 and last summer took match figures of 8-69 at Chester-le-Street to seal victory in the youth Test series against South Africa. He has been a consistent performer for Worcestershire Second XI for the past two years and was part of the Young Lions training camp in Bangalore over the winter before joining the U19 tour of Bangladesh

HARRY FINCH RHB / RM / R0 / W0

FULL NAME: Harry Zacariah Finch
BORN: February 10, 1995, Hastings, Sussex
SQUAD NO: 6
HEIGHT: 5ft 9in
NICKNAME: Chozza, Yoghurt Boy
EDUCATION: St Richard's Catholic College, Bexhill; Eastbourne College
TEAMS: Sussex
ROLE: Batsman
DEBUT: First-class: 2013; List A: 2013; T20: 2014

BEST BATTING: 135* Sussex vs Leeds/Bradford MCCU, Hove, 2016
BEST BOWLING: 1-9 Sussex vs Leeds/Bradford MCCU, Hove, 2016

WHAT WAS YOUR FIRST CRICKET CLUB? Hastings & St Leonards Priory CC, East Sussex
FAVOURITE CRICKET BAT? My MB Malik which I used in the garden as a kid
WHICH BOWLER WOULD YOU LEAST LIKE TO FACE? Steve Magoffin – too good and too sweaty
BEST INNINGS YOU'VE SEEN? Luke Wright's 92 off 53 balls in the T20 semi-final against Somerset last season
WHO WOULD YOU ASK TO BAT FOR YOUR LIFE? Luke 'Dave' Wells
WHICH RULE WOULD YOU CHANGE ABOUT CRICKET? Batsmen should have two lives
YOUR BIGGEST CRICKETING REGRET? Not being 7ft 1in – that would make my seamers useful
WHAT WILL YOU BE DOING IN THE YEAR 2040? Managing Wycombe Wanderers FC to back-to-back relegation
WHICH BOOK MEANS MOST TO YOU? Harry Kane – The Biography by Frank Worrall
TWITTER: @hfinch72

Batting	Mat	Inns	NO	Runs	HS	Ave	SR	100	50	Ct	St
First-class	39	63	5	1728	135*	29.79	52.86	3	11	50	0
List A	28	26	3	961	108	41.78	76.02	1	7	4	0
T20s	19	14	3	193	35*	17.54	106.04	0	0	6	0
Bowling	**Mat**	**Balls**	**Runs**	**Wkts**	**BBI**	**BBM**	**Ave**	**Econ**	**SR**	**5w**	**10**
First-class	39	156	109	2	1/9	1/9	54.50	4.19	78.0	0	0
List A	28	16	24	0	-	-	-	9.00	-	0	0
T20s	19	-	-	-	-	-	-	-	-	-	-

STEVEN FINN RHB / RFM / R0 / W2

FULL NAME: Steven Thomas Finn
BORN: April 4, 1989, Watford, Hertfordshire
SQUAD NO: 9
HEIGHT: 6ft 8in
NICKNAME: Finny, Cyril, Finndog
EDUCATION: Parmiter's School, Watford
TEAMS: England, Middlesex, Islamabad United, Otago
ROLE: Bowler
DEBUT: Test: 2010; ODI: 2011; T20I: 2011; First-class: 2005; List A: 2007; T20: 2008

BEST BATTING: 56 England vs New Zealand, Dunedin, 2013
BEST BOWLING: 9-37 Middlesex vs Worcestershire, Worcester, 2010
COUNTY CAP: 2009

FAMILY TIES? My father, Terry, played Minor Counties cricket for Hertfordshire
WHAT WAS YOUR FIRST CRICKET CLUB? Langlebury CC, Hertfordshire. The slope is more pronounced that it is at Lord's
CRICKETING HERO? Glenn McGrath
WHICH BOWLER WOULD YOU LEAST LIKE TO FACE? Tim Murtagh – I'd want to hit every ball for six
WHO WOULD YOU ASK TO BAT FOR YOUR LIFE? Jonathan Trott
TWITTER: @finnysteve

Batting	Mat	Inns	NO	Runs	HS	Ave	SR	100	50	Ct	St
Tests	36	47	22	279	56	11.16	30.96	0	1	8	0
ODIs	69	30	13	136	35	8.00	60.98	0	0	15	0
T20Is	21	3	3	14	8*	-	73.68	0	0	6	0
First-class	149	182	59	1111	56	9.03	38.13	0	1	47	0
List A	142	57	23	368	42*	10.82	64.67	0	0	31	0
T20s	88	17	12	55	8*	11.00	84.61	0	0	21	0
Bowling	**Mat**	**Balls**	**Runs**	**Wkts**	**BBI**	**BBM**	**Ave**	**Econ**	**SR**	**5w**	**10**
Tests	36	6412	3800	125	6/79	9/187	30.40	3.55	51.2	5	0
ODIs	69	3550	2996	102	5/33	5/33	29.37	5.06	34.8	2	0
T20Is	21	480	583	27	3/16	3/16	21.59	7.28	17.7	0	0
First-class	149	26646	15381	531	9/37	14/106	28.96	3.46	50.1	13	1
List A	142	6737	5762	200	5/33	5/33	28.81	5.13	33.6	3	0
T20s	88	1826	2323	104	4/24	4/24	22.33	7.63	17.5	0	0

MATTHEW FISHER RHB / RFM / R0 / W0

FULL NAME: Matthew David Fisher
BORN: November 9, 1997, York
SQUAD NO: 7
HEIGHT: 6ft 2in
NICKNAME: Fish, Nemo, Pup
EDUCATION: Easingwold School, North Yorkshire
TEAMS: Yorkshire, England Lions
ROLE: Bowler
DEBUT: First-class: 2015; List A: 2013; T20: 2015

BEST BATTING: 37 Yorkshire vs Warwickshire, Headingley, 2017
BEST BOWLING: 5-54 Yorkshire vs Warwickshire, Headingley, 2017

WHAT GOT YOU INTO CRICKET? Playing with my brothers at our local club. And the 2005 Ashes
'ROY OF THE ROVERS' MOMENT? Taking 5-22 against Derbyshire at Headingley on my T20 Blast debut for Yorkshire in 2015
BEST THING ABOUT YOUR HOME GROUND? The Dickie Bird Players' Balcony – all paid for by Dickie. Legend of Yorkshire cricket
SURPRISING FACT ABOUT YOU? I'm deaf in one ear
CRICKETING HERO? Andrew Flintoff – he played at his best when under pressure
NON-CRICKETING HERO? My dad – he taught me values and morals
TWITTER: @9M_Fisher

Batting	Mat	Inns	NO	Runs	HS	Ave	SR	100	50	Ct	St
First-class	9	12	2	131	37	13.10	32.42	0	0	3	0
List A	34	18	10	228	36*	28.50	98.70	0	0	10	0
T20s	22	5	4	24	17*	24.00	126.31	0	0	7	0
Bowling	**Mat**	**Balls**	**Runs**	**Wkts**	**BBI**	**BBM**	**Ave**	**Econ**	**SR**	**5w**	**10**
First-class	9	1430	789	20	5/54	5/89	39.45	3.31	71.5	1	0
List A	34	1384	1366	32	3/32	3/32	42.68	5.92	43.2	0	0
T20s	22	413	646	23	5/22	5/22	28.08	9.38	17.9	1	0

LUKE FLETCHER RHB / RFM / R0 / W0 / MVP22

FULL NAME: Luke Jack Fletcher
BORN: September 18, 1988, Nottingham
SQUAD NO: 19
HEIGHT: 6ft 6in
NICKNAME: Fletch
EDUCATION: Henry Mellish Comprehensive School, Nottingham
TEAMS: Nottinghamshire, Derbyshire, Surrey, Wellington
ROLE: Bowler
DEBUT: First-class: 2008; List A: 2008; T20: 2009

BEST BATTING: 92 Nottinghamshire vs Hampshire, Southampton, 2009
BEST BOWLING: 5-27 Nottinghamshire vs Worcestershire, Worcester, 2018
COUNTY CAP: 2014 (Nottinghamshire)

WHAT WAS YOUR FIRST CRICKET CLUB? Bulwell CC, Nottinghamshire
CRICKETING HERO? Andrew Flintoff
BEST ADVICE EVER RECEIVED? Enjoy yourself and get stuck in
WHICH BOWLER WOULD YOU LEAST LIKE TO FACE? Shoaib Akhtar – too fast
BEST INNINGS YOU'VE SEEN? Alex Hales: 187 not out to win the Lord's final in 2017
WHO WOULD YOU ASK TO BAT FOR YOUR LIFE? Alastair Cook
WHICH RULE WOULD YOU CHANGE ABOUT CRICKET? One hour for lunch
YOUR BIGGEST CRICKETING REGRET? Getting out on 92 – twice
SURPRISING FACT ABOUT YOU? My previous job was as a chef at Hooters
WHAT WILL YOU BE DOING IN THE YEAR 2040? Playing golf in Portugal
ODDEST SPORT YOU'VE PLAYED? Zorb football
TWITTER: @fletcherluke

Batting	Mat	Inns	NO	Runs	HS	Ave	SR	100	50	Ct	St
First-class	104	152	27	1820	92	14.56	49.25	0	4	26	0
List A	67	34	14	357	53*	17.85	100.84	0	1	11	0
T20s	68	24	10	103	27	7.35	111.95	0	0	9	0
Bowling	**Mat**	**Balls**	**Runs**	**Wkts**	**BBI**	**BBM**	**Ave**	**Econ**	**SR**	**5w**	**10**
First-class	104	17760	8728	308	5/27	9/108	28.33	2.94	57.6	4	0
List A	67	2733	2568	64	4/20	4/20	40.12	5.63	42.7	0	0
T20s	68	1410	1887	73	4/30	4/30	25.84	8.02	19.3	0	0

BEN FOAKES RHB / WK / R0 / W0 / MVP59

FULL NAME: Benjamin Thomas Foakes
BORN: February 15, 1993, Colchester, Essex
SQUAD NO: 7
HEIGHT: 6ft 2in
NICKNAME: Foakesey
EDUCATION: Tendring Technology College, Essex
TEAMS: England, Surrey, Essex
ROLE: Batsman/wicketkeeper
DEBUT: Test: 2018; First-class: 2011; List A: 2013; T20: 2014

BEST BATTING: 141* Surrey vs Hampshire, Southampton, 2016

COUNTY CAP: 2016 (Surrey)

WHAT GOT YOU INTO CRICKET? Growing up in a small town there wasn't a lot to do so I got involved with all the local sports clubs
FAMILY TIES? My brother plays in the East Anglian Premier League for Frinton-on-Sea
'ROY OF THE ROVERS' MOMENT? The quarter-final of the 2015 One-Day Cup: taking a skyer off Matt Coles to send us into the semis after his incredible innings and an amazing game. The emotion and joy as the team came together was quite something
SUPERSTITIONS? I touch my belly button and top and bottom lip between each ball
CRICKETING HERO? James Foster – he made me want to become a keeper when I first started watching Essex play as a kid
IF YOU WEREN'T A CRICKETER? I'd be exploring Asia
SURPRISING FACT? After I had a car crash a tooth was glued back together. It came unstuck while I was batting and was dangling, so I tore it out at lunch and batted with no front teeth

Batting	Mat	Inns	NO	Runs	HS	Ave	SR	100	50	Ct	St
Tests	5	10	2	332	107	41.50	53.80	1	1	10	2
First-class	95	147	27	4884	141*	40.70	53.11	9	25	184	17
List A	65	55	10	1552	92	34.48	86.60	0	14	76	7
T20s	55	39	9	710	75*	23.66	125.66	0	3	30	3
Bowling	**Mat**	**Balls**	**Runs**	**Wkts**	**BBI**	**BBM**	**Ave**	**Econ**	**SR**	**5w**	**10**
Tests	5	-	-	-	-	-	-	-	-	-	-
First-class	95	6	6	0	-	-	-	6.00	-	0	0
List A	65	-	-	-	-	-	-	-	-	-	-
T20s	55	-	-	-	-	-	-	-	-	-	-

MARK FOOTITT

RHB / LFM / R0 / W2

NOTTINGHAMSHIRE

FULL NAME: Mark Harold Alan Footitt
BORN: November 25, 1985, Nottingham
SQUAD NO: 7
HEIGHT: 6ft 2in
NICKNAME: Footy
EDUCATION: Carlton Le Willows School, Gedling; West Nottinghamshire College
TEAMS: Nottinghamshire, Derbyshire, Surrey
ROLE: Bowler
DEBUT: First-class: 2005; List A: 2002; T20: 2005

BEST BATTING: 34 Derbyshire vs Leicestershire, Leicester, 2015
BEST BOWLING: 7-62 Surrey vs Lancashire, The Oval, 2016
COUNTY CAP: 2014 (Derbyshire)

WHAT WAS YOUR FIRST CRICKET CLUB? Papplewick & Linby CC, Nottinghamshire
CRICKETING HERO? Brett Lee
WHICH BOWLER WOULD YOU LEAST LIKE TO FACE? Harry Gurney – because he's a frog in a blender
BEST INNINGS YOU'VE SEEN? Any of mine that have gone beyond two balls
WHO WOULD YOU ASK TO BAT FOR YOUR LIFE? Luke Fletcher – he's got the best defence in the world
WHICH RULE WOULD YOU CHANGE ABOUT CRICKET? Bowl as many bouncers as you want
SURPRISING FACT ABOUT YOU? I started bowling right-arm then changed to left-arm
WHAT WILL YOU BE DOING IN THE YEAR 2040? I'll be old and knackered. Umpiring?
FAVOURITE QUOTE OR SAYING? Ay up me duck
ODDEST SPORT YOU'VE PLAYED? Bubble football
TWITTER: @footitt_mark

Batting	Mat	Inns	NO	Runs	HS	Ave	SR	100	50	Ct	St
First-class	96	124	39	678	34	7.97	60.26	0	0	26	0
List A	36	10	4	28	11*	4.66	68.29	0	0	6	0
T20s	14	3	2	2	2*	2.00	66.66	0	0	1	0
Bowling	**Mat**	**Balls**	**Runs**	**Wkts**	**BBI**	**BBM**	**Ave**	**Econ**	**SR**	**5w**	**10**
First-class	96	15579	9227	352	7/62	10/155	26.21	3.55	44.2	21	1
List A	36	1331	1387	47	5/28	5/28	29.51	6.25	28.3	2	0
T20s	14	240	431	12	3/22	3/22	35.91	10.77	20.0	0	0

WILL FRAINE

RHB / RM / R0 / W0

FULL NAME: William Alan Richard Fraine
BORN: June 13, 1996, Huddersfield
SQUAD NO: 31
EDUCATION: Silcoates School, Wakefield, West Yorkshire; Bromsgrove Sixth Form College, Worcestershire; Durham University
TEAMS: Yorkshire, Nottinghamshire
ROLE: Batsman
DEBUT: First-class: 2017; List A: 2018; T20: 2018

BEST BATTING: 30 Nottinghamshire vs Surrey, Trent Bridge, 2018

NOTES: Fraine is a top-order batsman who turned down an offer from Nottinghamshire to sign for his home county Yorkshire last October. He was born in Huddersfield and played for Yorkshire's age-group sides up until representing the U19s in 2014. After moving to a boarding school in Bromsgrove, Fraine played Second XI cricket for Worcestershire and in 2016 he made his first-class debut for Durham MCCU against Gloucestershire at Bristol. Nottinghamshire then gave him a run in their Second XI and signed him on a short contract last May. He played in all three formats last summer, making his Championship debut against Surrey at Trent Bridge, before making the decision to return home. "There's always that pull of being a Yorkie lad," he said. "All my friends speak of one day playing for Yorkshire. I never thought it would happen because I made my own way elsewhere"

Batting	Mat	Inns	NO	Runs	HS	Ave	SR	100	50	Ct	St
First-class	5	5	0	97	30	19.40	37.89	0	0	0	0
List A	3	3	1	27	13	13.50	122.72	0	0	1	0
T20s	7	7	1	49	14	8.16	116.66	0	0	4	0
Bowling	**Mat**	**Balls**	**Runs**	**Wkts**	**BBI**	**BBM**	**Ave**	**Econ**	**SR**	**5w**	**10**
First-class	5	-	-	-	-	-	-	-	-	-	-
List A	3	-	-	-	-	-	-	-	-	-	-
T20s	7	-	-	-	-	-	-	-	-	-	-

JAMES FULLER RHB / RFM / R0 / W0 / MVP82

FULL NAME: James Kerr Fuller
BORN: January 24, 1990, Cape Town, South Africa
SQUAD NO: 26
HEIGHT: 6ft 2in
NICKNAME: Fuller, Foz
EDUCATION: Westlake Boys High School, Auckland; University of Otago
TEAMS: Hampshire, Auckland, England Lions, Gloucestershire, Middlesex, Otago
ROLE: Bowler
DEBUT: First-class: 2010; List A: 2011; T20: 2011

BEST BATTING: 93 Middlesex vs Somerset, Taunton, 2016
BEST BOWLING: 6-24 Otago vs Wellington, Dunedin, 2013
COUNTY CAP: 2011 (Gloucestershire)

WHAT GOT YOU INTO CRICKET? Watching the Black Caps play Australia on telly
'ROY OF THE ROVERS' MOMENT? The Glorious Glosters winning the 2015 one-day trophy
IF YOU WEREN'T A CRICKETER? I'd be a scientist
SURPRISING FACT ABOUT YOU? I have held my breath for over three minutes and 30 seconds
WHERE IS PARADISE? Hauraki Gulf, New Zealand. Line in the water
NON-CRICKETING HERO? Louis Zamperini – teenage Olympian, highly skilled bombardier and surviving POW. If you haven't read the book Unbroken, then I highly recommend it
TWITTER: @James_Fuller246
NOTES: The former Gloucestershire and Middlesex seamer signed a two-year contract with Hampshire in October. He said: "I'm looking forward to joining a strong team who have a great white-ball history and who are pushing to win the County Championship"

Batting	Mat	Inns	NO	Runs	HS	Ave	SR	100	50	Ct	St
First-class	49	64	8	1101	93	19.66	64.76	0	5	20	0
List A	52	41	14	597	45	22.11	98.02	0	0	15	0
T20s	76	44	18	547	46*	21.03	149.04	0	0	33	0
Bowling	**Mat**	**Balls**	**Runs**	**Wkts**	**BBI**	**BBM**	**Ave**	**Econ**	**SR**	**5w**	**10**
First-class	49	7858	4662	141	6/24	10/79	33.06	3.55	55.7	5	1
List A	52	2161	2082	70	6/35	6/35	29.74	5.78	30.8	1	0
T20s	76	1550	2248	94	6/28	6/28	23.91	8.70	16.4	1	0

GEORGE GARTON

LHB / LF / R0 / W0

FULL NAME: George Henry Simmons Garton
BORN: April 15, 1997, Brighton
SQUAD NO: 15
HEIGHT: 6ft 1in
NICKNAME: Garts
EDUCATION: Hurstpierpoint College, West Sussex
TEAMS: Sussex, England Lions
ROLE: Bowler
DEBUT: First-class: 2016; List A: 2016; T20: 2016

BEST BATTING: 22* Sussex vs Middlesex, Hove, 2018
BEST BOWLING: 3-20 Sussex vs Durham, Chester-le-Street, 2017

WHAT WAS YOUR FIRST CRICKET CLUB? Preston Nomads CC, West Sussex
FAVOURITE CRICKET BAT? Keeley Worx
WHICH BOWLER WOULD YOU LEAST LIKE TO FACE? Rashid Khan
BEST INNINGS YOU'VE SEEN? Phil Salt's Championship hundred against Derbyshire at Hove last summer – that was some serious ball-striking
WHO WOULD YOU ASK TO BAT FOR YOUR LIFE? Stuart Whittingham – strongest (and latest) forward defence going around
WHICH RULE WOULD YOU CHANGE ABOUT CRICKET? Remove the limit on bouncers
WHAT WILL YOU BE DOING IN THE YEAR 2040? I'll be trying to answer these questions
FAVOURITE QUOTE OR SAYING? Don't like training? Try losing
ODDEST SPORT YOU'VE PLAYED? Underwater hockey
TWITTER: @george_garton

Batting	Mat	Inns	NO	Runs	HS	Ave	SR	100	50	Ct	St
First-class	10	11	3	101	22*	12.62	53.43	0	0	4	0
List A	16	5	2	20	7*	6.66	90.90	0	0	7	0
T20s	12	1	1	2	2*	-	100.00	0	0	3	0
Bowling	**Mat**	**Balls**	**Runs**	**Wkts**	**BBI**	**BBM**	**Ave**	**Econ**	**SR**	**5w**	**10**
First-class	10	1387	942	24	3/20	5/109	39.25	4.07	57.7	0	0
List A	16	672	726	20	4/43	4/43	36.30	6.48	33.6	0	0
T20s	12	186	272	11	4/16	4/16	24.72	8.77	16.9	0	0

NATHAN GILCHRIST RHB / RFM / R0 / W0

FULL NAME: Nathan Nicholas Gilchrist
BORN: June 11, 2000, Harare, Zimbabwe
SQUAD NO: 21
HEIGHT: 6ft 5in
NICKNAME: Gilly, Melman
EDUCATION: St Stithians School, Johannesburg; King's College, Taunton
TEAMS: Somerset
ROLE: Bowler

WHAT WAS YOUR FIRST CRICKET CLUB? Staplegrove CC, Somerset. The cricket field was right next to a heard of cows
FAVOURITE CRICKET BAT? Gunn & Moore Icon – my first bat
WHICH BOWLER WOULD YOU LEAST LIKE TO FACE? Morne Morkel – that bounce!
BEST INNINGS YOU'VE SEEN? AB de Villiers making the fastest hundred in ODI cricket (31 balls) against West Indies at Johannesburg in 2015. Chaos
WHO WOULD YOU ASK TO BAT FOR YOUR LIFE? Virat Kohli
WHICH RULE WOULD YOU CHANGE ABOUT CRICKET? Allow more bumpers per over
WHAT WILL YOU BE DOING IN THE YEAR 2040? Travelling to cool places around the world
ODDEST SPORT YOU'VE PLAYED? Lacrosse
TWITTER: @nathgilchrist
NOTES: A genuinely quick bowler and clean striker of a ball, Gilchrist signed a one-year contract with Somerset last summer. The tall 18-year-old was born in Harare to an English father and first came to this country when he was involved in a cricket exchange between St Stithians in Johannesburg and King's College Taunton. He has represented Somerset in U17 and Second XI cricket and bowled some rapid spells last season, taking match figures of 9-52 against Surrey

ALFIE GLEADALL

RHB / RMF / R0 / W0

FULL NAME: Alfie Frank Gleadall
BORN: May 28, 2000, Chesterfield
SQUAD NO: 17
HEIGHT: 5ft 11in
NICKNAME: Alf
EDUCATION: Westfield Sports College, Sheffield
TEAMS: Derbyshire
ROLE: Bowler
DEBUT: First-class: 2018; List A: 2017

BEST BATTING: 27* Derbyshire vs Durham, Chester-le-Street, 2018
BEST BOWLING: 1-20 Derbyshire vs Durham, Chester-le-Street, 2018

TWITTER: @alfie_gleadall
NOTES: Gleadall signed a two-year professional contract with Derbyshire in June 2017. The 17-year-old pace bowler, who is also a handy lower-order batsman, has been a regular in the Second XI for the past two summers and made his first-team debut in the tour fixture against South Africa A in May 2017. Last summer he made his first-class debut in the Championship match against Durham at Chester-le-Street and also represented England U19 for the first time in the youth Test against South Africa at Scarborough

Batting	Mat	Inns	NO	Runs	HS	Ave	SR	100	50	Ct	St
First-class	1	2	1	29	27*	29.00	47.54	0	0	0	0
List A	1	-	-	-	-	-	-	-	-	0	0
Bowling	**Mat**	**Balls**	**Runs**	**Wkts**	**BBI**	**BBM**	**Ave**	**Econ**	**SR**	**5w**	**10**
First-class	1	81	59	1	1/20	1/59	59.00	4.37	81.0	0	0
List A	1	18	22	0	-	-	-	7.33	-	0	0

RICHARD GLEESON RHB / RFM / R0 / W0 / MVP95

FULL NAME: Richard James Gleeson
BORN: December 2, 1987, Blackpool, Lancashire
SQUAD NO: 33
HEIGHT: 6ft 3in
NICKNAME: Gleese
EDUCATION: Baines High School, Lancashire; University of Cumbria
TEAMS: Lancashire, England Lions, Northamptonshire, Rangpur Riders
ROLE: Bowler
DEBUT: First-class: 2015; List A: 2016; T20: 2016

BEST BATTING: 31 Northamptonshire vs Gloucestershire, Bristol, 2016
BEST BOWLING: 6-79 Northamptonshire vs Kent, Canterbury, 2018

FAMILY TIES? My father ran the bar at our local cricket club, my sister ran the kitchen, and my brother-in-law was the first XI captain
BEST ADVICE EVER RECEIVED? Just enjoy it maaaate (Steven Crook)
'ROY OF THE ROVERS' MOMENT? Becoming a pro at the age of 28
IF YOU WEREN'T A CRICKETER? I'd be on MasterChef
SURPRISING FACT ABOUT YOU? I am a published poet
WHERE IS PARADISE? Blackpool
CRICKETING HERO? Allan Donald – I loved the way he got fired up
NON-CRICKETING HERO? Steven Gerrard
UNUSUAL OBJECT AT HOME? A Buddha head
TWITTER: @RicGleeson

Batting	Mat	Inns	NO	Runs	HS	Ave	SR	100	50	Ct	St
First-class	24	30	12	219	31	12.16	34.59	0	0	6	0
List A	21	13	5	53	13	6.62	42.06	0	0	3	0
T20s	31	9	5	24	7*	6.00	92.30	0	0	6	0
Bowling	**Mat**	**Balls**	**Runs**	**Wkts**	**BBI**	**BBM**	**Ave**	**Econ**	**SR**	**5w**	**10**
First-class	24	3779	2053	93	6/79	9/95	22.07	3.25	40.6	5	0
List A	21	841	816	28	5/47	5/47	29.14	5.82	30.0	1	0
T20s	31	658	808	34	3/12	3/12	23.76	7.36	19.3	0	0

BILLY GODLEMAN

LHB / LB / R1 / W0 / MVP49

FULL NAME: Billy Ashley Godleman
BORN: February 11, 1989, Camden, London
SQUAD NO: 1
HEIGHT: 6ft 2in
NICKNAME: G, Chief
EDUCATION: Islington Green School, London
TEAMS: Derbyshire, Essex, Middlesex
ROLE: Batsman
DEBUT: First-class: 2005; List A: 2007; T20: 2006

BEST BATTING: 204 Derbyshire vs Worcestershire, Derby, 2016

WHAT WAS YOUR FIRST CRICKET CLUB? Hampstead CC, London
FAVOURITE CRICKET BAT? Slazenger V500 – because Alec Stewart used it
CRICKETING HERO? I admire Hashim Amla. He stands for something more than cricket. He shares his experience and inside knowledge with other players. And he scores runs consistently in all competitions. Top bloke
WHICH BOWLER WOULD YOU LEAST LIKE TO FACE? Wasim Akram
WHO WOULD YOU ASK TO BAT FOR YOUR LIFE? Brian Lara
SURPRISING FACT ABOUT YOU? I don't engage on social media
SURPRISING FACT ABOUT A TEAMMATE? My close friend Tony Palladino wears a Batman skin under his whites – and he has delivered many superhuman spells over the years
FAVOURITE QUOTE OR SAYING? What will be, will be
WHICH BOOK MEANS MOST TO YOU? Luck – A Fresh Look at Fortune by Ed Smith

Batting	Mat	Inns	NO	Runs	HS	Ave	SR	100	50	Ct	St
First-class	141	253	13	7667	204	31.94	45.55	17	36	95	0
List A	60	58	7	2026	137	39.72	76.07	3	11	21	0
T20s	65	60	4	1201	77	21.44	118.67	0	8	26	0
Bowling	**Mat**	**Balls**	**Runs**	**Wkts**	**BBI**	**BBM**	**Ave**	**Econ**	**SR**	**5w**	**10**
First-class	141	30	35	0	-	-	-	7.00	-	0	0
List A	60	-	-	-	-	-	-	-	-	-	-
T20s	65	-	-	-	-	-	-	-	-	-	-

BEN GREEN

RHB / RFM / R0 / W0

FULL NAME: Benjamin George Frederick Green
BORN: September 28, 1997, Exeter, Devon
SQUAD NO: 54
HEIGHT: 6ft 2in
NICKNAME: Greener, Neil
EDUCATION: Exeter School
TEAMS: Somerset
ROLE: Allrounder
DEBUT: First-class: 2018; List A: 2018; T20: 2016

BEST BATTING: 26 Somerset vs Hampshire, Southampton, 2018
BEST BOWLING: 1-8 Somerset vs Hampshire, Southampton, 2018

WHAT WAS YOUR FIRST CRICKET CLUB? Clyst St George CC, East Devon – my local village team. It was a brilliant starting point and I have fond memories of Friday-night training
WHICH BOWLER WOULD YOU LEAST LIKE TO FACE? Kagiso Rabada
BEST INNINGS YOU'VE SEEN? I saw Roelof van der Merwe hit 165 not out against Surrey at Taunton in the 2017 One-Day Cup
WHO WOULD YOU ASK TO BAT FOR YOUR LIFE? Don Bradman – he's a pretty safe bet
WHICH RULE WOULD YOU CHANGE ABOUT CRICKET? Allow more than two fielders behind square on the leg side
YOUR BIGGEST CRICKETING REGRET? Not deciding to bat left-handed
FAVOURITE QUOTE OR SAYING? Get busy living or get busy dying (The Shawshank Redemption)
WHICH BOOK MEANS MOST TO YOU? The Harry Potter books – my parents used to read a chapter to me and my sister every night
TWITTER: @Ben_Green28

Batting	Mat	Inns	NO	Runs	HS	Ave	SR	100	50	Ct	St
First-class	2	4	0	43	26	10.75	40.18	0	0	3	0
List A	3	3	2	35	26*	35.00	79.54	0	0	0	0
T20s	1	1	1	12	12*	-	92.30	0	0	0	0
Bowling	**Mat**	**Balls**	**Runs**	**Wkts**	**BBI**	**BBM**	**Ave**	**Econ**	**SR**	**5w**	**10**
First-class	2	42	17	1	1/8	1/17	17.00	2.42	42.0	0	0
List A	3	66	70	1	1/52	1/52	70.00	6.36	66.0	0	0
T20s	1	12	12	0	-	-	-	6.00	-	0	0

LEWIS GREGORY RHB / RFM / R0 / W0 / MVP4

FULL NAME: Lewis Gregory
BORN: May 24, 1992, Plymouth
SQUAD NO: 24
HEIGHT: 6ft
NICKNAME: Mowgli
EDUCATION: Hele's School, Plymouth
TEAMS: Somerset, England Lions
ROLE: Allrounder
DEBUT: First-class: 2011; List A: 2010; T20: 2011

BEST BATTING: 137 Somerset vs Middlesex, Lord's, 2017
BEST BOWLING: 6-47 Somerset vs Northamptonshire, Northampton, 2014
COUNTY CAP: 2015

WHAT GOT YOU INTO CRICKET? I saw it on TV and gave it a go
STRANGEST THING SEEN IN A GAME? Ryan Davies going out to bat in a 50-over game in the wrong shirt
'ROY OF THE ROVERS' MOMENT? Taking my maiden first-class five-wicket haul at Lord's and scoring my maiden first-class hundred at the same ground
CRICKETING HERO? Michael Vaughan
NON-CRICKETING HERO? Tiger Woods
SURPRISING FACT? I'm a black belt in taekwondo
TWITTER: @Lewisgregory23

Batting	Mat	Inns	NO	Runs	HS	Ave	SR	100	50	Ct	St
First-class	73	107	11	2000	137	20.83	55.14	1	7	37	0
List A	65	47	5	919	105*	21.88	92.54	1	4	23	0
T20s	79	59	17	969	62	23.07	148.39	0	3	28	0
Bowling	**Mat**	**Balls**	**Runs**	**Wkts**	**BBI**	**BBM**	**Ave**	**Econ**	**SR**	**5w**	**10**
First-class	73	10421	5855	205	6/47	11/122	28.56	3.37	50.8	9	1
List A	65	2506	2503	96	4/23	4/23	26.07	5.99	26.1	0	0
T20s	79	1399	2091	75	4/15	4/15	27.88	8.96	18.6	0	0

GAVIN GRIFFITHS

RHB / RFM / R0 / W0

FULL NAME: Gavin Timothy Griffiths
BORN: November 19, 1993, Ormskirk, Lancashire
SQUAD NO: 93
HEIGHT: 6ft 2in
NICKNAME: Gavlar
EDUCATION: St Michael's CE High School, Chorley; St Mary's College, Crosby
TEAMS: Leicestershire, Hampshire, Lancashire
ROLE: Bowler
DEBUT: First-class: 2017; List A: 2014; T20: 2015

BEST BATTING: 40 Leicestershire vs Middlesex, Leicester, 2018
BEST BOWLING: 6-49 Leicestershire vs Durham, Chester-le-Street, 2018

WHAT WAS YOUR FIRST CRICKET CLUB? Ormskirk CC, West Lancashire
FAVOURITE CRICKET BAT? Kookaburra Bubble. First bat I used, inspired by Graham Thorpe
CRICKETING HERO? Allan Donald
WHICH BOWLER WOULD YOU LEAST LIKE TO FACE? Mohammad Abbas – enough pace, line and length, seam movement
BEST INNINGS YOU'VE SEEN? Ben Stokes's 258 at Cape Town in 2016
WHICH RULE WOULD YOU CHANGE ABOUT CRICKET? Bowlers don't need to field
YOUR BIGGEST CRICKETING REGRET? Not learning more about my game as a teenager
SURPRISING FACT ABOUT YOU? I have played chess for England
FAVOURITE QUOTE OR SAYING? If you don't risk anything, you risk even more
WHICH BOOK MEANS MOST TO YOU? Bounce – The Myth of Talent and the Power of Practice by Matthew Syed
TWITTER: @Gavvlar

Batting	Mat	Inns	NO	Runs	HS	Ave	SR	100	50	Ct	St
First-class	18	26	11	262	40	17.46	35.54	0	0	2	0
List A	16	7	6	24	15*	24.00	52.17	0	0	9	0
T20s	27	8	7	28	11	28.00	75.67	0	0	6	0
Bowling	**Mat**	**Balls**	**Runs**	**Wkts**	**BBI**	**BBM**	**Ave**	**Econ**	**SR**	**5w**	**10**
First-class	18	2448	1316	44	6/49	10/83	29.90	3.22	55.6	1	1
List A	16	718	677	22	4/30	4/30	30.77	5.65	32.6	0	0
T20s	27	468	671	20	3/28	3/28	33.55	8.60	23.4	0	0

TIM GROENEWALD

RHB / RFM / R0 / W0

FULL NAME: Timothy Duncan Groenewald
BORN: January 10, 1984, Pietermaritzburg, South Africa
SQUAD NO: 5
HEIGHT: 6ft
NICKNAME: TimmyG, Groeners
EDUCATION: Maritzburg College; University of South Africa
TEAMS: Somerset, Derbyshire, Warwickshire
ROLE: Bowler
DEBUT: First-class: 2006; List A: 2006; T20: 2006

BEST BATTING: 78 Warwickshire vs Bangladesh A, Edgbaston, 2008
BEST BOWLING: 6-50 Derbyshire vs Surrey, Whitgift School, 2009
COUNTY CAP: 2011 (Derbyshire); 2016 (Somerset)

WHAT WAS YOUR FIRST CRICKET CLUB? Sutton Coldfield CC, Birmingham. The slope is twice as bad as at Lord's
FAVOURITE CRICKET BAT? My first one, a Duncan Fearnley. Everyone would use it in our U10 team, we would pass it to the next batter as we walked off. It was always an issue if I batted for most of the innings
WHICH BOWLER WOULD YOU LEAST LIKE TO FACE? Max Waller – love to whack him everywhere but couldn't face getting out to him
BEST INNINGS YOU'VE SEEN? Johann Myburgh's 42-ball hundred for Somerset against Essex in last season's T20 Blast
WHO WOULD YOU ASK TO BAT FOR YOUR LIFE? Jack Leach – he can't live without me
YOUR BIGGEST CRICKETING REGRET? Not being an opening bat in white-ball cricket
WHAT WILL YOU BE DOING IN THE YEAR 2040? Recovering from knee and hip operations
TWITTER: @timmyg12

Batting	Mat	Inns	NO	Runs	HS	Ave	SR	100	50	Ct	St
First-class	131	187	63	2275	78	18.34	51.55	0	6	42	0
List A	103	60	23	731	57	19.75	111.60	0	2	26	0
T20s	103	42	17	384	41	15.36	126.73	0	0	29	0
Bowling	**Mat**	**Balls**	**Runs**	**Wkts**	**BBI**	**BBM**	**Ave**	**Econ**	**SR**	**5w**	**10**
First-class	131	22030	11313	383	6/50	9/136	29.53	3.08	57.5	15	0
List A	103	4090	3798	116	4/22	4/22	32.74	5.57	35.2	0	0
T20s	103	1855	2535	87	4/21	4/21	29.13	8.19	21.3	0	0

NICK GUBBINS

LHB / LB / R1 / W0

FULL NAME: Nicholas Richard Trail Gubbins
BORN: December 31, 1993, Richmond, London
SQUAD NO: 18
HEIGHT: 6ft
NICKNAME: Gubbs, Gubbo, Cathy
EDUCATION: Radley College, Oxfordshire; University of Leeds
TEAMS: Middlesex, England Lions
ROLE: Batsman
DEBUT: First-class: 2013; List A: 2014; T20: 2015

BEST BATTING: 201* Middlesex vs Lancashire, Lord's, 2016

COUNTY CAP: 2016

FAMILY TIES? My dad played one ODI for Singapore
WHAT WAS YOUR FIRST CRICKET CLUB? Stirlands CC, Chichester, West Sussex. Joe Burns and Saeed Ajmal played as overseas players at the club when I was there
CRICKETING HERO? Marcus Trescothick – I used to get his GM bats when I was younger and I always tried to mimic him in the back garden
BEST INNINGS YOU'VE SEEN? Kevin Pietersen's 158 against Australia at The Oval in 2005. It was just mesmerising and made me want to become a professional
WHICH RULE WOULD YOU CHANGE ABOUT CRICKET? For DRS referrals, you can't be out on umpire's call. What happened to the benefit of the doubt?
WHAT WILL YOU BE DOING IN THE YEAR 2040? I'll be Middlesex's director of cricket (sorry Angus Fraser)
WHICH BOOK MEANS MOST TO YOU? The Forgotten Highlander – My Incredible Story of Survival During the War in the Far East by Alistair Urquhart
TWITTER: @ngubbins18

Batting	Mat	Inns	NO	Runs	HS	Ave	SR	100	50	Ct	St
First-class	58	103	2	3516	201*	34.81	48.72	6	23	24	0
List A	48	47	1	1650	141	35.86	91.41	5	8	9	0
T20s	29	27	0	391	46	14.48	121.05	0	0	11	0
Bowling	**Mat**	**Balls**	**Runs**	**Wkts**	**BBI**	**BBM**	**Ave**	**Econ**	**SR**	**5w**	**10**
First-class	58	66	52	0	-	-	-	4.72	-	0	0
List A	48	-	-	-	-	-	-	-	-	-	-
T20s	29	-	-	-	-	-	-	-	-	-	-

BROOKE GUEST

RHB / WK / R0 / W0

FULL NAME: Brooke David Guest
BORN: May 14, 1997, Whitworth Park, Manchester
SQUAD NO: 29
HEIGHT: 5ft 11in
NICKNAME: Guesty
EDUCATION: Kent Street Senior High School, Perth; Murdoch University, Perth
TEAMS: Lancashire
ROLE: Wicketkeeper
DEBUT: First-class: 2018

BEST BATTING: 8 Lancashire vs Hampshire, Southampton, 2018

WHAT WAS YOUR FIRST CRICKET CLUB? South Perth CC, Australia. I've played there my whole life
WHICH BOWLER WOULD YOU LEAST LIKE TO FACE? Jasprit Bumrah
BEST INNINGS YOU'VE SEEN? Graeme Smith against Australia in the 2009 Sydney Test – he showed a lot of guts to bat with a broken hand against Mitchell Johnson
WHO WOULD YOU ASK TO BAT FOR YOUR LIFE? Cheteshwar Pujara
NOTES: Born in Manchester, Guest moved to Australia as a young boy and made his Australia U19 debut in 2016. The wicketkeeper committed his future to England after returning to the UK in 2016 to play for Lancashire, where he turned out for the Second XI, and for Sale CC in the Cheshire County Cricket League. His 803 runs at 53.53, including two hundreds, were more than anyone else in the division. Guest did not make a senior appearance in 2017 but helped the Second XI reach T20 Finals Day and win the three-day Championship. He scored 395 runs from nine three-day matches and claimed 21 catches behind the stumps. Last season he scored 256 runs at an average of 53 with 18 dismissals in the Second XI Championship and made his first-class debut

Batting	Mat	Inns	NO	Runs	HS	Ave	SR	100	50	Ct	St
First-class	1	2	0	8	8	4.00	27.58	0	0	0	0
Bowling	**Mat**	**Balls**	**Runs**	**Wkts**	**BBI**	**BBM**	**Ave**	**Econ**	**SR**	**5w**	**10**
First-class	1	-	-	-	-	-	-	-	-	-	-

MARTIN GUPTILL RHB / OB / R0 / W0

FULL NAME: Martin James Guptill
BORN: September 30, 1986, Auckland, New Zealand
SQUAD NO: TBC
TEAMS: New Zealand, Worcestershire, Auckland, Barbados Tridents, Derbyshire, Guyana Amazon Warriors, Kings XI Punjab, Lancashire, Mumbai Indians, Sydney Thunder
ROLE: Batsman
DEBUT: Test: 2009; ODI: 2009; T20I: 2009; First-class: 2006; List A: 2006; T20: 2006

BEST BATTING: 227 Derbyshire vs Gloucestershire, Bristol, 2015
BEST BOWLING: 3-11 New Zealand vs Zimbabwe, Bulawayo, 2016
COUNTY CAP: 2012 (Derbyshire)

TWITTER: @Martyguptill
NOTES: Worcestershire have re-signed the powerful New Zealand opener for the 2019 T20 Blast. Guptill is available for 11 of the club's group games and for the knockout stages if necessary. He scored one hundred and two fifties in seven innings for the club in the Blast last summer, and has considerable experience of the major T20 leagues around the world. The 32-year-old has previously played for Lancashire and Derbyshire and holds the record for the highest score in ODI cricket – 237 not out against West Indies in the quarter-final of the 2015 World Cup. "It is a huge confidence boost and we are chuffed he is coming back," said first-team coach Alex Gidman. "Guppy was wonderful around the group last year, a fantastic bloke, and he showed how good he is in a handful of wonderful innings for us"

Batting	Mat	Inns	NO	Runs	HS	Ave	SR	100	50	Ct	St
Tests	47	89	1	2586	189	29.38	46.61	3	17	50	0
ODIs	169	166	18	6440	237*	43.51	87.44	16	34	82	0
T20Is	76	74	7	2272	105	33.91	132.71	2	14	40	0
First-class	108	196	13	6987	227	38.18	53.77	15	36	116	0
List A	224	219	21	8733	237*	44.10	87.36	26	43	109	0
T20s	217	212	21	6301	120*	32.98	128.53	4	42	130	0
Bowling	**Mat**	**Balls**	**Runs**	**Wkts**	**BBI**	**BBM**	**Ave**	**Econ**	**SR**	**5w**	**10**
Tests	47	428	298	8	3/11	3/11	37.25	4.17	53.5	0	0
ODIs	169	109	98	4	2/6	2/6	24.50	5.39	27.2	0	0
T20Is	76	6	11	0	-	-	-	11.00	-	0	0
First-class	108	842	670	11	3/11	3/11	60.90	4.77	76.5	0	0
List A	224	115	105	5	2/6	2/6	21.00	5.47	23.0	0	0
T20s	217	12	19	0	-	-	-	9.50	-	0	0

HARRY GURNEY RHB / LFM / R0 / W0 / MVP35

FULL NAME: Harry Frederick Gurney
BORN: October 20, 1986, Nottingham
SQUAD NO: 11
HEIGHT: 6ft 2in
NICKNAME: Gramps
EDUCATION: Loughborough Grammar School; University of Leeds
TEAMS: England, Nottinghamshire, Kolkata Knight Riders, Leicestershire, Melbourne Renegades
ROLE: Bowler
DEBUT: ODI: 2014; T20I: 2014; First-class: 2007; List A: 2009; T20: 2009

BEST BATTING: 42* Nottinghamshire vs Sussex, Hove, 2017
BEST BOWLING: 6-25 Nottinghamshire vs Lancashire, Old Trafford, 2018
COUNTY CAP: 2014 (Nottinghamshire)

WHAT WAS YOUR FIRST CRICKET CLUB? Loughborough Town CC, Leicestershire
FAVOURITE CRICKET BAT? Slazenger V500 – believe it or not I used to be able to bat
WHICH BOWLER WOULD YOU LEAST LIKE TO FACE? James Pattinson
BEST INNINGS YOU'VE SEEN? Alex Hales in the 2017 one-day final at Lord's. Pretty much single-handedly won the game for us
WHO WOULD YOU ASK TO BAT FOR YOUR LIFE? Jake Libby
WHICH RULE WOULD YOU CHANGE ABOUT CRICKET? The bouncer over head-height should be a wide like it is everywhere else in the world. Why do we have to be different?
WHICH BOOK MEANS MOST TO YOU? Carly Car (my son loves it)
TWITTER: @gurneyhf

Batting	Mat	Inns	NO	Runs	HS	Ave	SR	100	50	Ct	St
ODIs	10	6	4	15	6*	7.50	45.45	0	0	1	0
T20Is	2	-	-	-	-	-	-	-	-	0	0
First-class	103	131	63	424	42*	6.23	40.57	0	0	12	0
List A	92	28	17	60	13*	5.45	49.58	0	0	7	0
T20s	124	18	12	20	6	3.33	83.33	0	0	16	0
Bowling	**Mat**	**Balls**	**Runs**	**Wkts**	**BBI**	**BBM**	**Ave**	**Econ**	**SR**	**5w**	**10**
ODIs	10	455	432	11	4/55	4/55	39.27	5.69	41.3	0	0
T20Is	2	48	55	3	2/26	2/26	18.33	6.87	16.0	0	0
First-class	103	16909	9472	310	6/25	9/136	30.55	3.36	54.5	8	0
List A	92	3874	3784	113	5/24	5/24	33.48	5.86	34.2	3	0
T20s	124	2585	3325	145	4/17	4/17	22.93	7.71	17.8	0	0

CALUM HAGGETT

LHB / RM / R0 / W0

FULL NAME: Calum John Haggett
BORN: October 30, 1990, Taunton
SQUAD NO: 25
HEIGHT: 6ft 3in
NICKNAME: Haggs
EDUCATION: Crispin School, Somerset; Millfield School
TEAMS: Kent, Somerset
ROLE: Bowler
DEBUT: First-class: 2013; List A: 2013; T20: 2011

BEST BATTING: 80 Kent vs Surrey, The Oval, 2015
BEST BOWLING: 4-15 Kent vs Derbyshire, Derby, 2016

FAMILY TIES? My father played village cricket and my brother played for Somerset seconds
WHAT WAS YOUR FIRST CRICKET CLUB? Shapwick and Polden CC, a little village club in the heart of Somerset which formed as a merger between Ashcott & Shapwick CC and Chilton Polden CC
CRICKETING HERO? Chris March and Phil Hunt from Ashcott and Shapwick CC. They showed me what to do after the game
WHICH BOWLER WOULD YOU LEAST LIKE TO FACE? Mitchell Johnson
BEST INNINGS YOU'VE SEEN? Heino Kuhn's hundred to take us past Worcestershire in the 2018 One-Day Cup semi-final at New Road
WHO WOULD YOU ASK TO BAT FOR YOUR LIFE? Don Bradman
WHICH RULE WOULD YOU CHANGE ABOUT CRICKET? The minimum distance to the boundary should be bigger
SURPRISING FACT ABOUT YOU? I have a webbed toe
WHICH BOOK MEANS MOST TO YOU? 1984 by George Orwell

Batting	Mat	Inns	NO	Runs	HS	Ave	SR	100	50	Ct	St
First-class	41	54	13	926	80	22.58	39.60	0	2	10	0
List A	38	24	4	337	45	16.85	75.56	0	0	13	0
T20s	32	15	9	98	20	16.33	125.64	0	0	5	0
Bowling	**Mat**	**Balls**	**Runs**	**Wkts**	**BBI**	**BBM**	**Ave**	**Econ**	**SR**	**5w**	**10**
First-class	41	5884	3008	89	4/15	7/97	33.79	3.06	66.1	0	0
List A	38	1682	1662	47	4/59	4/59	35.36	5.92	35.7	0	0
T20s	32	534	824	26	2/12	2/12	31.69	9.25	20.5	0	0

SAM HAIN

RHB / RM / R0 / W0 / MVP73

FULL NAME: Samuel Robert Hain
BORN: July 16, 1995, Hong Kong
SQUAD NO: 16
HEIGHT: 6ft
NICKNAME: Ched, Hainy
EDUCATION: The Southport School, Queensland, Australia
TEAMS: Warwickshire, England Lions
ROLE: Batsman
DEBUT: First-class: 2014; List A: 2013; T20: 2016

BEST BATTING: 208 Warwickshire vs Northamptonshire, Edgbaston, 2014

WHAT GOT YOU INTO CRICKET? The battles with the brothers in the backyard. Always ended in tears
'ROY OF THE ROVERS' MOMENT? Winning the One-Day Cup at Lord's in 2016
BEST THING ABOUT YOUR HOME GROUND? What's not to love? It's got everything you'd want for your home ground
IF YOU WEREN'T A CRICKETER? I'd be opening a coffeehouse on the Gold Coast with my best mate
WHERE IS PARADISE? Any sunny afternoon on the first tee at Royal Pines on the Gold Coast
NON-CRICKETING HERO? Bryson DeChambeau – I've tried to copy his golf swing
TWITTER: @Sammiehain

Batting	Mat	Inns	NO	Runs	HS	Ave	SR	100	50	Ct	St
First-class	62	96	8	2983	208	33.89	47.88	8	15	47	0
List A	51	49	7	2425	145*	57.73	86.29	9	13	20	0
T20s	45	43	5	1233	95	32.44	126.72	0	7	32	0
Bowling	**Mat**	**Balls**	**Runs**	**Wkts**	**BBI**	**BBM**	**Ave**	**Econ**	**SR**	**5w**	**10**
First-class	62	42	31	0	-	-	-	4.42	-	0	0
List A	51	-	-	-	-	-	-	-	-	-	-
T20s	45	-	-	-	-	-	-	-	-	-	-

TOM HAINES

LHB / RM / R0 / W0

FULL NAME: Thomas Jacob Haines
BORN: October 28, 1998, Crawley, West Sussex
SQUAD NO: 20
HEIGHT: 5ft 11in
NICKNAME: Hainus
EDUCATION: Hurstpierpoint College
TEAMS: Sussex
ROLE: Batsman
DEBUT: First-class: 2016

BEST BATTING: 124 Sussex vs Durham, Arundel, 2018
BEST BOWLING: 1-13 Sussex vs Durham, Chester-le-Street, 2018

WHAT WAS YOUR FIRST CRICKET CLUB? Brockham Green CC, Surrey
CRICKETING HERO? Marcus Trescothick
WHICH BOWLER WOULD YOU LEAST LIKE TO FACE? Phil Salt
WHICH RULE WOULD YOU CHANGE ABOUT CRICKET? Sixes should be worth 10
YOUR BIGGEST CRICKETING REGRET? Not bowling leggies
WHAT WILL YOU BE DOING IN THE YEAR 2040? I'll be streaming Fortnite (online video game)
FAVOURITE QUOTE OR SAYING? Cheese on bread
TWITTER: @tomhaines

NOTES: Haines is a 20-year-old opening batsman from Crawley who has come through the Sussex Academy. He also bowls medium-pace. He signed a one-year professional contract in October 2017 after scoring two hundreds for the Second XI and helping the side win the T20 competition. Haines made his first-class debut in 2016 at the age of 17 and nailed down a first-team place last year, scoring his maiden first-class hundred at Arundel in June after receiving an unexpected call-up. In all he made 319 runs in 10 Championship innings. He signed a "multi-year" contract with Sussex last August

Batting	Mat	Inns	NO	Runs	HS	Ave	SR	100	50	Ct	St
First-class	9	13	0	331	124	25.46	59.96	1	1	3	0
Bowling	**Mat**	**Balls**	**Runs**	**Wkts**	**BBI**	**BBM**	**Ave**	**Econ**	**SR**	**5w**	**10**
First-class	9	198	82	1	1/13	1/13	82.00	2.48	198.0	0	0

ALEX HALES RHB / RM / R3 / W0

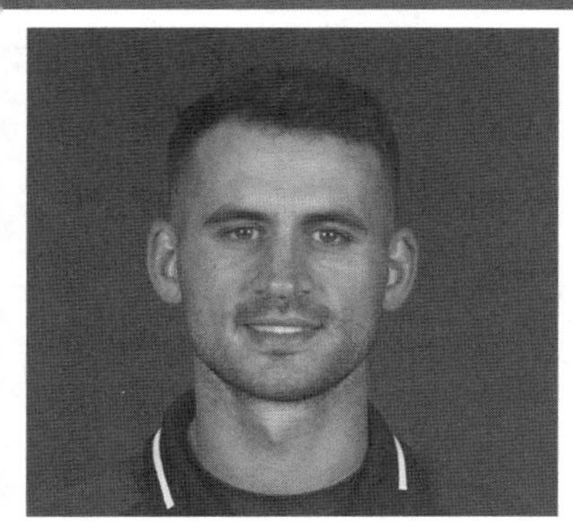

FULL NAME: Alexander Daniel Hales
BORN: January 3, 1989, Hillingdon, Middlesex
SQUAD NO: 10
HEIGHT: 6ft 4in
NICKNAME: Baz
EDUCATION: Chesham High School, Bucks
TEAMS: England, Nottinghamshire, Adelaide Strikers, Hobart Hurricanes, Melbourne Renegades, Sunrisers, Worcestershire
ROLE: Batsman
DEBUT: Test: 2015; ODI: 2014; T20I: 2011; First-class: 2008; List A: 2008; T20: 2009

BEST BATTING: 236 Nottinghamshire vs Yorkshire, Trent Bridge, 2015
BEST BOWLING: 2-63 Nottinghamshire vs Yorkshire, Trent Bridge, 2009
COUNTY CAP: 2011 (Nottinghamshire)

WHAT WAS YOUR FIRST CRICKET CLUB? Denham CC, Buckinghamshire. We lived in a bungalow on the cricket ground
FAVOURITE CRICKET BAT? A Gray-Nicolls Powerbow that I bought from a friend for £60. I scored a double ton with it on trial with Notts
WHO WOULD YOU ASK TO BAT FOR YOUR LIFE? Rahul Dravid – he faced more balls in Test cricket than anyone else (31,258)
WHICH BOOK MEANS MOST TO YOU? Fifty Shades of Grey by EL James
TWITTER: @AlexHales1
NOTES: Hales signed a one-year deal in February to play only white-ball cricket for Notts

Batting	Mat	Inns	NO	Runs	HS	Ave	SR	100	50	Ct	St
Tests	11	21	0	573	94	27.28	43.84	0	5	8	0
ODIs	70	67	3	2419	171	37.79	95.72	6	14	27	0
T20Is	60	60	7	1644	116*	31.01	136.65	1	8	32	0
First-class	107	182	6	6655	236	37.81	59.06	13	38	84	0
List A	172	167	6	6170	187*	38.32	99.14	17	31	63	0
T20s	202	201	13	5517	116*	29.34	143.55	3	34	94	0
Bowling	**Mat**	**Balls**	**Runs**	**Wkts**	**BBI**	**BBM**	**Ave**	**Econ**	**SR**	**5w**	**10**
Tests	11	18	2	0	-	-	-	0.66	-	0	0
ODIs	70	-	-	-	-	-	-	-	-	-	-
T20Is	60	-	-	-	-	-	-	-	-	-	-
First-class	107	311	173	3	2/63	2/63	57.66	3.33	103.6	0	0
List A	172	4	10	0	-	-	-	15.00	-	0	0
T20s	202	3	7	0	-	-	-	14.00	-	0	0

HASEEB HAMEED RHB / LB / R1 / W0

FULL NAME: Haseeb Hameed
BORN: January 17, 1997, Bolton, Lancashire
SQUAD NO: 23
HEIGHT: 6ft 2in
NICKNAME: Has
EDUCATION: Bolton School
TEAMS: England, Lancashire
ROLE: Batsman
DEBUT: Test: 2016; First-class: 2015; List A: 2017

BEST BATTING: 122 Lancashire vs Nottinghamshire, Trent Bridge, 2015

COUNTY CAP: 2016

TWITTER: @HaseebHameed97
NOTES: Tipped as one of the hottest batting prospects in England, Hameed hit 389 runs in five matches for England U19 against South Africa U19 in 2014, an international record for a batsman in a youth bilateral one-day series. He exceeded his growing reputation in 2016 by making more than 1,000 Championship runs in his first full season at Old Trafford – at 19 years of age becoming the youngest batsman to achieve the feat for Lancashire – and looking immediately at ease when scoring a fifty on his Test debut against India at Rajkot later that year. But an alarming dip in form since then has left him fighting for his spot in the Lancashire team. He hasn't scored a hundred since 2016 and last year 11 Championship matches produced only 170 runs at an average of 9.44. But Hameed has time on his side, having turned 22 in January

Batting	Mat	Inns	NO	Runs	HS	Ave	SR	100	50	Ct	St
Tests	3	6	1	219	82	43.80	34.21	0	2	4	0
First-class	53	91	8	2566	122	30.91	36.38	4	14	30	0
List A	11	11	2	388	88	43.11	79.50	0	3	1	0
Bowling	**Mat**	**Balls**	**Runs**	**Wkts**	**BBI**	**BBM**	**Ave**	**Econ**	**SR**	**5w**	**10**
Tests	3	-	-	-	-	-	-	-	-	-	-
First-class	53	42	21	0	-	-	-	3.00	-	0	0
List A	11	-	-	-	-	-	-	-	-	-	-

MILES HAMMOND

LHB / OB / R0 / W0

FULL NAME: Miles Arthur Halhead Hammond
BORN: January 11, 1996, Cheltenham, Gloucestershire
SQUAD NO: 88
HEIGHT: 6ft
NICKNAME: Hammo, Hammer, Wally, Cryles
EDUCATION: St Edward's School, Oxford; University of the Arts London
TEAMS: Gloucestershire
ROLE: Batsman
DEBUT: First-class: 2013; List A: 2013; T20: 2013

BEST BATTING: 123* Gloucestershire vs Middlesex, Bristol, 2018
BEST BOWLING: 1-96 Gloucestershire vs Glamorgan, Bristol, 2013

FAVOURITE CRICKET BAT? A Newbury Grizzly which I received aged 12
CRICKETING HERO? Marcus Trescothick
WHICH BOWLER WOULD YOU LEAST LIKE TO FACE? Daryl Mitchell
WHO WOULD YOU ASK TO BAT FOR YOUR LIFE? James Bracey – absolute badger
WHICH RULE WOULD YOU CHANGE ABOUT CRICKET? You can be out lbw if the ball pitches outside leg stump
YOUR BIGGEST CRICKETING REGRET? Choosing initially to bowl off-spin
WHAT WILL YOU BE DOING IN THE YEAR 2040? I'll be swimming in a sea of Donald Trump's fake tan
ODDEST SPORT YOU'VE PLAYED? Eton Fives
TWITTER: @hammo125

Batting	Mat	Inns	NO	Runs	HS	Ave	SR	100	50	Ct	St
First-class	11	19	2	510	123*	30.00	42.07	2	2	7	0
List A	3	1	0	0	0	0.00	0.00	0	0	0	0
T20s	16	13	0	313	51	24.07	155.72	0	1	9	0
Bowling	**Mat**	**Balls**	**Runs**	**Wkts**	**BBI**	**BBM**	**Ave**	**Econ**	**SR**	**5w**	**10**
First-class	11	312	210	1	1/96	1/155	210.00	4.03	312.0	0	0
List A	3	114	97	5	2/18	2/18	19.40	5.10	22.8	0	0
T20s	16	12	17	0	-	-	-	8.50	-	0	0

MIR HAMZA

LHB / LFM / R0 / W0

FULL NAME: Mir Hamza
BORN: September 10, 1992, Karachi, Pakistan
SQUAD NO: 92
TEAMS: Pakistan, Sussex, Baluchistan, Karachi Whites, National Bank of Pakistan, Sindh Knights, United Bank Limited
ROLE: Bowler
DEBUT: Test: 2018; First-class: 2012; List A: 2012; T20: 2014

BEST BATTING: 25 National Bank of Pakistan vs Peshawar, Faisalabad, 2018
BEST BOWLING: 7-59 United Bank Limited vs Sui Southern Gas Corporation, Sialkot, 2016

TWITTER: @mirhamza_k
NOTES: The Pakistan left-arm paceman signed for Sussex in January and will join the club in May for nine Championship fixtures and the tour match against Australia. "I'm very excited to have the chance to play county cricket with a great club like Sussex, following in the footsteps of Pakistan legends like Javed Miandad and Imran Khan," he said. At the time of writing Hamza had made only one appearance for Pakistan – a Test match against Australia in October 2018 when he clean-bowled Shaun Marsh for his first international wicket – but he has a superb domestic record, taking 125 wickets at an average of 15.28 for United Bank Limited. Over the last three seasons he has claimed 120 wickets at 12.41 in Pakistani first-class cricket

Batting	Mat	Inns	NO	Runs	HS	Ave	SR	100	50	Ct	St
Tests	1	2	2	4	4*	-	18.18	0	0	0	0
First-class	59	70	32	268	25	7.05	35.49	0	0	10	0
List A	54	27	18	179	49	19.88	83.25	0	0	9	0
T20s	23	6	4	7	5	3.50	46.66	0	0	6	0
Bowling	**Mat**	**Balls**	**Runs**	**Wkts**	**BBI**	**BBM**	**Ave**	**Econ**	**SR**	**5w**	**10**
Tests	1	90	67	1	1/40	1/67	67.00	4.46	90.0	0	0
First-class	59	11118	5173	282	7/59	12/137	18.34	2.79	39.4	26	6
List A	54	2606	2231	72	4/27	4/27	30.98	5.13	36.1	0	0
T20s	23	469	645	21	4/28	4/28	30.71	8.25	22.3	0	0

GEORGE HANKINS

RHB / OB / R0 / W0

FULL NAME: George Thomas Hankins
BORN: January 4, 1997, Bath
SQUAD NO: 21
HEIGHT: 6ft 1in
NICKNAME: Hanks, Hanko
EDUCATION: Kingswood School, Bath; Millfield School, Somerset
TEAMS: Gloucestershire
ROLE: Batsman
DEBUT: First-class: 2016; List A: 2017; T20: 2017

BEST BATTING: 116 Gloucestershire vs Northamptonshire, Northampton, 2016

WHAT WAS YOUR FIRST CRICKET CLUB? Bath CC, Somerset
FAVOURITE CRICKET BAT? My first, a GM Icon
CRICKETING HERO? Joe Root
WHICH BOWLER WOULD YOU LEAST LIKE TO FACE? Jasprit Bumrah – horrible angle
BEST INNINGS YOU'VE SEEN? Liam Norwell scoring a century as a nightwatchman in 2016 – amazing quality from a No.11
WHO WOULD YOU ASK TO BAT FOR YOUR LIFE? Rahul Dravid
SURPRISING FACT ABOUT YOU? I have no earlobes
FAVOURITE QUOTE OR SAYING? With great power comes great responsibilty
TWITTER: @hankins1997

Batting	Mat	Inns	NO	Runs	HS	Ave	SR	100	50	Ct	St
First-class	24	39	2	938	116	25.35	52.46	1	6	29	0
List A	10	10	1	418	92	46.44	75.58	0	4	7	0
T20s	7	3	0	17	14	5.66	60.71	0	0	1	0
Bowling	**Mat**	**Balls**	**Runs**	**Wkts**	**BBI**	**BBM**	**Ave**	**Econ**	**SR**	**5w**	**10**
First-class	24	13	13	0	-	-	-	6.00	-	0	0
List A	10	-	-	-	-	-	-	-	-	-	-
T20s	7	-	-	-	-	-	-	-	-	-	-

OLIVER HANNON-DALBY LHB / RMF / R0 / W0

FULL NAME: Oliver James Hannon-Dalby
BORN: June 20, 1989, Halifax, Yorkshire
SQUAD NO: 20
HEIGHT: 6ft 8in
NICKNAME: Owl Face, Owl Head, André Schürrle, Dizzle
EDUCATION: Brooksbank School; Leeds Metropolitan University
TEAMS: Warwickshire, Yorkshire
ROLE: Bowler
DEBUT: First-class: 2008; List A: 2011; T20: 2012

BEST BATTING: 40 Warwickshire vs Somerset, Taunton, 2014
BEST BOWLING: 5-68 Yorkshire vs Somerset, Headingley, 2010

WHAT WAS YOUR FIRST CRICKET CLUB? Copley CC, West Yorkshire. 'The Arches' is one of the most beautiful grounds in the Halifax League, defined by the Copley viaduct which runs along the north side of the ground. Well worth a visit for good cricket, great teas and the expert opinion of groundsman Tommy 'Topsoil' Thorpe on all things cricket
FAVOURITE CRICKET BAT? I did work experience at ACE Cricket Bats in Elland and the owner Alf gave me one of their top-range bats which I still have at home. It was a lovely gesture
WHICH RULE WOULD YOU CHANGE ABOUT CRICKET? Something which benefits bowlers more – wides, limited bouncers and batsmen dancing around like Fred Astaire means there are only a few spots where you can bowl it. Batter's game
FAVOURITE QUOTE OR SAYING? You Bears!
WHICH BOOK MEANS MOST TO YOU? Owls by Marianne Taylor
ODDEST SPORT YOU'VE PLAYED? Goalball – a sport for people who are visually impaired. It's a bit like dodgeball but using a big heavy ball with a bell in it. Tough but fun
TWITTER: @OHD_20

Batting	Mat	Inns	NO	Runs	HS	Ave	SR	100	50	Ct	St
First-class	57	68	23	294	40	6.53	24.09	0	0	5	0
List A	37	13	7	82	21*	13.66	101.23	0	0	12	0
T20s	53	11	7	52	14*	13.00	98.11	0	0	11	0
Bowling	**Mat**	**Balls**	**Runs**	**Wkts**	**BBI**	**BBM**	**Ave**	**Econ**	**SR**	**5w**	**10**
First-class	57	7925	4426	124	5/68	7/122	35.69	3.35	63.9	2	0
List A	37	1660	1750	54	5/27	5/27	32.40	6.32	30.7	1	0
T20s	53	1132	1652	73	4/20	4/20	22.63	8.75	15.5	0	0

GEORGE HARDING RHB / SLA / R0 / W0

FULL NAME: George Harvey Idris Harding
BORN: October 12, 1996, Poole, Dorset
SQUAD NO: 39
HEIGHT: 6ft 6in
NICKNAME: Hogster
EDUCATION: Brine Leas High School, Nantwich; Myerscough College, Preston
TEAMS: Durham
ROLE: Bowler
DEBUT: First-class: 2017; List A: 2017

BEST BATTING: 7 Durham vs Gloucestershire, Cheltenham, 2018
BEST BOWLING: 4-111 Durham vs Glamorgan, Swansea, 2017

WHAT WAS YOUR FIRST CRICKET CLUB? Crewe Vagrants CC, Cheshire
WHICH BOWLER WOULD YOU LEAST LIKE TO FACE? Mitchell Starc – I hate bouncers
BEST INNINGS YOU'VE SEEN? Matt Prior's century at Auckland in 2013 – grit and determination to pull off a draw with one wicket left
WHICH RULE WOULD YOU CHANGE ABOUT CRICKET? Bouncers allowed only to the top six batsmen
YOUR BIGGEST CRICKETING REGRET? Not being a fast bowler
SURPRISING FACT ABOUT YOU? I'm a big Chester FC fan
SURPRISING FACT ABOUT A TEAMMATE? Stuart Poynter has a dog called Wayne
WHAT WILL YOU BE DOING IN THE YEAR 2040? Farming
WHICH BOOK MEANS MOST TO YOU? Charlie and the Chocolate Factory by Roald Dahl
ODDEST SPORT YOU'VE PLAYED? Disc golf
TWITTER: @gharding96

Batting	Mat	Inns	NO	Runs	HS	Ave	SR	100	50	Ct	St
First-class	2	3	0	7	7	2.33	25.00	0	0	0	0
List A	8	4	4	23	18*	-	67.64	0	0	5	0
Bowling	**Mat**	**Balls**	**Runs**	**Wkts**	**BBI**	**BBM**	**Ave**	**Econ**	**SR**	**5w**	**10**
First-class	2	396	292	4	4/111	4/186	73.00	4.42	99.0	0	0
List A	8	438	431	6	2/52	2/52	71.83	5.90	73.0	0	0

ARUN HARINATH LHB / OB / R0 / W0

FULL NAME: Arun Harinath
BORN: April 3, 1987, Sutton, Surrey
SQUAD NO: 10
HEIGHT: 5ft 11in
NICKNAME: Baron
EDUCATION: Tiffin School, Kingston-upon-Thames; Loughborough University
TEAMS: Surrey, Leicestershire
ROLE: Batsman
DEBUT: First-class: 2007; List A: 2009

BEST BATTING: 154 Surrey vs Derbyshire, Derby, 2013
BEST BOWLING: 2-1 Surrey vs Middlesex, Lord's, 2013
COUNTY CAP: 2016 (Surrey)

FAMILY TIES? My dad played club cricket in Sri Lanka and my brother Muhunthan has also played for Surrey
WHAT WAS YOUR FIRST CRICKET CLUB? Sutton CC, London
FAVOURITE CRICKET BAT? Duncan Fearnley 405
CRICKETING HERO? Kumar Sangakkara
WHICH BOWLER WOULD YOU LEAST LIKE TO FACE? Corey Collymore
BEST INNINGS YOU'VE SEEN? Brian Lara's 375
WHO WOULD YOU ASK TO BAT FOR YOUR LIFE? Amar Virdi
WHICH RULE WOULD YOU CHANGE ABOUT CRICKET? Tea breaks need to be longer
YOUR BIGGEST CRICKETING REGRET? I haven't played cricket in the Caribbean yet
SURPRISING FACT ABOUT YOU? I have two university degrees
SURPRISING FACT ABOUT A TEAMMATE? Rory Burns plays the saxophone
FAVOURITE QUOTE OR SAYING? It is what it is
WHICH BOOK MEANS MOST TO YOU? The Catcher in the Rye by JD Salinger
TWITTER: @arunharinath

Batting	Mat	Inns	NO	Runs	HS	Ave	SR	100	50	Ct	St
First-class	75	131	6	3870	154	30.96	44.38	6	21	20	0
List A	7	7	2	108	52	21.60	78.83	0	1	1	0
Bowling	**Mat**	**Balls**	**Runs**	**Wkts**	**BBI**	**BBM**	**Ave**	**Econ**	**SR**	**5w**	**10**
First-class	75	351	195	5	2/1	2/1	39.00	3.33	70.2	0	0
List A	7	18	16	0	-	-	-	5.33	-	0	0

SIMON HARMER RHB / OB / R0 / W2 / MVP5

FULL NAME: Simon Ross Harmer
BORN: February 10, 1989, Pretoria, South Africa
SQUAD NO: 11
EDUCATION: Nelson Mandela Metropolitan University, Port Elizabeth
TEAMS: South Africa, Essex, Border, Eastern Province, Jozi Stars, Warriors
ROLE: Bowler
DEBUT: Test: 2015; First-class: 2009; List A: 2010; T20: 2011

BEST BATTING: 102* Essex vs Surrey, The Oval, 2018
BEST BOWLING: 9-95 Essex vs Middlesex, Chelmsford, 2017

TWITTER: @SimonHarmerRSA
NOTES: Essex were delighted to sign a proven Test off-spinner on a Kolpak deal ahead of the 2017 season but could not have envisaged the impact he would make: 72 Championship wickets to help the county to the title. Last year wasn't that bad either – 57 wickets at 24.46, plus a maiden Championship hundred. In November he signed a contract extension that ties him to the club until the end of the 2021 season. Harmer has played five Tests for South Africa but decided that his future was best served in county cricket after falling down the national pecking order. He took seven wickets on Test debut against West Indies at Newlands in 2015 and claimed 10 in two matches on South Africa's tour of India later that year

Batting	Mat	Inns	NO	Runs	HS	Ave	SR	100	50	Ct	St
Tests	5	6	1	58	13	11.60	33.33	0	0	1	0
First-class	130	197	40	3910	102*	24.90	49.53	2	20	124	0
List A	77	64	20	909	44*	20.65	97.84	0	0	50	0
T20s	78	45	16	592	43	20.41	129.82	0	0	32	0
Bowling	**Mat**	**Balls**	**Runs**	**Wkts**	**BBI**	**BBM**	**Ave**	**Econ**	**SR**	**5w**	**10**
Tests	5	1148	588	20	4/61	7/153	29.40	3.07	57.4	0	0
First-class	130	30895	15344	522	9/95	14/128	29.39	2.97	59.1	24	4
List A	77	3612	3062	74	4/42	4/42	41.37	5.08	48.8	0	0
T20s	78	1403	1741	51	3/22	3/22	34.13	7.44	27.5	0	0

JAMES HARRIS RHB / RFM / R0 / W3 / MVP51

FULL NAME: James Alexander Russell Harris
BORN: May 16, 1990, Morriston, Swansea, Wales
SQUAD NO: 5
HEIGHT: 6ft 1in
NICKNAME: Bones, Jimmy, Harry, Lance
EDUCATION: Pontarddulais Comprehensive School, Swansea; Gorseinon College, Swansea
TEAMS: Middlesex, England Lions, Glamorgan, Kent
ROLE: Bowler
DEBUT: First-class: 2007; List A: 2007; T20: 2008

BEST BATTING: 87* Glamorgan vs Nottinghamshire, Swansea, 2007
BEST BOWLING: 9-34 Middlesex vs Durham, Lord's, 2015
COUNTY CAP: 2010 (Glamorgan); 2015 (Middlesex)

WHAT WAS YOUR FIRST CRICKET CLUB? Pontarddulais CC, South Wales. It was next door to my secondary school, so we spent all our summers practising in the nets or playing in the outfield with a dustbin for stumps and a tennis ball covered in tape
FAVOURITE CRICKET BAT? Gray-Nicolls Millennium, which had scoops out of the back. Bought by my dad from Bill Edwards's old sports shop just around the corner from St Helen's cricket ground in Swansea
BEST INNINGS YOU'VE SEEN? Chris Rogers hitting a double hundred to chase down 472 against Yorkshire at Lord's in 2014. We did it in less than a day with relative ease
WHAT WILL YOU BE DOING IN THE YEAR 2040? I'll be still in the gym eating a kale salad coupled with a flat white
WHICH BOOK MEANS MOST TO YOU? Own the Day, Own Your Life – Optimized Practices for Waking, Working, Learning, Eating, Training, Playing, Sleeping and Sex by Aubrey Marcus
TWITTER: @James_Harris9

Batting	Mat	Inns	NO	Runs	HS	Ave	SR	100	50	Ct	St
First-class	134	192	45	3265	87*	22.21	40.46	0	15	40	0
List A	59	35	8	300	32	11.11	65.78	0	0	14	0
T20s	53	25	12	150	18	11.53	109.48	0	0	5	0
Bowling	**Mat**	**Balls**	**Runs**	**Wkts**	**BBI**	**BBM**	**Ave**	**Econ**	**SR**	**5w**	**10**
First-class	134	23441	12981	462	9/34	13/103	28.09	3.32	50.7	15	2
List A	59	2434	2324	80	4/38	4/38	29.05	5.72	30.4	0	0
T20s	53	970	1463	47	4/23	4/23	31.12	9.04	20.6	0	0

GARETH HARTE

RHB / RM / R0 / W0

FULL NAME: Gareth Jason Harte
BORN: March 15, 1993, Johannesburg, South Africa
SQUAD NO: 93
HEIGHT: 5ft 10in
NICKNAME: Gaz, Harty
EDUCATION: King Edward VII School, Johannesburg
TEAMS: Durham
ROLE: Batsman
DEBUT: First-class: 2018; List A: 2018; T20: 2017

BEST BATTING: 114 Durham vs Derbyshire, Chester-le-Street, 2018
BEST BOWLING: 2-26 Durham vs Leicestershire, Leicester, 2018

WHAT WAS YOUR FIRST CRICKET CLUB? Old Edwardians CC, Johannesburg, South Africa
FAVOURITE CRICKET BAT? SS Zulu Warrior, Lance Klusener edition. Scored my first hundred with it
WHICH BOWLER WOULD YOU LEAST LIKE TO FACE? Mohammad Abbas – he once got me out twice in a day and I don't want that to happen again!
WHICH RULE WOULD YOU CHANGE ABOUT CRICKET? The toss rule in the Championship
YOUR BIGGEST CRICKETING REGRET? Haven't got one – I love the great game
WHAT WILL YOU BE DOING IN THE YEAR 2040? Probably drinking whisky on my yacht
FAVOURITE QUOTE OR SAYING? Just do it
WHICH BOOK MEANS MOST TO YOU? The Obstacle is the Way – The Timeless Art of Turning Trials into Triumphs by Ryan Holiday
TWITTER: @HarteGareth

Batting	Mat	Inns	NO	Runs	HS	Ave	SR	100	50	Ct	St
First-class	8	15	0	382	114	25.46	41.61	2	0	4	0
List A	5	5	1	140	48	35.00	85.36	0	0	0	0
T20s	2	2	0	17	11	8.50	121.42	0	0	2	0
Bowling	**Mat**	**Balls**	**Runs**	**Wkts**	**BBI**	**BBM**	**Ave**	**Econ**	**SR**	**5w**	**10**
First-class	8	271	148	3	2/26	2/26	49.33	3.27	90.3	0	0
List A	5	102	91	3	2/35	2/35	30.33	5.35	34.0	0	0
T20s	2	-	-	-	-	-	-	-	-	-	-

JACK HAYNES

RHB / OB / R0 / W0

FULL NAME: Jack Alexander Haynes
BORN: January 30, 2001, Worcester
SQUAD NO: 17
HEIGHT: 6ft 1in
NICKNAME: Haynesy
EDUCATION: Malvern College
TEAMS: Worcestershire
ROLE: Batsman
DEBUT: List A: 2018

WHAT WAS YOUR FIRST CRICKET CLUB? Ombersley CC, Worcestershire
WHICH BOWLER WOULD YOU LEAST LIKE TO FACE? Shane Warne
BEST INNINGS YOU'VE SEEN? Alastair Cook's final Test innings at The Oval last summer
WHO WOULD YOU ASK TO BAT FOR YOUR LIFE? Daryl Mitchell
WHICH BOOK MEANS MOST TO YOU? Bounce – The Myth of Talent and the Power of Practice by Matthew Syed
TWITTER: @jack_haynes1
NOTES: Son of the former Worcestershire allrounder Gavin Haynes, who made more than 200 appearances for the club in the 1990s, Jack is a top-order batsman who was part of the Midlands U15 side that won the Bunbury T20 Schools competition in 2016 and then the U17 side that won the 50-over-and-T20 double the following season. He captained the England Schools U16 side and Worcestershire U17 before making his Second XI debut in 2017. Haynes made his England U19 debut last summer, scoring 74 as an opener against South Africa U19 in a youth ODI at Gosforth. Scored 33 on his first-team debut against West Indies A at New Road earlier in the season

Batting	Mat	Inns	NO	Runs	HS	Ave	SR	100	50	Ct	St
List A	1	1	0	33	33	33.00	86.84	0	0	1	0
Bowling	**Mat**	**Balls**	**Runs**	**Wkts**	**BBI**	**BBM**	**Ave**	**Econ**	**SR**	**5w**	**10**
List A	1	-	-	-	-	-	-	-	-	-	-

TOM HELM

RHB / RFM / R0 / W0

FULL NAME: Thomas George Helm
BORN: May 7, 1994, Aylesbury, Buckinghamshire
SQUAD NO: 7
HEIGHT: 6ft 4in
NICKNAME: Ched, Helmy
EDUCATION: The Misbourne School, Buckinghamshire
TEAMS: Middlesex, England Lions, Glamorgan
ROLE: Bowler
DEBUT: First-class: 2013; List A: 2013; T20: 2016

BEST BATTING: 52 Middlesex vs Derbyshire, Lord's, 2018
BEST BOWLING: 5-59 Middlesex vs Warwickshire, Edgbaston, 2017

FAMILY TIES? My brother Sam played Minor Counties for Buckinghamshire
WHAT WAS YOUR FIRST CRICKET CLUB? Chesham CC, Buckinghamshire
FAVOURITE CRICKET BAT? The blue Kwik Cricket bat – my kind of shape
CRICKETING HERO? James Anderson
WHICH BOWLER WOULD YOU LEAST LIKE TO FACE? Tymal Mills – he bowls like he snipes
BEST INNINGS YOU'VE SEEN? Tim Murtagh – take your pick
WHO WOULD YOU ASK TO BAT FOR YOUR LIFE? Martin Andersson, aka The Don
WHICH RULE WOULD YOU CHANGE ABOUT CRICKET? Make bats smaller
WHAT WILL YOU BE DOING IN THE YEAR 2040? Playing Fortnite (online video game)
FAVOURITE QUOTE OR SAYING? Oooooh like goats
ODDEST SPORT YOU'VE PLAYED? Shower curling
TWITTER: @tomhelm7

Batting	Mat	Inns	NO	Runs	HS	Ave	SR	100	50	Ct	St
First-class	22	30	7	343	52	14.91	45.07	0	1	8	0
List A	31	19	6	179	30	13.76	75.21	0	0	10	0
T20s	19	7	6	45	28*	45.00	145.16	0	0	1	0
Bowling	**Mat**	**Balls**	**Runs**	**Wkts**	**BBI**	**BBM**	**Ave**	**Econ**	**SR**	**5w**	**10**
First-class	22	3042	1693	54	5/59	7/140	31.35	3.33	56.3	1	0
List A	31	1306	1195	37	5/33	5/33	32.29	5.49	35.2	1	0
T20s	19	389	522	27	5/11	5/11	19.33	8.05	14.4	1	0

CHARLIE HEMPHREY RHB / OB / R0 / W0

FULL NAME: Charlie Richard Hemphrey
BORN: August 31, 1989, Doncaster, Yorkshire
SQUAD NO: 22
HEIGHT: 6ft 2in
NICKNAME: Bronson, Prince
EDUCATION: Harvey Grammar School, Folkestone, Kent
TEAMS: Glamorgan, Queensland
ROLE: Batsman
DEBUT: First-class: 2015; List A: 2015

BEST BATTING: 118 Queensland vs South Australia, Brisbane, 2015
BEST BOWLING: 2-56 Queensland vs South Australia, Adelaide, 2016

WHAT WAS YOUR FIRST CRICKET CLUB? Hythe CC, Kent. It used to be under the English Channel
WHICH BOWLER WOULD YOU LEAST LIKE TO FACE? Adam Hollioake
BEST INNINGS YOU'VE SEEN? Alastair Cook's 244 at the MCG during the 2017/18 Ashes. Grit and determination
WHO WOULD YOU ASK TO BAT FOR YOUR LIFE? Rahul Dravid – I enjoy life and he enjoyed batting
WHAT WILL YOU BE DOING IN THE YEAR 2040? Somewhere in the snow, flicking through the Racing Post
FAVOURITE QUOTE OR SAYING? Manyana
WHICH BOOK MEANS MOST TO YOU? Enemy Number One – The Secrets of the UK's Most Feared Professional Punter by Patrick Veitch

Batting	Mat	Inns	NO	Runs	HS	Ave	SR	100	50	Ct	St
First-class	30	57	5	1715	118	32.98	43.11	4	9	20	0
List A	13	13	0	288	58	22.15	72.91	0	1	3	0
Bowling	**Mat**	**Balls**	**Runs**	**Wkts**	**BBI**	**BBM**	**Ave**	**Econ**	**SR**	**5w**	**10**
First-class	30	564	411	6	2/56	3/91	68.50	4.37	94.0	0	0
List A	13	144	131	2	1/18	1/18	65.50	5.45	72.0	0	0

RYAN HIGGINS RHB / OB / RM / W0 / MVP13

FULL NAME: Ryan Francis Higgins
BORN: January 6, 1995, Harare, Zimbabwe
SQUAD NO: 29
HEIGHT: 5ft 10in
NICKNAME: Mad Bri, Brian, Higgo
EDUCATION: Peterhouse School, Marondera, Zimbabwe; Bradfield College, Reading
TEAMS: Gloucestershire, Middlesex
ROLE: Allrounder
DEBUT: First-class: 2017; List A: 2014; T20: 2014

BEST BATTING: 105 Gloucestershire vs Durham, Cheltenham, 2018
BEST BOWLING: 5-21 Gloucestershire vs Sussex, Hove, 2018

WHAT WAS YOUR FIRST CRICKET CLUB? Falkland CC, Berkshire. It was only five minutes from home
WHICH BOWLER WOULD YOU LEAST LIKE TO FACE? Rashid Khan
WHO WOULD YOU ASK TO BAT FOR YOUR LIFE? Nathan Sowter – gritty and tough. I could see him blasting a few over point and keeping it interesting
WHICH RULE WOULD YOU CHANGE ABOUT CRICKET? Have a maximum of 80 overs in a day
YOUR BIGGEST CRICKETING REGRET? My time in Sydney – I did not take the game as seriously out there
WHAT WILL YOU BE DOING IN THE YEAR 2040? I'd like to be involved in sports business and mentoring
FAVOURITE QUOTE OR SAYING? First learn the fundamentals (Larry Bird)
TWITTER: @ryanhiggins21

Batting	Mat	Inns	NO	Runs	HS	Ave	SR	100	50	Ct	St
First-class	19	32	3	655	105	22.58	58.27	1	2	6	0
List A	24	21	3	445	81*	24.72	92.70	0	2	3	0
T20s	51	45	11	815	68*	23.97	131.66	0	3	14	0
Bowling	**Mat**	**Balls**	**Runs**	**Wkts**	**BBI**	**BBM**	**Ave**	**Econ**	**SR**	**5w**	**10**
First-class	19	2747	1173	60	5/21	8/54	19.55	2.56	45.7	2	0
List A	24	496	457	14	4/50	4/50	32.64	5.52	35.4	0	0
T20s	51	430	623	23	5/13	5/13	27.08	8.69	18.6	1	0

JAMES HILDRETH

RHB / RM / R7 / W0 / MVP6

FULL NAME: James Charles Hildreth
BORN: September 9, 1984, Milton Keynes, Buckinghamshire
SQUAD NO: 25
HEIGHT: 5ft 10in
NICKNAME: Hildy, Hildz
EDUCATION: Millfield School, Somerset
TEAMS: Somerset, England Lions
ROLE: Batsman
DEBUT: First-class: 2003; List A: 2003; T20: 2004

BEST BATTING: 303* Somerset vs Warwickshire, Taunton, 2009
BEST BOWLING: 2-39 Somerset vs Hampshire, Taunton, 2009
COUNTY CAP: 2007; **BENEFIT:** 2017

'ROY OF THE ROVERS' MOMENT? Winning the T20 in 2005, captaining England Lions and captaining Somerset
CRICKETING HERO? Ricky Ponting
IF YOU WEREN'T A CRICKETER? I'd be travelling
SURPRISING FACT? I'm a big MK Dons fan
TWITTER: @dreth25
NOTES: At 34 years of age Hildreth is still one of the classiest batsmen on the circuit yet to play for England. He was in vintage form last summer, becoming one of only nine batsmen who passed 1,000 first-class runs in the season, as well as being Somerset's top run-scorer in the One-Day Cup and second-highest in the T20 Blast

Batting	Mat	Inns	NO	Runs	HS	Ave	SR	100	50	Ct	St
First-class	248	408	30	16427	303*	43.45	65.13	44	74	206	0
List A	201	188	35	5324	159	34.79	90.15	7	23	77	0
T20s	179	166	29	3359	107*	24.51	123.81	1	16	66	0
Bowling	**Mat**	**Balls**	**Runs**	**Wkts**	**BBI**	**BBM**	**Ave**	**Econ**	**SR**	**5w**	**10**
First-class	248	576	492	6	2/39	2/39	82.00	5.12	96.0	0	0
List A	201	150	185	6	2/26	2/26	30.83	7.40	25.0	0	0
T20s	179	169	247	10	3/24	3/24	24.70	8.76	16.9	0	0

LEWIS HILL RHB / WK / R0 / W0

FULL NAME: Lewis John Hill
BORN: October 5, 1990, Leicester
SQUAD NO: 23
HEIGHT: 5ft 8in
NICKNAME: Lew Show, Lew, Hilly
EDUCATION: Hastings High School, Hinckley; John Cleveland College, Hinckley
TEAMS: Leicestershire
ROLE: Wicketkeeper
DEBUT: First-class: 2015; List A: 2012; T20: 2015

BEST BATTING: 126 Leicestershire vs Surrey, The Oval, 2015

WHAT GOT YOU INTO CRICKET? Friends played it when we were nine years old, so I joined in at their club
FAMILY TIES? My dad and brother both play for Lutterworth CC
'ROY OF THE ROVERS' MOMENT? Scoring my maiden first-class century at The Oval and having Kumar Sangakkara and Kevin Pietersen shake my hand at the end of the day
IF YOU WEREN'T A CRICKETER? I'd be working for my dad in the family sports engineering business
SURPRISING FACT ABOUT YOU? I was targeted by armed robbers twice while working at my local newsagents
CRICKETING HERO? Karl Smith, Craig Wilson and Nathan Welham of Lutterworth CC
TWITTER: @lhjill23

Batting	Mat	Inns	NO	Runs	HS	Ave	SR	100	50	Ct	St
First-class	33	59	7	1227	126	23.59	47.50	1	4	68	2
List A	33	29	2	607	86	22.48	86.71	0	3	18	2
T20s	28	20	6	286	31*	20.42	123.80	0	0	11	0

Bowling	Mat	Balls	Runs	Wkts	BBI	BBM	Ave	Econ	SR	5w	10
First-class	33	12	6	0	-	-	-	3.00	-	0	0
List A	33	-	-	-	-	-	-	-	-	-	-
T20s	28	-	-	-	-	-	-	-	-	-	-

MICHAEL HOGAN RHB / RFM / R0 / W3 / MVP76

FULL NAME: Michael Garry Hogan
BORN: May 31, 1981, Newcastle, Australia
SQUAD NO: 31
HEIGHT: 6ft 5in
NICKNAME: Hulk, Hoges
TEAMS: Glamorgan, Hobart Hurricanes, Western Australia
ROLE: Bowler
DEBUT: First-class: 2009; List A: 2009; T20: 2010

BEST BATTING: 57 Glamorgan vs Lancashire, Colwyn Bay, 2015
BEST BOWLING: 7-92 Glamorgan vs Gloucestershire, Bristol, 2013
COUNTY CAP: 2013

BEST ADVICE EVER RECEIVED? If the grass looks greener on the other side, there's probably more shit there
'ROY OF THE ROVERS' MOMENT? Defending three when I was bowling the final over in a T20 game against Kent a few years ago
BEST THING ABOUT YOUR HOME GROUND? The Friday-night T20 atmosphere
SURPRISING FACT ABOUT YOU? I'm very boring
SURPRISING FACT ABOUT A TEAMMATE? Marchant de Lange drinks two litres of Coca-Cola every day
WHERE IS PARADISE? Fiji
CRICKETING HERO? Glenn McGrath
NON-CRICKETING HERO? Roger Federer
TWITTER: @hoges31

Batting	Mat	Inns	NO	Runs	HS	Ave	SR	100	50	Ct	St
First-class	144	206	79	2004	57	15.77	83.43	0	2	75	0
List A	66	26	16	159	27	15.90	80.30	0	0	23	0
T20s	92	19	12	75	17*	10.71	105.63	0	0	39	0
Bowling	**Mat**	**Balls**	**Runs**	**Wkts**	**BBI**	**BBM**	**Ave**	**Econ**	**SR**	**5w**	**10**
First-class	144	29825	13378	548	7/92	10/87	24.41	2.69	54.4	22	2
List A	66	3418	2877	99	5/44	5/44	29.06	5.05	34.5	1	0
T20s	92	1894	2448	104	5/17	5/17	23.53	7.75	18.2	1	0

MAX HOLDEN

LHB / OB / R0 / W0

FULL NAME: Max David Edward Holden
BORN: December 18, 1997, Cambridge
SQUAD NO: 4
HEIGHT: 6ft 1in
NICKNAME: Texas, Pepsi, Little Chef, Maxi
EDUCATION: Sawston Village College, Cambridge; Hills Road Sixth Form College, Cambridge
TEAMS: Middlesex, England Lions, Northamptonshire
ROLE: Batsman
DEBUT: First-class: 2017; List A: 2017; T20: 2018

BEST BATTING: 153 Northamptonshire vs Kent, Beckenham, 2017
BEST BOWLING: 2-59 Northamptonshire vs Kent, Beckenham, 2017

WHAT WAS YOUR FIRST CRICKET CLUB? Cambridge St Giles CC, Cambridgeshire. It had a 20-metre leg-side boundary
FAVOURITE CRICKET BAT? My Gray-Nicolls Powerbow. Had it when I was 10. Loved the stickers. I'm using one again in 2019
CRICKETING HERO? Brian Lara
WHICH BOWLER WOULD YOU LEAST LIKE TO FACE? Ethan Bamber – he gets me out every other ball in the nets
BEST INNINGS YOU'VE SEEN? Ben Duckett's hundred before lunch for Northants against Leicestershire in 2017. I watched it from the other end
WHO WOULD YOU ASK TO BAT FOR YOUR LIFE? James Harris – the man for a crisis
WHAT WILL YOU BE DOING IN THE YEAR 2040? Managing Arsenal (maybe)
WHICH BOOK MEANS MOST TO YOU? Harry Potter and the Goblet of Fire by JK Rowling
TWITTER: @maxholden_4

Batting	Mat	Inns	NO	Runs	HS	Ave	SR	100	50	Ct	St
First-class	28	50	4	1505	153	32.71	50.09	3	6	10	0
List A	6	5	1	187	71	46.75	82.74	0	2	0	0
T20s	6	6	0	169	84	28.16	137.39	0	1	3	0
Bowling	**Mat**	**Balls**	**Runs**	**Wkts**	**BBI**	**BBM**	**Ave**	**Econ**	**SR**	**5w**	**10**
First-class	28	498	348	5	2/59	3/94	69.60	4.19	99.6	0	0
List A	6	84	50	1	1/29	1/29	50.00	3.57	84.0	0	0
T20s	6	6	12	0	-	-	-	12.00	-	0	0

JASON HOLDER RHB / RMF / R0 / W0

FULL NAME: Jason Omar Holder
BORN: November 5, 1991, St George, Barbados
SQUAD NO: 98
HEIGHT: 6ft 7in
TEAMS: West Indies, Northamptonshire, Barbados, Chennai Super Kings, Kolkata Knight Riders, Otago, Sunrisers Hyderabad
ROLE: Allrounder
DEBUT: Test: 2014; ODI: 2013; T20I: 2014; First-class: 2009; List A: 2009; T20: 2010

BEST BATTING: 202* West Indies vs England, Barbados, 2019
BEST BOWLING: 6-59 West Indies vs Bangladesh, Jamaica, 2018

TWITTER: @Jaseholder98
NOTES: Northamptonshire have signed the West Indies captain for the first month of the campaign and he is due to play in two Championship fixtures and six One-Day Cup matches. "England is somewhere I've wanted to play for a long time and I'm looking forward to the experience of county cricket and testing myself in the different conditions," said Holder. The allrounder starred in West Indies' Test series win against England in the Caribbean in early 2019, hitting a maiden double century in a crushing victory on his home island of Barbados. That performance moved him to No.1 in the ICC's Test allrounder rankings. Holder was named West Indies captain in 2014 at the age of 23, making him the 15th-youngest Test skipper in history

Batting	Mat	Inns	NO	Runs	HS	Ave	SR	100	50	Ct	St
Tests	37	64	11	1783	202*	33.64	59.29	3	8	29	0
ODIs	90	73	17	1471	99*	26.26	93.45	0	7	35	0
T20Is	11	7	1	60	26*	10.00	107.14	0	0	3	0
First-class	65	102	11	2422	202*	26.61	57.09	3	10	47	0
List A	136	109	23	2077	99*	24.15	93.29	0	9	50	0
T20s	87	62	16	656	54	14.26	126.88	0	1	40	0
Bowling	**Mat**	**Balls**	**Runs**	**Wkts**	**BBI**	**BBM**	**Ave**	**Econ**	**SR**	**5w**	**10**
Tests	37	5904	2576	93	6/59	11/103	27.69	2.61	63.4	5	1
ODIs	90	4260	3934	119	5/27	5/27	33.05	5.54	35.7	2	0
T20Is	11	229	304	9	2/27	2/27	33.77	7.96	25.4	0	0
First-class	65	9361	4123	164	6/59	11/103	25.14	2.64	57.0	8	1
List A	136	6224	5324	193	5/27	5/27	27.58	5.13	32.2	2	0
T20s	87	1713	2205	63	4/27	4/27	35.00	7.72	27.1	0	0

IAN HOLLAND

RHB / RMF / R0 / W0

FULL NAME: Ian Gabriel Holland
BORN: October 3, 1990, Wisconsin, USA
SQUAD NO: 22
HEIGHT: 6ft
NICKNAME: Dutchy
EDUCATION: Ringwood Secondary College, Melbourne
TEAMS: Hampshire, Victoria
ROLE: Allrounder
DEBUT: First-class: 2016; List A: 2017; T20: 2017

BEST BATTING: 58* Hampshire vs Surrey, The Oval, 2017
BEST BOWLING: 4-16 Hampshire vs Somerset, Southampton, 2017

WHAT WAS YOUR FIRST CRICKET CLUB? Ringwood CC, Melbourne
FAVOURITE CRICKET BAT? Kookaburra Bubble – loved the shape
CRICKETING HERO? Jacques Kallis
WHICH BOWLER WOULD YOU LEAST LIKE TO FACE? Dale Steyn – he gets crazy eyes
BEST INNINGS YOU'VE SEEN? Ricky Ponting's 140 not out against India in the 2003 World Cup final – stood up as captain on the big occasion
WHO WOULD YOU ASK TO BAT FOR YOUR LIFE? Our former captain Jimmy Adams – he'd crab around for at least two days
WHICH RULE WOULD YOU CHANGE ABOUT CRICKET? No limit on the number of bouncers allowed per over
FAVOURITE QUOTE OR SAYING? Get comfortable being uncomfortable
WHICH BOOK MEANS MOST TO YOU? Green Bay Packers' Playbook
TWITTER: @IanHolland22

Batting	Mat	Inns	NO	Runs	HS	Ave	SR	100	50	Ct	St
First-class	17	25	5	393	58*	19.65	39.02	0	2	4	0
List A	2	1	1	11	11*	-	100.00	0	0	0	0
T20s	1	-	-	-	-	-	-	-	-	0	0
Bowling	**Mat**	**Balls**	**Runs**	**Wkts**	**BBI**	**BBM**	**Ave**	**Econ**	**SR**	**5w**	**10**
First-class	17	1908	818	35	4/16	6/39	23.37	2.57	54.5	0	0
List A	2	114	117	3	2/57	2/57	39.00	6.15	38.0	0	0
T20s	1	24	33	1	1/33	1/33	33.00	8.25	24.0	0	0

PAUL HORTON RHB / RM / R3 / W0

FULL NAME: Paul James Horton
BORN: September 20, 1982, Sydney, Australia
SQUAD NO: 2
HEIGHT: 5ft 10in
NICKNAME: Horts, Torts, Aussie, Custard
EDUCATION: Colo High School, Sydney; St Margaret's High School, Liverpool
TEAMS: Leicestershire, Lancashire, Matabeleland Tuskers
ROLE: Batsman
DEBUT: First-class: 2003; List A: 2003; T20: 2005

BEST BATTING: 209 Matabeleland Tuskers vs Southern Rocks, Masvingo, 2011
BEST BOWLING: 2-6 Leicestershire vs Sussex, Leicester, 2016
COUNTY CAP: 2007 (Lancashire)

STRANGEST THING SEEN IN A GAME? A team refuse to take the field because they weren't being paid enough
'ROY OF THE ROVERS' MOMENT? Nothing can top winning the County Championship in 2011 with Lancashire. Back-to-back Logan Cup trophies with Matabeleland Tuskers in 2010/11 and 2011/12 was also special
CRICKETING HERO? Dean Jones
NON-CRICKETING HERO? Robbie Fowler
SURPRISING FACT? I was a left-handed batsman as a kid. And I was once detained as an illegal immigrant
UNUSUAL OBJECT AT HOME? My French bulldog is pretty unusual at times
TWITTER: @PJHorton20

Batting	Mat	Inns	NO	Runs	HS	Ave	SR	100	50	Ct	St
First-class	203	346	25	11558	209	36.00	48.32	23	64	188	1
List A	115	106	13	2868	111*	30.83	77.91	3	14	46	0
T20s	82	76	14	1477	71*	23.82	108.52	0	5	32	0
Bowling	**Mat**	**Balls**	**Runs**	**Wkts**	**BBI**	**BBM**	**Ave**	**Econ**	**SR**	**5w**	**10**
First-class	203	118	80	2	2/6	2/6	40.00	4.06	59.0	0	0
List A	115	12	7	1	1/7	1/7	7.00	3.50	12.0	0	0
T20s	82	-	-	-	-	-	-	-	-	-	-

ADAM HOSE

RHB / RMF / R0 / W0

FULL NAME: Adam John Hose
BORN: October 25, 1992, Newport, Isle of Wight
SQUAD NO: 21
HEIGHT: 6ft 5in
NICKNAME: Pipe
EDUCATION: Carisbrooke School, Newport
TEAMS: Warwickshire, Somerset
ROLE: Batsman
DEBUT: First-class: 2016; List A: 2015; T20: 2015

BEST BATTING: 68 Somerset vs Yorkshire, Taunton, 2017

WHAT WAS YOUR FIRST CRICKET CLUB? Ventnor CC, Isle of Wight. Ever since I can remember I was down at my home club, watching and pestering all the players to throw me balls. The club's ground is a unique bowl
FAVOURITE CRICKET BAT? Slazenger V1200 – the bat everyone had when I was growing up
CRICKETING HERO? Kevin Pietersen
WHICH BOWLER WOULD YOU LEAST LIKE TO FACE? Darren Stevens on an early-season greentop
BEST INNINGS YOU'VE SEEN? Roelof van der Merwe's 165 not out to beat Surrey in the 2017 One-Day Cup. We were chasing 291 and it wasn't looking good at 22-5...
WHO WOULD YOU ASK TO BAT FOR YOUR LIFE? Jonathan Trott
WHAT WILL YOU BE DOING IN THE YEAR 2040? I'm still working out what I'm going to do this weekend, let alone in 2040
ODDEST SPORT YOU'VE PLAYED? Gaelic football
TWITTER: @adamhose21

Batting	Mat	Inns	NO	Runs	HS	Ave	SR	100	50	Ct	St
First-class	8	15	1	406	68	29.00	50.68	0	4	2	0
List A	29	24	1	761	101*	33.08	90.27	1	4	16	0
T20s	35	34	4	889	76	29.63	142.24	0	7	14	0
Bowling	**Mat**	**Balls**	**Runs**	**Wkts**	**BBI**	**BBM**	**Ave**	**Econ**	**SR**	**5w**	**10**
First-class	8	-	-	-	-	-	-	-	-	-	-
List A	29	-	-	-	-	-	-	-	-	-	-
T20s	35	-	-	-	-	-	-	-	-	-	-

HARVEY HOSEIN

RHB / WK / R0 / W0

FULL NAME: Harvey Richard Hosein
BORN: August 12, 1996, Chesterfield, Derbyshire
SQUAD NO: 16
HEIGHT: 5ft 11in
NICKNAME: General
EDUCATION: Denstone College, Staffordshire
TEAMS: Derbyshire
ROLE: Wicketkeeper
DEBUT: First-class: 2014; List A: 2016; T20: 2016

BEST BATTING: 108 Derbyshire vs Worcestershire, Worcester, 2016

WHAT WAS YOUR FIRST CRICKET CLUB? Matlock CC, Derbyshire. Shares just under half the outfield with the football club
FAVOURITE CRICKET BAT? Slazenger V800 – helped me score my maiden first-class century
WHICH BOWLER WOULD YOU LEAST LIKE TO FACE? Murali
BEST INNINGS YOU'VE SEEN? Brian Lara's 400 not out
WHO WOULD YOU ASK TO BAT FOR YOUR LIFE? Rahul Dravid
SURPRISING FACT ABOUT YOU? I played county-level tennis when I was younger
SURPRISING FACT ABOUT A TEAMMATE? Wayne Madsen was an international hockey player for South Africa before coming to England to play cricket
WHICH BOOK MEANS MOST TO YOU? The Champion's Mind – How Great Athletes Think, Train, and Thrive by Jim Afremow
TWITTER: @HarveyHosein16

Batting	Mat	Inns	NO	Runs	HS	Ave	SR	100	50	Ct	St
First-class	31	52	10	1259	108	29.97	42.46	1	9	75	2
List A	4	2	1	42	40	42.00	110.52	0	0	1	1
T20s	5	2	2	0	0*	-	-	0	0	7	0
Bowling	**Mat**	**Balls**	**Runs**	**Wkts**	**BBI**	**BBM**	**Ave**	**Econ**	**SR**	**5w**	**10**
First-class	31	-	-	-	-	-	-	-	-	-	-
List A	4	-	-	-	-	-	-	-	-	-	-
T20s	5	-	-	-	-	-	-	-	-	-	-

BENNY HOWELL RHB / RM / R0 / W0 / MVP58

FULL NAME: Benny Alexander Cameron Howell
BORN: October 5, 1988, Bordeaux, France
SQUAD NO: 13
HEIGHT: 6ft
NICKNAME: Novak, Trowell, Growler
EDUCATION: The Oratory School, Reading
TEAMS: Gloucestershire, Hampshire, Khulna Titans, Rangpur Riders
ROLE: Allrounder
DEBUT: First-class: 2011; List A: 2010; T20: 2011

BEST BATTING: 163 Gloucestershire vs Glamorgan, Cardiff, 2017
BEST BOWLING: 5-57 Gloucestershire vs Leicestershire, Leicester, 2013
COUNTY CAP: 2012 (Gloucestershire)

WHAT WAS YOUR FIRST CRICKET CLUB? Stoke Row CC, Oxfordshire. Beers were drank before and after the game. My brother Nicky was the best drunk batter I have seen
'ROY OF THE ROVERS' MOMENT? Winning league promotion with Goatacre CC (Wiltshire) – there was a pitch invasion after we won the deciding match in the last over
BEST INNINGS YOU'VE SEEN? Jack Taylor hitting 41 off 14 balls against Derbyshire in the 2015 One-Day Cup. We scored 69 in four overs to chase down the target off the last ball
SURPRISING FACT ABOUT A TEAMMATE? Jack Taylor is my brother-in-law
WHAT WILL YOU BE DOING IN THE YEAR 2040? Watching my son play for Miami Marlins in Major League Baseball
CRICKETING HERO? Michael Klinger – the ultimate professional and extremely humble. He never gave up on his dream to play for Australia
WHICH BOOK MEANS MOST TO YOU? Moneyball – The Art of Winning an Unfair Game by Michael Lewis
TWITTER: @bennyhowell510

Batting	Mat	Inns	NO	Runs	HS	Ave	SR	100	50	Ct	St
First-class	76	121	13	3009	163	27.86	54.88	2	16	40	0
List A	76	62	13	1789	122	36.51	89.58	1	11	24	0
T20s	109	89	25	1403	57	21.92	120.42	0	4	44	0
Bowling	**Mat**	**Balls**	**Runs**	**Wkts**	**BBI**	**BBM**	**Ave**	**Econ**	**SR**	**5w**	**10**
First-class	76	5871	2960	89	5/57	8/96	33.25	3.02	65.9	1	0
List A	76	2673	2267	64	3/37	3/37	35.42	5.08	41.7	0	0
T20s	109	1931	2227	115	4/26	4/26	19.36	6.91	16.7	0	0

ALEX HUGHES RHB / RM / R0 / W0 / MVP61

FULL NAME: Alex Lloyd Hughes
BORN: September 29, 1991, Wordsley, Staffordshire
SQUAD NO: 18
HEIGHT: 5ft 10in
NICKNAME: Yozza, Horse, Jude Law
EDUCATION: Ounsdale High School, Wolverhampton; University of Worcester
TEAMS: Derbyshire
ROLE: Allrounder
DEBUT: First-class: 2013; List A: 2012; T20: 2011

BEST BATTING: 142 Derbyshire vs Gloucestershire, Bristol, 2017
BEST BOWLING: 4-46 Derbyshire vs Glamorgan, Derby, 2014
COUNTY CAP: 2017

WHAT WAS YOUR FIRST CRICKET CLUB? Wombourne CC, Staffordshire
FAVOURITE CRICKET BAT? Slazenger V100. The red stickers
CRICKETING HERO? Mark Ealham
WHICH BOWLER WOULD YOU LEAST LIKE TO FACE? Ben Slater – because I don't want to hurt his feelings
BEST INNINGS YOU'VE SEEN? Harvey Hosein's maiden first-class ton at New Road in 2016
WHO WOULD YOU ASK TO BAT FOR YOUR LIFE? Batman
SURPRISING FACT ABOUT YOU? I got to The X Factor bootcamp in 2012
WHAT WILL YOU BE DOING IN THE YEAR 2040? Trolling cricketers on Twitter
FAVOURITE QUOTE OR SAYING? Anything that David Brent has ever said
WHICH BOOK MEANS MOST TO YOU? Any of the Mr Men books by Roger Hargreaves
TWITTER: @Yozza18

Batting	Mat	Inns	NO	Runs	HS	Ave	SR	100	50	Ct	St
First-class	58	101	10	2699	142	29.65	47.54	5	12	41	0
List A	56	37	7	695	96*	23.16	91.20	0	2	23	0
T20s	67	51	12	600	43*	15.38	117.41	0	0	27	0
Bowling	**Mat**	**Balls**	**Runs**	**Wkts**	**BBI**	**BBM**	**Ave**	**Econ**	**SR**	**5w**	**10**
First-class	58	2823	1496	32	4/46	4/75	46.75	3.17	88.2	0	0
List A	56	1757	1600	36	3/31	3/31	44.44	5.46	48.8	0	0
T20s	67	1031	1420	39	4/42	4/42	36.41	8.26	26.4	0	0

LIAM HURT

RHB / RFM / R0 / W0

FULL NAME: Liam Jack Hurt
BORN: March 15, 1994, Preston, Lancashire
SQUAD NO: 22
HEIGHT: 6ft 3in
NICKNAME: Hurty
EDUCATION: Balshaw's CE High School, Leyland, Lancashire
TEAMS: Lancashire, Leicestershire
ROLE: Bowler
DEBUT: List A: 2015

WHAT WAS YOUR FIRST CRICKET CLUB? Leyland CC, Lancashire
CRICKETING HERO? Andrew Flintoff
WHICH BOWLER WOULD YOU LEAST LIKE TO FACE? Jasprit Bumrah
WHO WOULD YOU ASK TO BAT FOR YOUR LIFE? Virat Kohli
WHICH RULE WOULD YOU CHANGE ABOUT CRICKET? No front-foot no-balls
YOUR BIGGEST CRICKETING REGRET? Not being a batter
IF YOU WEREN'T A CRICKETER? I'd be a plumber
TWITTER: @LiamHurt
NOTES: The Preston seamer signed his first professional contract with his home county ahead of the 2018 season. Hurt first represented the Lancashire Academy in 2011 but left the club in 2015 and went on trial for a number of counties. His only senior appearance is his List A debut for Leicestershire in 2015. He returned to Lancashire in 2017 and took 19 wickets for the Second XI in all formats, as well as making handy runs down the order. He also helped his club side in Manchester, Clifton CC, reach T20 Club Finals Day. Hurt took 19 wickets at 30.89 in the Second XI Championship last summer

Batting	Mat	Inns	NO	Runs	HS	Ave	SR	100	50	Ct	St
List A	1	1	0	15	15	15.00	68.18	0	0	1	0
Bowling	**Mat**	**Balls**	**Runs**	**Wkts**	**BBI**	**BBM**	**Ave**	**Econ**	**SR**	**5w**	**10**
List A	1	48	59	2	2/59	2/59	29.50	7.37	24.0	0	0

BRETT HUTTON RHB / RMF / R0 / W0 / MVP86

FULL NAME: Brett Alan Hutton
BORN: February 6, 1993, Doncaster, Yorkshire
SQUAD NO: 16
HEIGHT: 6ft 2in
NICKNAME: Bert
EDUCATION: Worksop College, Nottinghamshire
TEAMS: Northamptonshire, Nottinghamshire
ROLE: Bowler
DEBUT: First-class: 2011; List A: 2011; T20: 2016

BEST BATTING: 74 Nottinghamshire vs Durham, Trent Bridge, 2016
BEST BOWLING: 8-57 Northamptonshire vs Gloucestershire, Northampton, 2018

FAVOURITE CRICKET BAT? B3. Best bats I've ever had
CRICKETING HERO? Paul Franks – he had a very good career. I played cricket with him from a young age, watching him and learning
WHO WOULD YOU ASK TO BAT FOR YOUR LIFE? Luke Procter
WHICH RULE WOULD YOU CHANGE ABOUT CRICKET? Bring free hits into red-ball cricket
SURPRISING FACT ABOUT YOU? I have a stamp collection
SURPRISING FACT ABOUT A TEAMMATE? I won't name names, but one of my teammates has crashed his car more times than years he has been driving
WHAT WILL YOU BE DOING IN THE YEAR 2040? I'll be a dog-walker
TWITTER: @BrettAH26

Batting	Mat	Inns	NO	Runs	HS	Ave	SR	100	50	Ct	St
First-class	46	73	8	1168	74	17.96	44.46	0	4	25	0
List A	13	10	4	146	34*	24.33	94.80	0	0	4	0
T20s	9	7	4	50	18*	16.66	106.38	0	0	3	0
Bowling	**Mat**	**Balls**	**Runs**	**Wkts**	**BBI**	**BBM**	**Ave**	**Econ**	**SR**	**5w**	**10**
First-class	46	7562	4345	152	8/57	10/106	28.58	3.44	49.7	7	2
List A	13	620	662	15	3/72	3/72	44.13	6.40	41.3	0	0
T20s	9	172	255	5	2/28	2/28	51.00	8.89	34.4	0	0

COLIN INGRAM LHB / LB / R0 / W0 / MVP98

FULL NAME: Colin Alexander Ingram
BORN: July 3, 1985, Port Elizabeth, SA
SQUAD NO: 41
HEIGHT: 5ft 10in
NICKNAME: Bozie, Stingray, Farmer
EDUCATION: Woodbridge College, Eastern Cape, South Africa
TEAMS: South Africa, Glamorgan, Adelaide Strikers, Delhi Daredevils, Eastern Province, Kabul Zwanan, Somerset, Warriors
ROLE: Allrounder
DEBUT: ODI: 2010; T20I: 2010; First-class: 2004; List A: 2005; T20: 2007

BEST BATTING: 190 Eastern Province vs KwaZulu-Natal, Port Elizabeth, 2009
BEST BOWLING: 4-16 Eastern Province vs Boland, Port Elizabeth, 2006

WHAT WAS YOUR FIRST CRICKET CLUB? Old Grey CC, South Africa
FAVOURITE CRICKET BAT? Everybody knows that! My Gray-Nicolls Powerspot. A beauty
WHICH BOWLER WOULD YOU LEAST LIKE TO FACE? Lasith Malinga – he is a nightmare to face for left-handers
WHO WOULD YOU ASK TO BAT FOR YOUR LIFE? Michael Hogan – the best No.11 in the world and it would be edge-of-your-seat viewing
WHICH RULE WOULD YOU CHANGE ABOUT CRICKET? If it's hitting, it must be lbw!
SURPRISING FACT ABOUT A TEAMMATE? Andy Salter wants to start a business taking portable Jacuzzis to events with a Land Rover. He's going to call it Salty Tubs
WHAT WILL YOU BE DOING IN THE YEAR 2040? Hopefully the kids will be out the house so I can garden, mow and do some fishing
TWITTER: @CAIngram41

Batting	Mat	Inns	NO	Runs	HS	Ave	SR	100	50	Ct	St
ODIs	31	29	3	843	124	32.42	82.32	3	3	12	0
T20Is	9	9	1	210	78	26.25	129.62	0	1	2	0
First-class	111	195	17	6641	190	37.30	49.84	14	30	75	0
List A	186	178	18	7584	142	47.40	90.13	18	48	65	0
T20s	224	219	32	5769	127*	30.85	140.05	4	35	76	0
Bowling	**Mat**	**Balls**	**Runs**	**Wkts**	**BBI**	**BBM**	**Ave**	**Econ**	**SR**	**5w**	**10**
ODIs	31	6	17	0	-	-	-	17.00	-	0	0
T20Is	9	-	-	-	-	-	-	-	-	-	-
First-class	111	3516	2132	50	4/16	5/50	42.64	3.63	70.3	0	0
List A	186	1482	1345	40	4/39	4/39	33.62	5.44	37.0	0	0
T20s	224	931	1221	38	4/32	4/32	32.13	7.86	24.5	0	0

WILL JACKS RHB / OB / R0 / W0

FULL NAME: William George Jacks
BORN: November 21, 1998, Chertsey, Surrey
SQUAD NO: 9
HEIGHT: 6ft 1in
NICKNAME: Jacksy
EDUCATION: St George's College, Weybridge
TEAMS: Surrey, England Lions
ROLE: Batsman
DEBUT: First-class: 2018; List A: 2018; T20: 2018

BEST BATTING: 63 England Lions vs India A, Wayanad, 2019

WHAT WAS YOUR FIRST CRICKET CLUB? Valley End CC, Surrey
FAVOURITE CRICKET BAT? KP's Woodworm from the 2005 Ashes
CRICKETING HERO? Kevin Pietersen
WHICH BOWLER WOULD YOU LEAST LIKE TO FACE? Jasprit Bumrah
BEST INNINGS YOU'VE SEEN? Aaron Finch's 116 not out for Surrey against Middlesex in the T20 game at The Oval last summer. Best hitting I've ever seen
WHO WOULD YOU ASK TO BAT FOR YOUR LIFE? King Kohli
WHICH RULE WOULD YOU CHANGE ABOUT CRICKET? We should have a separate team for fielding so that batsmen don't have to do it
SURPRISING FACT ABOUT A TEAMMATE? Amar Virdi had a full beard at the age of 14
FAVOURITE QUOTE OR SAYING? Hakuna matata
ODDEST SPORT YOU'VE PLAYED? Head table-tennis
TWITTER: @Wjacks9

Batting	Mat	Inns	NO	Runs	HS	Ave	SR	100	50	Ct	St
First-class	8	12	2	301	63	30.10	50.75	0	2	8	0
List A	14	13	0	342	121	26.30	102.39	1	1	7	0
T20s	10	5	0	100	53	20.00	142.85	0	1	6	0
Bowling	**Mat**	**Balls**	**Runs**	**Wkts**	**BBI**	**BBM**	**Ave**	**Econ**	**SR**	**5w**	**10**
First-class	8	36	45	0	-	-	-	7.50	-	0	0
List A	14	312	269	6	2/33	2/33	44.83	5.17	52.0	0	0
T20s	10	12	26	0	-	-	-	13.00	-	0	0

ATEEQ JAVID

RHB / OB / R0 / W0

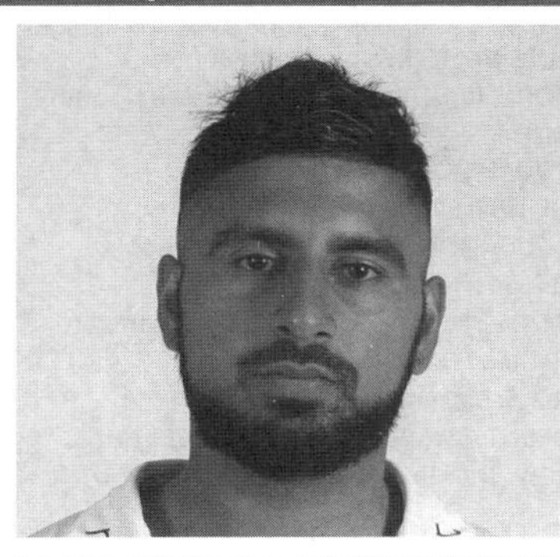

FULL NAME: Ateeq Javid
BORN: October 15, 1991, Birmingham
SQUAD NO: 99
HEIGHT: 5ft 7in
NICKNAME: King AJ
EDUCATION: Aston Manor Academy, Birmingham
TEAMS: Leicestershire, Warwickshire
ROLE: Allrounder
DEBUT: First-class: 2009; List A: 2011; T20: 2013

BEST BATTING: 133 Warwickshire vs Somerset, Edgbaston, 2013
BEST BOWLING: 1-1 Warwickshire vs Lancashire, Old Trafford, 2014

WHAT GOT YOU INTO CRICKET? While growing up all the kids used to play on streets so I joined in
'ROY OF THE ROVERS' MOMENT? When we celebrated winning the T20 Blast in 2014
IF YOU WEREN'T A CRICKETER? I'd be a businessman
SURPRISING FACT? I hate going to parties
CRICKETING HERO? Sachin Tendulkar
NON-CRICKETING HERO? Muhammad Ali
TWITTER: @ateeqjavid
NOTES: Ateeq made his first-class debut in 2009 when he was 17 after coming through the Warwickshire ranks but had to wait until 2013 to score his maiden first-class hundred. Opportunities to play four-day cricket were limited given the strength of Warwickshire's top order and he joined Leicestershire on a two-year deal at the end of the 2017 season. Ateeq, who is also a useful off-spin bowler, struggled in his first year at Grace Road, scoring 157 runs in 10 Championship innings

Batting	Mat	Inns	NO	Runs	HS	Ave	SR	100	50	Ct	St
First-class	38	61	6	1247	133	22.67	36.05	2	4	18	0
List A	43	35	13	613	43	27.86	84.66	0	0	6	0
T20s	59	41	18	527	51*	22.91	114.56	0	1	11	0
Bowling	**Mat**	**Balls**	**Runs**	**Wkts**	**BBI**	**BBM**	**Ave**	**Econ**	**SR**	**5w**	**10**
First-class	38	758	433	5	1/1	2/73	86.60	3.42	151.6	0	0
List A	43	1295	1283	27	4/42	4/42	47.51	5.94	47.9	0	0
T20s	59	711	875	30	4/17	4/17	29.16	7.38	23.7	0	0

KEATON JENNINGS LHB / RM / R1 / W0 / MVP45

FULL NAME: Keaton Kent Jennings
BORN: June 19, 1992, Johannesburg, South Africa
SQUAD NO: 1
HEIGHT: 6ft 4in
EDUCATION: King Edward VII School; University of South Africa
TEAMS: England, Lancashire, Durham, Gauteng
ROLE: Batsman
DEBUT: Test: 2016; First-class: 2011; List A: 2012; T20: 2014

BEST BATTING: 221* Durham vs Yorkshire, Chester-le-Street, 2016
BEST BOWLING: 3-37 Durham vs Sussex, Chester-le-Street, 2017

FAMILY TIES? My brother Dylan, uncle Kenneth and father Ray have all played first-class cricket
CRICKETING HERO? Mike Hussey
IF YOU WEREN'T A CRICKETER? I'd be working in some sort of accountancy job
TWITTER: @JetJennings
NOTES: Following a prolific 2016 season, Jennings found it tougher going the following year and left Durham for Old Trafford ahead of the 2018 season in a bid to regain an opening spot in the Test team. An impressive 709 runs at an average of 42.27 earnt him a place on England's winter tours to Sri Lanka and West Indies, but he was dropped from the Test side after a run of low scores. Jennings, who captained Durham in the One-Day Cup in 2017, has not played limited-overs cricket for England but has been a consistent performer in the short formats at domestic level

Batting	Mat	Inns	NO	Runs	HS	Ave	SR	100	50	Ct	St
Tests	17	32	1	781	146*	25.19	42.49	2	1	17	0
First-class	118	210	12	6712	221*	33.89	45.94	18	21	86	0
List A	58	57	12	1855	139	41.22	83.78	4	12	22	0
T20s	43	29	10	602	88	31.68	118.73	0	3	9	0
Bowling	**Mat**	**Balls**	**Runs**	**Wkts**	**BBI**	**BBM**	**Ave**	**Econ**	**SR**	**5w**	**10**
Tests	17	73	55	0	-	-	-	4.52	-	0	0
First-class	118	1515	892	28	3/37	4/48	31.85	3.53	54.1	0	0
List A	58	588	601	11	2/19	2/19	54.63	6.13	53.4	0	0
T20s	43	510	628	22	4/37	4/37	28.54	7.38	23.1	0	0

ROB JONES

RHB / LB / R0 / W0

FULL NAME: Robert Peter Jones
BORN: November 3, 1995, Warrington, Cheshire
SQUAD NO: 12
HEIGHT: 5ft 11in
NICKNAME: Jonesy, Jonah
EDUCATION: Bridgewater High School, Warrington
TEAMS: Lancashire
ROLE: Batsman
DEBUT: First-class: 2016; List A: 2018; T20: 2017

BEST BATTING: 106* Lancashire vs Middlesex, Old Trafford, 2016
BEST BOWLING: 1-18 Lancashire vs Worcestershire, Worcester, 2018

WHAT WAS YOUR FIRST CRICKET CLUB? Oakmere CC, Cheshire
CRICKETING HERO? Jos Buttler
WHICH BOWLER WOULD YOU LEAST LIKE TO FACE? Dale Steyn
BEST INNINGS YOU'VE SEEN? Jos Buttler's unbeaten hundred when England beat Australia by one wicket in an ODI at Old Trafford in 2018
WHO WOULD YOU ASK TO BAT FOR YOUR LIFE? Graeme Smith
WHAT WILL YOU BE DOING IN THE YEAR 2040? Saving lives at sea or with the SAS
FAVOURITE QUOTE OR SAYING? Difficult roads lead to beautiful destinations
WHICH BOOK MEANS MOST TO YOU? The Go-Giver – A Little Story About a Powerful Business Idea by Bob Burg and John David Mann
TWITTER: @robpeterjones

Batting	Mat	Inns	NO	Runs	HS	Ave	SR	100	50	Ct	St
First-class	13	21	3	474	106*	26.33	36.12	1	1	13	0
List A	3	2	0	19	17	9.50	55.88	0	0	2	0
T20s	2	-	-	-	-	-	-	-	-	0	0
Bowling	**Mat**	**Balls**	**Runs**	**Wkts**	**BBI**	**BBM**	**Ave**	**Econ**	**SR**	**5w**	**10**
First-class	13	42	20	1	1/18	1/18	20.00	2.85	42.0	0	0
List A	3	-	-	-	-	-	-	-	-	-	-
T20s	2	-	-	-	-	-	-	-	-	-	-

CHRIS JORDAN

RHB / RFM / R0 / W1

FULL NAME: Christopher James Jordan
BORN: October 4, 1988, Barbados
SQUAD NO: 8
HEIGHT: 6ft 2in
NICKNAME: CJ
EDUCATION: Combermere School, Barbados; Dulwich College
TEAMS: England, Sussex, Adelaide Strikers, Barbados, RC Bangalore, Sunrisers Hyderabad, Surrey, Sydney Thunder
ROLE: Allrounder
DEBUT: Test: 2014; ODI: 2013; T20I: 2013; First-class: 2007; List A: 2007; T20: 2008

BEST BATTING: 147 Sussex vs Nottinghamshire, Hove, 2017
BEST BOWLING: 7-43 Barbados vs Combined Campuses and Colleges, Bridgetown, 2013
COUNTY CAP: 2014 (Sussex)

TWITTER: @ChrisJordan94
NOTES: Born in Barbados, Jordan is eligible to represent England through his grandmother. An allrounder known for his brilliant close catching, he is a regular member of England's T20 side but hasn't played an ODI since 2016. His most recent Test was in 2015. Released by Surrey after the 2012 season, Jordan took 61 first-class wickets in his first summer at Hove. Injuries blighted the next couple of seasons but he has been a key figure in Championship and T20 cricket over the last two summers. He has featured in the the IPL but went unsold for this year's edition

Batting	Mat	Inns	NO	Runs	HS	Ave	SR	100	50	Ct	St
Tests	8	11	1	180	35	18.00	56.25	0	0	14	0
ODIs	31	21	7	169	38*	12.07	89.89	0	0	19	0
T20Is	38	23	10	168	27*	12.92	116.66	0	0	21	0
First-class	102	142	21	2999	147	24.78	52.89	2	14	119	0
List A	78	53	13	607	55	15.17	84.07	0	1	44	0
T20s	146	88	36	832	45*	16.00	119.88	0	0	85	0
Bowling	**Mat**	**Balls**	**Runs**	**Wkts**	**BBI**	**BBM**	**Ave**	**Econ**	**SR**	**5w**	**10**
Tests	8	1530	752	21	4/18	7/50	35.80	2.94	72.8	0	0
ODIs	31	1532	1521	43	5/29	5/29	35.37	5.95	35.6	1	0
T20Is	38	808	1156	46	4/6	4/6	25.13	8.58	17.5	0	0
First-class	102	17120	9758	304	7/43	9/58	32.09	3.41	56.3	9	0
List A	78	3580	3395	117	5/28	5/28	29.01	5.68	30.5	2	0
T20s	146	2834	3959	150	4/6	4/6	26.39	8.38	18.8	0	0

DIMUTH KARUNARATNE LHB / RM / R0 / W0

FULL NAME: Frank Dimuth Madushanka Karunaratne
BORN: April 21, 1988, Colombo, Sri Lanka
SQUAD NO: 21
HEIGHT: 6ft
TEAMS: Sri Lanka, Hampshire, Basnahira North, Dambulla District, Galle District, Kandurata and Uva, Kandy District, Sinhalese Sports Club, Wayamba, Western Troopers
ROLE: Batsman
DEBUT: Test: 2012; ODI: 2011; First-class: 2008; List A: 2008; T20: 2010

BEST BATTING: 212 Sri Lanka A vs England Lions, Dambulla, 2017
BEST BOWLING: 1-6 Sri Lanka A vs West Indies A, Pallekele, 2016

TWITTER: @IamDimuth
NOTES: Hampshire signed the left-handed opening batsman in February just days after he had led Sri Lanka to a shock 2-0 win in South Africa in his first series as Test captain. He will be available for the first half of the season in the Championship and the One-Day Cup. Karunaratne quickly became a fixture in Sri Lanka's Test team after making his debut in 2012 and was named in the ICC's 2018 Test Team of the Year. Hampshire director of cricket Giles White said: "He's a high-class player and in recent months we've seen his quality, not only as an opening batsman at the top of the order, but also as a leader as part of Sri Lanka's recent historic series win in South Africa"

Batting	Mat	Inns	NO	Runs	HS	Ave	SR	100	50	Ct	St
Tests	60	117	4	4074	196	36.05	49.18	8	22	47	0
ODIs	17	13	1	190	60	15.83	68.84	0	1	4	0
First-class	160	279	21	11780	212	45.65	57.68	37	53	160	1
List A	113	105	7	3229	132	32.94	74.76	5	19	51	0
T20s	34	33	1	543	80	16.96	108.81	0	3	17	1
Bowling	**Mat**	**Balls**	**Runs**	**Wkts**	**BBI**	**BBM**	**Ave**	**Econ**	**SR**	**5w**	**10**
Tests	60	231	138	2	1/12	1/12	69.00	3.58	115.5	0	0
ODIs	17	10	11	0	-	-	-	6.60	-	0	0
First-class	160	751	439	4	1/6	1/6	109.75	3.50	187.7	0	0
List A	113	64	46	3	2/13	2/13	15.33	4.31	21.3	0	0
T20s	34	-	-	-	-	-	-	-	-	-	-

ROB KEOGH

RHB / OB / R0 / W0

FULL NAME: Robert Ian Keogh
BORN: October 21, 1991, Dunstable, Bedfordshire
SQUAD NO: 14
HEIGHT: 6ft 2in
NICKNAME: Keezy, Key Dog, Chav
EDUCATION: Queensbury Upper School, Dunstable; Dunstable College
TEAMS: Northamptonshire
ROLE: Allrounder
DEBUT: First-class: 2012; List A: 2010; T20: 2011

BEST BATTING: 221 Northamptonshire vs Hampshire, Southampton, 2013
BEST BOWLING: 9-52 Northamptonshire vs Glamorgan, Northampton, 2016

WHAT WAS YOUR FIRST CRICKET CLUB? Dunstable Town CC, Bedfordshire. I got into cricket watching my dad play for the club. I owe a lot to DTCC – especially Brian Chapman
FAVOURITE CRICKET BAT? A Gray-Nicolls Powerbow. I scored my maiden first-class hundred with it, which turned out to be a double ton. I was gutted when it was beyond repair
WHICH BOWLER WOULD YOU LEAST LIKE TO FACE? Ben Duckett – he's got all the tricks!
BEST INNINGS YOU'VE SEEN? Josh Cobb in the 2016 T20 final. We were 9-3 and he scored 80 to win us the trophy
WHO WOULD YOU ASK TO BAT FOR YOUR LIFE? Ben Duckett – I've seen him score plenty of runs, and he is a good friend so I hope he would dig in for me
WHICH RULE WOULD YOU CHANGE ABOUT CRICKET? No slips allowed
YOUR BIGGEST CRICKETING REGRET? Choosing a locker next to David Murphy
TWITTER: @RobKeogh91

Batting	Mat	Inns	NO	Runs	HS	Ave	SR	100	50	Ct	St
First-class	64	106	8	2796	221	28.53	49.89	7	7	19	0
List A	38	34	3	913	134	29.45	87.45	1	8	6	0
T20s	47	25	6	348	41*	18.31	117.17	0	0	23	0
Bowling	**Mat**	**Balls**	**Runs**	**Wkts**	**BBI**	**BBM**	**Ave**	**Econ**	**SR**	**5w**	**10**
First-class	64	4962	2940	71	9/52	13/125	41.40	3.55	69.8	1	1
List A	38	804	740	5	2/26	2/26	148.00	5.52	160.8	0	0
T20s	47	180	267	6	2/27	2/27	44.50	8.90	30.0	0	0

RASHID KHAN RHB / LB / R0 / W0

FULL NAME: Rashid Khan Arman
BORN: September 20, 1998, Nangarhar, Afghanistan
SQUAD NO: 1
TEAMS: Afghanistan, Sussex, Adelaide Strikers, Durban Heat, Guyana Amazon Warriors, Kabul Zwanan, Quetta Gladiators, Sunrisers Hyderabad
ROLE: Bowler
DEBUT: Test: 2018; ODI: 2015; T20I: 2015; First-class: 2016; List A: 2015; T20: 2015

BEST BATTING: 52 Afghanistan vs England Lions, Abu Dhabi, 2016
BEST BOWLING: 8-74 Afghanistan vs England Lions, Abu Dhabi, 2016

TWITTER: @rashidkhan_19
NOTES: Sussex have re-signed the 20-year-old leg-spinner for the first half of the T20 Blast group stage. Rashid was the first Afghan to sign for an English county when he joined Sussex ahead of the 2018 season and he played a huge part in taking the club to the final of the competition, claiming 17 wickets at an average of 14.35 with an economy-rate of 6.59. Possessing a lethal googly, Rashid is the biggest talent to emerge from Afghanistan and has played in the major T20 leagues all over the world. At the time of writing he is the No.2 bowler in the ICC ODI rankings and No.1 in the T20I rankings

Batting	Mat	Inns	NO	Runs	HS	Ave	SR	100	50	Ct	St
Tests	1	2	0	19	12	9.50	82.60	0	0	0	0
ODIs	57	42	9	782	60*	23.69	100.77	0	4	18	0
T20Is	38	17	8	123	33	13.66	124.24	0	0	11	0
First-class	5	6	1	144	52	28.80	75.78	0	1	0	0
List A	59	43	9	803	60*	23.61	101.64	0	4	19	0
T20s	155	70	26	572	56*	13.00	152.12	0	1	44	0
Bowling	**Mat**	**Balls**	**Runs**	**Wkts**	**BBI**	**BBM**	**Ave**	**Econ**	**SR**	**5w**	**10**
Tests	1	209	154	2	2/154	2/154	77.00	4.42	104.5	0	0
ODIs	57	2833	1845	123	7/18	7/18	15.00	3.90	23.0	4	0
T20Is	38	864	867	75	5/3	5/3	11.56	6.02	11.5	2	0
First-class	5	1388	681	37	8/74	12/122	18.40	2.94	37.5	4	1
List A	59	2940	1933	127	7/18	7/18	15.22	3.94	23.1	4	0
T20s	155	3587	3644	237	5/3	5/3	15.37	6.09	15.1	2	0

FEROZE KHUSHI RHB / OB / R0 / W0

FULL NAME: Feroze Isa Nazir Khushi
BORN: June 23, 1999, Whipps Cross, Essex
SQUAD NO: 23
HEIGHT: 6ft 1in
NICKNAME: Fink
EDUCATION: Kelmscott School, Walthamstow, London
TEAMS: Essex
ROLE: Batsman

WHAT GOT YOU INTO CRICKET? My father introduced me to the sport at the age of three
BEST ADVICE EVER RECEIVED? Work hard and be dedicated
'ROY OF THE ROVERS' MOMENT? When I hit six sixes in the last over of a school match to win the game
BEST THING ABOUT YOUR HOME GROUND? Chelmsford has a good batting track, a fast outfield and short boundaries. And there is a great atmosphere for the T20 games
IF YOU WEREN'T A CRICKETER? I'd be a professional footballer
SURPRISING FACT ABOUT YOU? I went to the same school as Fabrice Muamba
CRICKETING HERO? Shahid Afridi
NON-CRICKETING HERO? Cristiano Ronaldo – he works very hard at his game and is a great role model of professionalism on and off the field
NOTES: Khushi is a 19-year-old batsman who signed a professional contract with Essex in October 2017 after a number of impressive performances for Essex Second XI, including an unbeaten 101 against Middlesex Second XI at Colchester in August. He played regularly for the Second XI last summer, and lined up with a number of first-team players for the tour match against a strong Indian side at Chelmsford, making an unbeaten 14 batting down the order. Later in the summer he made a Second XI hundred against Durham at Chester-le-Street

FRED KLAASSEN RHB / LMF / R0 / W0

FULL NAME: Frederick Jack Klaassen
BORN: November 13, 1992, Haywards Heath, Sussex
SQUAD NO: 18
TEAMS: Netherlands, Kent
ROLE: Bowler
DEBUT: ODI: 2018; T20I: 2018; List A: 2017; T20: 2018

TWITTER: @freddieklaassen
NOTES: Kent signed the Netherlands left-arm seamer on a two-year contract last October. The 26-year-old impressed for the Second XI last year, taking seven wickets in a match against Essex at Canterbury's Polo Farm. He made his ODI debut last year against Nepal, taking 3-30. "We are delighted to add Fred to our seam-bowling unit," said Paul Downton, Kent's director of cricket. "In the short time we have known Fred he has made a big impression around the group. His left-arm bowling will give us a different option and balance to our attack. He'll be a great addition"

Batting	Mat	Inns	NO	Runs	HS	Ave	SR	100	50	Ct	St
ODIs	2	2	0	24	13	12.00	52.17	0	0	0	0
T20Is	8	3	1	11	9	5.50	183.33	0	0	1	0
List A	11	9	4	66	16*	13.20	59.45	0	0	6	0
T20s	9	3	1	11	9	5.50	183.33	0	0	2	0
Bowling	**Mat**	**Balls**	**Runs**	**Wkts**	**BBI**	**BBM**	**Ave**	**Econ**	**SR**	**5w**	**10**
ODIs	2	120	68	6	3/30	3/30	11.33	3.40	20.0	0	0
T20Is	8	168	246	9	3/31	3/31	27.33	8.78	18.6	0	0
List A	11	554	416	19	3/30	3/30	21.89	4.50	29.1	0	0
T20s	9	180	258	10	3/31	3/31	25.80	8.60	18.0	0	0

DIETER KLEIN RHB / LFM / R0 / W0

FULL NAME: Dieter Klein
BORN: October 31, 1988, Lichtenburg, North West Province, South Africa
SQUAD NO: 77
HEIGHT: 5ft 9in
NICKNAME: Diets
EDUCATION: Hoërskool Lichtenberg, South Africa
TEAMS: Leicestershire, Lions, North West
ROLE: Bowler
DEBUT: First-class: 2008; List A: 2008; T20: 2013

BEST BATTING: 94 Leicestershire vs Glamorgan, Cardiff, 2018
BEST BOWLING: 8-72 North West vs Northerns, Potchefstroom, 2014

WHAT GOT YOU INTO CRICKET? I always had a love for all sports, but something had to give and eventually cricket won through
BEST ADVICE EVER RECEIVED? Nothing comes for free. What you put in is what you get out. Anything is possible
BEST THING ABOUT YOUR HOME GROUND? Our very own Barmy Army
IF YOU WEREN'T A CRICKETER? I'd be a pilot
SURPRISING FACT ABOUT A TEAMMATE? During a club game one of the players went in to bat with his mobile in his pocket. He was batting very poorly and one of his teammates called him on his mobile and asked if they could bring him a pair of glasses
WHERE IS PARADISE? On a beach
CRICKETING HERO? Jacques Kallis – very controlled and good at all aspects of the game
NON-CRICKETING HERO? My brother – just a hero. Nothing gets him down. One hell of a fighter

Batting	Mat	Inns	NO	Runs	HS	Ave	SR	100	50	Ct	St
First-class	58	85	18	1268	94	18.92	77.03	0	5	19	0
List A	26	13	3	118	26	11.80	76.12	0	0	1	0
T20s	14	7	3	49	16	12.25	106.52	0	0	3	0
Bowling	**Mat**	**Balls**	**Runs**	**Wkts**	**BBI**	**BBM**	**Ave**	**Econ**	**SR**	**5w**	**10**
First-class	58	8579	5572	196	8/72	10/125	28.42	3.89	43.7	10	1
List A	26	1215	964	37	5/35	5/35	26.05	4.76	32.8	1	0
T20s	14	250	297	15	3/27	3/27	19.80	7.12	16.6	0	0

MICHAEL KLINGER RHB / RM / R1 / W0

FULL NAME: Michael Klinger
BORN: July 4, 1980, Melbourne, Australia
SQUAD NO: 2
HEIGHT: 5ft 11in
NICKNAME: Maxy
EDUCATION: Deakin University, Victoria
TEAMS: Australia, Gloucestershire, Adelaide Strikers, Kochi Tuskers Kerala, Paarl Rocks, Perth Scorchers, South Australia, Victoria, Western Australia, Worcestershire
ROLE: Batsman
DEBUT: T20I: 2017; First-class: 1999; List A: 1999; T20: 2006

BEST BATTING: 255 South Australia vs Western Australia, Adelaide, 2008

COUNTY CAP: 2012 (Worcestershire); 2013 (Gloucestershire)

WHAT WAS YOUR FIRST CRICKET CLUB? Prahran CC, Melbourne, Australia
WHICH BOWLER WOULD YOU LEAST LIKE TO FACE? Rashid Khan – fast spinner who turns it both ways with great control
BEST INNINGS YOU'VE SEEN? Ricky Ponting's 140 not out in the 2003 World Cup final
WHO WOULD YOU ASK TO BAT FOR YOUR LIFE? Cameron Bancroft
WHICH RULE WOULD YOU CHANGE ABOUT CRICKET? We should have 90 overs a day in all first-class cricket
YOUR BIGGEST CRICKETING REGRET? Not playing in the first half of my career like I have in the second half
SURPRISING FACT ABOUT YOU? I used to have an afro
WHICH BOOK MEANS MOST TO YOU? Open by Andre Agassi
TWITTER: @maxyklinger
NOTES: Klinger will play exclusively in the T20 Blast and captain the side

Batting	Mat	Inns	NO	Runs	HS	Ave	SR	100	50	Ct	St
T20Is	3	3	0	143	62	47.66	127.67	0	1	2	0
First-class	182	321	33	11320	255	39.30	45.91	30	49	178	0
List A	177	174	23	7449	166*	49.33	76.64	18	44	72	0
T20s	193	186	24	5589	126*	34.50	123.13	7	32	73	0
Bowling	**Mat**	**Balls**	**Runs**	**Wkts**	**BBI**	**BBM**	**Ave**	**Econ**	**SR**	**5w**	**10**
T20Is	3	-	-	-	-	-	-	-	-	-	-
First-class	182	6	3	0	-	-	-	3.00	-	0	0
List A	177	-	-	-	-	-	-	-	-	-	-
T20s	193	-	-	-	-	-	-	-	-	-	-

TOM KOHLER-CADMORE RHB / OB / R0 / W0 / MVP65

FULL NAME: Tom Kohler-Cadmore
BORN: August 19, 1994, Chatham, Kent
SQUAD NO: 32
HEIGHT: 6ft 2in
NICKNAME: Pepsi, Herbert, Brother Bilo
EDUCATION: Malvern College, Worcestershire
TEAMS: Yorkshire, England Lions, Worcestershire
ROLE: Batsman
DEBUT: First-class: 2014; List A: 2013; T20: 2014

BEST BATTING: 169 Worcestershire vs Gloucestershire, Worcester, 2016

COUNTY CAP: 2019 (Yorkshire)

BEST ADVICE EVER RECEIVED? In cricket: hit the sightscreen. In life: never eat yellow snow
BEST THING ABOUT YOUR HOME GROUND? My dad works there – he does the washing so I don't have to
IF YOU WEREN'T A CRICKETER? I'd be an underwater fireman
SURPRISING FACT ABOUT YOU? I've been called the songbird of my generation by people who have heard me sing
SURPRISING FACT ABOUT A TEAMMATE? Ben Coad only eats chicken nuggets. I've never seen someone take down 20 nuggets so quickly and easily and come back for more
WHERE IS PARADISE? A McDonald's with Ben Coad
CRICKETING HERO? Dwayne Leverock – because of that one-handed screamer
TWITTER: @tomkcadmore

Batting	Mat	Inns	NO	Runs	HS	Ave	SR	100	50	Ct	St
First-class	46	77	6	2328	169	32.78	54.55	6	12	52	0
List A	48	47	1	1518	164	33.00	87.79	3	7	24	0
T20s	66	66	2	1580	127	24.68	140.31	1	9	37	0
Bowling	**Mat**	**Balls**	**Runs**	**Wkts**	**BBI**	**BBM**	**Ave**	**Econ**	**SR**	**5w**	**10**
First-class	46	-	-	-	-	-	-	-	-	-	-
List A	48	-	-	-	-	-	-	-	-	-	-
T20s	66	-	-	-	-	-	-	-	-	-	-

HEINO KUHN RHB / WK / R0 / W0 / MVP14

FULL NAME: Heino Gunther Kuhn
BORN: April 1, 1984, Piet Retief, South Africa
SQUAD NO: 4
TEAMS: South Africa, Kent, Dhaka Dynamites, Nelson Mandela Bay Giants, Northerns, Titans
ROLE: Batsman/wicketkeeper
DEBUT: Test: 2017; T20I: 2009; First-class: 2005; List A: 2005; T20: 2007

BEST BATTING: 244* Titans vs Lions, Benoni, 2015

COUNTY CAP: 2018

TWITTER: @HeinoKuhn
NOTES: Kent signed the South Africa top-order batsman on a Kolpak deal in March 2018 and Kuhn agreed a contract extension later that summer after making an incredible start in county cricket. He amassed a record 696 runs in the One-Day Cup, including four centuries in five matches to take Kent to the final at Lord's. An ever-present in all three formats, he also made 780 runs in Championship cricket and 310 in the T20 Blast. Kuhn, a competent wicketkeeper, made his Test debut in the series against England in 2017 but subsequently lost his place and decided to pursue his career in county cricket. In South African domestic cricket he has won three successive T20 titles with reigning champions Titans, as well as lifting four-day and one-day trophies with Northerns

Batting	Mat	Inns	NO	Runs	HS	Ave	SR	100	50	Ct	St
Tests	4	8	0	113	34	14.12	38.04	0	0	1	0
T20Is	7	6	2	49	29	12.25	116.66	0	0	5	0
First-class	159	279	27	10635	244*	42.20	58.06	23	53	358	18
List A	166	152	16	4611	141*	33.90	89.18	12	22	176	22
T20s	104	86	12	1912	83*	25.83	127.21	0	10	56	6
Bowling	**Mat**	**Balls**	**Runs**	**Wkts**	**BBI**	**BBM**	**Ave**	**Econ**	**SR**	**5w**	**10**
Tests	4	-	-	-	-	-	-	-	-	-	-
T20Is	7	-	-	-	-	-	-	-	-	-	-
First-class	159	6	12	0	-	-	-	12.00	-	0	0
List A	166	-	-	-	-	-	-	-	-	-	-
T20s	104	-	-	-	-	-	-	-	-	-	-

TOM LACE

RHB / WK / R0 / W0

FULL NAME: Thomas Cresswell Lace
BORN: May 27, 1998, Hammersmith, London
SQUAD NO: 27
HEIGHT: 5ft 9in
NICKNAME: Lacey
EDUCATION: Millfield School, Somerset; Royal Holloway, University of London
TEAMS: Derbyshire, Middlesex
ROLE: Wicketkeeper/batsman
DEBUT: First-class: 2018

BEST BATTING: 43 Derbyshire vs Kent, Derby, 2018

WHAT WAS YOUR FIRST CRICKET CLUB? Wimbledon CC, London
FAVOURITE CRICKET BAT? Millichamp and Hall F100
CRICKETING HERO? Andrew Flintoff
BEST INNINGS YOU'VE SEEN? Alastair Cook's 294 against India at Edgbaston in 2011
WHICH RULE WOULD YOU CHANGE ABOUT CRICKET? Scrap the extra half hour
SURPRISING FACT ABOUT YOU? I love Chelsea
WHAT WILL YOU BE DOING IN THE YEAR 2040? Discontinuing my shocking leggies
FAVOURITE QUOTE OR SAYING? Be interesting and interested
WHICH BOOK MEANS MOST TO YOU? To Kill a Mocking Bird by Harper Lee
ODDEST SPORT YOU'VE PLAYED? Crabbing (in Norfolk)
TWITTER: @tom_lace
NOTES: The 20-year-old Middlesex wicketkeeper-batsman will spend another season on loan at Derbyshire, where last summer he made his first-class debut and scored 219 runs in four appearances. Lace has been part of the Middlesex set-up since he was 10 and signed a three-year contract with the county after the 2017 season

Batting	Mat	Inns	NO	Runs	HS	Ave	SR	100	50	Ct	St
First-class	4	8	0	219	43	27.37	36.80	0	0	1	0
Bowling	**Mat**	**Balls**	**Runs**	**Wkts**	**BBI**	**BBM**	**Ave**	**Econ**	**SR**	**5w**	**10**
First-class	4	-	-	-	-	-	-	-	-	-	-

DANIEL LAMB

RHB / RFM / R0 / W0

FULL NAME: Daniel John Lamb
BORN: September 7, 1995, Preston, Lancashire
SQUAD NO: 26
HEIGHT: 6ft
NICKNAME: Lamby, Sherman, Wust
EDUCATION: St Michael's CE High School, Chorley; Cardinal Newman College, Preston; Edgehill University
TEAMS: Lancashire
ROLE: Allrounder
DEBUT: First-class: 2018; List A: 2017; T20: 2017

BEST BATTING: 20* Lancashire vs Somerset, Taunton, 2018

FAMILY TIES? My younger sister Emma plays for Lancashire and we have played together regularly for Bramhall in the Cheshire Premier League
WHAT WAS YOUR FIRST CRICKET CLUB? Hoghton CC, Lancashire. There's a massive hill on the outfield
CRICKETING HERO? Andrew Flintoff
WHICH BOWLER WOULD YOU LEAST LIKE TO FACE? Shane Warne
WHO WOULD YOU ASK TO BAT FOR YOUR LIFE? Matty Parkinson – I enjoy seeing him get into the battle
SURPRISING FACT ABOUT YOU? I was Blackburn Rovers FC Academy goalkeeper from U9 to U16 level
TWITTER: @lamby236

Batting	Mat	Inns	NO	Runs	HS	Ave	SR	100	50	Ct	St
First-class	4	6	2	57	20*	14.25	30.31	0	0	1	0
List A	2	2	2	5	4*	-	83.33	0	0	0	0
T20s	7	3	0	50	24	16.66	102.04	0	0	0	0
Bowling	**Mat**	**Balls**	**Runs**	**Wkts**	**BBI**	**BBM**	**Ave**	**Econ**	**SR**	**5w**	**10**
First-class	4	168	146	0	-	-	-	5.21	-	0	0
List A	2	120	108	4	2/51	2/51	27.00	5.40	30.0	0	0
T20s	7	96	130	8	3/30	3/30	16.25	8.12	12.0	0	0

MATT LAMB

RHB / RM / R0 / W0

FULL NAME: Matthew Lamb
BORN: July 19, 1996, Wolverhampton, Staffordshire
SQUAD NO: 7
HEIGHT: 6ft 2in
NICKNAME: Lambdog, Son
EDUCATION: North Bromsgrove High School, Worcestershire
TEAMS: Warwickshire
ROLE: Batsman
DEBUT: First-class: 2016; List A: 2017

BEST BATTING: 79 Warwickshire vs Derbyshire, Edgbaston, 2018
BEST BOWLING: 1-19 Warwickshire vs Somerset, Edgbaston, 2017

WHAT WAS YOUR FIRST CRICKET CLUB? Barnt Green CC, Worcestershire
FAVOURITE CRICKET BAT? Woodworm Globe – my first real bat
CRICKETING HERO? Andrew Flintoff
WHICH BOWLER WOULD YOU LEAST LIKE TO FACE? Morne Morkel – he bowls gas and is massive
BEST INNINGS YOU'VE SEEN? KP's hundred at The Oval in 2005
WHO WOULD YOU ASK TO BAT FOR YOUR LIFE? Jonathan Trott
WHICH RULE WOULD YOU CHANGE ABOUT CRICKET? Eight runs if you hit it out the stands
SURPRISING FACT ABOUT YOU? I was about to quit cricket until I was luckily selected for a Second XI game against Worcestershire in September 2015 and managed to score 142
WHAT WILL YOU BE DOING IN THE YEAR 2040? I'll own a club
WHICH BOOK MEANS MOST TO YOU? Muhammad Ali's autobiography
ODDEST SPORT YOU'VE PLAYED? Fencing
TWITTER: @Lamb_Matt

Batting	Mat	Inns	NO	Runs	HS	Ave	SR	100	50	Ct	St
First-class	11	20	1	482	79	25.36	39.25	0	3	4	0
List A	3	3	0	61	47	20.33	89.70	0	0	1	0
Bowling	**Mat**	**Balls**	**Runs**	**Wkts**	**BBI**	**BBM**	**Ave**	**Econ**	**SR**	**5w**	**10**
First-class	11	156	88	3	1/19	1/19	29.33	3.38	52.0	0	0
List A	3	6	9	0	-	-	-	9.00	-	0	0

TOM LAMMONBY

LHB / LMF / R0 / W0

FULL NAME: Thomas Alexander Lammonby
BORN: June 2, 2000, Exeter, Devon
SQUAD NO: 15
HEIGHT: 6ft
NICKNAME: Lammers
EDUCATION: Exeter School
TEAMS: Somerset, England U19
ROLE: Allrounder

WHAT WAS YOUR FIRST CRICKET CLUB? Exeter CC, Devon
FAVOURITE CRICKET BAT? My first one, which was a Kookaburra Kahuna – the same one that Ricky Ponting used
WHICH BOWLER WOULD YOU LEAST LIKE TO FACE? Shane Warne
BEST INNINGS YOU'VE SEEN? Chris Rogers hitting his maiden Test century against England at Chester-le-Street in the 2013 Ashes. Gritty and unconventional
WHO WOULD YOU ASK TO BAT FOR YOUR LIFE? Don Bradman
WHICH RULE WOULD YOU CHANGE ABOUT CRICKET? Hit it out of the ground = 12 runs
YOUR BIGGEST CRICKETING REGRET? Not playing at the U19 World Cup
WHAT WILL YOU BE DOING IN THE YEAR 2040? Hopefully doing a passable impression of Marcus Trescothick by still playing cricket
ODDEST SPORT YOU'VE PLAYED? Eton Fives
TWITTER: @TomLammonby
NOTES: An allrounder who has come through the Devon age-group system, Lammonby signed his first professional contract with Somerset in June 2018 after completing his A-Levels. He joined the Somerset Academy in 2015 and was named Player of the Series for England U19 against India two years later. He scored his maiden century for Somerset Second XI in 2018 and followed it up with a half-century in the Second XI Trophy final. In June he became one of only four Devon CCC players to have scored a century in each innings of a Minor Counties Championship match

GEORGE LAVELLE

LHB / WK / R0 / W0

FULL NAME: George Isaac Davies Lavelle
BORN: March 24, 2000
SQUAD NO: 24
HEIGHT: 5ft 8in
NICKNAME: Spizza
EDUCATION: Merchant Taylors' School, Crosby, Merseyside
TEAMS: Lancashire, England U19
ROLE: Wicketkeeper/batsman

WHAT WAS YOUR FIRST CRICKET CLUB? Ormskirk CC, Lancashire. I still play there now
FAVOURITE CRICKET BAT? My first was a Gray-Nicolls Powerbow with the yellow stickers and it is still my favourite
WHICH BOWLER WOULD YOU LEAST LIKE TO FACE? Morne Morkel – I would imagine that the amount of bounce he gets would be very tough to face
BEST INNINGS YOU'VE SEEN? Alastair Cook's 294 against India at Edgbaston in 2011. Just to be able to concentrate for nearly 13 hours is incredible
WHO WOULD YOU ASK TO BAT FOR YOUR LIFE? Cheteshwar Pujara
WHICH RULE WOULD YOU CHANGE ABOUT CRICKET? Byes down the leg side shouldn't go down against the wicketkeeper
YOUR BIGGEST CRICKETING REGRET? Losing the Royal London Club Championship final with Ormskirk against Wanstead and Snaresbrook at Chelmsford in 2017
WHAT WILL YOU BE DOING IN THE YEAR 2040? Hopefully I will be in the last few years of my cricket career...
FAVOURITE QUOTE OR SAYING? No one likes a whinger (Dad)
ODDEST SPORT YOU'VE PLAYED? Footgolf
TWITTER: @Glavelle_181

JEREMY LAWLOR

RHB / OB / R0 / W0

FULL NAME: Jeremy Lloyd Lawlor
BORN: November 4, 1995, Cardiff, Wales
SQUAD NO: 6
HEIGHT: 6ft
NICKNAME: Jez, King
EDUCATION: The Cathedral School, Llandaff; Cardiff Metropolitan University
TEAMS: Glamorgan
ROLE: Allrounder
DEBUT: First-class: 2015

BEST BATTING: 81 Cardiff MCCU vs Hampshire, Southampton, 2016
BEST BOWLING: 3-59 Glamorgan vs Sussex, Hove, 2018

FAMILY TIES? My dad Peter played for Glamorgan
WHAT WAS YOUR FIRST CRICKET CLUB? St Fagans CC, Cardiff. It has the most beautiful club ground in Wales
CRICKETING HERO? Sachin Tendulkar
WHICH BOWLER WOULD YOU LEAST LIKE TO FACE? Owen Morgan – he turns it too much
WHO WOULD YOU ASK TO BAT FOR YOUR LIFE? Kieran Bull – the Carmarthen Wall
WHICH RULE WOULD YOU CHANGE ABOUT CRICKET? Allow free hits in red-ball cricket
SURPRISING FACT ABOUT YOU? I was the inter-house chess champion at school
WHAT WILL YOU BE DOING IN THE YEAR 2040? Drinking rum on a beach
WHICH BOOK MEANS MOST TO YOU? Mental – Bad Behaviour, Ugly Truths and the Beautiful Game by Jermaine Pennant

Batting	Mat	Inns	NO	Runs	HS	Ave	SR	100	50	Ct	St
First-class	9	14	2	310	81	25.83	42.87	0	3	6	0
Bowling	**Mat**	**Balls**	**Runs**	**Wkts**	**BBI**	**BBM**	**Ave**	**Econ**	**SR**	**5w**	**10**
First-class	9	439	264	7	3/59	3/59	37.71	3.60	62.7	0	0

DAN LAWRENCE

RHB / LB / R1 / W0

FULL NAME: Daniel William Lawrence
BORN: July 12, 1997, Whipps Cross, Essex
SQUAD NO: 28
EDUCATION: Trinity Catholic High School, London
TEAMS: Essex, England Lions
ROLE: Batsman
DEBUT: First-class: 2015; List A: 2016; T20: 2015

BEST BATTING: 161 Essex vs Surrey, The Oval, 2015
BEST BOWLING: 2-63 Essex vs MCC, Barbados, 2018

FAMILY TIES? My dad is the groundsman at Chingford Cricket Club. My great uncle played for England
CRICKETING HEROES? Ricky Ponting, Graeme Smith, AB de Villiers
NON-CRICKETING HEROES? Martin Luther King, David Beckham
TWITTER: @Lawrenc28Daniel
NOTES: The top-order batsman has been on England's radar ever since he made 161 as a 17-year-old in 2015 in his second Championship appearance. The following year he passed 1,000 first-class runs in his first full season at Chelmsford and was the Cricket Writers' Young Player of the Year in 2017 after contributing three hundreds to Essex's title-winning campaign. He made his England Lions debut that year. Now he will want to come back strong after averaging just 24 last season. Lawrence has a more modest white-ball record, although he did make his first List A hundred in 2018

Batting	Mat	Inns	NO	Runs	HS	Ave	SR	100	50	Ct	St
First-class	54	86	8	2894	161	37.10	51.85	8	11	42	0
List A	20	17	0	400	115	23.52	85.10	1	0	7	0
T20s	37	33	4	700	86	24.13	137.25	0	1	12	0
Bowling	**Mat**	**Balls**	**Runs**	**Wkts**	**BBI**	**BBM**	**Ave**	**Econ**	**SR**	**5w**	**10**
First-class	54	456	292	9	2/63	2/8	32.44	3.84	50.6	0	0
List A	20	324	327	6	3/35	3/35	54.50	6.05	54.0	0	0
T20s	37	216	255	14	3/21	3/21	18.21	7.08	15.4	0	0

JACK LEACH

LHB / SLA / R0 / W2

FULL NAME: Matthew Jack Leach
BORN: June 22, 1991, Taunton, Somerset
SQUAD NO: 17
HEIGHT: 6ft
NICKNAME: Nut
EDUCATION: Bishop Fox's Community School; Richard Huish College; Cardiff Metropolitan University
TEAMS: England, Somerset
ROLE: Bowler
DEBUT: Test: 2018; First-class: 2012; List A: 2012

BEST BATTING: 66 Somerset vs Lancashire, Old Trafford, 2018
BEST BOWLING: 8-85 Somerset vs Essex, Taunton, 2018
COUNTY CAP: 2017

WHAT WAS YOUR FIRST CRICKET CLUB? Taunton Deane CC, Somerset
BEST INNINGS YOU'VE SEEN? Marcus Trescothick's 13-ball fifty in a T20 in 2010
WHO WOULD YOU ASK TO BAT FOR YOUR LIFE? My brother Ben – couldn't get him out in the garden
WHICH RULE WOULD YOU CHANGE ABOUT CRICKET? You can be given lbw even if you are hit outside the line
SURPRISING FACT ABOUT YOU? I wrote a letter to Marcus Trescothick asking for advice when I was about 10 years old. He sent me a long reply and I still have the letter. What a man
FAVOURITE QUOTE OR SAYING? You've got to learn your instrument. Then, you practise, practise, practise. And then when you finally get up there on the bandstand, forget all that and wail (Charlie Parker)
TWITTER: @jackleach1991

Batting	Mat	Inns	NO	Runs	HS	Ave	SR	100	50	Ct	St
Tests	4	7	1	55	16	9.16	36.91	0	0	2	0
First-class	70	94	22	866	66	12.02	35.63	0	2	24	0
List A	16	5	2	22	18	7.33	44.00	0	0	9	0
Bowling	**Mat**	**Balls**	**Runs**	**Wkts**	**BBI**	**BBM**	**Ave**	**Econ**	**SR**	**5w**	**10**
Tests	4	1162	498	20	5/83	8/153	24.90	2.57	58.1	1	0
First-class	70	13529	6056	236	8/85	12/102	25.66	2.68	57.3	17	3
List A	16	824	641	21	3/7	3/7	30.52	4.66	39.2	0	0

JOE LEACH

RHB / RFM / R0 / W3

FULL NAME: Joseph Leach
BORN: October 30, 1990, Stafford
SQUAD NO: 23
HEIGHT: 6ft
NICKNAME: Leachy, Lusty SSSB
EDUCATION: Shrewsbury School; University of Leeds
TEAMS: Worcestershire
ROLE: Allrounder
DEBUT: First-class: 2012; List A: 2012; T20: 2013

BEST BATTING: 114 Worcestershire vs Gloucestershire, Cheltenham, 2013
BEST BOWLING: 6-73 Worcestershire vs Warwickshire, Edgbaston, 2015
COUNTY CAP: 2012

WHAT WAS YOUR FIRST CRICKET CLUB? Stone CC, Staffordshire. Never play on the back foot at Stone!
WHICH BOWLER WOULD YOU LEAST LIKE TO FACE? Josh Tongue – wouldn't be able to stop staring at his ears
BEST INNINGS YOU'VE SEEN? Ben Cox's knock in the 2018 T20 Blast final to win us the trophy
WHO WOULD YOU ASK TO BAT FOR YOUR LIFE? Daryl Mitchell – he would bore the opposition bowlers into submission
WHICH RULE WOULD YOU CHANGE ABOUT CRICKET? It's far too much of a batsman's game, so I'd say three play-and-misses in a row and you're out
YOUR BIGGEST CRICKETING REGRET? Being injured for Finals Day last year
FAVOURITE QUOTE OR SAYING? Things always happen for a reason (from one of my nans)
TWITTER: @joeleach230

Batting	Mat	Inns	NO	Runs	HS	Ave	SR	100	50	Ct	St
First-class	75	111	12	2452	114	24.76	64.15	2	16	21	0
List A	38	28	8	539	63	26.95	100.00	0	1	13	0
T20s	51	32	8	260	24	10.83	114.03	0	0	10	0
Bowling	**Mat**	**Balls**	**Runs**	**Wkts**	**BBI**	**BBM**	**Ave**	**Econ**	**SR**	**5w**	**10**
First-class	75	11693	6980	269	6/73	10/122	25.94	3.58	43.4	12	1
List A	38	1707	1719	43	4/30	4/30	39.97	6.04	39.6	0	0
T20s	51	825	1296	52	5/33	5/33	24.92	9.42	15.8	1	0

JACK LEANING

RHB / RM / R0 / W0

FULL NAME: Jack Andrew Leaning
BORN: October 18, 1993, Bristol
SQUAD NO: 34
HEIGHT: 6ft
EDUCATION: Archbishop Holgate's School, York; York College
TEAMS: Yorkshire
ROLE: Batsman
DEBUT: First-class: 2013; List A: 2012; T20: 2013

BEST BATTING: 123 Yorkshire vs Somerset, Taunton, 2015
BEST BOWLING: 2-30 Yorkshire vs MCC, Abu Dhabi, 2016
COUNTY CAP: 2016

TWITTER: @JackLeaning1
NOTES: Son of former York City goalkeeper Andy, Leaning wrote himself into the Yorkshire record books when he hit an unbeaten 164 for the county's U14 side against Cheshire. He was Yorkshire's Academy Player of the Year in 2012 and made his List A debut in the same season. Leaning made his first-class debut in 2013 against Surrey at Headingley and played 10 Championship matches in 2014, top-scoring with 99. He scored his maiden Championship century in 2015 and added two more on his way to 922 runs, earning him the Cricket Writers' Club Young Player of the Year award. He stalled in 2016 (233 runs in 15 Championship innings) but managed a modest recovery the following summer (454 runs at 30.27). Leaning was one of the many Yorkshire batsmen who struggled last season, averaging 26.50 in 16 Championship innings, and was selected for just nine matches in limited-overs cricket

Batting	Mat	Inns	NO	Runs	HS	Ave	SR	100	50	Ct	St
First-class	59	95	10	2640	123	31.05	42.34	4	13	48	0
List A	45	40	7	1033	131*	31.30	80.26	2	5	20	0
T20s	46	41	11	839	64	27.96	134.45	0	2	21	0
Bowling	**Mat**	**Balls**	**Runs**	**Wkts**	**BBI**	**BBM**	**Ave**	**Econ**	**SR**	**5w**	**10**
First-class	59	454	327	4	2/30	2/30	81.75	4.32	113.5	0	0
List A	45	255	236	9	5/22	5/22	26.22	5.55	28.3	1	0
T20s	46	12	30	0	-	-	-	15.00	-	0	0

ALEX LEES

LHB / LB / R2 / W0

FULL NAME: Alexander Zak Lees
BORN: April 14, 1993, Halifax, Yorkshire
SQUAD NO: 19
HEIGHT: 6ft 3in
NICKNAME: Leesy
EDUCATION: Holy Trinity Senior School, Halifax
TEAMS: Durham, England Lions, Yorkshire
ROLE: Batsman
DEBUT: First-class: 2010; List A: 2011; T20: 2013

BEST BATTING: 275* Yorkshire vs Derbyshire, Chesterfield, 2013
BEST BOWLING: 2-51 Yorkshire vs Middlesex, Lord's, 2016
COUNTY CAP: 2014 (Yorkshire)

WHAT WAS YOUR FIRST CRICKET CLUB? Bradshaw & Illingworth CC, Halifax
CRICKETING HERO? Brian Lara
WHICH BOWLER WOULD YOU LEAST LIKE TO FACE? Joe Leach
SURPRISING FACT ABOUT YOU? I do a bit of magic on the side
TWITTER: @aleesy14
NOTES: The left-handed opener joined Durham on loan last August and has now signed a three-year permanent deal following a tough couple of seasons at Yorkshire. Lees made an instant impact at Headingley, scoring a century on his first-class debut in 2013 and then 275 not out at Chesterfield in the same year. In 2014 he made his England Lions debut and was voted the Cricket Writers' Club Young Player of the Year. He was Yorkshire's leading run-scorer in the Championship in 2016 (1,165 runs) and captained the side in limited-overs cricket. The runs have dried up since then, with just 306 runs in 19 Championship innings last summer. He has not played white-ball cricket since 2017

Batting	Mat	Inns	NO	Runs	HS	Ave	SR	100	50	Ct	St
First-class	95	163	12	5091	275*	33.71	48.55	12	23	66	0
List A	46	42	2	1172	102	29.30	73.34	1	8	16	0
T20s	37	36	2	857	67*	25.20	121.90	0	4	12	0
Bowling	**Mat**	**Balls**	**Runs**	**Wkts**	**BBI**	**BBM**	**Ave**	**Econ**	**SR**	**5w**	**10**
First-class	95	54	77	2	2/51	2/51	38.50	8.55	27.0	0	0
List A	46	-	-	-	-	-	-	-	-	-	-
T20s	37	-	-	-	-	-	-	-	-	-	-

TOBY LESTER

LHB / LFM / R0 / W0

FULL NAME: Toby James Lester
BORN: April 5, 1993, Blackpool
SQUAD NO: 5
HEIGHT: 6ft 4in
NICKNAME: Tobs
EDUCATION: Baines High School, Blackpool; Rossall School, Lancashire; Loughborough University
TEAMS: Lancashire
ROLE: Bowler
DEBUT: First-class: 2012; T20: 2018

BEST BATTING: 8 Lancashire vs Worcestershire, Southport, 2018
BEST BOWLING: 3-50 Lancashire vs Essex, Old Trafford, 2015

WHAT GOT YOU INTO CRICKET? Playing cricket in the back garden with my brothers
'ROY OF THE ROVERS' MOMENT? Making my debut for Lancashire and taking my first wicket
BEST THING ABOUT YOUR HOME GROUND? Being able to walk out onto the pitch and know how many unbelievable players have played there
WHERE IS PARADISE? Sydney
CRICKETING HERO? Andrew Flintoff
NON-CRICKETING HERO? Will Ferrell
TWITTER: @lobylester
NOTES: The left-arm pace bowler made his first-class debut for Loughborough MCCU in 2014. Lester impressed with his performances in Lancashire's Second XI in 2015, earning a first call-up to the senior side for two matches and a Championship debut against Essex at Old Trafford. He has played only three Championship matches since then but was a regular in the T20 side last season, taking 15 wickets at an average of 22.33

Batting	Mat	Inns	NO	Runs	HS	Ave	SR	100	50	Ct	St
First-class	11	13	7	22	8	3.66	19.29	0	0	2	0
T20s	11	4	2	8	7*	4.00	88.88	0	0	2	0
Bowling	**Mat**	**Balls**	**Runs**	**Wkts**	**BBI**	**BBM**	**Ave**	**Econ**	**SR**	**5w**	**10**
First-class	11	1441	899	12	3/50	3/73	74.91	3.74	120.0	0	0
T20s	11	226	335	15	4/25	4/25	22.33	8.89	15.0	0	0

RICHARD LEVI

RHB / RO / WO

FULL NAME: Richard Ernst Levi
BORN: January 14, 1988, Johannesburg, SA
SQUAD NO: 88
HEIGHT: 6ft
NICKNAME: Bear
EDUCATION: Wynberg Boys' High School, Cape Town; University of South Africa
TEAMS: South Africa, Northamptonshire, Cape Cobras, Mumbai Indians, Somerset, Western Province
ROLE: Batsman
DEBUT: T20I: 2012; First-class: 2006; List A: 2005; T20: 2008

BEST BATTING: 168 Northamptonshire vs Essex, Northampton, 2015

COUNTY CAP: 2017 (Northamptonshire)

WHAT WAS YOUR FIRST CRICKET CLUB? Claremont CC, Cape Town, South Africa. Feeder club for Wynberg Boys' and Western Province
FAVOURITE CRICKET BAT? My Laser 3 Star – made me love whacking the ball
CRICKETING HERO? Gary Kirsten
BEST INNINGS YOU'VE SEEN? Brian Lara's 400 not out against England at Antigua in 2004
WHO WOULD YOU ASK TO BAT FOR YOUR LIFE? Rahul Dravid
WHICH RULE WOULD YOU CHANGE ABOUT CRICKET? You should be able to shake hands on a draw earlier than is currently allowed
YOUR BIGGEST CRICKETING REGRET? Not bowling
WHAT WILL YOU BE DOING IN THE YEAR 2040? I'll be colonising Mars
ODDEST SPORT YOU'VE PLAYED? Extreme ironing
TWITTER: @RichardLevi88

Batting	Mat	Inns	NO	Runs	HS	Ave	SR	100	50	Ct	St
T20Is	13	13	2	236	117*	21.45	141.31	1	1	4	0
First-class	100	166	16	5544	168	36.96	68.62	10	31	85	0
List A	130	122	6	4412	166	38.03	105.55	8	28	40	0
T20s	198	189	12	5070	117*	28.64	144.81	3	33	54	0
Bowling	**Mat**	**Balls**	**Runs**	**Wkts**	**BBI**	**BBM**	**Ave**	**Econ**	**SR**	**5w**	**10**
T20Is	13	-	-	-	-	-	-	-	-	-	-
First-class	100	-	-	-	-	-	-	-	-	-	-
List A	130	-	-	-	-	-	-	-	-	-	-
T20s	198	-	-	-	-	-	-	-	-	-	-

JAKE LIBBY

RHB / OB / R0 / W0

FULL NAME: Jacob Daniel Libby
BORN: January 3, 1993, Plymouth, Devon
SQUAD NO: 2
HEIGHT: 5ft 8in
NICKNAME: Libbs
EDUCATION: Plymouth College; Truro College, Cornwall; Cardiff Metropolitan University
TEAMS: Nottinghamshire, Northamptonshire
ROLE: Batsman
DEBUT: First-class: 2014; T20: 2018

BEST BATTING: 144 Nottinghamshire vs Durham, Chester-le-Street, 2016
BEST BOWLING: 1-13 Northamptonshire vs Leicestershire, Leicester, 2016

FAMILY TIES? My brother captains Callington CC in the Cornish Premier League
WHAT WAS YOUR FIRST CRICKET CLUB? Menheniot & Looe CC, Cornwall – where I used to watch my dad play on Saturday
CRICKETING HERO? Marcus Trescothick – I grew up watching him at Taunton
WHICH BOWLER WOULD YOU LEAST LIKE TO FACE? My brother – bowls dibbly-dobblers
BEST INNINGS YOU'VE SEEN? Dave Waters when he was playing as a ringer for my club side Callington CC
WHO WOULD YOU ASK TO BAT FOR YOUR LIFE? Luke Fletcher – he has the best forward defence in the country
WHICH RULE WOULD YOU CHANGE ABOUT CRICKET? Ban the Dukes ball!
WHAT WILL YOU BE DOING IN THE YEAR 2040? I'll be an umpire or a director of cricket
WHICH BOOK MEANS MOST TO YOU? Relentless – From Good to Great to Unstoppable by Tim Grover
TWITTER: @JakeLibby1

Batting	Mat	Inns	NO	Runs	HS	Ave	SR	100	50	Ct	St
First-class	50	86	6	2385	144	29.81	42.65	5	10	16	0
T20s	11	11	3	284	58	35.50	142.71	0	1	1	0
Bowling	**Mat**	**Balls**	**Runs**	**Wkts**	**BBI**	**BBM**	**Ave**	**Econ**	**SR**	**5w**	**10**
First-class	50	436	264	4	1/13	1/22	66.00	3.63	109.0	0	0
T20s	11	-	-	-	-	-	-	-	-	-	-

CHRIS LIDDLE

RHB / LMF / R0 / W0

FULL NAME: Christopher John Liddle
BORN: February 1, 1984, Middlesbrough, Yorkshire
SQUAD NO: 23
HEIGHT: 6ft 4in
NICKNAME: Lids
EDUCATION: Nunthorpe Comprehensive, Middlesborough; Teeside Tertiary College
TEAMS: Gloucestershire, Dhaka Gladiators, Leicestershire, Sussex
ROLE: Bowler
DEBUT: First-class: 2005; List A: 2006; T20: 2008

BEST BATTING: 53 Sussex vs Worcestershire, Hove, 2007
BEST BOWLING: 3-42 Leicestershire vs Somerset, Leicester, 2006

WHAT WAS YOUR FIRST CRICKET CLUB? Marton CC, North Yorkshire
CRICKETING HERO? Ryan Sidebottom – fine bowler and a thoroughly nice guy
BEST ADVICE EVER RECEIVED? Always remember why you played cricket in the first place
WHICH BOWLER WOULD YOU LEAST LIKE TO FACE? Ben Brown – bowls filthy off-spin
WHO WOULD YOU ASK TO BAT FOR YOUR LIFE? Mike Yardy
WHICH RULE WOULD YOU CHANGE ABOUT CRICKET? If the batters cross in the middle during a dismissal then the new batter still has to face the next ball
YOUR BIGGEST CRICKETING REGRET? Trying to change my bowling to suit a more traditional left-armer
SURPRISING FACT ABOUT YOU? I occasionally DJ for friends
TWITTER: @chrisliddle11

Batting	Mat	Inns	NO	Runs	HS	Ave	SR	100	50	Ct	St
First-class	34	36	18	208	53	11.55	41.68	0	1	8	0
List A	75	30	9	126	18	6.00	69.61	0	0	19	0
T20s	83	17	9	54	16	6.75	69.23	0	0	21	0
Bowling	**Mat**	**Balls**	**Runs**	**Wkts**	**BBI**	**BBM**	**Ave**	**Econ**	**SR**	**5w**	**10**
First-class	34	4144	2326	48	3/42	4/82	48.45	3.36	86.3	0	0
List A	75	2969	2918	110	5/18	5/18	26.52	5.89	26.9	3	0
T20s	83	1558	2149	88	5/17	5/17	24.42	8.27	17.7	1	0

ARRON LILLEY

RHB / OB / R0 / W0

FULL NAME: Arron Mark Lilley
BORN: April 1, 1991, Tameside, Lancashire
SQUAD NO: 19
HEIGHT: 6ft 2in
NICKNAME: The Bigshow, Lill, Azza
EDUCATION: Mossley Hollins High School, Tameside; Ashton Sixth Form
TEAMS: Leicestershire, Lancashire
ROLE: Bowler
DEBUT: First-class: 2013; List A: 2012; T20: 2013

BEST BATTING: 63 Lancashire vs Derbyshire, Southport, 2015
BEST BOWLING: 5-23 Lancashire vs Derbyshire, Southport, 2015

WHAT WAS YOUR FIRST CRICKET CLUB? Micklehurst CC, Greater Manchester. My grandad and dad played there before me
FAVOURITE CRICKET BAT? My current one – a Kippax. Good slogger's bat
WHICH BOWLER WOULD YOU LEAST LIKE TO FACE? Keaton Jennings – he's just too quick
WHO WOULD YOU ASK TO BAT FOR YOUR LIFE? Virat Kohli
WHICH RULE WOULD YOU CHANGE ABOUT CRICKET? Ban the bouncer!
YOUR BIGGEST CRICKETING REGRET? Not winning the T20 Blast with Lancashire last season after getting to Finals Day
WHAT WILL YOU BE DOING IN THE YEAR 2040? Lying on a beach somewhere drinking red wine and gin (hopefully)
FAVOURITE QUOTE OR SAYING? Ohhhhh I'm lovin' it
WHICH BOOK MEANS MOST TO YOU? Blessed – The Autobiography by George Best
ODDEST SPORT YOU'VE PLAYED? Kabaddi
TWITTER: @Arronlilley20

Batting	Mat	Inns	NO	Runs	HS	Ave	SR	100	50	Ct	St
First-class	14	18	5	426	63	32.76	94.03	0	2	4	0
List A	12	5	1	36	16	9.00	116.12	0	0	7	0
T20s	70	42	9	499	47	15.12	153.53	0	0	33	0
Bowling	**Mat**	**Balls**	**Runs**	**Wkts**	**BBI**	**BBM**	**Ave**	**Econ**	**SR**	**5w**	**10**
First-class	14	2625	1385	38	5/23	6/151	36.44	3.16	69.0	2	0
List A	12	390	339	15	4/30	4/30	22.60	5.21	26.0	0	0
T20s	70	939	1145	40	3/31	3/31	28.62	7.31	23.4	0	0

LIAM LIVINGSTONE RHB / OB / R0 / W0 / MVP32

FULL NAME: Liam Stephen Livingstone
BORN: August 4, 1993, Barrow-in-Furness, Cumbria
SQUAD NO: 7
HEIGHT: 6ft 2in
NICKNAME: Livvy, Livvo
EDUCATION: Chetwynde School, Barrow-in-Furness
TEAMS: England, Lancashire, Karachi Kings, Rajasthan Royals
ROLE: Batsman
DEBUT: T20I: 2018; First-class: 2016; List A: 2015; T20: 2015

BEST BATTING: 224 Lancashire vs Warwickshire, Old Trafford, 2017
BEST BOWLING: 6-52 Lancashire vs Surrey, Old Trafford, 2017
COUNTY CAP: 2017

WHAT GOT YOU INTO CRICKET? Playing on the outfield at Barrow CC from a very early age
FAMILY TIES? My father and brother played low-level club cricket
'ROY OF THE ROVERS' MOMENT? Winning the T20 Blast in 2015
CRICKETING HEROES? Andrew Flintoff – so good to watch as a young kid. Shane Warne – I was a leg-spinner growing up
NON-CRICKETING HERO? David Beckham
SURPRISING FACT? I scored 350 in a club game. I support Blackburn Rovers FC
TWITTER: @liaml4893
NOTES: Livingstone will miss the early part of the season after he was bought by Rajasthan Royals for approximately £56,000 to play in the IPL

Batting	Mat	Inns	NO	Runs	HS	Ave	SR	100	50	Ct	St
T20Is	2	2	0	16	16	8.00	84.21	0	0	0	0
First-class	43	71	13	2356	224	40.62	58.69	6	10	61	0
List A	53	44	3	1526	129	37.21	99.54	1	10	25	0
T20s	60	56	6	1395	100	27.90	142.63	1	6	25	0
Bowling	**Mat**	**Balls**	**Runs**	**Wkts**	**BBI**	**BBM**	**Ave**	**Econ**	**SR**	**5w**	**10**
T20Is	2	-	-	-	-	-	-	-	-	-	-
First-class	43	1889	965	24	6/52	6/52	40.20	3.06	78.7	1	0
List A	53	1227	1064	22	3/51	3/51	48.36	5.20	55.7	0	0
T20s	60	183	235	14	4/17	4/17	16.78	7.70	13.0	0	0

DAVID LLOYD RHB / OB / R0 / W0

FULL NAME: David Liam Lloyd
BORN: June 15, 1992, St Asaph, Denbighshire, Wales
SQUAD NO: 73
HEIGHT: 5ft 10in
NICKNAME: Ram, Sergio, Ramos
EDUCATION: Darland High School, Wrexham; Shrewsbury School
TEAMS: Glamorgan
ROLE: Batsman
DEBUT: First-class: 2012; List A: 2014; T20: 2014

BEST BATTING: 119 Glamorgan vs Gloucestershire, Bristol, 2018
BEST BOWLING: 3-36 Glamorgan vs Northamptonshire, Swansea, 2016

WHAT WAS YOUR FIRST CRICKET CLUB? Brymbo CC, Clwyd, Wales
WHICH BOWLER WOULD YOU LEAST LIKE TO FACE? Shane Warne
BEST INNINGS YOU'VE SEEN? Mitchell Marsh's maiden Test hundred against England at Perth in the 2017/18 Ashes. Never seen anyone hit the ball so clean
WHO WOULD YOU ASK TO BAT FOR YOUR LIFE? Kieran Bull – his nickname is The Wall
WHICH RULE WOULD YOU CHANGE ABOUT CRICKET? Sessions should be one hour long
YOUR BIGGEST CRICKETING REGRET? Getting 97 not out in a T20 against Kent in 2016
SURPRISING FACT ABOUT YOU? I support Wrexham FC and I have a degree in Economics
FAVOURITE QUOTE OR SAYING? Work hard, play hard
WHICH BOOK MEANS MOST TO YOU? From Nowhere – My Story by Jamie Vardy
ODDEST SPORT YOU'VE PLAYED? Eton Fives
TWITTER: @lloyddl2010

Batting	Mat	Inns	NO	Runs	HS	Ave	SR	100	50	Ct	St
First-class	55	93	11	2271	119	27.69	61.69	4	7	18	0
List A	38	32	1	702	92	22.64	82.88	0	3	8	0
T20s	36	31	2	581	97*	20.03	118.81	0	2	13	0
Bowling	**Mat**	**Balls**	**Runs**	**Wkts**	**BBI**	**BBM**	**Ave**	**Econ**	**SR**	**5w**	**10**
First-class	55	3576	2375	51	3/36	3/53	46.56	3.98	70.1	0	0
List A	38	721	717	17	5/53	5/53	42.17	5.96	42.4	1	0
T20s	36	30	50	4	2/13	2/13	12.50	10.00	7.5	0	0

JAMES LOGAN

LHB / SLA / R0 / W0

FULL NAME: James Edwin Graham Logan
BORN: October 12, 1997, Wakefield, Yorkshire
SQUAD NO: 11
NICKNAME: Logi
EDUCATION: Normanton Freestone High School, West Yorkshire; Pontefract New College
TEAMS: Yorkshire
ROLE: Bowler
DEBUT: First-class: 2018

BEST BATTING: 6 Yorkshire vs Worcestershire, Worcester, 2018

NOTES: A left-arm spinner, Logan made his first-team debut in a Championship win over Worcestershire at New Road during the final round of 2018."I am aiming for more first-team appearances next year," he said. "But it's obviously tough for a spinner at the start of the year when it's cold and the pitches are green. I'll just try and do well for the seconds and go from there." The Wakefield-born 21-year-old first represented Yorkshire at U13 level in 2011 and has gone to play for every age-group, making his Second XI debut in 2014. The following summer he took 8-76 in the second innings of a rain-affected win over Leicestershire at Scarborough. He had made 50 appearances for the Second XI going into the new season. Over the previous five summers for the Yorkshire Academy Logan has taken 193 wickets, the most by any bowler, and he was part of the team that won a historic league-and-cup double in 2014

Batting	Mat	Inns	NO	Runs	HS	Ave	SR	100	50	Ct	St
First-class	1	1	0	6	6	6.00	16.66	0	0	1	0
Bowling	**Mat**	**Balls**	**Runs**	**Wkts**	**BBI**	**BBM**	**Ave**	**Econ**	**SR**	**5w**	**10**
First-class	1	72	44	0	-	-	-	3.66	-	0	0

ADAM LYTH LHB / OB / R3 / W0 / MVP20

FULL NAME: Adam Lyth
BORN: September 25, 1987, Whitby, Yorkshire
SQUAD NO: 9
HEIGHT: 5ft 9in
NICKNAME: Lythy, Budge, Peanut
EDUCATION: Caedmon School; Whitby Community School
TEAMS: England, Yorkshire, Rangpur Riders
ROLE: Batsman
DEBUT: Test: 2015; First-class: 2007; List A: 2006; T20: 2008

BEST BATTING: 251 Yorkshire vs Lancashire, Old Trafford, 2014
BEST BOWLING: 2-9 Yorkshire vs Middlesex, Scarborough, 2016
COUNTY CAP: 2010

FAMILY TIES? My brother and dad played for Scarborough and my grandad played for Whitby CC
CRICKETING HERO? Graham Thorpe
SURPRISING FACT? I had trials with Manchester City before choosing cricket
TWITTER: @lythy09
NOTES: The dashing left-handed opener has been one of Yorkshire's more consistent run-getters in the Championship over the last two seasons and has set the standard in white-ball cricket. He has been the club's leading run-scorer in T20 cricket for the past two seasons and last summer he made 433 runs at an average of 54.12 in the One-Day Cup, including two hundreds. A sharp fielder, Lyth scored his maiden Test hundred against New Zealand in 2015 but was dropped after a poor Ashes later that summer and has not been recalled since

Batting	Mat	Inns	NO	Runs	HS	Ave	SR	100	50	Ct	St
Tests	7	13	0	265	107	20.38	50.09	1	0	8	0
First-class	161	270	12	9858	251	38.20	53.63	23	50	204	0
List A	115	108	8	3564	144	35.64	93.10	5	16	52	0
T20s	103	94	3	2226	161	24.46	140.53	1	11	54	0
Bowling	**Mat**	**Balls**	**Runs**	**Wkts**	**BBI**	**BBM**	**Ave**	**Econ**	**SR**	**5w**	**10**
Tests	7	6	0	0	-	-	-	0.00	-	0	0
First-class	161	2519	1536	33	2/9	2/9	46.54	3.65	76.3	0	0
List A	115	342	346	4	1/6	1/6	86.50	6.07	85.5	0	0
T20s	103	144	174	5	2/5	2/5	34.80	7.25	28.8	0	0

WAYNE MADSEN RHB / OB / R5 / W0 / MVP33

FULL NAME: Wayne Lee Madsen
BORN: January 2, 1984, Durban, South Africa
SQUAD NO: 77
HEIGHT: 5ft 11in
NICKNAME: Madders, Mads
EDUCATION: Highbury Preparatory School; Kearsney College; University of South Africa
TEAMS: Derbyshire, KwaZulu-Natal
ROLE: Batsman
DEBUT: First-class: 2004; List A: 2004; T20: 2010

BEST BATTING: 231* Derbyshire vs Northamptonshire, Northampton, 2012
BEST BOWLING: 3-45 KwaZulu-Natal vs Eastern Province, Port Elizabeth, 2008
COUNTY CAP: 2011

FAMILY TIES? My uncles Trevor Madsen and Henry Fotheringham represented South Africa. My other uncle Mike Madsen played for Natal and so did my cousin Greg Fotheringham
WHAT WAS YOUR FIRST CRICKET CLUB? Crusaders CC, Durban, South Africa. Got a golden duck in my first game
BEST INNINGS YOU'VE SEEN? AB de Villiers scoring 162 off 66 balls against West Indies at Sydney in the 2015 World Cup. He was picking which part of the stands he wanted to hit each delivery – 360-degree batting
SURPRISING FACT ABOUT YOU? I hold the Guinness World Record for cricket's version of keepy-uppies: the most bat touches in one minute (282)
FAVOURITE QUOTE OR SAYING? It always seems impossible until it's done (Nelson Mandela)
WHICH BOOK MEANS MOST TO YOU? The Bible
TWITTER: @waynemadsen2017

Batting	Mat	Inns	NO	Runs	HS	Ave	SR	100	50	Ct	St
First-class	170	304	22	11047	231*	39.17	50.95	28	58	163	0
List A	96	88	16	2869	138	39.84	87.92	4	18	62	0
T20s	101	98	16	2347	86*	28.62	130.67	0	15	31	0
Bowling	**Mat**	**Balls**	**Runs**	**Wkts**	**BBI**	**BBM**	**Ave**	**Econ**	**SR**	**5w**	**10**
First-class	170	2725	1520	29	3/45	3/60	52.41	3.34	93.9	0	0
List A	96	440	354	14	3/27	3/27	25.28	4.82	31.4	0	0
T20s	101	396	517	17	2/20	2/20	30.41	7.83	23.2	0	0

SAQIB MAHMOOD

RHB / RFM / R0 / W0

FULL NAME: Saqib Mahmood
BORN: February 25, 1997, Birmingham
SQUAD NO: 25
HEIGHT: 6ft 3in
NICKNAME: Saq
EDUCATION: Matthew Moss High School, Rochdale
TEAMS: Lancashire, England Lions
ROLE: Bowler
DEBUT: First-class: 2016; List A: 2016; T20: 2015

BEST BATTING: 9 England Lions vs West Indies A, Antigua, 2018
BEST BOWLING: 4-50 Lancashire vs Surrey, Old Trafford, 2017

TWITTER: @SaqMahmood25
NOTES: Pace bowler Mahmood joined the Lancashire Academy four years ago. He made his England U19 debut in 2015, taking 3-12 to help rout South Africa for 77 at Northampton. He was part of the Lancashire U17 side that won the One-Day Cup and shared the two-day Championship in 2014. Mahmood made his full Lancashire debut in 2015. He impressed for England at the 2016 U19 World Cup and was a regular member of Lancashire's 50-over side that summer. He took 12 wickets in three Championship matches in 2017 but did not feature in the short formats. A groin injury put him on the sidelines at the start of last season, when he made only one competitive appearance for the club. Mahmood has been a regular for the England Lions since making his debut in 2016. However, he was unable to take part in the tour of India over the winter because of difficulties obtaining a visa to enter the country, something partly attributed to his Pakistan heritage

Batting	Mat	Inns	NO	Runs	HS	Ave	SR	100	50	Ct	St
First-class	7	8	5	18	9	6.00	28.12	0	0	1	0
List A	17	8	6	65	27*	32.50	89.04	0	0	7	0
T20s	8	-	-	-	-	-	-	-	-	0	0
Bowling	**Mat**	**Balls**	**Runs**	**Wkts**	**BBI**	**BBM**	**Ave**	**Econ**	**SR**	**5w**	**10**
First-class	7	957	554	21	4/50	5/120	26.38	3.47	45.5	0	0
List A	17	729	748	22	5/60	5/60	34.00	6.15	33.1	1	0
T20s	8	140	156	12	4/14	4/14	13.00	6.68	11.6	0	0

GAVIN MAIN

RHB / RFM / R0 / W0

FULL NAME: Gavin Thomas Main
BORN: February 28, 1995, Lanark, Scotland
SQUAD NO: 20
HEIGHT: 6ft 1in
NICKNAME: Gav
EDUCATION: The High School of Glasgow; University of Strathclyde
TEAMS: Scotland, Durham
ROLE: Bowler
DEBUT: T20I: 2015; First-class: 2014; List A: 2015; T20: 2015

BEST BATTING: 13 Durham vs Northamptonshire, Chester-le-Street, 2017
BEST BOWLING: 3-72 Durham vs Nottinghamshire, Trent Bridge, 2014

WHAT WAS YOUR FIRST CRICKET CLUB? Uddington CC, South Lanarkshire, Scotland. Quickest pitch in the north
CRICKETING HERO? Brett Lee
WHICH BOWLER WOULD YOU LEAST LIKE TO FACE? Ryan Pringle – I play a lot better against spinners who turn the ball
BEST INNINGS YOU'VE SEEN? Calum MacLeod's 140 not out for Scotland when they beat England at Edinburgh in 2018
WHO WOULD YOU ASK TO BAT FOR YOUR LIFE? Cameron Steel
YOUR BIGGEST CRICKETING REGRET? Not learning to swing the ball
SURPRISING FACT ABOUT YOU? I was the Scotland U8 swimming champion
WHICH BOOK MEANS MOST TO YOU? 1984 by George Orwell
TWITTER: @gmain95

Batting	Mat	Inns	NO	Runs	HS	Ave	SR	100	50	Ct	St
T20Is	4	-	-	-	-	-	-	-	-	1	0
First-class	4	4	2	13	13	6.50	40.62	0	0	1	0
List A	2	-	-	-	-	-	-	-	-	0	0
T20s	4	-	-	-	-	-	-	-	-	1	0
Bowling	**Mat**	**Balls**	**Runs**	**Wkts**	**BBI**	**BBM**	**Ave**	**Econ**	**SR**	**5w**	**10**
T20Is	4	24	34	2	1/13	1/13	17.00	8.50	12.0	0	0
First-class	4	402	319	8	3/72	3/72	39.87	4.76	50.2	0	0
List A	2	102	74	4	2/35	2/35	18.50	4.35	25.5	0	0
T20s	4	24	34	2	1/13	1/13	17.00	8.50	12.0	0	0

DAWID MALAN

LHB / LB / R2 / W0

FULL NAME: Dawid Johannes Malan
BORN: September 3, 1987, Roehampton
SQUAD NO: 29
HEIGHT: 6ft
NICKNAME: Mal, Mala
EDUCATION: Paarl Boys' High School; University of South Africa
TEAMS: England, Middlesex, Barisal Bulls, Boland, Cape Town Blitz, Khulna Titans, Peshawar Zalmi, Prime Doleshwar Sporting Club
ROLE: Batsman
DEBUT: Test: 2017; T20I: 2017; First-class: 2006; List A: 2006; T20: 2006

BEST BATTING: 182* Middlesex vs Nottinghamshire, Trent Bridge, 2015
BEST BOWLING: 5-61 Middlesex vs Lancashire, Liverpool, 2012
COUNTY CAP: 2010

FAMILY TIES? My dad Dawid played for Transvaal B and Western Province B and my brother Charl played for MCC Young Cricketers and Loughborough MCCU
SUPERSTITIONS? Too many to write down
CRICKETING HERO? Gary Kirsten
IF YOU WEREN'T A CRICKETER? I would like to have gone into sports psychology
SURPRISING FACT? I love to go to the cinema by myself
TWITTER: @DJMalan29

Batting	Mat	Inns	NO	Runs	HS	Ave	SR	100	50	Ct	St
Tests	15	26	0	724	140	27.84	41.08	1	6	11	0
T20Is	5	5	0	250	78	50.00	150.60	0	4	1	0
First-class	174	298	20	10170	182*	36.58	51.74	21	56	181	0
List A	143	139	21	4938	185*	41.84	83.52	10	24	47	0
T20s	165	160	26	4139	115*	30.88	124.18	2	23	58	0
Bowling	**Mat**	**Balls**	**Runs**	**Wkts**	**BBI**	**BBM**	**Ave**	**Econ**	**SR**	**5w**	**10**
Tests	15	156	70	0	-	-	-	2.69	-	0	0
T20Is	5	12	27	1	1/27	1/27	27.00	13.50	12.0	0	0
First-class	174	3775	2292	55	5/61	5/61	41.67	3.64	68.6	1	0
List A	143	1203	1150	38	4/25	4/25	30.26	5.73	31.6	0	0
T20s	165	525	647	23	2/10	2/10	28.13	7.39	22.8	0	0

SHAUN MARSH LHB / SLA / R0 / W0

FULL NAME: Shaun Edward Marsh
BORN: July 9, 1983, Narrogin, Western Australia, Australia
SQUAD NO: 43
HEIGHT: 6ft
NICKNAME: Sos
TEAMS: Australia, Glamorgan, Kings XI Punjab, Perth Scorchers, Western Australia, Yorkshire
ROLE: Batsman
DEBUT: Test: 2011; ODI: 2008; T20I: 2008; First-class: 2001; List A: 2002; T20: 2006

BEST BATTING: 182 Australia vs West Indies, Hobart, 2015
BEST BOWLING: 2-20 Western Australia vs New South Wales, Sydney, 2003

TWITTER: @shaunmarsh9
NOTES: Marsh has been a regular member of the Australian top-order for a number of years, scoring a hundred on Test debut against Sri Lanka in 2011 and starring in the 2017/18 Ashes series, scoring two centuries. The son of former Australia opener Geoff Marsh and brother of Mitchell Marsh, Shaun had a first taste of the County Championship in 2017, averaging 112.50 in his two games for Yorkshire, before later that year signing a two-year deal with Glamorgan as their overseas player for all formats. He was available for only 10 matches in all competitions last season, scoring one Championship hundred. It is unclear how much he will figure in Australia's plans for the World Cup and Ashes this summer, although he is expected to play for Glamorgan in the early season after going unsold in the IPL auction

Batting	Mat	Inns	NO	Runs	HS	Ave	SR	100	50	Ct	St
Tests	38	68	2	2265	182	34.31	43.85	6	10	23	0
ODIs	66	65	2	2565	151	40.71	81.53	7	13	18	0
T20Is	15	15	1	255	47*	18.21	102.82	0	0	3	0
First-class	157	277	28	10157	182	40.79	48.05	26	50	136	0
List A	155	151	8	6238	186	43.62	80.70	17	32	52	0
T20s	169	166	24	5589	115	39.35	128.98	2	43	57	0
Bowling	**Mat**	**Balls**	**Runs**	**Wkts**	**BBI**	**BBM**	**Ave**	**Econ**	**SR**	**5w**	**10**
Tests	38	-	-	-	-	-	-	-	-	-	-
ODIs	66	-	-	-	-	-	-	-	-	-	-
T20Is	15	-	-	-	-	-	-	-	-	-	-
First-class	157	216	155	2	2/20		77.50	4.30	108.0	0	0
List A	155	36	31	1	1/14	1/14	31.00	5.16	36.0	0	0
T20s	169	12	13	0	-	-	-	6.50	-	0	0

GLENN MAXWELL RHB / OB / R0 / W0

FULL NAME: Glenn James Maxwell
BORN: October 14, 1988, Kew, Melbourne, Australia
SQUAD NO: 32
TEAMS: Australia, Lancashire, Delhi Daredevils, Hampshire, Kings XI Punjab, Melbourne Stars, Mumbai Indians, Surrey, Victoria, Yorkshire
ROLE: Allrounder
DEBUT: Test: 2013; ODI: 2012; T20I: 2012; First-class: 2011; List A: 2010; T20: 2010

BEST BATTING: 278 Victoria vs New South Wales, Sydney, 2017
BEST BOWLING: 4-42 Victoria vs South Australia, Melbourne, 2012

TWITTER: @Gmaxi_32
NOTES: Described by Lancashire director of cricket Paul Allott as "one of the most exciting cricketers in the world", the Australian allrounder will be available in all three formats, including up to five Championship games. A key component in his country's limited-overs side but ignored for Test selection in recent times, Maxwell is hoping to make a late bid for this summer's Ashes series. "I have really enjoyed my spells in England before and I'm determined to put in some match-winning performances for Lancashire in all three formats of the game," said Maxwell. "I still have aspirations to play Test cricket for Australia so I felt it was important that I play some first-class cricket whilst I'm over in England"

Batting	Mat	Inns	NO	Runs	HS	Ave	SR	100	50	Ct	St
Tests	7	14	1	339	104	26.07	59.47	1	0	5	0
ODIs	94	85	9	2441	102	32.11	120.48	1	16	57	0
T20Is	59	53	9	1514	145*	34.40	158.20	3	6	30	0
First-class	61	104	10	3864	278	41.10	73.12	7	21	49	0
List A	155	140	16	4105	146	33.10	119.57	4	25	93	0
T20s	238	225	27	5222	145*	26.37	154.63	3	26	126	0
Bowling	**Mat**	**Balls**	**Runs**	**Wkts**	**BBI**	**BBM**	**Ave**	**Econ**	**SR**	**5w**	**10**
Tests	7	462	341	8	4/127	4/127	42.62	4.42	57.7	0	0
ODIs	94	2158	2021	47	4/46	4/46	43.00	5.61	45.9	0	0
T20Is	59	564	704	26	3/10	3/10	27.07	7.48	21.6	0	0
First-class	61	4655	2660	60	4/42	5/66	44.33	3.42	77.5	0	0
List A	155	3540	3189	80	4/46	4/46	39.86	5.40	44.2	0	0
T20s	238	1905	2501	79	3/10	3/10	31.65	7.87	24.1	0	0

CONOR MCKERR

RHB / RFM / R0 / W0

FULL NAME: Conor McKerr
BORN: January 19, 1998, Johannesburg, South Africa
SQUAD NO: 83
HEIGHT: 6ft 6in
NICKNAME: Fat Knees
EDUCATION: St John's College, Johannesburg
TEAMS: Surrey, Derbyshire
ROLE: Bowler
DEBUT: First-class: 2017

BEST BATTING: 29 Surrey vs Yorkshire, The Oval, 2018
BEST BOWLING: 5-54 Derbyshire vs Northamptonshire, Northampton, 2017

WHAT WAS YOUR FIRST CRICKET CLUB? Randburg CC, Johannesburg, South Africa. I remember the old concrete nets
FAVOURITE CRICKET BAT? GM Purist 505. Earnt a place in the regional side after making 77 with that gorgeous stick
CRICKETING HERO? Dale Steyn
BEST ADVICE EVER RECEIVED? Train harder than everyone so you can have more fun than everyone when you play
WHICH BOWLER WOULD YOU LEAST LIKE TO FACE? Mitchell Johnson from round the wicket
BEST INNINGS YOU'VE SEEN? Graeme Smith's double century against England at Lord's in 2003. My first memory of cricket
WHO WOULD YOU ASK TO BAT FOR YOUR LIFE? Amar Virdi
WHICH RULE WOULD YOU CHANGE ABOUT CRICKET? Remove stump mics
YOUR BIGGEST CRICKETING REGRET? Ducking into a short ball in the nets
FAVOURITE QUOTE OR SAYING? I always get to where I'm going by walking away from where I've been (Winnie the Pooh)
WHICH BOOK MEANS MOST TO YOU? The Alchemist by Paulo Coelho
TWITTER: @cemckerr83

Batting	Mat	Inns	NO	Runs	HS	Ave	SR	100	50	Ct	St
First-class	9	9	3	98	29	16.33	40.66	0	0	0	0
Bowling	**Mat**	**Balls**	**Runs**	**Wkts**	**BBI**	**BBM**	**Ave**	**Econ**	**SR**	**5w**	**10**
First-class	9	1069	638	28	5/54	10/141	22.78	3.58	38.1	2	1

MATTIE MCKIERNAN

RHB / LB / R0 / W0

FULL NAME: Matthew Henry McKiernan
BORN: June 14, 1994, Lancashire
SQUAD NO: 21
HEIGHT: 6ft 1in
NICKNAME: Macka
EDUCATION: Lowton High School, Leigh, Greater Manchester; St John Rigby College, Wigan; Edge Hill University, Ormskirk, Lancashire
TEAMS: Derbyshire
ROLE: Bowler
DEBUT: T20: 2018

WHAT WAS YOUR FIRST CRICKET CLUB? Leigh CC, Greater Manchester
WHICH BOWLER WOULD YOU LEAST LIKE TO FACE? Mitchell Starc
BEST INNINGS YOU'VE SEEN? George Bailey's 202 for South Hobart Sandy Bay vs North Hobart in the 2015/16 Cricket Tasmania Premier League. Manipulated the field effortlessly and made it look easy
WHO WOULD YOU ASK TO BAT FOR YOUR LIFE? Luis Reece – he values his wicket immensely. I've played in a four-day match in which he was on the field for every minute. I suppose Virat Kohli would also do
WHICH RULE WOULD YOU CHANGE ABOUT CRICKET? It should be five runs if the ball bounces once on its way to the boundary
YOUR BIGGEST CRICKETING REGRET? Missing the South Hobart Sandy Bay grand final week in 2015/16
WHAT WILL YOU BE DOING IN THE YEAR 2040? I'll be playing in Leigh CC's third XI
WHICH BOOK MEANS MOST TO YOU? What's a book?!
ODDEST SPORT YOU'VE PLAYED? I played a very weird version of cricket in Australia: you got double runs for hitting the ball between long-off and long-on
TWITTER: @MattieMcKiernan

Batting	Mat	Inns	NO	Runs	HS	Ave	SR	100	50	Ct	St
T20s	1	1	1	1	1*	-	100.00	0	0	0	0
Bowling	**Mat**	**Balls**	**Runs**	**Wkts**	**BBI**	**BBM**	**Ave**	**Econ**	**SR**	**5w**	**10**
T20s	1	24	27	0	-	-	-	6.75	-	0	0

LEWIS MCMANUS RHB / WK / R0 / W0

FULL NAME: Lewis David McManus
BORN: October 9, 1994, Poole, Dorset
SQUAD NO: 18
HEIGHT: 5ft 8in
NICKNAME: Lewy, King
EDUCATION: Clayesmore School, Bournemouth; University of Exeter
TEAMS: Hampshire
ROLE: Wicketkeeper/batsman
DEBUT: First-class: 2015; List A: 2016; T20: 2016

BEST BATTING: 132* Hampshire vs Surrey, Southampton, 2016

WHAT GOT YOU INTO CRICKET? It was a sport to play during the football off-season
STRANGEST THING SEEN IN A GAME? James Tomlinson's one-handed catch at fine-leg while holding a banana in the other hand during a first-class game
'ROY OF THE ROVERS' MOMENT? My maiden first-class century in 2016
CRICKETING HERO? Ricky Ponting
NON-CRICKETING HERO? Floyd Mayweather
IF YOU WEREN'T A CRICKETER? I'd be a gym junkie
SURPRISING FACT? I play in the same team as Batman
UNUSUAL OBJECT AT HOME? Golf putter
TWITTER: @lewis_mcmanus

Batting	Mat	Inns	NO	Runs	HS	Ave	SR	100	50	Ct	St
First-class	32	46	5	1147	132*	27.97	47.59	1	5	63	9
List A	32	25	5	430	47	21.50	88.47	0	0	24	8
T20s	27	22	4	289	59	16.05	129.01	0	1	8	5
Bowling	**Mat**	**Balls**	**Runs**	**Wkts**	**BBI**	**BBM**	**Ave**	**Econ**	**SR**	**5w**	**10**
First-class	32	-	-	-	-	-	-	-	-	-	-
List A	32	-	-	-	-	-	-	-	-	-	-
T20s	27	-	-	-	-	-	-	-	-	-	-

STUART MEAKER

RHB / RF / R0 / W1

FULL NAME: Stuart Christopher Meaker
BORN: January 21, 1989, Pietermaritzburg, South Africa
SQUAD NO: 18
HEIGHT: 5ft 11in
NICKNAME: Meaks, Ten Bears
EDUCATION: Cranleigh Senior School
TEAMS: England, Surrey, Auckland
ROLE: Bowler
DEBUT: ODI: 2011; T20I: 2012; First-class: 2008; List A: 2008; T20: 2010

BEST BATTING: 94 Surrey vs Bangladeshis, The Oval, 2010
BEST BOWLING: 8-52 Surrey vs Somerset, The Oval, 2012
COUNTY CAP: 2012

BEST THING ABOUT YOUR HOME GROUND? It has the best T20 crowds in the country
IF YOU WEREN'T A CRICKETER? I'd be a McDonald's manager
SURPRISING FACT ABOUT YOU? I have a certificate in corporate governance but still don't know what it means
CRICKETING HERO? Allan Donald
NON-CRICKETING HERO? My grandfather
TWITTER: @SMeaker18

Batting	Mat	Inns	NO	Runs	HS	Ave	SR	100	50	Ct	St
ODIs	2	2	0	2	1	1.00	12.50	0	0	0	0
T20Is	2	-	-	-	-	-	-	-	-	1	0
First-class	89	117	24	1445	94	15.53	37.43	0	6	20	0
List A	69	34	18	115	21*	7.18	52.03	0	0	19	0
T20s	32	11	6	46	17	9.20	121.05	0	0	13	0
Bowling	**Mat**	**Balls**	**Runs**	**Wkts**	**BBI**	**BBM**	**Ave**	**Econ**	**SR**	**5w**	**10**
ODIs	2	114	110	2	1/45	1/45	55.00	5.78	57.0	0	0
T20Is	2	47	70	2	1/28	1/28	35.00	8.93	23.5	0	0
First-class	89	13762	8701	279	8/52	11/167	31.18	3.79	49.3	11	2
List A	69	2565	2635	75	4/37	4/37	35.13	6.16	34.2	0	0
T20s	32	519	774	26	4/30	4/30	29.76	8.94	19.9	0	0

ALEX MELLOR

LHB / WK / R0 / W0

WARWICKSHIRE

FULL NAME: Alexander James Mellor
BORN: July 22, 1991, Stoke-on-Trent, Staffordshire
SQUAD NO: 15
HEIGHT: 5ft 10in
NICKNAME: Al, Mella, Jar Jar
EDUCATION: Westwood College; Staffordshire University
TEAMS: Warwickshire, Derbyshire
ROLE: Wicketkeeper
DEBUT: First-class: 2016; List A: 2016; T20: 2016

BEST BATTING: 59 Warwickshire vs Oxford MCCU, Oxford, 2017

FAMILY TIES? Dad represented Staffordshire age-groups and the senior side. My brother represented Staffordshire age-groups
WHAT WAS YOUR FIRST CRICKET CLUB? Leek CC, Staffordshire. Played in every age-group and senior team
FAVOURITE CRICKET BAT? Hunts County Insignia, my first bat, very well oiled
CRICKETING HERO? Bob Taylor – fantastic person, brilliant keeper. Albie Morkel – I've known him since I was 10, clean striker, matchwinner
BEST INNINGS YOU'VE SEEN? Jason Roy's 180 against Australia in the ODI at Melbourne in January 2018 – he positively took down the Aussies from the first ball
WHO WOULD YOU ASK TO BAT FOR YOUR LIFE? Jonathan Trott
WHAT WILL YOU BE DOING IN THE YEAR 2040? Playing club cricket and standing at slip
ODDEST SPORT YOU'VE PLAYED? Handball
TWITTER: @alexmellor22

Batting	Mat	Inns	NO	Runs	HS	Ave	SR	100	50	Ct	St
First-class	9	16	1	282	59	18.80	40.11	0	1	15	0
List A	3	1	1	3	3*	-	100.00	0	0	1	0
T20s	9	6	3	38	18*	12.66	102.70	0	0	4	0
Bowling	**Mat**	**Balls**	**Runs**	**Wkts**	**BBI**	**BBM**	**Ave**	**Econ**	**SR**	**5w**	**10**
First-class	9	-	-	-	-	-	-	-	-	-	-
List A	3	-	-	-	-	-	-	-	-	-	-
T20s	9	-	-	-	-	-	-	-	-	-	-

CRAIG MESCHEDE RHB / RMF / R0 / W0

FULL NAME: Craig Anthony Joseph Meschede
BORN: November 21, 1991, Johannesburg, South Africa
SQUAD NO: 44
HEIGHT: 6ft 2in
NICKNAME: Mesh, Meshy
EDUCATION: King's College, Taunton
TEAMS: Glamorgan, Somerset
ROLE: Allrounder
DEBUT: First-class: 2011; List A: 2011; T20: 2011

BEST BATTING: 107 Glamorgan vs Northamptonshire, Cardiff, 2015
BEST BOWLING: 5-84 Glamorgan vs Essex, Chelmsford, 2016

WHAT WAS YOUR FIRST CRICKET CLUB? Old Edwardians CC, Johannesburg
FAVOURITE CRICKET BAT? GM Purist Original LE – my first bat, bought for me by my father. It was a bit big and heavy for me and I didn't score any runs with it at first so my dad told me he would take it away and give it back to me when I was stronger. But I was determined to get some runs in the next game because I loved the bat so much... I got a fifty and ended up keeping the bat
WHICH BOWLER WOULD YOU LEAST LIKE TO FACE? Shoaib Akhtar
BEST INNINGS YOU'VE SEEN? Herschelle Gibbs' 175 against Australia at Joburg when South Africa scored 438-9 to beat Australia's 434-4 in 2006. I was very fortunate to be there
YOUR BIGGEST CRICKETING REGRET? Not giving it my all at the start of my career as a pro
FAVOURITE QUOTE OR SAYING? Dream as if you will live forever, live as if you will for today (LeBron James)
WHICH BOOK MEANS MOST TO YOU? Rich Dad Poor Dad by Robert Kiyosaki
TWITTER: @cmeschy

Batting	Mat	Inns	NO	Runs	HS	Ave	SR	100	50	Ct	St
First-class	70	101	13	2250	107	25.56	64.04	2	13	23	0
List A	52	36	5	462	45	14.90	92.95	0	0	11	0
T20s	91	66	16	832	77*	16.64	130.20	0	2	16	0
Bowling	**Mat**	**Balls**	**Runs**	**Wkts**	**BBI**	**BBM**	**Ave**	**Econ**	**SR**	**5w**	**10**
First-class	70	8866	5310	142	5/84	7/80	37.39	3.59	62.4	1	0
List A	52	1905	1763	51	4/5	4/5	34.56	5.55	37.3	0	0
T20s	91	1070	1549	54	3/9	3/9	28.68	8.68	19.8	0	0

BEN MIKE

RHB / RFM / R0 / W0

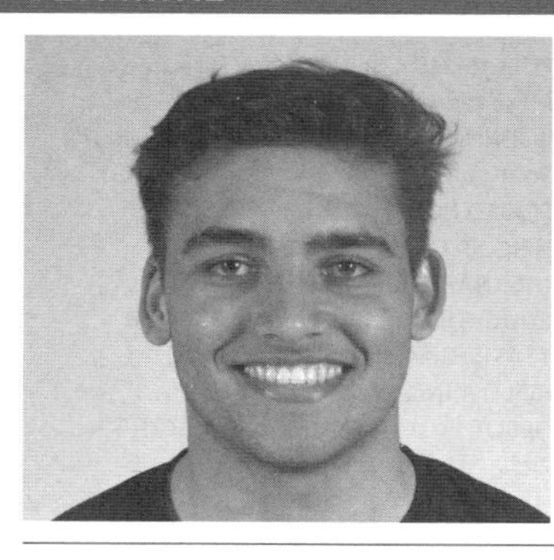

FULL NAME: Benjamin Wentworth Munro Mike
BORN: August 24, 1998, Nottingham
SQUAD NO: 8
HEIGHT: 6ft 1in
NICKNAME: Benny, Mikey
EDUCATION: Loughborough Grammar School
TEAMS: Leicestershire
ROLE: Bowler
DEBUT: First-class: 2018; List A: 2018

BEST BATTING: 39 Leicestershire vs Warwickshire, Leicester, 2018
BEST BOWLING: 5-37 Leicestershire vs Sussex, Hove, 2018

WHAT WAS YOUR FIRST CRICKET CLUB? Radcliffe-On-Trent CC, Nottingham. Runners-up in the U13 national cup – lost on net run-rate
FAVOURITE CRICKET BAT? SS Ton. It was the first bat I scored a hundred with. Bought it while on holiday in India
WHICH BOWLER WOULD YOU LEAST LIKE TO FACE? Brett Lee
BEST INNINGS YOU'VE SEEN? Chris Gayle's 175 not out off 66 bals for Royal Challengers Bangalore in the 2013 IPL. Universe boss
WHO WOULD YOU ASK TO BAT FOR YOUR LIFE? Shivnarine Chanderpaul
WHICH RULE WOULD YOU CHANGE ABOUT CRICKET? Be kinder to bowlers when calling leg-side wides
YOUR BIGGEST CRICKETING REGRET? Trying to be perfect
WHICH BOOK MEANS MOST TO YOU? Jamie's 30-Minute Meals – A Revolutionary Approach to Cooking Good Food Fast by Jamie Oliver
ODDEST SPORT YOU'VE PLAYED? Kabbadi

Batting	Mat	Inns	NO	Runs	HS	Ave	SR	100	50	Ct	St
First-class	4	7	0	96	39	13.71	54.23	0	0	2	0
List A	1	1	0	10	10	10.00	55.55	0	0	0	0
Bowling	**Mat**	**Balls**	**Runs**	**Wkts**	**BBI**	**BBM**	**Ave**	**Econ**	**SR**	**5w**	**10**
First-class	4	524	385	19	5/37	9/94	20.26	4.40	27.5	1	0
List A	1	18	46	0	-	-	-	15.33	-	0	0

CRAIG MILES RHB / RFM / R0 / W3 / MVP88

FULL NAME: Craig Neil Miles
BORN: July 20, 1994, Swindon, Wiltshire
SQUAD NO: 18
HEIGHT: 6ft 4in
NICKNAME: Milo, Miler
EDUCATION: Bradon Forest School, Purton, Wiltshire; SGS Filton College, Bristol
TEAMS: Warwickshire, Gloucestershire
ROLE: Bowler
DEBUT: First-class: 2011; List A: 2011; T20: 2013

BEST BATTING: 62* Gloucestershire vs Worcestershire, Cheltenham, 2014
BEST BOWLING: 6-63 Gloucestershire vs Northamptonshire, Northampton, 2015
COUNTY CAP: 2011 (Gloucestershire)

FAMILY TIES? My older brother Adam has played for Cardiff MCCU and for New Zealand side Otago in first-class cricket
WHAT WAS YOUR FIRST CRICKET CLUB? Purton CC, Swindon. The oldest club in Wiltshire
WHICH BOWLER WOULD YOU LEAST LIKE TO FACE? Kagiso Rabada – pace and swing
BEST INNINGS YOU'VE SEEN? Jack Taylor and Benny Howell scoring 69 off four overs to beat Derbyshire in the 2015 One-Day Cup. Every game that year was a thriller, especially the final
WHO WOULD YOU ASK TO BAT FOR YOUR LIFE? James Bracey – the Winterbourne Wall
WHICH RULE WOULD YOU CHANGE ABOUT CRICKET? Something to make T20 more bowler-friendly
SURPRISING FACT ABOUT YOU? I played football for Swindon Town Academy until I was 13
SURPRISING FACT ABOUT A TEAMMATE? Graeme van Buuren folds his dirty washing
ODDEST SPORT YOU'VE PLAYED? Kabbadi – played it at school. Weird wrestling game originating from Asia
TWITTER: @cmiles34

Batting	Mat	Inns	NO	Runs	HS	Ave	SR	100	50	Ct	St
First-class	68	94	14	1343	62*	16.78	46.39	0	5	17	0
List A	35	13	3	76	16	7.60	64.95	0	0	5	0
T20s	13	5	2	13	8	4.33	92.85	0	0	4	0
Bowling	**Mat**	**Balls**	**Runs**	**Wkts**	**BBI**	**BBM**	**Ave**	**Econ**	**SR**	**5w**	**10**
First-class	68	11005	6805	255	6/63	10/121	26.68	3.71	43.1	13	1
List A	35	1445	1489	43	4/29	4/29	34.62	6.18	33.6	0	0
T20s	13	265	351	15	3/25	3/25	23.40	7.94	17.6	0	0

TYMAL MILLS RHB / LF / R0 / W0

FULL NAME: Tymal Solomon Mills
BORN: August 12, 1992, Dewsbury, Yorkshire
SQUAD NO: 7
HEIGHT: 6ft 1in
NICKNAME: T, Tyrone
EDUCATION: Mildenhall College of Technology; University of East London
TEAMS: England, Sussex, Auckland, Brisbane Heat, Chittagong Vikings, Essex, Hobart Hurricanes, Kandahar Kings, RC Bangalore
ROLE: Bowler
DEBUT: T20I: 2016; First-class: 2011; List A: 2011; T20: 2012

BEST BATTING: 31* England Lions vs Sri Lanka Emerging Players, Colombo, 2014
BEST BOWLING: 4-25 Essex vs Glamorgan, Cardiff, 2012

WHAT WAS YOUR FIRST CRICKET CLUB? Tuddenham CC and then Mildenhall CC, both in Suffolk. Both clubs helped me a lot on and off the field
WHICH BOWLER WOULD YOU LEAST LIKE TO FACE? Anybody – I'm useless with the bat!
BEST INNINGS YOU'VE SEEN? Mohammad Shahzad's 74 from 16 balls during last winter's T10 League in the UAE
WHO WOULD YOU ASK TO BAT FOR YOUR LIFE? Phil Salt – at least I would go out entertained
WHICH RULE WOULD YOU CHANGE ABOUT CRICKET? Allow two bouncers per over in T20 cricket
FAVOURITE QUOTE OR SAYING? It's not the cards that you're dealt in life, it's how you play the hand (I've got this tattooed on my arm)
TWITTER: @tmills15

Batting	Mat	Inns	NO	Runs	HS	Ave	SR	100	50	Ct	St
T20Is	5	1	0	0	0	0.00	0.00	0	0	1	0
First-class	32	38	15	260	31*	11.30	57.77	0	0	9	0
List A	23	9	5	7	3*	1.75	31.81	0	0	3	0
T20s	99	22	10	51	8*	4.25	87.93	0	0	17	0
Bowling	**Mat**	**Balls**	**Runs**	**Wkts**	**BBI**	**BBM**	**Ave**	**Econ**	**SR**	**5w**	**10**
T20Is	5	114	129	3	1/27	1/27	43.00	6.78	38.0	0	0
First-class	32	3531	2008	55	4/25	5/79	36.50	3.41	64.2	0	0
List A	23	790	787	22	3/23	3/23	35.77	5.97	35.9	0	0
T20s	99	2045	2705	104	4/22	4/22	26.00	7.93	19.6	0	0

ADAM MILNE

RHB / RF / R0 / W0

FULL NAME: Adam Fraser Milne
BORN: April 13, 1992, Palmerston North, New Zealand
SQUAD NO: 20
HEIGHT: 6ft
TEAMS: New Zealand, Kent, Central Districts, Royal Challengers Bangalore
ROLE: Bowler
DEBUT: ODI: 2012; T20I: 2010; First-class: 2010; List A: 2011; T20: 2010

BEST BATTING: 97 Central Districts vs Otago, Napier, 2012
BEST BOWLING: 5-47 Central Districts vs Otago, Napier, 2012

TWITTER: @AdamMilne19
NOTES: The New Zealand fast bowler returns to Kent for a third consecutive season and will be available exclusively for the T20 Blast. Milne has an impressive T20 record for the Spitfires, having taken 28 wickets at a strike-rate of 14.42 and economy of 7.18, and was instrumental in helping them qualify for the quarter-finals last season. "I'm delighted to come back to Kent, a team of talented players, hungry for success," said Milne. "Last year we came close to reaching T20 Finals Day and there is a real belief in this squad that we can challenge again this season." The Kiwi is one of the fastest bowlers in the world and has been clocked at 95mph

Batting	Mat	Inns	NO	Runs	HS	Ave	SR	100	50	Ct	St
ODIs	40	17	7	168	36	16.80	101.81	0	0	21	0
T20Is	21	8	8	21	10*	-	91.30	0	0	5	0
First-class	30	45	14	756	97	24.38	53.65	0	4	10	0
List A	73	37	15	392	45	17.81	103.15	0	0	25	0
T20s	87	33	23	182	18*	18.20	117.41	0	0	20	0
Bowling	**Mat**	**Balls**	**Runs**	**Wkts**	**BBI**	**BBM**	**Ave**	**Econ**	**SR**	**5w**	**10**
ODIs	40	1801	1581	41	3/49	3/49	38.56	5.26	43.9	0	0
T20Is	21	437	541	25	4/37	4/37	21.64	7.42	17.4	0	0
First-class	30	5403	2872	88	5/47	8/154	32.63	3.18	61.3	2	0
List A	73	3516	3090	103	5/61	5/61	30.00	5.27	34.1	1	0
T20s	87	1840	2348	106	5/11	5/11	22.15	7.65	17.3	1	0

MATT MILNES

RHB / RFM / R0 / W0

FULL NAME: Matthew Edward Milnes
BORN: July 29, 1994, Nottingham
SQUAD NO: 29
HEIGHT: 6ft 1in
NICKNAME: Milnesy, Milner, Milno
EDUCATION: West Bridgford School; Durham University
TEAMS: Kent, Nottinghamshire
ROLE: Bowler
DEBUT: First-class: 2014

BEST BATTING: 43 Nottinghamshire vs Yorkshire, Trent Bridge, 2018
BEST BOWLING: 4-44 Nottinghamshire vs Essex, Chelmsford, 2018

WHAT GOT YOU INTO CRICKET? Having to bowl at my brother for hours on end in the garden
'ROY OF THE ROVERS' MOMENT? Taking a six-for on my Durham MCCU debut having been asked to come down to bowl in the nets for a trial that morning
IF YOU WEREN'T A CRICKETER? I'd be a teacher
SURPRISING FACT ABOUT YOU? I once scored a goal for Manchester United. It was a horror own goal when I was playing against them at U14 level, but I'm counting it
WHERE IS PARADISE? Loveshack Wednesdays (nightclub in Durham)
CRICKETING HERO? Jimmy Anderson
TWITTER: @mmilnes84
NOTES: The 24-year-old seamer left Nottinghamshire, his home club, to sign a three-year contract with Kent last September. Milnes made his Championship debut for Notts last summer and took 11 wickets in six first-class matches. Kent director of cricket Paul Downton said: "We are really delighted Matt has chosen to join us to continue his development in the game, and at a time when we are making progress. Since I arrived, my aim has been to build and develop a seam-bowling attack that grows to become the best in the country. We now have a crop of bowlers here in the squad with some immense potential. Matt has a very big future ahead of him"

Batting	Mat	Inns	NO	Runs	HS	Ave	SR	100	50	Ct	St
First-class	8	12	5	109	43	15.57	43.42	0	0	6	0
Bowling	**Mat**	**Balls**	**Runs**	**Wkts**	**BBI**	**BBM**	**Ave**	**Econ**	**SR**	**5w**	**10**
First-class	8	1158	635	14	4/44	5/64	45.35	3.29	82.7	0	0

ALEX MILTON RHB / WK / R0 / W0

FULL NAME: Alexander Geoffrey Milton
BORN: May 19, 1996, Redhill, Surrey
SQUAD NO: 12
HEIGHT: 5ft 7in
NICKNAME: Milts
EDUCATION: Malvern College; Cardiff Metropolitan University
TEAMS: Worcestershire
ROLE: Wicketkeeper/batsman
DEBUT: First-class: 2016; List A: 2018

BEST BATTING: 104* Worcestershire vs Somerset, Worcester, 2018

WHAT WAS YOUR FIRST CRICKET CLUB? Dormansland CC, Sussex. Played my first U12s match as an eight-year-old
FAVOURITE CRICKET BAT? A CC (Cricket Company) – scored 143 in a T20 with that bat
WHICH BOWLER WOULD YOU LEAST LIKE TO FACE? Morne Morkel – because he's reaching the height of two of me put on top of each other!
BEST INNINGS YOU'VE SEEN? Moeen Ali's double hundred at Scarborough last season
WHICH RULE WOULD YOU CHANGE ABOUT CRICKET? Give free hits for no-balls in Championship cricket
YOUR BIGGEST CRICKETING REGRET? Getting to 60 at Lord's in the MCCU final and not going on to score a hundred
SURPRISING FACT ABOUT YOU? I played a drum solo blindfolded in my school unplugged concert
FAVOURITE QUOTE OR SAYING? May the force be with you
WHICH BOOK MEANS MOST TO YOU? Who Wants to be a Batsman? by Simon Hughes
TWITTER: @alex_milton12

Batting	Mat	Inns	NO	Runs	HS	Ave	SR	100	50	Ct	St
First-class	10	15	2	267	104*	20.53	44.72	1	0	6	1
List A	1	1	0	0	0	0.00	-	0	0	0	0
Bowling	**Mat**	**Balls**	**Runs**	**Wkts**	**BBI**	**BBM**	**Ave**	**Econ**	**SR**	**5w**	**10**
First-class	10	-	-	-	-	-	-	-	-	-	-
List A	1	-	-	-	-	-	-	-	-	-	-

DARYL MITCHELL RHB / RM / R6 / W0 / MVP21

FULL NAME: Daryl Keith Henry Mitchell
BORN: November 25, 1983, Badsey, Worcestershire
SQUAD NO: 27
HEIGHT: 5ft 10in
NICKNAME: Mitch
EDUCATION: Prince Henry's High School, Evesham; University of Worcester
TEAMS: Worcestershire, Mountaineers
ROLE: Allrounder
DEBUT: First-class: 2005; List A: 2005; T20: 2005

BEST BATTING: 298 Worcestershire vs Somerset, Taunton, 2009
BEST BOWLING: 4-49 Worcestershire vs Yorkshire, Headingley, 2009
BENEFIT: 2016

WHAT WAS YOUR FIRST CRICKET CLUB? Bretforton CC (aka The Bughut), Worcestershire
CRICKETING HERO? Ian Botham and Graeme Hick – Worcester legends I grew up watching at New Road
WHICH BOWLER WOULD YOU LEAST LIKE TO FACE? Jack Shantry – awkward, accurate, swing, bounce, and doesn't wear any underwear
BEST INNINGS YOU'VE SEEN? Callum Ferguson against Leicestershire at New Road last summer. A match-winning 192 chasing 377 in 50 overs
WHO WOULD YOU ASK TO BAT FOR YOUR LIFE? Rory Burns
YOUR BIGGEST CRICKETING REGRET? Getting bowled slogging on 298
SURPRISING FACT ABOUT YOU? I was in the Aston Villa Academy
WHAT WILL YOU BE DOING IN THE YEAR 2040? Watching the Villa in the Champions League
FAVOURITE QUOTE OR SAYING? Things are never as good or as bad as they seem
WHICH BOOK MEANS MOST TO YOU? Jack Shantry's Benefit 2019 brochure
TWITTER: @mitchwccc

Batting	Mat	Inns	NO	Runs	HS	Ave	SR	100	50	Ct	St
First-class	192	347	37	12507	298	40.34	46.34	35	48	263	0
List A	128	113	17	3297	107	34.34	81.32	3	22	50	0
T20s	149	117	27	2126	68*	23.62	118.04	0	7	61	0
Bowling	**Mat**	**Balls**	**Runs**	**Wkts**	**BBI**	**BBM**	**Ave**	**Econ**	**SR**	**5w**	**10**
First-class	192	2336	1216	27	4/49	4/49	45.03	3.12	86.5	0	0
List A	128	2873	2657	75	4/19	4/19	35.42	5.54	38.3	0	0
T20s	149	1879	2443	85	5/28	5/28	28.74	7.80	22.1	1	0

TOM MOORES LHB / WK / R0 / W0 / MVP28

FULL NAME: Thomas James Moores
BORN: September 4, 1996, Brighton, Sussex
SQUAD NO: 23
HEIGHT: 5ft 9in
NICKNAME: Mooresy
EDUCATION: Loughborough Grammar School; Millfield School, Somerset
TEAMS: Nottinghamshire, Lancashire, Multan Sultans
ROLE: Wicketkeeper
DEBUT: First-class: 2016; List A: 2016; T20: 2016

BEST BATTING: 103 Nottinghamshire vs Somerset, Taunton, 2018

FAMILY TIES? My father Peter played for Sussex and was England head coach. He's now my coach at Nottinghamshire
WHAT WAS YOUR FIRST CRICKET CLUB? Barrow Town CC, Leicestershire. The club gave me my first opportunity to play men's cricket
FAVOURITE CRICKET BAT? Puma Ballistic. It was my first bat, and I wanted the same one as my cricketing hero
CRICKETING HERO? Adam Gilchrist
WHICH BOWLER WOULD YOU LEAST LIKE TO FACE? Jimmy Anderson
WHO WOULD YOU ASK TO BAT FOR YOUR LIFE? Virat Kohli
WHICH RULE WOULD YOU CHANGE ABOUT CRICKET? A batsman should have more than one life
TWITTER: @tommoores23

Batting	Mat	Inns	NO	Runs	HS	Ave	SR	100	50	Ct	St
First-class	20	34	1	818	103	24.78	52.06	1	2	46	0
List A	12	11	2	285	76	31.66	99.65	0	1	10	3
T20s	40	35	8	708	80*	26.22	138.28	0	4	22	3
Bowling	**Mat**	**Balls**	**Runs**	**Wkts**	**BBI**	**BBM**	**Ave**	**Econ**	**SR**	**5w**	**10**
First-class	20	-	-	-	-	-	-	-	-	-	-
List A	12	-	-	-	-	-	-	-	-	-	-
T20s	40	-	-	-	-	-	-	-	-	-	-

EOIN MORGAN LHB / RM / R1 / W0

FULL NAME: Eoin Joseph Gerard Morgan
BORN: September 10, 1986, Dublin, Ireland
SQUAD NO: 16
HEIGHT: 5ft 9in
NICKNAME: Moggie, Morgs, Iceman
EDUCATION: Catholic University School, Dublin; Dulwich College, London
TEAMS: England, Ireland, Middlesex, Kolkata KR, Peshawar Zalmi, RC Bangalore, Sunrisers Hyderabad, Sydney Thunder
ROLE: Batsman
DEBUT: Test: 2010; ODI: 2006; T20I: 2009; First-class: 2004; List A: 2003; T20: 2006

BEST BATTING: 209* Ireland vs UAE, Abu Dhabi, 2007
BEST BOWLING: 2-24 Middlesex vs Nottinghamshire, Lord's, 2007
COUNTY CAP: 2008

TWITTER: @Eoin16
NOTES: An Irishman by birth, Morgan switched his allegiance after he was named in England's provisional squad for the 2009 World T20. He made his ODI debut for his adopted nation against West Indies in 2009 and his T20I debut a month later in a shock defeat to Netherlands at Lord's. His Test debut followed against Bangladesh in May 2010. After a lean 2013, Morgan rediscovered his form in the ODI series against Australia in January 2014. Handed the ODI captaincy in 2014, he has turned England into serious contenders for this summer's World Cup. Also leads the T20I side. Rarely seen in four-day cricket

Batting	Mat	Inns	NO	Runs	HS	Ave	SR	100	50	Ct	St
Tests	16	24	1	700	130	30.43	54.77	2	3	11	0
ODIs	217	203	29	6813	124*	39.15	89.73	12	43	77	0
T20Is	80	78	15	1753	85*	27.82	130.14	0	9	35	0
First-class	99	164	16	4912	209*	33.18	50.90	11	23	75	1
List A	345	319	44	10667	161	38.78	90.01	20	64	116	0
T20s	267	253	34	5595	90	25.54	127.79	0	28	126	0

Bowling	Mat	Balls	Runs	Wkts	BBI	BBM	Ave	Econ	SR	5w	10
Tests	16	-	-	-	-	-	-	-	-	-	-
ODIs	217	-	-	-	-	-	-	-	-	-	-
T20Is	80	-	-	-	-	-	-	-	-	-	-
First-class	99	102	90	2	2/24	2/24	45.00	5.29	51.0	0	0
List A	345	42	49	0	-	-	-	7.00	-	0	0
T20s	267	-	-	-	-	-	-	-	-	-	-

OWEN MORGAN

RHB / SLA / R0 / W0

FULL NAME: Alan Owen Morgan
BORN: April 14, 1994, Swansea, Wales
SQUAD NO: 29
HEIGHT: 5ft 11in
NICKNAME: Morgs, Ows, Strawbs
EDUCATION: Ysgol Gyfun Y Strade, Llanelli; Cardiff University
TEAMS: Glamorgan
ROLE: Allrounder
DEBUT: First-class: 2014; List A: 2016

BEST BATTING: 103* Glamorgan vs Worcestershire, Worcester, 2016
BEST BOWLING: 2-37 Glamorgan vs Northamptonshire, Northampton, 2016

WHAT GOT YOU INTO CRICKET? A local volunteer came into primary school to start a local village side which I joined
'ROY OF THE ROVERS' MOMENT? My maiden first-class hundred – as a nightwatchman – against Worcestershire in 2016
BEST THING ABOUT YOUR HOME GROUND? It's an international venue
IF YOU WEREN'T A CRICKETER? I'd be working in finance
SURPRISING FACT ABOUT YOU? I'm fluent in Welsh, grew up on a farm, and have a degree in Accounting and Finance
CRICKETING HERO? Ricky Ponting
NON-CRICKETING HERO? My grandfather – he had the greatest influence on me as I was growing up and taught me a lot
UNUSUAL OBJECT AT HOME? A tractor
TWITTER: @owenmorgan14

Batting	Mat	Inns	NO	Runs	HS	Ave	SR	100	50	Ct	St
First-class	17	31	5	556	103*	21.38	38.03	1	1	5	0
List A	3	2	0	32	29	16.00	76.19	0	0	0	0
Bowling	**Mat**	**Balls**	**Runs**	**Wkts**	**BBI**	**BBM**	**Ave**	**Econ**	**SR**	**5w**	**10**
First-class	17	1699	895	15	2/37	3/57	59.66	3.16	113.2	0	0
List A	3	84	81	2	2/49	2/49	40.50	5.78	42.0	0	0

MORNE MORKEL LHB / RFM / R0 / W1 / MVP18

FULL NAME: Morne Morkel
BORN: October 6, 1984, Vereeniging, Transvaal, South Africa
SQUAD NO: 65
TEAMS: South Africa, Surrey, Delhi Daredevils, Easterns, Kent, Kolkata Knight Riders, Rajasthan Royals, St Lucia Zouks, Titans, Yorkshire
ROLE: Bowler
DEBUT: Test: 2006; ODI: 2007; T20I: 2007; First-class: 2004; List A: 2005; T20: 2005

BEST BATTING: 82* Titans vs Warriors, East London, 2008
BEST BOWLING: 6-23 South Africa vs New Zealand, Wellington, 2012

TWITTER: @mornemorkel65
NOTES: The South Africa fast bowler signed for Surrey on a two-year Kolpak contract in April 2018 and was hugely influential in the county winning their first Championship title for 16 years last summer, claiming 59 wickets at an exceptional average of 14.32. His best return of the season came in Surrey's dramatic win over Lancashire at The Oval when he took 6-57 in the second innings to bowl his team to a six-run win. Morkel announced he would be retiring from international duty in February 2018 and finished his Test career with 309 wickets, putting him fifth on South Africa's all-time list. He is also his country's seventh-highest wicket-taker in ODIs, with 180 victims. In March he extended his contract with Surrey to the end of next season

Batting	Mat	Inns	NO	Runs	HS	Ave	SR	100	50	Ct	St
Tests	86	104	23	944	40	11.65	50.80	0	0	25	0
ODIs	117	47	18	268	32*	9.24	75.70	0	0	31	0
T20Is	44	8	5	22	8*	7.33	122.22	0	0	5	0
First-class	137	167	32	1895	82*	14.03	51.81	0	4	48	0
List A	150	60	22	374	35	9.84	82.56	0	0	40	0
T20s	174	48	25	207	23*	9.00	113.11	0	0	25	0
Bowling	**Mat**	**Balls**	**Runs**	**Wkts**	**BBI**	**BBM**	**Ave**	**Econ**	**SR**	**5w**	**10**
Tests	86	16498	8550	309	6/23	9/110	27.66	3.10	53.3	8	0
ODIs	117	5760	4761	188	5/21	5/21	25.32	4.95	30.6	2	0
T20Is	44	952	1191	47	4/17	4/17	25.34	7.50	20.2	0	0
First-class	137	25167	13028	522	6/23	12/91	24.95	3.10	48.2	20	2
List A	150	7173	5906	226	5/21	5/21	26.13	4.94	31.7	3	0
T20s	174	3874	4880	190	4/17	4/17	25.68	7.55	20.3	0	0

CHARLIE MORRIS

RHB / RMF / R0 / W2

FULL NAME: Charles Andrew John Morris
BORN: July 6, 1992, Hereford
SQUAD NO: 31
HEIGHT: 6ft
NICKNAME: Moz, Tim, Dug, Mr Beige, Tintin
EDUCATION: Kingswood School, Bath; King's College, Taunton; Oxford Brookes University
TEAMS: Worcestershire
ROLE: Bowler
DEBUT: First-class: 2012; List A: 2013; T20: 2013

BEST BATTING: 33* Oxford MCCU vs Warwickshire, Oxford, 2013
BEST BOWLING: 5-54 Worcestershire vs Derbyshire, Derby, 2014

WHAT WAS YOUR FIRST CRICKET CLUB? Yelverton CC, Devon, on the edge of Dartmoor between Tavistock and Plymouth. Played from the U10s to the first XI
FAVOURITE CRICKET BAT? Any of the Spyder bats – good sticks used by Dravid, Dhoni, Kohli
WHICH BOWLER WOULD YOU LEAST LIKE TO FACE? Mitchell Johnson – quick, so hard to pick up the ball because of his action, and fired at the body
BEST INNINGS YOU'VE SEEN? Callum Ferguson making 192 against Leicestershire in the One-Day Cup last summer to help us chase down 370-odd
YOUR BIGGEST CRICKETING REGRET? Not backing myself 100 per cent in certain match scenarios. Take the risk and seize the opportunity
FAVOURITE QUOTE OR SAYING? I will persist until I succeed, always will take another step. If that is of no avail, I will take another and yet another. In truth, one step at a time is not too difficult, and many steps repeated will complete any undertaking (OG Mandino)
WHICH BOOK MEANS MOST TO YOU? Hard to choose one. I enjoy military reading. It puts perspective into daily life and is humbling to read the sacrifices made by individuals
TWITTER: @morris_9

Batting	Mat	Inns	NO	Runs	HS	Ave	SR	100	50	Ct	St
First-class	48	67	38	305	33*	10.51	28.37	0	0	12	0
List A	26	13	9	49	16*	12.25	65.33	0	0	4	0
T20s	4	2	1	5	3	5.00	83.33	0	0	1	0
Bowling	**Mat**	**Balls**	**Runs**	**Wkts**	**BBI**	**BBM**	**Ave**	**Econ**	**SR**	**5w**	**10**
First-class	48	8594	4429	136	5/54	9/109	32.56	3.09	63.1	2	0
List A	26	1079	1075	29	4/33	4/33	37.06	5.97	37.2	0	0
T20s	4	84	126	4	2/30	2/30	31.50	9.00	21.0	0	0

STEVEN MULLANEY RHB / RM / R1 / W0 / MVP10

FULL NAME: Steven John Mullaney
BORN: November 19, 1986, Warrington, Cheshire
SQUAD NO: 5
HEIGHT: 5ft 8in
NICKNAME: Mull, Tev
EDUCATION: St Mary's Catholic High School, Greater Manchester
TEAMS: Nottinghamshire, England Lions, Khelaghar Samaj Kallyan Samity, Lancashire
ROLE: Allrounder
DEBUT: First-class: 2006; List A: 2006; T20: 2006

BEST BATTING: 168 Nottinghamshire vs Kent, Trent Bridge, 2017
BEST BOWLING: 5-32 Nottinghamshire vs Gloucestershire, Trent Bridge, 2017
COUNTY CAP: 2013 (Nottinghamshire)

WHAT WAS YOUR FIRST CRICKET CLUB? Golborne CC, Cheshire
CRICKETING HERO? Luke Fletcher
WHICH BOWLER WOULD YOU LEAST LIKE TO FACE? Rashid Khan – so hard to pick
BEST INNINGS YOU'VE SEEN? Alex Hales's 187 not out to win the 2017 Lord's final
WHICH RULE WOULD YOU CHANGE ABOUT CRICKET? No-balls to be free hits in any format
SURPRISING FACT ABOUT YOU? I played England schoolboy rugby league
WHAT WILL YOU BE DOING IN THE YEAR 2040? Hopefully coaching
FAVOURITE QUOTE OR SAYING? Fear has two meanings – Forget Everything And Run or Face Everything And Rise. The choice is yours (Zig Ziglar)
WHICH BOOK MEANS MOST TO YOU? Legacy – What the All Blacks Can Teach Us About The Business of Life by James Kerr
TWITTER: @mull05

Batting	Mat	Inns	NO	Runs	HS	Ave	SR	100	50	Ct	St
First-class	124	208	9	6668	168	33.50	57.67	13	36	118	0
List A	114	83	15	2306	124	33.91	101.99	2	16	55	0
T20s	125	88	22	1150	55	17.42	141.80	0	2	57	0
Bowling	**Mat**	**Balls**	**Runs**	**Wkts**	**BBI**	**BBM**	**Ave**	**Econ**	**SR**	**5w**	**10**
First-class	124	6459	3356	95	5/32	7/46	35.32	3.11	67.9	1	0
List A	114	3777	3215	97	4/29	4/29	33.14	5.10	38.9	0	0
T20s	125	2036	2702	90	4/19	4/19	30.02	7.96	22.6	0	0

JACK MURPHY

LHB / LFM / R0 / W0

FULL NAME: Jack Roger Murphy
BORN: July 15, 1995, Haverfordwest, Pembrokeshire, Wales
SQUAD NO: 7
HEIGHT: 6ft 7in
NICKNAME: Smurf, J Rock
EDUCATION: Ysgol Greenhill School, Pembrokeshire; Cardiff Metropolitan University
TEAMS: Glamorgan
ROLE: Allrounder
DEBUT: First-class: 2015; List A: 2016

BEST BATTING: 80 Glamorgan vs Kent, Canterbury, 2018
BEST BOWLING: 2-90 Cardiff MCCU vs Glamorgan, Cardiff, 2015

WHAT WAS YOUR FIRST CRICKET CLUB? Kilgetty CC, Pembrokeshire
CRICKETING HERO? Simon Jones
WHICH BOWLER WOULD YOU LEAST LIKE TO FACE? Darren Stevens
BEST INNINGS YOU'VE SEEN? Aneurin Donald's double hundred against Derbyshire at Colwyn Bay in 2016 – the joint-fastest in first-class cricket. Shows what you can do when you close your eyes and swing!
WHO WOULD YOU ASK TO BAT FOR YOUR LIFE? Kieran Bull
WHICH RULE WOULD YOU CHANGE ABOUT CRICKET? Thirty minutes for lunch, 30 minutes for tea
WHAT WILL YOU BE DOING IN THE YEAR 2040? Battling away at the start of my 27th season
FAVOURITE QUOTE OR SAYING? How'z it
TWITTER: @Jrock6ft7

Batting	Mat	Inns	NO	Runs	HS	Ave	SR	100	50	Ct	St
First-class	18	32	2	669	80	22.30	40.32	0	2	6	0
List A	3	3	0	25	10	8.33	47.16	0	0	0	0
Bowling	**Mat**	**Balls**	**Runs**	**Wkts**	**BBI**	**BBM**	**Ave**	**Econ**	**SR**	**5w**	**10**
First-class	18	339	208	3	2/90	2/90	69.33	3.68	113.0	0	0
List A	3	60	64	0	-	-	-	6.40	-	0	0

TIM MURTAGH LHB / RMF / R0 / W7 / MVP77

FULL NAME: Timothy James Murtagh
BORN: August 2, 1981, Lambeth, London
SQUAD NO: 34
HEIGHT: 6ft
NICKNAME: Murts, Jack, Brow
EDUCATION: The John Fisher School, London; St Mary's College, Twickenham
TEAMS: Ireland, Middlesex, Surrey
ROLE: Bowler
DEBUT: Test: 2018; ODI: 2012; T20I: 2012; First-class: 2000; List A: 2000; T20: 2003

BEST BATTING: 74* Surrey vs Middlesex, The Oval, 2004
BEST BOWLING: 7-82 Middlesex vs Derbyshire, Derby, 2009
COUNTY CAP: 2008 (Middlesex); BENEFIT: 2015 (Middlesex)

FAMILY TIES? My brother Chris played for Surrey and uncle Andrew played for Hampshire
WHAT WAS YOUR FIRST CRICKET CLUB? Purley CC, London
WHICH BOWLER WOULD YOU LEAST LIKE TO FACE? Me – I'd just try to hit every ball for four
WHICH RULE WOULD YOU CHANGE ABOUT CRICKET? No play past 6pm
YOUR BIGGEST CRICKETING REGRET? Missing the 2015 World Cup through injury
SUPERSTITIONS? I bat with my lucky horseshoe inside my box
WHAT WILL YOU BE DOING IN THE YEAR 2040? I'll be still waddling in from the Nursery End
NON-CRICKETING HEROES? Jürgen Klopp, followed closely by my wife
WHICH BOOK MEANS MOST TO YOU? Shoe Dog – A Memoir by the Creator of Nike by Phil Knight
TWITTER: @tjmurtagh

Batting	Mat	Inns	NO	Runs	HS	Ave	SR	100	50	Ct	St
Tests	1	2	1	10	5*	10.00	100.00	0	0	0	0
ODIs	50	31	9	161	23*	7.31	63.88	0	0	15	0
T20Is	14	5	3	26	12*	13.00	104.00	0	0	3	0
First-class	218	289	83	3923	74*	19.04	54.74	0	10	62	0
List A	199	120	42	792	35*	10.15	66.11	0	0	52	0
T20s	102	38	14	227	40*	9.45	106.57	0	0	22	0
Bowling	**Mat**	**Balls**	**Runs**	**Wkts**	**BBI**	**BBM**	**Ave**	**Econ**	**SR**	**5w**	**10**
Tests	1	246	100	6	4/45	6/100	16.66	2.43	41.0	0	0
ODIs	50	2571	1940	62	4/30	4/30	31.29	4.52	41.4	0	0
T20Is	14	268	324	13	3/23	3/23	24.92	7.25	20.6	0	0
First-class	218	38308	19613	760	7/82	10/77	25.80	3.07	50.4	30	4
List A	199	9089	7641	256	4/14	4/14	29.84	5.04	35.5	0	0
T20s	102	1984	2727	106	6/24	6/24	25.72	8.24	18.7	1	0

BLESSING MUZARABANI RHB / RFM / R0 / W0

FULL NAME: Blessing Muzarabani
BORN: October 2, 1996, Harare, Zimbabwe
SQUAD NO: 40
HEIGHT: 6ft 6in
EDUCATION: Churchill School, Harare
TEAMS: Zimbabwe, Northamptonshire, Rising Stars
ROLE: Bowler
DEBUT: Test: 2017; ODI: 2017; T20I: 2018; First-class: 2017; List A: 2017; T20: 2018

BEST BATTING: 23 Rising Stars vs Midlands Rhinos, Kwekwe, 2017
BEST BOWLING: 5-32 Rising Stars vs Bulawayo Metropolitan Tuskers, Kwekwe, 2017

TWITTER: @BMuzarabani
NOTES: Northants pulled off a major coup by signing the tall, young Zimbabwean fast bowler on a three-year Kolpak deal last September. "I've come here to chase my dreams," said Muzarabani, who represented his country on 25 occasions before deciding to put his international career on hold last August. He played for Northamptonshire's Second XI last summer and is a valuable addition to the first team following the departures of pacemen Richard Gleeson and Rory Kleinveldt. "We've been talking to Blessing for quite some time and were impressed by the way he plays," said David Ripley, Northamptonshire's head coach. "He's got a lot to learn and he knows it, but we're looking forward to helping him achieve his potential over the next few years"

Batting	Mat	Inns	NO	Runs	HS	Ave	SR	100	50	Ct	St
Tests	1	2	1	14	10	14.00	100.00	0	0	0	0
ODIs	18	15	7	16	7	2.00	17.97	0	0	7	0
T20Is	6	3	2	1	1*	1.00	20.00	0	0	2	0
First-class	6	12	2	138	23	13.80	54.11	0	0	2	0
List A	19	16	8	16	7	2.00	17.97	0	0	7	0
T20s	6	3	2	1	1*	1.00	20.00	0	0	2	0
Bowling	**Mat**	**Balls**	**Runs**	**Wkts**	**BBI**	**BBM**	**Ave**	**Econ**	**SR**	**5w**	**10**
Tests	1	78	48	0	-	-	-	3.69	-	0	0
ODIs	18	786	733	18	4/47	4/47	40.72	5.59	43.6	0	0
T20Is	6	144	220	9	3/21	3/21	24.44	9.16	16.0	0	0
First-class	6	625	372	18	5/32	6/48	20.66	3.57	34.7	1	0
List A	19	834	764	19	4/47	4/47	40.21	5.49	43.8	0	0
T20s	6	144	220	9	3/21	3/21	24.44	9.16	16.0	0	0

MOHAMMAD NABI

RHB / OB / R0 / W0

FULL NAME: Mohammad Nabi
BORN: January 1, 1985, Loger, Afghanistan
SQUAD NO: 7
TEAMS: Afghanistan, Kent, Balkh Legends, Chittagong Vikings, Comilla Victorians, Leicestershire, Melbourne Renegades, Quetta Gladiators, St Kitts and Nevis Patriots, Sunrisers Hyderabad, Sylhet Royals
ROLE: Allrounder
DEBUT: Test: 2018; ODI: 2009; T20I: 2010; First-class: 2007; List A: 2008; T20: 2010

BEST BATTING: 117 Afghanistan vs United Arab Emirates, Sharjah, 2011
BEST BOWLING: 6-33 Afghanistan vs Namibia, Windhoek, 2013

TWITTER: @MohammadNabi007
NOTES: Nabi was among the first wave of Afghan cricketers to play county cricket last summer, scoring 246 runs and taking nine wickets in 13 T20s for Leicestershire, and has joined Kent to play 11 matches in the T20 Blast. The veteran off-spinning allrounder has been a mainstay of the Afghanistan side which has shot to prominence over the last decade. He is his country's second-highest run-scorer in ODIs and second-highest wicket-taker in T20Is, and he played in Afghanistan's inaugural Test last year. "We are thrilled to have beaten several other counties to sign Nabi," said Paul Downton, Kent's director of cricket. "He has been an outstanding performer in T20 international cricket as well the global T20 competitions for a number of years"

Batting	Mat	Inns	NO	Runs	HS	Ave	SR	100	50	Ct	St
Tests	1	2	0	24	24	12.00	50.00	0	0	2	0
ODIs	111	99	11	2565	116	29.14	87.18	1	13	50	0
T20Is	68	63	10	1161	89	21.90	145.12	0	3	37	0
First-class	33	53	4	1275	117	26.02	51.76	2	5	20	0
List A	146	132	14	3569	146	30.24	89.85	3	16	66	0
T20s	207	169	34	3060	89	22.66	141.79	0	8	95	0
Bowling	**Mat**	**Balls**	**Runs**	**Wkts**	**BBI**	**BBM**	**Ave**	**Econ**	**SR**	**5w**	**10**
Tests	1	78	65	1	1/65	1/65	65.00	5.00	78.0	0	0
ODIs	111	5279	3747	118	4/30	4/30	31.75	4.25	44.7	0	0
T20Is	68	1432	1705	69	4/10	4/10	24.71	7.14	20.7	0	0
First-class	33	4380	1989	87	6/33	8/85	22.86	2.72	50.3	3	0
List A	146	7080	4987	166	5/12	5/12	30.04	4.22	42.6	1	0
T20s	207	4148	4792	217	4/10	4/10	22.08	6.93	19.1	0	0

CHRIS NASH RHB / OB / R4 / W0

FULL NAME: Christopher David Nash
BORN: May 19, 1983, Cuckfield, Sussex
SQUAD NO: 3
HEIGHT: 6ft
NICKNAME: Nashy, Knocker, Beaut, Wig
EDUCATION: Collyer's Sixth Form College; Loughborough University
TEAMS: Nottinghamshire, Auckland, England Lions, Otago, Prime Doleshwar Sporting Club, Sussex
ROLE: Allrounder
DEBUT: First-class: 2002; List A: 2006; T20: 2006

BEST BATTING: 184 Sussex vs Leicestershire, Leicester, 2010
BEST BOWLING: 4-12 Sussex vs Glamorgan, Cardiff, 2010
COUNTY CAP: 2008 (Sussex); **BENEFIT:** 2017 (Sussex)

WHAT WAS YOUR FIRST CRICKET CLUB? Horsham CC, West Sussex. Venue of the legendary Beer Olympics, played annually after the last home game and soon to gain IOC status
FAVOURITE CRICKET BAT? Gray-Nicolls Legend. It arrived on the morning of a game and I used it straight out the wrapper and got 220 runs in the match
CRICKETING HERO? Michael Slater – he tried to whack the first over for as many as possible and that's what made me want to open the batting
WHICH BOWLER WOULD YOU LEAST LIKE TO FACE? Paul Hacker of Eastbourne CC, aka 'table manners'. He will always get you in the end during one of his 29 overs
BEST INNINGS YOU'VE SEEN? Harry Gurney's 42 not out against Sussex in 2017 – purity in an innings
WHO WOULD YOU ASK TO BAT FOR YOUR LIFE? Harry Gurney
FAVOURITE QUOTE OR SAYING? Don't take life too seriously, you'll never get out alive (Van Wilder)
TWITTER: @chrisnash23

Batting	Mat	Inns	NO	Runs	HS	Ave	SR	100	50	Ct	St
First-class	193	331	19	11807	184	37.84	57.92	24	61	118	0
List A	124	116	5	3391	124*	30.54	88.65	2	22	28	0
T20s	155	147	19	3396	112*	26.53	125.35	1	20	47	0
Bowling	**Mat**	**Balls**	**Runs**	**Wkts**	**BBI**	**BBM**	**Ave**	**Econ**	**SR**	**5w**	**10**
First-class	193	5797	3271	78	4/12	5/67	41.93	3.38	74.3	0	0
List A	124	1603	1477	45	4/40	4/40	32.82	5.52	35.6	0	0
T20s	155	1022	1222	49	4/7	4/7	24.93	7.17	20.8	0	0

ROB NEWTON

RHB / LB / R1 / W0

FULL NAME: Robert Irving Newton
BORN: January 18, 1990, Taunton
SQUAD NO: 10
HEIGHT: 5ft 8in
NICKNAME: Ewok, KOTL, Newts
EDUCATION: Framlingham College, Suffolk
TEAMS: Northamptonshire
ROLE: Batsman
DEBUT: First-class: 2010; List A: 2009; T20: 2010

BEST BATTING: 202* Northamptonshire vs Leicestershire, Northampton, 2016
BEST BOWLING: 1-82 Northamptonshire vs Derbyshire, Derby, 2017
COUNTY CAP: 2017

BEST ADVICE EVER RECEIVED? Don't touch that – it's hot!
'ROY OF THE ROVERS' MOMENT? Every game of warm-up football. Or winning the 'stump game' at Northamptonshire's end-of-season celebrations
BEST THING ABOUT YOUR HOME GROUND? There's a pub attached
IF YOU WEREN'T A CRICKETER? I'd be a pub landlord
WHERE IS PARADISE? My couch
CRICKETING HERO? Ajaz Akhtar
NON-CRICKETING HERO? Gazza
TWITTER: @robbienewts77

Batting	Mat	Inns	NO	Runs	HS	Ave	SR	100	50	Ct	St
First-class	87	152	11	5161	202*	36.60	57.29	13	23	27	0
List A	42	38	2	1072	107	29.77	92.49	1	5	7	0
T20s	21	18	1	214	38	12.58	102.88	0	0	0	0
Bowling	**Mat**	**Balls**	**Runs**	**Wkts**	**BBI**	**BBM**	**Ave**	**Econ**	**SR**	**5w**	**10**
First-class	87	73	107	1	1/82	1/82	107.00	8.79	73.0	0	0
List A	42	-	-	-	-	-	-	-	-	-	-
T20s	21	-	-	-	-	-	-	-	-	-	-

ARON NIJJAR LHB / SLA / R0 / W0

FULL NAME: Aron Stuart Singh Nijjar
BORN: September 24, 1994, Goodmayes, Essex
SQUAD NO: 24
EDUCATION: Ilford County High School
TEAMS: Essex
ROLE: Bowler
DEBUT: First-class: 2015; List A: 2015; T20: 2018

BEST BATTING: 53 Essex vs Northamptonshire, Chelmsford, 2015
BEST BOWLING: 2-33 Essex vs Lancashire, Chelmsford, 2015

TWITTER: @aronnijjar
NOTES: A left-arm orthodox spinner and a fluent left-handed strokemaker, Nijjar has yet to establish himself at his hometown club despite playing a handful of Championship matches in 2015. He made his T20 debut for the club last summer. Nijjar, who plays for the hugely successful Wanstead & Snaresbrook club, is highly regarded at Essex and is expected to have more opportunities soon – although it won't be easy to break into such a successful side. He spent most of the last two seasons in the Second XI, also turning out for Cardiff MCCU. He made a pretty 30 against a strong West Indies attack in the tour match at Chelmsford in 2017 and an unbeaten 29 in last summer's tour match against India

Batting	Mat	Inns	NO	Runs	HS	Ave	SR	100	50	Ct	St
First-class	11	14	5	235	53	26.11	45.10	0	1	1	0
List A	3	1	0	21	21	21.00	70.00	0	0	4	0
T20s	1	-	-	-	-	-	-	-	-	0	0
Bowling	**Mat**	**Balls**	**Runs**	**Wkts**	**BBI**	**BBM**	**Ave**	**Econ**	**SR**	**5w**	**10**
First-class	11	1113	739	16	2/33	3/48	46.18	3.98	69.5	0	0
List A	3	126	107	1	1/39	1/39	107.00	5.09	126.0	0	0
T20s	1	18	30	1	1/30	1/30	30.00	10.00	18.0	0	0

SAM NORTHEAST RHB / OB / R3 / W0

FULL NAME: Sam Alexander Northeast
BORN: October 16, 1989, Ashford, Kent
SQUAD NO: 17
HEIGHT: 5ft 11in
NICKNAME: North, Bam, Nick Knight
EDUCATION: Harrow School, London
TEAMS: Hampshire, England Lions, Kent
ROLE: Batsman
DEBUT: First-class: 2007; List A: 2007; T20: 2010

BEST BATTING: 191 Kent vs Derbyshire, Canterbury, 2016
BEST BOWLING: 1-60 Kent vs Gloucestershire, Cheltenham, 2013
COUNTY CAP: 2012 (Kent)

TWITTER: @sanortheast
NOTES: Northeast made a much publicised move to Hampshire in February 2018 after 10 seasons at Canterbury, hoping that Division One cricket is the platform he needs to attract the England selectors. But he suffered a finger injury early last season and wasn't able to find form when he returned to the side, averaging 25.06 in 10 Championship matches, and his performances in the T20 Blast were also below his high standards. His most significant innings was an unbeaten 75 in Hampshire's victory over his old club in the Lord's one-day final, an innings which began with Kent fans booing him to the crease. Hotly tipped from his early teens, Northeast scored his maiden first-class hundred for Kent in 2009 and hit three Championship centuries in 2012. He struggled in 2013 and was dropped in 2014 but soon returned to the side and made four Championship hundreds. He scored 1,000 first-class runs in three successive seasons from 2015-2017 and has also been dominant in the short formats. Kent appointed him four-day captain at the end of 2015, but relationships were strained by the time Northeast decided to leave the club

Batting	Mat	Inns	NO	Runs	HS	Ave	SR	100	50	Ct	St
First-class	149	255	18	9060	191	38.22	55.51	20	46	78	0
List A	96	88	7	2706	132	33.40	76.74	3	15	33	0
T20s	103	94	12	2538	114	30.95	133.22	1	18	26	0
Bowling	**Mat**	**Balls**	**Runs**	**Wkts**	**BBI**	**BBM**	**Ave**	**Econ**	**SR**	**5w**	**10**
First-class	149	178	147	1	1/60	1/60	147.00	4.95	178.0	0	0
List A	96	-	-	-	-	-	-	-	-	-	-
T20s	103	-	-	-	-	-	-	-	-	-	-

LIAM NORWELL RHB / RFM / R0 / W2

FULL NAME: Liam Connor Norwell
BORN: December 27, 1991, Bournemouth
SQUAD NO: 24
HEIGHT: 6ft 3in
NICKNAME: Pasty
EDUCATION: Redruth School, Cornwall
TEAMS: Warwickshire, Gloucestershire
ROLE: Bowler
DEBUT: First-class: 2011; List A: 2012; T20: 2012

BEST BATTING: 102 Gloucestershire vs Derbyshire, Bristol, 2016
BEST BOWLING: 8-43 Gloucestershire vs Leicestershire, Leicester, 2017
COUNTY CAP: 2011 (Gloucestershire)

WHAT WAS YOUR FIRST CRICKET CLUB? Redruth CC, Cornwall
FAVOURITE CRICKET BAT? Kookaburra Kahuna – it has the fibre glass on the back
BEST INNINGS YOU'VE SEEN? Michael Klinger's match-winning hundred at Headingley in the 2015 One-Day Cup semi-final. That was a special win
WHICH RULE WOULD YOU CHANGE ABOUT CRICKET? Let each team make one tactical sub at the interval in T20 cricket
YOUR BIGGEST CRICKETING REGRET? Not learning enough from the senior players in the first years of my career
SURPRISING FACT ABOUT YOU? I was born in Bournemouth but everyone thinks I was born in Cornwall because that's where I grew up
ODDEST SPORT YOU'VE PLAYED? The game in which a number of different types of sports balls are on the pitch and whichever ball is deemed to be in play determines the sport
TWITTER: @icnorwell24

Batting	Mat	Inns	NO	Runs	HS	Ave	SR	100	50	Ct	St
First-class	68	86	34	703	102	13.51	41.72	1	1	15	0
List A	17	10	2	47	16	5.87	69.11	0	0	2	0
T20s	24	5	5	5	2*	-	71.42	0	0	10	0
Bowling	**Mat**	**Balls**	**Runs**	**Wkts**	**BBI**	**BBM**	**Ave**	**Econ**	**SR**	**5w**	**10**
First-class	68	11922	6690	248	8/43	10/65	26.97	3.36	48.0	10	3
List A	17	780	716	23	6/52	6/52	31.13	5.50	33.9	2	0
T20s	24	422	653	12	3/27	3/27	54.41	9.28	35.1	0	0

DUANNE OLIVIER

RHB / RFM / R0 / W0

FULL NAME: Duanne Olivier
BORN: May 9, 1992, Groblersdal, Limpopo, South Africa
SQUAD NO: 74
TEAMS: South Africa, Yorkshire, Derbyshire, Free State, Jozi Stars, Knights
ROLE: Bowler
DEBUT: Test: 2017; ODI: 2019; First-class: 2011; List A: 2011; T20: 2011

BEST BATTING: 72 Free State vs Namibia, Bloemfontein, 2014
BEST BOWLING: 6-37 South Africa vs Pakistan, Centurion, 2018

TWITTER: @Duanne992
NOTES: Olivier caused a shock in February when Yorkshire announced they had signed the rib-tickling fast bowler on a three-year Kolpak deal, making him ineligible to play for South Africa. He had been playing Test cricket just three days earlier. Olivier, who turns 27 in May, had become a key member of a new generation of hostile South African quicks, having taken 48 wickets at an average of just 19.25 in 10 Tests. He took 31 Championship wickets for Derbyshire last summer. "I would be lying if I said this wasn't a difficult decision to make," he said. "But at the end of the day I needed to be true to myself. I've only got this one chance to see where my talent can take me and Yorkshire just felt right to me. I was originally looking to come back as an overseas player but, when I got a long-term offer from Yorkshire as a Kolpak, I knew that signing would be the best option for both myself and my family"

Batting	Mat	Inns	NO	Runs	HS	Ave	SR	100	50	Ct	St
Tests	10	12	5	26	10*	3.71	27.95	0	0	2	0
ODIs	2	-	-	-	-	-	-	-	-	0	0
First-class	96	126	36	1100	72	12.22	43.30	0	3	27	0
List A	44	22	7	184	25*	12.26	66.42	0	0	6	0
T20s	34	11	8	62	15*	20.66	86.11	0	0	5	0
Bowling	**Mat**	**Balls**	**Runs**	**Wkts**	**BBI**	**BBM**	**Ave**	**Econ**	**SR**	**5w**	**10**
Tests	10	1440	924	48	6/37	11/96	19.25	3.85	30.0	3	1
ODIs	2	114	124	3	2/73	2/73	41.33	6.52	38.0	0	0
First-class	96	16745	8722	399	6/37	11/96	21.85	3.12	41.9	22	4
List A	44	1779	1515	61	4/34	4/34	24.83	5.10	29.1	0	0
T20s	34	665	862	38	4/28	4/28	22.68	7.77	17.5	0	0

GRAHAM ONIONS RHB / RMF / R0 / W8 / MVP40

FULL NAME: Graham Onions
BORN: September 9, 1982, Gateshead, County Durham
SQUAD NO: 99
HEIGHT: 6ft 2in
NICKNAME: Bunny, Wills
EDUCATION: St Thomas More Roman Catholic School, Blaydon, Gateshead
TEAMS: England, Lancashire, Dolphins, Durham
ROLE: Bowler
DEBUT: Test: 2009; ODI: 2009; First-class: 2004; List A: 2003; T20: 2004

BEST BATTING: 65 Durham vs Nottinghamshire, Chester-le-Street, 2016
BEST BOWLING: 9-67 Durham vs Nottinghamshire, Trent Bridge, 2012
COUNTY CAP: 2018 (Lancashire); **BENEFIT:** 2015 (Durham)

'ROY OF THE ROVERS' MOMENT? My Test debut, taking nine wickets against Nottinghamshire and returning to Test cricket against West Indies in 2012 after my serious back injury
SUPERSTITIONS? I lick my fingers before I bowl
CRICKETING HERO? Darren Gough
IF YOU WEREN'T A CRICKETER? I'd be struggling! Maybe a PE teacher
TWITTER: @BunnyOnions
NOTES: The veteran former England fast bowler, plagued by injury for much of his career, returned to form at the end of the 2017 season with 32 Championship wickets at 22.66. After 14 seasons at Durham, Onions moved to Lancashire ahead of the last campaign and immediately formed a deadly new-ball pairing with Tom Bailey, taking 57 wickets at 21.77

Batting	Mat	Inns	NO	Runs	HS	Ave	SR	100	50	Ct	St
Tests	9	10	7	30	17*	10.00	30.92	0	0	0	0
ODIs	4	1	0	1	1	1.00	50.00	0	0	1	0
First-class	182	238	85	2035	65	13.30	52.03	0	1	34	0
List A	91	34	12	162	30*	7.36	76.77	0	0	13	0
T20s	47	14	7	62	31	8.85	103.33	0	0	10	0
Bowling	**Mat**	**Balls**	**Runs**	**Wkts**	**BBI**	**BBM**	**Ave**	**Econ**	**SR**	**5w**	**10**
Tests	9	1606	957	32	5/38	7/102	29.90	3.57	50.1	1	0
ODIs	4	204	185	4	2/58	2/58	46.25	5.44	51.0	0	0
First-class	182	31637	17702	678	9/67	11/95	26.10	3.35	46.6	28	3
List A	91	3784	3224	104	4/45	4/45	31.00	5.11	36.3	0	0
T20s	47	990	1133	38	3/15	3/15	29.81	6.86	26.0	0	0

FELIX ORGAN

RHB / OB / R0 / W0

FULL NAME: Felix Spencer Organ
BORN: June 2, 1999, Sydney, Australia
SQUAD NO: 3
EDUCATION: Canford School, Dorset
TEAMS: Hampshire
ROLE: Batsman
DEBUT: First-class: 2017; List A: 2018

BEST BATTING: 16 Hampshire vs Middlesex, Uxbridge, 2018

NOTES: The 19-year-old top-order batsman signed his first professional contract with Hampshire in early 2018 after making his first-class debut in the Championship match against Middlesex the previous summer. Born in Sydney, Organ has come through the Hampshire youth system and was vice-captain of the side which won the U17 County Championship in 2015. He put in a number of impressive performances for Hampshire Second XI last season, averaging nearly 50 in the three-day Championship and scoring 189 against Surrey at New Malden in July. He also scored 843 runs at an average of 56.20 in 18 games for the Hampshire Academy in the Southern Premier League. Organ signed a new two-year contract with the club in October

Batting	Mat	Inns	NO	Runs	HS	Ave	SR	100	50	Ct	St
First-class	1	1	0	16	16	16.00	44.44	0	0	0	0
List A	4	2	0	0	0	0.00	0.00	0	0	2	0
Bowling	**Mat**	**Balls**	**Runs**	**Wkts**	**BBI**	**BBM**	**Ave**	**Econ**	**SR**	**5w**	**10**
First-class	1	-	-	-	-	-	-	-	-	-	-
List A	4	63	33	2	1/6	1/6	16.50	3.14	31.5	0	0

CRAIG OVERTON RHB / RFM / R0 / W0 / MVP53

FULL NAME: Craig Overton
BORN: April 10, 1994, Barnstaple, Devon
SQUAD NO: 12
HEIGHT: 6ft 5in
NICKNAME: Goober
EDUCATION: West Buckland School, Devon
TEAMS: England, Somerset
ROLE: Allrounder
DEBUT: Test: 2017; ODI: 2018; First-class: 2012; List A: 2012; T20: 2014

BEST BATTING: 138 Somerset vs Hampshire, Taunton, 2016
BEST BOWLING: 6-74 Somerset vs Warwickshire, Edgbaston, 2015
COUNTY CAP: 2016

FAMILY TIES? My father played Minor Counties and my twin Jamie also plays for Somerset
WHAT WAS YOUR FIRST CRICKET CLUB? North Devon CC, Bideford
WHICH BOWLER WOULD YOU LEAST LIKE TO FACE? My brother – he'd want to hurt me!
BEST INNINGS YOU'VE SEEN? Chris Gayle's 151 not out for Somerset against Kent in the 2015 T20 Blast
WHICH RULE WOULD YOU CHANGE ABOUT CRICKET? If the batsman edges it through the slips then they can't score any runs
YOUR BIGGEST CRICKETING REGRET? Not winning the Championship
TWITTER: @craigoverton12

Batting	Mat	Inns	NO	Runs	HS	Ave	SR	100	50	Ct	St
Tests	3	6	2	98	41*	24.50	53.26	0	0	1	0
ODIs	1	-	-	-	-	-	-	-	-	2	0
First-class	76	111	15	2074	138	21.60	66.30	1	8	46	0
List A	58	41	10	543	60*	17.51	111.95	0	1	24	0
T20s	32	17	7	194	35*	19.40	121.25	0	0	15	0
Bowling	**Mat**	**Balls**	**Runs**	**Wkts**	**BBI**	**BBM**	**Ave**	**Econ**	**SR**	**5w**	**10**
Tests	3	504	296	7	3/105	4/116	42.28	3.52	72.0	0	0
ODIs	1	42	55	0	-	-	-	7.85	-	0	0
First-class	76	12269	6402	239	6/74	9/134	26.78	3.13	51.3	4	0
List A	58	2680	2418	70	4/27	4/27	34.54	5.41	38.2	0	0
T20s	32	589	923	25	3/17	3/17	36.92	9.40	23.5	0	0

JAMIE OVERTON RHB / RF / R0 / W0 / MVP55

FULL NAME: Jamie Overton
BORN: April 10, 1994, Barnstaple, Devon
SQUAD NO: 8
HEIGHT: 6ft 5in
NICKNAME: Goober, J
EDUCATION: West Buckland School, Devon
TEAMS: Somerset, England Lions
ROLE: Bowler
DEBUT: First-class: 2012; List A: 2012; T20: 2015

BEST BATTING: 56 Somerset vs Warwickshire, Edgbaston, 2014
BEST BOWLING: 6-95 Somerset vs Middlesex, Taunton, 2013

FAMILY TIES? My dad played for Devon and my twin brother Craig plays for Somerset too
WHAT WAS YOUR FIRST CRICKET CLUB? North Devon CC, situated on the splitting of the Taw-Torridge Estuary
FAVOURITE CRICKET BAT? Millichamp and Hall F100
CRICKETING HERO? James Anderson
WHICH BOWLER WOULD YOU LEAST LIKE TO FACE? Craig Overton, for obvious reasons
BEST INNINGS YOU'VE SEEN? Matt Renshaw's hundred before lunch against Yorkshire at Taunton in 2018
WHO WOULD YOU ASK TO BAT FOR YOUR LIFE? Me – I wouldn't let anyone else do it
SURPRISING FACT ABOUT YOU? I was in a film when I was younger
ODDEST SPORT YOU'VE PLAYED? Croquet
TWITTER: @JamieOverton

Batting	Mat	Inns	NO	Runs	HS	Ave	SR	100	50	Ct	St
First-class	54	75	19	968	56	17.28	80.33	0	5	11	0
List A	37	28	7	360	40*	17.14	112.50	0	0	17	0
T20s	44	21	11	136	31	13.60	160.00	0	0	23	0
Bowling	**Mat**	**Balls**	**Runs**	**Wkts**	**BBI**	**BBM**	**Ave**	**Econ**	**SR**	**5w**	**10**
First-class	54	7166	4319	130	6/95	8/143	33.22	3.61	55.1	2	0
List A	37	1434	1514	49	4/42	4/42	30.89	6.33	29.2	0	0
T20s	44	877	1369	56	5/47	5/47	24.44	9.36	15.6	1	0

TONY PALLADINO RHB / RMF / R0 / W3

FULL NAME: Antonio Paul Palladino
BORN: June 29, 1983, Tower Hamlets, London
SQUAD NO: 28
HEIGHT: 6ft 4in
NICKNAME: Battler, Pallas, Dino
EDUCATION: Cardinal Pole Sixth Form, London; Anglia Polytechnic University
TEAMS: Namibia, Derbyshire, Essex
ROLE: Bowler
DEBUT: First-class: 2003; List A: 2003; T20: 2005

BEST BATTING: 106 Derbyshire vs Australia A, Derby, 2012
BEST BOWLING: 7-53 Derbyshire vs Kent, Derby, 2012
COUNTY CAP: 2012 (Derbyshire)

WHAT WAS YOUR FIRST CRICKET CLUB? Wanstead CC, London. I played and won league and cup titles in the men's team
FAVOURITE CRICKET BAT? OptiMax Pyro – got my one and only first-class ton with it
WHICH BOWLER WOULD YOU LEAST LIKE TO FACE? Darren Stevens – not enough pockets in the world for the amount of times he's got me
BEST INNINGS YOU'VE SEEN? Martin Guptill's double century for us against Gloucestershire in 2015. It was like watching Stick Cricket
WHO WOULD YOU ASK TO BAT FOR YOUR LIFE? Billy Godleman
YOUR BIGGEST CRICKETING REGRET? Not moving to Derbyshire earlier
FAVOURITE QUOTE OR SAYING? Never say die
ODDEST SPORT YOU'VE PLAYED? Rugby – didn't see the fun in having 10 bells knocked out of me for 80 minutes
TWITTER: @apalladino28

Batting	Mat	Inns	NO	Runs	HS	Ave	SR	100	50	Ct	St
First-class	155	223	47	2781	106	15.80	48.42	1	7	40	0
List A	56	32	7	267	31	10.68	92.06	0	0	6	0
T20s	26	12	5	48	14*	6.85	81.35	0	0	5	0
Bowling	**Mat**	**Balls**	**Runs**	**Wkts**	**BBI**	**BBM**	**Ave**	**Econ**	**SR**	**5w**	**10**
First-class	155	25594	12569	437	7/53	10/81	28.76	2.94	58.5	16	1
List A	56	2231	1998	54	5/49	5/49	37.00	5.37	41.3	1	0
T20s	26	490	614	28	4/21	4/21	21.92	7.51	17.5	0	0

GEORGE PANAYI

RHB / RFM / R0 / W0

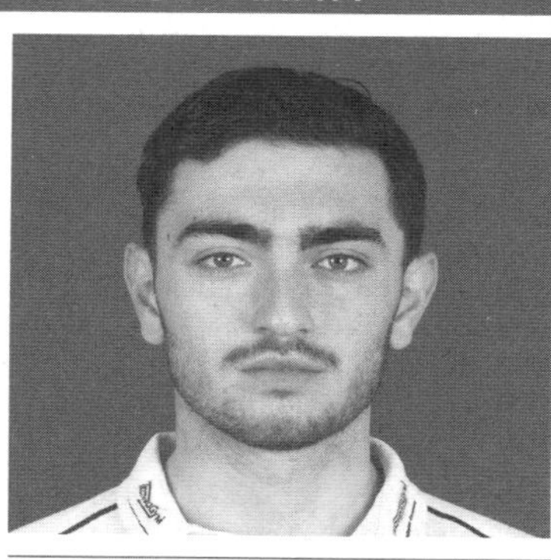

FULL NAME: George David Panayi
BORN: September 23, 1997, Enfield, Middlesex
SQUAD NO: 33
HEIGHT: 6ft 2in
NICKNAME: Poon
EDUCATION: Shrewsbury School
TEAMS: Warwickshire
ROLE: Bowler
DEBUT: First-class: 2017; List A: 2018

BEST BATTING: 16 Warwickshire vs Lancashire, Edgbaston, 2017
BEST BOWLING: 3-41 Warwickshire vs Lancashire, Edgbaston, 2017

WHAT WAS YOUR FIRST CRICKET CLUB? Southgate CC, London. There's a great pub next door called The Orange Tree
FAVOURITE CRICKET BAT? The Asda plastic – for pure bat speed
WHICH BOWLER WOULD YOU LEAST LIKE TO FACE? Liam Banks – I struggle with his floaty straight-breaks
BEST INNINGS YOU'VE SEEN? Andy Umeed's hundred against Lancashire at Edgbaston in 2017. It was the slowest Championship century ever (429 minutes). True patience
YOUR BIGGEST CRICKETING REGRET? Not adjusting to professional life sooner
SURPRISING FACT ABOUT YOU? I'm a big fan of jazz and I have a diploma in saxophone performance
WHAT WILL YOU BE DOING IN THE YEAR 2040? Hopefully I'll be retired in Lanzarote drinking oversized tax-free gin
FAVOURITE QUOTE OR SAYING? This time next year, we'll be millionaires (Del Boy)
WHICH BOOK MEANS MOST TO YOU? The Very Hungry Caterpillar by Eric Carle
ODDEST SPORT YOU'VE PLAYED? Kiss chase
TWITTER: @Gpanayi

Batting	Mat	Inns	NO	Runs	HS	Ave	SR	100	50	Ct	St
First-class	2	3	0	17	16	5.66	29.31	0	0	0	0
List A	1	-	-	-	-	-	-	-	-	0	0
Bowling	**Mat**	**Balls**	**Runs**	**Wkts**	**BBI**	**BBM**	**Ave**	**Econ**	**SR**	**5w**	**10**
First-class	2	231	141	4	3/41	3/75	35.25	3.66	57.7	0	0
List A	1	12	17	0	-	-	-	8.50	-	0	0

CALLUM PARKINSON RHB / SLA / R0 / W0

FULL NAME: Callum Francis Parkinson
BORN: October 24, 1996, Bolton, Lancashire
SQUAD NO: 10
HEIGHT: 5ft 7in
NICKNAME: Parky
EDUCATION: Bolton School; Canon Slade, Bolton
TEAMS: Leicestershire, Derbyshire
ROLE: Bowler
DEBUT: First-class: 2016; List A: 2017; T20: 2017

BEST BATTING: 75 Leicestershire vs Kent, Canterbury, 2017
BEST BOWLING: 8-148 Leicestershire vs Worcestershire, Worcester, 2017

FAMILY TIES? My dad played in the Bolton League and my twin brother Matt is at Lancashire
WHAT WAS YOUR FIRST CRICKET CLUB? Heaton CC, Greater Manchester
WHICH BOWLER WOULD YOU LEAST LIKE TO FACE? Duanne Olivier – he kept hitting me on the head last year
BEST INNINGS YOU'VE SEEN? Colin Ackerman's 66 not out in a T20 at Northampton last season. Dragged us from certain defeat to a great win
WHO WOULD YOU ASK TO BAT FOR YOUR LIFE? Gavin Griffiths – best technique in cricket
WHICH RULE WOULD YOU CHANGE ABOUT CRICKET? Five men outside the ring in List A cricket. Having only four is killing spinners!
YOUR BIGGEST CRICKETING REGRET? Not bowling spin when I was younger – only started when I was 16
WHICH BOOK MEANS MOST TO YOU? Not a massive reader so I'm going to say the Bolton Wanderers Season Review 2005
TWITTER: @cal_parky

Batting	Mat	Inns	NO	Runs	HS	Ave	SR	100	50	Ct	St
First-class	21	32	7	435	75	17.40	44.56	0	1	4	0
List A	8	6	2	122	52*	30.50	80.26	0	1	1	0
T20s	29	12	7	62	27*	12.40	96.87	0	0	3	0
Bowling	**Mat**	**Balls**	**Runs**	**Wkts**	**BBI**	**BBM**	**Ave**	**Econ**	**SR**	**5w**	**10**
First-class	21	3342	1911	41	8/148	10/185	46.60	3.43	81.5	1	1
List A	8	396	421	2	1/34	1/34	210.50	6.37	198.0	0	0
T20s	29	534	700	30	4/20	4/20	23.33	7.86	17.8	0	0

MATT PARKINSON RHB / LB / R0 / W0 / MVP64

FULL NAME: Matthew William Parkinson
BORN: October 24, 1996, Bolton, Lancashire
SQUAD NO: 28
HEIGHT: 5ft 9in
NICKNAME: Daddy, Parky
EDUCATION: Canon Slade School, Bolton
TEAMS: Lancashire, England Lions
ROLE: Bowler
DEBUT: First-class: 2016; List A: 2018; T20: 2017

BEST BATTING: 13 Lancashire vs Middlesex, Lord's, 2017
BEST BOWLING: 5-49 Lancashire vs Warwickshire, Old Trafford, 2016

FAMILY TIES? Dad played for Lancashire Federation U19 and league cricket in Bolton. My twin Callum plays for Leicestershire
WHAT WAS YOUR FIRST CRICKET CLUB? Heaton CC, Bolton, Greater Manchester
FAVOURITE CRICKET BAT? New Balance – wasted on me
CRICKETING HERO? Stuart MacGill
WHICH BOWLER WOULD YOU LEAST LIKE TO FACE? Callum Parkinson
BEST INNINGS YOU'VE SEEN? Sam Hain's 144 for England Lions against West Indies A in Antigua last year. Smacked it
WHO WOULD YOU ASK TO BAT FOR YOUR LIFE? Chris Martin – get it over with
SURPRISING FACT ABOUT YOU? I lost my front four teeth in a cricket accident when I was 12 and recently underwent implant surgery
FAVOURITE QUOTE OR SAYING? Don't kick it or snick it (Matt Parkinson, 2018)
TWITTER: @mattypark96

Batting	Mat	Inns	NO	Runs	HS	Ave	SR	100	50	Ct	St
First-class	16	22	9	71	13	5.46	23.74	0	0	3	0
List A	16	8	6	30	15*	15.00	42.25	0	0	1	0
T20s	24	7	4	14	7*	4.66	87.50	0	0	3	0
Bowling	**Mat**	**Balls**	**Runs**	**Wkts**	**BBI**	**BBM**	**Ave**	**Econ**	**SR**	**5w**	**10**
First-class	16	2166	1183	42	5/49	8/181	28.16	3.27	51.5	2	0
List A	16	839	679	30	5/68	5/68	22.63	4.85	27.9	1	0
T20s	24	532	609	39	4/23	4/23	15.61	6.86	13.6	0	0

WAYNE PARNELL LHB / LFM / R0 / W0

FULL NAME: Wayne Dillon Parnell
BORN: July 30, 1989, Port Elizabeth, SA
SQUAD NO: 7
HEIGHT: 6ft 2in
NICKNAME: Parny, Parnygram
EDUCATION: Nelson Mandela University
TEAMS: South Africa, Worcestershire, Cape Cobras, Delhi Daredevils, Eastern Province, Glamorgan, Kent, Pune Warriors, Sussex, Warriors, Western Province
ROLE: Allrounder
DEBUT: Test: 2010; ODI: 2009; T20I: 2009; First-class: 2006; List A: 2007; T20: 2008

BEST BATTING: 111* Cape Cobras vs Warriors, Paarl, 2016
BEST BOWLING: 7-51 Cape Cobras vs Dolphins, Cape Town, 2016

WHAT WAS YOUR FIRST CRICKET CLUB? Northville CC, Port Elizabeth, South Africa. I was recruited aged 14 to play in the first XI and that's where I learned to be mentally tough. The older guys really helped me cope with the pressure
FAVOURITE CRICKET BAT? A Steve Waugh GM which my dad bought me when I was eight
WHICH BOWLER WOULD YOU LEAST LIKE TO FACE? Rashid Khan – amazing competitor who never wants to give you anything
BEST INNINGS YOU'VE SEEN? Hashim Amla's triple century against England at The Oval in 2012. I've been fortunate to play alongside him and his concentration is on another level
WHICH BOOK MEANS MOST TO YOU? The Quran
TWITTER: @WayneParnell

Batting	Mat	Inns	NO	Runs	HS	Ave	SR	100	50	Ct	St
Tests	6	4	0	67	23	16.75	37.22	0	0	3	0
ODIs	65	38	14	508	56	21.16	78.39	0	1	12	0
T20Is	40	13	9	114	29*	28.50	118.75	0	0	5	0
First-class	68	93	11	2297	111*	28.01	52.91	2	14	21	0
List A	156	109	30	1953	129	24.72	86.26	2	5	30	0
T20s	194	111	45	1282	99	19.42	122.56	0	3	34	0
Bowling	**Mat**	**Balls**	**Runs**	**Wkts**	**BBI**	**BBM**	**Ave**	**Econ**	**SR**	**5w**	**10**
Tests	6	556	414	15	4/51	6/89	27.60	4.46	37.0	0	0
ODIs	65	2911	2738	94	5/48	5/48	29.12	5.64	30.9	2	0
T20Is	40	749	1038	41	4/13	4/13	25.31	8.31	18.2	0	0
First-class	68	10485	6035	198	7/51	12/105	30.47	3.45	52.9	6	1
List A	156	6989	6335	211	6/51	6/51	30.02	5.43	33.1	3	0
T20s	194	3784	4894	196	4/13	4/13	24.96	7.76	19.3	0	0

STEPHEN PARRY RHB / SLA / R0 / W0

FULL NAME: Stephen David Parry
BORN: January 12, 1986, Manchester
SQUAD NO: 4
HEIGHT: 6ft
NICKNAME: Pazza
EDUCATION: Audenshaw High School, Manchester
TEAMS: England, Lancashire, Brisbane Heat
ROLE: Bowler
DEBUT: ODI: 2014; T20I: 2014; First-class: 2007; List A: 2009; T20: 2009

BEST BATTING: 44 Lancashire vs Somerset, Old Trafford, 2017
BEST BOWLING: 5-23 Lancashire vs Durham UCCE, Durham University, 2007
COUNTY CAP: 2015

NON-CRICKETING HERO? Muhammad Ali
IF YOU WEREN'T A CRICKETER? I'd be fishing
SURPRISING FACT? I'm an elite table-tennis player
TWITTER: @SDParry86
NOTES: Left-arm spinner known as a white-ball specialist, Parry played a handful of limited-overs matches for England in 2014 and 2015. He has well over 200 wickets in List A and T20 cricket combined. After not playing a first-class match for nearly three years, Parry made a return to Championship action in 2017, taking 25 wickets at 31.08. Last summer he played just 13 games across all formats, in part due to injury

Batting	Mat	Inns	NO	Runs	HS	Ave	SR	100	50	Ct	St
ODIs	2	-	-	-	-	-	-	-	-	0	0
T20Is	5	1	0	1	1	1.00	100.00	0	0	2	0
First-class	26	32	2	452	44	15.06	45.79	0	0	7	0
List A	95	48	21	341	31	12.62	78.57	0	0	32	0
T20s	125	35	22	140	15*	10.76	106.87	0	0	27	0
Bowling	**Mat**	**Balls**	**Runs**	**Wkts**	**BBI**	**BBM**	**Ave**	**Econ**	**SR**	**5w**	**10**
ODIs	2	114	92	4	3/32	3/32	23.00	4.84	28.5	0	0
T20Is	5	96	138	3	2/33	2/33	46.00	8.62	32.0	0	0
First-class	26	3863	1716	50	5/23	6/101	34.32	2.66	77.2	2	0
List A	95	4126	3462	115	5/17	5/17	30.10	5.03	35.8	1	0
T20s	125	2598	3135	122	5/13	5/13	25.69	7.24	21.2	1	0

JEETAN PATEL RHB / OB / R0 / W6 / MVP23

FULL NAME: Jeetan Shashi Patel
BORN: May 7, 1980, Wellington, New Zealand
SQUAD NO: 5
HEIGHT: 5ft 8in
NICKNAME: Dave
TEAMS: New Zealand, Warwickshire, North Island, Wellington
ROLE: Bowler
DEBUT: Test: 2006; ODI: 2005; T20I: 2005; First-class: 1999; List A: 1999; T20: 2005

BEST BATTING: 120 Warwickshire vs Yorkshire, Edgbaston, 2014
BEST BOWLING: 7-38 Warwickshire vs Somerset, Taunton, 2015
COUNTY CAP: 2012

WHAT GOT YOU INTO CRICKET? My old man – he's a cricket badger
WHAT WAS YOUR FIRST CRICKET CLUB? Eastern Suburbs CC, Wellington, New Zealand
BEST THING ABOUT YOUR HOME GROUND? Edgbaston has the best dressing rooms in the country
WHICH BOWLER WOULD YOU LEAST LIKE TO FACE? Courtney Walsh
CRICKETING HERO? Saqlain Mushtaq
NON-CRICKETING HERO? Tiger Woods

Batting	Mat	Inns	NO	Runs	HS	Ave	SR	100	50	Ct	St
Tests	24	38	8	381	47	12.70	51.62	0	0	13	0
ODIs	43	15	8	95	34	13.57	58.64	0	0	13	0
T20Is	11	4	1	9	5	3.00	64.28	0	0	4	0
First-class	278	368	75	6321	120	21.57	67.64	3	26	145	0
List A	218	114	35	748	50	9.46	91.55	0	1	89	0
T20s	218	89	29	417	34*	6.95	127.13	0	0	79	0
Bowling	**Mat**	**Balls**	**Runs**	**Wkts**	**BBI**	**BBM**	**Ave**	**Econ**	**SR**	**5w**	**10**
Tests	24	5833	3078	65	5/110	6/151	47.35	3.16	89.7	1	0
ODIs	43	2014	1691	49	3/11	3/11	34.51	5.03	41.1	0	0
T20Is	11	199	269	16	3/20	3/20	16.81	8.11	12.4	0	0
First-class	278	56874	27380	824	7/38	10/106	33.22	2.88	69.0	34	5
List A	218	10485	8135	267	5/43	5/43	30.46	4.65	39.2	1	0
T20s	218	4493	5228	218	4/11	4/11	23.98	6.98	20.6	0	0

RISHI PATEL

RHB / LB / R0 / W0

FULL NAME: Rishi Ketan Patel
BORN: July 26, 1998, Chigwell, Essex
SQUAD NO: 12
EDUCATION: Brentwood School, Essex
TEAMS: Essex
ROLE: Batsman

NOTES: The 20-year-old batsman signed his first professional contract in September and will remain with Essex until at least the end of the 2020 season. Patel was in prolific form for the second team last year, equalling the club record of five centuries in a Second XI Championship season. He was selected to face India in the tour match last July, scoring 19 runs. "I'm really excited to be part of such a great club and sign for the side that I have been involved with since I was seven years old," said Patel. "I'm extremely thankful to the coaching staff that have helped me achieve my dreams of becoming a professional, and I'd like to thank my parents who have supported me throughout this journey and have been there every step of the way"

RYAN PATEL

LHB / RMF / R0 / W0

FULL NAME: Ryan Patel
BORN: October 26, 1997, Sutton, Surrey
SQUAD NO: 26
HEIGHT: 5ft 10in
NICKNAME: FP
EDUCATION: Whitgift School, Croydon
TEAMS: Surrey
ROLE: Allrounder
DEBUT: First-class: 2017

BEST BATTING: 81 Surrey vs Hampshire, Southampton, 2017
BEST BOWLING: 6-5 Surrey vs Somerset, Guildford, 2018

WHAT WAS YOUR FIRST CRICKET CLUB? Old Rutlishians CC, London
CRICKETING HERO? Jacques Kallis
WHICH BOWLER WOULD YOU LEAST LIKE TO FACE? Pat Cummins
BEST INNINGS YOU'VE SEEN? Kumar Sangakkara's double hundred against Essex at Chelmsford in 2017
WHO WOULD YOU ASK TO BAT FOR YOUR LIFE? Amar Virdi
WHICH RULE WOULD YOU CHANGE ABOUT CRICKET? Make the stumps bigger
YOUR BIGGEST CRICKETING REGRET? Realising that hair-loss treatment doesn't work
SURPRISING FACT ABOUT YOU? I was an opening bowler who batted down the order until I was 15 but have since become an opening batsman who bowls
SURPRISING FACT ABOUT A TEAMMATE? Matt Dunn used to live in Norway
WHAT WILL YOU BE DOING IN THE YEAR 2040? I'll be running one of Arun Harinath's BP garages
FAVOURITE QUOTE OR SAYING? I am the master of my fate: I am the captain of my soul (William Ernest Henley)
WHICH BOOK MEANS MOST TO YOU? The Obstacle is the Way – The Timeless Art of Turning Trials into Triumph by Ryan Holiday

Batting	Mat	Inns	NO	Runs	HS	Ave	SR	100	50	Ct	St
First-class	14	21	3	520	81	28.88	40.27	0	1	6	0
Bowling	**Mat**	**Balls**	**Runs**	**Wkts**	**BBI**	**BBM**	**Ave**	**Econ**	**SR**	**5w**	**10**
First-class	14	835	437	10	6/5	6/12	43.70	3.14	83.5	1	0

SAMIT PATEL

RHB / SLA / R4 / W0 / MVP25

FULL NAME: Samit Rohit Patel
BORN: November 30, 1984, Leicester
SQUAD NO: 21
HEIGHT: 5ft 8in
NICKNAME: Sarnie, Slippery
EDUCATION: Worksop College, Nottinghamshire
TEAMS: England, Nottinghamshire, Islamabad United, Mohammedan Sporting Club, Rajshahi Kings, Warriors, Wellington
ROLE: Allrounder
DEBUT: Test: 2012; ODI: 2008; T20I: 2011; First-class: 2002; List A: 2002; T20: 2003

BEST BATTING: 257* Nottinghamshire vs Gloucestershire, Bristol, 2017
BEST BOWLING: 7-68 Nottinghamshire vs Hampshire, Southampton, 2011
COUNTY CAP: 2008; BENEFIT: 2017

FAMILY TIES? My brother Akhil played for Nottinghamshire for two years
WHAT WAS YOUR FIRST CRICKET CLUB? Kimberley Institute CC, Nottinghamshire
CRICKETING HERO? Stephen Fleming
WHICH BOWLER WOULD YOU LEAST LIKE TO FACE? Morne Morkel – so awkward
BEST INNINGS YOU'VE SEEN? Sachin Tendulkar's double century in the 2004 Sydney Test – for the mental strength he showed in not playing a cover-drive
WHICH RULE WOULD YOU CHANGE ABOUT CRICKET? Being run out backing up
FAVOURITE QUOTE OR SAYING? If you don't believe in yourself nobody else will
TWITTER: @Samitpatel21

Batting	Mat	Inns	NO	Runs	HS	Ave	SR	100	50	Ct	St
Tests	6	9	0	151	42	16.77	44.67	0	0	3	0
ODIs	36	22	7	482	70*	32.13	93.23	0	1	7	0
T20Is	18	14	2	189	67	15.75	109.24	0	1	3	0
First-class	212	345	18	11976	257*	36.62	63.27	26	59	134	0
List A	236	205	32	6060	129*	35.02	85.43	7	33	68	0
T20s	246	215	38	4577	90*	25.85	124.61	0	28	73	0
Bowling	**Mat**	**Balls**	**Runs**	**Wkts**	**BBI**	**BBM**	**Ave**	**Econ**	**SR**	**5w**	**10**
Tests	6	858	421	7	2/27	3/164	60.14	2.94	122.5	0	0
ODIs	36	1187	1091	24	5/41	5/41	45.45	5.51	49.4	1	0
T20Is	18	252	321	7	2/6	2/6	45.85	7.64	36.0	0	0
First-class	212	24465	12558	322	7/68	11/111	39.00	3.07	75.9	5	1
List A	236	7940	7127	217	6/13	6/13	32.84	5.38	36.5	2	0
T20s	246	4469	5420	203	4/20	4/20	26.69	7.27	22.0	0	0

STEVEN PATTERSON RHB / RMF / R0 / W2 / MVP63

FULL NAME: Steven Andrew Patterson
BORN: October 3, 1983, Beverley, Yorkshire
SQUAD NO: 17
HEIGHT: 6ft 4in
NICKNAME: Dead Man, Patto
EDUCATION: Malet Lambert School, Hull; St Mary's Sixth Form College, Hull; University of Leeds
TEAMS: Yorkshire
ROLE: Bowler
DEBUT: First-class: 2005; List A: 2003; T20: 2009

BEST BATTING: 63* Yorkshire vs Warwickshire, Edgbaston, 2016
BEST BOWLING: 6-40 Yorkshire vs Essex, Chelmsford, 2018
COUNTY CAP: 2012

FAMILY TIES? My grandad played for Durham before World War II
'ROY OF THE ROVERS' MOMENT? Making my Championship debut at Scarborough, receiving my first XI cap, and winning the County Championship
CRICKETING HERO? Shaun Pollock
NON-CRICKETING HERO? My grandad
IF YOU WEREN'T A CRICKETER? I'd be working in finance
NOTES: In February the veteran Yorkshire seamer was appointed the club's full-time captain across all formats, having deputised last summer when Gary Ballance was given a break from the game in mid-season. "He did fantastically well both on and off the field," said director of cricket Martyn Moxon. "He's relishing the role and has got his feet under the table now. It's an easy decision for him to continue as club captain for the foreseeable future. When you're under pressure and a couple of decisions go against you, you need that calm head to calm everyone down and not panic. Steve's very good at that"

Batting	Mat	Inns	NO	Runs	HS	Ave	SR	100	50	Ct	St
First-class	140	165	41	2044	63*	16.48	38.53	0	3	25	0
List A	90	37	20	231	25*	13.58	72.78	0	0	17	0
T20s	62	9	4	9	3*	1.80	42.85	0	0	9	0
Bowling	**Mat**	**Balls**	**Runs**	**Wkts**	**BBI**	**BBM**	**Ave**	**Econ**	**SR**	**5w**	**10**
First-class	140	22553	10359	372	6/40	8/94	27.84	2.75	60.6	7	0
List A	90	3858	3261	114	6/32	6/32	28.60	5.07	33.8	2	0
T20s	62	1278	1784	61	4/30	4/30	29.24	8.37	20.9	0	0

DAVID PAYNE

RHB / LFM / R0 / W0

GLOUCESTERSHIRE

FULL NAME: David Alan Payne
BORN: February 15, 1991, Poole, Dorset
SQUAD NO: 14
HEIGHT: 6ft 3in
NICKNAME: Sid, Payney
EDUCATION: Lytchett Minster Secondary and Sixth Form, Poole, Dorset
TEAMS: Gloucestershire
ROLE: Bowler
DEBUT: First-class: 2011; List A: 2009; T20: 2010

BEST BATTING: 67* Gloucestershire vs Glamorgan, Cardiff, 2016
BEST BOWLING: 6-26 Gloucestershire vs Leicestershire, Bristol, 2011
COUNTY CAP: 2011

WHAT WAS YOUR FIRST CRICKET CLUB? Parley CC, Dorset
FAVOURITE CRICKET BAT? Gray-Nicolls Powerbow – I loved the yellow-wrap grip
WHICH BOWLER WOULD YOU LEAST LIKE TO FACE? Ben Stokes – pace, bounce, swings it both ways
BEST INNINGS YOU'VE SEEN? Michael Klinger and Jack Taylor scoring hundreds to chase down 320 in 50-odd overs in a Championship match at New Road in 2016
WHO WOULD YOU ASK TO BAT FOR YOUR LIFE? Chris Dent – he makes it look easy
WHICH RULE WOULD YOU CHANGE ABOUT CRICKET? Set a maximum of 75 overs per day for four-day cricket
SURPRISING FACT ABOUT YOU? I cut my own hair
WHAT WILL YOU BE DOING IN THE YEAR 2040? I'll be a bowling coach or a graphic designer
FAVOURITE QUOTE OR SAYING? Look good, feel good, play good
TWITTER: @sidpayne7

Batting	Mat	Inns	NO	Runs	HS	Ave	SR	100	50	Ct	St
First-class	83	102	34	1423	67*	20.92	47.84	0	6	27	0
List A	59	24	14	108	23	10.80	69.23	0	0	16	0
T20s	69	19	11	46	10	5.75	90.19	0	0	14	0
Bowling	**Mat**	**Balls**	**Runs**	**Wkts**	**BBI**	**BBM**	**Ave**	**Econ**	**SR**	**5w**	**10**
First-class	83	13170	7101	220	6/26	9/96	32.27	3.23	59.8	3	0
List A	59	2477	2330	101	7/29	7/29	23.06	5.64	24.5	3	0
T20s	69	1328	1905	83	5/24	5/24	22.95	8.60	16.0	1	0

DILLON PENNINGTON

RHB / RFM / R0 / W0

FULL NAME: Dillon Young Pennington
BORN: February 26, 1999, Shrewsbury, Shropshire
SQUAD NO: 22
HEIGHT: 6ft 2in
NICKNAME: Dill
EDUCATION: Wrekin College, Shropshire; University of Worcester
TEAMS: Worcestershire
ROLE: Bowler
DEBUT: First-class: 2018; List A: 2018; T20: 2018

BEST BATTING: 37 Worcestershire vs Somerset, Worcester, 2018
BEST BOWLING: 4-53 Worcestershire vs Yorkshire, Scarborough, 2018

WHAT WAS YOUR FIRST CRICKET CLUB? Shrewsbury CC, Shropshire
WHICH BOWLER WOULD YOU LEAST LIKE TO FACE? Mitchell Starc – I don't want to get hit on the head
WHICH RULE WOULD YOU CHANGE ABOUT CRICKET? Outlaw the lbw rule! I get hit on the front pad quite a lot
YOUR BIGGEST CRICKETING REGRET? Being injured a lot of the time and causing the Worcestershire staff hell
FAVOURITE QUOTE OR SAYING? I've missed more than 9,000 shots in my career. I've lost almost 300 games. Twenty-six times I've been trusted to take the game-winning shot and missed. I've failed over and over and over again in my life. And that is why I succeed (Michael Jordan)
ODDEST SPORT YOU'VE PLAYED? Rugby – everyone just gets injured. I've never come away from a game without a broken nose
TWITTER: @DillonPenningt4

Batting	Mat	Inns	NO	Runs	HS	Ave	SR	100	50	Ct	St
First-class	8	14	3	94	37	8.54	36.86	0	0	4	0
List A	3	2	1	7	4*	7.00	28.00	0	0	2	0
T20s	4	2	1	6	6*	6.00	75.00	0	0	0	0
Bowling	**Mat**	**Balls**	**Runs**	**Wkts**	**BBI**	**BBM**	**Ave**	**Econ**	**SR**	**5w**	**10**
First-class	8	1122	778	22	4/53	6/80	35.36	4.16	51.0	0	0
List A	3	156	178	8	5/67	5/67	22.25	6.84	19.5	1	0
T20s	4	72	86	7	4/9	4/9	12.28	7.16	10.2	0	0

MICHAEL PEPPER

RHB / WK / R0 / W0

ESSEX

FULL NAME: Michael-Kyle Steven Pepper
BORN: June 25, 1998, Harlow, Essex
SQUAD NO: 19
EDUCATION: The Perse School, Cambridge
TEAMS: Essex
ROLE: Wicketkeeper/batsman
DEBUT: First-class: 2018; T20: 2018

BEST BATTING: 22 Essex vs Somerset, Chelmsford, 2018

NOTES: The 20-year-old wicketkeeper/batsman signed a summer contract with Essex in April 2018 after a string of impressive performances for the Second XI. He went on to make two Championship appearances and also played four matches in Essex's T20 Blast campaign, signing a new two-year deal with the club in September. Head coach Anthony McGrath said: "Michael is a great young wicketkeeper who is also very handy with a bat. He has heaps of talent and we're excited about seeing him progress at the club." Pepper has also played for Cambridgeshire in Minor Counties cricket and for Cambridge Granta in the East Anglian Premier League

Batting	Mat	Inns	NO	Runs	HS	Ave	SR	100	50	Ct	St
First-class	2	4	0	53	22	13.25	42.06	0	0	0	0
T20s	4	3	2	53	27	53.00	98.14	0	0	1	0
Bowling	**Mat**	**Balls**	**Runs**	**Wkts**	**BBI**	**BBM**	**Ave**	**Econ**	**SR**	**5w**	**10**
First-class	2	-	-	-	-	-	-	-	-	-	-
T20s	4	-	-	-	-	-	-	-	-	-	-

MATHEW PILLANS

RHB / RF / R0 / W0

FULL NAME: Mathew William Pillans
BORN: July 4, 1991, Pretoria, South Africa
SQUAD NO: 47
HEIGHT: 6ft 4in
NICKNAME: Matty P
EDUCATION: Pretoria Boys High School
TEAMS: Yorkshire, Dolphins, KwaZulu-Natal, Leicestershire, Northerns, Surrey
ROLE: Bowler
DEBUT: First-class: 2012; List A: 2013; T20: 2014

BEST BATTING: 56 Leicestershire vs Northamptonshire, Northampton, 2017
BEST BOWLING: 6-67 Dolphins vs Knights, Durban, 2015

FAMILY TIES? My mum played for the Springbok hockey team for 13 years and my dad played rugby in Zimbabwe and represented the World XV
'ROY OF THE ROVERS' MOMENT? Bowling the final over for Leicestershire against Notts in the 2017 T20 Blast and defending eight runs
IF YOU WEREN'T A CRICKETER? I'd be a fly-fisherman
SURPRISING FACT ABOUT YOU? I had open-heart surgery when I was 12
CRICKETING HERO? Brett Lee. He is an amazingly dedicated cricketer and a great man both on and off the field to anyone he meets
NON-CRICKETING HERO? Nelson Mandela
TWITTER: @matwilpil

Batting	Mat	Inns	NO	Runs	HS	Ave	SR	100	50	Ct	St
First-class	41	58	5	727	56	13.71	64.67	0	1	20	0
List A	12	8	4	79	20*	19.75	91.86	0	0	3	0
T20s	34	17	9	166	34*	20.75	105.06	0	0	7	0

Bowling	Mat	Balls	Runs	Wkts	BBI	BBM	Ave	Econ	SR	5w	10
First-class	41	6421	3651	129	6/67	10/129	28.30	3.41	49.7	3	1
List A	12	420	344	16	3/14	3/14	21.50	4.91	26.2	0	0
T20s	34	643	904	35	3/15	3/15	25.82	8.43	18.3	0	0

JACK PLOM

LHB / RFM / R0 / W0

FULL NAME: Jack Henry Plom
BORN: August 27, 1999, Basildon, Essex
SQUAD NO: 77
HEIGHT: 6ft 3in
NICKNAME: Plommy
EDUCATION: Gable Hall School, Corringham; South Essex College, Southend-on-Sea
TEAMS: Essex
ROLE: Bowler
DEBUT: First-class: 2018

FAVOURITE CRICKET BAT? Chase Platinum – you just know once it hits the middle it will go
WHICH BOWLER WOULD YOU LEAST LIKE TO FACE? Adam Milne – if he hits you anywhere in the body it's going to leave a nice bruise
WHO WOULD YOU ASK TO BAT FOR YOUR LIFE? Alastair Cook – best England batsman of all time
WHICH RULE WOULD YOU CHANGE ABOUT CRICKET? In T20, allow a 'last-man-stands' rule so that the not-out batsman can bat on his own
WHAT WILL YOU BE DOING IN THE YEAR 2040? I'll probably be working a nine-to-five job, although hopefully not
WHICH BOOK MEANS MOST TO YOU? Thinking Out Loud – Love, Grief and Being Mum and Dad by Rio Ferdinand
NOTES: The 19-year-old seamer signed his first professional contract in October 2018. He said: "I've now been on three England U19 tours which was really good for my development, and I want to crack on from that and progress further as a player with Essex"

Batting	Mat	Inns	NO	Runs	HS	Ave	SR	100	50	Ct	St
First-class	1	-	-	-	-	-	-	-	-	-	-
Bowling	**Mat**	**Balls**	**Runs**	**Wkts**	**BBI**	**BBM**	**Ave**	**Econ**	**SR**	**5w**	**10**
First-class	1	-	-	-	-	-	-	-	-	-	-

LIAM PLUNKETT RHB / RFM / R0 / W3

FULL NAME: Liam Edward Plunkett
BORN: April 6, 1985, Middlesbrough
SQUAD NO: 28
HEIGHT: 6ft 3in
NICKNAME: Pudsy
EDUCATION: Nunthorpe Comprehensive School; Teesside Tertiary College
TEAMS: England, Surrey, Delhi Daredevils, Dolphins, Durham, Melbourne Stars, Sylhet Sixers, Yorkshire
ROLE: Bowler
DEBUT: Test: 2005; ODI: 2005; T20I: 2006; First-class: 2003; List A: 2003; T20: 2003

BEST BATTING: 126 Yorkshire vs Hampshire, Headingley, 2016
BEST BOWLING: 6-33 Durham vs Leeds/Bradford MCCU, Headingley, 2013
COUNTY CAP: 2013 (Yorkshire)

TWITTER: @Liam628
NOTES: The England fast bowler signed a three-year contract with Surrey last year after six years at Yorkshire. Plunkett is only the second player to record a five-wicket haul on his Championship debut for Durham in 2003 and he made his England Test debut two years later. He signed for Yorkshire in 2012 and in 2014 played his first Test for seven years, picking up 18 wickets in four Tests before injury ended his summer. He has not played a Test since but continues to be a regular in England's limited-overs teams. Niggling injuries and international duty have severely limited Plunkett's county appearances – he has played two Championship matches since 2016 – and Surrey are likely to see little of him until the World Cup ends in July

Batting	Mat	Inns	NO	Runs	HS	Ave	SR	100	50	Ct	St
Tests	13	20	5	238	55*	15.86	46.75	0	1	3	0
ODIs	78	45	15	584	56	19.46	99.31	0	1	25	0
T20Is	22	11	4	42	18	6.00	123.52	0	0	7	0
First-class	155	213	39	4376	126	25.14	54.57	3	22	86	0
List A	200	124	45	1586	72	20.07	100.69	0	3	61	0
T20s	146	87	34	777	41	14.66	131.25	0	0	39	0
Bowling	**Mat**	**Balls**	**Runs**	**Wkts**	**BBI**	**BBM**	**Ave**	**Econ**	**SR**	**5w**	**10**
Tests	13	2659	1536	41	5/64	9/176	37.46	3.46	64.8	1	0
ODIs	78	3627	3557	116	5/52	5/52	30.66	5.88	31.2	1	0
T20Is	22	476	627	25	3/21	3/21	25.08	7.90	19.0	0	0
First-class	155	23711	14273	452	6/33	11/119	31.57	3.61	52.4	11	1
List A	200	8574	7912	257	5/52	5/52	30.78	5.53	33.3	1	0
T20s	146	2782	3723	136	5/31	5/31	27.37	8.02	20.4	1	0

HARRY PODMORE RHB / RMF / R0 / W0 / MVP100

FULL NAME: Harry William Podmore
BORN: July 23, 1994, Hammersmith, Middlesex
SQUAD NO: 1
HEIGHT: 6ft 3in
NICKNAME: Podders, Pods, Pongo, Chav
EDUCATION: Twyford CE High School, London
TEAMS: Kent, Derbyshire, Glamorgan, Middlesex
ROLE: Bowler
DEBUT: First-class: 2016; List A: 2014; T20: 2014

BEST BATTING: 66* Derbyshire vs Sussex, Hove, 2017
BEST BOWLING: 6-36 Kent vs Middlesex, Canterbury, 2018

WHAT GOT YOU INTO CRICKET? Ealing CC, London
STRANGEST THING SEEN IN A GAME? Ryan Higgins hit a bird out of the sky
'ROY OF THE ROVERS' MOMENT? Playing at Lord's for the first time (on TV!)
SUPERSTITIONS? The volume has to be on 23 on any electrical device
CRICKETING HERO? Ian Botham
SURPRISING FACT? I have my family crest tattooed on my chest
TWITTER: @harrypod16
NOTES: The 24-year-old seam bowler came through the Middlesex youth system and spent four years at Lord's before signing for Kent ahead of last season in a bid for more first-team opportunities. He seized his opportunity with 43 Championship wickets at an average of 23.30 to help take Kent into Division One. It included a career-best of 6-36 against his old club at Canterbury. Podmore also served notice of his batting potential with a hundred for the Second XI. In November he signed a new three-year deal with Kent. "Harry has fitted into the squad brilliantly both on and off the pitch," said director of cricket Paul Downton. "His capabilities with both bat and ball are there for all to see"

Batting	Mat	Inns	NO	Runs	HS	Ave	SR	100	50	Ct	St
First-class	27	40	11	494	66*	17.03	44.26	0	2	6	0
List A	10	3	2	8	6*	8.00	100.00	0	0	1	0
T20s	21	8	3	32	9	6.40	57.14	0	0	9	0
Bowling	**Mat**	**Balls**	**Runs**	**Wkts**	**BBI**	**BBM**	**Ave**	**Econ**	**SR**	**5w**	**10**
First-class	27	3815	2005	76	6/36	8/110	26.38	3.15	50.1	1	0
List A	10	440	499	10	4/57	4/57	49.90	6.80	44.0	0	0
T20s	21	367	572	18	3/13	3/13	31.77	9.35	20.3	0	0

ED POLLOCK

LHB / OB / R0 / W0 /

FULL NAME: Edward John Pollock
BORN: July 10, 1995, High Wycombe, Buckinghamshire
SQUAD NO: 28
HEIGHT: 5ft 10in
EDUCATION: Royal Grammar School, Worcester; Shrewsbury School; Durham University
TEAMS: Warwickshire
ROLE: Batsman
DEBUT: First-class: 2015; List A: 2018; T20: 2017

BEST BATTING: 52 Durham MCCU vs Gloucestershire, Bristol, 2017

FAMILY TIES? My dad and brother have both captained Cambridge University
WHAT WAS YOUR FIRST CRICKET CLUB? Barnt Green CC, Worcestershire. Andy and Grant Flower have both played for the club
FAVOURITE CRICKET BAT? My first: a Hunts County size three-quarters. Still have it at home
WHICH BOWLER WOULD YOU LEAST LIKE TO FACE? Jeetan Patel
BEST INNINGS YOU'VE SEEN? Brian Lara's 400 not out
WHO WOULD YOU ASK TO BAT FOR YOUR LIFE? Me – no one else would have such a big incentive not to get myself out as me
WHICH RULE WOULD YOU CHANGE ABOUT CRICKET? Hitting the ball out the ground should be worth 10 runs
YOUR BIGGEST CRICKETING REGRET? Letting my bowling decline
SURPRISING FACT ABOUT YOU? I am a published poet
TWITTER: @kcollopde

Batting	Mat	Inns	NO	Runs	HS	Ave	SR	100	50	Ct	St
First-class	5	7	1	184	52	30.66	50.13	0	1	1	0
List A	9	7	0	174	56	24.85	155.35	0	1	2	0
T20s	23	23	0	534	66	23.21	179.79	0	3	6	0
Bowling	**Mat**	**Balls**	**Runs**	**Wkts**	**BBI**	**BBM**	**Ave**	**Econ**	**SR**	**5w**	**10**
First-class	5	-	-	-	-	-	-	-	-	-	-
List A	9	-	-	-	-	-	-	-	-	-	-
T20s	23	-	-	-	-	-	-	-	-	-	-

OLLIE POPE RHB / WK / R1 / W0 / MVP67

FULL NAME: Oliver John Douglas Pope
BORN: January 2, 1998, Chelsea, London
SQUAD NO: 32
HEIGHT: 5ft 10in
NICKNAME: Pope-dog
EDUCATION: Cranleigh School, Surrey
TEAMS: England, Surrey
ROLE: Batsman/wicketkeeper
DEBUT: Test: 2018; First-class: 2017; List A: 2016; T20: 2017

BEST BATTING: 158* Surrey vs Yorkshire, The Oval, 2018

WHAT WAS YOUR FIRST CRICKET CLUB? Grayshott CC, Hampshire
FAVOURITE CRICKET BAT? GM Noir – the stickers are flair
CRICKETING HERO? My former teammate Kumar Sangakkara – he just didn't stop scoring runs and was amazing to watch
WHICH BOWLER WOULD YOU LEAST LIKE TO FACE? Morne Morkel
BEST INNINGS YOU'VE SEEN? Aaron Finch's hundred against Middlesex in last season's T20 Blast. Made the boundaries look 30 yards away
WHO WOULD YOU ASK TO BAT FOR YOUR LIFE? Rory Burns
WHICH RULE WOULD YOU CHANGE ABOUT CRICKET? First ball: free hit
SURPRISING FACT ABOUT A TEAMMATE? Sam Curran is a useless footballer
FAVOURITE QUOTE OR SAYING? Alright my son
TWITTER: @opope32

Batting	Mat	Inns	NO	Runs	HS	Ave	SR	100	50	Ct	St
Tests	2	3	0	54	28	18.00	54.54	0	0	2	0
First-class	25	37	6	1481	158*	47.77	61.73	5	4	33	0
List A	25	22	5	666	93*	39.17	80.72	0	5	6	0
T20s	24	22	6	434	46	27.12	135.20	0	0	7	0
Bowling	**Mat**	**Balls**	**Runs**	**Wkts**	**BBI**	**BBM**	**Ave**	**Econ**	**SR**	**5w**	**10**
Tests	2	-	-	-	-	-	-	-	-	-	-
First-class	25	-	-	-	-	-	-	-	-	-	-
List A	25	-	-	-	-	-	-	-	-	-	-
T20s	24	-	-	-	-	-	-	-	-	-	-

JAMIE PORTER RHB / RMF / R0 / W4 / MVP34

FULL NAME: James Alexander Porter
BORN: May 25, 1993, Leytonstone, Essex
SQUAD NO: 44
HEIGHT: 6ft 1in
NICKNAME: Ports
EDUCATION: Oaks Park High School, Ilford; Epping Forest College, Essex
TEAMS: Essex, England Lions
ROLE: Bowler
DEBUT: First-class: 2014; List A: 2015; T20: 2017

BEST BATTING: 34 Essex vs Glamorgan, Cardiff, 2015
BEST BOWLING: 7-41 Essex vs Worcestershire, Chelmsford, 2018
COUNTY CAP: 2015

WHAT WAS YOUR FIRST CRICKET CLUB? Chingford CC, London
FAVOURITE CRICKET BAT? New Balance TC 1260 – makes me bat like Mark Wood
BEST INNINGS YOU'VE SEEN? Dan Lawrence's 161 against Surrey in 2015. It was only his second first-class match and Surrey were coming at him hard, but he got the last laugh
WHO WOULD YOU ASK TO BAT FOR YOUR LIFE? Nick Browne – he has a better defence than Rahul Dravid
WHICH RULE WOULD YOU CHANGE ABOUT CRICKET? Three misses and you're out
YOUR BIGGEST CRICKETING REGRET? Not being a better batsman
WHAT WILL YOU BE DOING IN THE YEAR 2040? I'll be telling the kids how tough we were back in my day
FAVOURITE QUOTE OR SAYING? Top of off with an occasional bumper
WHICH BOOK MEANS MOST TO YOU? The Cat in the Hat by Dr. Seuss
TWITTER: @jamieporter93

Batting	Mat	Inns	NO	Runs	HS	Ave	SR	100	50	Ct	St
First-class	69	81	29	325	34	6.25	26.20	0	0	21	0
List A	25	9	5	21	6	5.25	43.75	0	0	3	0
T20s	15	5	4	5	1*	5.00	71.42	0	0	4	0
Bowling	**Mat**	**Balls**	**Runs**	**Wkts**	**BBI**	**BBM**	**Ave**	**Econ**	**SR**	**5w**	**10**
First-class	69	11759	6625	276	7/41	12/95	24.00	3.38	42.6	10	2
List A	25	1078	941	29	4/29	4/29	32.44	5.23	37.1	0	0
T20s	15	248	354	9	4/20	4/20	39.33	8.56	27.5	0	0

MATTY POTTS

RHB / RFM / R0 / W0

FULL NAME: Matthew James Potts
BORN: October 29, 1998, Sunderland, County Durham
SQUAD NO: 35
HEIGHT: 6ft 2in
NICKNAME: Harry, Junior, Pottsy
EDUCATION: St Robert of Newminster Catholic School, Sunderland
TEAMS: Durham
ROLE: Allrounder
DEBUT: First-class: 2017; List A: 2018

BEST BATTING: 53* Durham vs Derbyshire, Chester-le-Street, 2017
BEST BOWLING: 3-48 Durham vs Glamorgan, Chester-le-Street, 2017

WHAT WAS YOUR FIRST CRICKET CLUB? Philadelphia CC, Tyne and Wear
CRICKETING HERO? Kevin Pietersen
WHICH BOWLER WOULD YOU LEAST LIKE TO FACE? Shoaib Akhtar
BEST INNINGS YOU'VE SEEN? Ben Stokes's double hundred against South Africa in the 2016 Cape Town Test
WHO WOULD YOU ASK TO BAT FOR YOUR LIFE? The Great Wall of (Matt) Salisbury
WHICH RULE WOULD YOU CHANGE ABOUT CRICKET? DRS: if it's hitting the stumps, it's out
YOUR BIGGEST CRICKETING REGRET? Bottling a double hundred playing a reverse-sweep
WHICH BOOK MEANS MOST TO YOU? Brave Two Zero – The Harrowing True Story of a Special Forces Patrol Behind the Lines in Iraq by Andy McNab
TWITTER: @mattyjpotts

Batting	Mat	Inns	NO	Runs	HS	Ave	SR	100	50	Ct	St
First-class	6	8	3	120	53*	24.00	48.78	0	1	0	0
List A	2	2	0	31	30	15.50	62.00	0	0	1	0
Bowling	**Mat**	**Balls**	**Runs**	**Wkts**	**BBI**	**BBM**	**Ave**	**Econ**	**SR**	**5w**	**10**
First-class	6	1008	502	15	3/48	5/106	33.46	2.98	67.2	0	0
List A	2	60	83	3	3/69	3/69	27.66	8.30	20.0	0	0

STUART POYNTER RHB / WK / R0 / W0

FULL NAME: Stuart William Poynter
BORN: October 18, 1990, Hammersmith, London
SQUAD NO: 90
HEIGHT: 5ft 8in
NICKNAME: Stuey, Points
EDUCATION: Teddington School, London
TEAMS: Ireland, Durham, Middlesex, Warwickshire
ROLE: Wicketkeeper
DEBUT: ODI: 2014; T20I: 2015; First-class: 2010; List A: 2012; T20: 2015

BEST BATTING: 170 Durham vs Derbyshire, Derby, 2018

FAMILY TIES? My uncle Deryck and brother Andrew both played for Ireland
BEST ADVICE EVER RECEIVED? Play with a smile on your face
'ROY OF THE ROVERS' MOMENT? Making my debut for Ireland
BEST THING ABOUT YOUR HOME GROUND? Playing T20 under the lights at the Riverside
IF YOU WEREN'T A CRICKETER? I'd be working at Tesco
SURPRISING FACT ABOUT YOU? I'm a massive Westlife fan and play the ukulele
SURPRISING FACT ABOUT A TEAMMATE? Graham Clark is a massive Westlife fan too
WHERE IS PARADISE? At home on the sofa with my family watching Harry Potter
CRICKETING HERO? Jack Russell – the best keeper I have ever seen and one of the first I saw standing up to pace bowling
TWITTER: @spoynter_90

Batting	Mat	Inns	NO	Runs	HS	Ave	SR	100	50	Ct	St
ODIs	21	19	5	185	36	13.21	66.54	0	0	22	1
T20Is	25	21	6	240	39	16.00	112.67	0	0	13	2
First-class	36	56	2	1281	170	23.72	64.63	2	3	103	3
List A	47	40	9	581	109	18.74	85.94	1	0	42	3
T20s	55	42	17	643	61*	25.72	125.09	0	1	34	8
Bowling	**Mat**	**Balls**	**Runs**	**Wkts**	**BBI**	**BBM**	**Ave**	**Econ**	**SR**	**5w**	**10**
ODIs	21	-	-	-	-	-	-	-	-	-	-
T20Is	25	-	-	-	-	-	-	-	-	-	-
First-class	36	-	-	-	-	-	-	-	-	-	-
List A	47	-	-	-	-	-	-	-	-	-	-
T20s	55	-	-	-	-	-	-	-	-	-	-

JOSH POYSDEN LHB / LB / R0 / W0

FULL NAME: Joshua Edward Poysden
BORN: August 8, 1991, Shoreham-by-Sea, Sussex
SQUAD NO: 14
HEIGHT: 5ft 10in
NICKNAME: Dobby, Bendicii
EDUCATION: Cardinal Newman School, Hove; Anglia Ruskin University
TEAMS: Yorkshire, England Lions, Warwickshire
ROLE: Bowler
DEBUT: First-class: 2011; List A: 2013; T20: 2014

BEST BATTING: 47 Cambridge MCCU vs Surrey, Cambridge, 2011
BEST BOWLING: 5-29 Warwickshire vs Glamorgan, Edgbaston, 2018

WHAT WAS YOUR FIRST CRICKET CLUB? Brighton and Hove CC, coached by the great man Dick Roberts
CRICKETING HERO? Shane Warne
BEST INNINGS YOU'VE SEEN? Brendon McCullum's 158 not out off 64 balls for Warwickshire against Derbyshire at Edgbaston in the 2015 T20 Blast
WHICH RULE WOULD YOU CHANGE ABOUT CRICKET? Set a minimum temperature that it is acceptable to play at
YOUR BIGGEST CRICKETING REGRET? Deciding to bat left-handed
SURPRISING FACT ABOUT YOU? I have a mild obsession with sausage dogs – I can't walk past one in the street without stroking it, and one day I hope to have one called Frank
WHICH BOOK MEANS MOST TO YOU? The Alchemist by Paulo Coelho
ODDEST SPORT YOU'VE PLAYED? Golf at a military base in Sri Lanka
TWITTER: @JoshPoysden14

Batting	Mat	Inns	NO	Runs	HS	Ave	SR	100	50	Ct	St
First-class	14	14	4	96	47	9.60	36.22	0	0	2	0
List A	24	12	5	33	10*	4.71	60.00	0	0	7	0
T20s	26	10	8	13	9*	6.50	118.18	0	0	6	0
Bowling	**Mat**	**Balls**	**Runs**	**Wkts**	**BBI**	**BBM**	**Ave**	**Econ**	**SR**	**5w**	**10**
First-class	14	1549	1084	33	5/29	8/133	32.84	4.19	46.9	2	0
List A	24	951	945	24	3/33	3/33	39.37	5.96	39.6	0	0
T20s	26	474	590	20	4/51	4/51	29.50	7.46	23.7	0	0

RYAN PRINGLE RHB / OB / R0 / W0

FULL NAME: Ryan David Pringle
BORN: April 17, 1992, Sunderland
SQUAD NO: 17
HEIGHT: 6ft 1in
NICKNAME: Rhino
EDUCATION: Hetton Comprehensive School, Sunderland; Durham Sixth Form Centre; University of Sunderland
TEAMS: Durham
ROLE: Allrounder
DEBUT: First-class: 2014; List A: 2012; T20: 2013

BEST BATTING: 99 Durham vs Hampshire, Chester-le-Street, 2015
BEST BOWLING: 7-107 Durham vs Hampshire, Southampton, 2016

FAVOURITE CRICKET BAT? I love all my Kippax bats equally
WHICH BOWLER WOULD YOU LEAST LIKE TO FACE? Graham Clark – he's a genius
BEST INNINGS YOU'VE SEEN? No.11 Ben Whitehead blocking out for a draw in the 2018 Second XI final to secure the Championship for Durham
WHO WOULD YOU ASK TO BAT FOR YOUR LIFE? Ben Whitehead
WHICH RULE WOULD YOU CHANGE ABOUT CRICKET? A no-ball should be a free hit in any format
YOUR BIGGEST CRICKETING REGRET? Not being a left-handed batter
SURPRISING FACT ABOUT YOU? I've never seen Titanic
WHAT WILL YOU BE DOING IN THE YEAR 2040? Hopefully another Cricketers' Who's Who questionnaire
FAVOURITE QUOTE OR SAYING? Fours and sixes, no risks
TWITTER: @RyanPringle

Batting	Mat	Inns	NO	Runs	HS	Ave	SR	100	50	Ct	St
First-class	37	58	8	1292	99	25.84	52.75	0	8	22	0
List A	40	31	0	492	125	15.87	101.44	1	0	12	0
T20s	70	49	6	463	35	10.76	120.25	0	0	24	0
Bowling	**Mat**	**Balls**	**Runs**	**Wkts**	**BBI**	**BBM**	**Ave**	**Econ**	**SR**	**5w**	**10**
First-class	37	3902	2360	61	7/107	10/260	38.68	3.62	63.9	2	1
List A	40	987	919	14	2/39	2/39	65.64	5.58	70.5	0	0
T20s	70	744	1061	29	3/30	3/30	36.58	8.55	25.6	0	0

LUKE PROCTER LHB / RMF / R0 / W0

FULL NAME: Luke Anthony Procter
BORN: June 24, 1988, Oldham, Lancashire
SQUAD NO: 2
HEIGHT: 5ft 11in
NICKNAME: Proccy
EDUCATION: Counthill School, Oldham
TEAMS: Northamptonshire, Lancashire
ROLE: Allrounder
DEBUT: First-class: 2010; List A: 2009; T20: 2011

BEST BATTING: 137 Lancashire vs Hampshire, Old Trafford, 2016
BEST BOWLING: 7-71 Lancashire vs Surrey, Liverpool, 2012

BEST ADVICE EVER RECEIVED? Never settle for second-best
'ROY OF THE ROVERS' MOMENT? Winning the County Championship in 2011
IF YOU WEREN'T A CRICKETER? I'd be single and on the dole
SURPRISING FACT ABOUT YOU? I'm a level-two umpire
WHERE IS PARADISE? Oldham
CRICKETING HERO? Shivnarine Chanderpaul
TWITTER: @vvsprocter
NOTES: The 30-year-old allrounder was part of the Lancashire side that won the Championship back in 2011. He joined Northamptonshire on a three-year contract at the end of 2017, having struggled to hold down a first-team spot at Old Trafford. He made 124 appearances for Lancashire in all competitions. Procter scored 442 runs and took 14 wickets in 10 Championship matches last summer. He played six games in the One-Day Cup and six in the T20 Blast without making any serious impact with bat or ball

Batting	Mat	Inns	NO	Runs	HS	Ave	SR	100	50	Ct	St
First-class	79	126	7	3549	137	29.82	43.56	3	20	19	0
List A	37	27	7	535	97	26.75	85.73	0	4	4	0
T20s	31	18	6	170	25*	14.16	98.83	0	0	10	0
Bowling	**Mat**	**Balls**	**Runs**	**Wkts**	**BBI**	**BBM**	**Ave**	**Econ**	**SR**	**5w**	**10**
First-class	79	5359	3097	89	7/71	8/79	34.79	3.46	60.2	3	0
List A	37	732	746	18	3/29	3/29	41.44	6.11	40.6	0	0
T20s	31	230	364	12	3/22	3/22	30.33	9.49	19.1	0	0

HAMIDULLAH QADRI RHB / OB / R0 / W0

FULL NAME: Hamidullah Qadri
BORN: December 5, 2000, Kandahar, Afghanistan
SQUAD NO: 75
HEIGHT: 5ft 5in
NICKNAME: Hammy
EDUCATION: Chellaston Academy, Derby; Derby Moor Academy
TEAMS: Derbyshire
ROLE: Bowler
DEBUT: First-class: 2017; List A: 2017; T20: 2017

BEST BATTING: 15* Derbyshire vs Kent, Derby, 2018
BEST BOWLING: 5-60 Derbyshire vs Glamorgan, Cardiff, 2017

WHAT WAS YOUR FIRST CRICKET CLUB? Alvaston & Boulton CC, Derbyshire
CRICKETING HERO? Saqlain Mushtaq – inventor of the doosra
BEST ADVICE EVER RECEIVED? Keep practising until you get it right
WHICH BOWLER WOULD YOU LEAST LIKE TO FACE? Mitchell Starc
BEST INNINGS YOU'VE SEEN? Kevin Pietersen's 186 in Mumbai in 2012
WHO WOULD YOU ASK TO BAT FOR YOUR LIFE? Virat Kohli
WHICH RULE WOULD YOU CHANGE ABOUT CRICKET? Hitting the ball out the ground should be worth eight runs
SURPRISING FACT ABOUT YOU? I learnt the art of off-spin by watching YouTube clips
ODDEST SPORT YOU'VE PLAYED? Rugby
TWITTER: @Hamid_Qadri2000

Batting	Mat	Inns	NO	Runs	HS	Ave	SR	100	50	Ct	St
First-class	7	14	6	53	15*	6.62	30.11	0	0	4	0
List A	3	1	0	4	4	4.00	50.00	0	0	1	0
T20s	1	-	-	-	-	-	-	-	-	0	0
Bowling	**Mat**	**Balls**	**Runs**	**Wkts**	**BBI**	**BBM**	**Ave**	**Econ**	**SR**	**5w**	**10**
First-class	7	1078	607	18	5/60	6/76	33.72	3.37	59.8	1	0
List A	3	61	61	1	1/31	1/31	61.00	6.00	61.0	0	0
T20s	1	6	12	0	-	-	-	12.00	-	0	0

IMRAN QAYYUM RHB / SLA / R0 / W0

FULL NAME: Imran Qayyum
BORN: May 23, 1993, Ealing, London
SQUAD NO: 11
HEIGHT: 5ft 11in
NICKNAME: Imy, IQ
EDUCATION: Villiers High School, Ealing; Greenford High School, Ealing; City University of London
TEAMS: Kent
ROLE: Bowler
DEBUT: First-class: 2016; List A: 2017; T20: 2017

BEST BATTING: 39 Kent vs Leicestershire, Canterbury, 2017
BEST BOWLING: 3-158 Kent vs Northamptonshire, Northampton, 2016

FAMILY TIES? Dad played in Pakistan, my brother plays club cricket in Hertfordshire
BEST ADVICE EVER RECEIVED? Try coffee
'ROY OF THE ROVERS' MOMENT? Playing alongside Geraint Jones
BEST THING ABOUT YOUR HOME GROUND? It's less than a mile away from my bed
IF YOU WEREN'T A CRICKETER? I'd be a finance analyst
SURPRISING FACT ABOUT YOU? I talk in my sleep
SURPRISING FACT ABOUT A TEAMMATE? Ivan Thomas eats two dinners every night
WHERE IS PARADISE? Heaven
CRICKETING HERO? Virat Kohli
NON-CRICKETING HERO? J Hus – check out the track 'Spirit'
TWITTER: @ImranQC

Batting	Mat	Inns	NO	Runs	HS	Ave	SR	100	50	Ct	St
First-class	5	7	2	40	39	8.00	42.55	0	0	3	0
List A	19	12	4	53	18	6.62	60.22	0	0	5	0
T20s	23	3	1	27	21*	13.50	150.00	0	0	6	0
Bowling	**Mat**	**Balls**	**Runs**	**Wkts**	**BBI**	**BBM**	**Ave**	**Econ**	**SR**	**5w**	**10**
First-class	5	775	481	12	3/158	3/46	40.08	3.72	64.5	0	0
List A	19	972	812	20	4/33	4/33	40.60	5.01	48.6	0	0
T20s	23	397	570	17	3/40	3/40	33.52	8.61	23.3	0	0

MATT QUINN RHB / RMF / R0 / W0

FULL NAME: Matthew Richard Quinn
BORN: February 28, 1993, Auckland, New Zealand
SQUAD NO: 94
HEIGHT: 6ft 5in
NICKNAME: Quinny
EDUCATION: Sacred Heart College, Auckland; Auckland University of Technology
TEAMS: Essex, Auckland
ROLE: Bowler
DEBUT: First-class: 2013; List A: 2013; T20: 2012

BEST BATTING: 50 Auckland vs Canterbury, Auckland, 2013
BEST BOWLING: 7-76 Essex vs Gloucestershire, Cheltenham, 2016

FAMILY TIES? My great grandad played social cricket in Yorkshire
WHAT WAS YOUR FIRST CRICKET CLUB? Cornwall CC, Auckland – the largest cricket club in New Zealand
FAVOURITE CRICKET BAT? A Slazenger V100 – the first hard-ball bat I had
CRICKETING HERO? Martin Crowe – a fantastic cricketer and even better man
WHICH BOWLER WOULD YOU LEAST LIKE TO FACE? Lockie Ferguson – because he's gas
BEST INNINGS YOU'VE SEEN? Colin Munro scoring 281 from 167 balls for Auckland at Napier in 2015 – including 23 sixes, a record for a first-class innings
WHO WOULD YOU ASK TO BAT FOR YOUR LIFE? Jeet Raval – he has so much patience
WHICH RULE WOULD YOU CHANGE ABOUT CRICKET? The one which says you can only have two fielders behind square on the leg side
SURPRISING FACT ABOUT YOU? I was once attacked by a goose
ODDEST SPORT YOU'VE PLAYED? Nashball
TWITTER: @quinny_cricket

Batting	Mat	Inns	NO	Runs	HS	Ave	SR	100	50	Ct	St
First-class	30	39	9	324	50	10.80	53.64	0	1	5	0
List A	32	18	11	124	36	17.71	72.94	0	0	3	0
T20s	53	10	9	27	8*	27.00	117.39	0	0	11	0
Bowling	**Mat**	**Balls**	**Runs**	**Wkts**	**BBI**	**BBM**	**Ave**	**Econ**	**SR**	**5w**	**10**
First-class	30	5784	3175	113	7/76	11/163	28.09	3.29	51.1	1	1
List A	32	1606	1538	44	4/71	4/71	34.95	5.74	36.5	0	0
T20s	53	1037	1543	54	4/20	4/20	28.57	8.92	19.2	0	0

BEN RAINE LHB / RMF / R0 / W2 / MVP7

FULL NAME: Benjamin Alexander Raine
BORN: September 14, 1991, Sunderland
SQUAD NO: 44
HEIGHT: 6ft
NICKNAME: Ranger, Reindeer, Slush Puppy
EDUCATION: St Aidan's Catholic Academy, Sunderland
TEAMS: Durham, Leicestershire
ROLE: Bowler
DEBUT: First-class: 2011; List A: 2011; T20: 2014

BEST BATTING: 72 Leicestershire vs Lancashire, Old Trafford, 2013
BEST BOWLING: 6-66 Leicestershire vs Nottinghamshire, Leicester, 2017

WHAT WAS YOUR FIRST CRICKET CLUB? Murton CC, County Durham. They drew lots for the batting order in the second team and as a nine-year-old I drew No.4 so that's where I batted
WHICH BOWLER WOULD YOU LEAST LIKE TO FACE? Darren Stevens – he blows my front pad off every year
BEST INNINGS YOU'VE SEEN? Charlie Shreck's maiden fifty in the 2014 Championship match between Surrey and Leicestershire. He bludgeoned it all around The Oval. It delayed our departure from London until the rush hour but was worth every second of traffic
WHO WOULD YOU ASK TO BAT FOR YOUR LIFE? Charlie Schreck
YOUR BIGGEST CRICKETING REGRET? Taking far too long to realise that it doesn't really matter if I have a bad game
FAVOURITE QUOTE OR SAYING? Grab your spuds and give it a crack
ODDEST SPORT YOU'VE PLAYED? Really weird sports exist only in posh schools which sadly I missed out on
TWITTER: @BenRaine88

Batting	Mat	Inns	NO	Runs	HS	Ave	SR	100	50	Ct	St
First-class	64	105	9	1979	72	20.61	49.61	0	8	15	0
List A	20	16	0	330	83	20.62	112.24	0	1	5	0
T20s	51	38	9	665	113	22.93	137.11	1	1	13	0
Bowling	**Mat**	**Balls**	**Runs**	**Wkts**	**BBI**	**BBM**	**Ave**	**Econ**	**SR**	**5w**	**10**
First-class	64	10944	5741	207	6/66	8/107	27.73	3.14	52.8	5	0
List A	20	940	941	20	3/31	3/31	47.05	6.00	47.0	0	0
T20s	51	987	1487	54	3/7	3/7	27.53	9.03	18.2	0	0

RAVI RAMPAUL LHB / RFM / R0 / W0

FULL NAME: Ravindranath Rampaul
BORN: October 15, 1984, Preysal, Trinidad
SQUAD NO: 41
NICKNAME: Frisco Kid
EDUCATION: Presentation College, Trinidad
TEAMS: West Indies, Ireland, Derbyshire, Barbados Tridents, Royal Challengers Bangalore, Surrey, Trinidad & Tobago
ROLE: Bowler
DEBUT: Test: 2009; ODI: 2003; T20I: 2007; First-class: 2002; List A: 2003; T20: 2007

BEST BATTING: 64* West Indies A vs Sri Lanka A, Basseterre, 2006
BEST BOWLING: 7-51 Trinidad & Tobago vs Barbados, Point-a-Pierre, 2007

TWITTER: @RaviRampaul14
NOTES: Veteran West Indies seamer who joined Derbyshire in October 2017 after spending two seasons at Surrey as a Kolpak player. Rampaul is available to play in all formats, adding consistency and experience to the county's seam attack. He struggled with the red ball last season, taking 13 wickets in eight matches, but was more impressive in the shorter formats and was Derbyshire's joint-top wicket-taker in the One-Day Cup. Rampaul made his international debut in 2003 and last played for West Indies in 2015

Batting	Mat	Inns	NO	Runs	HS	Ave	SR	100	50	Ct	St
Tests	18	31	8	335	40*	14.56	53.25	0	0	3	0
ODIs	92	40	11	362	86*	12.48	76.69	0	1	14	0
T20Is	23	6	5	12	8	12.00	57.14	0	0	2	0
First-class	79	116	28	1131	64*	12.85	53.75	0	2	23	0
List A	183	87	31	637	86*	11.37	77.03	0	1	32	0
T20s	139	43	25	173	23*	9.61	103.59	0	0	25	0
Bowling	**Mat**	**Balls**	**Runs**	**Wkts**	**BBI**	**BBM**	**Ave**	**Econ**	**SR**	**5w**	**10**
Tests	18	3440	1705	49	4/48	7/75	34.79	2.97	70.2	0	0
ODIs	92	4033	3434	117	5/49	5/49	29.35	5.10	34.4	2	0
T20Is	23	497	705	29	3/16	3/16	24.31	8.51	17.1	0	0
First-class	79	12442	6980	225	7/51	11/125	31.02	3.36	55.2	9	1
List A	183	8318	6768	277	5/48	5/48	24.43	4.88	30.0	3	0
T20s	139	2950	3773	169	5/9	5/9	22.32	7.67	17.4	1	0

ADIL RASHID

RHB / LB / R0 / W2

FULL NAME: Adil Usman Rashid
BORN: February 17, 1988, Bradford, Yorkshire
SQUAD NO: 3
HEIGHT: 5ft 8in
NICKNAME: Dilly, Dilo, Rash
EDUCATION: Heaton School, Bradford; Bellevue Sixth Form College, Bradford
TEAMS: England, Yorkshire, Adelaide Strikers, Dhaka Dynamites, South Australia
ROLE: Allrounder
DEBUT: Test: 2015; ODI: 2009; T20I: 2009; First-class: 2006; List A: 2006; T20: 2008

BEST BATTING: 180 Yorkshire vs Somerset, Headingley, 2013
BEST BOWLING: 7-107 Yorkshire vs Hampshire, Southampton, 2008
COUNTY CAP: 2008

CRICKETING HEROES? Sachin Tendulkar, Shane Warne
NON-CRICKETING HERO? Muhammad Ali
IF YOU WEREN'T A CRICKETER? I'd be a taxi driver
SURPRISING FACT? I have a big FIFA (video game) rivalry with Moeen Ali
TWITTER: @AdilRashid03
NOTES: Rashid agreed a deal to play only white-ball cricket in 2018 but in September he signed a one-year contract to play in all formats of the game after regaining his place in the England Test team. Yorkshire director of cricket Martyn Moxon said: "For now, it will just be for a year because it's still not clear what career path he's going to take. He's back in the Test team and continues to do well, so we'll see where that takes us"

Batting	Mat	Inns	NO	Runs	HS	Ave	SR	100	50	Ct	St
Tests	19	33	5	540	61	19.28	42.51	0	2	4	0
ODIs	83	36	9	529	69	19.59	100.57	0	1	25	0
T20Is	36	14	8	47	9*	7.83	85.45	0	0	10	0
First-class	175	251	41	6822	180	32.48	52.65	10	37	79	0
List A	198	116	33	1626	71	19.59	90.23	0	2	63	0
T20s	163	85	32	682	36*	12.86	105.24	0	0	47	0
Bowling	**Mat**	**Balls**	**Runs**	**Wkts**	**BBI**	**BBM**	**Ave**	**Econ**	**SR**	**5w**	**10**
Tests	19	3816	2390	60	5/49	7/178	39.83	3.75	63.6	2	0
ODIs	83	4090	3807	128	5/27	5/27	29.74	5.58	31.9	2	0
T20Is	36	708	863	36	3/11	3/11	23.97	7.31	19.6	0	0
First-class	175	29901	17949	512	7/107	11/114	35.05	3.60	58.4	20	1
List A	198	9063	8177	272	5/27	5/27	30.06	5.41	33.3	3	0
T20s	163	3321	4086	186	4/19	4/19	21.96	7.38	17.8	0	0

DELRAY RAWLINS LHB / SLA / R0 / W0

FULL NAME: Delray Millard Wendell Rawlins
BORN: September 14, 1997, Bermuda
SQUAD NO: 9
HEIGHT: 6ft 2in
NICKNAME: Del
EDUCATION: St Bede's School, East Sussex
TEAMS: Sussex
ROLE: Allrounder
DEBUT: First-class: 2017; List A: 2017; T20: 2018

BEST BATTING: 96 Sussex vs South Africa A, Arundel, 2017
BEST BOWLING: 1-46 Sussex vs Kent, Hove, 2017

WHAT WAS YOUR FIRST CRICKET CLUB? Warwick Workmen's Club, Bermuda. Helped me grow a love for the sport
FAVOURITE CRICKET BAT? Can't remember the brand, but it was given to me by an ex-coach for scoring my first half-century in senior cricket aged about 13. It lasted me a long time
CRICKETING HERO? Brian Lara
WHICH BOWLER WOULD YOU LEAST LIKE TO FACE? Ollie Robinson – he's got all the skills
WHO WOULD YOU ASK TO BAT FOR YOUR LIFE? My dad – because I know he'll keep anything out to keep me alive
SURPRISING FACT ABOUT YOU? I eat pineapple slices out of the tin
WHAT WILL YOU BE DOING IN THE YEAR 2040? Living back in Bermuda, enjoying the sun
FAVOURITE QUOTE OR SAYING? If it's up, it's off
ODDEST SPORT YOU'VE PLAYED? Handball
TWITTER: @Delraw90

Batting	Mat	Inns	NO	Runs	HS	Ave	SR	100	50	Ct	St
First-class	7	12	0	245	96	20.41	42.98	0	2	0	0
List A	6	6	0	133	53	22.16	125.47	0	1	5	0
T20s	9	9	1	203	49	25.37	146.04	0	0	6	0
Bowling	**Mat**	**Balls**	**Runs**	**Wkts**	**BBI**	**BBM**	**Ave**	**Econ**	**SR**	**5w**	**10**
First-class	7	240	161	1	1/46	1/46	161.00	4.02	240.0	0	0
List A	6	162	161	1	1/33	1/33	161.00	5.96	162.0	0	0
T20s	9	-	-	-	-	-	-	-	-	-	-

OLLIE RAYNER RHB / OB / R0 / W1

FULL NAME: Oliver Philip Rayner
BORN: November 1, 1985, Bad Fallingbostel, Lower Saxony, Germany
SQUAD NO: 2
HEIGHT: 6ft 6in
NICKNAME: Draynes, Vaynes, Great Raynes, Ashton Kutcher
EDUCATION: St Bede's School, East Sussex
TEAMS: Middlesex, England Lions, Hampshire, Mid West Rhinos, Sussex
ROLE: Bowler
DEBUT: First-class: 2006; List A: 2006; T20: 2006

BEST BATTING: 143* Middlesex vs Nottinghamshire, Trent Bridge, 2012
BEST BOWLING: 8-46 Middlesex vs Surrey, The Oval, 2013
COUNTY CAP: 2015 (Middlesex)

WHAT WAS YOUR FIRST CRICKET CLUB? Eastbourne CC, East Sussex. Peter Bibby, dirty pint, spoof
FAVOURITE CRICKET BAT? A Duncan Fearnley which was shared round the family for car-park and beach cricket, 20% wood, 80% linseed oil
WHO WOULD YOU ASK TO BAT FOR YOUR LIFE? Nick Compton
WHICH RULE WOULD YOU CHANGE ABOUT CRICKET? No reverse-sweeps allowed
YOUR BIGGEST CRICKETING REGRET? Not bowling left-arm spin
SURPRISING FACT ABOUT YOU? Online gamers call me "the dentist"
SURPRISING FACT ABOUT A TEAMMATE? Tim Murtagh has a bath every morning
FAVOURITE QUOTE OR SAYING? Everything I'm not makes me everything I am (Kanye West)
WHICH BOOK MEANS MOST TO YOU? Harry Potter and the Philosopher's Stone by JK Rowling
TWITTER: @ollie2rayner

Batting	Mat	Inns	NO	Runs	HS	Ave	SR	100	50	Ct	St
First-class	141	187	30	3251	143*	20.70	50.98	2	13	189	0
List A	61	42	19	508	61	22.08	90.07	0	1	32	0
T20s	71	43	16	343	41*	12.70	103.00	0	0	17	0
Bowling	Mat	Balls	Runs	Wkts	BBI	BBM	Ave	Econ	SR	5w	10
First-class	141	21078	9936	298	8/46	15/118	33.34	2.82	70.7	10	1
List A	61	2346	2017	53	4/35	4/35	38.05	5.15	44.2	0	0
T20s	71	1323	1620	41	5/18	5/18	39.51	7.34	32.2	1	0

LUIS REECE

LHB / LM / R0 / W0

FULL NAME: Luis Michael Reece
BORN: August 4, 1990, Taunton
SQUAD NO: 10
HEIGHT: 6ft 1in
NICKNAME: Reecey, Rexy, Red Rum
EDUCATION: St Michael's School; Myerscough College; Leeds Metropolitan University
TEAMS: Derbyshire, Lancashire
ROLE: Allrounder
DEBUT: First-class: 2012; List A: 2011; T20: 2016

BEST BATTING: 168 Derbyshire vs Northamptonshire, Derby, 2017
BEST BOWLING: 7-20 Derbyshire vs Gloucestershire, Derby, 2018

WHAT WAS YOUR FIRST CRICKET CLUB? Vernon Carus CC, Lancashire
CRICKETING HERO? AB de Villiers
WHICH BOWLER WOULD YOU LEAST LIKE TO FACE? Jasprit Bumrah – so hard to pick up
BEST INNINGS YOU'VE SEEN? Kevin Pietersen's 158 against Australia at The Oval in 2005
WHO WOULD YOU ASK TO BAT FOR YOUR LIFE? Shivnarine Chanderpaul
WHICH RULE WOULD YOU CHANGE ABOUT CRICKET? It should be a no-ball if the bowler hits the bails at the non-striker's end with his hand
YOUR BIGGEST CRICKETING REGRET? Breaking my hand
SURPRISING FACT ABOUT YOU? As a kid I played chess at national level
SURPRISING FACT ABOUT A TEAMMATE? Matt Critchley went to the same school as me
FAVOURITE QUOTE OR SAYING? Don't be afraid to change it up
WHICH BOOK MEANS MOST TO YOU? Of Mice and Men by John Steinbeck
TWITTER: @lreece17

Batting	Mat	Inns	NO	Runs	HS	Ave	SR	100	50	Ct	St
First-class	47	83	7	2584	168	34.00	49.24	4	18	23	0
List A	32	28	5	598	92	26.00	84.46	0	4	8	0
T20s	26	25	4	622	97*	29.61	130.67	0	5	9	0
Bowling	**Mat**	**Balls**	**Runs**	**Wkts**	**BBI**	**BBM**	**Ave**	**Econ**	**SR**	**5w**	**10**
First-class	47	2038	1201	33	7/20	7/38	36.39	3.53	61.7	1	0
List A	32	620	630	14	4/35	4/35	45.00	6.09	44.2	0	0
T20s	26	192	255	10	3/33	3/33	25.50	7.96	19.2	0	0

MATT RENSHAW

LHB / OB / R0 / W0

FULL NAME: Matthew Thomas Renshaw
BORN: March 28, 1996, Middlesbrough, Yorkshire
SQUAD NO: 77
TEAMS: Australia, Kent, Brisbane Heat, Queensland, Somerset
ROLE: Batsman
DEBUT: Test: 2016; First-class: 2015; List A: 2016; T20: 2018

BEST BATTING: 184 Australia vs Pakistan, Sydney, 2017
BEST BOWLING: 1-12 Queensland vs Victoria, Melbourne, 2018

TWITTER: @MattRenshaw449
NOTES: Kent have signed the Australian opener for the early stages of the Championship campaign and the duration of the One-Day Cup. They will hope he makes a similar impact to that he made during a brief stint at Somerset last season, when he hit 513 runs in six Championship matches, including three centuries. One of those, against Yorkshire at Taunton, was scored before lunch on day one. "Matt is a young talent who is very hungry for success," said Paul Downton, Kent's director of cricket. "He has the ability to strengthen our batting line-up, which will be key at the beginning of the season with both Sam [Billings] and Joe [Denly] away playing in the IPL." Renshaw will be hoping to catch the eye of the Australian selectors ahead of this summer's Ashes having fallen out of favour in recent times

Batting	Mat	Inns	NO	Runs	HS	Ave	SR	100	50	Ct	St
Tests	11	20	1	636	184	33.47	42.48	1	3	8	0
First-class	51	95	5	3363	184	37.36	48.94	10	11	45	0
List A	18	18	2	553	88	34.56	84.55	0	5	6	0
T20s	10	9	1	201	90*	25.12	130.51	0	1	4	0
Bowling	**Mat**	**Balls**	**Runs**	**Wkts**	**BBI**	**BBM**	**Ave**	**Econ**	**SR**	**5w**	**10**
Tests	11	24	13	0	-	-	-	3.25	-	0	0
First-class	51	186	112	2	1/12	1/12	56.00	3.61	93.0	0	0
List A	18	72	54	0	-	-	-	4.50	-	0	0
T20s	10	84	97	2	1/15	1/15	48.50	6.92	42.0	0	0

GEORGE RHODES

RHB / OB / R0 / W0

FULL NAME: George Harry Rhodes
BORN: October 26, 1993, Birmingham
SQUAD NO: 34
HEIGHT: 6ft
NICKNAME: Sherlock, Gnomey
EDUCATION: The Chase School, Malvern; University of Worcester
TEAMS: Worcestershire
ROLE: Allrounder
DEBUT: First-class: 2016; List A: 2016; T20: 2016

BEST BATTING: 59 Worcestershire vs Essex, Chelmsford, 2016
BEST BOWLING: 2-83 Worcestershire vs Kent, Canterbury, 2016

FAMILY TIES? My father Steve played for England and Worcestershire for 20 years and my grandfather William played first-class cricket for Nottinghamshire
WHAT WAS YOUR FIRST CRICKET CLUB? Rushwick CC, Worcestershire. Grass is long, the walk-off much longer
WHICH BOWLER WOULD YOU LEAST LIKE TO FACE? Olly Stone – nasty and fast
BEST INNINGS YOU'VE SEEN? Tom Kohler-Cadmore vs Harbourne at Evesham. Gutsy red-inker, proper cricket
WHO WOULD YOU ASK TO BAT FOR YOUR LIFE? Easy question: Mark 'The Wall' Hooper
YOUR BIGGEST CRICKETING REGRET? Not persevering with my raw pace
WHAT WILL YOU BE DOING IN THE YEAR 2040? Living on Mars drinking piña coladas
WHICH BOOK MEANS MOST TO YOU? Sapiens – A Brief History of Humankind by Yuval Noah Harari
ODDEST SPORT YOU'VE PLAYED? Onslow Ball (also the greatest sport I have played)
TWITTER: @Ghrhodes

Batting	Mat	Inns	NO	Runs	HS	Ave	SR	100	50	Ct	St
First-class	17	32	4	675	59	24.10	40.73	0	4	9	0
List A	7	4	1	102	95	34.00	91.07	0	1	5	0
T20s	13	9	4	57	17*	11.40	105.55	0	0	5	0
Bowling	**Mat**	**Balls**	**Runs**	**Wkts**	**BBI**	**BBM**	**Ave**	**Econ**	**SR**	**5w**	**10**
First-class	17	617	465	6	2/83	2/83	77.50	4.52	102.8	0	0
List A	7	228	243	5	2/34	2/34	48.60	6.39	45.6	0	0
T20s	13	96	143	8	4/13	4/13	17.87	8.93	12.0	0	0

WILL RHODES

LHB / RMF / R0 / W0

FULL NAME: William Michael Harry Rhodes
BORN: March 2, 1995, Nottingham
SQUAD NO: 35
HEIGHT: 6ft 1in
NICKNAME: Codhead, Besty
EDUCATION: Cottingham High School, Hull
TEAMS: Warwickshire, Essex, Yorkshire
ROLE: Allrounder
DEBUT: First-class: 2015; List A: 2013; T20: 2013

BEST BATTING: 137 Warwickshire vs Gloucestershire, Edgbaston, 2018
BEST BOWLING: 3-42 Yorkshire vs Middlesex, Headingley, 2015

FAMILY TIES? My dad played a bit of Nottinghamshire junior cricket
WHAT WAS YOUR FIRST CRICKET CLUB? Cottingham CC, East Riding of Yorkshire
FAVOURITE CRICKET BAT? A GM which I stole off my dad
CRICKETING HERO? My brother Dom Rhodes – he hits it miles
BEST ADVICE EVER RECEIVED? Always hit the middle of the ball
BEST INNINGS YOU'VE SEEN? Adam Lyth's 161 from 73 balls against Northamptonshire at Headingley in the 2017 T20 Blast
WHO WOULD YOU ASK TO BAT FOR YOUR LIFE? Ian Bell
WHICH RULE WOULD YOU CHANGE ABOUT CRICKET? If it pitches outside leg stump then it can still be given out lbw
SURPRISING FACT ABOUT YOU? I once did one million keepie-uppies with a balloon
WHAT WILL YOU BE DOING IN THE YEAR 2040? Playing golf every day
TWITTER: @willrhodes_152

Batting	Mat	Inns	NO	Runs	HS	Ave	SR	100	50	Ct	St
First-class	34	52	3	1667	137	34.02	48.10	4	7	14	0
List A	23	19	2	390	69	22.94	84.59	0	2	9	0
T20s	20	17	3	149	45	10.64	107.97	0	0	2	0
Bowling	**Mat**	**Balls**	**Runs**	**Wkts**	**BBI**	**BBM**	**Ave**	**Econ**	**SR**	**5w**	**10**
First-class	34	1895	1011	26	3/42	4/114	38.88	3.20	72.8	0	0
List A	23	485	445	12	2/22	2/22	37.08	5.50	40.4	0	0
T20s	20	205	312	14	3/27	3/27	22.28	9.13	14.6	0	0

KANE RICHARDSON RHB / RFM / R0 / W0

FULL NAME: Kane William Richardson
BORN: February 12, 1991, Eudunda, South Australia, Australia
SQUAD NO: TBC
TEAMS: Australia, Derbyshire, Adelaide Strikers, Melbourne Renegades, Pune Warriors, Rajasthan Royals, Royal Challengers Bangalore, South Australia
ROLE: Bowler
DEBUT: ODI: 2013; T20I: 2014; First-class: 2011; List A: 2009; T20: 2009

BEST BATTING: 49 South Australia vs Tasmania, Adelaide, 2013
BEST BOWLING: 5-69 South Australia vs Western Australia, Adelaide, 2017

NOTES: Derbyshire have signed the 28-year-old Australian fast bowler for the whole of this summer's T20 Blast campaign, subject to international commitments. Richardson has established himself as a short-format specialist over the last few years and was the leading wicket-taker in the 2018/19 Big Bash, taking 24 scalps for tournament winners Melbourne Renegades. He has represented three different IPL franchises. Richardson has also played white-ball cricket for Australia, although at the time of writing he hadn't featured for his country since June 2018. "Kane is a top-level T20 bowler and that is what we were looking for with our second overseas signing," said Derbyshire T20 coach Dominic Cork. "He's quick and with his international experience I'm looking forward to seeing him lead the line for Derbyshire"

Batting	Mat	Inns	NO	Runs	HS	Ave	SR	100	50	Ct	St
ODIs	18	8	3	45	19	9.00	84.90	0	0	4	0
T20Is	9	2	0	9	9	4.50	112.50	0	0	4	0
First-class	32	51	4	661	49	14.06	58.13	0	0	10	0
List A	76	45	14	377	36	12.16	87.26	0	0	14	0
T20s	90	33	16	275	45	16.17	116.52	0	0	35	0
Bowling	**Mat**	**Balls**	**Runs**	**Wkts**	**BBI**	**BBM**	**Ave**	**Econ**	**SR**	**5w**	**10**
ODIs	18	935	854	27	5/68	5/68	31.62	5.48	34.6	1	0
T20Is	9	204	299	9	3/33	3/33	33.22	8.79	22.6	0	0
First-class	32	6739	3341	99	5/69	9/124	33.74	2.97	68.0	1	0
List A	76	4066	3523	123	6/48	6/48	28.64	5.19	33.0	6	0
T20s	90	1933	2612	107	4/22	4/22	24.41	8.10	18.0	0	0

MICHAEL RICHARDSON

RHB / WK / R2 / W0

FULL NAME: Michael John Richardson
BORN: October 4, 1986, Port Elizabeth, SA
SQUAD NO: 10
HEIGHT: 5ft 10in
NICKNAME: Richie, Rory, Chelsea
EDUCATION: Rondebosch Boys High School, South Africa; Stonyhurst College, Lancashire; University of Nottingham
TEAMS: Durham, Badureliya Sports Club, Colombo
ROLE: Wicketkeeper/batsman
DEBUT: First-class: 2010; List A: 2012; T20: 2013

BEST BATTING: 148 Durham vs Yorkshire, Chester-le-Street, 2014

FAMILY TIES? My father David played for South Africa, my grandfather John played for Northern Transvaal, my cousin Matthew played for Border, my uncle Ralph played for Western Province
WHAT WAS YOUR FIRST CRICKET CLUB? Datchett CC, Berkshire. I was their opening bowler and would bowl from one end through the whole innings
CRICKETING HERO? Sachin Tendulkar – loved watching him as a kid
WHICH BOWLER WOULD YOU LEAST LIKE TO FACE? Mohammad Abbas – very skilful
BEST INNINGS YOU'VE SEEN? Rahul Dravid and VVS Laxman batting the whole day against Australia at Kolkata in 2001
WHO WOULD YOU ASK TO BAT FOR YOUR LIFE? Brian Lara
WHICH RULE WOULD YOU CHANGE ABOUT CRICKET? Bring back the toss in the County Championship
YOUR BIGGEST CRICKETING REGRET? Getting my pad in the way
TWITTER: @richo18howu

Batting	Mat	Inns	NO	Runs	HS	Ave	SR	100	50	Ct	St
First-class	102	174	11	4816	148	29.54	53.58	6	26	181	5
List A	25	23	3	1089	111	54.45	85.27	2	9	12	0
T20s	46	34	10	514	53	21.41	115.76	0	1	23	0
Bowling	**Mat**	**Balls**	**Runs**	**Wkts**	**BBI**	**BBM**	**Ave**	**Econ**	**SR**	**5w**	**10**
First-class	102	24	13	0	-	-	-	3.25	-	0	0
List A	25	-	-	-	-	-	-	-	-	-	-
T20s	46	-	-	-	-	-	-	-	-	-	-

ADAM RILEY

RHB / OB / R0 / W1

FULL NAME: Adam Edward Nicholas Riley
BORN: March 23, 1992, Sidcup, Kent
SQUAD NO: 33
HEIGHT: 6ft 2in
NICKNAME: Jenny, General, Gen, Riles
EDUCATION: Beths Grammar School, Bexley, London; Loughborough University
TEAMS: Kent, England Lions
ROLE: Bowler
DEBUT: First-class: 2011; List A: 2011; T20: 2011

BEST BATTING: 34 Kent vs Derbyshire, Canterbury, 2015
BEST BOWLING: 7-150 Kent vs Hampshire, Southampton, 2013

WHAT WAS YOUR FIRST CRICKET CLUB? Bexley CC, London. Will always be my only club
FAVOURITE CRICKET BAT? GM Purist. Lovely bat, I just wasn't very good at using it
WHICH BOWLER WOULD YOU LEAST LIKE TO FACE? Darren Stevens in April (and May, June, July, August, September)
BEST INNINGS YOU'VE SEEN? Heino Kuhn's hundred at New Road in last season's One-Day Cup semi-final
WHO WOULD YOU ASK TO BAT FOR YOUR LIFE? Probably not Mitch Claydon. He has been known to get caught at long-on as nightwatchman
WHICH RULE WOULD YOU CHANGE ABOUT CRICKET? You shouldn't need to tell the umpire when you decide to bowl around the wicket – batsmen don't declare a switch-hit, do they?
WHAT WILL YOU BE DOING IN THE YEAR 2040? Following around Charlton Athletic in the depths of the Football League
WHICH BOOK MEANS MOST TO YOU? The ones that got me through university
TWITTER: @AdamRiley92

Batting	Mat	Inns	NO	Runs	HS	Ave	SR	100	50	Ct	St
First-class	58	72	26	485	34	10.54	28.05	0	0	33	0
List A	33	12	5	61	21*	8.71	62.24	0	0	11	0
T20s	29	8	5	18	5*	6.00	85.71	0	0	5	0
Bowling	**Mat**	**Balls**	**Runs**	**Wkts**	**BBI**	**BBM**	**Ave**	**Econ**	**SR**	**5w**	**10**
First-class	58	7701	4586	126	7/150	9/123	36.39	3.57	61.1	5	0
List A	33	1284	1098	32	4/40	4/40	34.31	5.13	40.1	0	0
T20s	29	532	687	23	4/22	4/22	29.86	7.74	23.1	0	0

NATHAN RIMMINGTON RHB / RFM / R0 / W0

FULL NAME: Nathan John Rimmington
BORN: November 11, 1982, Redcliffe, Queensland, Australia
SQUAD NO: 11
HEIGHT: 5ft 9in
NICKNAME: Rimmo
EDUCATION: Queensland University of Technology, Brisbane
TEAMS: Durham, Derbyshire, Hampshire, Kings XI Punjab, Melbourne Renegades, Perth Scorchers, Queensland, Western Australia
ROLE: Bowler
DEBUT: First-class: 2006; List A: 2006; T20: 2006

BEST BATTING: 102* Western Australia vs New South Wales, Sydney, 2011
BEST BOWLING: 5-27 Western Australia vs Queensland, Perth, 2014

WHAT WAS YOUR FIRST CRICKET CLUB? Wamuran CC, Queensland, Australia. Tiny country town with only two junior teams
FAVOURITE CRICKET BAT? Slazenger V100. Used it for at least five years
WHICH BOWLER WOULD YOU LEAST LIKE TO FACE? Rashid Khan – good wrong 'un
BEST INNINGS YOU'VE SEEN? Steve Waugh's hundred at The Oval in 2001, 19 days after tearing his calf. Sheer mental toughness
WHICH RULE WOULD YOU CHANGE ABOUT CRICKET? No leg byes
YOUR BIGGEST CRICKETING REGRET? Not being taller
FAVOURITE QUOTE OR SAYING? She'll be chooks
WHICH BOOK MEANS MOST TO YOU? The God Delusion by Richard Dawkins
ODDEST SPORT YOU'VE PLAYED? Football
TWITTER: @nrimmo11

Batting	Mat	Inns	NO	Runs	HS	Ave	SR	100	50	Ct	St
First-class	46	66	14	989	102*	19.01	53.17	1	2	12	0
List A	56	39	9	534	55	17.80	91.28	0	1	10	0
T20s	96	37	18	203	26	10.68	105.18	0	0	22	0
Bowling	**Mat**	**Balls**	**Runs**	**Wkts**	**BBI**	**BBM**	**Ave**	**Econ**	**SR**	**5w**	**10**
First-class	46	7482	3789	116	5/27	7/90	32.66	3.03	64.5	3	0
List A	56	2970	2337	74	4/34	4/34	31.58	4.72	40.1	0	0
T20s	96	1905	2573	110	5/27	5/27	23.39	8.10	17.3	1	0

OLLIE ROBINSON

RHB / WK / R0 / W0

FULL NAME: Oliver Graham Robinson
BORN: December 1, 1998, Sidcup, Kent
SQUAD NO: 21
HEIGHT: 5ft 9in
NICKNAME: Robbo
EDUCATION: Hurstmere School; Chislehurst and Sidcup Grammar
TEAMS: Kent
ROLE: Wicketkeeper
DEBUT: First-class: 2018; List A: 2017

BEST BATTING: 26 Kent vs Leicestershire, Leicester, 2018

WHAT WAS YOUR FIRST CRICKET CLUB? Sidcup CC, London. Played with my dad for two seasons in the first team
FAVOURITE CRICKET BAT? Gray-Nicolls Powerbow
WHICH BOWLER WOULD YOU LEAST LIKE TO FACE? Darren Stevens – he's a genius
BEST INNINGS YOU'VE SEEN? Alastair Cook's final Test innings
WHO WOULD YOU ASK TO BAT FOR YOUR LIFE? Cheteshwar Pujara
YOUR BIGGEST CRICKETING REGRET? Not bowling fast
FAVOURITE QUOTE OR SAYING? You get out what you put in
WHICH BOOK MEANS MOST TO YOU? Any of the Harry Potter books
ODDEST SPORT YOU'VE PLAYED? Danish longball
TWITTER: @ollierobinson7

Batting	Mat	Inns	NO	Runs	HS	Ave	SR	100	50	Ct	St
First-class	3	4	0	59	26	14.75	56.19	0	0	1	0
List A	1	-	-	-	-	-	-	-	-	1	0
Bowling	**Mat**	**Balls**	**Runs**	**Wkts**	**BBI**	**BBM**	**Ave**	**Econ**	**SR**	**5w**	**10**
First-class	3	-	-	-	-	-	-	-	-	-	-
List A	1	-	-	-	-	-	-	-	-	-	-

OLLIE ROBINSON RHB / RMF / R0 / W1 / MVP26

FULL NAME: Oliver Edward Robinson
BORN: December 1, 1993, Margate, Kent
SQUAD NO: 25
HEIGHT: 6ft 5in
NICKNAME: Robbo, Rig, Riggy, Ols
EDUCATION: King's School, Canterbury
TEAMS: Sussex, Hampshire, Yorkshire
ROLE: Allrounder
DEBUT: First-class: 2015; List A: 2013; T20: 2014

BEST BATTING: 110 Sussex vs Durham, Chester-le-Street, 2015
BEST BOWLING: 7-23 Sussex vs Loughborough MCCU, Hove, 2018

WHAT GOT YOU INTO CRICKET? I started with a wind ball in my grandparents' garden at the age of two. I played my first hard-ball game aged six, taking 5-5 (including a hat-trick)
'ROY OF THE ROVERS' MOMENT? Scoring a hundred against Durham on my first-class debut
BEST THING ABOUT YOUR HOME GROUND? The location – it's a great place to celebrate
SURPRISING FACT ABOUT YOU? I was county champion at discus and shot put at the age of 13 and came fourth at the nationals
WHERE IS PARADISE? Hamilton Island, Australia
UNUSUAL OBJECT AT HOME? A dressmakers' mannequin (my girlfriend is a fashion designer)
TWITTER: @ollierobinson25

Batting	Mat	Inns	NO	Runs	HS	Ave	SR	100	50	Ct	St
First-class	42	62	11	1094	110	21.45	65.58	1	4	14	0
List A	14	10	3	122	30	17.42	89.70	0	0	6	0
T20s	24	10	4	34	10	5.66	70.83	0	0	10	0
Bowling	**Mat**	**Balls**	**Runs**	**Wkts**	**BBI**	**BBM**	**Ave**	**Econ**	**SR**	**5w**	**10**
First-class	42	7517	3912	165	7/23	10/67	23.70	3.12	45.5	7	1
List A	14	576	568	14	3/31	3/31	40.57	5.91	41.1	0	0
T20s	24	416	630	20	3/16	3/16	31.50	9.08	20.8	0	0

SAM ROBSON

RHB / LB / R2 / W0

FULL NAME: Samuel David Robson
BORN: July 1, 1989, Sydney, Australia
SQUAD NO: 12
HEIGHT: 6ft
NICKNAME: Bronco
EDUCATION: Marcellin College, Sydney
TEAMS: England, Middlesex
ROLE: Batsman
DEBUT: Test: 2014; First-class: 2009; List A: 2008; T20: 2011

BEST BATTING: 231 Middlesex vs Warwickshire, Lord's, 2016
BEST BOWLING: 1-4 England Lions vs Sri Lanka A, Dambulla, 2014
COUNTY CAP: 2013

WHAT WAS YOUR FIRST CRICKET CLUB? Randwick Junior CC, New South Wales, Australia
BEST INNINGS YOU'VE SEEN? Hashim Amla scoring 80-odd against us at The Oval in 2013 on a disgraceful pitch which was turning square and going up and down. The best innings I have seen up close
WHO WOULD YOU ASK TO BAT FOR YOUR LIFE? Geoff Boycott circa 1975
YOUR BIGGEST CRICKETING REGRET? Not learning to bowl slow left-arm – very handy bowlers for any team even if they are rarely champion bowlers
WHAT WILL YOU BE DOING IN THE YEAR 2040? Drinking solidly behind the pavilion at the Lord's Test match with Tim Murtagh, Ollie Rayner, Steven Finn, Daniel Rootes, Angus Robson, Nathan Rowe, Mitch Jones, James Campbell and Jason Hood
WHICH BOOK MEANS MOST TO YOU? Harry Potter and the Goblet of Fire by JK Rowling
ODDEST SPORT YOU'VE PLAYED? Fuzzy Duck (ask Chris Rogers)

Batting	Mat	Inns	NO	Runs	HS	Ave	SR	100	50	Ct	St
Tests	7	11	0	336	127	30.54	44.50	1	1	5	0
First-class	142	251	17	8850	231	37.82	51.46	21	35	134	0
List A	16	14	0	407	88	29.07	68.17	0	2	5	0
T20s	4	4	2	53	28*	26.50	103.92	0	0	2	0
Bowling	**Mat**	**Balls**	**Runs**	**Wkts**	**BBI**	**BBM**	**Ave**	**Econ**	**SR**	**5w**	**10**
Tests	7	-	-	-	-	-	-	-	-	-	-
First-class	142	164	137	2	1/4	1/4	68.50	5.01	82.0	0	0
List A	16	-	-	-	-	-	-	-	-	-	-
T20s	4	-	-	-	-	-	-	-	-	-	-

GARETH RODERICK

RHB / WK / R0 / W0

FULL NAME: Gareth Hugh Roderick
BORN: August 29, 1991, Durban, South Africa
SQUAD NO: 27
HEIGHT: 6ft
NICKNAME: Roders, Pear
EDUCATION: Maritzburg College, South Africa
TEAMS: Gloucestershire, KwaZulu-Natal
ROLE: Batsman/wicketkeeper
DEBUT: First-class: 2011; List A: 2011; T20: 2011

BEST BATTING: 171 Gloucestershire vs Leicestershire, Bristol, 2014

COUNTY CAP: 2013

WHAT WAS YOUR FIRST CRICKET CLUB? Northwood Crusaders CC, Durban, South Africa
CRICKETING HERO? Steve Waugh
BEST INNINGS YOU'VE SEEN? Hashim Amla's triple century against England at The Oval in 2012. Pretty much a chanceless innings
WHO WOULD YOU ASK TO BAT FOR YOUR LIFE? Rahul Dravid
YOUR BIGGEST CRICKETING REGRET? That Gloucestershire haven't reached T20 Finals Day
WHAT WILL YOU BE DOING IN THE YEAR 2040? Hopefully on a club cricket field somewhere
ODDEST SPORT YOU'VE PLAYED? Underwater hockey
TWITTER: @Roders369

Batting	Mat	Inns	NO	Runs	HS	Ave	SR	100	50	Ct	St
First-class	82	132	17	4147	171	36.06	51.18	5	30	224	4
List A	43	33	5	882	104	31.50	81.14	1	6	42	4
T20s	41	24	8	213	32	13.31	119.66	0	0	20	1
Bowling	**Mat**	**Balls**	**Runs**	**Wkts**	**BBI**	**BBM**	**Ave**	**Econ**	**SR**	**5w**	**10**
First-class	82	-	-	-	-	-	-	-	-	-	-
List A	43	-	-	-	-	-	-	-	-	-	-
T20s	41	-	-	-	-	-	-	-	-	-	-

TOBY ROLAND-JONES RHB / RMF / R0 / W2

FULL NAME: Tobias Skelton Roland-Jones
BORN: January 29, 1988, Ashford, Middlesex
SQUAD NO: 21
HEIGHT: 6ft 3in
NICKNAME: Rojo, TRJ
EDUCATION: Hampton School, Greater London; University of Leeds
TEAMS: England, Middlesex
ROLE: Bowler
DEBUT: Test: 2017; ODI: 2017; First-class: 2010; List A: 2010; T20: 2011

BEST BATTING: 103* Middlesex vs Yorkshire, Lord's, 2015
BEST BOWLING: 6-50 Middlesex vs Northamptonshire, Northampton, 2014
COUNTY CAP: 2012

FAMILY TIES? My older brother Olly played for Leeds/Bradford MCCU and Middlesex Second XI. My dad is a coach
'ROY OF THE ROVERS' MOMENT? Winning the 2016 County Championship in the final session of the season will take some beating
CRICKETING HERO? Ian Botham
NON-CRICKETING HEROES? Ricky Gervais, Alan Partridge, Paul Scholes
IF YOU WEREN'T A CRICKETER? I'd be working in my friends' wine investment company
SURPRISING FACT? I actually live in Surrey
UNUSUAL OBJECT AT HOME? A stuffed panda
TWITTER: @tobyrj21

Batting	Mat	Inns	NO	Runs	HS	Ave	SR	100	50	Ct	St
Tests	4	6	2	82	25	20.50	69.49	0	0	0	0
ODIs	1	1	1	37	37*	-	100.00	0	0	0	0
First-class	102	141	26	2488	103*	21.63	58.66	1	9	30	0
List A	71	42	13	553	65	19.06	90.35	0	1	12	0
T20s	40	24	10	196	30	14.00	130.66	0	0	8	0
Bowling	**Mat**	**Balls**	**Runs**	**Wkts**	**BBI**	**BBM**	**Ave**	**Econ**	**SR**	**5w**	**10**
Tests	4	536	334	17	5/57	8/129	19.64	3.73	31.5	1	0
ODIs	1	42	34	1	1/34	1/34	34.00	4.85	42.0	0	0
First-class	102	17624	9343	366	6/50	12/105	25.52	3.18	48.1	16	3
List A	71	3230	2745	113	4/10	4/10	24.29	5.09	28.5	0	0
T20s	40	800	1171	45	4/25	4/25	26.02	8.78	17.7	0	0

BILLY ROOT LHB / OB / R0 / W0

FULL NAME: William Thomas Root
BORN: August 5, 1992, Sheffield
SQUAD NO: 66
HEIGHT: 5ft 10in
NICKNAME: Rooty, Rootfish, Junior
EDUCATION: Worksop College, Nottinghamshire; Leeds Metropolitan University
TEAMS: Glamorgan, Nottinghamshire
ROLE: Batsman
DEBUT: First-class: 2015; List A: 2017; T20: 2017

BEST BATTING: 133 Leeds/Bradford MCCU vs Sussex, Hove, 2016
BEST BOWLING: 3-29 Nottinghamshire vs Sussex, Hove, 2017

FAMILY TIES? My dad was a good cricketer and my brother plays the occasional game
WHAT WAS YOUR FIRST CRICKET CLUB? Sheffield Collegiate CC. It's got exactly the same slope as the one at Lord's
FAVOURITE CRICKET BAT? New Balance DC – too good for me
WHICH BOWLER WOULD YOU LEAST LIKE TO FACE? Wasim Akram
BEST INNINGS YOU'VE SEEN? Chris Read's hundred against Sussex in 2017 in his final game before retiring. It helped win promotion for my former county Notts
WHO WOULD YOU ASK TO BAT FOR YOUR LIFE? Joe Root – because he'd want to save it
WHICH RULE WOULD YOU CHANGE ABOUT CRICKET? Only two stumps
WHAT WILL YOU BE DOING IN THE YEAR 2040? I'll be fishing
FAVOURITE QUOTE OR SAYING? You shall not pass (Gandalf)
WHICH BOOK MEANS MOST TO YOU? Jamie's 30-Minute Meals – A Revolutionary Approach to Cooking Good Food Fast by Jamie Oliver
TWITTER: @Rootdog22

Batting	Mat	Inns	NO	Runs	HS	Ave	SR	100	50	Ct	St
First-class	14	24	1	697	133	30.30	55.53	2	2	3	0
List A	16	13	3	387	107*	38.70	90.00	1	1	3	0
T20s	23	15	6	277	40	30.77	114.93	0	0	4	0
Bowling	**Mat**	**Balls**	**Runs**	**Wkts**	**BBI**	**BBM**	**Ave**	**Econ**	**SR**	**5w**	**10**
First-class	14	155	107	6	3/29	3/29	17.83	4.14	25.8	0	0
List A	16	172	195	3	1/27	1/27	65.00	6.80	57.3	0	0
T20s	23	18	37	0	-	-	-	12.33	-	0	0

JOE ROOT

RHB / OB / R3 / W0

FULL NAME: Joseph Edward Root
BORN: December 30, 1990, Sheffield
SQUAD NO: 66
HEIGHT: 6ft
NICKNAME: Rooty, Roota, Rootfish
EDUCATION: King Ecgbert School, Sheffield; Worksop College, Nottinghamshire
TEAMS: England, Yorkshire, Sydney Thunder
ROLE: Batsman
DEBUT: Test: 2012; ODI: 2013; T20I: 2012; First-class: 2010; List A: 2009; T20: 2011

BEST BATTING: 254 England vs Pakistan, Old Trafford, 2016
BEST BOWLING: 4-5 Yorkshire vs Lancashire, Old Trafford, 2018
COUNTY CAP: 2012

FAMILY TIES? My dad played club cricket and represented Nottinghamshire Second XI and Colts. My brother Billy has played for Notts and is currently at Glamorgan
'ROY OF THE ROVERS' MOMENT? Winning the Ashes in 2015
CRICKETING HERO? Michael Vaughan
NON-CRICKETING HEROES? Seve Ballesteros, Alan Shearer
IF YOU WEREN'T A CRICKETER? I'd be studying Art and Design at college or university
SURPRISING FACT? I taught myself to play the ukulele on tour with England
TWITTER: @root66

Batting	Mat	Inns	NO	Runs	HS	Ave	SR	100	50	Ct	St
Tests	80	147	12	6685	254	49.51	55.43	16	41	91	0
ODIs	126	119	19	5090	133*	50.90	86.69	14	29	57	0
T20Is	31	29	5	846	90*	35.25	127.21	0	5	18	0
First-class	137	239	22	10474	254	48.26	56.26	25	56	128	0
List A	165	157	25	6374	133*	48.28	85.30	15	38	69	0
T20s	71	65	13	1572	92*	30.23	126.16	0	9	32	0
Bowling	**Mat**	**Balls**	**Runs**	**Wkts**	**BBI**	**BBM**	**Ave**	**Econ**	**SR**	**5w**	**10**
Tests	80	1968	986	20	2/9	2/9	49.30	3.00	98.4	0	0
ODIs	126	1342	1299	20	3/52	3/52	64.95	5.80	67.1	0	0
T20Is	31	84	139	6	2/9	2/9	23.16	9.92	14.0	0	0
First-class	137	3613	1840	40	4/5	4/5	46.00	3.05	90.3	0	0
List A	165	1929	1798	34	3/52	3/52	52.88	5.59	56.7	0	0
T20s	71	264	415	10	2/9	2/9	41.50	9.43	26.4	0	0

ADAM ROSSINGTON

RHB / WK / R0 / W0

NORTHAMPTONSHIRE

FULL NAME: Adam Matthew Rossington
BORN: May 5, 1993, Edgware, Middlesex
SQUAD NO: 7
HEIGHT: 6ft
NICKNAME: Rosso
EDUCATION: Belmont Preparatory School, Surrey; Mill Hill School, London
TEAMS: Northamptonshire, Middlesex
ROLE: Wicketkeeper/batsman
DEBUT: First-class: 2010; List A: 2012; T20: 2011

BEST BATTING: 138* Northamptonshire vs Sussex, Arundel, 2016

WHAT WAS YOUR FIRST CRICKET CLUB? Barnet CC, London
CRICKETING HERO? Alec Stewart
WHICH BOWLER WOULD YOU LEAST LIKE TO FACE? Kieran Noema-Barnett
BEST INNINGS YOU'VE SEEN? Every one played by Ben Sanderson
WHO WOULD YOU ASK TO BAT FOR YOUR LIFE? Geoffrey Boycott
WHICH RULE WOULD YOU CHANGE ABOUT CRICKET? Introduce a free hit for a no-ball in all formats of the game
YOUR BIGGEST CRICKETING REGRET? That I've never played in the Hong Kong Sixes tournament
SURPRISING FACT ABOUT YOU? I can't ride a bicycle. I support Barnet FC
WHAT WILL YOU BE DOING IN THE YEAR 2040? I'll be a cricket coach
FAVOURITE QUOTE OR SAYING? Just quietly
TWITTER: @rossington17

Batting	Mat	Inns	NO	Runs	HS	Ave	SR	100	50	Ct	St
First-class	63	102	10	3100	138*	33.69	70.47	6	20	133	9
List A	43	38	6	1197	97	37.40	95.99	0	10	28	5
T20s	65	61	5	1153	85	20.58	143.05	0	6	33	10
Bowling	**Mat**	**Balls**	**Runs**	**Wkts**	**BBI**	**BBM**	**Ave**	**Econ**	**SR**	**5w**	**10**
First-class	63	90	66	0	-	-	-	4.40	-	0	0
List A	43	-	-	-	-	-	-	-	-	-	-
T20s	65	-	-	-	-	-	-	-	-	-	-

RILEE ROSSOUW LHB / OB / R0 / W0 / MVP81

FULL NAME: Rilee Roscoe Rossouw
BORN: October 9, 1989, Bloemfontein, South Africa
SQUAD NO: 30
NICKNAME: Rudi
EDUCATION: Grey College, Bloemfontein
TEAMS: South Africa, Hampshire, Basnahira Cricket Dundee, Eagles, Free State, Knights, Quetta Gladiators, Royal Challengers Bangalore, Tshwane Spartans
ROLE: Batsman
DEBUT: ODI: 2014; T20I: 2014; First-class: 2007; List A: 2007; T20: 2008

BEST BATTING: 319 Eagles vs Titans, Centurion, 2010
BEST BOWLING: 1-1 Knights vs Cape Cobras, Cape Town, 2013

TWITTER: @Rileerr
NOTES: A top-order batsman, Rossouw quit international cricket ahead of the 2017 season to take up a three-year Kolpak deal with Hampshire to play in all formats. He scored just one fifty from 13 Championship innings in his first season at the club, although a one-day hundred served notice of his talent. The left-hander scored his first Championship hundred last summer, scoring 489 runs at an average of 34.93. But his starring role came in the One-Day Cup, making a hundred in the final at Lord's to help Hampshire lift the trophy. Rossouw's South Africa career got off to a shaky start in 2014, with ducks in four of his first six ODI innings, but he soon established himself as one of his country's most consistent white-ball performers. His highest first-class score, a 291-ball innings of 319 which included 47 fours, is indicative of his pedigree in the longer format

Batting	Mat	Inns	NO	Runs	HS	Ave	SR	100	50	Ct	St
ODIs	36	35	3	1239	132	38.71	94.36	3	7	22	0
T20Is	15	14	3	327	78	29.72	137.97	0	2	9	0
First-class	97	171	9	6743	319	41.62	62.66	19	28	117	0
List A	142	140	7	5258	156	39.53	95.32	12	30	74	0
T20s	163	157	18	4021	100*	28.92	133.76	1	22	66	0
Bowling	**Mat**	**Balls**	**Runs**	**Wkts**	**BBI**	**BBM**	**Ave**	**Econ**	**SR**	**5w**	**10**
ODIs	36	45	44	1	1/17	1/17	44.00	5.86	45.0	0	0
T20Is	15	-	-	-	-	-	-	-	-	-	-
First-class	97	78	70	3	1/1	1/1	23.33	5.38	26.0	0	0
List A	142	45	44	1	1/17	1/17	44.00	5.86	45.0	0	0
T20s	163	17	19	1	1/8	1/8	19.00	6.70	17.0	0	0

ADAM ROUSE

RHB / WK / R0 / W0

FULL NAME: Adam Paul Rouse
BORN: June 30, 1992, Harare, Zimbabwe
SQUAD NO: 12
EDUCATION: Perins Community Sports College, Hampshire; Peter Symonds College, Winchester
TEAMS: Kent, Gloucestershire, Hampshire
ROLE: Wicketkeeper/batsman
DEBUT: First-class: 2013; List A: 2013; T20: 2014

BEST BATTING: 95* Kent vs Derbyshire, Canterbury, 2017

TWITTER: @Rousie20
NOTES: A former England U19 wicketkeeper/batsman, Zimbabwean-born Rouse had a trial with Kent in 2015 and also played for their Second XI the previous summer. He has also had brief spells with Gloucestershire and Hampshire. Rouse agreed a deal with Kent ahead of the 2016 season, in which he played six Championship matches but only one game of white-ball cricket. In 2017 he played 10 Championship matches, making his highest first-class score of 95 not out. The 26-year-old was a bit-part player again last summer, scoring just one fifty in 11 Championship innings and playing five One-Day Cup games

Batting	Mat	Inns	NO	Runs	HS	Ave	SR	100	50	Ct	St
First-class	34	48	4	1070	95*	24.31	52.01	0	5	106	4
List A	31	27	8	551	75*	29.00	70.73	0	3	29	2
T20s	8	7	2	61	35*	12.20	117.30	0	0	4	4
Bowling	**Mat**	**Balls**	**Runs**	**Wkts**	**BBI**	**BBM**	**Ave**	**Econ**	**SR**	**5w**	**10**
First-class	34	-	-	-	-	-	-	-	-	-	-
List A	31	-	-	-	-	-	-	-	-	-	-
T20s	8	-	-	-	-	-	-	-	-	-	-

TIM ROUSE RHB / OB / R0 / W0

FULL NAME: Timothy David Rouse
BORN: April 9, 1996, Sheffield
SQUAD NO: 44
HEIGHT: 6ft
NICKNAME: Rousey, Chunk
EDUCATION: Kingswood School, Bath; Cardiff University
TEAMS: Somerset
ROLE: Allrounder
DEBUT: First-class: 2015; T20: 2016

BEST BATTING: 69 Somerset vs Yorkshire, Scarborough, 2017
BEST BOWLING: 2-31 Cardiff MCCU vs Glamorgan, Cardiff, 2017

FAMILY TIES? My older brother Harry has played first-class cricket for Leeds/Bradford MCCU and represented Somerset Second XI
BEST ADVICE EVER RECEIVED? Smile
BEST THING ABOUT YOUR HOME GROUND? The supporters
IF YOU WEREN'T A CRICKETER? I'd hopefully be a lawyer
SURPRISING FACT ABOUT YOU? I'm 22 but am yet to attempt a driving test
WHERE IS PARADISE? Taunton
CRICKETING HERO? Marcus Trescothick – well, it had to be, didn't it? Legend of the 2005 Ashes and still loves the game
NON-CRICKETING HERO? Christopher Hitchens – great speaker
TWITTER: @tim_rouse

Batting	Mat	Inns	NO	Runs	HS	Ave	SR	100	50	Ct	St
First-class	9	13	1	205	69	17.08	40.83	0	1	5	0
T20s	1	1	0	9	9	9.00	90.00	0	0	1	0
Bowling	**Mat**	**Balls**	**Runs**	**Wkts**	**BBI**	**BBM**	**Ave**	**Econ**	**SR**	**5w**	**10**
First-class	9	228	185	5	2/31	2/31	37.00	4.86	45.6	0	0
T20s	1	-	-	-	-	-	-	-	-	-	-

JASON ROY RHB / RM / R1 / W0

SURREY

FULL NAME: Jason Jonathan Roy
BORN: July 21, 1990, Durban, South Africa
SQUAD NO: 20
HEIGHT: 6ft
NICKNAME: JRoy, Roy the Boy
EDUCATION: Whitgift School, Croydon
TEAMS: England, Surrey, Chittagong Kings, Delhi Daredevils, Gujarat Lions, Lahore Qalanders, Nelson Mandela Bay Giants, Sydney Sixers, Sylhet Sixers
ROLE: Batsman
DEBUT: ODI: 2015; T20I: 2014; First-class: 2010; List A: 2008; T20: 2008

BEST BATTING: 143 Surrey vs Lancashire, The Oval, 2015
BEST BOWLING: 3-9 Surrey vs Gloucestershire, Bristol, 2014
COUNTY CAP: 2014

'ROY OF THE ROVERS' MOMENT? Winning the Championship with Surrey, my England T20 and ODI debuts and my first century for England in ODI cricket
CRICKETING HERO? Jacques Kallis
NON-CRICKETING HERO? Superman
IF YOU WEREN'T A CRICKETER? I'd be a professional surfer and living on a beach
TWITTER: @JasonRoy20

Batting	Mat	Inns	NO	Runs	HS	Ave	SR	100	50	Ct	St
ODIs	73	71	2	2661	180	38.56	105.51	7	12	29	0
T20Is	32	32	0	743	78	23.21	145.11	0	4	5	0
First-class	81	132	11	4645	143	38.38	82.11	9	22	73	0
List A	166	159	7	5658	180	37.22	106.57	14	28	66	0
T20s	192	188	9	4882	122*	27.27	145.77	4	31	83	0
Bowling	**Mat**	**Balls**	**Runs**	**Wkts**	**BBI**	**BBM**	**Ave**	**Econ**	**SR**	**5w**	**10**
ODIs	73	-	-	-	-	-	-	-	-	-	-
T20Is	32	-	-	-	-	-	-	-	-	-	-
First-class	81	712	495	14	3/9	4/47	35.35	4.17	50.8	0	0
List A	166	6	12	0	-	-	-	12.00	-	0	0
T20s	192	18	39	1	1/23	1/23	39.00	13.00	18.0	0	0

CHRIS RUSHWORTH RHB / RFM / R0 / W4 / MVP31

FULL NAME: Christopher Rushworth
BORN: July 11, 1986, Sunderland
SQUAD NO: 22
HEIGHT: 6ft 2in
NICKNAME: Rushy, Sponge
EDUCATION: Castle View Comprehensive School, Sunderland
TEAMS: Durham
ROLE: Bowler
DEBUT: First-class: 2010; List A: 2004; T20: 2011

BEST BATTING: 57 Durham vs Kent, Canterbury, 2017
BEST BOWLING: 9-52 Durham vs Northamptonshire, Chester-le-Street, 2014
BENEFIT: 2019

FAMILY TIES? My brother Lee represented England U19 and my cousin Phil Mustard has played for England, Durham and Gloucestershire
WHAT WAS YOUR FIRST CRICKET CLUB? Hylton Colliery CC, Sunderland
BEST INNINGS YOU'VE SEEN? Michael Vaughan's 183 at Sydney in the 2002/03 Ashes. England were really up against it but he was batting on another planet
WHO WOULD YOU ASK TO BAT FOR YOUR LIFE? You can't look past Paul Collingwood in Brigadier mode. Once he gets in that zone...
WHICH RULE WOULD YOU CHANGE ABOUT CRICKET? More fielders! Or at least one extra fielder outside the circle in the first six overs of T20
YOUR BIGGEST CRICKETING REGRET? Trying to sweep Liam Dawson while my partner was on 99 at the other end. I was the last man. Oops
ODDEST SPORT YOU'VE PLAYED? Well, The Hundred hasn't started yet...
TWITTER: @ChrisRush22

Batting	Mat	Inns	NO	Runs	HS	Ave	SR	100	50	Ct	St
First-class	112	159	48	1394	57	12.55	64.77	0	1	24	0
List A	72	30	15	188	38*	12.53	87.85	0	0	18	0
T20s	84	15	9	20	5	3.33	50.00	0	0	17	0
Bowling	**Mat**	**Balls**	**Runs**	**Wkts**	**BBI**	**BBM**	**Ave**	**Econ**	**SR**	**5w**	**10**
First-class	112	19663	9959	419	9/52	15/95	23.76	3.03	46.9	21	3
List A	72	3139	2765	111	5/31	5/31	24.90	5.28	28.2	2	0
T20s	84	1611	2102	78	3/14	3/14	26.94	7.82	20.6	0	0

ABI SAKANDE

RHB / RFM / R0 / W0

FULL NAME: Abidine Sakande
BORN: September 22, 1994, Chester, Cheshire
SQUAD NO: 11
HEIGHT: 6ft 4in
NICKNAME: Abi
EDUCATION: Ardingly College; St John's College, Oxford University
TEAMS: Sussex
ROLE: Bowler
DEBUT: First-class: 2014; List A: 2016

BEST BATTING: 33 Oxford MCCU vs Cambridge MCCU, Cambridge, 2015
BEST BOWLING: 5-43 Sussex vs South Africa A, Arundel, 2017

WHAT WAS YOUR FIRST CRICKET CLUB? Lindfield CC, Sussex. Home of the infamous ridge where I learnt the basics of the game
FAVOURITE CRICKET BAT? The Willostix Stick (with curved shoulders)
CRICKETING HERO? Michael Holding
BEST INNINGS YOU'VE SEEN? Alastair Cook's final Test innings. You could see what it meant to him, the emotion of his story was so clear on his face and everyone around him
WHO WOULD YOU ASK TO BAT FOR YOUR LIFE? Me – I'm a solid nightwatchman
YOUR BIGGEST CRICKETING REGRET? Not claiming that I was a top-order batsman when I was younger
WHAT WILL YOU BE DOING IN THE YEAR 2040? Running an international not-for-profit scaling-up development program in Sub-Saharan Africa
FAVOURITE QUOTE OR SAYING? Well, if you look at it another way...
WHICH BOOK MEANS MOST TO YOU? Guns, Germs, and Steel by Jared Diamond
ODDEST SPORT YOU'VE PLAYED? Wallball
TWITTER: @AbiSakande

Batting	Mat	Inns	NO	Runs	HS	Ave	SR	100	50	Ct	St
First-class	11	13	5	104	33	13.00	31.51	0	0	4	0
List A	5	3	2	8	7*	8.00	44.44	0	0	0	0
Bowling	**Mat**	**Balls**	**Runs**	**Wkts**	**BBI**	**BBM**	**Ave**	**Econ**	**SR**	**5w**	**10**
First-class	11	1516	857	27	5/43	6/87	31.74	3.39	56.1	1	0
List A	5	191	225	5	2/53	2/53	45.00	7.06	38.2	0	0

OLLIE SALE

RHB / RFM / R0 / W0

FULL NAME: Oliver Richard Trethowan Sale
BORN: September 30, 1995, Newcastle-under-Lyme, Staffordshire
SQUAD NO: 82
HEIGHT: 6ft 2in
NICKNAME: Saler, Snail, Salestorm
EDUCATION: Sherborne School, Dorset; Newcastle University
TEAMS: Somerset
ROLE: Allrounder
DEBUT: T20: 2016

WHAT WAS YOUR FIRST CRICKET CLUB? Tavistock CC, Devon. The pitch is in the middle of Dartmoor and play is often interrupted by ponies and sheep
WHICH BOWLER WOULD YOU LEAST LIKE TO FACE? Jofra Archer – pace out of nowhere
BEST INNINGS YOU'VE SEEN? James Hildreth making a hundred with a broken foot to put us in first place during the 2016 season
WHO WOULD YOU ASK TO BAT FOR YOUR LIFE? Jack Leach – he's an absolute wall
SURPRISING FACT ABOUT YOU? I'm scared of sponges… when I say "scared" I mean I literally cannot deal with the feel of them
WHAT WILL YOU BE DOING IN THE YEAR 2040? I'll be the captain of a large sea vessel to fit my nickname
FAVOURITE QUOTE OR SAYING? Don't sweat on the small stuff
WHICH BOOK MEANS MOST TO YOU? I Am Pilgrim – A Thriller by Terry Hayes
ODDEST SPORT YOU'VE PLAYED? Quidditch
TWITTER: @olliesale1

Batting	Mat	Inns	NO	Runs	HS	Ave	SR	100	50	Ct	St
T20s	1	1	0	1	1	1.00	33.33	0	0	0	0
Bowling	**Mat**	**Balls**	**Runs**	**Wkts**	**BBI**	**BBM**	**Ave**	**Econ**	**SR**	**5w**	**10**
T20s	1	18	40	0	-	-	-	13.33	-	0	0

MATT SALISBURY

RHB / RMF / R0 / W0

FULL NAME: Matthew Edward Thomas Salisbury
BORN: April 18, 1993, Chelmsford, Essex
SQUAD NO: 32
HEIGHT: 6ft 2in
NICKNAME: Sals, Great Wall
EDUCATION: Shenfield High School, Essex; Anglia Ruskin University, Cambridge
TEAMS: Durham, Essex, Hampshire
ROLE: Bowler
DEBUT: First-class: 2012; List A: 2014; T20: 2014

BEST BATTING: 37 Durham vs Warwickshire, Edgbaston, 2018
BEST BOWLING: 6-37 Durham vs Middlesex, Chester-le-Street, 2018

WHAT WAS YOUR FIRST CRICKET CLUB? Shenfield CC, Essex
FAVOURITE CRICKET BAT? MRF Prodigy, size six. Made me feel like Sachin Tendulkar
WHICH BOWLER WOULD YOU LEAST LIKE TO FACE? Mitchell Johnson
WHO WOULD YOU ASK TO BAT FOR YOUR LIFE? Kane Williamson
FAVOURITE QUOTE OR SAYING? He's thrown a kettle over a pub, what have you done? (Gareth from The Office)
WHICH BOOK MEANS MOST TO YOU? The dictionary
ODDEST SPORT YOU'VE PLAYED? Bat and trap
TWITTER: @mattsalisbury10

Batting	Mat	Inns	NO	Runs	HS	Ave	SR	100	50	Ct	St
First-class	26	43	10	298	37	9.03	31.40	0	0	4	0
List A	7	2	1	6	5*	6.00	27.27	0	0	2	0
T20s	8	2	2	2	1*	-	100.00	0	0	2	0
Bowling	**Mat**	**Balls**	**Runs**	**Wkts**	**BBI**	**BBM**	**Ave**	**Econ**	**SR**	**5w**	**10**
First-class	26	3772	2356	71	6/37	7/107	33.18	3.74	53.1	1	0
List A	7	198	213	5	4/55	4/55	42.60	6.45	39.6	0	0
T20s	8	172	256	10	2/19	2/19	25.60	8.93	17.2	0	0

PHIL SALT RHB / OB / R0 / W0 / MVP83

FULL NAME: Philip Dean Salt
BORN: August 28, 1996, Bodelwyddan, Denbighshire, Wales
SQUAD NO: 28
HEIGHT: 6ft
NICKNAME: Salty, Hotdog, Knock 'Em Flat Salt
EDUCATION: Harrison College, Barbados; Reed's School, Surrey
TEAMS: Sussex
ROLE: Batsman
DEBUT: First-class: 2016; List A: 2015; T20: 2016

BEST BATTING: 148 Sussex vs Derbyshire, Hove, 2018
BEST BOWLING: 1-32 Sussex vs Warwickshire, Hove, 2018

WHAT WAS YOUR FIRST CRICKET CLUB? St Asaph CC, North Wales
CRICKETING HERO? Growing up in Barbados, I didn't look past Sir Garry Sobers
WHICH BOWLER WOULD YOU LEAST LIKE TO FACE? Jofra Archer – because he bowls off 17 yards in the nets
BEST INNINGS YOU'VE SEEN? My favourite shot was the huge six by Tymal Mills against Gloucestershire at Arundel in the 2016 T20 Blast. I'm pretty sure the ball is still going up
SURPRISING FACT ABOUT YOU? I once picked up Sir Garry Sobers' Indian takeaway by accident
WHAT WILL YOU BE DOING IN THE YEAR 2040? I'll be a managing director of an up-and-coming software firm
FAVOURITE QUOTE OR SAYING? If it ain't gone in three, it ain't meant to be
WHICH BOOK MEANS MOST TO YOU? Cats Galore – A Compendium of Cultured Cats by Susan Herbert
TWITTER: @PhilSalt1

Batting	Mat	Inns	NO	Runs	HS	Ave	SR	100	50	Ct	St
First-class	22	35	1	950	148	27.94	70.57	2	3	14	0
List A	9	9	0	253	81	28.11	96.56	0	2	2	0
T20s	35	33	3	706	74	23.53	151.50	0	4	9	1
Bowling	**Mat**	**Balls**	**Runs**	**Wkts**	**BBI**	**BBM**	**Ave**	**Econ**	**SR**	**5w**	**10**
First-class	22	54	32	1	1/32	1/32	32.00	3.55	54.0	0	0
List A	9	-	-	-	-	-	-	-	-	-	-
T20s	35	-	-	-	-	-	-	-	-	-	-

ANDREW SALTER RHB / OB / R0 / W0

FULL NAME: Andrew Graham Salter
BORN: June 1, 1993, Haverfordwest, Pembrokeshire, Wales
SQUAD NO: 21
HEIGHT: 5ft 10in
NICKNAME: Beak, Salty
EDUCATION: Milford Haven School, Pembrokeshire; Cardiff Metropolitan University
TEAMS: Glamorgan
ROLE: Allrounder
DEBUT: First-class: 2012; List A: 2012; T20: 2014

BEST BATTING: 88 Glamorgan vs Gloucestershire, Cardiff, 2017
BEST BOWLING: 4-80 Glamorgan vs Warwickshire, Edgbaston, 2018

WHAT GOT YOU INTO CRICKET? Trying to bowl my brother out in the garden
FAMILY TIES? My father and brother both played, my mum made teas and scored
'ROY OF THE ROVERS' MOMENT? Hitting six sixes in an over for St Ishmaels U15
BEST THING ABOUT YOUR HOME GROUND? The warm Welsh welcome
IF YOU WEREN'T A CRICKETER? I'd be a Steve McQueen wannabe
SURPRISING FACT ABOUT YOU? I co-manage a motorcycle initiative called Baffle Culture which aims at "seizing the opportunity to bring like-minded riders together"
SURPRISING FACT ABOUT A TEAMMATE? Kiran Carlson can't reach the sweet jar in the kitchen
WHERE IS PARADISE? Pembrokeshire
CRICKETING HERO? Nathan Lyon – appreciation from one off-spinner to another
NON-CRICKETING HERO? Charley Boorman (TV presenter and motorbike enthusiast)
TWITTER: @AndySalts

Batting	Mat	Inns	NO	Runs	HS	Ave	SR	100	50	Ct	St
First-class	54	84	17	1582	88	23.61	43.12	0	8	28	0
List A	36	28	10	371	51	20.61	88.12	0	1	9	0
T20s	56	33	16	241	37*	14.17	115.86	0	0	17	0
Bowling	**Mat**	**Balls**	**Runs**	**Wkts**	**BBI**	**BBM**	**Ave**	**Econ**	**SR**	**5w**	**10**
First-class	54	6907	4027	82	4/80	6/69	49.10	3.49	84.2	0	0
List A	36	1288	1155	17	2/41	2/41	67.94	5.38	75.7	0	0
T20s	56	702	956	29	3/34	3/34	32.96	8.17	24.2	0	0

BEN SANDERSON RHB / RMF / R0 / W2 / MVP52

FULL NAME: Ben William Sanderson
BORN: January 3, 1989, Sheffield
SQUAD NO: 26
HEIGHT: 6ft
NICKNAME: Sandoooo
EDUCATION: Ecclesfield School, Sheffield; Sheffield College
TEAMS: Northamptonshire, Yorkshire
ROLE: Bowler
DEBUT: First-class: 2008; List A: 2010; T20: 2010

BEST BATTING: 42 Northamptonshire vs Kent, Canterbury, 2015
BEST BOWLING: 8-73 Northamptonshire vs Gloucestershire, Northampton, 2016
COUNTY CAP: 2018 (Northamptonshire)

WHAT WAS YOUR FIRST CRICKET CLUB? Whitley Hall CC, Sheffield. Very good drinkers
FAVOURITE CRICKET BAT? Blue Dog Wizard
BEST ADVICE EVER RECEIVED? Bite the apple and brush your ear when bowling
WHICH BOWLER WOULD YOU LEAST LIKE TO FACE? My dad. He always gets me out
BEST INNINGS YOU'VE SEEN? Josh Cobb's 80 to win us the 2016 T20 Blast
WHO WOULD YOU ASK TO BAT FOR YOUR LIFE? No one in the Northants dressing room (they're all sloggers)
YOUR BIGGEST CRICKETING REGRET? Being a bowler
WHAT WILL YOU BE DOING IN THE YEAR 2040? Still opening the bowling for Northants I suppose
FAVOURITE QUOTE OR SAYING? The cheaper the better
WHICH BOOK MEANS MOST TO YOU? My chequebook
TWITTER: @sando567

Batting	Mat	Inns	NO	Runs	HS	Ave	SR	100	50	Ct	St
First-class	45	60	24	259	42	7.19	40.65	0	0	9	0
List A	25	10	6	54	19*	13.50	75.00	0	0	7	0
T20s	26	10	8	30	12*	15.00	111.11	0	0	0	0
Bowling	**Mat**	**Balls**	**Runs**	**Wkts**	**BBI**	**BBM**	**Ave**	**Econ**	**SR**	**5w**	**10**
First-class	45	7860	3479	172	8/73	10/89	20.22	2.65	45.6	9	1
List A	25	930	935	23	3/36	3/36	40.65	6.03	40.4	0	0
T20s	26	497	762	28	4/21	4/21	27.21	9.19	17.7	0	0

GEORGE SCOTT

RHB / RM / R0 / W0

FULL NAME: George Frederick Buchan Scott
BORN: November 6, 1995, Hemel Hempstead, Hertfordshire
SQUAD NO: 17
HEIGHT: 6ft 2in
NICKNAME: Scotty
EDUCATION: Beechwood Park School, St Albans; St Albans School; University of Leeds
TEAMS: Middlesex
ROLE: Allrounder
DEBUT: First-class: 2015; List A: 2015; T20: 2015

BEST BATTING: 16* Leeds/Bradford MCCU vs Sussex, Hove, 2016
BEST BOWLING: 2-67 Leeds/Bradford MCCU vs Sussex, Hove, 2015

FAMILY TIES? I have an older brother and younger brother who play Minor Counties cricket for Hertfordshire, and another younger brother in the Middlesex Academy
BEST ADVICE EVER RECEIVED? The stiller you are, the easier it is to see
'ROY OF THE ROVERS' MOMENT? Playing in front of a full house of 28,000 at Lord's
SURPRISING FACT ABOUT YOU? I was a music scholar at St Albans School, playing the piano and the bassoon
CRICKETING HERO? Kumar Sangakarra – having a degree in Law and being one of the best cricketers ever shows he must be a very intelligent and well-rounded individual
NON-CRICKETING HEROES? My brothers
TWITTER: @georgefbscott

Batting	Mat	Inns	NO	Runs	HS	Ave	SR	100	50	Ct	St
First-class	5	7	2	53	16*	10.60	26.36	0	0	2	0
List A	2	2	0	6	4	3.00	28.57	0	0	0	0
T20s	15	13	4	207	38*	23.00	100.48	0	0	3	0
Bowling	**Mat**	**Balls**	**Runs**	**Wkts**	**BBI**	**BBM**	**Ave**	**Econ**	**SR**	**5w**	**10**
First-class	5	198	144	2	2/67	2/67	72.00	4.36	99.0	0	0
List A	2	18	28	0	-	-	-	9.33	-	0	0
T20s	15	42	68	2	1/14	1/14	34.00	9.71	21.0	0	0

GEORGE SCRIMSHAW RHB / RFM / R0 / W0

FULL NAME: George Louis Sheridan Scrimshaw
BORN: February 10, 1998, Burton-on-Trent, Staffordshire
SQUAD NO: 9
HEIGHT: 6ft 6in
NICKNAME: Scrim, Scrimmy, Groot
EDUCATION: Thomas Russel Junior School; John Taylor High School, Burton-on-Trent
TEAMS: Worcestershire
ROLE: Bowler
DEBUT: T20: 2017

FAMILY TIES? My dad and grandad both played county age-group cricket
WHAT WAS YOUR FIRST CRICKET CLUB? Dunstall CC, Burton-upon-Trent, Staffordshire – aka Deer Park, home of the Stags
FAVOURITE CRICKET BAT? Gray-Nicolls Dynadrive. Hit many a six with that bat
CRICKETING HERO? Dale Steyn – I love his aggression. For a fast bowler like myself, he's a role model
'ROY OF THE ROVERS' MOMENT? Taking 5-12 in a Second XI T20 match for Worcestershire against Yorkshire in 2017
BEST THING ABOUT YOUR HOME GROUND? The balcony at New Road
WHICH BOWLER WOULD YOU LEAST LIKE TO FACE? Jofra Archer – because he bowls at the speed of light
BEST INNINGS YOU'VE SEEN? AB de Villiers smashing the fastest hundred in ODI cricket (31 balls). Such skill and variety of shot. Not many bowlers know where to bowl at him
SURPRISING FACT ABOUT YOU? I once hit 16 sixes in a row in Kwik Cricket
TWITTER: @Gscrimshaw98

Batting	Mat	Inns	NO	Runs	HS	Ave	SR	100	50	Ct	St
T20s	4	1	1	1	1*	-	50.00	0	0	0	0
Bowling	**Mat**	**Balls**	**Runs**	**Wkts**	**BBI**	**BBM**	**Ave**	**Econ**	**SR**	**5w**	**10**
T20s	4	60	90	3	1/20	1/20	30.00	9.00	20.0	0	0

NICK SELMAN

RHB / RM / R0 / W0

GLAMORGAN

FULL NAME: Nicholas James Selman
BORN: October 18, 1995, Brisbane, Australia
SQUAD NO: 9
HEIGHT: 6ft 3in
NICKNAME: Salmon
EDUCATION: Matthew Flinders Anglican College, Queensland, Australia
TEAMS: Glamorgan
ROLE: Batsman
DEBUT: First-class: 2016; List A: 2016; T20: 2016

BEST BATTING: 142* Glamorgan vs Gloucestershire, Cardiff, 2017

WHAT GOT YOU INTO CRICKET? Playing in the backyard with my mum and dad
BEST ADVICE EVER RECEIVED? Play straight, leave well
'ROY OF THE ROVERS' MOMENT? Hitting 14 off the last over to beat Durham in a Championship game in 2017
BEST THING ABOUT YOUR HOME GROUND? The all-you-can-eat lunches
IF YOU WEREN'T A CRICKETER? I'd be a groundsman
SURPRISING FACT ABOUT YOU? I name my bats after greyhounds
WHERE IS PARADISE? Coogee Beach
CRICKETING HERO? Virat Kohli – he's on a different level when it comes to batting. Works extremely hard on and off the field
NON-CRICKETING HERO? Hugh Bowman (jockey) – always finds a way to win
TWITTER: @nickselman22

Batting	Mat	Inns	NO	Runs	HS	Ave	SR	100	50	Ct	St
First-class	37	69	4	1775	142*	27.30	46.61	6	5	44	0
List A	9	9	0	242	92	26.88	67.78	0	1	3	0
T20s	9	6	1	127	66	25.40	132.29	0	1	3	0
Bowling	**Mat**	**Balls**	**Runs**	**Wkts**	**BBI**	**BBM**	**Ave**	**Econ**	**SR**	**5w**	**10**
First-class	37	24	14	0	-	-	-	3.50	-	0	0
List A	9	-	-	-	-	-	-	-	-	-	-
T20s	9	-	-	-	-	-	-	-	-	-	-

JOSH SHAW

RHB / RMF / R0 / W0

FULL NAME: Joshua Shaw
BORN: January 3, 1996, Wakefield, Yorkshire
SQUAD NO: 25
HEIGHT: 6ft 1in
NICKNAME: Shawy
EDUCATION: Crofton Academy, West Yorkshire; Skills Exchange College, Wakefield
TEAMS: Yorkshire, Gloucestershire
ROLE: Bowler
DEBUT: First-class: 2016; T20: 2015

BEST BATTING: 42 Yorkshire vs Somerset, Headingley, 2018
BEST BOWLING: 5-79 Gloucestershire vs Sussex, Bristol, 2016

WHAT GOT YOU INTO CRICKET? My father Chris played for Yorkshire. We also lived on the back of Streethouse CC so I was always around cricket from a young age
'ROY OF THE ROVERS' MOMENT? Taking a hat-trick for Yorkshire Academy in the Yorkshire League Cup final in 2014
BEST THING ABOUT YOUR HOME GROUND? It's so homely
IF YOU WEREN'T A CRICKETER? I'd be working in the joinery trade
SURPRISING FACT ABOUT YOU? I passed my driving test with no minors
CRICKETING HERO? Andrew Flintoff – for his ability to perform with bat and ball when it mattered most
NON-CRICKETING HERO? Tiger Woods – for his natural ability but also his willingness to work hard to improve his game
TWITTER: @joshuashaw1

Batting	Mat	Inns	NO	Runs	HS	Ave	SR	100	50	Ct	St
First-class	24	32	7	298	42	11.92	37.81	0	0	5	0
T20s	4	2	1	1	1	1.00	50.00	0	0	1	0
Bowling	**Mat**	**Balls**	**Runs**	**Wkts**	**BBI**	**BBM**	**Ave**	**Econ**	**SR**	**5w**	**10**
First-class	24	3669	2396	59	5/79	5/79	40.61	3.91	62.1	2	0
T20s	4	60	99	0	-	-	-	9.90	-	0	0

D'ARCY SHORT

LHB / SLW / R0 / W0

DURHAM

FULL NAME: D'Arcy John Matthew Short
BORN: August 9, 1990, Katherine, Northern Territory, Australia
SQUAD NO: TBC
TEAMS: Australia, Durham, Hobart Hurricanes, Rajasthan Royal, Western Australia
ROLE: Batsman
DEBUT: ODI: 2018; T20I: 2018; First-class: 2016; List A: 2011; T20: 2016

BEST BATTING: 66 Western Australia vs South Australia, Adelaide, 2018
BEST BOWLING: 3-78 Western Australia vs Victoria, Melbourne, 2017

TWITTER: @ShortDarcy
NOTES: Durham have signed the Australian top-order batsman and left-arm wrist-spinner for the 2019 T20 Blast. Short made his ODI debut against England at Cardiff in 2018 and featured regularly for Australia in white-ball cricket last year. His 76 from 44 balls helped the Aussies record the highest T20I run-chase of 244 against New Zealand last year. Known for his early-order aggression with the bat and unusual bowling style, the 28-year-old has been voted Player of the Tournament in the last two editions of the Big Bash, hitting 637 runs and taking 10 wickets for Hobart Hurricanes in the 2018/19 competition. He was described as "one of the finest T20 batsmen in world cricket" by Durham director of cricket Marcus North

Batting	Mat	Inns	NO	Runs	HS	Ave	SR	100	50	Ct	St
ODIs	4	4	1	83	47*	27.66	83.83	0	0	1	0
T20Is	20	20	2	592	76	32.88	120.81	0	4	8	0
First-class	11	20	0	452	66	22.60	52.68	0	2	9	0
List A	26	22	2	890	257	44.50	112.94	2	3	9	0
T20s	62	62	6	2114	122*	37.75	136.21	1	16	21	0
Bowling	**Mat**	**Balls**	**Runs**	**Wkts**	**BBI**	**BBM**	**Ave**	**Econ**	**SR**	**5w**	**10**
ODIs	4	42	59	0	-	-	-	8.42	-	0	0
T20Is	20	114	151	3	1/13	1/13	50.33	7.94	38.0	0	0
First-class	11	891	606	18	3/78	4/43	33.66	4.08	49.5	0	0
List A	26	700	683	17	3/53	3/53	40.17	5.85	41.1	0	0
T20s	62	518	706	21	2/17	2/17	33.61	8.17	24.6	0	0

JACK SHUTT

RHB / OB / R0 / W0

FULL NAME: Jack William Shutt
BORN: June 24, 1997, Barnsley
SQUAD NO: 24
EDUCATION: Kirk Balk School, Barnsley; Thomas Rotherham College, South Yorkshire
TEAMS: Yorkshire
ROLE: Bowler

NOTES: The Barnsley-born off-spinner has yet to make his first-team debut but was named in the squad for a late-season Championship match against Surrey at The Oval in 2017 having impressed in Yorkshire's second team. Earlier that summer he had returned a Man-of-the-Match display in the Second XI Trophy final win over Middlesex at Headingley, taking 4-19 from 3.3 overs to mop up the tail. Shutt first played for the Academy in 2013, shortly after his 16th birthday. He has represented Yorkshire at U17 and U19 level, making his Second XI debut in a four-day friendly against Kent in Canterbury in 2015. He played eight matches for the Second XI last summer. Shutt said: "I definitely didn't think I would be a professional cricketer when I was 12, 13 or 14. It wasn't even in my mind because I wasn't good enough for the Yorkshire age-group teams. It's a dream come true to be in this position and now I just want to make the most of it. I think I've been helped by having a big growth-spurt when I was 16 and also by playing men's cricket week in, week out for Elsecar CC"

DOMINIC SIBLEY RHB / OB / R0 / W0

FULL NAME: Dominic Peter Sibley
BORN: September 5, 1995, Epsom, Surrey
SQUAD NO: 45
HEIGHT: 6ft 3in
NICKNAME: Frocko, Big Tree
EDUCATION: Whitgift School, Croydon
TEAMS: Warwickshire, Surrey
ROLE: Batsman
DEBUT: First-class: 2013; List A: 2013; T20: 2016

BEST BATTING: 242 Surrey vs Yorkshire, The Oval, 2013
BEST BOWLING: 2-103 Surrey vs Hampshire, Southampton, 2016

WHAT WAS YOUR FIRST CRICKET CLUB? Ashtead CC, Surrey
CRICKETING HERO? Virat Kohli
WHICH BOWLER WOULD YOU LEAST LIKE TO FACE? Shoaib Akhtar
BEST INNINGS YOU'VE SEEN? Kevin Pietersen's hundred against South Africa in the 2012 Headingley Test
WHICH RULE WOULD YOU CHANGE ABOUT CRICKET? Introduce free hits for no-balls in four-day cricket
YOUR BIGGEST CRICKETING REGRET? Playing while I did my A-Levels
SURPRISING FACT ABOUT YOU? I am half-French
WHICH BOOK MEANS MOST TO YOU? The Alchemist by Paulo Coelho
ODDEST SPORT YOU'VE PLAYED? Hurling
TWITTER: @DomSibley

Batting	Mat	Inns	NO	Runs	HS	Ave	SR	100	50	Ct	St
First-class	51	87	9	2622	242	33.61	40.81	6	14	43	0
List A	14	12	2	301	115	30.10	84.31	1	0	6	0
T20s	24	21	3	598	74*	33.22	120.80	0	5	11	0
Bowling	**Mat**	**Balls**	**Runs**	**Wkts**	**BBI**	**BBM**	**Ave**	**Econ**	**SR**	**5w**	**10**
First-class	51	374	264	4	2/103	2/117	66.00	4.23	93.5	0	0
List A	14	54	62	1	1/20	1/20	62.00	6.88	54.0	0	0
T20s	24	222	324	5	2/33	2/33	64.80	8.75	44.4	0	0

PETER SIDDLE RHB / RFM / R0 / W0

FULL NAME: Peter Matthew Siddle
BORN: November 25, 1984, Traralgon, Victoria, Australia
SQUAD NO: 64
HEIGHT: 6ft 2in
NICKNAME: Vicious, Dermie
TEAMS: Australia, Essex, Adelaide Strikers, Lancashire, Melbourne Renegades, Nottinghamshire, Victoria
ROLE: Bowler
DEBUT: Test: 2008; ODI: 2009; T20I: 2009; First-class: 2005; List A: 2005; T20: 2006

BEST BATTING: 103* Australia A vs Scotland, Edinburgh, 2013
BEST BOWLING: 8-54 Victoria vs South Australia, Adelaide, 2015
COUNTY CAP: 2014 (Nottinghamshire)

TWITTER: @petersiddle403
NOTES: Essex first signed Siddle for their T20 campaign in 2012 but he pulled out with injury. He then played county cricket for Nottinghamshire in 2014 before switching to Lancashire in 2015. Siddle had a devastating impact for Essex last summer, taking 37 wickets at 16.41 in seven Championship matches. He has agreed a two-year deal to be the club's overseas player until the end of next season, although the Ashes may restrict his appearances this summer. Siddle was a junior wood-chopping champion before giving up the pursuit because he feared that slicing off a toe could end his cricket career. He is a vegan and has said he eats "between 15-20 bananas a day"

Batting	Mat	Inns	NO	Runs	HS	Ave	SR	100	50	Ct	St
Tests	64	90	14	1080	51	14.21	47.05	0	2	17	0
ODIs	20	6	3	31	10*	10.33	103.33	0	0	1	0
T20Is	2	1	1	1	1*	-	100.00	0	0	0	0
First-class	156	209	36	2876	103*	16.62	50.80	1	5	50	0
List A	55	29	10	240	62	12.63	99.17	0	1	6	0
T20s	46	14	9	31	9*	6.20	83.78	0	0	9	0
Bowling	**Mat**	**Balls**	**Runs**	**Wkts**	**BBI**	**BBM**	**Ave**	**Econ**	**SR**	**5w**	**10**
Tests	64	13325	6482	214	6/54	9/104	30.28	2.91	62.2	8	0
ODIs	20	901	743	17	3/55	3/55	43.70	4.94	53.0	0	0
T20Is	2	48	58	3	2/24	2/24	19.33	7.25	16.0	0	0
First-class	156	30068	14723	527	8/54	9/77	27.93	2.93	57.0	20	0
List A	55	2764	2140	59	4/27	4/27	36.27	4.64	46.8	0	0
T20s	46	936	1143	40	4/29	4/29	28.57	7.32	23.4	0	0

RYAN SIDEBOTTOM RHB / RMF / R0 / W0

FULL NAME: Ryan Nathan Sidebottom
BORN: August 14, 1989, Shepparton, Victoria, Australia
SQUAD NO: 22
HEIGHT: 6ft 2in
NICKNAME: Sidey, Sid, Siddy
EDUCATION: Wanganui Park Secondary College, Victoria, Australia
TEAMS: Warwickshire, Victoria
ROLE: Bowler
DEBUT: First-class: 2013

BEST BATTING: 13 Warwickshire vs Hampshire, Edgbaston, 2017
BEST BOWLING: 6-35 Warwickshire vs Northamptonshire, Northampton, 2018

WHAT WAS YOUR FIRST CRICKET CLUB? Northerners CC, Victoria, Australia. Formed after a merger of two clubs called Tallygaroopna and Congupna in the early 2000s
FAVOURITE CRICKET BAT? My Kookaburra Kahuna. First bat I owned and I basically carried it everywhere
CRICKETING HERO? Glenn McGrath
WHICH BOWLER WOULD YOU LEAST LIKE TO FACE? Olly Stone – he's quick!
BEST INNINGS YOU'VE SEEN? Ian Bell's double hundred against Glamorgan last summer. It was a pleasure to watch
WHO WOULD YOU ASK TO BAT FOR YOUR LIFE? Mike Hussey
WHICH RULE WOULD YOU CHANGE ABOUT CRICKET? The one that says only two bouncers are allowed per over
SURPRISING FACT ABOUT YOU? I've got four brothers, one of whom plays Aussie rules for Collingwood. We grew up in Tallygaroopna near Melbourne, but I have a British passport because my mum moved to Devon
WHAT WILL YOU BE DOING IN THE YEAR 2040? Living back home in Australia
TWITTER: @ryansidebottom2

Batting	Mat	Inns	NO	Runs	HS	Ave	SR	100	50	Ct	St
First-class	17	26	12	56	13	4.00	23.14	0	0	5	0
Bowling	**Mat**	**Balls**	**Runs**	**Wkts**	**BBI**	**BBM**	**Ave**	**Econ**	**SR**	**5w**	**10**
First-class	17	2051	1247	49	6/35	10/96	25.44	3.64	41.8	1	1

JOHN SIMPSON

LHB / WK / R0 / W0

FULL NAME: John Andrew Simpson
BORN: July 13, 1988, Bury, Lancashire
SQUAD NO: 20
HEIGHT: 5ft 10in
NICKNAME: Simmo
EDUCATION: St Gabriel's RC High School, Bury; Holy Cross College, Bury
TEAMS: Middlesex
ROLE: Wicketkeeper
DEBUT: First-class: 2009; List A: 2009; T20: 2009

BEST BATTING: 143 Middlesex vs Surrey, Lord's, 2011

COUNTY CAP: 2011

FAMILY TIES? Dad played for England Amateurs and Lancashire Cricket Board and holds club and league records in the Lancashire/Central Lancashire leagues. Grandad captained the Army XI. My uncle plays for Woodbank CC. Two cousins play for Lancashire Second XI
WHAT WAS YOUR FIRST CRICKET CLUB? Ramsbottom CC, Greater Manchester. One of the most picturesque grounds in the UK
BEST ADVICE EVER RECEIVED? There are no fielders in the air
WHICH BOWLER WOULD YOU LEAST LIKE TO FACE? Nick Gubbins – I would be required to hit every ball for six
SURPRISING FACT ABOUT YOU? I don't drink tea or coffee
FAVOURITE QUOTE OR SAYING? Swing hard
WHICH BOOK MEANS MOST TO YOU? The Exhaustive Guide to Club Cricket by Dan Whiting. I wrote the foreword to it
TWITTER: @johnsimpson_88

Batting	Mat	Inns	NO	Runs	HS	Ave	SR	100	50	Ct	St
First-class	140	221	33	5827	143	30.99	47.23	5	33	430	24
List A	84	63	10	1355	82*	25.56	83.59	0	7	70	16
T20s	94	82	14	1557	84*	22.89	128.57	0	7	46	17
Bowling	**Mat**	**Balls**	**Runs**	**Wkts**	**BBI**	**BBM**	**Ave**	**Econ**	**SR**	**5w**	**10**
First-class	140	12	21	0	-	-	-	10.50	-	0	0
List A	84	-	-	-	-	-	-	-	-	-	-
T20s	94	-	-	-	-	-	-	-	-	-	-

PREM SISODIYA RHB / SLA / R0 / W0

FULL NAME: Prem Sisodiya
BORN: September 21, 1998, Cardiff, Wales
SQUAD NO: 32
HEIGHT: 5ft 11in
NICKNAME: Prince
EDUCATION: Clifton College, Bristol; Cardiff Metropolitan University
TEAMS: Glamorgan
ROLE: Bowler
DEBUT: First-class: 2018

BEST BATTING: 38 Glamorgan vs Derbyshire, Swansea, 2018
BEST BOWLING: 3-54 Glamorgan vs Derbyshire, Swansea, 2018

WHAT WAS YOUR FIRST CRICKET CLUB? Cardiff CC. In 2014 we won the league-and-cup double with a team whose average age was 19
FAVOURITE CRICKET BAT? GM Purist (Michael Vaughan Edition) – an absolute weapon
WHICH BOWLER WOULD YOU LEAST LIKE TO FACE? Darren Stevens
BEST INNINGS YOU'VE SEEN? MS Dhoni's match-winning 91 not out against Sri Lanka in the 2011 World Cup final. He's an unbelievable finisher
WHO WOULD YOU ASK TO BAT FOR YOUR LIFE? Monty Panesar – look at that incredible innings he played at Cardiff in 2009
WHICH RULE WOULD YOU CHANGE ABOUT CRICKET? I would introduce free hits in Tests
YOUR BIGGEST CRICKETING REGRET? Trying to switch-hit when I was on 97
WHAT WILL YOU BE DOING IN THE YEAR 2040? Hopefully coaching at a school
WHICH BOOK MEANS MOST TO YOU? Playing It My Way by Sachin Tendulkar
TWITTER: @PremSisodiya

Batting	Mat	Inns	NO	Runs	HS	Ave	SR	100	50	Ct	St
First-class	2	4	1	41	38	13.66	54.66	0	0	1	0
Bowling	**Mat**	**Balls**	**Runs**	**Wkts**	**BBI**	**BBM**	**Ave**	**Econ**	**SR**	**5w**	**10**
First-class	2	380	151	7	3/54	5/73	21.57	2.38	54.2	0	0

BEN SLATER LHB / OB / R1 / W0 / MVP80

FULL NAME: Benjamin Thomas Slater
BORN: August 26, 1991, Chesterfield, Derbyshire
SQUAD NO: 26
HEIGHT: 5ft 11in
NICKNAME: BennySlats, Slats, Slatsy
EDUCATION: Netherthorpe School, Staveley; Leeds Metropolitan University
TEAMS: Nottinghamshire, Derbyshire, Southern Rocks
ROLE: Batsman
DEBUT: First-class: 2012; List A: 2012; T20: 2012

BEST BATTING: 119 Derbyshire vs Leicestershire, Derby, 2014

WHAT WAS YOUR FIRST CRICKET CLUB? Chesterfield CC, Derbyshire. They play at Queen's Park – nicest outground in the country
CRICKETING HEROES? Brian Lara, Marcus Trescothick, Matthew Hayden, my grandad (all left-handed batsmen)
WHICH BOWLER WOULD YOU LEAST LIKE TO FACE? Duanne Olivier
BEST INNINGS YOU'VE SEEN? Harvey Hosein's maiden first-class fifty in 2015. After setting off for his 50th run, his knees buckled mid-pitch, and watching him scramble along the floor to the other end was one of the funniest things I've seen
WHO WOULD YOU ASK TO BAT FOR YOUR LIFE? Luke Fletcher
WHICH RULE WOULD YOU CHANGE ABOUT CRICKET? Tea should be longer than 20 minutes
YOUR BIGGEST CRICKETING REGRET? Getting out for 99 against Middlesex in the first game of last season
FAVOURITE QUOTE OR SAYING? Get rich or die trying
TWITTER: @BennySlats

Batting	Mat	Inns	NO	Runs	HS	Ave	SR	100	50	Ct	St
First-class	69	129	6	4003	119	32.54	45.36	4	24	24	0
List A	32	29	4	1296	148*	51.84	86.68	4	6	3	0
T20s	11	11	0	236	57	21.45	105.82	0	1	0	0
Bowling	**Mat**	**Balls**	**Runs**	**Wkts**	**BBI**	**BBM**	**Ave**	**Econ**	**SR**	**5w**	**10**
First-class	69	105	113	0	-	-	-	6.45	-	0	0
List A	32	-	-	-	-	-	-	-	-	-	-
T20s	11	-	-	-	-	-	-	-	-	-	-

DARYN SMIT RHB / LB / WK / R0 / W0

FULL NAME: Daryn Smit
BORN: January 28, 1984, Durban, South Africa
SQUAD NO: 11
HEIGHT: 6ft 3in
NICKNAME: Smitty, Speech, Dazza
EDUCATION: Northwood School, Durban; University of South Africa
TEAMS: Derbyshire, Dolphins, KwaZulu-Natal
ROLE: Batsman
DEBUT: First-class: 2004; List A: 2004; T20: 2004

BEST BATTING: 156* KwaZulu-Natal vs North West, Durban, 2015
BEST BOWLING: 7-27 KwaZulu-Natal vs South Western Districts, Durban, 2014

WHAT WAS YOUR FIRST CRICKET CLUB? Delta CC, South Africa. I played there for 16 years and it was my one and only club until I had one season at my school's old boys' club the year before emigrating to the UK in 2016
FAVOURITE CRICKET BAT? Kookaburra Bubble. My mum brought it back from Australia and it was my first proper English willow bat. The Bubble was the thing back then
WHICH BOWLER WOULD YOU LEAST LIKE TO FACE? Waqar Younis – I like my toes
BEST INNINGS YOU'VE SEEN? Jacques Kallis's final Test innings, when he scored a hundred at Kingsmead. A fitting farewell to a master of his trade. Got goosebumps witnessing it live
YOUR BIGGEST CRICKETING REGRET? Not moving to England earlier. My career at the Dolphins had run its course about three years earlier, but making that decision to move is so difficult
ODDEST SPORT YOU'VE PLAYED? Jukskei
TWITTER: @darynsmit

Batting	Mat	Inns	NO	Runs	HS	Ave	SR	100	50	Ct	St
First-class	137	208	37	6077	156*	35.53	46.73	9	33	361	22
List A	123	93	26	2139	109	31.92	79.57	1	11	115	13
T20s	98	58	22	886	57	24.61	123.39	0	2	53	11
Bowling	**Mat**	**Balls**	**Runs**	**Wkts**	**BBI**	**BBM**	**Ave**	**Econ**	**SR**	**5w**	**10**
First-class	137	6749	3501	106	7/27	8/30	33.02	3.11	63.6	3	0
List A	123	2107	1718	45	4/39	4/39	38.17	4.89	46.8	0	0
T20s	98	630	721	28	3/19	3/19	25.75	6.86	22.5	0	0

JAMIE SMITH

RHB / WK / R0 / W0

FULL NAME: Jamie Luke Smith
BORN: July 12, 2000, Epsom, Surrey
SQUAD NO: 11
HEIGHT: 6ft 1in
NICKNAME: Smudger
EDUCATION: Whitgift School, Croydon
TEAMS: Surrey
ROLE: Wicketkeeper
DEBUT: T20: 2018

WHAT WAS YOUR FIRST CRICKET CLUB? Sutton CC, Surrey
FAVOURITE CRICKET BAT? A Woodworm Torch – my first bat
WHICH BOWLER WOULD YOU LEAST LIKE TO FACE? Brett Lee – he bowled too fast
BEST INNINGS YOU'VE SEEN? An opening partnership of nearly 200 between Aaron Finch and Jason Roy in the T20 against Middlesex at The Oval last summer
WHO WOULD YOU ASK TO BAT FOR YOUR LIFE? Ricky Ponting
WHICH RULE WOULD YOU CHANGE ABOUT CRICKET? Longer lunch, longer tea
WHAT WILL YOU BE DOING IN THE YEAR 2040? I'll be manager of West Ham United
FAVOURITE QUOTE OR SAYING? The best preparation for tomorrow is doing your best today
WHICH BOOK MEANS MOST TO YOU? Legacy – What the All Blacks Can Teach Us About the Business of Life by James Kerr
ODDEST SPORT YOU'VE PLAYED? Zorb football
TWITTER: @Jamiesm148

Batting	Mat	Inns	NO	Runs	HS	Ave	SR	100	50	Ct	St
T20s	2	2	1	7	7*	7.00	70.00	0	0	1	0
Bowling	**Mat**	**Balls**	**Runs**	**Wkts**	**BBI**	**BBM**	**Ave**	**Econ**	**SR**	**5w**	**10**
T20s	2	-	-	-	-	-	-	-	-	-	-

RUAIDHRI SMITH

RHB / RM / R0 / W0

FULL NAME: Ruaidhri Alexander James Smith
BORN: August 5, 1994, Glasgow, Scotland
SQUAD NO: 20
HEIGHT: 6ft 1in
NICKNAME: Trigger
EDUCATION: The Cathedral School, Llandaff; Shrewsbury School; University of Bristol
TEAMS: Scotland, Glamorgan
ROLE: Allrounder
DEBUT: ODI: 2016; T20I: 2019; First-class: 2013; List A: 2013; T20: 2014

BEST BATTING: 57* Glamorgan vs Gloucestershire, Bristol, 2014
BEST BOWLING: 5-87 Glamorgan vs Durham, Cardiff, 2018

WHAT WAS YOUR FIRST CRICKET CLUB? St Fagans CC, Cardiff. Provides the best teas in south Wales
BEST INNINGS YOU'VE SEEN? AB de Villiers's 169 in the 2012 Perth Test
WHO WOULD YOU ASK TO BAT FOR YOUR LIFE? Cheteshwar Pujara
WHICH RULE WOULD YOU CHANGE ABOUT CRICKET? Lbws can be given if it pitches outside leg stump
SURPRISING FACT ABOUT YOU? Born in Scotland, Irish mother, English mother, raised in Wales
ODDEST SPORT YOU'VE PLAYED? Bike polo
TWITTER: @ruaidhrismith

Batting	Mat	Inns	NO	Runs	HS	Ave	SR	100	50	Ct	St
ODIs	2	1	0	10	10	10.00	166.66	0	0	0	0
T20Is	2	1	1	9	9*	-	128.57	0	0	0	0
First-class	26	37	6	620	57*	20.00	59.21	0	2	4	0
List A	18	11	3	71	14	8.87	92.20	0	0	4	0
T20s	15	9	6	80	22*	26.66	133.33	0	0	5	0
Bowling	**Mat**	**Balls**	**Runs**	**Wkts**	**BBI**	**BBM**	**Ave**	**Econ**	**SR**	**5w**	**10**
ODIs	2	90	97	1	1/34	1/34	97.00	6.46	90.0	0	0
T20Is	2	41	66	0	-	-	-	9.65	-	0	0
First-class	26	3090	2064	58	5/87	7/148	35.58	4.00	53.2	1	0
List A	18	572	591	18	4/7	4/7	32.83	6.19	31.7	0	0
T20s	15	213	296	10	4/6	4/6	29.60	8.33	21.3	0	0

TOM SMITH

RHB / SLA / R0 / W0

FULL NAME: Thomas Michael John Smith
BORN: August 29, 1987, Eastbourne, Sussex
SQUAD NO: 6
HEIGHT: 5ft 9in
NICKNAME: Smudge
EDUCATION: Seaford Head Community College, East Sussex; Sussex Downs College
TEAMS: Gloucestershire, Middlesex, Surrey, Sussex
ROLE: Bowler
DEBUT: First-class: 2007; List A: 2006; T20: 2007

BEST BATTING: 80 Gloucestershire vs Surrey, Bristol, 2014
BEST BOWLING: 4-35 Gloucestershire vs Kent, Canterbury, 2014
COUNTY CAP: 2013 (Gloucestershire)

WHAT WAS YOUR FIRST CRICKET CLUB? Eastbourne CC, East Sussex. I started aged four on Sunday mornings and went on to captain the club and play a professional match there (Gloucestershire against Sussex)
FAVOURITE CRICKET BAT? Woodstock Air Stream – I got 270 in a second-team game with it
CRICKETING HERO? Daniel Vettori
BEST ADVICE EVER RECEIVED? Peel ginger with a teaspoon
WHICH BOWLER WOULD YOU LEAST LIKE TO FACE? Benny Howell – he has 25 variations
BEST INNINGS YOU'VE SEEN? A last-wicket stand of 137 between Liam Norwell and Craig Miles at Cheltenham in 2014. We still lost but it was amazing to watch
WHO WOULD YOU ASK TO BAT FOR YOUR LIFE? Murray Goodwin – I watched him all the time when I started at Sussex and he never seemed to get out
SURPRISING FACT ABOUT YOU? I'm a qualified plumber
FAVOURITE QUOTE OR SAYING? The darkest nights produce the brightest stars
WHICH BOOK MEANS MOST TO YOU? Outliers – The Story of Success by Malcolm Gladwell

Batting	Mat	Inns	NO	Runs	HS	Ave	SR	100	50	Ct	St
First-class	43	59	12	1055	80	22.44	39.04	0	2	12	0
List A	73	36	16	468	65	23.40	76.59	0	1	33	0
T20s	114	43	29	276	36*	19.71	112.65	0	0	37	0
Bowling	**Mat**	**Balls**	**Runs**	**Wkts**	**BBI**	**BBM**	**Ave**	**Econ**	**SR**	**5w**	**10**
First-class	43	6359	3641	74	4/35	6/155	49.20	3.43	85.9	0	0
List A	73	2614	2391	57	4/26	4/26	41.94	5.48	45.8	0	0
T20s	114	2112	2612	115	5/24	5/24	22.71	7.42	18.3	2	0

WILL SMITH

RHB / OB / R1 / W0

FULL NAME: William Rew Smith
BORN: September 28, 1982, Luton
SQUAD NO: 2
HEIGHT: 5ft 9in
NICKNAME: Smudger, Jiggy
EDUCATION: Bedford School; Durham University
TEAMS: Durham, Hampshire, Nottinghamshire
ROLE: Batsman
DEBUT: First-class: 2002; List A: 2002; T20: 2003

BEST BATTING: 210 Hampshire vs Lancashire, Southampton, 2016
BEST BOWLING: 3-34 Durham UCCE vs Leicestershire, Leicester, 2005
COUNTY CAP: 2015 (Hampshire)

WHAT WAS YOUR FIRST CRICKET CLUB? Harrold CC, Bedfordshire
CRICKETING HERO? Graeme Fowler – he was my mentor at university and has a brilliant outlook on cricket and life
WHICH BOWLER WOULD YOU LEAST LIKE TO FACE? Malcolm Marshall
BEST INNINGS YOU'VE SEEN? Michael Atherton's match-saving 185 not out at Johannesburg in 1995. Sheer iron-willed belligerence
WHAT WILL YOU BE DOING IN THE YEAR 2040? Managing a successful race-horse ownership empire
FAVOURITE QUOTE OR SAYING? Don't get bitter, get better (Ottis Gibson)
WHICH BOOK MEANS MOST TO YOU? Any of the Calvin & Hobbes comic strips – I loved them as a kid
ODDEST SPORT YOU'VE PLAYED? Orienteering – pre-season team-building exercise
TWITTER: @WillSmith_2

Batting	Mat	Inns	NO	Runs	HS	Ave	SR	100	50	Ct	St
First-class	181	309	21	9343	210	32.44	42.69	17	37	114	0
List A	118	102	8	2782	120*	29.59	76.26	3	20	39	0
T20s	116	94	23	1160	55	16.33	116.58	0	3	48	0
Bowling	**Mat**	**Balls**	**Runs**	**Wkts**	**BBI**	**BBM**	**Ave**	**Econ**	**SR**	**5w**	**10**
First-class	181	2774	1598	32	3/34	3/68	49.93	3.45	86.6	0	0
List A	118	605	570	14	2/19	2/19	40.71	5.65	43.2	0	0
T20s	116	995	1192	47	3/15	3/15	25.36	7.18	21.1	0	0

SHANE SNATER

RHB / RM / R0 / W0

FULL NAME: Shane Snater
BORN: March 24, 1996, Harare, Zimbabwe
SQUAD NO: 29
EDUCATION: St John's College, Harare
TEAMS: Netherlands, Essex
ROLE: Bowler
DEBUT: ODI: 2018; T20I: 2018; First-class: 2016; List A: 2017; T20: 2018

BEST BATTING: 50* Netherlands vs Namibia, Dubai, 2017
BEST BOWLING: 5-88 Netherlands vs Namibia, Dubai, 2017

TWITTER: @ShaneSnater
NOTES: Essex signed the 23-year-old Netherlands seamer in September on a one-year deal following a successful trial period at the club in 2018. He took five wickets in three One-Day Cup matches for the club last year and also played in one T20 Blast game. Snater said: "I've really enjoyed my time here so far and hopefully I can push on next year, make a further impression and play as many games as possible." Snater grew up in Harare and played for Zimbabwe U17 back in 2014. He holds a Dutch passport and made his ODI and T20I debuts for Netherlands last year

Batting	Mat	Inns	NO	Runs	HS	Ave	SR	100	50	Ct	St
ODIs	2	2	0	12	12	6.00	85.71	0	0	3	0
T20Is	6	2	0	8	6	4.00	114.28	0	0	1	0
First-class	3	4	1	73	50*	24.33	90.12	0	1	1	0
List A	15	10	3	56	23*	8.00	75.67	0	0	9	0
T20s	7	2	0	8	6	4.00	114.28	0	0	2	0
Bowling	**Mat**	**Balls**	**Runs**	**Wkts**	**BBI**	**BBM**	**Ave**	**Econ**	**SR**	**5w**	**10**
ODIs	2	71	63	1	1/41	1/41	63.00	5.32	71.0	0	0
T20Is	6	102	170	6	2/25	2/25	28.33	10.00	17.0	0	0
First-class	3	550	324	12	5/88	7/129	27.00	3.53	45.8	2	0
List A	15	567	493	13	5/60	5/60	37.92	5.21	43.6	1	0
T20s	7	120	212	7	2/25	2/25	30.28	10.60	17.1	0	0

OLI SOAMES

RHB / RM / R0 / W0

FULL NAME: Oliver Courtney Soames
BORN: October 27, 1995, Kingston upon Thames, Surrey
SQUAD NO: 27
HEIGHT: 5ft 9in
NICKNAME: Soamsey
EDUCATION: Cheltenham College; Loughborough University
TEAMS: Hampshire
ROLE: Batsman
DEBUT: First-class: 2018

BEST BATTING: 29 Hampshire vs Lancashire, Southampton, 2018

WHAT WAS YOUR FIRST CRICKET CLUB? Yateley CC, Hampshire. I joined when I was 12 and we made it to the club national finals three times in four years
FAVOURITE CRICKET BAT? Chase Vortex – incredible pick-up and balance
WHICH BOWLER WOULD YOU LEAST LIKE TO FACE? Wasim Akram – because of his lethal reverse-swing
BEST INNINGS YOU'VE SEEN? JP Duminy's 166 for South Africa against Australia at the MCG in 2008. He carried South Africa from 184-7 to 459 all out to set up victory
WHO WOULD YOU ASK TO BAT FOR YOUR LIFE? Virat Kohli
WHICH RULE WOULD YOU CHANGE ABOUT CRICKET? A batsman cannot be dismissed from his first ball
YOUR BIGGEST CRICKETING REGRET? Not winning the club national finals, despite having the best team on the day
WHAT WILL YOU BE DOING IN THE YEAR 2040? Hopefully getting my money's worth on my degree in Accountancy
FAVOURITE QUOTE OR SAYING? If you don't believe in yourself, why should anybody else?
WHICH BOOK MEANS MOST TO YOU? Mind Gym – An Athlete's Guide to Inner Excellence by Gary Mack
TWITTER: @ozza50

Batting	Mat	Inns	NO	Runs	HS	Ave	SR	100	50	Ct	St
First-class	6	9	0	90	29	10.00	33.58	0	0	1	0
Bowling	**Mat**	**Balls**	**Runs**	**Wkts**	**BBI**	**BBM**	**Ave**	**Econ**	**SR**	**5w**	**10**
First-class	6	-	-	-	-	-	-	-	-	-	-

TOM SOLE

RHB / OB / R0 / W0

FULL NAME: Thomas Barclay Sole
BORN: June 21, 1996, Edinburgh, Scotland
SQUAD NO: 90
HEIGHT: 5ft 11in
NICKNAME: Soley, Stollers
EDUCATION: Merchiston Castle School, Edinburgh
TEAMS: Scotland, Northamptonshire
ROLE: Allrounder
DEBUT: ODI: 2018; List A: 2017; T20: 2018

WHAT WAS YOUR FIRST CRICKET CLUB? Grange CC, Edinburgh – where Scotland beat England for the first time in the summer of 2018!
WHICH BOWLER WOULD YOU LEAST LIKE TO FACE? My brother Chris Sole – because he'd have bragging rights over me if he got me out
BEST INNINGS YOU'VE SEEN? Calum MacLeod's 140 not out to set up an historical win against England in 2018
WHICH RULE WOULD YOU CHANGE ABOUT CRICKET? Free hits for no-balls in all cricket
YOUR BIGGEST CRICKETING REGRET? Not getting Northants over the line on my county debut in 2017 against South Africa in a tour match
FAVOURITE QUOTE OR SAYING? Yolo
WHICH BOOK MEANS MOST TO YOU? My dad's autobiography about his rugby union career for Scotland, even though I wasn't born when he wrote it so didn't get a dedication
TWITTER: @TomSole1

Batting	Mat	Inns	NO	Runs	HS	Ave	SR	100	50	Ct	St
ODIs	5	2	0	24	20	12.00	126.31	0	0	3	0
List A	7	3	0	78	54	26.00	125.80	0	1	3	0
T20s	1	1	1	7	7*	-	140.00	0	0	1	0
Bowling	**Mat**	**Balls**	**Runs**	**Wkts**	**BBI**	**BBM**	**Ave**	**Econ**	**SR**	**5w**	**10**
ODIs	5	246	187	6	4/15	4/15	31.16	4.56	41.0	0	0
List A	7	366	284	8	4/15	4/15	35.50	4.65	45.7	0	0
T20s	1	24	32	0	-	-	-	8.00	-	0	0

NATHAN SOWTER RHB / LB / R0 / W0

FULL NAME: Nathan Adam Sowter
BORN: October 12, 1992, Penrith, New South Wales, Australia
SQUAD NO: 72
HEIGHT: 5ft 10in
NICKNAME: Sowts, Racing Snake, Goblin
EDUCATION: Hills Sport High School, New South Wales
TEAMS: Middlesex
ROLE: Bowler
DEBUT: First-class: 2017; List A: 2016; T20: 2015

BEST BATTING: 37 Middlesex vs Warwickshire, Lord's, 2017
BEST BOWLING: 1-23 Middlesex vs Warwickshire, Lord's, 2017

WHAT WAS YOUR FIRST CRICKET CLUB? Rooty Hill RSL CC – a small club not far from where I grew up in western Sydney
WHICH BOWLER WOULD YOU LEAST LIKE TO FACE? Dale Steyn – because he seems to bowl quicker at tailenders
'ROY OF THE ROVERS' MOMENT? Playing at Lord's and being part of the Middlesex squad that won the Championship in 2016
IF YOU WEREN'T A CRICKETER? I'd be a groundsman
SURPRISING FACT ABOUT YOU? I'm a glazier by trade
SURPRISING FACT ABOUT A TEAMMATE? Steve Eskinazi doesn't wash his bedsheets – he just buys new ones when needed
UNUSUAL OBJECT AT HOME? A red chicken
TWITTER: @nsowter

Batting	Mat	Inns	NO	Runs	HS	Ave	SR	100	50	Ct	St
First-class	1	2	0	37	37	18.50	148.00	0	0	0	0
List A	10	7	2	79	29	15.80	72.47	0	0	8	0
T20s	39	11	5	48	12	8.00	104.34	0	0	11	0
Bowling	**Mat**	**Balls**	**Runs**	**Wkts**	**BBI**	**BBM**	**Ave**	**Econ**	**SR**	**5w**	**10**
First-class	1	61	25	1	1/23	1/25	25.00	2.45	61.0	0	0
List A	10	472	407	11	3/43	3/43	37.00	5.17	42.9	0	0
T20s	39	670	910	30	4/23	4/23	30.33	8.14	22.3	0	0

CAMERON STEEL

RHB / LB / R0 / W0

FULL NAME: Cameron Tate Steel
BORN: September 13, 1995, Greenbrae, California, USA
SQUAD NO: 14
HEIGHT: 5ft 10in
NICKNAME: Steely, Lex
EDUCATION: Millfield Prep School, Somerset; Scotch College, Perth, Australia; Durham University
TEAMS: Durham
ROLE: Batsman
DEBUT: First-class: 2014; List A: 2017; T20: 2017

BEST BATTING: 224 Durham vs Leicestershire, Leicester, 2017
BEST BOWLING: 2-7 Durham vs Glamorgan, Cardiff, 2018

FAMILY TIES? My sister played youth cricket for Somerset and Western Australia
WHAT WAS YOUR FIRST CRICKET CLUB? Glastonbury CC, Somerset
FAVOURITE CRICKET BAT? I once put an Apple sticker that came with an old iPod on the back of my GM Cannon. I scored my first hundred the next day so I kept it on for good luck
WHICH BOWLER WOULD YOU LEAST LIKE TO FACE? Stevie Eskinazi, if he ever gets a bowl. I'd hate to get out to him
BEST INNINGS YOU'VE SEEN? No.10 Matt Salisbury scoring 25 off 147 balls against Derbyshire on his Durham debut. Best leaver in the game
WHICH RULE WOULD YOU CHANGE ABOUT CRICKET? Umpires should not rule that leg-spinners must be taken out of the attack for bowling waist-high no-balls – sadly it's happened to me twice
YOUR BIGGEST CRICKETING REGRET? Not learning to bowl slow left-arm as a kid
FAVOURITE QUOTE OR SAYING? Live fast, die old (David Brent)
TWITTER: @CameronSteel2

Batting	Mat	Inns	NO	Runs	HS	Ave	SR	100	50	Ct	St
First-class	31	55	2	1852	224	34.94	40.71	3	11	16	0
List A	11	10	1	181	77	20.11	67.03	0	1	1	0
T20s	6	6	0	93	37	15.50	125.67	0	0	2	0
Bowling	**Mat**	**Balls**	**Runs**	**Wkts**	**BBI**	**BBM**	**Ave**	**Econ**	**SR**	**5w**	**10**
First-class	31	784	595	18	2/7	4/99	33.05	4.55	43.5	0	0
List A	11	30	47	0	-	-	-	9.40	-	0	0
T20s	6	48	88	2	2/60	2/60	44.00	11.00	24.0	0	0

SCOTT STEEL

RHB / OB / R0 / W0

FULL NAME: Scott Steel
BORN: April 20, 1999, Durham
SQUAD NO: 55
HEIGHT: 5ft 10in
NICKNAME: Steely
EDUCATION: Belmont Community School, Durham
TEAMS: Durham
ROLE: Allrounder

WHAT WAS YOUR FIRST CRICKET CLUB? Durham City CC
FAVOURITE CRICKET BAT? Gray-Nicolls Legend when I was a junior
WHICH BOWLER WOULD YOU LEAST LIKE TO FACE? Kagiso Rabada – bowls rockets
BEST INNINGS YOU'VE SEEN? AB de Villers: 149 off 44 balls vs West Indies at Johannesburg in 2015
WHO WOULD YOU ASK TO BAT FOR YOUR LIFE? Virat Kohli
WHICH RULE WOULD YOU CHANGE ABOUT CRICKET? Remove the stumping rule (I always get stumped)
FAVOURITE QUOTE OR SAYING? Can happen
ODDEST SPORT YOU'VE PLAYED? Badminton
TWITTER: @scottsteel102
NOTES: The young allrounder has come through the Durham Academy and scored 590 runs at 42.14 with one century in the 2018 Second XI Championship, as well as taking 12 wickets at 26.66 with his off-spin. Has yet to make his first-team debut but was included in the 13-man squad for the T20 match against Sussex at Chester-le-Street last summer

DARREN STEVENS RHB / RM / R3 / W3 / MVP42

FULL NAME: Darren Ian Stevens
BORN: April 30, 1976, Leicester
SQUAD NO: 3
HEIGHT: 5ft 11in
NICKNAME: Stevo
EDUCATION: John Cleveland College, Hinckley; Charles Keene College, Leicester
TEAMS: Kent, Comilla Victorians, Dhaka Gladiators, Leicestershire, Mid West Rhinos, Otago
ROLE: Allrounder
DEBUT: First-class: 1997; List A: 1997; T20: 2003

BEST BATTING: 208 Kent vs Middlesex, Canterbury, 2009
BEST BOWLING: 8-75 Kent vs Leicestershire, Canterbury, 2017
COUNTY CAP: 2002 (Leicestershire); 2005 (Kent); **BENEFIT:** 2016 (Kent)

WHAT GOT YOU INTO CRICKET? My dad pestered me to play. I preferred football but gave in after a year
CRICKETING HERO? Sir Viv Richards
NON-CRICKETING HERO? Fred Couples
IF YOU WEREN'T A CRICKETER? I'd be a professional golfer
SURPRISING FACT? I am colour blind with browns, reds and greens. I struggled when I was with Otago in New Zealand because there were no sightscreens!
TWITTER: @Stevo208

Batting	Mat	Inns	NO	Runs	HS	Ave	SR	100	50	Ct	St
First-class	290	456	29	15036	208	35.21	67.75	33	77	194	0
List A	311	286	31	7571	147	29.69	88.68	7	46	127	0
T20s	208	187	39	3970	90	26.82	136.66	0	17	65	0
Bowling	**Mat**	**Balls**	**Runs**	**Wkts**	**BBI**	**BBM**	**Ave**	**Econ**	**SR**	**5w**	**10**
First-class	290	25193	12083	463	8/75	11/70	26.09	2.87	54.4	21	1
List A	311	6227	4984	157	6/25	6/25	31.74	4.80	39.6	3	0
T20s	208	2224	2925	114	4/14	4/14	25.65	7.89	19.5	0	0

RYAN STEVENSON

RHB / RFM / R0 / W0

FULL NAME: Ryan Anthony Stevenson
BORN: April 2, 1992, Torquay
SQUAD NO: 47
HEIGHT: 6ft 2in
NICKNAME: Raz, Stevo
EDUCATION: King Edward VI Community College, Devon
TEAMS: Hampshire
ROLE: Bowler
DEBUT: First-class: 2015; List A: 2016; T20: 2016

BEST BATTING: 30 Hampshire vs Durham, Chester-le-Street, 2015
BEST BOWLING: 1-15 Hampshire vs Nottinghamshire, Trent Bridge, 2015

WHAT GOT YOU INTO CRICKET? My dad taking me to nets
FAMILY TIES? My dad has played for Devon Over-50s
'ROY OF THE ROVERS' MOMENT? My first-class debut in 2015 – I was absolutely clueless about what I was doing!
BEST THING ABOUT YOUR HOME GROUND? The facilities: hotel, golf course and two cricket pitches. Plus a curry house on site!
IF YOU WEREN'T A CRICKETER? I'd be a farmer
SURPRISING FACT ABOUT YOU? I gave up cricket for a year as a teenager to do other things
WHERE IS PARADISE? Devon – nowhere else comes close
CRICKETING HERO? Shaun Pollock – an unbelievable bowler and one of the first cricketers I saw playing live
TWITTER: @ryanstevenson47

Batting	Mat	Inns	NO	Runs	HS	Ave	SR	100	50	Ct	St
First-class	4	5	1	73	30	18.25	57.48	0	0	0	0
List A	3	1	0	0	0	0.00	0.00	0	0	0	0
T20s	11	7	3	15	4*	3.75	88.23	0	0	2	0
Bowling	**Mat**	**Balls**	**Runs**	**Wkts**	**BBI**	**BBM**	**Ave**	**Econ**	**SR**	**5w**	**10**
First-class	4	431	270	3	1/15	1/46	90.00	3.75	143.6	0	0
List A	3	120	142	2	1/28	1/28	71.00	7.10	60.0	0	0
T20s	11	215	329	11	2/28	2/28	29.90	9.18	19.5	0	0

GRANT STEWART

RHB / RFM / R0 / W0

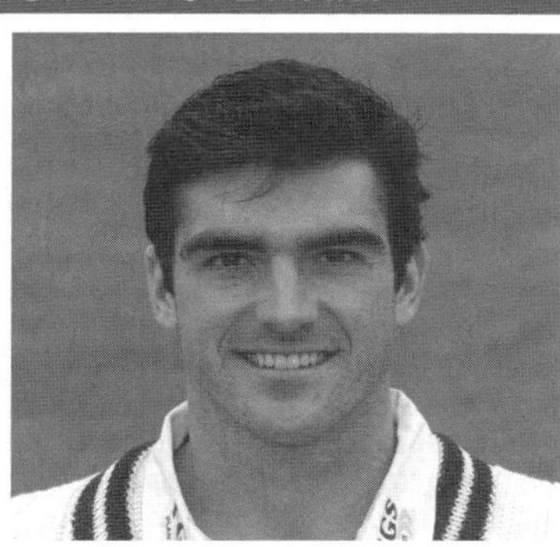

FULL NAME: Grant Stewart
BORN: February 19, 1994, Kalgoorlie, Western Australia, Australia
SQUAD NO: 9
HEIGHT: 6ft 3in
NICKNAME: Stewie
EDUCATION: All Saints College, New South Wales; University of Newcastle, NSW
TEAMS: Kent
ROLE: Allrounder
DEBUT: First-class: 2017; List A: 2018; T20: 2018

BEST BATTING: 103 Kent vs Middlesex, Canterbury, 2018
BEST BOWLING: 6-22 Kent vs Middlesex, Canterbury, 2018

WHAT GOT YOU INTO CRICKET? My older brothers
'ROY OF THE ROVERS' MOMENT? My first-class debut for Kent against Glamorgan at Canterbury in 2017
BEST THING ABOUT YOUR HOME GROUND? The slope at Canterbury really adds to the home advantage
IF YOU WEREN'T A CRICKETER? I'd be a civil engineer
SURPRISING FACT ABOUT YOU? I was a wicketkeeper until I was 16
WHERE IS PARADISE? Barcelona
CRICKETING HERO? Steve Waugh
NON-CRICKETING HERO? Hugh Jackman
TWITTER: @GStewart195

Batting	Mat	Inns	NO	Runs	HS	Ave	SR	100	50	Ct	St
First-class	12	19	2	429	103	25.23	68.97	1	2	3	0
List A	5	4	1	69	44	23.00	62.72	0	0	1	0
T20s	2	2	1	5	5*	5.00	166.66	0	0	2	0
Bowling	**Mat**	**Balls**	**Runs**	**Wkts**	**BBI**	**BBM**	**Ave**	**Econ**	**SR**	**5w**	**10**
First-class	12	1109	594	24	6/22	8/58	24.75	3.21	46.2	1	0
List A	5	242	152	8	3/17	3/17	19.00	3.76	30.2	0	0
T20s	2	32	68	1	1/40	1/40	68.00	12.75	32.0	0	0

PAUL STIRLING RHB / OB / R0 / W0 / MVP38

FULL NAME: Paul Robert Stirling
BORN: September 3, 1990, Belfast, Northern Ireland
SQUAD NO: 39
HEIGHT: 5ft 9in
NICKNAME: Stirlo
EDUCATION: Belfast High School
TEAMS: Ireland, Middlesex, Kandahar Kings, Khulna Titans, Sylhet Royals
ROLE: Allrounder
DEBUT: Test: 2018; ODI: 2008; T20I: 2009; First-class: 2008; List A: 2008; T20: 2008

BEST BATTING: 146 Ireland vs UAE, Malahide, 2015
BEST BOWLING: 2-27 Ireland vs Namibia, Windhoek, 2015
COUNTY CAP: 2016

FAMILY TIES? My brother Richard represented Ireland in the U19 World Cup in Sri Lanka
STRANGEST THING SEEN IN A GAME? A pigeon hit out of the sky
'ROY OF THE ROVERS' MOMENT? Getting a first-class wicket with a flipper while bowling leg-spin, and scoring a century at Lord's
SUPERSTITIONS? Don't walk in shadows
CRICKETING HERO? Damien Martyn – pleasing to watch
NON-CRICKETING HERO? George Best – a Belfast legend
SURPRISING FACT? My father is an ex-international rugby referee
TWITTER: @stirlo90

Batting	Mat	Inns	NO	Runs	HS	Ave	SR	100	50	Ct	St
Tests	1	2	0	28	17	14.00	52.83	0	0	3	0
ODIs	105	102	2	3536	177	35.36	88.35	7	18	40	0
T20Is	58	57	4	1433	91	27.03	136.47	0	11	18	0
First-class	65	102	4	2706	146	27.61	61.96	5	14	37	0
List A	185	179	8	6159	177	36.01	91.28	15	27	70	0
T20s	185	184	7	4544	109	25.67	142.22	1	32	57	0
Bowling	**Mat**	**Balls**	**Runs**	**Wkts**	**BBI**	**BBM**	**Ave**	**Econ**	**SR**	**5w**	**10**
Tests	1	12	11	0	-	-	-	5.50	-	0	0
ODIs	105	2320	1849	40	6/55	6/55	46.22	4.78	58.0	1	0
T20Is	58	444	548	16	3/21	3/21	34.25	7.40	27.7	0	0
First-class	65	2290	1089	25	2/27	3/31	43.56	2.85	91.6	0	0
List A	185	3170	2626	65	6/55	6/55	40.40	4.97	48.7	1	0
T20s	185	1403	1682	66	4/10	4/10	25.48	7.19	21.2	0	0

BEN STOKES LHB / RFM / R0 / W0

FULL NAME: Benjamin Andrew Stokes
BORN: June 4, 1991, Christchurch, New Zealand
SQUAD NO: 38
HEIGHT: 6ft 2in
NICKNAME: Stokesy, Benji, Stoker
EDUCATION: Cockermouth School, Cumbria
TEAMS: England, Durham, Canterbury, Melbourne Renegades, Rajasthan Royals, Rising Pune Supergiant
ROLE: Allrounder
DEBUT: Test: 2013; ODI: 2011; T20I: 2011; First-class: 2010; List A: 2009; T20: 2010

BEST BATTING: 258 England vs South Africa, Cape Town, 2016
BEST BOWLING: 7-67 Durham vs Sussex, Chester-le-Street, 2014

SUPERSTITIONS? Swiping my bat across the crease at the end of every over
CRICKETING HERO? Herschelle Gibbs
IF YOU WEREN'T A CRICKETER? I'd be on the dole
SURPRISING FACT? My father played one Test match for New Zealand at rugby league. I was a right-handed batsman when I was younger
TWITTER: @benstokes38

Batting	Mat	Inns	NO	Runs	HS	Ave	SR	100	50	Ct	St
Tests	52	95	2	3152	258	33.89	58.69	6	17	55	0
ODIs	79	68	11	2088	102*	36.63	93.84	3	14	39	0
T20Is	23	20	5	232	38	15.46	130.33	0	0	9	0
First-class	127	215	10	6942	258	33.86	63.24	14	36	96	0
List A	150	132	20	3989	164	35.61	96.91	7	21	70	0
T20s	111	101	15	2134	103*	24.81	135.75	1	8	45	0
Bowling	**Mat**	**Balls**	**Runs**	**Wkts**	**BBI**	**BBM**	**Ave**	**Econ**	**SR**	**5w**	**10**
Tests	52	7328	4054	127	6/22	8/161	31.92	3.31	57.7	4	0
ODIs	79	2505	2562	63	5/61	5/61	40.66	6.13	39.7	1	0
T20Is	23	334	496	10	3/26	3/26	49.60	8.91	33.4	0	0
First-class	127	15101	8719	296	7/67	10/121	29.45	3.46	51.0	7	1
List A	150	4180	4049	127	5/61	5/61	31.88	5.81	32.9	1	0
T20s	111	1382	1892	58	4/16	4/16	32.62	8.21	23.8	0	0

OLLY STONE RHB / RFM / R0 / W0 / MVP71

FULL NAME: Oliver Peter Stone
BORN: October 9, 1993, Norwich
SQUAD NO: 6
HEIGHT: 6ft 2in
NICKNAME: Stoney
EDUCATION: Thorpe St Andrew High School, Norwich; Moulton College, Northamptonshire
TEAMS: England, Warwickshire, Northamptonshire
ROLE: Bowler
DEBUT: ODI: 2018; First-class: 2012; List A: 2012; T20: 2011

BEST BATTING: 60 Northamptonshire vs Kent, Northampton, 2016
BEST BOWLING: 8-80 Warwickshire vs Sussex, Edgbaston, 2018

WHAT WAS YOUR FIRST CRICKET CLUB? Vauxhall Mallards CC, Norfolk. Home of the ducks
BEST ADVICE EVER RECEIVED? Don't celebrate your wickets
BEST INNINGS YOU'VE SEEN? David Willey's 27-ball 60 for my former county Northants in the 2013 final of the T20 Blast
WHO WOULD YOU ASK TO BAT FOR YOUR LIFE? Chris Wright – especially against spin, he's one of the best around
WHICH RULE WOULD YOU CHANGE ABOUT CRICKET? Allow bowlers to put their feet up after a spell
SURPRISING FACT ABOUT YOU? My great-grandad created the Twix chocolate bar
FAVOURITE QUOTE OR SAYING? Go hard or go home
TWITTER: @ollystone2

Batting	Mat	Inns	NO	Runs	HS	Ave	SR	100	50	Ct	St
ODIs	4	1	1	9	9*	-	128.57	0	0	0	0
First-class	34	42	10	532	60	16.62	47.62	0	1	14	0
List A	30	14	9	122	24*	24.40	70.93	0	0	13	0
T20s	42	11	7	24	8*	6.00	109.09	0	0	10	0
Bowling	**Mat**	**Balls**	**Runs**	**Wkts**	**BBI**	**BBM**	**Ave**	**Econ**	**SR**	**5w**	**10**
ODIs	4	96	97	1	1/23	1/23	97.00	6.06	96.0	0	0
First-class	34	5125	2809	116	8/80	11/96	24.21	3.28	44.1	5	1
List A	30	1125	1023	24	4/71	4/71	42.62	5.45	46.8	0	0
T20s	42	756	1131	33	3/22	3/22	34.27	8.97	22.9	0	0

MARK STONEMAN

LHB / OB / R5 / W0

FULL NAME: Mark Daniel Stoneman
BORN: June 26, 1987, Newcastle
SQUAD NO: 23
HEIGHT: 5ft 10in
NICKNAME: Rocky
EDUCATION: Whickham Comprehensive School, Newcastle Upon Tyne
TEAMS: England, Surrey, Durham
ROLE: Batsman
DEBUT: Test: 2017; First-class: 2007; List A: 2008; T20: 2010

BEST BATTING: 197 Surrey vs Sussex, Guildford, 2017

WHAT GOT YOU INTO CRICKET? Following my dad everywhere as soon as I could, carrying my little plastic bat along with me
FAMILY TIES? Grandfather played and umpired locally for many years. Dad played all over the north-east as a local pro
'ROY OF THE ROVERS' MOMENT? Captaining the Durham side which won the 2014 One-Day Cup at Lord's
SUPERSTITIONS? Nervous wee box goes on first
CRICKETING HEROES? Dad – he got me into the game and gave me every opportunity to be successful. Michael Di Venuto – the best role model a young county cricketer could have
IF YOU WEREN'T A CRICKETER? I'd be a fisherman
SURPRISING FACT? The Lion King makes me cry
TWITTER: @mark23stone

Batting	Mat	Inns	NO	Runs	HS	Ave	SR	100	50	Ct	St
Tests	11	20	1	526	60	27.68	44.27	0	5	1	0
First-class	176	307	8	10474	197	35.03	57.91	22	54	83	0
List A	74	70	5	2601	144*	40.01	93.76	6	16	21	0
T20s	63	59	4	1140	89*	20.72	121.14	0	6	26	0
Bowling	**Mat**	**Balls**	**Runs**	**Wkts**	**BBI**	**BBM**	**Ave**	**Econ**	**SR**	**5w**	**10**
Tests	11	-	-	-	-	-	-	-	-	-	-
First-class	176	204	150	0	-	-	-	4.41	-	0	0
List A	74	4	8	1	1/8	1/8	8.00	12.00	4.0	0	0
T20s	63	-	-	-	-	-	-	-	-	-	-

HARRY SWINDELLS RHB / WK / R0 / W0

FULL NAME: Harry John Swindells
BORN: February 21, 1999, Leicester
SQUAD NO: 28
HEIGHT: 5ft 8in
NICKNAME: Dumbo
EDUCATION: Brockington College, Leicestershire; Lutterworth College; Loughborough College
TEAMS: Leicestershire
ROLE: Wicketkeeper/batsman
DEBUT: List A: 2018; T20: 2018

WHAT GOT YOU INTO CRICKET? The 2005 Ashes
'ROY OF THE ROVERS' MOMENT? Playing for England in an U19 Test match against India and playing against West Indies in a tour match
BEST THING ABOUT YOUR HOME GROUND? The great atmosphere – especially for the T20 Blast games
SURPRISING FACT ABOUT YOU? I'm a Leicester City FC supporter and go to both the home and away matches
SURPRISING FACT ABOUT A TEAMMATE? I've played with Sam Evans since we were 10
WHERE IS PARADISE? Phillip Island, Australia
CRICKETING HERO? Adam Gilchrist – the best wicketkeeper/batsman of all time
NON-CRICKETING HERO? Muhammad Ali – he overcame adversity and stuck to what he believed in, as well as being one of the greatest boxers
TWITTER: @harryswindells1

Batting	Mat	Inns	NO	Runs	HS	Ave	SR	100	50	Ct	St
List A	2	1	0	28	28	28.00	112.00	0	0	2	0
T20s	5	3	0	31	15	10.33	91.17	0	0	2	0
Bowling	**Mat**	**Balls**	**Runs**	**Wkts**	**BBI**	**BBM**	**Ave**	**Econ**	**SR**	**5w**	**10**
List A	2	-	-	-	-	-	-	-	-	-	-
T20s	5	-	-	-	-	-	-	-	-	-	-

JONATHAN TATTERSALL RHB / WK / R0 / W0

FULL NAME: Jonathan Andrew Tattersall
BORN: December 15, 1994, Harrogate, Yorkshire
SQUAD NO: 12
HEIGHT: 5ft 8in
NICKNAME: Tatts
EDUCATION: King James's School, Knaresborough
TEAMS: Yorkshire
ROLE: Wicketkeeper/batsman
DEBUT: First-class: 2018; List A: 2013; T20: 2018

BEST BATTING: 70 Yorkshire vs Surrey, Scarborough, 2018

BEST ADVICE EVER RECEIVED? Always remember why you played the game in the first place
'ROY OF THE ROVERS' MOMENT? Being released from Yorkshire and then getting another contract with Yorkshire
BEST THING ABOUT YOUR HOME GROUND? The Western Terrace
SURPRISING FACT ABOUT YOU? I have a handicap of nine in golf
SURPRISING FACT ABOUT A TEAMMATE? Ed Barnes loves a glass of rosé
WHERE IS PARADISE? South Africa
CRICKETING HERO? Rahul Dravid – for his temperament
NON-CRICKETING HERO? Steve Coogan – for being Alan Partridge
TWITTER: @JonnyTatts

Batting	Mat	Inns	NO	Runs	HS	Ave	SR	100	50	Ct	St
First-class	7	12	1	350	70	31.81	37.15	0	2	19	0
List A	8	5	1	143	89	35.75	102.14	0	2	6	1
T20s	15	10	2	191	53*	23.87	134.50	0	1	8	2
Bowling	**Mat**	**Balls**	**Runs**	**Wkts**	**BBI**	**BBM**	**Ave**	**Econ**	**SR**	**5w**	**10**
First-class	7	-	-	-	-	-	-	-	-	-	-
List A	8	-	-	-	-	-	-	-	-	-	-
T20s	15	-	-	-	-	-	-	-	-	-	-

WILLIAM TAVARÉ

RHB / RMF / R1 / W0

GLOUCESTERSHIRE

FULL NAME: William Andrew Tavaré
BORN: January 1, 1990, Bristol
SQUAD NO: 4
HEIGHT: 6ft
NICKNAME: Tav, Tekkers, Postman, Mezut, Zukkers
EDUCATION: Bristol Grammar School; Loughborough University
TEAMS: Gloucestershire, Tamil Union Cricket & Athletic Club
ROLE: Batsman
DEBUT: First-class: 2010; List A 2014

BEST BATTING: 139 Gloucestershire vs Hampshire, Bristol, 2014

FAMILY TIES? My dad played for Gloucestershire Second XI and my uncle Chris played for England, Kent and Somerset
WHAT WAS YOUR FIRST CRICKET CLUB? Bristol CC – my dad won the national knockout with the club in 1992. Still my club today
FAVOURITE CRICKET BAT? Slazenger Viz. My first bat, which my brother buried on a beach in Portugal and was never to be seen again
CRICKETING HERO? Mike Hussey
WHICH BOWLER WOULD YOU LEAST LIKE TO FACE? Mark Thorburn (Gloucestershire bowling coach) with the slinger
WHICH RULE WOULD YOU CHANGE ABOUT CRICKET? You can't be caught down the leg side
YOUR BIGGEST CRICKETING REGRET? Leaving a straight one
SURPRISING FACT ABOUT YOU? I lived in Dallas, Texas
FAVOURITE QUOTE OR SAYING? Winners see possibilities, losers see problems
WHICH BOOK MEANS MOST TO YOU? SAS Rogue Heroes by Ben MacIntyre
TWITTER: @wtav90

Batting	Mat	Inns	NO	Runs	HS	Ave	SR	100	50	Ct	St
First-class	54	92	6	2721	139	31.63	45.17	6	14	36	0
List A	8	8	0	221	77	27.62	72.22	0	2	1	0
Bowling	**Mat**	**Balls**	**Runs**	**Wkts**	**BBI**	**BBM**	**Ave**	**Econ**	**SR**	**5w**	**10**
First-class	54	102	82	0	-	-	-	4.82	-	0	0
List A	8	-	-	-	-	-	-	-	-	-	-

BRAD TAYLOR

RHB / OB / R0 / W0

FULL NAME: Bradley Jacob Taylor
BORN: March 14, 1997, Winchester, Hampshire
SQUAD NO: 93
HEIGHT: 6ft
NICKNAME: Bradders
EDUCATION: Alton College, Hampshire
TEAMS: Hampshire
ROLE: Bowler
DEBUT: First-class: 2013; List A: 2013; T20: 2014

BEST BATTING: 36 Hampshire vs Cardiff MCCU, Southampton, 2016
BEST BOWLING: 4-64 Hampshire vs Lancashire, Southport, 2013

FAMILY TIES? My dad is a Level 3 coach
WHAT WAS YOUR FIRST CRICKET CLUB? Holybourne CC, Hampshire
CRICKETING HERO? Daniel Vettori
NON-CRICKETING HERO? LeBron James – he works hard and is always motivated to become better even though he is the best in the world at his sport
SURPRISING FACT ABOUT YOU? I'm a massive Southampton fan and I go to the home games whenever I can
TWITTER: @bradtay93

Batting	Mat	Inns	NO	Runs	HS	Ave	SR	100	50	Ct	St
First-class	6	10	3	133	36	19.00	44.63	0	0	2	0
List A	17	15	5	355	69	35.50	65.74	0	3	7	0
T20s	6	3	1	21	9*	10.50	84.00	0	0	2	0
Bowling	**Mat**	**Balls**	**Runs**	**Wkts**	**BBI**	**BBM**	**Ave**	**Econ**	**SR**	**5w**	**10**
First-class	6	798	544	13	4/64	4/106	41.84	4.09	61.3	0	0
List A	17	834	635	15	4/26	4/26	42.33	4.56	55.6	0	0
T20s	6	68	84	3	2/20	2/20	28.00	7.41	22.6	0	0

JACK TAYLOR

RHB / OB / R0 / W0

FULL NAME: Jack Martin Robert Taylor
BORN: November 12, 1991, Banbury, Oxfordshire
SQUAD NO: 10
HEIGHT: 6ft
NICKNAME: Tails, JT, Jacko
EDUCATION: Chipping Norton School, Oxfordshire
TEAMS: Gloucestershire
ROLE: Allrounder
DEBUT: First-class: 2010; List A: 2011; T20: 2011

BEST BATTING: 156 Gloucestershire vs Northamptonshire, Cheltenham, 2015
BEST BOWLING: 4-16 Gloucestershire vs Glamorgan, Bristol, 2016
COUNTY CAP: 2010

WHAT WAS YOUR FIRST CRICKET CLUB? Great and Little Tew CC, Oxfordshire. My family have always played there
FAVOURITE CRICKET BAT? A Woodstock I had in 2015 – absolute rocket
WHICH BOWLER WOULD YOU LEAST LIKE TO FACE? Liam Norwell in the nets – horrible angle
BEST INNINGS YOU'VE SEEN? Hamish Marshall and Kevin O'Brien both hitting hundreds in a T20 against Middlesex in 2011
WHO WOULD YOU ASK TO BAT FOR YOUR LIFE? James Bracey
WHICH RULE WOULD YOU CHANGE ABOUT CRICKET? You can be out if the ball pitches outside leg stump
YOUR BIGGEST CRICKETING REGRET? Not turning to leg-spin sooner
WHAT WILL YOU BE DOING IN THE YEAR 2040? I'll be on a golf course in Australia
ODDEST SPORT YOU'VE PLAYED? Royal Tennis

Batting	Mat	Inns	NO	Runs	HS	Ave	SR	100	50	Ct	St
First-class	68	105	9	2950	156	30.72	66.27	7	8	36	0
List A	42	32	5	836	68	30.96	121.68	0	7	16	0
T20s	67	51	14	735	80	19.86	152.48	0	2	19	0
Bowling	**Mat**	**Balls**	**Runs**	**Wkts**	**BBI**	**BBM**	**Ave**	**Econ**	**SR**	**5w**	**10**
First-class	68	5661	3290	75	4/16	5/140	43.86	3.48	75.4	0	0
List A	42	1184	1021	29	4/38	4/38	35.20	5.17	40.8	0	0
T20s	67	634	862	26	4/16	4/16	33.15	8.15	24.3	0	0

JAMES TAYLOR RHB / RM / R0 / W0

FULL NAME: James Philip Arthur Taylor
BORN: January 19, 2001, Stoke-on-Trent, Staffordshire
SQUAD NO: 32
HEIGHT: 6ft 4in
NICKNAME: JT
EDUCATION: Trentham High School, Stoke-on-Trent
TEAMS: Derbyshire
ROLE: Bowler
DEBUT: First-class: 2017

BEST BOWLING: 1-14 Derbyshire vs West Indians, Derby, 2017

WHAT WAS YOUR FIRST CRICKET CLUB? Barlaston CC, Staffordshire. Always stay on the front foot because the wicket is slow and low at Barlaston
FAVOURITE CRICKET BAT? A Spyder which I scored plenty of runs with
CRICKETING HERO? Andrew Flintoff
BEST ADVICE EVER RECEIVED? Play late and straight, be great
WHICH BOWLER WOULD YOU LEAST LIKE TO FACE? Olly Stone – because he'd hit me in the face
BEST INNINGS YOU'VE SEEN? Wayne Madsen's Championship hundred against Northants at Chesterfield last summer. On a turning wicket, he made it look easy
WHO WOULD YOU ASK TO BAT FOR YOUR LIFE? Tom Taylor #thewall
WHICH RULE WOULD YOU CHANGE ABOUT CRICKET? Introduce one hand one bounce
YOUR BIGGEST CRICKETING REGRET? Being a bowler. It hurts
FAVOURITE QUOTE OR SAYING? Yolo
WHICH BOOK MEANS MOST TO YOU? Biff, Chip and Kipper by Roderick Hunt and Alex Brychta
TWITTER: @_Jamestaylor19

Batting	Mat	Inns	NO	Runs	HS	Ave	SR	100	50	Ct	St
First-class	1	1	1	0	0*	-	0.00	0	0	0	0
Bowling	**Mat**	**Balls**	**Runs**	**Wkts**	**BBI**	**BBM**	**Ave**	**Econ**	**SR**	**5w**	**10**
First-class	1	102	77	1	1/14	1/77	77.00	4.52	102.0	0	0

JEROME TAYLOR

RHB / RFM / R0 / W0

FULL NAME: Jerome Everton Taylor
BORN: June 22, 1984, St Elizabeth, Jamaica
SQUAD NO: 74
TEAMS: West Indies, Somerset, Hobart Hurricanes, Jamaica, Leicestershire, Pune Warriors, Rahuna Royals, St Lucia Zouks, Sussex
ROLE: Bowler
DEBUT: Test: 2003; ODI: 2003; T20I: 2006; First-class: 2003; List A: 2003; T20: 2006

BEST BATTING: 106 West Indies vs New Zealand, Dunedin, 2008
BEST BOWLING: 8-59 Jamaica vs Trinidad and Tobago, Trinidad, 2003

NOTES: The experienced Jamaican fast bowler returns to Somerset for this season's T20 Blast after helping propel them to Finals Day in 2018. Taylor took 22 wickets at 16.63 in the last campaign, including a sensational spell of 5-15 – his second T20 five-wicket haul – against Hampshire. He called time on an injury-blighted Test career in 2016, his finest hour coming against England on his home ground of Sabina Park in 2009 when he returned figures of 9-4-11-5. "Jerome's experience and expertise were exactly what we needed last year," said Lewis Gregory, Somerset's T20 captain. "We have an outstanding bowling unit here and he complemented that perfectly"

Batting	Mat	Inns	NO	Runs	HS	Ave	SR	100	50	Ct	St
Tests	46	73	7	856	106	12.96	62.57	1	1	8	0
ODIs	90	42	9	278	43*	8.42	86.06	0	0	20	0
T20Is	30	15	6	118	21	13.11	128.26	0	0	9	0
First-class	103	161	25	1595	106	11.72	63.37	1	1	25	0
List A	135	68	17	518	43*	10.15	89.75	0	0	27	0
T20s	101	41	19	228	21	10.36	117.52	0	0	20	0
Bowling	**Mat**	**Balls**	**Runs**	**Wkts**	**BBI**	**BBM**	**Ave**	**Econ**	**SR**	**5w**	**10**
Tests	46	7757	4480	130	6/47	9/95	34.46	3.46	59.6	4	0
ODIs	90	4341	3780	128	5/48	5/48	29.53	5.22	33.9	1	0
T20Is	30	600	863	33	3/6	3/6	26.15	8.63	18.1	0	0
First-class	103	15824	8401	326	8/59	10/81	25.76	3.18	48.5	16	2
List A	135	6431	5414	203	5/40	5/40	26.66	5.05	31.6	2	0
T20s	101	2152	2952	126	5/10	5/10	23.42	8.23	17.0	2	0

MATT TAYLOR RHB / LMF / R0 / W1

FULL NAME: Matthew David Taylor
BORN: July 8, 1994, Banbury, Oxfordshire
SQUAD NO: 36
HEIGHT: 6ft 2in
NICKNAME: MT, Bomber, Melon, Swede
EDUCATION: Chipping Norton Secondary School, Oxfordshire
TEAMS: Gloucestershire
ROLE: Bowler
DEBUT: First-class: 2013; List A: 2011; T20: 2015

BEST BATTING: 48 Gloucestershire vs Glamorgan, Bristol, 2018
BEST BOWLING: 5-15 Gloucestershire vs Cardiff MCCU, Bristol, 2018
COUNTY CAP: 2013

FAMILY TIES? My older brother Jack also plays for Gloucestershire. My dad and grandad played Minor Counties for Oxfordshire
WHAT WAS YOUR FIRST CRICKET CLUB? Great and Little Tew CC, Oxfordshire
CRICKETING HERO? Darren Gough
WHICH BOWLER WOULD YOU LEAST LIKE TO FACE? Graeme van Buuren (in the marquee)
WHO WOULD YOU ASK TO BAT FOR YOUR LIFE? James Bracey – he just loves cricket
WHICH RULE WOULD YOU CHANGE ABOUT CRICKET? No extra balls
YOUR BIGGEST CRICKETING REGRET? Not being a batsman
WHAT WILL YOU BE DOING IN THE YEAR 2040? Bowling left-arm wrist spin
FAVOURITE QUOTE OR SAYING? When all is said and done, more is always said than done
TWITTER: @matt_taylor94

Batting	Mat	Inns	NO	Runs	HS	Ave	SR	100	50	Ct	St
First-class	43	57	21	447	48	12.41	40.56	0	0	7	0
List A	22	8	6	38	16	19.00	90.47	0	0	4	0
T20s	30	8	5	28	9*	9.33	84.84	0	0	6	0
Bowling	**Mat**	**Balls**	**Runs**	**Wkts**	**BBI**	**BBM**	**Ave**	**Econ**	**SR**	**5w**	**10**
First-class	43	6555	3974	113	5/15	7/133	35.16	3.63	58.0	4	0
List A	22	981	961	15	3/48	3/48	64.06	5.87	65.4	0	0
T20s	30	526	755	26	3/16	3/16	29.03	8.61	20.2	0	0

TOM TAYLOR

RHB / RMF / R0 / W0

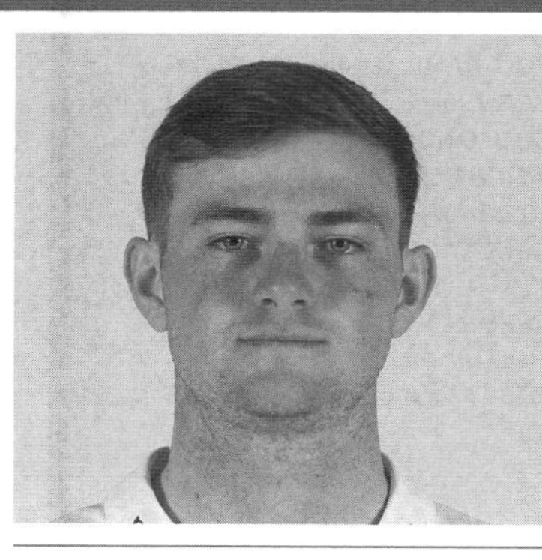

FULL NAME: Thomas Alexander Ian Taylor
BORN: December 21, 1994, Stoke-on-Trent, Staffordshire
SQUAD NO: 16
HEIGHT: 6ft 3in
NICKNAME: Audi, Anne Robinson
EDUCATION: Trentham High School, Stoke-on-Trent; Newcastle-under-Lyme College; Leeds Metropolitan University
TEAMS: Leicestershire, Derbyshire
ROLE: Bowler
DEBUT: First-class: 2014; List A 2014

BEST BATTING: 80 Derbyshire vs Kent, Derby, 2016
BEST BOWLING: 6-61 Derbyshire vs Lancashire, Derby, 2015

FAMILY TIES? Father, cousins, uncles all play cricket; other family members used to run my home club
'ROY OF THE ROVERS' MOMENT? Probably my maiden first-class five-wicket haul against Lancashire. Getting Hashim Amla as my maiden first-class wicket wasn't bad either
STRANGEST THING SEEN IN A GAME? Match abandoned because all the balls were lost
CRICKETING HERO? Brett Lee
SURPRISING FACT? I drink a lot of milk
TWITTER: @TomTaylor43
NOTES: The former Derbyshire seamer joined Leicestershire ahead of the 2018 season and signed a two-year extension to his contract last August. Taylor impressed in his only Championship appearance last summer, taking six wickets in a late-season match against Glamorgan at Cardiff, including second-innings figures of 4-15. Head coach Paul Nixon said: "It is vital to have strength in depth and competition for places in the seam department, an area we have thrived in under [bowling coach] Matt Mason. We rate Tom very highly, as he also adds value with the bat and in the field too"

Batting	Mat	Inns	NO	Runs	HS	Ave	SR	100	50	Ct	St
First-class	26	41	6	618	80	17.65	42.18	0	2	5	0
List A	5	-	-	-	-	-	-	-	-	0	0
Bowling	**Mat**	**Balls**	**Runs**	**Wkts**	**BBI**	**BBM**	**Ave**	**Econ**	**SR**	**5w**	**10**
First-class	26	3920	2427	70	6/61	8/116	34.67	3.71	56.0	2	0
List A	5	218	225	5	3/48	3/48	45.00	6.19	43.6	0	0

RYAN TEN DOESCHATE RHB / RMF / R1 / W0 / MVP93

FULL NAME: Ryan Neil ten Doeschate
BORN: June 30, 1980, Port Elizabeth, SA
SQUAD NO: 27
HEIGHT: 5ft 11in
EDUCATION: University of Cape Town
TEAMS: Netherlands, Essex, Adelaide Strikers, Canterbury, Chittagong Kings, Comilla Victorians, Dhaka Dynamites, Impi, Kolkata Knight Riders, Mashonaland Eagles, Otago, Tasmania, Western Province
ROLE: Allrounder
DEBUT: ODI: 2006; T20I: 2008; First-class: 2003; List A: 2003; T20: 2003

BEST BATTING: 259* Netherlands vs Canada, Pretoria, 2006
BEST BOWLING: 6-20 Netherlands vs Canada, Pretoria, 2006
COUNTY CAP: 2006

TWITTER: @rtendo27
NOTES: The veteran Netherlands allrounder took on the captaincy across all formats in 2016 and led Essex to Championship promotion and then the title in successive seasons. This will be his 17th season at Chelmsford. He has played T20 cricket all over the globe, including for Kolkata Knight Riders in the IPL. For Netherlands he scored 686 runs at an average of 228.66 in the ICC Intercontinental Cup in 2006, recording four consecutive hundreds, including a competition record 259* vs Canada in Pretoria. He made a century (119) against England at Nagpur in the 2011 World Cup, becoming the first batsman from the Netherlands to make a hundred in the World Cup finals, and scored a second hundred against Ireland at Kolkata. He then retired from international cricket, only to reverse his decision in 2017

Batting	Mat	Inns	NO	Runs	HS	Ave	SR	100	50	Ct	St
ODIs	33	32	9	1541	119	67.00	87.70	5	9	13	0
T20Is	13	13	6	300	56	42.85	131.00	0	1	4	0
First-class	174	256	38	10283	259*	47.16	68.12	27	48	110	0
List A	219	183	55	5826	180	45.51	99.46	11	30	67	0
T20s	332	294	66	6677	121*	29.28	135.05	2	28	123	0
Bowling	**Mat**	**Balls**	**Runs**	**Wkts**	**BBI**	**BBM**	**Ave**	**Econ**	**SR**	**5w**	**10**
ODIs	33	1580	1327	55	4/31	4/31	24.12	5.03	28.7	0	0
T20Is	13	210	245	13	3/23	3/23	18.84	7.00	16.1	0	0
First-class	174	10910	7172	212	6/20	9/112	33.83	3.94	51.4	7	0
List A	219	5457	5241	173	5/50	5/50	30.29	5.76	31.5	1	0
T20s	332	2147	2922	114	4/24	4/24	25.63	8.16	18.8	0	0

IVAN THOMAS

RHB / RMF / R0 / W0

FULL NAME: Ivan Alfred Astley Thomas
BORN: September 25, 1991, Greenwich, Kent
SQUAD NO: 5
HEIGHT: 6ft 4in
NICKNAME: Big Red, The Viking, Goober, JK
EDUCATION: The John Roan School, Greenwich; University of Leeds
TEAMS: Kent
ROLE: Bowler
DEBUT: First-class: 2012; List A: 2014; T20: 2015

BEST BATTING: 13 Kent vs Australians, Canterbury, 2015
BEST BOWLING: 5-91 Kent vs Leicestershire, Leicester, 2018

WHAT WAS YOUR FIRST CRICKET CLUB? Blackheath CC, Kent
FAVOURITE CRICKET BAT? A Slazenger V1200 which cost me £20 from JD Sports
CRICKETING HERO? Andrew Flintoff
WHICH BOWLER WOULD YOU LEAST LIKE TO FACE? Mitchell Starc
WHO WOULD YOU ASK TO BAT FOR YOUR LIFE? Imran Qayyum
YOUR BIGGEST CRICKETING REGRET? Not being a spinner
SURPRISING FACT ABOUT YOU? I have clicking bones, and I can tear an apple in half
WHAT WILL YOU BE DOING IN THE YEAR 2040? Running away from responsibility
FAVOURITE QUOTE OR SAYING? People say nothing is impossible but I do nothing every day
WHICH BOOK MEANS MOST TO YOU? The Lord of the Rings by JRR Tolkien
ODDEST SPORT YOU'VE PLAYED? Carrom
TWITTER: @ivanthomas_5

Batting	Mat	Inns	NO	Runs	HS	Ave	SR	100	50	Ct	St
First-class	33	44	22	114	13	5.18	22.52	0	0	9	0
List A	21	8	5	18	6	6.00	37.50	0	0	8	0
T20s	12	3	2	3	3*	3.00	60.00	0	0	4	0
Bowling	**Mat**	**Balls**	**Runs**	**Wkts**	**BBI**	**BBM**	**Ave**	**Econ**	**SR**	**5w**	**10**
First-class	33	4159	2124	70	5/91	9/126	30.34	3.06	59.4	1	0
List A	21	1036	964	31	4/30	4/30	31.09	5.58	33.4	0	0
T20s	12	210	320	9	2/42	2/42	35.55	9.14	23.3	0	0

AARON THOMASON

RHB / RFM / R0 / W0

FULL NAME: Aaron Dean Thomason
BORN: June 26, 1997, Birmingham
SQUAD NO: 26
HEIGHT: 5ft 10in
NICKNAME: Thomo
EDUCATION: Barr Beacon School, Walsall
TEAMS: Warwickshire
ROLE: Allrounder
DEBUT: List A: 2014; T20: 2016

FAMILY TIES? We are members of Sutton Coldfield CC, where my brother plays and my whole family go and watch each Saturday
'ROY OF THE ROVERS' MOMENT? Making my Warwickshire debut at Lord's
CRICKETING HERO? Andrew Flintoff
NON-CRICKETING HERO? My great-grandad watched us play all the time. He left me some medals he was awarded for service in the war which I treasure
IF YOU WEREN'T A CRICKETER? I'd be window-cleaning with my dad
SURPRISING FACT? Me and Chris Woakes went to the same school – it was a non-cricket-playing school

Batting	Mat	Inns	NO	Runs	HS	Ave	SR	100	50	Ct	St
List A	16	12	5	153	28	21.85	93.29	0	0	6	0
T20s	28	20	5	236	42	15.73	129.67	0	0	13	0
Bowling	**Mat**	**Balls**	**Runs**	**Wkts**	**BBI**	**BBM**	**Ave**	**Econ**	**SR**	**5w**	**10**
List A	16	340	408	13	4/45	4/45	31.38	7.20	26.1	0	0
T20s	28	372	670	24	3/33	3/33	27.91	10.80	15.5	0	0

JORDAN THOMPSON

LHB / RM / R0 / W0

FULL NAME: Jordan Aaron Thompson
BORN: October 9, 1996, Leeds, Yorkshire
SQUAD NO: 44
HEIGHT: 6ft 1in
NICKNAME: Tommo, Lizard
EDUCATION: Benton Park School, Leeds
TEAMS: Yorkshire
ROLE: Allrounder
DEBUT: T20: 2018

'ROY OF THE ROVERS' MOMENT? Scoring 146 not out in a Second XI Championship match for Yorkshire against Worcestershire at Scarborough in 2016
BEST THING ABOUT YOUR HOME GROUND? On a Friday night under the lights the Western Terrace is electric
IF YOU WEREN'T A CRICKETER? I'd be a professional goalkeeper
SURPRISING FACT ABOUT YOU? I'm a Type 1 diabetic
SURPRISING FACT ABOUT A TEAMMATE? Matthew Waite has the nickname 'Pingu' because we all think he walks like a penguin
WHERE IS PARADISE? Dover Beach, Barbados
CRICKETING HERO? Ben Stokes – because of his aggressive style on the field
NON-CRICKETING HERO? Pontus Jansson – Leeds United footballer. Love his aggression and passion on the football field
TWITTER: @Tommo455

Batting	Mat	Inns	NO	Runs	HS	Ave	SR	100	50	Ct	St
T20s	9	6	3	22	12*	7.33	129.41	0	0	4	0
Bowling	**Mat**	**Balls**	**Runs**	**Wkts**	**BBI**	**BBM**	**Ave**	**Econ**	**SR**	**5w**	**10**
T20s	9	144	208	8	3/23	3/23	26.00	8.66	18.0	0	0

ALEX THOMSON

RHB / OB / R0 / W0

FULL NAME: Alexander Thomas Thomson
BORN: October 30, 1993, Stoke-on-Trent, Staffordshire
SQUAD NO: 29
HEIGHT: 6ft 5in
NICKNAME: Tommo, Big Al
EDUCATION: Denstone College; Cardiff Metropolitan University
TEAMS: Warwickshire
ROLE: Allrounder
DEBUT: First-class: 2014; List A: 2018; T20: 2018

BEST BATTING: 26 Warwickshire vs Hampshire, Edgbaston, 2017
BEST BOWLING: 6-138 Cardiff MCCU vs Hampshire, Southampton, 2017

WHAT WAS YOUR FIRST CRICKET CLUB? Leek CC, Staffordshire
CRICKETING HERO? Jacques Kallis
WHICH BOWLER WOULD YOU LEAST LIKE TO FACE? Matt Bowcock on a green seamer
BEST INNINGS YOU'VE SEEN? Alastair Cook's final Test innings at The Oval last year
WHO WOULD YOU ASK TO BAT FOR YOUR LIFE? Tim Tweats – never practises anymore but still bats like Lara
WHICH RULE WOULD YOU CHANGE ABOUT CRICKET? You should be allowed to play in shorts
SURPRISING FACT ABOUT YOU? I'm an avid angler
FAVOURITE QUOTE OR SAYING? Leave nothing in the tank
WHICH BOOK MEANS MOST TO YOU? The Story of Cricket – A Ladybird Easy-Reading Book by Vera Southgate and Jack Matthew
TWITTER: @tommo1039

Batting	Mat	Inns	NO	Runs	HS	Ave	SR	100	50	Ct	St
First-class	6	7	0	113	26	16.14	43.29	0	0	2	0
List A	1	1	0	19	19	19.00	86.36	0	0	0	0
T20s	1	1	0	14	14	14.00	200.00	0	0	0	0
Bowling	**Mat**	**Balls**	**Runs**	**Wkts**	**BBI**	**BBM**	**Ave**	**Econ**	**SR**	**5w**	**10**
First-class	6	475	326	9	6/138	7/176	36.22	4.11	52.7	1	0
List A	1	60	53	3	3/53	3/53	17.66	5.30	20.0	0	0
T20s	1	24	35	4	4/35	4/35	8.75	8.75	6.0	0	0

CHARLIE THURSTON

RHB / RM / R0 / W0

FULL NAME: Charlie Oliver Thurston
BORN: August 17, 1996, Cambridge
SQUAD NO: 96
HEIGHT: 6ft
NICKNAME: Chazzy, Deano, Baloo
EDUCATION: Bedford School; Loughborough University
TEAMS: Northamptonshire
ROLE: Batsman
DEBUT: First-class: 2016; List A: 2018; T20: 2018

BEST BATTING: 126 Loughborough MCCU vs Northamptonshire, Northampton, 2017

WHAT WAS YOUR FIRST CRICKET CLUB? Shenley Village CC, Hertfordshire. I can just about remember meeting Brian Lara when West Indies and Pakistan once played a warm-up there
WHICH BOWLER WOULD YOU LEAST LIKE TO FACE? Murali
BEST INNINGS YOU'VE SEEN? Alastair Cook's 244 not out at the MCG in the 2017/18 Ashes
WHICH RULE WOULD YOU CHANGE ABOUT CRICKET? I'd implement a proper Test championship table to allow casual fans to buy into it more
WHAT WILL YOU BE DOING IN THE YEAR 2040? I'll be a geography teacher
FAVOURITE QUOTE OR SAYING? It always seems impossible until it's done (Nelson Mandela)
WHICH BOOK MEANS MOST TO YOU? To Kill a Mockingbird by Harper Lee
ODDEST SPORT YOU'VE PLAYED? Tiddlywinks
TWITTER: @ThurstonCharlie

Batting	Mat	Inns	NO	Runs	HS	Ave	SR	100	50	Ct	St
First-class	8	10	0	236	126	23.60	59.14	1	0	2	0
List A	1	1	0	53	53	53.00	85.48	0	1	0	0
T20s	6	5	0	87	41	17.40	112.98	0	0	3	0
Bowling	**Mat**	**Balls**	**Runs**	**Wkts**	**BBI**	**BBM**	**Ave**	**Econ**	**SR**	**5w**	**10**
First-class	8	18	16	0	-	-	-	5.33	-	0	0
List A	1	-	-	-	-	-	-	-	-	-	-
T20s	6	-	-	-	-	-	-	-	-	-	-

JOSH TONGUE

RHB / RMF / R0 / W0

FULL NAME: Joshua Charles Tongue
BORN: November 15, 1997, Redditch, Worcestershire
SQUAD NO: 24
HEIGHT: 6ft 2in
NICKNAME: Tonguey
EDUCATION: King's School, Worcester; Christopher Whitehead Language College, Worcester
TEAMS: Worcestershire
ROLE: Bowler
DEBUT: First-class: 2016; List A: 2017; T20: 2017

BEST BATTING: 41 Worcestershire vs Glamorgan, Worcester, 2017
BEST BOWLING: 6-97 Worcestershire vs Glamorgan, Worcester, 2017

FAMILY TIES? My dad is a coach and my mum used to be manager for different age-groups in Worcester
WHAT WAS YOUR FIRST CRICKET CLUB? Redditch CC, Worcestershire. I started out by watching my dad play for the club
CRICKETING HERO? Andrew Flintoff
BEST ADVICE EVER RECEIVED? Don't change who you are
WHICH BOWLER WOULD YOU LEAST LIKE TO FACE? Mitchell Starc
BEST INNINGS YOU'VE SEEN? Moeen Ali's double hundred at Scarborough last year –he whacked it everywhere
WHO WOULD YOU ASK TO BAT FOR YOUR LIFE? Dillon Pennington
TWITTER: @JoshTongue

Batting	Mat	Inns	NO	Runs	HS	Ave	SR	100	50	Ct	St
First-class	26	37	6	339	41	10.93	45.56	0	0	4	0
List A	7	3	2	12	11*	12.00	66.66	0	0	1	0
T20s	5	2	2	3	2*	-	150.00	0	0	2	0
Bowling	**Mat**	**Balls**	**Runs**	**Wkts**	**BBI**	**BBM**	**Ave**	**Econ**	**SR**	**5w**	**10**
First-class	26	3980	2272	91	6/97	9/98	24.96	3.42	43.7	4	0
List A	7	273	299	8	2/46	2/46	37.37	6.57	34.1	0	0
T20s	5	84	122	3	2/32	2/32	40.66	8.71	28.0	0	0

PETER TREGO RHB / RM / R1 / W1

FULL NAME: Peter David Trego
BORN: June 12, 1981, Weston-super-Mare
SQUAD NO: 7
HEIGHT: 6ft
NICKNAME: Tregs, Pirate, Tony Dorigo
EDUCATION: Wyvern School, Weston-super-Mare
TEAMS: Somerset, Central Districts, England Lions, Kent, Mashonaland Eagles, Middlesex, Sylhet Royals
ROLE: Allrounder
DEBUT: First-class: 2000; List A: 1999; T20: 2003

BEST BATTING: 154* Somerset vs Lancashire, Old Trafford, 2016
BEST BOWLING: 7-84 Somerset vs Yorkshire, Headingley, 2014
COUNTY CAP: 2007 (Somerset); **BENEFIT:** 2015 (Somerset)

WHAT WAS YOUR FIRST CRICKET CLUB? Two clubs: Weston-super-Mare CC and Uphill Castle CC. I played juniors in the morning for WSM and then walked over the road in the afternoon to play men's cricket for Uphill
FAVOURITE CRICKET BAT? My Gray-Nicolls from 2013, when I scored 1,000 runs in one-day and T20 cricket. I got it signed by John Cleese after he watched me score a century at Lord's
WHICH BOWLER WOULD YOU LEAST LIKE TO FACE? Andre van Troost. The Flying Dutchman was rapid and let's just say his length alternated between bouncer and beamer far too often!
BEST INNINGS YOU'VE SEEN? Mohammad Shazad: 74 off 16 balls in the T10 League last November
WHO WOULD YOU ASK TO BAT FOR YOUR LIFE? Darren Lehmann
YOUR BIGGEST CRICKETING REGRET? Afraid there's not enough space here
TWITTER: @tregs140
NOTES: Trego has signed a contract to play only white-ball cricket this season

Batting	Mat	Inns	NO	Runs	HS	Ave	SR	100	50	Ct	St
First-class	217	322	37	9510	154*	33.36	71.10	15	54	87	0
List A	187	165	25	4573	147	32.66	103.42	9	25	55	0
T20s	197	182	21	3855	94*	23.94	125.73	0	21	53	0
Bowling	**Mat**	**Balls**	**Runs**	**Wkts**	**BBI**	**BBM**	**Ave**	**Econ**	**SR**	**5w**	**10**
First-class	217	24301	13973	382	7/84	11/153	36.57	3.44	63.6	5	1
List A	187	6001	5564	171	5/40	5/40	32.53	5.56	35.0	2	0
T20s	197	1728	2451	78	4/27	4/27	31.42	8.51	22.1	0	0

MARCUS TRESCOTHICK

LHB / RM / R8 / W0

FULL NAME: Marcus Edward Trescothick
BORN: December 25, 1975, Keynsham, Somerset
SQUAD NO: 2
HEIGHT: 6ft 3in
NICKNAME: Banger, Tresco
EDUCATION: Sir Bernard Lovell School, Bristol
TEAMS: England, Somerset
ROLE: Batsman
DEBUT: Test: 2000; ODI: 2000; T20I: 2005; First-class: 1993; List A: 1993; T20: 2004

BEST BATTING: 284 Somerset vs Northamptonshire, Northampton, 2007
BEST BOWLING: 4-36 Somerset vs Young Australia, Taunton, 1995
COUNTY CAP: 1999; **BENEFIT:** 2008

TWITTER: @Trescricket
NOTES: Trescothick's maiden Test appearance came against West Indies at Old Trafford in 2000. His highest Test score was 219 against South Africa in a decisive nine-wicket victory at The Oval. He played his 76th and final Test against Pakistan at the same ground in 2006. Wisden Cricketer of the Year in 2005 and PCA Player of the Year in 2000, 2009 and 2011. He held the English record for ODI hundreds (12) until Joe Root passed him last year. After retiring from international cricket Trescothick scored 1,000 runs five years in a row between 2007 and 2011 and then for three successive seasons between 2014 and 2016. He stood down as captain in January 2016 after six years in charge. He now plays Championship cricket only. This summer is his 27th as a Somerset player

Batting	Mat	Inns	NO	Runs	HS	Ave	SR	100	50	Ct	St
Tests	76	143	10	5825	219	43.79	54.51	14	29	95	0
ODIs	123	122	6	4335	137	37.37	85.21	12	21	49	0
T20Is	3	3	0	166	72	55.33	126.71	0	2	2	0
First-class	385	665	36	26089	284	41.47	57.59	66	127	550	0
List A	372	357	29	12229	184	37.28	95.14	28	63	149	0
T20s	89	87	5	2363	108*	28.81	150.60	2	17	29	0
Bowling	**Mat**	**Balls**	**Runs**	**Wkts**	**BBI**	**BBM**	**Ave**	**Econ**	**SR**	**5w**	**10**
Tests	76	300	155	1	1/34	1/34	155.00	3.10	300.0	0	0
ODIs	123	232	219	4	2/7	2/7	54.75	5.66	58.0	0	0
T20Is	3	-	-	-	-	-	-	-	-	-	-
First-class	385	2704	1551	36	4/36	7/106	43.08	3.44	75.1	0	0
List A	372	2010	1644	57	4/50	4/50	28.84	4.90	35.2	0	0
T20s	89	-	-	-	-	-	-	-	-	-	-

LIAM TREVASKIS

RHB / SLA / R0 / W0

FULL NAME: Liam Trevaskis
BORN: April 18, 1999, Carlisle, Cumberland
SQUAD NO: 80
HEIGHT: 5ft 10in
NICKNAME: T-rev, Trav, Trevor
EDUCATION: Queen Elizabeth Grammar School, Penrith, Cumbria
TEAMS: Durham
ROLE: Allrounder
DEBUT: First-class: 2017; T20: 2017

BEST BATTING: 9 Durham vs Worcestershire, Worcester, 2017
BEST BOWLING: 1-69 Durham vs Worcestershire, Worcester, 2017

WHAT WAS YOUR FIRST CRICKET CLUB? Penrith CC, Cumbria
FAVOURITE CRICKET BAT? Gray-Nicolls Powerbow (the yellow one) which I played with about five years ago. It was just a cannon of a bat
CRICKETING HERO? Steve Waugh – because he changed his game for the good of the team
WHICH BOWLER WOULD YOU LEAST LIKE TO FACE? Ravi Ashwin – he can make you look like you don't know which end of the bat to hold
BEST INNINGS YOU'VE SEEN? Ben Stokes against South Africa at Cape Town in 2016. Aggressive batting at its finest against a strong bowling attack
WHO WOULD YOU ASK TO BAT FOR YOUR LIFE? Matt Salisbury (The Great Wall of Salisbury). Just for his leave
WHICH RULE WOULD YOU CHANGE ABOUT CRICKET? You should get more than six runs for hitting it out the ground
FAVOURITE QUOTE OR SAYING? You've got to risk it for a chocolate biscuit
WHICH BOOK MEANS MOST TO YOU? Fantastic Mr Fox by Roald Dahl
TWITTER: @LiamTrevaskis

Batting	Mat	Inns	NO	Runs	HS	Ave	SR	100	50	Ct	St
First-class	1	2	0	14	9	7.00	18.91	0	0	0	0
T20s	9	8	2	67	26	11.16	100.00	0	0	9	0
Bowling	**Mat**	**Balls**	**Runs**	**Wkts**	**BBI**	**BBM**	**Ave**	**Econ**	**SR**	**5w**	**10**
First-class	1	156	126	1	1/69	1/126	126.00	4.84	156.0	0	0
T20s	9	66	70	5	4/16	4/16	14.00	6.36	13.2	0	0

BEN TWOHIG

RHB / SLA / R0 / W0

FULL NAME: Benjamin Jake Twohig
BORN: April 13, 1998, Dewsbury, Yorkshire
SQUAD NO: 42
HEIGHT: 5ft 9in
NICKNAME: Twiggy, The Owl, Twiglet
EDUCATION: Malvern College
TEAMS: Worcestershire
ROLE: Bowler
DEBUT: First-class: 2018; List A: 2018

BEST BATTING: 35 Worcestershire vs Nottinghamshire, Trent Bridge, 2018
BEST BOWLING: 2-47 Worcestershire vs Yorkshire, Worcester, 2018

WHAT WAS YOUR FIRST CRICKET CLUB? Batley CC, West Yorkshire. Best cuppa in the north
FAVOURITE CRICKET BAT? Stac Hammerhead. Great middle
CRICKETING HERO? Daniel Vettori – someone I look up to as a fellow slow left-armer
BEST ADVICE EVER RECEIVED? Fours and sixes, and don't get out
WHO WOULD YOU ASK TO BAT FOR YOUR LIFE? Charlie Morris – solid
WHICH RULE WOULD YOU CHANGE ABOUT CRICKET? Nobody is allowed to hit me for six
YOUR BIGGEST CRICKETING REGRET? Not becoming a seamer
SURPRISING FACT ABOUT YOU? I played Dorothy in a school production of The Wizard of Oz
WHICH BOOK MEANS MOST TO YOU? 1984 by George Orwell
ODDEST SPORT YOU'VE PLAYED? Racquets
TWITTER: @Ben_Twohig

Batting	Mat	Inns	NO	Runs	HS	Ave	SR	100	50	Ct	St
First-class	7	13	2	145	35	13.18	36.89	0	0	3	0
List A	1	1	0	1	1	1.00	50.00	0	0	1	0
Bowling	**Mat**	**Balls**	**Runs**	**Wkts**	**BBI**	**BBM**	**Ave**	**Econ**	**SR**	**5w**	**10**
First-class	7	966	598	10	2/47	3/84	59.80	3.71	96.6	0	0
List A	1	60	55	0	-	-	-	5.50	-	0	0

MUJEEB UR RAHMAN

RHB / OB / R0 / W0

FULL NAME: Mujeeb ur Rahman
BORN: March 28, 2001, Khost, Afghanistan
SQUAD NO: 88
TEAMS: Afghanistan, Middlesex, Boost Defenders, Brisbane Heat, Comilla Victorians, Hampshire, Kings XI Punjab, Nangarhar Leopards
ROLE: Bowler
DEBUT: Test: 2018; ODI: 2017; T20I: 2018; First-class: 2018; List A: 2017; T20: 2017

BEST BATTING: 15 Afghanistan vs India, Bengaluru, 2018
BEST BOWLING: 1-75 Afghanistan vs India, Bengaluru, 2018

NOTES: The Afghan teenager has been snapped up by Middlesex for the T20 Blast campaign having impressed for Hampshire last season when he took nine wickets with an economy-rate of 7.09. Still just 18, Mujeeb has also impressed in the Indian Premier League and Big Bash League for Kings XI Punjab and Brisbane Heat respectively. An off-spinner with a leg-break and googly in his locker, he burst onto the scene at the 2018 U19 World Cup and has since been a regular at senior level. In February 2018 he became the youngest player to take an ODI five-wicket haul, returning figures of 5-50 against Zimbabwe in Sharjah. "His unique style of spin has proven to be difficult to play against and his record is outstanding in the T20 format," said Middlesex head coach Stuart Law

Batting	Mat	Inns	NO	Runs	HS	Ave	SR	100	50	Ct	St
Tests	1	2	0	18	15	9.00	105.88	0	0	0	0
ODIs	28	12	6	41	15	6.83	91.11	0	0	3	0
T20Is	9	2	2	0	0*	-	-	0	0	3	0
First-class	1	2	0	18	15	9.00	105.88	0	0	0	0
List A	35	14	8	45	15	7.50	95.74	0	0	4	0
T20s	60	17	10	78	27	11.14	101.29	0	0	11	0
Bowling	**Mat**	**Balls**	**Runs**	**Wkts**	**BBI**	**BBM**	**Ave**	**Econ**	**SR**	**5w**	**10**
Tests	1	90	75	1	1/75	1/75	75.00	5.00	90.0	0	0
ODIs	28	1536	959	51	5/50	5/50	18.80	3.74	30.1	1	0
T20Is	9	210	187	11	3/17	3/17	17.00	5.34	19.0	0	0
First-class	1	90	75	1	1/75	1/75	75.00	5.00	90.0	0	0
List A	35	1920	1206	59	5/50	5/50	20.44	3.76	32.5	1	0
T20s	60	1339	1497	63	4/16	4/16	23.76	6.70	21.2	0	0

LOGAN VAN BEEK

RHB / RFM / R0 / W0

FULL NAME: Logan Verjus van Beek
BORN: September 7, 1990, Christchurch, New Zealand
SQUAD NO: 37
TEAMS: Netherlands, Derbyshire, Canterbury, Wellington
ROLE: Allrounder
DEBUT: T20I: 2014; First-class: 2010; List A: 2010; T20: 2012

BEST BATTING: 111* Canterbury vs Otago, Christchurch, 2015
BEST BOWLING: 6-46 Canterbury vs Otago, Christchurch, 2015

TWITTER: @loganvanbeek
NOTES: Derbyshire have signed the New Zealand-born allrounder for the duration of the season and he will be available across all formats. A former Netherlands international, van Beek returned figures of 3-9 in the famous victory over England at the 2014 World T20 in Bangladesh before switching his allegiance to the country of his birth, taking the new ball and scoring a half-century from No.10 during New Zealand A's series against Pakistan A in the UAE last October. "We were looking for a specific type of cricketer, someone to enhance our bowling attack," said Derbyshire head of cricket Dave Houghton. "He gets his wickets with balls that are pitched up and that's a good length in England, especially in the early season. He's on the verge of the New Zealand side and bursting to try and get in. That's the type of cricketer we want – guys who are here with a point to prove"

Batting	Mat	Inns	NO	Runs	HS	Ave	SR	100	50	Ct	St
T20Is	8	4	1	7	4*	2.33	46.66	0	0	3	0
First-class	41	57	12	1212	111*	26.93	54.84	1	7	29	0
List A	54	35	6	420	64*	14.48	83.66	0	2	29	0
T20s	64	36	8	206	24*	7.35	110.75	0	0	29	0
Bowling	**Mat**	**Balls**	**Runs**	**Wkts**	**BBI**	**BBM**	**Ave**	**Econ**	**SR**	**5w**	**10**
T20Is	8	102	160	5	3/9	3/9	32.00	9.41	20.4	0	0
First-class	41	6187	3489	111	6/46	10/117	31.43	3.38	55.7	6	1
List A	54	1985	1833	61	6/18	6/18	30.04	5.54	32.5	1	0
T20s	64	977	1489	55	3/9	3/9	27.07	9.14	17.7	0	0

GRAEME VAN BUUREN

RHB / SLA / R0 / W0

FULL NAME: Graeme Lourens van Buuren
BORN: August 22, 1990, Pretoria, South Africa
SQUAD NO: 12
HEIGHT: 5ft 7in
NICKNAME: GVB, Buggers
EDUCATION: Pretoria Boys High School, South Africa
TEAMS: Gloucestershire, Northerns, Titans
ROLE: Allrounder
DEBUT: First-class: 2010; List A: 2010; T20: 2011

BEST BATTING: 235 Northerns vs Eastern Province, Centurion, 2015
BEST BOWLING: 4-12 Northerns vs South Western Districts, Oudtshoorn, 2013

WHAT WAS YOUR FIRST CRICKET CLUB? Tuks CC, University of Pretoria, South Africa. It's both a public club and university team
FAVOURITE CRICKET BAT? IXU Nexus. It's sweet
CRICKETING HERO? AB de Villiers
WHICH BOWLER WOULD YOU LEAST LIKE TO FACE? Liam Norwell – because he hits you all over the body
WHO WOULD YOU ASK TO BAT FOR YOUR LIFE? Kane Williamson
WHICH RULE WOULD YOU CHANGE ABOUT CRICKET? Make the tea break longer
FAVOURITE QUOTE OR SAYING? Work hard in silence and let the success make the noise
WHICH BOOK MEANS MOST TO YOU? The Bible
ODDEST SPORT YOU'VE PLAYED? Gaelic football
TWITTER: @GraemeGVB

Batting	Mat	Inns	NO	Runs	HS	Ave	SR	100	50	Ct	St
First-class	75	119	18	4348	235	43.04	62.48	10	26	42	0
List A	63	56	11	1312	119*	29.15	81.08	1	6	17	0
T20s	48	36	11	548	64	21.92	109.16	0	3	24	0
Bowling	**Mat**	**Balls**	**Runs**	**Wkts**	**BBI**	**BBM**	**Ave**	**Econ**	**SR**	**5w**	**10**
First-class	75	5171	2469	84	4/12	6/87	29.39	2.86	61.5	0	0
List A	63	1914	1512	48	5/35	5/35	31.50	4.73	39.8	1	0
T20s	48	661	721	29	5/8	5/8	24.86	6.54	22.7	1	0

FREDDIE VAN DEN BERGH RHB / SLA / R0 / W0

FULL NAME: Freddie Oliver Edward van den Bergh
BORN: June 14, 1992, Bickley, Kent
SQUAD NO: 5
HEIGHT: 6ft 4in
NICKNAME: Vanders, Fruba
EDUCATION: Whitgift School, Croydon; Durham University
TEAMS: Surrey
ROLE: Bowler
DEBUT: First-class: 2011; List A 2014; T20: 2018

BEST BATTING: 34 Surrey vs Nottinghamshire, Trent Bridge, 2013
BEST BOWLING: 4-84 Surrey vs Nottinghamshire, Trent Bridge, 2013

FAMILY TIES? My dad used to work for the ECB
WHAT WAS YOUR FIRST CRICKET CLUB? Bickley Park CC, Bromley, London
FAVOURITE CRICKET BAT? My first, a Gray-Nicolls Sabre
CRICKETING HERO? Andrew Flintoff
WHICH BOWLER WOULD YOU LEAST LIKE TO FACE? Morne Morkel
BEST INNINGS YOU'VE SEEN? Any knock by Kumar Sangakkara
WHO WOULD YOU ASK TO BAT FOR YOUR LIFE? Arun Harinath
YOUR BIGGEST CRICKETING REGRET? Not getting a bat from Sanga!
FAVOURITE QUOTE OR SAYING? The harder I practise, the luckier I get
ODDEST SPORT YOU'VE PLAYED? Kabaddi
TWITTER: @freddievdb15

Batting	Mat	Inns	NO	Runs	HS	Ave	SR	100	50	Ct	St
First-class	7	9	1	62	34	7.75	48.06	0	0	1	0
List A	3	1	1	29	29*	-	107.40	0	0	0	0
T20s	4	3	1	27	19*	13.50	103.84	0	0	1	0
Bowling	**Mat**	**Balls**	**Runs**	**Wkts**	**BBI**	**BBM**	**Ave**	**Econ**	**SR**	**5w**	**10**
First-class	7	1159	667	15	4/84	5/145	44.46	3.45	77.2	0	0
List A	3	156	122	0	-	-	-	4.69	-	0	0
T20s	4	36	67	0	-	-	-	11.16	-	0	0

TIMM VAN DER GUGTEN RHB / RFM / R0 / W1 / MVP57

FULL NAME: Timm van der Gugten
BORN: February 25, 1991, Sydney, Australia
SQUAD NO: 64
HEIGHT: 6ft 2in
NICKNAME: Windsock, Bull
EDUCATION: St Pius X College, Sydney; Swinburn University
TEAMS: Netherlands, Glamorgan, Hobart Hurricanes, New South Wales, Northern Districts, Tasmania
ROLE: Bowler
DEBUT: ODI: 2012; T20I: 2012; First-class: 2011; List A: 2011; T20: 2012

BEST BATTING: 60* Glamorgan vs Gloucestershire, Cardiff, 2018
BEST BOWLING: 7-42 Glamorgan vs Kent, Cardiff, 2018

WHAT WAS YOUR FIRST CRICKET CLUB? University of New South Wales CC, Australia. Same club where Geoff Lawson played
WHICH BOWLER WOULD YOU LEAST LIKE TO FACE? Tymal Mills – I'm his bunny: faced two balls from him and got out both times
BEST INNINGS YOU'VE SEEN? Watching records tumble as Netherlands chased down 193 in 13.5 overs against Ireland in the 2014 World T20
WHICH RULE WOULD YOU CHANGE ABOUT CRICKET? I would love an hour for lunch and half an hour for tea
FAVOURITE QUOTE OR SAYING? The more you weigh, the harder you are to kidnap. Stay safe, eat cake
WHICH BOOK MEANS MOST TO YOU? My passport
ODDEST SPORT YOU'VE PLAYED? Lawn bowls – underrated

Batting	Mat	Inns	NO	Runs	HS	Ave	SR	100	50	Ct	St
ODIs	4	2	0	4	2	2.00	66.66	0	0	0	0
T20Is	29	10	3	69	13	9.85	115.00	0	0	3	0
First-class	35	52	11	517	60*	12.60	47.78	0	3	6	0
List A	53	31	10	327	36	15.57	93.16	0	0	6	0
T20s	78	30	10	178	21*	8.90	114.83	0	0	16	0
Bowling	**Mat**	**Balls**	**Runs**	**Wkts**	**BBI**	**BBM**	**Ave**	**Econ**	**SR**	**5w**	**10**
ODIs	4	126	85	8	5/24	5/24	10.62	4.04	15.7	1	0
T20Is	29	545	672	28	3/18	3/18	24.00	7.39	19.4	0	0
First-class	35	6337	3399	138	7/42	10/121	24.63	3.21	45.9	10	1
List A	53	2373	2191	64	5/24	5/24	34.23	5.53	37.0	1	0
T20s	78	1427	1906	88	5/21	5/21	21.65	8.01	16.2	1	0

ROELOF VAN DER MERWE RHB/SLA/R0/W0

FULL NAME: Roelof Erasmus van der Merwe
BORN: December 31, 1984, Johannesburg, South Africa
SQUAD NO: 52
HEIGHT: 5ft 8in
NICKNAME: Roela
EDUCATION: Pretoria High School
TEAMS: Netherlands, South Africa, Somerset, Brisbane Heat, Delhi Daredevils, Northerns, RC Bangalore, St Lucia Zouks, Titans
ROLE: Allrounder
DEBUT: ODIs: 2009; T20I: 2009; First-class: 2006; List A: 2006; T20: 2008

BEST BATTING: 205* Titans vs Warriors, Benoni, 2014
BEST BOWLING: 4-22 Somerset vs Middlesex, Taunton, 2017
COUNTY CAP: 2018

WHAT WAS YOUR FIRST CRICKET CLUB? Pretoria CC, South Africa. Worst pitch in the league
FAVOURITE CRICKET BAT? SS Jumbo. It was used by everybody in my U11 team. We loved that bat
CRICKETING HERO? Jonty Rhodes
WHICH BOWLER WOULD YOU LEAST LIKE TO FACE? Mitchell Starc
YOUR BIGGEST CRICKETING REGRET? Dropping Kumar Sangakkara when he was on 20 at The Oval in 2017. Let's just say he made us field for a long time
WHAT WILL YOU BE DOING IN THE YEAR 2040? I'll be retired, drinking Thatchers while watching Marcus Trescothick play for Somerset at Taunton
TWITTER: @Roela52

Batting	Mat	Inns	NO	Runs	HS	Ave	SR	100	50	Ct	St
ODIs	13	7	3	39	12	9.75	95.12	0	0	3	0
T20Is	28	17	6	211	48	19.18	132.70	0	0	13	0
First-class	63	102	14	3053	205*	34.69	70.07	6	18	46	0
List A	173	142	42	2652	165*	26.52	99.77	1	10	66	0
T20s	192	141	43	2109	89*	21.52	131.97	0	8	79	0
Bowling	**Mat**	**Balls**	**Runs**	**Wkts**	**BBI**	**BBM**	**Ave**	**Econ**	**SR**	**5w**	**10**
ODIs	13	705	561	17	3/27	3/27	33.00	4.77	41.4	0	0
T20Is	28	576	641	33	2/3	2/3	19.42	6.67	17.4	0	0
First-class	63	8738	4342	123	4/22	8/104	35.30	2.98	71.0	0	0
List A	173	7626	6136	236	5/26	5/26	26.00	4.82	32.3	4	0
T20s	192	3771	4523	176	3/13	3/13	25.69	7.19	21.4	0	0

PAUL VAN MEEKEREN RHB / RFM / R0 / W0

FULL NAME: Paul Adriaan van Meekeren
BORN: January 15, 1993, Amsterdam, Netherlands
SQUAD NO: 47
HEIGHT: 6ft 4in
NICKNAME: Meerkat, Smacky, Meeks
TEAMS: Netherlands, Somerset
ROLE: Bowler
DEBUT: ODI: 2013; T20I: 2013; First-class: 2013; List A: 2013; T20: 2013

BEST BATTING: 34 Netherlands vs Papua New Guinea, Amstelveen, 2015
BEST BOWLING: 4-60 Somerset vs Essex, Chelmsford, 2017

WHAT WAS YOUR FIRST CRICKET CLUB? Haarlesmsche CC Rood en Wit, Netherlands
BEST INNINGS YOU'VE SEEN? James Hildreth's hundred against Notts in the last Championship game of the 2016 season. He was batting with a broken foot
WHICH RULE WOULD YOU CHANGE ABOUT CRICKET? The no-ball bouncer. Anyone with common sense knows it should be a wide
YOUR BIGGEST CRICKETING REGRET? When we bowled out a side for such a low total (50-over game) that I thought we'd win by lunch, so as I walked off the field I shook hands with the opposition. We tied the game and I got a first-baller
FAVOURITE QUOTE OR SAYING? Hakuna matata
ODDEST SPORT YOU'VE PLAYED? Fierljeppen
TWITTER: @paulvanmeekeren

Batting	Mat	Inns	NO	Runs	HS	Ave	SR	100	50	Ct	St
ODIs	4	3	3	30	15*	-	75.00	0	0	0	0
T20Is	25	6	0	33	18	5.50	117.85	0	0	4	0
First-class	8	14	3	106	34	9.63	34.98	0	0	2	0
List A	44	26	13	118	15*	9.07	61.78	0	0	10	0
T20s	40	14	3	51	18	4.63	104.08	0	0	12	0
Bowling	**Mat**	**Balls**	**Runs**	**Wkts**	**BBI**	**BBM**	**Ave**	**Econ**	**SR**	**5w**	**10**
ODIs	4	156	131	2	1/21	1/21	65.50	5.03	78.0	0	0
T20Is	25	456	528	24	4/11	4/11	22.00	6.94	19.0	0	0
First-class	8	1346	785	21	4/60	5/75	37.38	3.49	64.0	0	0
List A	44	1553	1232	42	3/21	3/21	29.33	4.75	36.9	0	0
T20s	40	698	893	29	4/11	4/11	30.79	7.67	24.0	0	0

STIAAN VAN ZYL

LHB / RM / R1 / W0

FULL NAME: Stiaan van Zyl
BORN: September 19, 1987, Cape Town, SA
SQUAD NO: 74
HEIGHT: 5ft 11in
NICKNAME: Stigo
EDUCATION: Kenridge Primary School, Western Cape; Boland Agricultural School
TEAMS: South Africa, Sussex, Boland, Cape Cobras, Chittagong Vikings, Western Province
ROLE: Allrounder
DEBUT: Test: 2014; First-class: 2006; List A: 2006; T20: 2008

BEST BATTING: 228 Cape Cobras vs Lions, Paarl, 2018
BEST BOWLING: 5-32 Boland vs Northerns, Paarl, 2011

BEST ADVICE EVER RECEIVED? Play with a smile on your face
'ROY OF THE ROVERS' MOMENT? Making 101 not out on my Test debut for South Africa against West Indies at Centurion in 2014
BEST THING ABOUT YOUR HOME GROUND? The crowd – they come even in terrible weather
IF YOU WEREN'T A CRICKETER? I'd be a pilot
WHERE IS PARADISE? Cape Town
CRICKETING HERO? Kumar Sangakkara – a legend and a leftie
TWITTER: @laggies74

Batting	Mat	Inns	NO	Runs	HS	Ave	SR	100	50	Ct	St
Tests	12	17	2	395	101*	26.33	50.77	1	0	6	0
First-class	162	271	39	10201	228	43.96	52.13	24	46	95	0
List A	116	106	12	3350	114*	35.63	74.76	5	18	32	0
T20s	68	61	7	1434	86*	26.55	119.59	0	9	20	0
Bowling	**Mat**	**Balls**	**Runs**	**Wkts**	**BBI**	**BBM**	**Ave**	**Econ**	**SR**	**5w**	**10**
Tests	12	403	148	6	3/20	3/22	24.66	2.20	67.1	0	0
First-class	162	5564	2535	68	5/32	7/82	37.27	2.73	81.8	1	0
List A	116	1056	927	20	4/24	4/24	46.35	5.26	52.8	0	0
T20s	68	120	160	7	2/14	2/14	22.85	8.00	17.1	0	0

RICARDO VASCONCELOS

LHB / WK / R0 / W0

FULL NAME: Ricardo Surrador Vasconcelos
BORN: October 27, 1997, Johannesburg, South Africa
SQUAD NO: 27
HEIGHT: 5ft 5in
NICKNAME: Vasco, Dave
EDUCATION: St Stithians College, Johannesburg; Stellenbosch University, Western Cape
TEAMS: Northamptonshire, Boland
ROLE: Batsman/wicketkeeper
DEBUT: First-class: 2016; List A: 2016; T20: 2017

BEST BATTING: 140 Boland vs Namibia, Windhoek, 2017

WHAT WAS YOUR FIRST CRICKET CLUB? Old Edwardians CC, Johannesburg, South Africa. Graeme Smith, Quinton de Kock, Stephen Cook and Neil McKenzie all played there
WHICH BOWLER WOULD YOU LEAST LIKE TO FACE? Facing Blessing Muzarabani indoors is never fun
BEST INNINGS YOU'VE SEEN? Herschelle Gibbs in the 438 game between South Africa and Australia at Johannesburg in 2006
WHO WOULD YOU ASK TO BAT FOR YOUR LIFE? Ben Sanderson – he's an absolute wall
WHICH RULE WOULD YOU CHANGE ABOUT CRICKET? Batsmen shouldn't have to field
WHAT WILL YOU BE DOING IN THE YEAR 2040? I'll be retired on a game farm somewhere in Africa
FAVOURITE QUOTE OR SAYING? The lyrics of the poem 'If' by Rudyard Kipling
WHICH BOOK MEANS MOST TO YOU? Any of the Harry Potter books

Batting	Mat	Inns	NO	Runs	HS	Ave	SR	100	50	Ct	St
First-class	22	41	3	1252	140	32.94	57.14	3	8	28	4
List A	19	18	0	439	56	24.38	73.90	0	2	16	2
T20s	10	9	3	126	45*	21.00	122.33	0	0	6	0
Bowling	**Mat**	**Balls**	**Runs**	**Wkts**	**BBI**	**BBM**	**Ave**	**Econ**	**SR**	**5w**	**10**
First-class	22	-	-	-	-	-	-	-	-	-	-
List A	19	-	-	-	-	-	-	-	-	-	-
T20s	10	-	-	-	-	-	-	-	-	-	-

DANE VILAS RHB / WK / R0 / W0 / MVP16

FULL NAME: Dane James Vilas
BORN: June 10, 1985, Johannesburg, SA
SQUAD NO: 33
HEIGHT: 6ft
NICKNAME: Vili
EDUCATION: King Edward VII School, Johannesburg
TEAMS: South Africa, Lancashire, Cape Cobras, Dolphins, Gauteng, Lions, South Western Districts, Western Province
ROLE: Batsman/wicketkeeper
DEBUT: Test: 2015; T20I: 2012; First-class: 2006; List A: 2006; T20: 2009

BEST BATTING: 244 Lancashire vs Hampshire, Old Trafford, 2017

TWITTER: @DaneVilas
NOTES: The former Test wicketkeeper was another South African to announce his international retirement in early 2017 and take up a two-year Kolpak deal with Lancashire to play across all formats. The highlights of his first season at Old Trafford were a career-best 244 against Hampshire in the Championship and a brace of hundreds in the One-Day Cup. Vilas scored another double hundred last summer, when he was the club's leading run-scorer in the Championship (792 runs at an average of 37.71). He has appeared in every game across all three formats since his arrival at Old Trafford. The last of his six Tests came against England in 2016, after which the emergence of Quinton de Kock pushed him down the pecking order

Batting	Mat	Inns	NO	Runs	HS	Ave	SR	100	50	Ct	St
Tests	6	9	0	94	26	10.44	44.76	0	0	13	0
T20Is	1	-	-	-	-	-	-	-	-	0	0
First-class	142	222	25	7836	244	39.77	65.49	19	34	382	19
List A	156	144	22	4372	120	35.83	97.13	8	21	153	29
T20s	132	107	25	2451	71*	29.89	125.17	0	11	75	23
Bowling	**Mat**	**Balls**	**Runs**	**Wkts**	**BBI**	**BBM**	**Ave**	**Econ**	**SR**	**5w**	**10**
Tests	6	-	-	-	-	-	-	-	-	-	-
T20Is	1	-	-	-	-	-	-	-	-	-	-
First-class	142	6	3	0	-	-	-	3.00	-	0	0
List A	156	-	-	-	-	-	-	-	-	-	-
T20s	132	-	-	-	-	-	-	-	-	-	-

JAMES VINCE

RHB / RM / R2 / W0 / MVP11

FULL NAME: James Michael Vince
BORN: March 14, 1991, Cuckfield, Sussex
SQUAD NO: 14
HEIGHT: 6ft 2in
NICKNAME: JV, Vincey
EDUCATION: Warminster School, Wiltshire
TEAMS: England, Hampshire, Auckland, Karachi Kings, Sydney Thunder
ROLE: Batsman
DEBUT: Test: 2016; ODI: 2015; T20I: 2015; First-class: 2009; List A: 2009; T20: 2010

BEST BATTING: 240 Hampshire vs Essex, Southampton, 2014
BEST BOWLING: 5-41 Hampshire vs Loughborough MCCU, Southampton, 2013
COUNTY CAP: 2013

WHAT WAS YOUR FIRST CRICKET CLUB? Erlestoke CC, Wiltshire. A very small village club
FAVOURITE CRICKET BAT? GM Purist – was a favourite when I was growing up
WHICH BOWLER WOULD YOU LEAST LIKE TO FACE? Tom Westley – I really struggle to pick which way the ball will spin
BEST INNINGS YOU'VE SEEN? Alastair Cook's farewell century at The Oval last summer. What a way to finish an incredible career
WHICH RULE WOULD YOU CHANGE ABOUT CRICKET? Instead of the coin toss, have a catching competition between two nominated players from each team
TWITTER: @vincey14

Batting	Mat	Inns	NO	Runs	HS	Ave	SR	100	50	Ct	St
Tests	13	22	0	548	83	24.90	49.81	0	3	8	0
ODIs	6	5	0	131	51	26.20	87.33	0	1	4	0
T20Is	7	7	0	194	46	27.71	117.57	0	0	0	0
First-class	155	258	19	9188	240	38.44	61.54	23	35	133	0
List A	122	114	7	4205	178	39.29	96.97	8	20	45	0
T20s	172	166	16	4458	107*	29.72	133.07	1	28	83	0
Bowling	**Mat**	**Balls**	**Runs**	**Wkts**	**BBI**	**BBM**	**Ave**	**Econ**	**SR**	**5w**	**10**
Tests	13	24	13	0	-	-	-	3.25	-	0	0
ODIs	6	-	-	-	-	-	-	-	-	-	-
T20Is	7	-	-	-	-	-	-	-	-	-	-
First-class	155	1633	1014	22	5/41	6/56	46.09	3.72	74.2	1	0
List A	122	132	124	2	1/18	1/18	62.00	5.63	66.0	0	0
T20s	172	72	81	3	1/5	1/5	27.00	6.75	24.0	0	0

AMAR VIRDI

RHB / OB / R0 / W0

FULL NAME: Guramar Singh Virdi
BORN: July 19, 1998, Chiswick, Middlesex
SQUAD NO: 19
HEIGHT: 5ft 10in
NICKNAME: Virds
EDUCATION: Guru Nanak Sikh Academy, Middlesex
TEAMS: Surrey
ROLE: Bowler
DEBUT: First-class: 2017

BEST BATTING: 21* Surrey vs Somerset, Taunton, 2018
BEST BOWLING: 6-105 Surrey vs Worcestershire, The Oval, 2018

WHAT WAS YOUR FIRST CRICKET CLUB? Indian Gymkhana CC, London. It's the oldest South Asian cricket club in the UK
CRICKETING HERO? Saqlain Mushtaq
BEST ADVICE EVER RECEIVED? Treat everyone the way you wish to be treated
WHICH BOWLER WOULD YOU LEAST LIKE TO FACE? Ryan Patel – he's fast and swings it round corners
WHO WOULD YOU ASK TO BAT FOR YOUR LIFE? Arun Harinath
WHICH RULE WOULD YOU CHANGE ABOUT CRICKET? Make boundaries longer
YOUR BIGGEST CRICKETING REGRET? Dropping a catch in a club cricket final
FAVOURITE QUOTE OR SAYING? You come to this world with nothing and you leave with nothing. But you can leave something behind for others to remember
WHICH BOOK MEANS MOST TO YOU? The Alchemist by Paulo Coelho
ODDEST SPORT YOU'VE PLAYED? Swimming
TWITTER: @amarsinghvirdi

Batting	Mat	Inns	NO	Runs	HS	Ave	SR	100	50	Ct	St
First-class	18	21	9	97	21*	8.08	57.39	0	0	5	0
Bowling	**Mat**	**Balls**	**Runs**	**Wkts**	**BBI**	**BBM**	**Ave**	**Econ**	**SR**	**5w**	**10**
First-class	18	2829	1534	46	6/105	6/105	33.34	3.25	61.5	1	0

GRAHAM WAGG

RHB / LM / R0 / W2

FULL NAME: Graham Grant Wagg
BORN: April 28, 1983, Rugby, Warwickshire
SQUAD NO: 8
HEIGHT: 6ft
NICKNAME: Waggy
EDUCATION: Ashlawn School, Rugby
TEAMS: Glamorgan, Derbyshire, Warwickshire
ROLE: Allrounder
DEBUT: First-class: 2002; List A: 2000; T20: 2003

BEST BATTING: 200 Glamorgan vs Surrey, Guildford, 2015
BEST BOWLING: 6-29 Glamorgan vs Surrey, The Oval, 2014
COUNTY CAP: 2007 (Derbyshire); 2013 (Glamorgan)

FAMILY TIES? My dad played Second XI cricket and Minor Counties – he could bowl a heavy ball and hit a long ball. Watch out for my little man Brayden Wagg
WHAT WAS YOUR FIRST CRICKET CLUB? GEC CC, Rugby, Warwickshire
FAVOURITE CRICKET BAT? A Duncan Fearnley – my first sponsor. It was a toothpick
CRICKETING HERO? Allan Donald
WHICH BOWLER WOULD YOU LEAST LIKE TO FACE? Mitchell Johnson. Talking to guys who have faced him, they say he was very quick and could hit you at will. Not for me, thank you. I'll stick to facing Stevo on a flat one
WHICH RULE WOULD YOU CHANGE ABOUT CRICKET? Bowlers can decide to bowl with either arm without telling the umpire. After all, batsmen are allowed to switch hands without saying anything
ODDEST SPORT YOU'VE PLAYED? Any one of the many games which your strength and conditioning coach will get you to play in the morning as a warm-up
TWITTER: @GGWagg

Batting	Mat	Inns	NO	Runs	HS	Ave	SR	100	50	Ct	St
First-class	151	224	22	5386	200	26.66	64.72	4	31	49	0
List A	132	109	15	1853	62*	19.71	101.92	0	3	43	0
T20s	129	97	31	1274	62	19.30	125.39	0	4	35	0
Bowling	**Mat**	**Balls**	**Runs**	**Wkts**	**BBI**	**BBM**	**Ave**	**Econ**	**SR**	**5w**	**10**
First-class	151	25740	14975	437	6/29	10/133	34.26	3.49	58.9	12	1
List A	132	5138	5054	147	4/35	4/35	34.38	5.90	34.9	0	0
T20s	129	2181	3041	121	5/14	5/14	25.13	8.36	18.0	1	0

MATTHEW WAITE

RHB / RFM / R0 / W0

FULL NAME: Matthew James Waite
BORN: December 24, 1995, Leeds
SQUAD NO: 6
NICKNAME: Pingu
EDUCATION: Brigshaw High School, West Yorkshire
TEAMS: Yorkshire
ROLE: Allrounder
DEBUT: First-class: 2017; List A: 2014; T20: 2015

BEST BATTING: 42 Yorkshire vs Nottinghamshire, Trent Bridge, 2018
BEST BOWLING: 3-91 Yorkshire vs Nottinghamshire, Trent Bridge, 2018

TWITTER: @mat_waite
NOTES: A seam-bowling allrounder, Waite signed a two-year junior professional contract with Yorkshire at the end of 2015. He made his senior debut in the One-Day Cup in 2014 and played his first T20 Blast game the following year. In 2016 he made two appearances for Yorkshire in white-ball cricket, doing well on both occasions. First he hit 19* and took 1-6 from two overs in the T20 quarter-final against Glamorgan at Cardiff, and then he made 38 and took 3-48 from 10 overs in the One-Day Cup semi-final against Surrey at Headingley. Waite made his Championship debut against Somerset at Taunton in 2017 but his brief career has been hampered by a recurring ankle injury. He impressed last year with eight wickets at an average of 27.62 in a handful of four-day matches but he did not play limited-overs cricket

Batting	Mat	Inns	NO	Runs	HS	Ave	SR	100	50	Ct	St
First-class	5	8	0	118	42	14.75	48.76	0	0	0	0
List A	11	9	2	246	71	35.14	90.44	0	1	0	0
T20s	5	3	3	34	19*	-	147.82	0	0	3	0
Bowling	**Mat**	**Balls**	**Runs**	**Wkts**	**BBI**	**BBM**	**Ave**	**Econ**	**SR**	**5w**	**10**
First-class	5	462	291	11	3/91	3/70	26.45	3.77	42.0	0	0
List A	11	411	424	13	4/65	4/65	32.61	6.18	31.6	0	0
T20s	5	48	67	2	1/6	1/6	33.50	8.37	24.0	0	0

ALEX WAKELY

RHB / RM / R0 / W0 / MVP92

FULL NAME: Alex George Wakely
BORN: November 3, 1988, London
SQUAD NO: 8
HEIGHT: 6ft 2in
NICKNAME: Wakers, Baby Seal
EDUCATION: Bedford School
TEAMS: Northamptonshire
ROLE: Batsman
DEBUT: First-class: 2007; List A: 2005; T20: 2009

BEST BATTING: 123 Northamptonshire vs Leicestershire, Northampton, 2015
BEST BOWLING: 2-62 Northamptonshire vs Somerset, Taunton, 2007
COUNTY CAP: 2012

WHAT GOT YOU INTO CRICKET? My grandad made me a bat when I was five. Then watching my dad play for Ampthill Town CC for many years
'ROY OF THE ROVERS' MOMENT? Winning the T20 Cup in 2013
BEST THING ABOUT YOUR HOME GROUND? It's my home town and I am proud to be associated with Northampton
SURPRISING FACT ABOUT YOU? I play the piano
WHERE IS PARADISE? Anywhere with my family
CRICKETING HERO? David Sales – he was captain when I made my debut and took me under his wing. Best batsman I have watched
UNUSUAL OBJECT AT HOME? A gekko
TWITTER: @AlexWakely1

Batting	Mat	Inns	NO	Runs	HS	Ave	SR	100	50	Ct	St
First-class	134	217	15	6317	123	31.27	48.14	8	35	84	0
List A	81	76	8	2191	109*	32.22	85.02	2	14	30	0
T20s	114	107	22	2318	64	27.27	120.72	0	14	36	0
Bowling	**Mat**	**Balls**	**Runs**	**Wkts**	**BBI**	**BBM**	**Ave**	**Econ**	**SR**	**5w**	**10**
First-class	134	509	426	6	2/62	2/62	71.00	5.02	84.8	0	0
List A	81	136	131	5	2/14	2/14	26.20	5.77	27.2	0	0
T20s	114	12	29	0	-	-	-	14.50	-	0	0

MAX WALLER RHB / LB / R0 / W0

FULL NAME: Maximilian Thomas Charles Waller
BORN: March 3, 1988, Salisbury, Wiltshire
SQUAD NO: 10
HEIGHT: 6ft
NICKNAME: Goose, Jun Jun, Maxy
EDUCATION: Millfield School, Somerset; Bournemouth University
TEAMS: Somerset
ROLE: Bowler
DEBUT: First-class: 2009; List A: 2009; T20: 2009

BEST BATTING: 28 Somerset vs Hampshire, Southampton, 2009
BEST BOWLING: 3-33 Somerset vs Cambridge MCCU, Taunton, 2012

WHAT WAS YOUR FIRST CRICKET CLUB? Bashley CC, Hampshire – great village club based in the New Forest
CRICKETING HERO? Shane Warne
WHICH BOWLER WOULD YOU LEAST LIKE TO FACE? Morne Morkel – every ball he has bowled at me has been at my head
BEST INNINGS YOU'VE SEEN? James Hildreth's T20 hundred against Glamorgan in 2012. Robert Croft needed at least 15 fielders!
WHO WOULD YOU ASK TO BAT FOR YOUR LIFE? Brian Lara
WHICH RULE WOULD YOU CHANGE ABOUT CRICKET? Bigger boundaries in T20
YOUR BIGGEST CRICKETING REGRET? Not yet winning a T20 final for Somerset
SURPRISING FACT ABOUT YOU? I've sold paintings in an art shop
SURPRISING FACT ABOUT A TEAMMATE? Lewis Gregory is a black belt in judo but couldn't hurt a fly
TWITTER: @MaxTCWaller
NOTES: Waller signed a contract to play only white-ball cricket until the end of the 2020 season

Batting	Mat	Inns	NO	Runs	HS	Ave	SR	100	50	Ct	St
First-class	9	10	1	91	28	10.11	42.32	0	0	5	0
List A	58	22	15	109	25*	15.57	70.77	0	0	32	0
T20s	111	28	18	79	17	7.90	74.52	0	0	65	0
Bowling	**Mat**	**Balls**	**Runs**	**Wkts**	**BBI**	**BBM**	**Ave**	**Econ**	**SR**	**5w**	**10**
First-class	9	840	493	10	3/33	3/57	49.30	3.52	84.0	0	0
List A	58	1801	1696	45	3/37	3/37	37.68	5.65	40.0	0	0
T20s	111	2103	2569	111	4/16	4/16	23.14	7.32	18.9	0	0

PAUL WALTER LHB / LM / R0 / W0

FULL NAME: Paul Ian Walter
BORN: May 28, 1994, Basildon, Essex
SQUAD NO: 22
HEIGHT: 6ft 7in
EDUCATION: Billericay School, Essex
TEAMS: Essex
ROLE: Allrounder
DEBUT: First-class: 2016; List A: 2017; T20: 2016

BEST BATTING: 68* Essex vs West Indians, Chelmsford, 2017
BEST BOWLING: 3-44 Essex vs Derbyshire, Derby, 2016

TWITTER: @PWalter_22
NOTES: Walter signed a professional contract with his hometown club midway through the 2016 season after impressing in club cricket for Hornchurch and for Essex Second XI. An allrounder with Premier League hundreds under his belt allied to a series of thrusting spells of high-quality pace bowling, Walter offers Essex options, especially in one-day cricket. At 6ft 7in, he brings considerable physical presence to the Essex attack. He played five Championship matches as Essex romped to the Championship title in 2017, and took 15 wickets in 13 games in the T20 Blast. Last season he was restricted to just one Championship match and seven T20 games

Batting	Mat	Inns	NO	Runs	HS	Ave	SR	100	50	Ct	St
First-class	10	10	3	240	68*	34.28	55.29	0	1	0	0
List A	6	4	2	37	19	18.50	105.71	0	0	2	0
T20s	27	20	8	235	40	19.58	136.62	0	0	8	0
Bowling	**Mat**	**Balls**	**Runs**	**Wkts**	**BBI**	**BBM**	**Ave**	**Econ**	**SR**	**5w**	**10**
First-class	10	924	540	13	3/44	4/68	41.53	3.50	71.0	0	0
List A	6	256	267	12	4/37	4/37	22.25	6.25	21.3	0	0
T20s	27	408	654	19	3/24	3/24	34.42	9.61	21.4	0	0

JARED WARNER RHB / RFM / R0 / W0

FULL NAME: Jared David Warner
BORN: November 14, 1996, Wakefield, Yorkshire
SQUAD NO: 45
HEIGHT: 6ft 1in
NICKNAME: Jazz
EDUCATION: Silcoates School, West Yorkshire; Kettlethorpe High School, Wakefield
TEAMS: Yorkshire, England U19
ROLE: Bowler

WHAT WAS YOUR FIRST CRICKET CLUB? Wakefield Thornes CC, West Yorkshire
BEST ADVICE EVER RECEIVED? Have no fear
'ROY OF THE ROVERS' MOMENT? Winning the double with Yorkshire Academy. Taking figures of 9-19 from 10.2 overs for Yorkshire Academy against Castleford in a Yorkshire Premier League North match in 2016. Representing England U19
BEST THING ABOUT YOUR HOME GROUND? It has a great atmosphere
IF YOU WEREN'T A CRICKETER? I'd be involved in sport in some capacity
SURPRISING FACT ABOUT YOU? I'm a big Sheffield United fan
WHERE IS PARADISE? Top of the Kop at Bramall Lane
CRICKETING HERO? Andrew Flintoff – my first memories of watching cricket are of him winning the Ashes in 2005
NON-CRICKETING HERO? Michael Owen – he got me into football
TWITTER: @JaredWarner96

JOE WEATHERLEY RHB / OB / R0 / W0

FULL NAME: Joe James Weatherley
BORN: January 19, 1997, Winchester, Hampshire
SQUAD NO: 5
HEIGHT: 6ft 2in
NICKNAME: Lord, Weathers
EDUCATION: King Edward VI School, Southampton
TEAMS: Hampshire
ROLE: Batsman
DEBUT: First-class: 2016; List A: 2016; T20: 2016

BEST BATTING: 126* Hampshire vs Lancashire, Old Trafford, 2018
BEST BOWLING: 1-2 Hampshire vs Nottinghamshire, Southampton, 2018

WHAT WAS YOUR FIRST CRICKET CLUB? St Cross Symondians CC, Hampshire. Still play for them every now and again
FAVOURITE CRICKET BAT? A Salix bought from the Dummer Cricket Centre in Basingstoke when I was about 12. Felt like the best bat of all time
CRICKETING HERO? Marcus Trescothick
WHICH BOWLER WOULD YOU LEAST LIKE TO FACE? Mitchell Starc – I like my toes how they are, thanks
WHICH RULE WOULD YOU CHANGE ABOUT CRICKET? You are allowed to come off the field if temperatures dip below 10 degrees
SURPRISING FACT ABOUT YOU? My dad Ken played at Wimbledon in the 1972 Championships
SURPRISING FACT ABOUT A TEAMMATE? Mason Crane has pet tortoises
FAVOURITE QUOTE OR SAYING? Roosevelt's 'The Man in the Arena' speech, 1910
ODDEST SPORT YOU'VE PLAYED? 'Bat and Trap' in the pubs in Kent
TWITTER: @Joe_Weatherley

Batting	Mat	Inns	NO	Runs	HS	Ave	SR	100	50	Ct	St
First-class	23	37	1	817	126*	22.69	44.81	1	3	6	0
List A	19	19	4	497	105*	33.13	73.52	1	3	5	0
T20s	11	9	0	117	43	13.00	112.50	0	0	4	0
Bowling	**Mat**	**Balls**	**Runs**	**Wkts**	**BBI**	**BBM**	**Ave**	**Econ**	**SR**	**5w**	**10**
First-class	23	198	161	3	1/2	1/2	53.66	4.87	66.0	0	0
List A	19	327	221	8	4/25	4/25	27.62	4.05	40.8	0	0
T20s	11	6	9	0	-	-	-	9.00	-	0	0

JAMES WEIGHELL LHB / RMF / R0 / W0

FULL NAME: William James Weighell
BORN: January 28, 1994, Middlesbrough, Yorkshire
SQUAD NO: 28
HEIGHT: 6ft 4in
NICKNAME: Wheely
EDUCATION: Stokesley School, North Yorkshire
TEAMS: Durham
ROLE: Allrounder
DEBUT: First-class: 2015; List A: 2017; T20: 2017

BEST BATTING: 84 Durham vs Kent, Chester-le-Street, 2018
BEST BOWLING: 7-32 Durham vs Leicestershire, Chester-le-Street, 2018

WHAT WAS YOUR FIRST CRICKET CLUB? Stokesley CC, North Yorkshire
CRICKETING HERO? Andrew Flintoff
WHICH BOWLER WOULD YOU LEAST LIKE TO FACE? Graham Onions – because he's my godfather
WHO WOULD YOU ASK TO BAT FOR YOUR LIFE? Not sure, but definitely not Ryan Pringle
WHICH RULE WOULD YOU CHANGE ABOUT CRICKET? Make the boundaries shorter
SURPRISING FACT ABOUT A TEAMMATE? Graham Clark can fit 26 grapes into his mouth at once
FAVOURITE QUOTE OR SAYING? Money doesn't make the world go round, I'm searching for a higher ground (Des'ree)
WHICH BOOK MEANS MOST TO YOU? My Story by Steven Gerrrard
TWITTER: @jamesweighell

Batting	Mat	Inns	NO	Runs	HS	Ave	SR	100	50	Ct	St
First-class	12	20	4	469	84	29.31	70.84	0	3	3	0
List A	10	5	1	48	23	12.00	76.19	0	0	3	0
T20s	25	14	7	99	28	14.14	132.00	0	0	16	0
Bowling	**Mat**	**Balls**	**Runs**	**Wkts**	**BBI**	**BBM**	**Ave**	**Econ**	**SR**	**5w**	**10**
First-class	12	2116	1250	43	7/32	9/130	29.06	3.54	49.2	2	0
List A	10	510	549	20	5/57	5/57	27.45	6.45	25.5	1	0
T20s	25	441	678	22	3/28	3/28	30.81	9.22	20.0	0	0

LUKE WELLS LHB / OB / R2 / W0

FULL NAME: Luke William Peter Wells
BORN: December 29, 1990, Eastbourne, Sussex
SQUAD NO: 31
HEIGHT: 6ft 4in
NICKNAME: Dave, Rinser
EDUCATION: St Bede's, Hailsham; Loughborough University
TEAMS: Sussex, Colombo
ROLE: Batsman
DEBUT: First-class: 2010; List A: 2010; T20: 2011

BEST BATTING: 258 Sussex vs Durham, Hove, 2017
BEST BOWLING: 4-81 Sussex vs Leicestershire, Leicester, 2018
COUNTY CAP: 2016

FAMILY TIES? My dad Alan played for Sussex, Kent and England. My uncle Colin played for Sussex, Derbyshire and England
WHAT WAS YOUR FIRST CRICKET CLUB? Glynde & Beddingham CC, Sussex
FAVOURITE CRICKET BAT? Gray-Nicolls Powerbow Carbo. It had carbon on the handle – no idea what effect that had but I loved it
CRICKETING HERO? Matthew Hayden
WHICH BOWLER WOULD YOU LEAST LIKE TO FACE? Jofra Archer – he can bowl 90mph-plus, swings it both ways, has yorkers on tap, and a deadly bumper
WHICH RULE WOULD YOU CHANGE ABOUT CRICKET? Allow more than two fielders behind square on the leg side
FAVOURITE QUOTE OR SAYING? Grant me the serenity to accept the things I cannot change, courage to change the things I can and wisdom to know the difference (Serenity Prayer)
WHICH BOOK MEANS MOST TO YOU? The Harry Potter books by JK Rowling
TWITTER: @luke_wells07

Batting	Mat	Inns	NO	Runs	HS	Ave	SR	100	50	Ct	St
First-class	125	208	12	7159	258	36.52	46.93	18	30	57	0
List A	26	20	0	232	62	11.60	63.21	0	1	5	0
T20s	5	5	0	18	11	3.60	66.66	0	0	1	0
Bowling	**Mat**	**Balls**	**Runs**	**Wkts**	**BBI**	**BBM**	**Ave**	**Econ**	**SR**	**5w**	**10**
First-class	125	4392	2601	54	4/81	5/119	48.16	3.55	81.3	0	0
List A	26	437	384	10	3/19	3/19	38.40	5.27	43.7	0	0
T20s	5	1	4	0	-	-	-	24.00	-	0	0

RIKI WESSELS RHB / WK / R2 / W0 / MVP75

FULL NAME: Mattheus Hendrik Wessels
BORN: November 12, 1985, Queensland, Aus
SQUAD NO: 9
HEIGHT: 5ft 11in
NICKNAME: Weaz, Blood
EDUCATION: Woodridge College, Port Elizabeth; University of Northampton
TEAMS: Nottinghamshire, Kandahar Kings, Mid West Rhinos, Nondescripts, Northamptonshire, Sydney Sixers
ROLE: Batsman
DEBUT: First-class: 2004; List A: 2005; T20: 2005

BEST BATTING: 202* Nottinghamshire vs Sussex, Trent Bridge, 2017
BEST BOWLING: 1-10 Mid West Rhinos vs Matabeleland Tuskers, Bulawayo, 2009
COUNTY CAP: 2014 (Nottinghamshire)

WHAT WAS YOUR FIRST CRICKET CLUB? United Brothers CC, Eastern Cape, South Africa – a township-based club with some serious talent
FAVOURITE CRICKET BAT? Slazenger V500. I had it back in 1994, because that was the bat that my dad was using at the time
CRICKETING HERO? Justin Langer
BEST INNINGS YOU'VE SEEN? Alex Hales's 187 not out in the 2017 One-Day Cup final
WHO WOULD YOU ASK TO BAT FOR YOUR LIFE? Kane Williamson
WHICH RULE WOULD YOU CHANGE ABOUT CRICKET? Lunch and tea should be an hour
SURPRISING FACT ABOUT YOU? I lived in Colombo for six months. I love hunting
WHAT WILL YOU BE DOING IN THE YEAR 2040? I'll be umpiring perhaps
FAVOURITE QUOTE OR SAYING? If you're not first, you're last
ODDEST SPORT YOU'VE PLAYED? Mixed martial arts
TWITTER: @rikiwessels

Batting	Mat	Inns	NO	Runs	HS	Ave	SR	100	50	Ct	St
First-class	197	327	29	10740	202*	36.04	63.39	22	55	311	16
List A	170	159	14	4452	146	30.70	99.21	4	25	118	0
T20s	205	192	26	4840	110	29.15	137.69	1	22	76	16

Bowling	Mat	Balls	Runs	Wkts	BBI	BBM	Ave	Econ	SR	5w	10
First-class	197	240	130	3	1/10	1/10	43.33	3.25	80.0	0	0
List A	170	49	48	1	1/0	1/0	48.00	5.87	49.0	0	0
T20s	205	-	-	-	-	-	-	-	-	-	-

OLLY WESTBURY

RHB / OB / R0 / W0

FULL NAME: Oliver Edward Westbury
BORN: July 2, 1997, Dudley, West Midlands
SQUAD NO: 19
HEIGHT: 5ft 11in
NICKNAME: Wes, Westy
EDUCATION: Ellowes Hall Sports College, Dudley; Shrewsbury School
TEAMS: Worcestershire
ROLE: Batsman
DEBUT: First-class: 2018; List A: 2018; T20: 2018

BEST BATTING: 22 Worcestershire vs Surrey, Worcester, 2018

WHAT WAS YOUR FIRST CRICKET CLUB? Himley CC, Staffordshire
CRICKETING HERO? Andrew Flintoff
'ROY OF THE ROVERS' MOMENT? Scoring a century on my England U19 debut against Sri Lanka U19 in 2016
WHICH BOWLER WOULD YOU LEAST LIKE TO FACE? Shane Warne
WHICH RULE WOULD YOU CHANGE ABOUT CRICKET? Have a longer tea break
IF YOU WEREN'T A CRICKETER? I'd be on a ski season somewhere in Europe, working in a bar or restaurant by night and skiing during the day
SURPRISING FACT ABOUT YOU? I know all the lyrics to 'We Didn't Start The Fire' by Billy Joel
FAVOURITE QUOTE OR SAYING? Anything from Only Fools and Horses
TWITTER: @ollywestbury

Batting	Mat	Inns	NO	Runs	HS	Ave	SR	100	50	Ct	St
First-class	2	4	0	49	22	12.25	32.66	0	0	1	0
List A	1	1	0	8	8	8.00	34.78	0	0	0	0
T20s	1	1	0	24	24	24.00	150.00	0	0	0	0
Bowling	**Mat**	**Balls**	**Runs**	**Wkts**	**BBI**	**BBM**	**Ave**	**Econ**	**SR**	**5w**	**10**
First-class	2	6	6	0	-	-	-	6.00	-	0	0
List A	1	-	-	-	-	-	-	-	-	-	-
T20s	1	-	-	-	-	-	-	-	-	-	-

TOM WESTLEY RHB / OB / R1 / W0 / MVP89

FULL NAME: Thomas Westley
BORN: March 13, 1989, Cambridge
SQUAD NO: 21
HEIGHT: 6ft 2in
NICKNAME: Westie, Shellsy, Wezzo
EDUCATION: Linton Valley College, South Cambridgeshire; Hills Road College, Cambridge; Durham University
TEAMS: England, Essex, Bloomfield Cricket & Athletic Club
ROLE: Batsman
DEBUT: Test: 2017; First-class: 2007; List A: 2006; T20: 2010

BEST BATTING: 254 Essex vs Worcestershire, Chelmsford, 2016
BEST BOWLING: 4-55 Durham MCCU vs Durham, Durham University, 2010
COUNTY CAP: 2013

FAMILY TIES? My dad, uncle and brother all play for Weston Colville CC. My dad also harbours ambitions to play for England Over-50s
CRICKETING HEROES? Jacques Kallis, Sachin Tendulkar, Ben Matthews, Max Nolan, Dave Babbage, James Bunbury, Ben Lawrence
NON-CRICKETING HERO? Giovanni Colussi
SURPRISING FACT? I was one of the first students to study Harry Potter academically
TWITTER: @Westley21

Batting	Mat	Inns	NO	Runs	HS	Ave	SR	100	50	Ct	St
Tests	5	9	1	193	59	24.12	42.60	0	1	1	0
First-class	164	272	20	9151	254	36.31	52.29	20	44	104	0
List A	80	74	4	2480	134	35.42	87.29	5	18	17	0
T20s	65	59	6	1611	109*	30.39	129.50	2	5	23	0
Bowling	**Mat**	**Balls**	**Runs**	**Wkts**	**BBI**	**BBM**	**Ave**	**Econ**	**SR**	**5w**	**10**
Tests	5	24	12	0	-	-	-	3.00	-	0	0
First-class	164	4993	2635	59	4/55	5/122	44.66	3.16	84.6	0	0
List A	80	1006	830	20	4/60	4/60	41.50	4.95	50.3	0	0
T20s	65	246	311	7	2/27	2/27	44.42	7.58	35.1	0	0

BRAD WHEAL RHB / RFM / R0 / W0

FULL NAME: Bradley Thomas James Wheal
BORN: August 28, 1996, Durban, South Africa
SQUAD NO: 58
EDUCATION: Clifton School, Durban
TEAMS: Scotland, Hampshire
ROLE: Bowler
DEBUT: ODI: 2016; T20I: 2016; First-class: 2015; List A: 2016; T20: 2016

BEST BATTING: 25* Hampshire vs Somerset, Taunton, 2018
BEST BOWLING: 6-51 Hampshire vs Nottinghamshire, Trent Bridge, 2016

TWITTER: @Brad_wheal
NOTES: Born in South Africa, Wheal's mother is Scottish and he holds a British passport. He made his Hampshire debut in 2015 and is contracted to the county until the end of the 2019 season. His Scotland debut came in January 2016, when he was just 19. The fast bowler chipped in with key contributions in one-day and Championship cricket in 2016, taking a career-best 6-51 against Nottinghamshire, but he played just four Championship games the following summer, with stiff competition for places in Hampshire's star-studded attack. Wheal took 11 wickets in five four-day matches last summer before a stress fracture of the back ended his season in July

Batting	Mat	Inns	NO	Runs	HS	Ave	SR	100	50	Ct	St
ODIs	11	6	3	16	14	5.33	51.61	0	0	3	0
T20Is	5	2	2	2	2*	-	100.00	0	0	1	0
First-class	25	29	8	157	25*	7.47	24.37	0	0	11	0
List A	23	13	6	60	18*	8.57	68.96	0	0	5	0
T20s	12	5	3	22	16	11.00	95.65	0	0	1	0
Bowling	**Mat**	**Balls**	**Runs**	**Wkts**	**BBI**	**BBM**	**Ave**	**Econ**	**SR**	**5w**	**10**
ODIs	11	579	410	19	3/34	3/34	21.57	4.24	30.4	0	0
T20Is	5	104	143	5	3/20	3/20	28.60	8.25	20.8	0	0
First-class	25	3352	2080	56	6/51	7/71	37.14	3.72	59.8	1	0
List A	23	1098	894	38	4/38	4/38	23.52	4.88	28.8	0	0
T20s	12	224	317	11	3/20	3/20	28.81	8.49	20.3	0	0

ADAM WHEATER RHB / WK / R0 / W0 / MVP94

FULL NAME: Adam Jack Aubrey Wheater
BORN: February 13, 1990, Whipps Cross Hospital, London
SQUAD NO: 31
EDUCATION: Millfield School, Somerset; Anglia Ruskin University
TEAMS: Essex, Badureliya Sports Club, Hampshire, Matabeleland Tuskers
ROLE: Batsman/wicketkeeper
DEBUT: First-class: 2008; List A: 2010; T20: 2009

BEST BATTING: 204* Hampshire vs Warwickshire, Edgbaston, 2016
BEST BOWLING: 1-86 Essex vs Leicestershire, Leicester, 2012

'ROY OF THE ROVERS' MOMENT? On a broader scale, having the opportunity to see the world through cricket
CRICKETING HEROES? Alec Stewart, Nasser Hussain, Adam Gilchrist
IF YOU WEREN'T A CRICKETER? I'd find myself a very wealthy girlfriend I could sponge off
NOTES: The hard-hitting wicketkeeper signed an extension to his contract in October, keeping him at Essex until the end of the 2020 season. Wheater was part of the side which won the County Championship in 2017, having re-joined his old club after a spell at Hampshire. Essex head coach Anthony McGrath said: "After the retirement of James Foster, it is now time for Adam to make the position his own and highlight to everyone what a valuable performer he can be"

Batting	Mat	Inns	NO	Runs	HS	Ave	SR	100	50	Ct	St
First-class	127	189	23	6066	204*	36.54	65.71	11	35	208	11
List A	80	65	5	1713	135	28.55	97.38	2	9	41	12
T20s	99	78	13	1214	78	18.67	125.28	0	3	39	20
Bowling	**Mat**	**Balls**	**Runs**	**Wkts**	**BBI**	**BBM**	**Ave**	**Econ**	**SR**	**5w**	**10**
First-class	127	24	86	1	1/86	1/86	86.00	21.50	24.0	0	0
List A	80	-	-	-	-	-	-	-	-	-	-
T20s	99	-	-	-	-	-	-	-	-	-	-

GRAEME WHITE RHB / SLA / R0 / W0

FULL NAME: Graeme Geoffrey White
BORN: April 18, 1987, Milton Keynes, Buckinghamshire
SQUAD NO: 87
HEIGHT: 5ft 10in
NICKNAME: Whitey, G
EDUCATION: Royal Latin School, Buckinghamshire; Stowe School
TEAMS: Northamptonshire
ROLE: Bowler
DEBUT: First-class: 2006; List A: 2007; T20: 2007

BEST BATTING: 65 Northamptonshire vs Glamorgan, Colwyn Bay, 2007
BEST BOWLING: 6-44 Northamptonshire vs Glamorgan, Northampton, 2016

WHAT WAS YOUR FIRST CRICKET CLUB? Milton Keynes CC, Buckinghamshire. My sister was my age-group captain
FAVOURITE CRICKET BAT? Duncan Fearnley Magnum
BEST ADVICE EVER RECEIVED? You need a steak and a Guiness to fill out lad (told to me by Nick Cook when I was 13)
BEST INNINGS YOU'VE SEEN? David Sales hitting 161 for Northants in a one-day match against Yorkshire at Northampton in 2006. I was 12th man
WHO WOULD YOU ASK TO BAT FOR YOUR LIFE? My mum – she's good off her legs
WHICH RULE WOULD YOU CHANGE ABOUT CRICKET? The distance of the boundary should be set at 120 metres
YOUR BIGGEST CRICKETING REGRET? Sitting next to Nathan Buck in the changing room
SURPRISING FACT ABOUT YOU? I have 35 tattoos
WHICH BOOK MEANS MOST TO YOU? Leading – Learning from Life and My Years at Manchester United by Alex Ferguson and Michael Moritz

Batting	Mat	Inns	NO	Runs	HS	Ave	SR	100	50	Ct	St
First-class	39	55	5	659	65	13.18	48.85	0	2	12	0
List A	84	51	16	539	41*	15.40	86.51	0	0	29	0
T20s	95	35	17	240	34	13.33	136.36	0	0	36	0
Bowling	**Mat**	**Balls**	**Runs**	**Wkts**	**BBI**	**BBM**	**Ave**	**Econ**	**SR**	**5w**	**10**
First-class	39	4776	2730	65	6/44	7/89	42.00	3.42	73.4	1	0
List A	84	3156	2663	92	6/37	6/37	28.94	5.06	34.3	2	0
T20s	95	1373	1881	70	5/22	5/22	26.87	8.21	19.6	1	0

ROBBIE WHITE

RHB / WK / R0 / W0

FULL NAME: Robert George White
BORN: September 15, 1995, Ealing, London
SQUAD NO: 14
HEIGHT: 5ft 10in
NICKNAME: Whitey
EDUCATION: Harrow School, London; Loughborough University
TEAMS: Middlesex
ROLE: Batsman/wicketkeeper
DEBUT: First-class: 2015

BEST BATTING: 69 Loughborough MCCU vs Northamptonshire, Northampton, 2017

WHAT WAS YOUR FIRST CRICKET CLUB? Ealing CC, London
FAVOURITE CRICKET BAT? Kookaburra Bubble – classic
WHICH BOWLER WOULD YOU LEAST LIKE TO FACE? Tom Barber – he is horrendous to face in the nets
BEST INNINGS YOU'VE SEEN? Aaron Finch's 117 not out off 52 balls against us at The Oval last year – best hitting I've seen close up
WHO WOULD YOU ASK TO BAT FOR YOUR LIFE? Tom Lace – lovely technique and values my friendship
WHICH RULE WOULD YOU CHANGE ABOUT CRICKET? If you are caught off a free hit then the ball should be called dead
YOUR BIGGEST CRICKETING REGRET? Leaving my first Championship ball at Lord's
WHAT WILL YOU BE DOING IN THE YEAR 2040? Playing in the Ryder Cup
FAVOURITE QUOTE OR SAYING? There's no such thing as a free lunch
TWITTER: @rwhitey15

Batting	Mat	Inns	NO	Runs	HS	Ave	SR	100	50	Ct	St
First-class	12	17	1	211	69	13.18	45.86	0	1	20	0
List A	1	1	0	12	12	12.00	70.58	0	0	1	0
T20s	3	2	1	11	11*	11.00	100.00	0	0	1	0
Bowling	**Mat**	**Balls**	**Runs**	**Wkts**	**BBI**	**BBM**	**Ave**	**Econ**	**SR**	**5w**	**10**
First-class	12	-	-	-	-	-	-	-	-	-	-
List A	1	-	-	-	-	-	-	-	-	-	-
T20s	3	-	-	-	-	-	-	-	-	-	-

BEN WHITEHEAD

RHB / LB / R0 / W0

FULL NAME: Benjamin Guy Whitehead
BORN: April 28, 1997, Sunderland
SQUAD NO: 97
HEIGHT: 6ft
NICKNAME: Benji
EDUCATION: Hetton School, Sunderland
TEAMS: Durham
ROLE: Bowler
DEBUT: T20: 2018

WHAT WAS YOUR FIRST CRICKET CLUB? Hetton Lyons CC, Sunderland. It had the best tuckshop in the league
FAVOURITE CRICKET BAT? Gray-Nicolls Powerbow. My first one, so it was pretty special even though it was way too heavy and big
WHICH BOWLER WOULD YOU LEAST LIKE TO FACE? Jimmy Anderson
BEST INNINGS YOU'VE SEEN? Ben Stokes's 258 at Cape Town in 2016
WHO WOULD YOU ASK TO BAT FOR YOUR LIFE? Alastair Cook
WHICH RULE WOULD YOU CHANGE ABOUT CRICKET? Give the bowlers a chance: have another stump
YOUR BIGGEST CRICKETING REGRET? Messing around in my younger years and not taking the game seriously enough
WHICH BOOK MEANS MOST TO YOU? No Spin by Shane Warne. So much information on how to bowl leg-spin
ODDEST SPORT YOU'VE PLAYED? Aussie Rules
TWITTER: @Benwhitehead97

Batting	Mat	Inns	NO	Runs	HS	Ave	SR	100	50	Ct	St
T20s	6	1	1	2	2*	-	66.66	0	0	3	0
Bowling	**Mat**	**Balls**	**Runs**	**Wkts**	**BBI**	**BBM**	**Ave**	**Econ**	**SR**	**5w**	**10**
T20s	6	120	144	5	2/23	2/23	28.80	7.20	24.0	0	0

ROSS WHITELEY

LHB / LM / R0 / W0

FULL NAME: Ross Andrew Whiteley
BORN: September 13, 1988, Sheffield
SQUAD NO: 44
HEIGHT: 6ft 2in
NICKNAME: Rossco, Pico, Shaggy
EDUCATION: Repton School, Derbyshire; Leeds Metropolitan University
TEAMS: Worcestershire, Derbyshire, England Lions
ROLE: Batsman
DEBUT: First-class: 2008; List A: 2008; T20: 2011

BEST BATTING: 130* Derbyshire vs Kent, Derby, 2011
BEST BOWLING: 2-6 Derbyshire vs Hampshire, Derby, 2012

WHAT WAS YOUR FIRST CRICKET CLUB? Eckington CC, South Yorkshire
WHICH BOWLER WOULD YOU LEAST LIKE TO FACE? Daryl Mitchell – he's got a fearsome record against Test batsmen and is a true golden arm
BEST INNINGS YOU'VE SEEN? Martin Guptill's 35-ball hundred for Worcestershire in a T20 match at Northampton last summer. Some of the cleanest hitting I have ever seen
SURPRISING FACT ABOUT YOU? I have 11 sheep with each squad number of the 2012 Derbyshire side which won Division Two shaved onto them
FAVOURITE QUOTE OR SAYING? Fear of failure doesn't exist if your preparation is right
ODDEST SPORT YOU'VE PLAYED? Ice hockey
TWITTER: @rosswhiteley44

Batting	Mat	Inns	NO	Runs	HS	Ave	SR	100	50	Ct	St
First-class	77	126	12	3152	130*	27.64	50.20	3	16	55	0
List A	71	61	10	1319	77	25.86	95.57	0	9	21	0
T20s	105	98	26	1880	91*	26.11	143.95	0	4	36	0
Bowling	**Mat**	**Balls**	**Runs**	**Wkts**	**BBI**	**BBM**	**Ave**	**Econ**	**SR**	**5w**	**10**
First-class	77	2475	1761	32	2/6	4/43	55.03	4.26	77.3	0	0
List A	71	435	481	12	4/58	4/58	40.08	6.63	36.2	0	0
T20s	105	96	168	4	1/10	1/10	42.00	10.50	24.0	0	0

STUART WHITTINGHAM

RHB / RFM / R0 / W0

GLOUCESTERSHIRE

FULL NAME: Stuart Gordon Whittingham
BORN: February 10, 1994, Derby
SQUAD NO: 19
HEIGHT: 6ft 2in
NICKNAME: The Jug
EDUCATION: Christ's Hospital, Horsham; Loughborough University
TEAMS: Scotland, Gloucestershire, Sussex
ROLE: Bowler
DEBUT: ODI: 2017; T20I: 2018; First-class: 2015; List A: 2017; T20: 2018

BEST BATTING: 22 Sussex vs Nottinghamshire, Hove, 2017
BEST BOWLING: 5-70 Scotland vs Ireland, Dubai, 2017

BEST ADVICE EVER RECEIVED? Respect the game and it will look after you (Russell Cobb)
'ROY OF THE ROVERS' MOMENT? My first Championship five-for
IF YOU WEREN'T A CRICKETER? I'd be a scientist
SURPRISING FACT ABOUT YOU? I have a brother who is a celebrity in South Korea
CRICKETING HERO? Dale Steyn
NON-CRICKETING HERO? Bradley Wiggins
TWITTER: @Stuartwhitt10

Batting	Mat	Inns	NO	Runs	HS	Ave	SR	100	50	Ct	St
ODIs	4	3	2	6	3*	6.00	66.66	0	0	3	0
T20Is	3	-	-	-	-	-	-	-	-	0	0
First-class	15	16	6	68	22	6.80	35.23	0	0	3	0
List A	5	3	2	6	3*	6.00	66.66	0	0	3	0
T20s	3	-	-	-	-	-	-	-	-	0	0
Bowling	**Mat**	**Balls**	**Runs**	**Wkts**	**BBI**	**BBM**	**Ave**	**Econ**	**SR**	**5w**	**10**
ODIs	4	203	174	7	3/58	3/58	24.85	5.14	29.0	0	0
T20Is	3	60	79	3	2/33	2/33	26.33	7.90	20.0	0	0
First-class	15	1993	1389	46	5/70	8/93	30.19	4.18	43.3	2	0
List A	5	263	209	10	3/35	3/35	20.90	4.76	26.3	0	0
T20s	3	60	79	3	2/33	2/33	26.33	7.90	20.0	0	0

DAVID WIESE

RHB / RMF / R0 / W0 / MVP27

FULL NAME: David Wiese
BORN: May 18, 1985, Roodepoort, Transvaal, South Africa
SQUAD NO: 96
HEIGHT: 6ft 3in
NICKNAME: Weez
EDUCATION: Witbank High School, SA
TEAMS: South Africa, Sussex, Barbados Tridents, Easterns, Guyana Amazon Warriors, Paarl Rocks, RC Bangalore, Titans
ROLE: Allrounder
DEBUT: ODI: 2015; T20I: 2013; First-class: 2005; List A: 2005; T20: 2008

BEST BATTING: 208 Easterns vs Griqualand West, Benoni, 2008
BEST BOWLING: 6-58 Titans vs Knights, Centurion, 2015

WHAT WAS YOUR FIRST CRICKET CLUB? SACE CC, Mpumalanga, South Africa
FAVOURITE CRICKET BAT? An old GM Autograph – I never used it but was given it by my school when I scored my first hundred
WHICH BOWLER WOULD YOU LEAST LIKE TO FACE? Jofra Archer – I have seen what he does to other batsmen
BEST INNINGS YOU'VE SEEN? Too many to mention – you see some special knocks playing in the same IPL team as de Villiers, Gayle and Kohli
WHO WOULD YOU ASK TO BAT FOR YOUR LIFE? Jacques Kallis
WHICH RULE WOULD YOU CHANGE ABOUT CRICKET? No switch-hits
YOUR BIGGEST CRICKETING REGRET? Not taking cricket seriously and not backing myself when I started playing
TWITTER: @David_Wiese

Batting	Mat	Inns	NO	Runs	HS	Ave	SR	100	50	Ct	St
ODIs	6	6	1	102	41*	20.40	88.69	0	0	0	0
T20Is	20	11	4	92	28	13.14	122.66	0	0	9	0
First-class	108	171	20	5087	208	33.68	70.99	10	26	68	0
List A	140	118	24	3184	106	33.87	115.07	1	18	44	0
T20s	197	134	50	1798	71*	21.40	143.95	0	4	64	0
Bowling	**Mat**	**Balls**	**Runs**	**Wkts**	**BBI**	**BBM**	**Ave**	**Econ**	**SR**	**5w**	**10**
ODIs	6	294	316	9	3/50	3/50	35.11	6.44	32.6	0	0
T20Is	20	392	497	24	5/23	5/23	20.70	7.60	16.3	1	0
First-class	108	15916	8529	312	6/58	10/111	27.33	3.21	51.0	8	1
List A	140	5142	4563	127	5/25	5/25	35.92	5.32	40.4	1	0
T20s	197	2970	4113	154	5/19	5/19	26.70	8.30	19.2	4	0

DAVID WILLEY

LHB / LFM / R0 / W0 / MVP72

FULL NAME: David Jonathan Willey
BORN: February 28, 1990, Northampton
SQUAD NO: 72
HEIGHT: 6ft 1in
NICKNAME: Will, Wills, Wildman
EDUCATION: Northampton School for Boys
TEAMS: England, Yorkshire, Chennai Super Kings, Northamptonshire, Perth Scorchers
ROLE: Allrounder
DEBUT: ODI: 2015; T20I: 2015; First-class: 2009; List A: 2009; T20: 2009

BEST BATTING: 104* Northamptonshire vs Gloucestershire, Northampton, 2015
BEST BOWLING: 5-29 Northamptonshire vs Gloucestershire, Northampton, 2011
COUNTY CAP: 2013 (Northamptonshire); 2016 (Yorkshire)

FAMILY TIES? My dad Peter played for England, Northamptonshire and Leicestershire
BEST ADVICE EVER RECEIVED? Hard to pick one, but most of it came from my dad
'ROY OF THE ROVERS' MOMENT? Making my England debut in 2015
SURPRISING FACT ABOUT YOU? My wife Carolynne is a country singer and was a two-time X Factor contestant
CRICKETING HERO? My dad – I always wanted to follow in his footsteps
NON-CRICKETING HERO? Karl Pilkington
TWITTER: @david_willey

Batting	Mat	Inns	NO	Runs	HS	Ave	SR	100	50	Ct	St
ODIs	42	25	12	245	50	18.84	84.48	0	1	19	0
T20Is	27	19	7	166	29*	13.83	131.74	0	0	11	0
First-class	66	93	11	2179	104*	26.57	64.12	2	14	14	0
List A	121	86	19	1606	167	23.97	95.53	3	5	42	0
T20s	174	130	25	2559	118	24.37	140.60	2	11	68	0
Bowling	**Mat**	**Balls**	**Runs**	**Wkts**	**BBI**	**BBM**	**Ave**	**Econ**	**SR**	**5w**	**10**
ODIs	42	1761	1665	48	4/34	4/34	34.68	5.67	36.6	0	0
T20Is	27	539	736	34	4/7	4/7	21.64	8.19	15.8	0	0
First-class	66	9324	5100	167	5/29	10/75	30.53	3.28	55.8	5	1
List A	121	4396	4145	131	5/62	5/62	31.64	5.65	33.5	1	0
T20s	174	2880	3773	166	4/7	4/7	22.72	7.86	17.3	0	0

CHRIS WOAKES

RHB / RFM / R0 / W3

FULL NAME: Christopher Roger Woakes
BORN: March 2, 1989, Birmingham
SQUAD NO: 19
HEIGHT: 6ft 1in
NICKNAME: Woaksy, Woako, Wiz, GB
EDUCATION: Barr Beacon Language College, Walsall
TEAMS: England, Warwickshire, Kolkata Knight Riders, Royal Challengers Bangalore, Sydney Thunder, Wellington
ROLE: Allrounder
DEBUT: Test: 2013; ODI: 2011; T20I: 2011; First-class: 2006; List A: 2007; T20: 2008

BEST BATTING: 152* Warwickshire vs Derbyshire, Derby, 2013
BEST BOWLING: 9-36 Warwickshire vs Durham, Edgbaston, 2016
COUNTY CAP: 2009

FAMILY TIES? My brothers played Birmingham League cricket
STRANGEST THING SEEN IN A GAME? Jonathan Trott catching a ball in his pocket (though not on purpose)
'ROY OF THE ROVERS' MOMENT? Receiving my first England cap
SUPERSTITIONS? Only one: always turn off my left shoulder at the end of my run-up
CRICKETING HERO? Jacques Kallis
NON-CRICKETING HERO? Paul 'God' McGrath
SURPRISING FACT? I won a keep-uppy competition when I was 10 (70 keepy-ups)
TWITTER: @chriswoakes

Batting	Mat	Inns	NO	Runs	HS	Ave	SR	100	50	Ct	St
Tests	26	43	10	1012	137*	30.66	50.07	1	4	12	0
ODIs	84	57	18	1039	95*	26.64	90.42	0	4	35	0
T20Is	8	7	4	91	37	30.33	144.44	0	0	1	0
First-class	140	207	48	5620	152*	35.34	56.28	10	23	59	0
List A	162	106	34	1697	95*	23.56	89.74	0	4	49	0
T20s	111	69	36	803	57*	24.33	136.10	0	2	41	0
Bowling	**Mat**	**Balls**	**Runs**	**Wkts**	**BBI**	**BBM**	**Ave**	**Econ**	**SR**	**5w**	**10**
Tests	26	4600	2372	72	6/70	11/102	32.94	3.09	63.8	2	1
ODIs	84	3924	3669	116	6/45	6/45	31.62	5.61	33.8	2	0
T20Is	8	162	253	7	2/40	2/40	36.14	9.37	23.1	0	0
First-class	140	23651	12181	474	9/36	11/97	25.69	3.09	49.8	19	4
List A	162	6966	6446	190	6/45	6/45	33.92	5.55	36.6	2	0
T20s	111	2175	3040	121	4/21	4/21	25.12	8.38	17.9	0	0

CHRIS WOOD

RHB / LMF / R0 / W0

FULL NAME: Christopher Philip Wood
BORN: June 27, 1990, Basingstoke, Hampshire
SQUAD NO: 25
HEIGHT: 6ft 3in
NICKNAME: Woody, Nuts
EDUCATION: St Lawrence CE Primary School; Amery Hill School; Alton College, Hampshire
TEAMS: Hampshire
ROLE: Bowler
DEBUT: First-class: 2010; List A: 2010; T20: 2010

BEST BATTING: 105* Hampshire vs Leicestershire, Leicester, 2012
BEST BOWLING: 5-39 Hampshire vs Kent, Canterbury, 2014

STRANGEST THING SEEN IN A GAME? The final over of the 2010 T20 final
'ROY OF THE ROVERS' MOMENT? Winning the 2012 One-Day Cup at Lord's
CRICKETING HERO? Nathan Bracken
NON-CRICKETING HERO? Novak Djokovic
SURPRISING FACT? I played football at semi-professional level
TWITTER: @CWoody27
NOTES: The left-armer signed a new contract with Hampshire in October which will keep him at the Ageas Bowl until the end of the 2020 season. Director of cricket Giles White said: "Chris has done particularly well in white-ball cricket this year and was a standout performer for us during our T20 campaign. He's a product of the Academy here, so we know him very well, and he's become a very smart bowler who has a sense of what the batsman's looking to do. Hopefully he plays a big part in our campaigns over the coming two years"

Batting	Mat	Inns	NO	Runs	HS	Ave	SR	100	50	Ct	St
First-class	43	62	6	1326	105*	23.67	64.65	1	6	14	0
List A	75	42	13	383	41	13.20	95.75	0	0	23	0
T20s	108	39	15	271	27	11.29	105.03	0	0	33	0
Bowling	**Mat**	**Balls**	**Runs**	**Wkts**	**BBI**	**BBM**	**Ave**	**Econ**	**SR**	**5w**	**10**
First-class	43	6169	3174	105	5/39	7/49	30.22	3.08	58.7	3	0
List A	75	3136	2797	103	5/22	5/22	27.15	5.35	30.4	2	0
T20s	108	2186	3040	117	5/32	5/32	25.98	8.34	18.6	1	0

LUKE WOOD

LHB / LM / R0 / W0

FULL NAME: Luke Wood
BORN: August 2, 1995, Sheffield
SQUAD NO: 14
HEIGHT: 5ft 9in
NICKNAME: Biscuit
EDUCATION: Portland Comprehensive School, Worksop; Outwood Post 16 Centre Worksop
TEAMS: Nottinghamshire, Worcestershire
ROLE: Bowler
DEBUT: First-class: 2014; List A: 2016; T20: 2016

BEST BATTING: 100 Nottinghamshire vs Sussex, Trent Bridge, 2015
BEST BOWLING: 5-40 Nottinghamshire vs Cambridge MCCU, Cambridge, 2016

WHAT WAS YOUR FIRST CRICKET CLUB? Cuckney CC, Nottinghamshire
FAVOURITE CRICKET BAT? Loved my Woodworm as a kid, pretending to be Andrew Flintoff or Kevin Pietersen
CRICKETING HERO? Ryan Sidebottom
WHICH BOWLER WOULD YOU LEAST LIKE TO FACE? Rashid Khan
BEST INNINGS YOU'VE SEEN? Alex Hales's 187 not out against Surrey in the 2017 One-Day Cup final at Lord's
WHO WOULD YOU ASK TO BAT FOR YOUR LIFE? Virat Kohli
WHAT WILL YOU BE DOING IN THE YEAR 2040? Rolling out some slow seamers in club cricket on a Saturday
WHICH BOOK MEANS MOST TO YOU? Believe and Achieve – The World's Most Motivational Quotes by Chris Naylor
TWITTER: @lwood_95

Batting	Mat	Inns	NO	Runs	HS	Ave	SR	100	50	Ct	St
First-class	30	47	11	989	100	27.47	67.92	1	3	11	0
List A	3	2	1	56	52	56.00	160.00	0	1	0	0
T20s	21	6	2	25	11	6.25	96.15	0	0	7	0
Bowling	**Mat**	**Balls**	**Runs**	**Wkts**	**BBI**	**BBM**	**Ave**	**Econ**	**SR**	**5w**	**10**
First-class	30	4000	2496	73	5/40	8/83	34.19	3.74	54.7	1	0
List A	3	96	89	3	2/44	2/44	29.66	5.56	32.0	0	0
T20s	21	334	496	13	2/15	2/15	38.15	8.91	25.6	0	0

MARK WOOD

RHB / RF / R0 / W0

DURHAM

FULL NAME: Mark Andrew Wood
BORN: January 11, 1990, Ashington, Northumberland
SQUAD NO: 33
HEIGHT: 6ft
NICKNAME: Woody
EDUCATION: Ashington High School; Newcastle College
TEAMS: England, Durham
ROLE: Bowler
DEBUT: Test: 2015; ODI: 2015; T20I: 2015; First-class: 2011; List A: 2011; T20: 2013

BEST BATTING: 72* Durham vs Kent, Chester-le-Street, 2017
BEST BOWLING: 6-46 Durham vs Derbyshire, Derby, 2018

FAMILY TIES? My dad Derek and uncle Neil played for Ashington CC and Minor Counties for Northumberland
CRICKETING HEROES? Graham Onions, Stephen Harmison, Ben Harmison, Michael Holding, Ian Botham
NON-CRICKETING HERO? Lennox Lewis
SURPRISING FACT? I was in the Newcastle United FC Academy
TWITTER: @MAWood33

Batting	Mat	Inns	NO	Runs	HS	Ave	SR	100	50	Ct	St
Tests	13	23	5	297	52	16.50	60.24	0	1	5	0
ODIs	40	13	8	45	13	9.00	88.23	0	0	9	0
T20Is	5	2	2	10	5*	-	83.33	0	0	0	0
First-class	51	84	17	1433	72*	21.38	55.69	0	5	14	0
List A	72	29	13	107	24	6.68	79.85	0	0	19	0
T20s	25	12	6	100	27*	16.66	100.00	0	0	4	0
Bowling	**Mat**	**Balls**	**Runs**	**Wkts**	**BBI**	**BBM**	**Ave**	**Econ**	**SR**	**5w**	**10**
Tests	13	2408	1345	36	5/41	6/93	37.36	3.35	66.8	1	0
ODIs	40	1987	1851	41	4/33	4/33	45.14	5.58	48.4	0	0
T20Is	5	105	148	11	3/9	3/9	13.45	8.45	9.5	0	0
First-class	51	8052	4435	162	6/46	8/117	27.37	3.30	49.7	9	0
List A	72	3366	2991	87	4/33	4/33	34.37	5.33	38.6	0	0
T20s	25	501	671	30	4/25	4/25	22.36	8.03	16.7	0	0

DAN WORRALL

RHB / RFM / R0 / W0

FULL NAME: Daniel James Worrall
BORN: July 10, 1991, Melbourne, Australia
SQUAD NO: 41
TEAMS: Australia, Gloucestershire, Melbourne Stars, South Australia
ROLE: Bowler
DEBUT: ODI: 2016; First-class: 2012; List A: 2012; T20: 2014

BEST BATTING: 50 Gloucestershire vs Glamorgan, Bristol, 2018
BEST BOWLING: 7-64 South Australia vs Western Australia, Adelaide, 2018

NOTES: Worrall is a 27-year-old Australian pace bowler who plays for South Australia in the Sheffield Shield and for the Melbourne Stars in the Big Bash. He was signed for Gloucestershire as an overseas player ahead of the 2018 season and impressed with 16 wickets at 21.75 in his first four Championship matches before he was sidelined for the rest of the season with a foot injury. The club have re-signed him to play across all formats in 2019 in the hope that the injury-stricken bowler can stay fit. Worrall made his first-class debut in 2012 but his career really lifted off during the 2015/16 season, when he finished as the second-highest wicket-taker in the Sheffield Shield. He played three ODIs for Australia in 2016 and many pundits have said that he may be in line for a Test call-up for this summer's Ashes

Batting	Mat	Inns	NO	Runs	HS	Ave	SR	100	50	Ct	St
ODIs	3	1	1	6	6*	-	150.00	0	0	1	0
First-class	43	65	28	430	50	11.62	41.06	0	1	14	0
List A	26	11	8	43	16	14.33	72.88	0	0	8	0
T20s	19	7	4	49	16	16.33	125.64	0	0	4	0
Bowling	**Mat**	**Balls**	**Runs**	**Wkts**	**BBI**	**BBM**	**Ave**	**Econ**	**SR**	**5w**	**10**
ODIs	3	158	171	1	1/43	1/43	171.00	6.49	158.0	0	0
First-class	43	9079	4741	172	7/64	10/148	27.56	3.13	52.7	6	1
List A	26	1364	1192	31	5/62	5/62	38.45	5.24	44.0	1	0
T20s	19	393	574	19	4/23	4/23	30.21	8.76	20.6	0	0

CHRIS WRIGHT

RHB / RFM / R0 / W1

FULL NAME: Christopher Julian Clement Wright
BORN: July 14, 1985, Chipping Norton, Oxfordshire
SQUAD NO: 31
HEIGHT: 6ft 3in
NICKNAME: Wrighty, Dog, Wrightdog
EDUCATION: Eggars Grammar School, Alton
TEAMS: Leicestershire, England Lions, Essex, Middlesex, Tamil Union, Warwickshire
ROLE: Bowler
DEBUT: First-class: 2004; List A: 2004; T20: 2004

BEST BATTING: 77 Essex vs Cambridge MCCU, Cambridge, 2011
BEST BOWLING: 6-22 Essex vs Leicestershire, Leicester, 2008
COUNTY CAP: 2013 (Warwickshire)

WHAT GOT YOU INTO CRICKET? Watching my father play for Liphook & Ripsley CC
STRANGEST THING SEEN IN A GAME? Instead of a traditional coin toss, two coach/captains played a game of tossing objects closest to the stumps at the other end. It lasted 15 minutes
'ROY OF THE ROVERS' MOMENT? Bowling out Worcestershire in a morning session in 2012. Keith Barker and I each got five wickets and effectively sealed the title for Warwickshire
CRICKETING HEROES? Jason Gillespie – amazing action, quick, moved it away, long hair. Mark Ramprakash – my favourite batter to watch as a boy. Great technique
NON-CRICKETING HERO? James Richardson – former presenter of Gazzetta Football Italia
SURPRISING FACT? I once (a long time ago but as a professional) missed a pre-season game to play in the Irish Open Poker tournament. I got knocked out early on and as a result got very drunk! I then overslept and missed my flight home. I was £10,000 poorer and very ill but it was a good life experience. The captain and coach of the club didn't think so
TWITTER: @chriswright1985

Batting	Mat	Inns	NO	Runs	HS	Ave	SR	100	50	Ct	St
First-class	146	187	42	2699	77	18.61	49.39	0	11	25	0
List A	99	39	18	229	42	10.90	77.36	0	0	17	0
T20s	58	14	9	28	6*	5.60	103.70	0	0	13	0
Bowling	**Mat**	**Balls**	**Runs**	**Wkts**	**BBI**	**BBM**	**Ave**	**Econ**	**SR**	**5w**	**10**
First-class	146	23128	13608	406	6/22	9/89	33.51	3.53	56.9	11	0
List A	99	3833	3568	100	4/20	4/20	35.68	5.58	38.3	0	0
T20s	58	1167	1739	52	4/24	4/24	33.44	8.94	22.4	0	0

LUKE WRIGHT

RHB / RMF / R1 / W0 / MVP91

FULL NAME: Luke James Wright
BORN: March 7, 1985, Grantham, Lincolnshire
SQUAD NO: 10
HEIGHT: 5ft 10in
NICKNAME: Bammers, Bam Bam
EDUCATION: Loughborough University
TEAMS: England, Sussex, Abhani Limited, Auckland, Dhaka Gladiators, Impi, Leicestershire, Melbourne Stars, Pune Warriors, Quetta Gladiators, Wellington
ROLE: Allrounder
DEBUT: ODI: 2007; T20I: 2007; First-class: 2003; List A 2002; T20: 2004

BEST BATTING: 226* Sussex vs Worcestershire, Worcester, 2015
BEST BOWLING: 5-65 Sussex vs Derbyshire, Derby, 2010
COUNTY CAP: 2007 (Sussex); BENEFIT: 2017 (Sussex)

WHAT WAS YOUR FIRST CRICKET CLUB? Bottesford CC, Leicestershire. I played men's cricket at a really young age, which helped me develop. Lots of great memories
BEST INNINGS YOU'VE SEEN? I played in the IPL match when Chris Gayle hit 175 not out
WHICH RULE WOULD YOU CHANGE ABOUT CRICKET? I would introduce substitute fielders in four-day cricket
YOUR BIGGEST CRICKETING REGRET? Not playing the red-ball nip-backer very well in 2018
FAVOURITE QUOTE OR SAYING? I spent 90 percent of my money on women and drink. The rest I wasted (George Best)
WHICH BOOK MEANS MOST TO YOU? Where's Wally? by Martin Handford
TWITTER: @lukewright204

Batting	Mat	Inns	NO	Runs	HS	Ave	SR	100	50	Ct	St
ODIs	50	39	4	707	52	20.20	86.21	0	2	18	0
T20Is	51	45	5	759	99*	18.97	137.00	0	4	14	0
First-class	144	223	23	7622	226*	38.11	65.54	17	38	58	0
List A	204	169	21	4717	143*	31.87	105.02	10	17	63	0
T20s	300	279	26	7199	153*	28.45	144.09	7	38	94	0
Bowling	**Mat**	**Balls**	**Runs**	**Wkts**	**BBI**	**BBM**	**Ave**	**Econ**	**SR**	**5w**	**10**
ODIs	50	1038	884	15	2/34	2/34	58.93	5.10	69.2	0	0
T20Is	51	330	465	18	2/24	2/24	25.83	8.45	18.3	0	0
First-class	144	8264	4862	120	5/65	7/127	40.51	3.53	68.8	3	0
List A	204	4752	4231	111	4/12	4/12	38.11	5.34	42.8	0	0
T20s	300	1799	2563	79	3/17	3/17	32.44	8.54	22.7	0	0

ROB YATES LHB / OB / R0 / W0

FULL NAME: Robert Michael Yates
BORN: September 19, 1999, Solihull, Warwickshire
SQUAD NO: 17
HEIGHT: 6ft 1in
EDUCATION: Warwick School; University of Birmingham
TEAMS: Warwickshire
ROLE: Batsman

WHAT WAS YOUR FIRST CRICKET CLUB? Moseley CC, Solihull, West Midlands. I've been there since I was eight years old
FAVOURITE CRICKET BAT? Hawk XB 300 Short Blade 2016 – the ball flew off it and the bat felt like a toothpick. I loved it so much that I used it even when half the face was hanging off
WHICH BOWLER WOULD YOU LEAST LIKE TO FACE? Usman Awan (Moseley CC) – drifts it in and spins it away at 60mph
BEST INNINGS YOU'VE SEEN? AB de Villiers breaking the record for the fastest ODI hundred of all time (31 balls), against West Indies at Johannesburg in 2015. Every ball was going for four and six
WHO WOULD YOU ASK TO BAT FOR YOUR LIFE? Dean Elgar
WHICH RULE WOULD YOU CHANGE ABOUT CRICKET? Batters should have two lives
YOUR BIGGEST CRICKETING REGRET? Dropping someone on 10 who went on to make 190. The match would have been over a day earlier if I'd taken that catch
FAVOURITE QUOTE OR SAYING? Winners never quit, quitters never win
WHICH BOOK MEANS MOST TO YOU? The Inner Game of Tennis by W Timothy Gallwey

SAIF ZAIB

LHB / SLA / R0 / W0

FULL NAME: Saif Ali Zaib
BORN: May 22, 1998, High Wycombe, Buckinghamshire
SQUAD NO: 5
HEIGHT: 5ft 8in
NICKNAME: Saify, Zaiby
EDUCATION: Royal Grammar School, High Wycombe
TEAMS: Northamptonshire
ROLE: Bowler
DEBUT: First-class: 2015; List A: 2014; T20: 2017

BEST BATTING: 65* Northamptonshire vs Glamorgan, Swansea, 2016
BEST BOWLING: 6-115 Northamptonshire vs Loughborough MCCU, Northampton, 2017

WHAT WAS YOUR FIRST CRICKET CLUB? High Wycombe CC, Buckinghamshire
CRICKETING HERO? Brian Lara – for the way he could turn a game in half an hour
WHICH BOWLER WOULD YOU LEAST LIKE TO FACE? My new Northamptonshire teammate Blessing Muzarabani – he's just too tall!
BEST INNINGS YOU'VE SEEN? Ben Duckett's 282 not out against Sussex at Northampton in 2016 – awesome to watch
WHO WOULD YOU ASK TO BAT FOR YOUR LIFE? Virat Kohli
SURPRISING FACT ABOUT YOU? I'm scared of swimming in open water due to my fear of sharks and crocodiles
FAVOURITE QUOTE OR SAYING? Never give up, no matter the circumstances
ODDEST SPORT YOU'VE PLAYED? Aussie Rules
TWITTER: @zaib_05

Batting	Mat	Inns	NO	Runs	HS	Ave	SR	100	50	Ct	St
First-class	13	19	3	331	65*	20.68	43.09	0	2	3	0
List A	8	5	0	56	17	11.20	76.71	0	0	0	0
T20s	5	2	0	7	6	3.50	50.00	0	0	2	0
Bowling	**Mat**	**Balls**	**Runs**	**Wkts**	**BBI**	**BBM**	**Ave**	**Econ**	**SR**	**5w**	**10**
First-class	13	637	397	13	6/115	6/115	30.53	3.73	49.0	2	0
List A	8	120	128	3	2/22	2/22	42.66	6.40	40.0	0	0
T20s	5	48	76	0	-	-	-	9.50	-	0	0

ADAM ZAMPA

RHB / LB / R0 / W0

FULL NAME: Adam Zampa
BORN: March 31, 1992, Shellharbour, New South Wales, Australia
SQUAD NO: 88
TEAMS: Australia, Essex, Adelaide Strikers, Guyana Amazon Warriors, Jamaica Tallawahs, Melbourne Stars, New South Wales, Rising Pune Supergiant, South Australia, Sydney Thunder
ROLE: Bowler
DEBUT: ODI: 2016; T20I: 2016; First-class: 2012; List A: 2012; T20: 2012

BEST BATTING: 74 South Australia vs Western Australia, Adelaide, 2015
BEST BOWLING: 6-62 South Australia vs Queensland, Adelaide, 2017

NOTES: An Australian leg-spinner, Zampa has played in multiple T20 leagues around the world including the IPL, the Caribbean Premier League and the Big Bash, having represented four different teams in the latter. In 2016 he claimed the second-best figures in IPL history – 6-19 for Rising Pune Supergiant against Sunrisers Hyderabad. He made his T20 international debut against South Africa in 2016 and is a regular in Australia's limited-over sides. Last summer he was the only standout performer among the the Essex bowlers, taking 12 wickets with an economy-rate of 7.90. He will be available for the whole of the T20 Blast

Batting	Mat	Inns	NO	Runs	HS	Ave	SR	100	50	Ct	St
ODIs	38	18	4	99	22	7.07	63.46	0	0	9	0
T20Is	22	6	4	23	9	11.50	88.46	0	0	1	0
First-class	36	59	7	1118	74	21.50	71.34	0	6	9	0
List A	72	45	10	562	66	16.05	97.40	0	3	17	0
T20s	115	40	17	138	17*	6.00	89.03	0	0	15	0
Bowling	**Mat**	**Balls**	**Runs**	**Wkts**	**BBI**	**BBM**	**Ave**	**Econ**	**SR**	**5w**	**10**
ODIs	38	1930	1820	50	3/16	3/16	36.40	5.65	38.6	0	0
T20Is	22	444	447	23	3/16	3/16	19.43	6.04	19.3	0	0
First-class	36	7348	4804	102	6/62	10/119	47.09	3.92	72.0	2	1
List A	72	3821	3427	103	4/18	4/18	33.27	5.38	37.0	0	0
T20s	115	2319	2780	127	6/19	6/19	21.88	7.19	18.2	1	0

England
Women

ENGLAND WOMEN

CAPTAIN: Heather Knight
COACH: Mark Robinson

2019 SUMMER FIXTURES

June 6
England vs West Indies
1st ODI
Leicester

June 9
England vs West Indies
2nd ODI
Worcester

June 13
England vs West Indies
3rd ODI
Chelmsford

June 18
England vs West Indies
1st T20I
Northampton

June 21
England vs West Indies
2nd T20I
Northampton

June 25
England vs West Indies
3rd T20I
Derby

July 2
England vs Australia
1st ODI
Leicester

July 4
England vs Australia
2nd ODI
Leicester

July 7
England vs Australia
3rd ODI
Canterbury

July 18
England vs Australia
Only Test
Taunton

July 26
England vs Australia
1st T20I
Chelmsford

July 28
England vs Australia
2nd T20I
Hove

July 31
England vs Australia
3rd T20I
Bristol

TAMMY BEAUMONT RHB/WK

FULL NAME: Tamsin Tilley Beaumont
BORN: March 11, 1991, Dover, Kent
SQUAD NO: 12
HEIGHT: 5ft 3in
NICKNAME: Tambeau, Little Mitts
EDUCATION: Sir Roger Manwood's School, Kent; Loughborough University
TEAMS: England, Kent, Southern Vipers, Adelaide Strikers, Emeralds, Sapphires, Surrey Stars, Diamonds
ROLE: Batsman
DEBUT: Test: 2013; ODI: 2009; T20I: 2009

BEST ODI BATTING: 168* England vs Pakistan, Taunton, 2016

WHAT WAS YOUR FIRST CRICKET CLUB? Sandwich Town CC, Kent. Played in the U11 boys' team when I was eight and a few years later I opened the batting with Sam Northeast in age-group cricket
FAVOURITE CRICKET BAT? My first Salix when I was 10. It would travel home on the backseat with a seatbelt on
WHICH BOWLER WOULD YOU LEAST LIKE TO FACE? Michael Holding – because of the bounce!
BEST INNINGS YOU'VE SEEN? Alastair Cook's final hundred at The Oval last year. I was so lucky to be there and I even cried when he got out (not ashamed to admit that!)
WHO WOULD YOU ASK TO BAT FOR YOUR LIFE? Sarah Taylor – I'd trust her with my life any day, and she'd look good doing it
WHICH RULE WOULD YOU CHANGE ABOUT CRICKET? You can't be run out while backing up
YOUR BIGGEST CRICKETING REGRET? Letting nerves get the better of me in the early part of my career
WHICH BOOK MEANS MOST TO YOU? My scrapbook with family photos
TWITTER: @Tammy_Beaumont

Batting	Mat	Inns	NO	Runs	HS	Ave	SR	100	50	Ct	St
Tests	3	5	0	132	70	26.40	40.74	0	1	1	0
ODIs	59	52	6	1845	168*	40.10	70.98	5	7	13	4
T20Is	65	51	5	982	116	21.34	105.81	1	5	13	4
Bowling	**Mat**	**Balls**	**Runs**	**Wkts**	**BBI**	**BBM**	**Ave**	**Econ**	**SR**	**5w**	**10**
Tests	3	-	-	-	-	-	-	-	-	-	-
ODIs	59	-	-	-	-	-	-	-	-	-	-
T20Is	65	-	-	-	-	-	-	-	-	-	-

KATHERINE BRUNT RHB / RFM

FULL NAME: Katherine Helen Brunt
BORN: July 2, 1985, Barnsley
SQUAD NO: 26
HEIGHT: 5ft 5in
NICKNAME: Brunty, Nunny, Ethel
EDUCATION: Penistone Grammar School, South Yorkshire
TEAMS: England, Yorkshire, Yorkshire Diamonds, Braves, Knight Riders, Perth Scorchers, Sapphires
ROLE: Allrounder
DEBUT: Test: 2004; ODI: 2005; T20I: 2005

BEST ODI BATTING: 72* England vs South Africa, Worcester, 2018
BEST ODI BOWLING: 5-18 England vs Australia, Wormsley, 2011

WHAT WAS YOUR FIRST CRICKET CLUB? Barnsley CC, South Yorkshire. Same club where Darren Gough and Arnie Sidebottom played
FAVOURITE CRICKET BAT? My first real willow bat, a Slazenger V100. It's signed by Darren Gough, who I met as a kid at Barnsley CC. Vintage
WHICH BOWLER WOULD YOU LEAST LIKE TO FACE? Jasprit Bumrah – because he's quicker than you think and his action would do me all over
WHO WOULD YOU ASK TO BAT FOR YOUR LIFE? Don Bradman
WHICH RULE WOULD YOU CHANGE ABOUT CRICKET? Five referrals per team in the women's game!
YOUR BIGGEST CRICKETING REGRET? Being born in the wrong era. I would have had a safer bowling action earlier because I would have had a proper coach in this day and age. Then I wouldn't have had a chronic back issue
FAVOURITE QUOTE OR SAYING? To live will be an awfully big adventure
WHICH BOOK MEANS MOST TO YOU? The Hobbit by JRR Tolkien
TWITTER: @KBrunt26

Batting	Mat	Inns	NO	Runs	HS	Ave	SR	100	50	Ct	St
Tests	11	14	4	156	52	15.60	30.83	0	1	3	0
ODIs	115	63	16	771	72*	16.40	78.27	0	2	32	0
T20Is	67	36	18	302	42*	16.77	109.02	0	0	19	0
Bowling	**Mat**	**Balls**	**Runs**	**Wkts**	**BBI**	**BBM**	**Ave**	**Econ**	**SR**	**5w**	**10**
Tests	11	2082	852	39	6/69	9/111	21.84	2.45	53.3	2	0
ODIs	115	5679	3297	141	5/18	5/18	23.38	3.48	40.2	5	0
T20Is	67	1461	1253	66	3/6	3/6	18.98	5.14	22.1	0	0

KATE CROSS RHB/RMF

FULL NAME: Kathryn Laura Cross
BORN: October 3, 1991, Manchester
SQUAD NO: 16
HEIGHT: 5ft 8in
NICKNAME: Crossy, Sunny
EDUCATION: Bury Grammar School; University of Leeds
TEAMS: England, Lancashire, Lancashire Thunder, Brisbane Heat, Perth Scorchers, Western Australia
ROLE: Bowler
DEBUT: Test: 2014; ODI: 2013; T20I: 2013

BEST ODI BATTING: 4* England vs India, Scarborough, 2014
BEST ODI BOWLING: 5-24 England vs New Zealand, Lincoln, 2015

WHAT WAS YOUR FIRST CRICKET CLUB? Heywood CC, Greater Manchester. Andy Flower played a few seasons at the club
FAVOURITE CRICKET BAT? My first was a Peak Sport bat, which I loved. Peak Sport is a northern brand and I wanted one because my brother had one
WHICH BOWLER WOULD YOU LEAST LIKE TO FACE? Dwayne Bravo
BEST INNINGS YOU'VE SEEN? I was there when Brian Lara scored 400 not out at Antigua in 2004
WHO WOULD YOU ASK TO BAT FOR YOUR LIFE? Amy Jones
YOUR BIGGEST CRICKETING REGRET? Bowling seam at a time when T20 is very popular
WHICH BOOK MEANS MOST TO YOU? My sister made me a scrapbook of my first year in international cricket which took her a long time to create and has some amazing memories
ODDEST SPORT YOU'VE PLAYED? Tedball – introduced to Lancashire Thunder by Alex Blackwell last summer
TWITTER: @katecross16

Batting	Mat	Inns	NO	Runs	HS	Ave	SR	100	50	Ct	St
Tests	3	6	3	15	4*	5.00	24.19	0	0	0	0
ODIs	15	5	3	11	4*	5.50	39.28	0	0	3	0
T20Is	7	-	-	-	-	-	-	-	-	2	0
Bowling	**Mat**	**Balls**	**Runs**	**Wkts**	**BBI**	**BBM**	**Ave**	**Econ**	**SR**	**5w**	**10**
Tests	3	554	209	14	3/29	6/70	14.92	2.26	39.5	0	0
ODIs	15	678	507	16	5/24	5/24	31.68	4.48	42.3	1	0
T20Is	7	144	141	7	2/18	2/18	20.14	5.87	20.5	0	0

ALICE DAVIDSON-RICHARDS RHB / RFM

FULL NAME: Alice Natica Davidson-Richards
BORN: May 29, 1994, Tunbridge Wells, Kent
SQUAD NO: 36
HEIGHT: 5ft 8in
NICKNAME: ADR, AD
EDUCATION: Epsom College, Surrey; University of Leeds
TEAMS: England, Kent, Yorkshire Diamonds, Emeralds, Otago, Sapphires
ROLE: Allrounder
DEBUT: ODI: 2018; T20I: 2018

BEST ODI BATTING: 9 England vs India, Nagpur, 2018

WHAT WAS YOUR FIRST CRICKET CLUB? Tunbridge Wells CC, Kent, where I grew up
WHICH BOWLER WOULD YOU LEAST LIKE TO FACE? Katie Levick – she loves bowling at me
FAVOURITE CRICKET BAT? My Salix Pod – perfect weight and balance
BEST INNINGS YOU'VE SEEN? For sentimental value, Alastair Cook's final Test innings
WHO WOULD YOU ASK TO BAT FOR YOUR LIFE? Tammy Beaumont
WHICH RULE WOULD YOU CHANGE ABOUT CRICKET? Every club has to have a brew ready at the end of an innings. I'd also like to see some rule changes which will help the bowlers a bit more
WHAT WILL YOU BE DOING IN THE YEAR 2040? Going on an adventure with my dog
FAVOURITE QUOTE OR SAYING? Why fit in when you were born to stand out? (Dr Seuss)
WHICH BOOK MEANS MOST TO YOU? Any of the Harry Potter series

Batting	Mat	Inns	NO	Runs	HS	Ave	SR	100	50	Ct	St
ODIs	1	1	0	9	9	9.00	28.12	0	0	0	0
T20Is	5	3	0	28	24	9.33	82.35	0	0	2	0
Bowling	**Mat**	**Balls**	**Runs**	**Wkts**	**BBI**	**BBM**	**Ave**	**Econ**	**SR**	**5w**	**10**
ODIs	1	-	-	-	-	-	-	-	-	-	-
T20Is	5	24	44	0	-	-	-	11.00	-	0	0

FREYA DAVIES RHB / RFM

FULL NAME: Freya Ruth Davies
BORN: October 27, 1995, Chichester, Sussex
SQUAD NO: 61
HEIGHT: 5ft 9in
EDUCATION: Brighton College; Exeter University
TEAMS: England, Sussex, Western Storm
ROLE: Bowler

WHAT WAS YOUR FIRST CRICKET CLUB? Singleton CC, West Sussex. A small village club where I started aged seven with my dad. Known as one of the prettiest grounds around – not that I noticed this aged seven
WHICH BOWLER WOULD YOU LEAST LIKE TO FACE? Rashid Khan – I can't even pick him on TV
BEST INNINGS YOU'VE SEEN? Smriti Mandhana smashing 52 off 19 balls for Western Storm against Loughborough Lightning in last season's Kia Super League
WHO WOULD YOU ASK TO BAT FOR YOUR LIFE? Alex Hartley – she wasn't dismissed in her first 11 international innings!
YOUR BIGGEST CRICKETING REGRET? That neither of my grandfathers got to see me play
WHAT WILL YOU BE DOING IN THE YEAR 2040? Sitting at a desk all day attempting to be a lawyer
FAVOURITE QUOTE OR SAYING? Grant me the serenity to accept the things I cannot change, the courage to change the things I can, and the wisdom to know the difference (Serenity Prayer)
WHICH BOOK MEANS MOST TO YOU? To Kill a Mocking Bird by Harper Lee
TWITTER: @FreyaRuth

SOPHIA DUNKLEY RHB / LB

FULL NAME: Sophia Ivy Dunkley
BORN: July 16, 1998, Lambeth, London
SQUAD NO: 47
HEIGHT: 5ft 7in
NICKNAME: Dunks, Dunkers, Flippers
EDUCATION: Mill Hill School, London
TEAMS: England, Middlesex, Surrey Stars
ROLE: Allrounder
DEBUT: T20I: 2018

WHAT WAS YOUR FIRST CRICKET CLUB? Finchley CC, London. Couldn't wait to get there after school, and they did great ham-and-cheese toasties
WHICH BOWLER WOULD YOU LEAST LIKE TO FACE? Mitchell Johnson – it looks terrifying
BEST INNINGS YOU'VE SEEN? Alastair Cook's final Test innings at The Oval at the end of last summer. What a special day
WHO WOULD YOU ASK TO BAT FOR YOUR LIFE? Beth Morgan – you can trust her with anything
WHICH RULE WOULD YOU CHANGE ABOUT CRICKET? You should get more runs if you hit a boundary in a certain area
YOUR BIGGEST CRICKETING REGRET? Not going to watch more games live – there's still time!
WHAT WILL YOU BE DOING IN THE YEAR 2040? Living somewhere sunny with a pet dog and maybe a goat
FAVOURITE QUOTE OR SAYING? Everything happens for a reason
WHICH BOOK MEANS MOST TO YOU? Private Peaceful by Michael Morpurgo
ODDEST SPORT YOU'VE PLAYED? Eton Fives
TWITTER: @dunkleysophia

Batting	Mat	Inns	NO	Runs	HS	Ave	SR	100	50	Ct	St
T20Is	7	3	1	49	35	24.50	100.00	0	0	3	0
Bowling	**Mat**	**Balls**	**Runs**	**Wkts**	**BBI**	**BBM**	**Ave**	**Econ**	**SR**	**5w**	**10**
T20Is	7	-	-	-	-	-	-	-	-	-	-

SOPHIE ECCLESTONE RHB / SLA

FULL NAME: Sophie Ecclestone
BORN: May 6, 1999, Chester, Cheshire
SQUAD NO: 71
HEIGHT: 5ft 10in
NICKNAME: Ecclescake
EDUCATION: Helsby High School, Cheshire
TEAMS: England, Lancashire, Lancashire Thunder, Cheshire
ROLE: Bowler
DEBUT: Test: 2017; ODI: 2016; T20I: 2016

BEST ODI BATTING: 12* England vs South Africa, Worcester, 2018
BEST ODI BOWLING: 4-14 England vs India, Nagpur, 2018

WHAT WAS YOUR FIRST CRICKET CLUB? Alvanley CC, Cheshire
WHICH BOWLER WOULD YOU LEAST LIKE TO FACE? Anya Shrubsole – she seems horrible to face when watching highlights back, as well as from watching her from mid-on and mid-off
WHO WOULD YOU ASK TO BAT FOR YOUR LIFE? Definitely Heather Knight because nothing seems to faze her, no matter the situation
WHAT WILL YOU BE DOING IN THE YEAR 2040? I'd love to be a pilot but it takes a lot of hard work and commitment
FAVOURITE QUOTE OR SAYING? All the England girls tease me because I speak too fast and they can't understand me! I often use the words "sick" or "buzzing" to describe a good situation
WHICH BOOK MEANS MOST TO YOU? I don't have the concentration to be able to read!
ODDEST SPORT YOU'VE PLAYED? I do love a game of crown green bowling. It's such a hard sport to be good at
TWITTER: @sophecc19

Batting	Mat	Inns	NO	Runs	HS	Ave	SR	100	50	Ct	St
Tests	1	1	1	8	8*	-	42.10	0	0	0	0
ODIs	15	11	3	28	12*	3.50	41.79	0	0	4	0
T20Is	19	5	1	26	9*	6.50	92.85	0	0	3	0
Bowling	**Mat**	**Balls**	**Runs**	**Wkts**	**BBI**	**BBM**	**Ave**	**Econ**	**SR**	**5w**	**10**
Tests	1	222	107	3	3/107	3/107	35.66	2.89	74.0	0	0
ODIs	15	786	474	25	4/14	4/14	18.96	3.61	31.4	0	0
T20Is	19	434	481	24	4/18	4/18	20.04	6.64	18.0	0	0

GEORGIA ELWISS RHB / RMF

FULL NAME: Georgia Amanda Elwiss
BORN: May 31, 1991, Wolverhampton
SQUAD NO: 34
HEIGHT: 5ft 7in
NICKNAME: G, George, G Dog
EDUCATION: Wolverhampton Girls' High School; Loughborough University
TEAMS: England, Sussex, Loughborough Lightning, Diamonds, Emeralds, Knight Riders, Melbourne Stars, Rubies, Staffordshire, Sapphires
ROLE: Allrounder
DEBUT: Test: 2015; ODI: 2011; T20I: 2011

BEST ODI BATTING: 77 England vs Pakistan, Taunton, 2016
BEST ODI BOWLING: 3-17 England vs India, Wormsley, 2012

WHAT WAS YOUR FIRST CRICKET CLUB? Wolverhampton CC, West Midlands. The same club where Rachael Heyhoe Flint played
WHICH BOWLER WOULD YOU LEAST LIKE TO FACE? Elyse Villani (Australia batter) – I'd never hear the end of it if she got me out
BEST INNINGS YOU'VE SEEN? Danni Wyatt's T20 hundred at Canberra in 2017
WHICH RULE WOULD YOU CHANGE ABOUT CRICKET? Do the warm-up after the toss
YOUR BIGGEST CRICKETING REGRET? Not trying to hit bigger sixes
WHAT WILL YOU BE DOING IN THE YEAR 2040? I'll be running a coffee shop in Melbourne
FAVOURITE QUOTE OR SAYING? Strength does not come from winning. Your struggles develop your strengths
WHICH BOOK MEANS MOST TO YOU? Lean in 15 – 15 Minute Meals and Workouts to Keep You Lean and Healthy by Joe Wicks
ODDEST SPORT YOU'VE PLAYED? Hybrid – a mix of AFL and NFL
TWITTER: @gelwiss

Batting	Mat	Inns	NO	Runs	HS	Ave	SR	100	50	Ct	St
Tests	2	4	1	131	46	43.66	28.60	0	0	0	0
ODIs	36	24	5	388	77	20.42	73.20	0	2	11	0
T20Is	13	4	2	24	18	12.00	100.00	0	0	3	0
Bowling	**Mat**	**Balls**	**Runs**	**Wkts**	**BBI**	**BBM**	**Ave**	**Econ**	**SR**	**5w**	**10**
Tests	2	96	51	1	1/40	1/40	51.00	3.18	96.0	0	0
ODIs	36	1097	679	26	3/17	3/17	26.11	3.71	42.1	0	0
T20Is	13	151	139	8	2/9	2/9	17.37	5.52	18.8	0	0

KATIE GEORGE LHB / LFM

FULL NAME: Katie Louise George
BORN: April 7, 1999, Haywards Heath, Sussex
SQUAD NO: 46
HEIGHT: 5ft 6in
EDUCATION: The Mountbatten School, Hampshire; Richard Taunton Sixth Form, Southampton
TEAMS: England, Hampshire, Southern Vipers
ROLE: Bowler
DEBUT: ODI: 2018; T20I: 2018

BEST ODI BATTING: 9 England vs New Zealand, Derby, 2018
BEST ODI BOWLING: 3-36 England vs New Zealand, Derby, 2018

WHAT WAS YOUR FIRST CRICKET CLUB? Cove CC, Hampshire. I'd go along with my dad and brother and play football along the boundary. Then one day I joined in
FAVOURITE CRICKET BAT? M&H – I was buzzing when I went with my dad to a cricket shop to get it. It was kept together by tape for a long time
WHICH BOWLER WOULD YOU LEAST LIKE TO FACE? Danni 'Pet' Hazell – absolute warrior. You know you're going to be in a battle with her. Something I aspire to
BEST INNINGS YOU'VE SEEN? Jos Buttler dismantling the Aussies in Sydney during the 2017/18 tour
WHO WOULD YOU ASK TO BAT FOR YOUR LIFE? Virat Kohli – he'd give everything but also play with his natural flair. I want my last innings to be remembered
WHICH RULE WOULD YOU CHANGE ABOUT CRICKET? One hand one bounce
YOUR BIGGEST CRICKETING REGRET? Concentrating too much on football and not enough on cricket when I was younger
FAVOURITE QUOTE OR SAYING? Hakuna matata
ODDEST SPORT YOU'VE PLAYED? Ultimate Frisbee
TWITTER: @KaTie_George46

Batting	Mat	Inns	NO	Runs	HS	Ave	SR	100	50	Ct	St
ODIs	2	1	0	9	9	9.00	47.36	0	0	1	0
T20Is	5	1	0	0	0	0.00	0.00	0	0	0	0
Bowling	**Mat**	**Balls**	**Runs**	**Wkts**	**BBI**	**BBM**	**Ave**	**Econ**	**SR**	**5w**	**10**
ODIs	2	75	70	4	3/36	3/36	17.50	5.60	18.7	0	0
T20Is	5	78	117	2	1/22	1/22	58.50	9.00	39.0	0	0

KIRSTIE GORDON RHB / SLA

FULL NAME: Kirstie Louise Gordon
BORN: October 20, 1997, Huntly, Aberdeenshire, Scotland
SQUAD NO: 48
HEIGHT: 5ft 4in
NICKNAME: Gordo, Scotty
EDUCATION: Loughborough University
TEAMS: England, Nottinghamshire, Loughborough Lightning, Scotland
ROLE: Bowler
DEBUT: T20I: 2018

WHAT WAS YOUR FIRST CRICKET CLUB? Huntly CC, Aberdeenshire. Formed in 1854 and one of the oldest cricket clubs in Scotland
FAVOURITE CRICKET BAT? A GM 505. My mum bought it for me for my 12th birthday
WHICH BOWLER WOULD YOU LEAST LIKE TO FACE? Dale Steyn – not sure I'd even see it
WHO WOULD YOU ASK TO BAT FOR YOUR LIFE? Alastair Cook
WHICH RULE WOULD YOU CHANGE ABOUT CRICKET? The No.11 can't be out first ball
YOUR BIGGEST CRICKETING REGRET? Not working hard enough through my first year at university
WHAT WILL YOU BE DOING IN THE YEAR 2040? Coaching or commentating maybe
FAVOURITE QUOTE OR SAYING? There's no elevator to success, you've got to take the stairs (Zig Ziglar)
WHICH BOOK MEANS MOST TO YOU? Unbelievable by Jessica Ennis-Hill
ODDEST SPORT YOU'VE PLAYED? Lawn bowls
TWITTER: @kirstiegordon97

Batting	Mat	Inns	NO	Runs	HS	Ave	SR	100	50	Ct	St
T20Is	5	1	1	1	1*	-	100.00	0	0	0	0
Bowling	**Mat**	**Balls**	**Runs**	**Wkts**	**BBI**	**BBM**	**Ave**	**Econ**	**SR**	**5w**	**10**
T20Is	5	114	98	8	3/16	3/16	12.25	5.15	14.2	0	0

JENNY GUNN

RHB / RM

FULL NAME: Jennifer Louise Gunn
BORN: May 9, 1986, Nottingham
SQUAD NO: 24
HEIGHT: 5ft 10in
NICKNAME: Chuckie
EDUCATION: Rushcliffe School; South Nottingham College
TEAMS: England, Warwickshire, Loughborough Lightning, Knight Riders, Nottinghamshire, South Australia, Super Strikers, Western Australia, Yorkshire Diamonds
ROLE: Allrounder
DEBUT: Test: 2004; ODI: 2004; T20I: 2004

BEST ODI BATTING: 73 England vs New Zealand, Taunton, 2007
BEST ODI BOWLING: 5-22 England vs Pakistan, Louth, 2013

FAMILY TIES? Dad was a professional footballer. And no, I'm not related to the Gunns that played for Notts years ago
WHAT WAS YOUR FIRST CRICKET CLUB? Lady Bay Boots CC, Nottingham. Played alongside my dad and my brother. Always fun getting men out
CRICKETING HERO? Glenn McGrath – he was medium pace but excelled nevertheless
BEST INNINGS YOU'VE SEEN? Claire Taylor and Beth Morgan chasing down 164 in the World T20 semi-final at The Oval in 2009
WHO WOULD YOU ASK TO BAT FOR YOUR LIFE? Heather Knight. She's a wall
WHICH RULE WOULD YOU CHANGE ABOUT CRICKET? Bring back the rule that allows five fielders outside the inner circle in women's T20
ODDEST SPORT YOU'VE PLAYED? American football. I tried it, loved it, but it's a little rough
TWITTER: @GunnJenny

Batting	Mat	Inns	NO	Runs	HS	Ave	SR	100	50	Ct	St
Tests	11	19	2	391	62*	23.00	30.38	0	1	6	0
ODIs	143	111	28	1629	73	19.62	57.19	0	5	48	0
T20Is	104	67	18	682	69	13.91	100.44	0	1	58	0
Bowling	**Mat**	**Balls**	**Runs**	**Wkts**	**BBI**	**BBM**	**Ave**	**Econ**	**SR**	**5w**	**10**
Tests	11	2189	645	29	5/19	5/59	22.24	1.76	75.4	1	0
ODIs	143	5864	3788	135	5/22	5/22	28.05	3.87	43.4	2	0
T20Is	104	1385	1487	75	5/18	5/18	19.82	6.44	18.4	1	0

ALEX HARTLEY RHB / SLA

FULL NAME: Alexandra Hartley
BORN: September 26, 1993, Blackburn, Lancashire
SQUAD NO: 65
HEIGHT: 5ft 4in
EDUCATION: Ribblesdale High School; Loughborough College
TEAMS: England, Lancashire, Lancashire Thunder, Emeralds, Hobart Hurricanes, Middlesex, Rubies, Surrey Stars, Tasmania
ROLE: Bowler
DEBUT: ODI: 2016; T20I: 2016

BEST ODI BATTING: 3* England vs India, Nagpur, 2018
BEST ODI BOWLING: 4-24 England vs West Indies, Kingston, 2016

WHAT WAS YOUR FIRST CRICKET CLUB? Read CC, Lancashire. Where I started playing cricket with the boys, a very small ground with a famous slope
BEST INNINGS YOU'VE SEEN? Ellyse Perry's 213 not out for Australia at Sydney in the 2017/18 Ashes
WHO WOULD YOU ASK TO BAT FOR YOUR LIFE? Heather Knight – gritty player and I'm hoping she doesn't leave a straight one
WHICH RULE WOULD YOU CHANGE ABOUT CRICKET? Flip the batting order (so that I get to bat more)
YOUR BIGGEST CRICKETING REGRET? Not working hard enough from a young age
WHAT WILL YOU BE DOING IN THE YEAR 2040? Having a pint
FAVOURITE QUOTE OR SAYING? Strength isn't staying on your feet, it's getting back up after you fall
ODDEST SPORT YOU'VE PLAYED? I tried AFL once. Didn't understand it and I just ran away from everyone who tried to flatten me
TWITTER: @alexhartley93

Batting	Mat	Inns	NO	Runs	HS	Ave	SR	100	50	Ct	St
ODIs	26	12	11	10	3*	10.00	19.60	0	0	3	0
T20Is	4	1	1	2	2*	-	100.00	0	0	0	0
Bowling	**Mat**	**Balls**	**Runs**	**Wkts**	**BBI**	**BBM**	**Ave**	**Econ**	**SR**	**5w**	**10**
ODIs	26	1282	875	34	4/24	4/24	25.73	4.09	37.7	0	0
T20Is	4	70	79	3	2/19	2/19	26.33	6.77	23.3	0	0

AMY JONES RHB/WK

FULL NAME: Amy Ellen Jones
BORN: June 13, 1993, Solihull, Warwickshire
SQUAD NO: 40
HEIGHT: 5ft 9in
NICKNAME: Jonesy
EDUCATION: John Willmott School; Loughborough College
TEAMS: England, Warwickshire, Loughborough Lightning, Diamonds, Emeralds, Perth Scorchers, Rubies, Sydney Sixers, Western Australia
ROLE: Wicketkeeper/batsman
DEBUT: ODI: 2013; T20I: 2013

BEST ODI BATTING: 94 England vs India, Nagpur, 2018

FAMILY TIES? My younger sister played for Warwickshire U13. My mum played two games for Walmley when we were short
WHAT WAS YOUR FIRST CRICKET CLUB? Walmley CC, West Midlands
WHICH BOWLER WOULD YOU LEAST LIKE TO FACE? Katherine Brunt when she's angry
BEST INNINGS YOU'VE SEEN? Danni Wyatt's 52-ball hundred in a T20 against India last year
WHO WOULD YOU ASK TO BAT FOR YOUR LIFE? Heather Knight – because she has great mental strength to go with her skill
WHICH RULE WOULD YOU CHANGE ABOUT CRICKET? You can't be out first ball
YOUR BIGGEST CRICKETING REGRET? Not being a left-arm spinner
SURPRISING FACT ABOUT YOU? I used to play football for Aston Villa
WHAT WILL YOU BE DOING IN THE YEAR 2040? Enjoying life without fitness testing
ODDEST SPORT YOU'VE PLAYED? Footgolf
TWITTER: @amyjones313

Batting	Mat	Inns	NO	Runs	HS	Ave	SR	100	50	Ct	St
ODIs	32	26	2	529	94	22.04	72.76	0	3	20	6
T20Is	31	21	4	253	53*	14.88	104.97	0	1	16	3
Bowling	**Mat**	**Balls**	**Runs**	**Wkts**	**BBI**	**BBM**	**Ave**	**Econ**	**SR**	**5w**	**10**
ODIs	32	-	-	-	-	-	-	-	-	-	-
T20Is	31	-	-	-	-	-	-	-	-	-	-

HEATHER KNIGHT RHB / OB

FULL NAME: Heather Clare Knight
BORN: December 26, 1990, Plymouth
SQUAD NO: 5
HEIGHT: 5ft 7in
NICKNAME: Trev
EDUCATION: Plymstock School; Cardiff University
TEAMS: England, Berkshire, Western Storm, Devon, Emeralds, Hobart Hurricanes, Rubies, Sapphires, Tasmania
ROLE: Allrounder
DEBUT: Test: 2011; ODI: 2010; T20I: 2010

BEST ODI BATTING: 106 England vs Pakistan, Leicester, 2017
BEST ODI BOWLING: 5-26 England vs Pakistan, Leicester, 2016

WHAT WAS YOUR FIRST CRICKET CLUB? Plymstock CC, Plymouth. Played there with my brother. It was an uncovered wicket which played better when it was wet!
WHICH BOWLER WOULD YOU LEAST LIKE TO FACE? Tammy Beaumont – her filthy off-spin from 3ft high is a nightmare to face. She bowls off the wrong foot too
BEST INNINGS YOU'VE SEEN? Lydia Greenway's unbeaten 80 off 64 balls in the T20 against Australia at Southampton in 2013 – it won us the Ashes
WHO WOULD YOU ASK TO BAT FOR YOUR LIFE? Nat Sciver – cool as a cucumber
WHICH RULE WOULD YOU CHANGE ABOUT CRICKET? You're not allowed to bowl in a hat
YOUR BIGGEST CRICKETING REGRET? The 2015 Ashes
WHAT WILL YOU BE DOING IN THE YEAR 2040? Sitting back and sipping some vino while watching the women's game become as big as the men's game
FAVOURITE QUOTE OR SAYING? Ever tried, ever failed? No matter. Try again, fail again. Fail better (Samuel Beckett)
ODDEST SPORT YOU'VE PLAYED? Octopush
TWITTER: @heatherknight55

Batting	Mat	Inns	NO	Runs	HS	Ave	SR	100	50	Ct	St
Tests	6	12	1	358	157	32.54	41.38	1	2	6	0
ODIs	89	85	19	2419	106	36.65	69.23	1	16	29	0
T20Is	56	49	12	642	51	17.35	110.49	0	1	21	0
Bowling	**Mat**	**Balls**	**Runs**	**Wkts**	**BBI**	**BBM**	**Ave**	**Econ**	**SR**	**5w**	**10**
Tests	6	179	80	2	1/7	1/7	40.00	2.68	89.5	0	0
ODIs	89	1439	1035	44	5/26	5/26	23.52	4.31	32.7	1	0
T20Is	56	399	384	17	3/9	3/9	22.58	5.77	23.4	0	0

LAURA MARSH RHB / OB

FULL NAME: Laura Alexandra Marsh
BORN: December 5, 1986, Pembury, Kent
SQUAD NO: 7
HEIGHT: 5ft 5in
NICKNAME: Boggy, Marshy
EDUCATION: Brighton College; Loughborough University
TEAMS: England, Kent, Surrey Stars, Braves, Emeralds, New South Wales, Otago, Rubies, Sapphires, Sussex, Sydney Sixers
ROLE: Bowler
DEBUT: Test: 2006; ODI: 2006; T20I: 2007

BEST ODI BATTING: 67 England vs Ireland, Kibworth, 2010
BEST ODI BOWLING: 5-15 England vs Pakistan, Sydney, 2009

WHAT WAS YOUR FIRST CRICKET CLUB? Brighton and Hove CC
FAVOURITE CRICKET BAT? Gray-Nicolls Powerspot – light, great middle and simple stickers
WHICH BOWLER WOULD YOU LEAST LIKE TO FACE? Mitchell Starc
BEST INNINGS YOU'VE SEEN? Alastair Cook's hundred at The Oval last summer in his final Test innings
WHO WOULD YOU ASK TO BAT FOR YOUR LIFE? Rahul Dravid
SURPRISING FACT ABOUT YOU? I was the U13 national javelin champion
WHAT WILL YOU BE DOING IN THE YEAR 2040? I might be involved in marketing or running a business
FAVOURITE QUOTE OR SAYING? Everything happens for a reason
ODDEST SPORT YOU'VE PLAYED? Real tennis
TWITTER: @lauramarsh7

Batting	Mat	Inns	NO	Runs	HS	Ave	SR	100	50	Ct	St
Tests	8	11	0	123	55	11.18	22.61	0	1	4	0
ODIs	95	57	11	629	67	13.67	66.98	0	1	23	0
T20Is	62	51	6	729	54	16.20	99.31	0	1	6	0
Bowling	**Mat**	**Balls**	**Runs**	**Wkts**	**BBI**	**BBM**	**Ave**	**Econ**	**SR**	**5w**	**10**
Tests	8	1763	679	20	3/44	4/83	33.95	2.31	88.1	0	0
ODIs	95	4914	3184	118	5/15	5/15	26.98	3.88	41.6	1	0
T20Is	62	1395	1215	61	3/12	3/12	19.91	5.22	22.8	0	0

NATALIE SCIVER RHB/RM

FULL NAME: Natalie Ruth Sciver
BORN: August 20, 1992, Tokyo, Japan
SQUAD NO: 39
HEIGHT: 5ft 10in
NICKNAME: Sciv
EDUCATION: Epsom College; Loughborough University
TEAMS: England, Surrey, Surrey Stars, Emeralds, Melbourne Stars, Perth Scorchers, Rubies
ROLE: Allrounder
DEBUT: Test: 2014; ODI: 2013; T20I: 2013

BEST ODI BATTING: 137 England vs Pakistan, Leicester, 2017
BEST ODI BOWLING: 3-3 England vs West Indies, Bristol, 2017

WHAT WAS YOUR FIRST CRICKET CLUB? Stoke d'Abernon CC, Surrey. I made my sister join for the first year so that I would have a friend
BEST INNINGS YOU'VE SEEN? Hard to choose which AB de Villiers innings. Some of those in the IPL were insane
WHO WOULD YOU ASK TO BAT FOR YOUR LIFE? Kane Williamson – he's a great batter and looks like a nice man
WHICH RULE WOULD YOU CHANGE ABOUT CRICKET? When there's a free hit, the batter gets to nominate who bowls it
YOUR BIGGEST CRICKETING REGRET? Being right-handed
WHAT WILL YOU BE DOING IN THE YEAR 2040? I'll be a ski bum
FAVOURITE QUOTE OR SAYING? Work hard in silence, let your success be your noise (Frank Ocean)
WHICH BOOK MEANS MOST TO YOU? Any of the Harry Potter books
TWITTER: @natsciver

Batting	Mat	Inns	NO	Runs	HS	Ave	SR	100	50	Ct	St
Tests	4	7	0	140	49	20.00	30.97	0	0	3	0
ODIs	56	49	9	1536	137	38.40	97.03	2	11	25	0
T20Is	58	55	12	954	68*	22.18	109.15	0	4	31	0
Bowling	**Mat**	**Balls**	**Runs**	**Wkts**	**BBI**	**BBM**	**Ave**	**Econ**	**SR**	**5w**	**10**
Tests	4	269	130	1	1/30	1/30	130.00	2.89	269.0	0	0
ODIs	56	1409	1043	38	3/3	3/3	27.44	4.44	37.0	0	0
T20Is	58	792	870	45	4/15	4/15	19.33	6.59	17.6	0	0

ANYA SHRUBSOLE RHB / RFM

FULL NAME: Anya Shrubsole
BORN: December 7, 1991, Bath
SQUAD NO: 41
HEIGHT: 5ft 10in
NICKNAME: Hoof
EDUCATION: Hayesfield School; Loughborough University
TEAMS: England, Somerset, Western Storm, Braves, Emeralds, Perth Scorchers, Rubies
ROLE: Bowler
DEBUT: Test: 2013; ODI: 2008; T20I: 2008

BEST ODI BATTING: 29 England vs New Zealand, Mount Maunganui, 2015
BEST ODI BOWLING: 6-46 England vs India, Lord's, 2017

WHAT WAS YOUR FIRST CRICKET CLUB? Bath CC, which is located in the city centre opposite The Rec where Bath Rugby play their home games
BEST INNINGS YOU'VE SEEN? Nat Sciver's hundred against New Zealand in the 2017 World Cup – she made batting look ridiculously easy on a really difficult pitch. Also saw the unveiling of the "Natmeg"
WHO WOULD YOU ASK TO BAT FOR YOUR LIFE? Nat Sciver – looks unbelievably calm in any circumstance
WHICH RULE WOULD YOU CHANGE ABOUT CRICKET? Might need the extra fielder out of the fielding circle in T20 again soon
YOUR BIGGEST CRICKETING REGRET? Not being fit enough early in my career
WHICH BOOK MEANS MOST TO YOU? I Love You to the Moon and Back – had it since I was a child
TWITTER: @anya_shrubsole

Batting	Mat	Inns	NO	Runs	HS	Ave	SR	100	50	Ct	St
Tests	5	8	0	51	20	6.37	25.12	0	0	3	0
ODIs	58	26	9	188	29	11.05	85.84	0	0	15	0
T20Is	62	14	6	99	29	12.37	110.00	0	0	18	0
Bowling	**Mat**	**Balls**	**Runs**	**Wkts**	**BBI**	**BBM**	**Ave**	**Econ**	**SR**	**5w**	**10**
Tests	5	1098	417	17	4/51	7/99	24.52	2.27	64.5	0	0
ODIs	58	2792	1982	72	6/46	6/46	27.52	4.25	38.7	2	0
T20Is	62	1270	1181	84	5/11	5/11	14.05	5.57	15.1	1	0

BRYONY SMITH RHB/OB

FULL NAME: Bryony Frances Smith
BORN: December 12, 1997, Sutton, Surrey
SQUAD NO: 43
HEIGHT: 5ft 6in
NICKNAME: Bry, Smithy
EDUCATION: St Andrews High School, London; Archbishop Tenison's Sixth Form, London
TEAMS: England, Surrey, Surrey Stars
ROLE: Batsman
DEBUT: T20I: 2018

WHAT WAS YOUR FIRST CRICKET CLUB? Wallington CC, London. I was the only girl in the league throughout age-group cricket and I captained the boys' teams in every age group
FAVOURITE CRICKET BAT? Gray-Nicolls Kaboom. I was devastated when it broke during a game. Sent my dad out to get another one
WHICH BOWLER WOULD YOU LEAST LIKE TO FACE? Rashid Khan – too many variations
WHO WOULD YOU ASK TO BAT FOR YOUR LIFE? Virat Kohli – scores runs for fun even when he is being defensive
WHICH RULE WOULD YOU CHANGE ABOUT CRICKET? You can't be out first ball
YOUR BIGGEST CRICKETING REGRET? Not making the most of opportunities when I was younger
WHAT WILL YOU BE DOING IN THE YEAR 2040? If I'm not playing then coaching. Or going back to school to help promote women's cricket
WHICH BOOK MEANS MOST TO YOU? Bounce – The Myth of Talent and the Power of Practice by Matthew Syed
TWITTER: @BrySmith97

Batting	Mat	Inns	NO	Runs	HS	Ave	SR	100	50	Ct	St
T20Is	3	3	0	16	15	5.33	100.00	0	0	0	0
Bowling	**Mat**	**Balls**	**Runs**	**Wkts**	**BBI**	**BBM**	**Ave**	**Econ**	**SR**	**5w**	**10**
T20Is	3	-	-	-	-	-	-	-	-	-	-

LINSEY SMITH LHB / SLA

FULL NAME: Linsey Claire Neale Smith
BORN: March 10, 1995, Hillingdon, Middlesex
SQUAD NO: 50
HEIGHT: 5ft 2in
NICKNAME: Smithy, Neal
EDUCATION: Loughborough College
TEAMS: England, Sussex, Loughborough Lightning, Berkshire, Emeralds, Rubies, Southern Vipers
ROLE: Bowler
DEBUT: T20I: 2018

WHAT WAS YOUR FIRST CRICKET CLUB? Aston Rowant CC, Oxfordshire. They have supported me since I first went there aged 12
FAVOURITE CRICKET BAT? My Blueroom – first time I've actually had a bat made specially for me
WHICH BOWLER WOULD YOU LEAST LIKE TO FACE? Anya Shrubsole – she swings it round corners
WHO WOULD YOU ASK TO BAT FOR YOUR LIFE? Heather Knight or Alastair Cook. Solid
WHICH RULE WOULD YOU CHANGE ABOUT CRICKET? The players should come off if it's cold or windy
YOUR BIGGEST CRICKETING REGRET? No regrets – everything's a learning curve
WHAT WILL YOU BE DOING IN THE YEAR 2040? Hopefully having a well-earned rest after a long and successful cricket career – fingers crossed!
TWITTER: @LinseySmith95

Batting	Mat	Inns	NO	Runs	HS	Ave	SR	100	50	Ct	St
T20Is	5	-	-	-	-	-	-	-	-	0	0
Bowling	**Mat**	**Balls**	**Runs**	**Wkts**	**BBI**	**BBM**	**Ave**	**Econ**	**SR**	**5w**	**10**
T20Is	5	102	96	7	2/11	2/11	13.71	5.64	14.5	0	0

SARAH TAYLOR RHB / WK

FULL NAME: Sarah Jane Taylor
BORN: May 20, 1989, London
SQUAD NO: 30
HEIGHT: 5ft 8in
NICKNAME: Sezzie, Squirt, Staylor
EDUCATION: St Bede's School; Brighton College
TEAMS: England, Sussex, Surrey Stars, Adelaide Strikers, Emeralds, Lancashire Thunder, Rubies, South Australia, Super Strikers, Wellington
ROLE: Wicketkeeper/batsman
DEBUT: Test: 2006; ODI: 2006; T20I: 2006

BEST ODI BATTING: 147 England vs South Africa, Bristol, 2017

FAMILY TIES? None. My dad caught a ball once. Apparently
WHAT WAS YOUR FIRST CRICKET CLUB? Roffey CC, Sussex. Everyone's name ended in 'bo'
FAVOURITE CRICKET BAT? A GM Zona. It's framed in my spare room
BEST INNINGS YOU'VE SEEN? Beth Morgan in the 2009 World T20 against Australia at The Oval. Helped chase down a huge total against Australia. Gutsy
WHICH RULE WOULD YOU CHANGE ABOUT CRICKET? A Dukes ball to be used in all Test matches
YOUR BIGGEST CRICKETING REGRET? Losing any World Cup final
SURPRISING FACT ABOUT YOU? I travel with a teddy bear called Bephy
FAVOURITE QUOTE OR SAYING? You must do the things you cannot do (Theodore Roosevelt)
WHICH BOOK MEANS MOST TO YOU? F*** It: The Ultimate Spiritual Way by John Parkin
ODDEST SPORT YOU'VE PLAYED? Bicycle football
TWITTER: @sarah_taylor30

Batting	Mat	Inns	NO	Runs	HS	Ave	SR	100	50	Ct	St
Tests	9	16	1	295	40	19.66	49.74	0	0	18	2
ODIs	121	114	13	3958	147	39.18	82.04	7	19	83	50
T20Is	89	86	11	2175	77	29.00	110.68	0	16	23	50
Bowling	**Mat**	**Balls**	**Runs**	**Wkts**	**BBI**	**BBM**	**Ave**	**Econ**	**SR**	**5w**	**10**
Tests	9	-	-	-	-	-	-	-	-	-	-
ODIs	121	-	-	-	-	-	-	-	-	-	-
T20Is	89	-	-	-	-	-	-	-	-	-	-

FRAN WILSON RHB / OB

FULL NAME: Frances Claire Wilson
BORN: November 7, 1991, Farnham, Surrey
SQUAD NO: 35
HEIGHT: 5ft 4in
EDUCATION: University of Bath; Loughborough University
TEAMS: England, Middlesex, Western Storm, Diamonds, Emeralds, Rubies, Somerset, Sydney Thunder, Wellington
ROLE: Batsman
DEBUT: Test: 2017; ODI: 2010; T20I: 2010

BEST ODI BATTING: 81 England vs India, Derby, 2017

WHAT WAS YOUR FIRST CRICKET CLUB? Bath CC. Played alongside Anya Shrubsole throughout my youth and was coached by her dad
BEST INNINGS YOU'VE SEEN? Danni Wyatt's maiden T20 hundred against the Aussies in 2017 – because she's one of my best friends and helped us win the series
WHO WOULD YOU ASK TO BAT FOR YOUR LIFE? Heather Knight
YOUR BIGGEST CRICKETING REGRET? Giving up leg-spin aged 13
SURPRISING FACT ABOUT YOU? I didn't play international cricket for five years after my England debut. I have an MSc in Sport and Exercise Nutrition and run a business delivering nutrition workshops in schools
FAVOURITE QUOTE OR SAYING? Everything in moderation
WHICH BOOK MEANS MOST TO YOU? The Tale of Peter Rabbit by Beatrix Potter
TWITTER: @fwilson07

Batting	Mat	Inns	NO	Runs	HS	Ave	SR	100	50	Ct	St
Tests	1	1	0	13	13	13.00	24.52	0	0	0	0
ODIs	20	15	0	319	81	21.26	83.94	0	1	8	0
T20Is	14	12	5	152	43*	21.71	93.82	0	0	3	0
Bowling	**Mat**	**Balls**	**Runs**	**Wkts**	**BBI**	**BBM**	**Ave**	**Econ**	**SR**	**5w**	**10**
Tests	1	-	-	-	-	-	-	-	-	-	-
ODIs	20	-	-	-	-	-	-	-	-	-	-
T20Is	14	-	-	-	-	-	-	-	-	-	-

LAUREN WINFIELD RHB / WK

FULL NAME: Lauren Winfield
BORN: August 16, 1990, York
SQUAD NO: 58
HEIGHT: 5ft 7in
NICKNAME: Loz
EDUCATION: Lougborough University
TEAMS: England, Yorkshire, Yorkshire Diamonds, Brisbane Heat, Diamonds, Hobart Hurricanes, Rubies, Sapphires
ROLE: Batsman
DEBUT: Tests: 2014; ODI: 2013; T20I: 2013

BEST ODI BATTING: 123 England vs Pakistan, Worcester, 2016

FAMILY TIES? My dad plays and we spent many a Saturday afternoon down at my local club Stamford Bridge
CRICKETING HERO? Graham Dilley – my former coach at Loughborough, my mentor and a good friend
WHO WOULD YOU ASK TO BAT FOR YOUR LIFE? Heather Knight
WHICH RULE WOULD YOU CHANGE ABOUT CRICKET? You can't be run out when the ball deflects off the bowler's hand at the non-striker's end
YOUR BIGGEST CRICKETING REGRET? Dropping a catch
SURPRISING FACT ABOUT YOU? I love classical music
FAVOURITE QUOTE OR SAYING? Hard work beats talent when talent doesn't work (Tim Notke)
TWITTER: @Lozwinfield

Batting	Mat	Inns	NO	Runs	HS	Ave	SR	100	50	Ct	St
Tests	3	6	0	94	35	15.66	25.06	0	0	1	0
ODIs	39	39	3	817	123	22.69	64.58	1	3	14	0
T20Is	26	23	2	443	74	21.09	111.30	0	3	10	0
Bowling	**Mat**	**Balls**	**Runs**	**Wkts**	**BBI**	**BBM**	**Ave**	**Econ**	**SR**	**5w**	**10**
Tests	3	-	-	-	-	-	-	-	-	-	-
ODIs	39	-	-	-	-	-	-	-	-	-	-
T20Is	26	-	-	-	-	-	-	-	-	-	-

DANNI WYATT

RHB / OB

FULL NAME: Danielle Nicole Wyatt
BORN: April 22, 1991, Stoke-on-Trent, Staffordshire
SQUAD NO: 28
HEIGHT: 5ft 4in
NICKNAME: Chesney, Waggy
EDUCATION: St Peter's High School; Stoke-On-Trent Sixth Form College
TEAMS: England, Sussex, Southern Vipers, Lancashire Thunder, Melbourne Renegades, Nottinghamshire, Sapphires, Staffordshire
ROLE: Batsman
DEBUT: ODI: 2010; T20I: 2010

BEST ODI BATTING: 56 England vs India, Mumbai, 2019
BEST ODI BOWLING: 3-7 England vs South Africa, Cuttack, 2013

WHAT WAS YOUR FIRST CRICKET CLUB? Whitmore CC, Staffordshire. Played there since I was 10 and still play there now. There's nowhere better
WHICH BOWLER WOULD YOU LEAST LIKE TO FACE? Grace Harris – because she's now bowling donkey drops
WHO WOULD YOU ASK TO BAT FOR YOUR LIFE? Virat Kohli – he's the king
YOUR BIGGEST CRICKETING REGRET? Not believing in myself earlier and not listening to myself and doing what works for me
WHAT WILL YOU BE DOING IN THE YEAR 2040? On my boat with my kids in Barbados listening to Rihanna
WHICH BOOK MEANS MOST TO YOU? The Subtle Art of Not Giving a F*** – A Counterintuitive Approach to Living a Good Life by Mark Manson
ODDEST SPORT YOU'VE PLAYED? Badminton
TWITTER: @Danni_wyatt

Batting	Mat	Inns	NO	Runs	HS	Ave	SR	100	50	Ct	St
ODIs	63	51	7	803	56	18.25	75.11	0	1	13	0
T20Is	91	70	9	1196	124	19.60	122.54	2	4	21	0
Bowling	**Mat**	**Balls**	**Runs**	**Wkts**	**BBI**	**BBM**	**Ave**	**Econ**	**SR**	**5w**	**10**
ODIs	63	888	748	27	3/7	3/7	27.70	5.05	32.8	0	0
T20Is	91	741	699	46	4/11	4/11	15.19	5.65	16.1	0	0

The
Umpires

ROB BAILEY

NAME: Robert John Bailey
BORN: October 28, 1963, Biddulph, Staffordshire
HEIGHT: 6ft 3in
NICKNAME: Bailers
APPOINTED TO FIRST-CLASS LIST: 2006
INTERNATIONAL PANEL: 2011-
ELITE PANEL: 2014
TESTS UMPIRED: 1 (1 as TV)
ODIS UMPIRED: 33 (4 as TV)
T20IS UMPIRED: 35 (8 as TV)
COUNTIES AS PLAYER: Northamptonshire, Derbyshire
ROLE: Batsman; RHB OB
COUNTY DEBUT: 1982 (Northamptonshire), 2000 (Derbyshire)
TEST DEBUT: 1988
ODI DEBUT: 1985

Batting	Mat	Inns	NO	Runs	HS	Ave	SR	100	50	Ct	St
Tests	4	8	0	119	43	14.87	36.50	0	0	0	0
ODIs	4	4	2	137	43*	68.50	69.89	0	0	1	0
First-class	374	628	89	21844	224*	40.52		47	111	272	0
List A	396	376	65	12076	153*	38.82		10	79	111	0
Bowling	**Mat**	**Balls**	**Runs**	**Wkts**	**BBI**	**BBM**	**Ave**	**Econ**	**SR**	**5w**	**10**
Tests	4	-	-	-	-	-	-	-	-	-	-
ODIs	4	36	25	0	-	-	-	4.16	-	0	0
First-class	374	9713	5144	121	5/54		42.51	3.17	80.2	2	0
List A	396	3092	2564	72	5/45	5/45	35.61	4.97	42.9	1	0

NEIL BAINTON

NAME: Neil Laurence Bainton
BORN: October 2, 1970, Romford, Essex
HEIGHT: 5ft 8in
APPOINTED TO FIRST-CLASS LIST: 2006
ODIS UMPIRED: 8 (3 as TV)
T20IS UMPIRED: 4 (1 as TV)

FAVOURITE OUTGROUND? Colwyn Bay. Lovely little ground, great pitch, friendly people
TRICKS TO MAINTAIN CONCENTRATION? Split sessions into 15-minute segments
STRANGEST LOCATION WHERE UMPIRED? I'm lucky to have umpired in Mozambique and Uganda on MCC tours
FAVOURITE UMPIRE AS A PLAYER? As a non-player, I always looked up to Nigel Plews – he was a great help to recreational umpires
HIGHLIGHT OF YOUR PLAYING CAREER? I kept wicket for South of England U15 at the England Schools Festival in 1986
FAVOURITE PASTIMES OUTSIDE OF CRICKET? Playing golf badly
SURPRISING FACT? I still work for the Royal Mail as a postman during the winter months

PAUL BALDWIN

NAME: Paul Kerr Baldwin
BORN: July 18, 1973, Epsom, Surrey
APPOINTED TO FIRST-CLASS LIST: 2015
ODIS UMPIRED: 23 (2 as TV)
T20IS UMPIRED: 12 (1 as TV)

UNUSUAL ITEM RECEIVED FROM A BOWLER? Teeth
HIGHLIGHT OF YOUR PLAYING CAREER? Being selected to captain RAF Brüggen, my club side in Germany in 1996, which I captained for the next four years
FAVOURITE PASTIMES OUTSIDE OF CRICKET? Equestrian photography – mostly when our horses compete. And walking with our two black labs in the Lincolnshire countryside
SURPRISING FACT? I was the English voice on BFBS Forces radio of DJ Ötzi who sung Hey Baby! in the '90s

IAN BLACKWELL

NAME: Ian David Blackwell
BORN: June 10, 1978, Chesterfield, Derbyshire
HEIGHT: 6ft 2in
NICKNAME: Blackdog
APPOINTED TO FIRST-CLASS LIST: 2014
COUNTIES AS PLAYER: Derbyshire, Durham, Somerset, Warwickshire
ROLE: Allrounder; LHB SLA
COUNTY DEBUT: 1997 (Derbyshire), 2000 (Somerset), 2009 (Durham), 2012 (Warwickshire)
TEST DEBUT: 2006
ODI DEBUT: 2002

Batting	Mat	Inns	NO	Runs	HS	Ave	SR	100	50	Ct	St
Tests	1	1	0	4	4	4.00	25.00	0	0	0	0
ODIs	34	29	2	403	82	14.92	86.66	0	1	8	0
First-class	210	319	26	11595	247*	39.57		27	64	66	0
List A	254	233	21	5765	134*	27.19		3	34	64	0
T20s	77	69	9	1281	82	21.35	131.79	0	5	17	0

Bowling	Mat	Balls	Runs	Wkts	BBI	BBM	Ave	Econ	SR	5w	10
Tests	1	114	71	0	-	-	-	3.73	-	0	0
ODIs	34	1230	877	24	3/26	3/26	36.54	4.27	51.2	0	0
First-class	210	31618	14295	398	7/52		35.91	2.71	79.4	14	0
List A	254	8885	7102	207	5/26	5/26	34.30	4.79	42.9	1	0
T20s	77	1273	1508	50	4/26	4/26	30.16	7.10	25.4	0	0

MIKE BURNS

NAME: Mike Burns
BORN: February 6, 1969, Barrow-in-Furness, Cumbria
APPOINTED TO F-C LIST: 2016
ODIS UMPIRED: 3 (1 as TV)
COUNTIES AS PLAYER: Warwickshire, Somerset
ROLE: Allrounder; RHB RM
COUNTY DEBUT: 1992 (War), 1997 (Som)

Batting	Mat	Inns	NO	Runs	HS	Ave	SR	100	50	Ct	St
First-class	154	248	14	7648	221	32.68		8	51	142	7
List A	221	207	21	4802	115*	25.81		3	31	101	15
T20s	9	7	0	108	36	15.42	108.00	0	0	3	0

Bowling	Mat	Balls	Runs	Wkts	BBI	BBM	Ave	Econ	SR	5w	10
First-class	154	4751	2885	68	6/54		42.42	3.64	69.8	1	0
List A	221	1844	1769	58	4/39	4/39	30.50	5.75	31.7	0	0
T20s	9	36	55	2	1/15	1/15	27.50	9.16	18.0	0	0

NICK COOK

NAME: Nicholas Grant Billson Cook
BORN: June 17, 1956, Leicester
NICKNAME: Beast
APPOINTED TO FIRST-CLASS LIST: 2009
TESTS UMPIRED: 1
ODIS UMPIRED: 4
T20IS UMPIRED: 7
COUNTIES AS PLAYER: Leicestershire, Northamptonshire
ROLE: Bowler; RHB SLA
COUNTY DEBUT: 1978 (Leicestershire), 1986 (Northamptonshire)
TEST DEBUT: 1983
ODI DEBUT: 1984

Batting	Mat	Inns	NO	Runs	HS	Ave	SR	100	50	Ct	St
Tests	15	25	4	179	31	8.52	23.58	0	0	5	0
ODIs	3	-	-	-	-	-	-	-	-	2	0
First-class	356	365	96	3137	75	11.66		0	4	197	0
List A	223	89	36	491	23	9.26		0	0	74	0

Bowling	Mat	Balls	Runs	Wkts	BBI	BBM	Ave	Econ	SR	5w	10
Tests	15	4174	1689	52	6/65	11/83	32.48	2.42	80.2	4	1
ODIs	3	144	95	5	2/18	2/18	19.00	3.95	28.8	0	0
First-class	356	64460	25507	879	7/34		29.01	2.37	73.3	31	4
List A	223	10077	6812	200	4/22	4/22	34.06	4.05	50.3	0	0

BEN DEBENHAM

NAME: Benjamin John Debenham
BORN: October 11, 1967, Chelmsford, Essex
APPOINTED TO FIRST-CLASS LIST: 2012
ODIS UMPIRED: 1
T20IS UMPIRED: 1

FAVOURITE OUTGROUND? Radlett CC – a good ground, great food and only 45 minutes from home
TRICKS TO MAINTAIN CONCENTRATION? Enjoying the cricket helps to retain focus
UNUSUAL ITEM RECEIVED FROM A BOWLER? A mobile phone – the bowler's friends were saying he was bowling rubbish on Snapchat
STRANGEST LOCATION WHERE UMPIRED? At a coffee plantation in Arusha North Tanzania
HIGHLIGHT OF YOUR PLAYING CAREER? Captaining MCC against Melbourne CC at the MCG
FAVOURITE PASTIMES OUTSIDE OF CRICKET? Skiing in Australia with my family
UNUSUAL OBJECT AT HOME? A dog from Madagascar

JEFF EVANS

NAME: Jeffrey Howard Evans
BORN: August 7, 1954, Llanelli, Carmarthenshire, Wales
HEIGHT: 5ft 8in
APPOINTED TO FIRST-CLASS LIST: 2001
ODIS UMPIRED: 5
T20IS UMPIRED: 5 (2 as TV)

FAVOURITE OUTGROUND? Scarborough for its atmosphere and excellent support
TRICKS TO MAINTAIN CONCENTRATION? Healthy body, healthy mind
MOST MEMORABLE DISMISSAL? Giving Brian Lara out first ball in the Indian Cricket League. Thankfully the replays showed the decision was correct
FUNNIEST MOMENT AS AN UMPIRE? Watching the band of the Royal Gurkha Regiment march towards the boundary in Canterbury only for them to immediately turn around and march towards the pitch. At this point my colleague Vanburn Holder called "play" with the band situated at mid-off

MICHAEL GOUGH

NAME: Michael Andrew Gough
BORN: December 18, 1978, Hartlepool
HEIGHT: 6ft 5in
NICKNAME: Goughy
APPOINTED TO FIRST-CLASS LIST: 2009
INTERNATIONAL PANEL: 2013-
ELITE PANEL: 2014
TESTS UMPIRED: 13 (4 as TV)
ODIS UMPIRED: 76 (21 as TV)
T20IS UMPIRED: 34 (10 as TV)
COUNTY AS PLAYER: Durham
ROLE: Batsman; RHB OB
COUNTY DEBUT: 1998

Batting	Mat	Inns	NO	Runs	HS	Ave	SR	100	50	Ct	St
First-class	67	119	3	2952	123	25.44	-	2	15	57	0
List A	49	45	4	974	132	23.75	-	1	3	14	0
Bowling	**Mat**	**Balls**	**Runs**	**Wkts**	**BBI**	**BBM**	**Ave**	**Econ**	**SR**	**5w**	**10**
First-class	67	2486	1350	30	5/66		45.00	3.25	82.8	1	0
List A	49	1136	947	21	3/26	3/26	45.09	5.00	54.0	0	0

IAN GOULD

NAME: Ian James Gould
BORN: August 19, 1957, Taplow, Buckinghamshire
HEIGHT: 5ft 7in
NICKNAME: Gunner
APPOINTED TO FIRST-CLASS LIST: 2002
INTERNATIONAL PANEL: 2006-
ELITE PANEL: 2009-
TESTS UMPIRED: 99 (25 as TV)
ODIS UMPIRED: 181 (44 as TV)
T20IS UMPIRED: 60 (19 as TV)
COUNTIES AS PLAYER: Middlesex, Sussex
ROLE: Wicketkeeper; LHB
COUNTY DEBUT: 1975 (Middlesex), 1981 (Sussex)
ODI DEBUT: 1983

Batting	Mat	Inns	NO	Runs	HS	Ave	SR	100	50	Ct	St
ODIs	18	14	2	155	42	12.91	63.78	0	0	15	3
First-class	298	399	63	8756	128	26.05		4	47	536	67
List A	315	270	41	4377	88	19.11		0	20	242	37
Bowling	**Mat**	**Balls**	**Runs**	**Wkts**	**BBI**	**BBM**	**Ave**	**Econ**	**SR**	**5w**	**10**
ODIs	18	-	-	-	-	-	-	-	-	-	-
First-class	298	478	365	7	3/10		52.14	4.58	68.2	0	0
List A	315	20	16	1	1/0	1/0	16.00	4.80	20.0	0	0

PETER HARTLEY

NAME: Peter John Hartley
BORN: April 18, 1960, Keighley, Yorkshire
HEIGHT: 6ft
NICKNAME: Jack
APPOINTED TO FIRST-CLASS LIST: 2003
INTERNATIONAL PANEL: 2006-2009
TESTS UMPIRED: 10 (9 as TV)
ODIS UMPIRED: 21 (10 as TV)
T20IS UMPIRED: 16 (6 as TV)
COUNTIES AS PLAYER: Warwickshire, Yorkshire, Hampshire
ROLE: Bowler; RHB RFM
COUNTY DEBUT: 1982 (Warwickshire), 1985 (Yorkshire), 1998 (Hampshire)

Batting	Mat	Inns	NO	Runs	HS	Ave	SR	100	50	Ct	St
First-class	232	283	66	4321	127*	19.91		2	14	68	0
List A	269	170	62	1765	83	16.34		0	4	46	0
Bowling	**Mat**	**Balls**	**Runs**	**Wkts**	**BBI**	**BBM**	**Ave**	**Econ**	**SR**	**5w**	**10**
First-class	232	37108	20635	683	9/41	11/168	30.21	3.33	54.3	23	3
List A	269	12636	9069	356	5/20	5/20	25.47	4.30	35.4	5	0

RICHARD ILLINGWORTH

NAME: Richard Keith Illingworth
BORN: August 23, 1963, Greengates, Bradford
NICKNAME: Harry, Lucy
APPOINTED TO FIRST-CLASS LIST: 2006
INTERNATIONAL PANEL: 2009-
ELITE PANEL: 2013-
TESTS UMPIRED: 58 (16 as TV)
ODIS UMPIRED: 154 (49 as TV)
T20IS UMPIRED: 37 (8 as TV)
COUNTIES AS PLAYER: Worcestershire, Derbyshire
ROLE: Bowler; RHB SLA
COUNTY DEBUT: 1982 (Worcestershire), 2001 (Derbyshire)
TEST DEBUT: 1991
ODI DEBUT: 1991

Batting	Mat	Inns	NO	Runs	HS	Ave	SR	100	50	Ct	St
Tests	9	14	7	128	28	18.28	32.08	0	0	5	0
ODIs	25	11	5	68	14	11.33	57.14	0	0	8	0
First-class	376	435	122	7027	120*	22.45		4	21	161	0
List A	381	185	87	1458	53*	14.87		0	1	93	0
Bowling	**Mat**	**Balls**	**Runs**	**Wkts**	**BBI**	**BBM**	**Ave**	**Econ**	**SR**	**5w**	**10**
Tests	9	1485	615	19	4/96	6/150	32.36	2.48	78.1	0	0
ODIs	25	1501	1059	30	3/33	3/33	35.30	4.23	50.0	0	0
First-class	376	65868	26213	831	7/50		31.54	2.38	79.2	27	6
List A	381	16918	11157	412	5/24	5/24	27.08	3.95	41.0	2	0

RICHARD KETTLEBOROUGH

NAME: Richard Allan Kettleborough
BORN: March 15, 1973, Sheffield
HEIGHT: 5ft 10in
NICKNAME: Ketts
APPOINTED TO FIRST-CLASS LIST: 2006
INTERNATIONAL PANEL: 2008-
ELITE PANEL: 2011-
TESTS UMPIRED: 80 (22 as TV)
ODIS UMPIRED: 116 (36 as TV)
T20IS UMPIRED: 34 (10 as TV)
COUNTIES AS PLAYER: Yorkshire, Middlesex
ROLE: Batsman; LHB RM
COUNTY DEBUT: 1994 (Yorkshire), 1998 (Middlesex)

Batting	Mat	Inns	NO	Runs	HS	Ave	SR	100	50	Ct	St
First-class	33	56	6	1258	108	25.16	-	1	7	20	0
List A	21	16	4	290	58	24.16	-	0	1	6	0
Bowling	**Mat**	**Balls**	**Runs**	**Wkts**	**BBI**	**BBM**	**Ave**	**Econ**	**SR**	**5w**	**10**
First-class	33	378	243	3	2/26		81.00	3.85	126.0	0	0
List A	21	270	230	6	2/43	2/43	38.33	5.11	45.0	0	0

NIGEL LLONG

NAME: Nigel James Llong
BORN: February 11, 1969, Ashford, Kent
HEIGHT: 6ft
NICKNAME: Nidge
APPOINTED TO FIRST-CLASS LIST: 2002
INTERNATIONAL PANEL: 2004-2006 (TV umpire), 2006-present (full member)
ELITE PANEL: 2012-
TESTS UMPIRED: 82 (26 as TV)
ODIS UMPIRED: 199 (73 as TV)
T20IS UMPIRED: 65 (14 as TV)
COUNTY AS PLAYER: Kent
ROLE: Allrounder; LHB OB
COUNTY DEBUT: 1990

Batting	Mat	Inns	NO	Runs	HS	Ave	SR	100	50	Ct	St
First-class	68	108	11	3024	130	31.17	-	6	16	59	0
List A	136	115	24	2302	123	25.29	-	2	8	41	0
Bowling	**Mat**	**Balls**	**Runs**	**Wkts**	**BBI**	**BBM**	**Ave**	**Econ**	**SR**	**5w**	**10**
First-class	68	2273	1259	35	5/21		35.97	3.32	64.9	2	0
List A	136	1317	1210	40	4/24	4/24	30.25	5.51	32.9	0	0

GRAHAM LLOYD

NAME: Graham David Lloyd
BORN: July 1, 1969, Accrington, Lancashire
APPOINTED TO FIRST-CLASS LIST: 2014
ODIS UMPIRED: 1
T20IS UMPIRED: 2
COUNTY AS PLAYER: Lancashire
ROLE: Batsman; RHB RM
COUNTY DEBUT: 1988
ODI DEBUT: 1996

Batting	Mat	Inns	NO	Runs	HS	Ave	SR	100	50	Ct	St
ODIs	6	5	1	39	22	9.75	48.75	0	0	2	0
First-class	203	323	28	11279	241	38.23		24	64	140	0
List A	295	258	48	6117	134	29.12		4	29	67	0
Bowling	**Mat**	**Balls**	**Runs**	**Wkts**	**BBI**	**BBM**	**Ave**	**Econ**	**SR**	**5w**	**10**
ODIs	6	-	-	-	-	-	-	-	-	-	-
First-class	203	339	440	2	1/4		220.00	7.78	169.5	0	0
List A	295	72	103	1	1/23	1/23	103.00	8.58	72.0	0	0

JEREMY LLOYDS

NAME: Jeremy William Lloyds
BORN: November 17, 1954, Penang, Malaysia
HEIGHT: 5ft 11in
NICKNAME: Jerry
APPOINTED TO FIRST-CLASS LIST: 1998
INTERNATIONAL PANEL: 2002-2004 (TV umpire); 2004-2006 (full member)
TESTS UMPIRED: 16 (10 as TV)
ODIS UMPIRED: 43 (22 as TV)
T20IS UMPIRED: 4
COUNTIES AS PLAYER: Somerset, Gloucestershire
ROLE: Allrounder; LHB OB
COUNTY DEBUT: 1979 (Somerset), 1985 (Gloucestershire)

Batting	Mat	Inns	NO	Runs	HS	Ave	SR	100	50	Ct	St
First-class	267	408	64	10679	132*	31.04	-	10	62	229	0
List A	177	150	26	1982	73*	15.98	-	0	5	58	0
Bowling	**Mat**	**Balls**	**Runs**	**Wkts**	**BBI**	**BBM**	**Ave**	**Econ**	**SR**	**5w**	**10**
First-class	267	24175	12943	333	7/88		38.86	3.21	72.5	13	1
List A	177	1522	1129	26	3/14	3/14	43.42	4.45	58.5	0	0

NEIL MALLENDER

NAME: Neil Alan Mallender
BORN: August 13, 1961, Kirk Sandall, Yorkshire
HEIGHT: 6ft
NICKNAME: Ghostie
APPOINTED TO FIRST-CLASS LIST: 1999
INTERNATIONAL PANEL: 2002-2004
TESTS UMPIRED: 11 (5 as TV)
ODIS UMPIRED: 36 (10 as TV)
T20IS UMPIRED: 2 (1 as TV)
COUNTIES AS PLAYER: Northamptonshire, Somerset
ROLE: Bowler; RHB RFM
COUNTY DEBUT: 1980 (Northamptonshire), 1987 (Somerset)
TEST DEBUT: 1992

Batting	Mat	Inns	NO	Runs	HS	Ave	SR	100	50	Ct	St
Tests	2	3	0	8	4	2.66	36.36	0	0	0	0
First-class	345	396	122	4709	100*	17.18		1	10	111	0
List A	325	163	75	1146	38*	13.02		0	0	60	0
Bowling	**Mat**	**Balls**	**Runs**	**Wkts**	**BBI**	**BBM**	**Ave**	**Econ**	**SR**	**5w**	**10**
Tests	2	449	215	10	5/50	8/122	21.50	2.87	44.9	1	0
First-class	345	53215	24654	937	7/27		26.31	2.77	56.7	36	5
List A	325	15488	9849	387	7/37	7/37	25.44	3.81	40.0	3	0

DAVID MILLNS

NAME: David James Millns
BORN: February 7, 1965, Clipstone, Nottinghamshire
HEIGHT: 6ft 3in
NICKNAME: Rocket Man
APPOINTED TO FIRST-CLASS LIST: 2009
TESTS UMPIRED: 1
ODIS UMPIRED: 9
T20IS UMPIRED: 8 (1 as TV)
COUNTIES AS PLAYER: Nottinghamshire, Leicestershire
ROLE: Bowler; LHB RF
COUNTY DEBUT: 1988 (Nottinghamshire), 1990 (Leicestershire)

Batting	Mat	Inns	NO	Runs	HS	Ave	SR	100	50	Ct	St
First-class	171	203	63	3082	121	22.01	-	3	8	76	0
List A	91	49	26	338	39*	14.69	-	0	0	18	0
Bowling	**Mat**	**Balls**	**Runs**	**Wkts**	**BBI**	**BBM**	**Ave**	**Econ**	**SR**	**5w**	**10**
First-class	171	26571	15129	553	9/37		27.35	3.41	48.0	23	4
List A	91	3931	3144	83	4/26	4/26	37.87	4.79	47.3	0	0

STEVE O'SHAUGHNESSY

NAME: Steven Joseph O'Shaughnessy
BORN: September 9, 1961, Bury, Lancashire
APPOINTED TO FIRST-CLASS LIST: 2011
ODIS UMPIRED: 9 (1 as TV)
T20IS UMPIRED: 2 (1 as TV)
COUNTIES AS PLAYER: Lancashire, Worcestershire
ROLE: Allrounder; RHB RM
COUNTY DEBUT: 1980 (Lancashire), 1988 (Worcestershire)

Batting	Mat	Inns	NO	Runs	HS	Ave	SR	100	50	Ct	St
First-class	112	181	28	3720	159*	24.31	-	5	16	57	0
List A	176	151	23	2999	101*	23.42	-	1	15	44	0
Bowling	**Mat**	**Balls**	**Runs**	**Wkts**	**BBI**	**BBM**	**Ave**	**Econ**	**SR**	**5w**	**10**
First-class	112	7179	4108	114	4/66		36.03	3.43	62.9	0	0
List A	176	5389	4184	115	4/17	4/17	36.38	4.65	46.8	0	0

PAUL POLLARD

NAME: Paul Raymond Pollard
BORN: September 24, 1968, Nottingham
APPOINTED TO FIRST-CLASS LIST: 2018
T20IS UMPIRED: 1 (1 as TV)
COUNTIES AS PLAYER: Nottinghamshire, Worcestershire
ROLE: Batsman; LHB RM
COUNTY DEBUT: 1987 (Nottinghamshire), 2004 (Worcestershire)

Batting	Mat	Inns	NO	Runs	HS	Ave	SR	100	50	Ct	St
First-class	192	332	24	9685	180	31.44	-	15	48	158	0
List A	187	173	17	5233	132*	33.54	-	5	33	66	0
Bowling	**Mat**	**Balls**	**Runs**	**Wkts**	**BBI**	**BBM**	**Ave**	**Econ**	**SR**	**5w**	**10**
First-class	192	275	272	4	2/79		68.00	5.93	68.7	0	0
List A	187	18	9	0	-	-	-	3.00	-	0	0

TIM ROBINSON

NAME: Robert Timothy Robinson
BORN: November 21, 1958, Sutton-in-Ashfield, Nottinghamshire
HEIGHT: 6ft
NICKNAME: Robbo, Chop
APPOINTED TO FIRST-CLASS LIST: 2007
INTERNATIONAL PANEL: 2013-
TESTS UMPIRED: 1 (1 as TV)
ODIS UMPIRED: 24 (1 as TV)
T20IS UMPIRED: 28 (11 as TV)
COUNTY AS PLAYER: Nottinghamshire
ROLE: Batsman; RHB RM
COUNTY DEBUT: 1978
TEST DEBUT: 1984
ODI DEBUT: 1984

Batting	Mat	Inns	NO	Runs	HS	Ave	SR	100	50	Ct	St
Tests	29	49	5	1601	175	36.38	41.62	4	6	8	0
ODIs	26	26	0	597	83	22.96	58.18	0	3	6	0
First-class	425	739	85	27571	220*	42.15		63	141	257	0
List A	397	386	40	11879	139	34.33		9	75	120	0
Bowling	**Mat**	**Balls**	**Runs**	**Wkts**	**BBI**	**BBM**	**Ave**	**Econ**	**SR**	**5w**	**10**
Tests	29	6	0	0	-	-	-	0.00	-	0	0
ODIs	26	-	-	-	-	-	-	-	-	-	-
First-class	425	259	289	4	1/22		72.25	6.69	64.7	0	0
List A	397	-	-	-	-	-	-	-	-	-	-

MARTIN SAGGERS

NAME: Martin John Saggers
BORN: May 23, 1972, King's Lynn, Norfolk
HEIGHT: 6ft 2in
NICKNAME: Saggs
APPOINTED TO FIRST-CLASS LIST: 2012
TESTS UMPIRED: 1 (1 as TV)
ODIS UMPIRED: 10 (3 as TV)
T20IS UMPIRED: 6
COUNTIES AS PLAYER: Durham, Kent
ROLE: Bowler; RHB RFM
COUNTY DEBUT: 1996 (Durham), 1999 (Kent)
TEST DEBUT: 2003

Batting	Mat	Inns	NO	Runs	HS	Ave	SR	100	50	Ct	St
Tests	3	3	0	1	1	0.33	3.33	0	0	1	0
First-class	119	147	43	1165	64	11.20		0	2	27	0
List A	124	68	34	313	34*	9.20		0	0	23	0
T20s	10	1	0	5	5	5.00	62.50	0	0	2	0
Bowling	**Mat**	**Balls**	**Runs**	**Wkts**	**BBI**	**BBM**	**Ave**	**Econ**	**SR**	**5w**	**10**
Tests	3	493	247	7	2/29	3/62	35.28	3.00	70.4	0	0
First-class	119	20676	10513	415	7/79		25.33	3.05	49.8	18	0
List A	124	5622	4229	166	5/22	5/22	25.47	4.51	33.8	2	0
T20s	10	186	256	6	2/14	2/14	42.66	8.25	31.0	0	0

BILLY TAYLOR

NAME: Billy Victor Taylor
BORN: January 11, 1977, Southampton, Hampshire
APPOINTED TO FIRST-CLASS LIST: 2016
TESTS UMPIRED: 1
ODIS UMPIRED: 1
COUNTIES AS PLAYER: Sussex, Hampshire
ROLE: Bowler; LHB RMF
COUNTY DEBUT: 1999 (Sussex), 2004 (Hampshire)

Batting	Mat	Inns	NO	Runs	HS	Ave	SR	100	50	Ct	St
First-class	54	68	26	431	40	10.26		0	0	6	0
List A	142	58	28	191	21*	6.36		0	0	26	0
T20s	37	9	8	22	12*	22.00	84.61	0	0	3	0
Bowling	**Mat**	**Balls**	**Runs**	**Wkts**	**BBI**	**BBM**	**Ave**	**Econ**	**SR**	**5w**	**10**
First-class	54	8412	4535	136	6/32		33.34	3.23	61.8	4	0
List A	142	6311	4699	182	5/28	5/28	25.81	4.46	34.6	1	0
T20s	37	713	883	30	2/9	2/9	29.43	7.43	23.7	0	0

RUSSELL WARREN

NAME: Russell John Warren
BORN: September 10, 1971, Northampton
HEIGHT: 6ft 2in
NICKNAME: Rabbit
APPOINTED TO FIRST-CLASS LIST: 2014
ODIS UMPIRED: 1
T20IS UMPIRED: 3
COUNTIES AS PLAYER: Northamptonshire, Nottinghamshire
ROLE: Wicketkeeper/batsman; RHB
COUNTY DEBUT: 1992 (Northamptonshire), 2003 (Nottinghamshire)

Batting	Mat	Inns	NO	Runs	HS	Ave	SR	100	50	Ct	St
First-class	146	238	26	7776	201*	36.67		15	41	128	5
List A	177	162	25	3363	100*	24.54		1	15	135	11
T20s	2	1	0	26	26	26.00	86.66	0	0	0	0
Bowling	**Mat**	**Balls**	**Runs**	**Wkts**	**BBI**	**BBM**	**Ave**	**Econ**	**SR**	**5w**	**10**
First-class	146	6	0	0	-	-	-	0.00	-	0	0
List A	177	-	-	-	-	-	-	-	-	-	-
T20s	2	-	-	-	-	-	-	-	-	-	-

ALEX WHARF

NAME: Alexander George Wharf
BORN: June 4, 1975, Bradford, Yorkshire
HEIGHT: 6ft 4in
NICKNAME: Gangster
APPOINTED TO FIRST-CLASS LIST: 2014
INTERNATIONAL PANEL: 2018-
TESTS UMPIRED: 1
ODIS UMPIRED: 10 (3 as TV)
T20IS UMPIRED: 13 (3 as TV)
COUNTIES AS PLAYER: Yorkshire, Nottinghamshire, Glamorgan
ROLE: Allrounder; RHB RMF
COUNTY DEBUT: 1994 (Yorkshire), 1998 (Notts), 2000 (Glamorgan)
ODI DEBUT: 2004

Batting	Mat	Inns	NO	Runs	HS	Ave	SR	100	50	Ct	St
ODIs	13	5	3	19	9	9.50	67.85	0	0	1	0
First-class	121	184	29	3570	128*	23.03		6	14	63	0
List A	155	109	22	1411	72	16.21		0	1	42	0
T20s	34	20	7	157	19	12.07	120.76	0	0	5	0
Bowling	**Mat**	**Balls**	**Runs**	**Wkts**	**BBI**	**BBM**	**Ave**	**Econ**	**SR**	**5w**	**10**
ODIs	13	584	428	18	4/24	4/24	23.77	4.39	32.4	0	0
First-class	121	16825	10941	293	6/59		37.34	3.90	57.4	5	1
List A	155	6497	5552	192	6/5	6/5	28.91	5.12	33.8	1	0
T20s	34	644	1028	39	4/39	4/39	26.35	9.57	16.5	0	0

Roll *of*
Honour

SPECSAVERS COUNTY CHAMPIONSHIP TABLES

Division One

Team	Mat	Won	Lost	Tied	Draw	Aban	Pts
Surrey	14	10	1	0	3	0	254
Somerset	14	7	2	1	4	0	208
Essex	14	7	4	0	2	1	187
Yorkshire	14	5	5	0	3	1	158
Hampshire	14	4	5	0	5	0	144
Nottinghamshire	14	4	8	0	2	0	133
Lancashire	14	3	7	1	3	0	133
Worcestershire	14	2	10	0	2	0	104

Division Two

Team	Mat	Won	Lost	Tied	Draw	Aban	Pts
Warwickshire	14	9	2	0	3	0	242
Kent	14	10	3	0	1	0	221
Sussex	14	6	4	0	4	0	186
Middlesex	14	7	4	0	3	0	179
Gloucestershire	14	5	4	0	5	0	157
Leicestershire	14	5	7	0	2	0	149
Derbyshire	14	4	7	0	3	0	147
Durham	14	4	7	0	2	1	130
Northamptonshire	14	4	8	0	1	1	126
Glamorgan	14	2	10	0	2	0	92

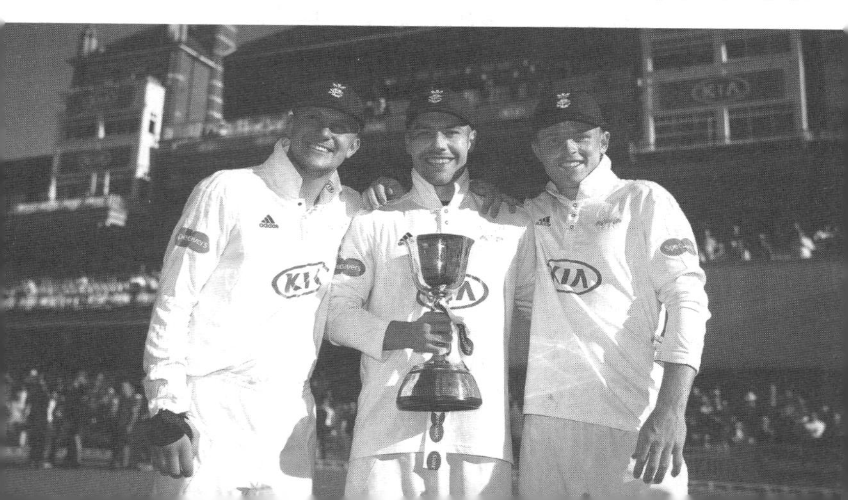

KIA
KIA

ROYAL LONDON ONE-DAY CUP

North Group

Team	Mat	Won	Lost	Tied	N/R	Pts	Net RR
Worcestershire	8	6	2	0	0	12	0.26
Nottinghamshire	8	5	2	0	1	11	0.675
Yorkshire	8	5	2	0	1	11	0.513
Warwickshire	8	4	2	0	2	10	0.446
Derbyshire	8	4	4	0	0	8	-0.552
Lancashire	8	3	4	0	1	7	0.969
Northamptonshire	8	2	5	0	1	5	-0.339
Leicestershire	8	2	6	0	0	4	-0.704
Durham	8	2	6	0	0	4	-1.088

South Group

Team	Mat	Won	Lost	Tied	N/R	Pts	Net RR
Hampshire	8	5	2	0	1	11	0.327
Essex	8	5	3	0	0	10	0.791
Kent	8	5	3	0	0	10	0.01
Somerset	8	4	3	0	1	9	0.548
Surrey	8	4	3	0	1	9	-0.848
Middlesex	8	4	4	0	0	8	0.089
Gloucestershire	8	2	3	0	3	7	-0.25
Sussex	8	2	4	0	2	6	0.075
Glamorgan	8	1	7	0	0	2	-0.784

QUARTER-FINALS

Nottinghamshire v Kent at Trent Bridge

June 14 –*Kent won by 9 wickets*

Nottinghamshire 255-8 (50/50 ov); Kent 257-1 (35.5/50 ov)

Essex v Yorkshire at Chelmsford

June 14 – *Yorkshire won by 25 runs*

Yorkshire 259-7 (50/50 ov); Essex 234 (49.1/50 ov)

The two group winners progressed straight into the semi-finals; the second- and third-placed teams played two 'quarter-finals'

SEMI-FINALS

Worcestershire v Kent at Worcester

June 17 – *Kent won by 2 wickets*

Worcestershire 306-6 (50/50 ov); Kent 307-8 (49.4/50 ov)

Hampshire v Yorkshire at Southampton

June 17 – *Hampshire won by 107 runs*

Hampshire 348-9 (50/50 ov); Yorkshire 241 (43.4/50 ov)

FINAL

Hampshire v Kent at Lord's

June 30 – *Hampshire won by 61 runs*

Hampshire 330-7 (50/50 ov); Kent 269 (47.1/50 ov) (47.5/50 ov)

Vanilla
adidas
ROYAL LONDON
Hampshire Cricket
adidas
82

North Group

Team	Mat	Won	Lost	Tied	N/R	Pts	Net RR
Worcestershire	14	9	4	0	1	19	0.595
Durham	14	9	4	0	1	19	0.556
Lancashire	14	8	5	0	1	17	0.683
Nottinghamshire	14	8	6	0	0	16	0.073
Yorkshire	14	7	7	0	0	14	-0.035
Warwickshire	14	6	7	1	0	13	0.033
Derbyshire	14	5	7	0	2	12	-0.047
Leicestershire	14	5	8	0	1	11	-0.38
Northamptonshire	14	2	11	1	0	5	-1.398

South Group

Team	Mat	Won	Lost	Tied	N/R	Pts	Net RR
Somerset	14	10	4	0	0	20	0.786
Kent	14	8	2	0	4	20	0.627
Sussex	14	7	3	0	4	18	0.737
Gloucestershire	14	8	4	0	2	18	0.381
Surrey	14	7	5	0	2	16	0.989
Glamorgan	14	7	6	0	1	15	-0.144
Essex	14	2	8	1	3	8	-1.035
Hampshire	14	2	9	1	2	7	-0.824
Middlesex	14	2	12	0	0	4	-1.128

QUARTER-FINALS

Kent v Lancashire at Canterbury

August 23 – *Lancashire won by 6 wickets*
Kent 133-9 (20/20 ov); Lancashire 134-4 (18.4/20 ov)

Durham v Sussex at Chester-le-Street

August 24 – *Sussex won by 5 wickets*
Durham 140-7 (20/20 ov); Sussex 144-5 (18.2/20 ov)

Worcestershire v Gloucestershire at Worcester

August 25 – *Worcestershire won by 5 wickets*
Gloucestershire 136-8 (20/20 ov); Worcestershire 137-5 (18.4/20 ov)

Somerset v Nottinghamshire at Taunton

August 26-27 – *Somerset won by 19 runs*
Somerset 209-5 (20/20 ov); Nottinghamshire 190 (20/20 ov)

SEMI-FINALS

Worcestershire v Lancashire at Edgbaston

September 15 – *Worcestershire won by 20 runs*
Worcestershire 169-6 (20/20 ov); Lancashire 149-9 (20/20 ov)

Sussex v Somerset at Edgbaston

September 15 – *Sussex won by 35 runs*
Sussex 202-8 (20/20 ov); Somerset 167-8 (20/20 ov)

FINAL

Sussex v Worcestershire at Edgbaston

September 15 – *Worcestershire won by 5 wickets*
Sussex 157-6 (20/20 ov); Worcestershire 158-5 (18.3/20 ov)

RAPIDS
Vitality
BLAST

COUNTY CHAMPIONSHIP BATTING AVERAGES *Minimum of 500 runs*

Name	Mat	Inns	NO	Runs	HS	Ave	BF	SR	100	50	0	4s	6s
OJ Pope	13	16	2	986	158*	70.42	1545	63.81	4	1	0	148	2
RJ Burns	14	22	1	1359	193	64.71	2637	51.53	4	7	0	178	1
IR Bell	14	23	4	1027	204	54.05	1838	55.87	5	2	2	140	3
MT Renshaw	6	11	1	513	112	51.3	812	63.17	3	1	0	69	9
KK Jennings	10	16	1	709	177	47.26	1463	48.46	3	1	1	110	0
IJL Trott	14	23	3	935	170*	46.75	1650	56.66	2	6	1	113	0
JC Hildreth	14	26	2	1089	184	45.37	1661	65.56	3	6	1	155	4
WMH Rhodes	14	23	1	972	137	44.18	1829	53.14	4	4	1	124	3
BC Brown	14	24	3	912	116	43.42	1538	59.29	1	7	2	117	0
BT Slater	9	17	1	676	99	42.25	1405	48.11	0	6	1	93	1
RS Bopara	13	22	4	751	133*	41.72	1404	53.49	2	4	2	87	4
TB Abell	14	26	4	883	132*	40.13	1727	51.12	1	5	1	124	2
JM Vince	14	25	1	962	201*	40.08	1681	57.22	3	2	2	147	3
CN Ackermann	14	24	2	876	196*	39.81	1617	54.17	2	3	2	116	8
GS Ballance	12	23	0	906	194	39.39	1503	60.27	3	4	1	142	3
RN ten Doeschate	12	20	2	680	173*	37.77	1052	64.63	1	4	0	84	6
DJ Vilas	14	23	2	792	235*	37.71	1448	54.69	3	1	3	104	5
WL Madsen	14	27	0	1016	144	37.62	1631	62.29	2	7	4	133	2
DP Sibley	14	23	2	777	144*	37	1825	42.57	4	1	2	82	0
DKH Mitchell	14	26	0	957	178	36.8	1893	50.55	4	1	3	130	0
BT Foakes	12	18	1	624	90	36.7	1257	49.64	0	4	2	80	1
SR Hain	12	17	1	566	90	35.37	1154	49.04	0	6	1	75	0
SS Eskinazi	12	22	1	740	97	35.23	1271	58.22	0	5	1	102	0
TR Ambrose	14	20	1	656	103	34.52	1260	52.06	1	3	0	80	1
JL Denly	14	24	0	828	119	34.5	1517	54.58	3	3	3	110	2
NJ Dexter	12	20	3	585	87	34.41	1193	49.03	0	3	1	81	2
NRT Gubbins	9	17	0	585	107	34.41	1125	52	1	2	0	90	1
JM Clarke	14	26	1	853	177*	34.12	1359	62.76	3	1	3	116	0
CDJ Dent	14	28	3	851	214*	34.04	1861	45.72	1	4	2	110	2
HG Kuhn	14	26	3	780	96*	33.91	1334	58.47	0	6	2	108	4
LRPL Taylor	8	15	0	506	146	33.73	665	76.09	1	4	4	68	6
J Clark	10	16	0	538	82	33.62	893	60.24	0	5	4	68	3
D Wiese	13	20	4	538	106	33.62	683	78.77	1	2	4	68	6
MD Stoneman	13	21	1	660	144	33	1139	57.94	1	4	3	101	1
SM Davies	14	25	2	756	92*	32.86	1323	57.14	0	5	0	115	1
JR Bracey	14	27	3	785	125*	32.7	1932	40.63	2	2	3	98	0
Z Crawley	14	24	0	755	168	31.45	1282	58.89	1	4	1	100	4
R Clarke	13	17	1	500	111	31.25	735	68.02	1	2	2	79	6
T Westley	13	23	1	687	134	31.22	1449	47.41	2	2	5	106	0
PD Salt	14	24	0	739	148	30.79	953	77.54	2	2	4	102	8
R Vasconcelos	10	18	0	554	140	30.77	1052	52.66	1	4	3	76	1
MGK Burgess	12	19	1	551	101*	30.61	771	71.46	1	2	0	70	2
AL Davies	14	24	0	732	115	30.5	1128	64.89	1	5	3	125	1
MDE Holden	13	24	3	632	119*	30.09	1173	53.87	1	3	3	84	1
HZ Finch	14	24	0	722	103	30.08	1358	53.16	1	5	3	103	5
SJ Mullaney	11	20	0	601	130	30.05	1041	57.73	1	4	3	80	7
TJ Moores	13	22	1	616	103	29.33	1072	57.46	1	2	0	88	14
DJ Malan	12	22	1	613	119	29.19	1161	52.79	1	4	3	78	1
CT Steel	12	22	0	638	160	29	1703	37.46	1	4	2	69	0
AG Wakely	12	22	1	600	106	28.57	1107	54.2	1	4	1	75	7
MH Wessels	12	23	3	568	75*	28.4	959	59.22	0	4	3	79	2

COUNTY CHAMPIONSHIP BOWLING AVERAGES *Minimum of 20 wickets*

Player	Mat	Overs	Mdns	Runs	Wkts	BBI	BBM	Ave	Econ	SR	5	10
OP Stone	7	160.2	26	525	43	8/80	11/96	12.2	3.27	22.3	3	1
M Morkel	10	315.4	82	845	59	6/57	9/120	14.32	2.67	32.1	4	0
TJ Murtagh	11	359.5	95	888	58	5/38	8/63	15.31	2.46	37.2	2	0
MJ Henry	11	382.4	83	1161	75	7/42	12/73	15.48	3.03	30.6	5	3
BO Coad	9	272.5	87	784	48	6/81	10/130	16.33	2.87	34.1	3	1
PM Siddle	7	234.4	47	607	37	5/37	8/72	16.4	2.58	38	3	0
BW Sanderson	13	422	112	1002	60	5/16	8/108	16.7	2.37	42.2	2	0
KHD Barker	10	254.1	69	672	40	5/32	9/96	16.8	2.64	38.1	2	0
Mohammad Abbas	10	345.1	101	886	50	6/48	10/52	17.72	2.56	41.4	5	1
JC Archer	8	273.5	67	750	42	5/69	8/46	17.85	2.73	39.1	1	0
RF Higgins	14	353.5	99	882	48	5/21	8/54	18.37	2.49	44.2	2	0
JL Denly	14	160.1	28	426	23	4/36	5/121	18.52	2.65	41.7	0	0
OE Robinson	14	485	92	1381	74	7/58	10/67	18.66	2.84	39.3	4	1
DI Stevens	11	295.4	76	799	42	6/26	8/83	19.02	2.7	42.2	2	0
DW Steyn	5	142.3	30	382	20	5/66	7/71	19.1	2.68	42.7	1	0
TE Bailey	14	439.4	106	1258	64	5/53	8/67	19.65	2.86	41.2	1	0
AP Palladino	12	369	94	1006	51	6/29	10/81	19.72	2.72	43.4	3	1
C Rushworth	12	386.4	83	1201	60	8/51	12/100	20.01	3.1	38.6	3	1
ER Bamber	6	203.5	37	567	28	4/81	6/70	20.25	2.78	43.6	0	0
JAR Harris	12	384.5	67	1253	61	7/83	9/48	20.54	3.25	37.8	3	0
CN Miles	13	328.1	61	1180	56	5/50	8/90	21.07	3.59	35.1	2	0
JM Mennie	7	192.5	44	601	28	4/43	6/50	21.46	3.11	41.3	0	0
R Clarke	13	363.1	87	1012	47	5/29	8/75	21.53	2.78	46.3	1	0
T van der Gugten	10	287	69	936	43	7/42	8/71	21.76	3.26	40	2	0
G Onions	12	379.3	72	1241	57	6/55	9/77	21.77	3.27	39.9	2	0
J Leach	5	157.5	28	508	23	4/42	7/97	22.08	3.21	41.1	0	0
JT Ball	6	171.5	38	623	28	5/43	9/57	22.25	3.62	36.8	2	0
HJH Brookes	5	142	22	470	21	4/54	8/119	22.38	3.3	40.5	0	0
BA Raine	11	395.1	90	1146	51	4/44	7/89	22.47	2.9	46.4	0	0
MG Hogan	13	393.3	101	1014	45	5/49	8/102	22.53	2.57	52.4	2	0
JS Patel	14	431.4	108	1276	56	7/83	10/106	22.78	2.95	46.2	4	2
G Stewart	10	164.5	26	505	22	6/22	8/58	22.95	3.06	44.9	1	0
KJ Abbott	14	348.3	70	1182	51	6/39	11/71	23.17	3.39	41	4	1
EG Barnard	13	368.3	93	1138	49	6/37	11/89	23.22	3.08	45.1	4	1
MJ Leach	11	255.4	57	722	30	8/85	12/102	24.06	2.82	51.1	3	2
TD Groenewald	7	173	41	509	21	4/85	5/63	24.23	2.94	49.4	0	0
SM Curran	7	192.2	37	608	25	6/54	10/101	24.32	3.16	46.1	1	1
SR Harmer	13	526.2	136	1394	57	6/87	7/69	24.45	2.64	55.4	3	0
JA Porter	13	432.3	81	1429	58	7/41	11/98	24.63	3.3	44.7	3	1
SA Patterson	8	235	63	594	24	6/40	7/63	24.75	2.52	58.7	1	0
J Overton	8	177.3	34	646	26	4/25	8/143	24.84	3.63	40.9	0	0
L Gregory	12	305.5	75	928	37	4/33	7/86	25.08	3.03	49.5	0	0
JC Tongue	11	304.4	52	1011	40	5/53	9/98	25.27	3.31	45.7	2	0
SJ Cook	10	219.3	60	684	27	5/28	5/84	25.33	3.11	48.7	1	0
JH Davey	11	290.4	73	862	34	5/65	7/111	25.35	2.96	51.2	1	0
LJ Fletcher	13	347.3	86	977	38	5/27	7/55	25.71	2.81	54.8	1	0
FH Edwards	14	362.2	55	1443	54	6/50	7/122	26.72	3.98	40.2	2	0
HF Gurney	11	325.3	52	1137	42	6/25	8/43	27.07	3.49	46.5	2	0
C Overton	11	321.3	72	1014	37	4/27	7/95	27.4	3.15	52.1	0	0

COUNTY CHAMPIONSHIP WICKETKEEPING *Minimum of 20 dismissals*

Name	Mat	Inns	Dis	Ct	St	Max Dis Inns	Dis/Inn
TR Ambrose	14	26	57	57	0	6 (6ct 0st)	2.192
BC Brown	14	27	53	52	1	6 (6ct 0st)	1.962
GH Roderick	12	21	48	48	0	4 (4ct 0st)	2.285
DJ Vilas	14	16	46	42	4	6 (5ct 1st)	2.875
CB Cooke	14	23	42	41	1	5 (5ct 0st)	1.826
SM Davies	14	25	41	38	3	4 (4ct 0st)	1.64
TJ Moores	13	21	39	39	0	5 (5ct 0st)	1.857
BT Foakes	12	22	38	37	1	5 (5ct 0st)	1.727
OB Cox	12	22	35	35	0	4 (4ct 0st)	1.59
SW Poynter	11	20	35	34	1	5 (5ct 0st)	1.75
AM Rossington	11	21	34	34	0	4 (4ct 0st)	1.619
LJ Hill	9	14	29	29	0	5 (5ct 0st)	2.071
EJH Eckersley	7	12	26	26	0	5 (5ct 0st)	2.166
JA Simpson	8	15	26	23	3	4 (3ct 1st)	1.733
AJA Wheater	8	16	24	23	1	4 (4ct 0st)	1.5
AP Rouse	7	14	24	24	0	3 (3ct 0st)	1.714
TP Alsop	8	12	22	22	0	4 (4ct 0st)	1.833
SW Billings	8	13	21	19	2	4 (3ct 1st)	1.615

COUNTY CHAMPIONSHIP FIELDING *Minimum of 13 catches*

Name	Mat	Inns	Ct	Max	Ct/Inn
WL Madsen	14	26	25	3	0.961
SR Dickson	14	27	25	3	0.925
HZ Finch	14	27	22	3	0.814
DKH Mitchell	14	26	21	3	0.807
NJ Selman	12	19	21	3	1.105
HG Kuhn	14	27	21	2	0.777
R Clarke	13	25	19	3	0.76
DP Sibley	14	26	18	3	0.692
ME Trescothick	10	18	16	3	0.888
A Lyth	13	22	16	2	0.727
LS Livingstone	10	20	15	2	0.75
JHK Adams	14	23	15	3	0.652
RE Levi	11	21	15	3	0.714
OP Rayner	9	17	14	4	0.823
SG Borthwick	8	14	13	2	0.928
LRPL Taylor	8	15	13	3	0.866
RN ten Doeschate	12	23	13	3	0.565
SR Harmer	13	25	13	2	0.52
JC Hildreth	14	25	13	2	0.52
IR Bell	14	26	13	3	0.5

MVP TOP 100

#	Name	County	Batting	Bowling	Field	Capt.	Wins	Pld	Pts	Avg.
1	Joe Denly	Kent	340.53	190.43	16.40	7	25	38	579.36	15.25
2	Rikki Clarke	Surrey	136.52	309.14	34.00	0	21	35	500.66	14.30
3	Ed Barnard	Worcestershire	120.99	301.57	35.00	0	20	38	477.56	12.57
4	Lewis Gregory	Somerset	172.83	249.83	19.00	13	20	33	474.66	14.38
5	Simon Harmer	Essex	95.85	287.09	25.00	0	14	35	421.94	12.06
6	James Hildreth	Somerset	365.73	0.00	23.00	0	22	38	410.73	10.81
7	Ben Raine	Leicestershire	165.26	223.39	10.80	0	11	30	410.45	13.68
8	Moeen Ali	Worcestershire	203.89	174.95	7.00	8	12	17	405.84	23.87
9	Alex Davies	Lancashire	336.41	0.00	39.00	0	15	37	390.41	10.55
10	Steven Mullaney	Nottinghamshire	233.78	109.40	23.00	8	16	34	390.18	11.48
11	James Vince	Hampshire	336.40	6.68	19.00	13	13	36	388.08	10.78
12	Matt Henry	Kent	47.23	314.40	10.20	0	15	22	386.83	17.58
13	Ryan Higgins	Gloucestershire	139.57	222.07	9.80	0	15	34	386.44	11.37
14	Heino Kuhn	Kent	331.56	0.00	29.80	0	25	38	386.36	10.17
15	Ian Bell	Warwickshire	351.40	0.00	15.40	0	19	36	385.80	10.72
16	Dane Vilas	Lancashire	215.84	0.00	147.00	5	15	37	382.84	10.35
17	Rory Burns	Surrey	326.10	0.00	18.00	14	17	31	375.10	12.10
18	Morne Morkel	Surrey	30.01	325.96	4.00	0	14	23	373.97	16.26
19	Tom Bailey	Lancashire	56.86	302.00	7.00	0	4	18	369.86	20.55
20	Adam Lyth	Yorkshire	299.79	23.79	24.00	0	18	36	365.58	10.15
21	Daryl Mitchell	Worcestershire	242.72	67.27	29.00	0	19	38	357.99	9.42
22	Luke Fletcher	Nottinghamshire	87.24	244.86	6.00	0	16	33	354.10	10.73
23	Jeetan Patel	Warwickshire	25.56	281.88	14.20	13	19	36	353.64	9.82
24	Ravi Bopara	Essex	246.68	75.51	16.00	0	14	35	352.19	10.06
25	Samit Patel	Nottinghamshire	177.96	147.10	10.00	0	17	37	352.06	9.52
26	Ollie Robinson	Sussex	40.74	291.02	6.80	0	11	23	349.56	15.20
27	David Wiese	Sussex	145.16	177.42	6.60	0	16	33	345.19	10.46
28	Tom Moores	Nottinghamshire	255.88	0.00	72.00	0	17	36	344.88	9.58
29	Jack Brooks	Yorkshire	50.98	271.96	10.00	0	11	23	343.94	14.95
30	Joe Clarke	Worcestershire	306.58	0.00	16.00	0	20	38	342.58	9.02
31	Chris Rushworth	Durham	15.31	307.10	5.60	0	14	30	342.00	11.40
32	Liam Livingstone	Lancashire	223.93	72.01	26.00	10	10	25	341.94	13.68
33	Wayne Madsen	Derbyshire	274.24	23.42	28.00	0	13	35	338.67	9.68
34	Jamie Porter	Essex	17.23	305.85	4.00	0	11	25	338.08	13.52
35	Harry Gurney	Nottinghamshire	14.46	301.57	4.00	0	14	30	334.03	11.13
36	Colin Ackermann	Leicestershire	253.53	40.32	20.00	6	12	36	331.85	9.22
37	Matthew Critchley	Derbyshire	155.05	139.65	14.80	0	13	35	322.50	9.21
38	Paul Stirling	Middlesex	260.60	36.47	16.20	0	9	28	322.27	11.51
39	Kyle Abbott	Hampshire	80.15	234.98	0.00	0	4	17	319.13	18.77
40	Graham Onions	Lancashire	30.35	280.99	1.00	0	6	19	318.34	16.75
41	Gary Ballance	Yorkshire	288.63	0.00	8.00	2	17	32	315.63	9.86
42	Darren Stevens	Kent	63.07	231.50	3.60	0	14	22	312.18	14.19
43	Tim Bresnan	Yorkshire	98.38	180.63	18.00	0	14	30	311.01	10.37
44	Ben Cox	Worcestershire	201.16	0.00	88.00	0	20	37	309.16	8.36
45	Keaton Jennings	Lancashire	262.15	21.84	14.00	0	9	25	306.99	12.28
46	Jordan Clark	Lancashire	143.61	131.65	13.00	0	14	31	302.26	9.75
47	Liam Dawson	Hampshire	144.98	137.06	12.00	0	8	26	302.04	11.62
48	Tom Abell	Somerset	202.71	52.89	17.00	9	20	32	301.60	9.43
49	Billy Godleman	Derbyshire	269.12	0.00	9.40	8	13	31	299.52	9.66
50	Jofra Archer	Sussex	50.36	225.43	8.80	0	14	26	298.59	11.48

#	Name	County	Batting	Bowling	Field	Capt.	Wins	Pld	Pts	Avg.
51	James Harris	Middlesex	55.22	229.84	4.80	0	8	18	297.86	16.55
52	Ben Sanderson	Northamptonshire	14.73	271.56	4.40	0	7	29	297.69	10.27
53	Craig Overton	Somerset	63.82	208.70	12.00	0	12	20	296.52	14.83
54	Hardus Viljoen	Derbyshire	78.50	194.32	4.80	0	11	29	288.62	9.95
55	Jamie Overton	Somerset	41.00	213.00	17.00	0	16	29	287.00	9.90
56	Danny Briggs	Sussex	30.20	222.57	12.80	2	17	34	284.58	8.37
57	Timm van der Gugten	Glamorgan	38.95	228.93	7.60	0	9	30	284.48	9.48
58	Benny Howell	Gloucestershire	139.61	115.01	16.20	0	13	30	283.82	9.46
59	Ben Foakes	Surrey	198.78	0.00	65.00	0	19	34	282.78	8.32
60	Steve Davies	Somerset	184.71	0.00	78.00	0	20	36	282.71	7.85
61	Alex Hughes	Derbyshire	132.73	122.53	14.20	0	13	35	282.46	8.07
62	Ben Coad	Yorkshire	20.98	246.01	2.00	0	8	15	276.99	18.47
63	Steven Patterson	Yorkshire	32.62	200.91	11.00	15	16	28	275.53	9.84
64	Matthew Parkinson	Lancashire	7.25	250.92	3.00	0	12	29	273.17	9.42
65	Tom Kohler-Cadmore	Yorkshire	237.86	0.00	19.00	0	15	28	271.86	9.71
66	Daniel Bell-Drummond	Kent	231.76	3.80	10.40	0	25	37	270.97	7.32
67	Ollie Pope	Surrey	226.39	0.00	26.00	0	18	30	270.39	9.01
68	Chris Cooke	Glamorgan	171.18	0.00	84.80	2	10	35	267.98	7.66
69	Neil Dexter	Leicestershire	156.82	88.53	11.20	0	11	32	267.55	8.36
70	Varun Chopra	Essex	239.00	0.00	11.00	0	11	29	261.00	9.00
71	Olly Stone	Warwickshire	14.33	226.31	9.80	0	10	20	260.44	13.02
72	David Willey	Yorkshire	141.48	105.72	4.00	1	7	15	259.20	17.28
73	Sam Hain	Warwickshire	224.86	0.00	13.20	0	18	34	256.06	7.53
74	Fidel Edwards	Hampshire	12.34	232.00	4.00	0	6	19	254.34	13.39
75	Riki Wessels	Nottinghamshire	211.86	0.00	26.00	0	16	34	253.86	7.47
76	Michael Hogan	Glamorgan	25.99	202.67	11.40	2	9	28	251.06	8.97
77	Tim Murtagh	Middlesex	31.02	211.43	2.40	0	6	11	250.86	22.81
78	Jade Dernbach	Surrey	26.08	185.99	13.00	7	18	30	250.07	8.34
79	Tom Latham	Durham	207.03	0.00	19.40	11	12	26	249.43	9.59
80	Ben Slater	Derbyshire	237.23	0.00	5.40	0	6	26	248.63	9.56
81	Rilee Rossouw	Hampshire	217.35	0.00	19.00	0	11	31	247.35	7.98
82	James Fuller	Middlesex	90.86	134.95	13.00	0	7	22	245.81	11.17
83	Philip Salt	Sussex	211.52	3.07	12.80	0	15	30	242.39	8.08
84	Mohammad Abbas	Leicestershire	14.45	217.35	2.80	0	7	19	241.60	12.72
85	Brett D'Oliveira	Worcestershire	122.25	82.84	12.00	6	18	34	241.09	7.09
86	Brett Hutton	Northamptonshire	45.65	174.78	12.00	0	7	24	239.43	9.98
87	Gareth Berg	Hampshire	90.43	125.85	12.00	0	11	27	239.28	8.86
88	Craig Miles	Gloucestershire	23.97	202.24	3.40	0	5	16	234.61	14.66
89	Tom Westley	Essex	211.59	6.93	3.00	0	13	28	234.52	8.38
90	Sam Billings	Kent	132.97	0.00	63.00	18	18	27	231.97	8.59
91	Luke Wright	Sussex	207.00	0.00	4.80	7	13	28	231.80	8.28
92	Alex Wakely	Northamptonshire	200.53	0.00	15.20	8	8	34	231.73	6.82
93	Ryan ten Doeschate	Essex	175.70	8.62	19.00	14	14	32	231.32	7.23
94	Adam Wheater	Essex	160.18	0.00	57.00	0	12	30	229.18	7.64
95	Keith Barker	Warwickshire	36.74	180.53	2.80	0	9	17	229.07	13.47
96	Jonathan Trott	Warwickshire	191.90	11.93	11.80	0	13	22	228.63	10.39
97	Ben Duckett	Northamptonshire	199.78	0.00	21.00	0	6	33	226.78	6.87
98	Colin Ingram	Glamorgan	172.87	33.97	7.00	6	6	19	225.84	11.89
99	Laurie Evans	Sussex	205.66	0.00	7.80	0	11	23	224.46	9.76
100	Harry Podmore	Kent	35.93	170.22	3.60	0	14	19	223.76	11.78

NOTES

NOTES

NOTES

NOTES

NOTES